Lecture Notes in Computer Science   8958

Commenced Publication in 1973
Founding and Former Series Editors:
Gerhard Goos, Juris Hartmanis, and Jan van Leeuwen

Editorial Board

More information about this series at http://www.springer.com/series/7410

Lucas C.K. Hui · S.H. Qing
Elaine Shi · S.M. Yiu (Eds.)

Information and Communications Security

16th International Conference, ICICS 2014
Hong Kong, China, December 16–17, 2014
Revised Selected Papers

 Springer

Editors
Lucas C.K. Hui
The University of Hong Kong
Hong Kong
China

Elaine Shi
University of Maryland
College Park
USA

S.H. Qing
Peking University
Beijing
China

S.M. Yiu
The University of Hong Kong
Hong Kong
China

ISSN 0302-9743   ISSN 1611-3349 (electronic)
Lecture Notes in Computer Science
ISBN 978-3-319-21965-3   ISBN 978-3-319-21966-0 (eBook)
DOI 10.1007/978-3-319-21966-0

Library of Congress Control Number: 2015944432

LNCS Sublibrary: SL4 – Security and Cryptology

Printed on acid-free paper

Springer International Publishing AG Switzerland is part of Springer Science+Business Media
(www.springer.com)

Preface

The ICICS conference series is a well-established forum for researchers in universities, research institutes, and industry to get together to share the latest research results and exchange ideas in the areas of information and communication security. ICICS has taken place in a number of different countries including China (1997, 2001, 2003, 2005, 2007, 2009, 2011, 2013), Australia (1999), Hong Kong (2012), Singapore (2002), Spain (2004, 2010), USA (2006), and UK (2008). This was the second time the ICICS conference (the 16th event in the series) was hosted by the Center for Information Security and Cryptography (CISC) of the University of Hong Kong (December 16–17, 2014). We received 87 submissions and the committee decided to accept 22 papers covering various aspects of information security. The program also included two remarkable invited talks given by Andrei Sabelfeld titled "Securing Web Applications" and by K.P. Chow titled "Occupy Central and Cyber Wars: The Technologies Behind the Political Event in Hong Kong."

We would like to thank all authors who submitted their papers to ICICS 2014 and the 33 Program Committee members as well as the external reviewers for their excellent work in reviewing the papers. We would also like to thank the Information Security and Forensics Society (ISFS), our co-organizer the Institute of Software of the Chinese Academy of Sciences (ISCAS), and the National Natural Science Foundation of China (Grant No. 61170282) for their valuable support and sponsorship. Last, but not the least, we give special thanks to the local organizing team led by Catherine Chan. The conference would not have been so successful without their assistance.

December 2014

Lucas C.K. Hui
S.H. Qing
Elaine Shi
S.M. Yiu

Organization

Program Committee

Man Ho Au	University of Wollongong, Australia
Alex Biryukov	University of Luxembourg
Zhenfu Cao	Shanghai Jiao Tong University, China
Chin-Chen Chang	Feng Chia University, Taiwan
Xiaolin Chang	Beijing Jiaotong University, China
Kefei Chen	Shanghai Jiaotong University, China
Zhong Chen	Peking University, China
Tat Wing Chim	The University of Hong Kong, SAR China
Sherman S.M. Chow	Chinese University of Hong Kong, SAR China
Cas Cremers	University of Oxford, UK
Reza Curtmola	New Jersey Institute of Technology, USA
Dieter Gollmann	Hamburg University of Technology, Germany
Hsu-Chun Hsiao	National Taiwan University, Taiwan
Kwangjo Kim	KAIST, South Korea
Tiffany Kim	HRL Laboratories, USA
Ming Li	Utah State University, USA
Joseph Liu	Institute for Infocomm Research, Singapore
Di Ma	University of Michigan-Dearborn, USA
Damon McCoy	George Mason University, USA
Andrew Miller	University of Maryland, USA
Chris Mitchell	Royal Holloway, University of London, UK
Raphael C.-W. Phan	Loughborough University, UK
Pierangela Samarati	Università degli Studi di Milano, Italy
Elaine Shi	University of Maryland, USA
Willy Susilo	University of Wollongong, Australia
Abhradeep Thakurta	Pennsylvania State University, USA
Wen-Guey Tzeng	National Chiao Tung University, Taiwan
Zhihui Wang	Dalian University of Technology, China
Andreas Wespi	IBM Zurich Research Laboratory, Switzerland
Yang Xiang	Deakin University, Australia
S.M. Yiu	The University of Hong Kong, SAR China
Shucheng Yu	University of Arkansas at Little Rock, USA
Tsz Hon Yuen	The University of Hong Kong, SAR China
Fangguo Zhang	Sun Yat-sen University, China
Jianqing Zhang	Intel
Wen Tao Zhu	Institute of Information Engineering, Chinese Academy of Sciences, China

Additional Reviewers

Bassily, Raef
Chow, Sherman S.M.
Dai, Shuguang
Derbez, Patrick
Ding, Daniel C.
Dixit, Kashyap
Dong, Xiaolei
Fan, Xiong
Han, Jinguang
Horvat, Marko
Huang, Xinyi
Khovratovich, Dmitry
Lai, Russell W.F.
Li, Huige
Li, Yanlin
Liang, Kaitai
Liu, Feng-Hao
Liu, Zhen
Livraga, Giovanni
Mohassel, Payman
Pan, Jiaxin
Pelosi, Gerardo

Peris-Lopez, Pedro
Perrin, Léo
Phong, Le Trieu
Pustogarov, Ivan
Servant, Victor
Shao, Jun
Sharad, Kumar
Velichkov, Vesselin
Wang, Boyang
Wang, Meiqin
Wang, Xinlei
Wang, Yang
Wei, Yongzhuang
Xiong, Weiwei
Xue, Hui
Yeh, Kuo-Hui
Zhang, Huang
Zhang, Kai
Zhang, Tao
Zhang, Yuexin
Zhao, Yongjun

Contents

Error-Tolerant Algebraic Side-Channel Attacks Using BEE

Ling Song[1,2,4(✉)], Lei Hu[1,2], Siwei Sun[1,2], Zhang Zhang[3], Danping Shi[1,2], and Ronglin Hao[1,2]

[1] State Key Laboratory of Information Security, Institute of Information Engineering, Chinese Academy of Sciences, Beijing 100093, China
{lsong,hu,swsun,dpshi,rlhao}@is.ac.cn
[2] Data Assurance and Communication Security Research Center, Chinese Academy of Sciences, Beijing 100093, China
[3] Institute of Information Engineering, Chinese Academy of Sciences, Beijing 100093, China
zhangzhang@iie.ac.cn
[4] University of Chinese Academy of Sciences, Beijing 100049, China

Abstract. Algebraic side-channel attacks are a type of side-channel analysis which can recover the secret information with a small number of samples (e.g., power traces). However, this type of side-channel analysis is sensitive to measurement errors which may make the attacks fail. In this paper, we propose a new method of algebraic side-channel attacks which considers noisy leakages as integers restricted to intervals and finds out the secret information with the help of a constraint programming compiler named BEE. To demonstrate the efficiency of this new method in algebraic side-channel attacks, we analyze some popular implementations of block ciphers—PRESENT, AES, and SIMON under the Hamming weight or Hamming distance leakage model. For AES, our method requires the least leakages compared with existing works under the same error model. For both PRESENT and SIMON, we provide the first analytical results of them under algebraic side-channel attacks in the presence of errors. To further demonstrate the wide applicability of this new method, we also extend it to cold boot attacks. In the cold boot attacks against AES, our method increases the success rate by over 25 % than previous works.

Keywords: Algebraic side-channel attack · Hamming weight leakage · Error-tolerance · Cold boot attack

1 Introduction

In recent years side-channel cryptanalysis has been an active topic of cryptanalysis, in which an attacker targets a certain implementation of a cipher and exploits the physical information during the encryption of the cipher such as computation traces and power traces. In 2002 Suresh Chari et al. proposed template attacks [9]

© Springer International Publishing Switzerland 2015
L.C.K. Hui et al. (Eds.): ICICS 2014, LNCS 8958, pp. 1–15, 2015.
DOI: 10.1007/978-3-319-21966-0_1

which are usually considered as the most powerful type of side-channel attacks in an information theoretical sense, since a template attack only requires minimum traces.

Combining template attacks with algebraic cryptanalysis, Renauld and Standaert proposed algebraic side-channel cryptanalysis [25]. Their analysis composes of two stages. First, the implementation of the cipher is profiled in advance as a template, and a decoding process is devised to map a single power consumption trace or electromagnetic trace to a vector of leaks (e.g., the Hamming weight) on the intermediate values of the encryption of the cipher. In the second stage, the cipher as well as the leaks is represented with a system of equations and the system is solved with a SAT solver, assuming the leaks derived from the first stage are accurate.

In fact, due to interference and the limitations of measurement setups, the side-channel information usually involves noise. However, the algebraic cryptanalysis is sensitive to errors and even small errors may make the key recovery attack fail, i.e., the attack finds no or wrong solutions. In the literature, there are several works that have explored error-tolerant algebraic side-channel attacks under some leakage models like Hamming weight leakage model. In [23], a cryptosystem and the corresponding Hamming weight leakages are transformed naturally into a pseudo-Boolean optimization (PBOPT) problem which was then solved with the mixed integer programming (MIP) solver SCIP [5]. Nevertheless, the method in [23] can not fully attack AES in the presence of errors. Later, an enhanced error-tolerant algebraic side-channel attack named MDASCA was introduced in [30], where the leakage is treated as a set of values rather than a single value, so that the correct leakage can be included with great confidence. In MDASCA, the cryptosystem and leakages are transformed into Conjunctive Normal Form (CNF) and then solved with a SAT solver. The MDASCA method outperforms the the SCIP-based method in [23] in dealing with errors. More techniques under a framework similar to MDASCA were discussed in [21].

Our Contribution. Inspired by the idea of MDASCA that models the leakage as a set of values to trade robustness for informativeness, we propose a new method of algebraic side-channel attacks that considers noisy leakages as integers restricted to an interval and finds secret information with BEE (Ben-Gurion Equi-propagation Encoder) [4,20]. BEE is a constraint programming compiler for problems represented with Boolean variables and integer variables and provides a high-level descriptive language for use and automatically generates low-level executable CNF for the underlying SAT solver. Using this method, we analyze some popular implementations for three block ciphers—PRESENT, AES and SIMON under the Hamming weight or Hamming distance leakage model where side-channel leakages are modeled as integers (constraints for BEE). We provide the first analytical results of PRESENT and SIMON under the Hamming weight and the Hamming distance leakage model respectively in the presence of errors, and our attack against the AES is better than MDASCA and other existing attacks under the same error model with respect to the error-tolerance and leakages required.

To further show the flexibility of the new method in algebraic side-channel attacks, we extend its use in cold boot attacks [15] and also other applications where the side-channel information can be described as *constraints* for BEE. In the cold boot attacks against AES, our method increases the success rate by over 25 % than previous works. Furthermore, all of our experiments are done within several seconds even in the worst case.

Organization. The paper is organized as follows. We briefly describe the process of our method of algebraic side-channel attacks using BEE in Sect. 2 and present algebraic side-channel attacks on two block ciphers in Sect. 3. In Sect. 4 we extend the use of our method into cold boot attacks and other attacks, and discuss the features of BEE in Sect. 5. Finally, we conclude the paper in the last section.

2 Algebraic Side-Channel Attacks Using BEE

In this section, we elaborate on the new method of algebraic side-channel attacks using BEE. As can be seen in Fig. 1, an attacker needs to build a system of polynomial equations from the target cipher, and then add the side-channel information he obtained to the equation system as constraints and solve it to recover the secret key. A more detailed description is provided below.

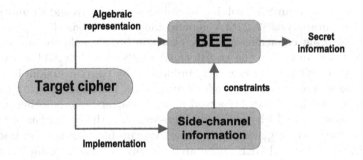

Fig. 1. Algebraic side-channel attacks using BEE

2.1 Building an Equation System

Theoretically, each cipher can be represented with a system of Boolean polynomial equations which involve the bits of the cipher key, plaintext and ciphertext as unknown variables. However, since a block cipher usually iterates a nonlinear function many times (e.g., AES iterates 10 or more rounds), it is unlikely to obtain a low degree polynomial representation on the bits of the cipher key, plaintext and ciphertext. To get a system of low degree Boolean equations, intermediate variables (e.g., standing for input and output bits of the nonlinear operations in intermediate round operations) are needed. To build quadratic equations for the nonlinear layer composed of S-boxes, techniques in [6,10,18] can be referred.

2.2   Extracting Side-Channel Information

Usually, it is difficult to solve the system of polynomial equations of a block cipher even when the plaintext and ciphertext are known, since there are too many unknown variables in the system [10]. However, under the circumstance of a side-channel attack, partial information related to the key, plaintext or ciphertext may be known, e.g., physical leakage of the intermediate states in the encryption or key schedule of a block cipher, and this so-called side-channel information can be plugged into the equation system to help to solve it. Unfortunately, the side-channel information usually involves noise in practice, which may make the attack fail, i.e., the attacker finds no or wrong solutions.

To deal with the noise, it is needed to profile a device (similar to the target one) which executes the encryptions and modulates the measurement errors in advance. Once the leakages of the target device are obtained, the side-channel information can be added to the equation system in an error-tolerant way according to a priori error model. In this paper we assume that the error model has been built and the leakages can be extracted in some way. Hence, we focus on the procedure of solving the system of equations and noisy side-channel information.

2.3   Solving the System of Equations and Noisy Side-Channel Information with BEE

In recent years, Boolean SAT solving techniques were improved dramatically in the field of cryptanalysis [2, 22]. A general idea of SAT-based cryptanalysis is to encode algebraic equations (usually over the binary field $\mathbb{F}_2$) into Boolean formulae in CNF and solve the transformed problem with a SAT solver. Since the efficiency of SAT solving is greatly influenced by the conversion, it is crucial to choose proper conversion methods. Truth table, Karnaugh map [17] and the methods proposed in [2] can be served as such conversions. Another way is to use a SAT-based tool which provides a high-level descriptive language for problems and automatically generates low-level executable files for the underlying SAT solver. STP [14] and BEE [4, 20] are this sort of known examples. In these tools specific techniques are used to optimize the problem before invoking the underlying SAT solver.

BEE is a compiler in constraint programming which facilitates users to translate problem instances involving Boolean and integral variables into CNF. The generated CNF is then solved by an underlying SAT solver such as CryptoMiniSat [27] and MiniSat [13]. A brief description of its syntax can be referred to [20]. Compared with a pure SAT solver, its ability to deal with integers and maintain the structure of the original problem instance opens a door for more complex applications.

For example, in an algebraic side-channel attack under the Hamming weight leakage model, a byte $X = x_7 x_6 \cdots x_0$ with x_0 as the least significant bit and its Hamming weight can be represented in the BEE syntax as

$$\text{new\_int}(I, w - i, w + j),$$
$$\text{bool\_array\_sum\_eq}([x_0, x_1, x_2, x_3, x_4, x_5, x_6, x_7], I),$$

where the i and j in the first sentence are used to define the interval of integer I around the most likely value w which includes the correct Hamming weight of X with great confidence, and the second sentence represents the Hamming weight of X as I. With additional information of the Hamming weight, the whole equation system of the target cipher ended with the functional sentence as *solve satisfy* can be fed into BEE, and BEE returns an assignment or reports UNSAT. Other functional sentences *solve minimize w* or *solve maximize w* can also be used, which means BEE returns UNSAT or solutions that minimize or maximize the objective integer variable w.

Hence, as long as the side-channel information can be modeled as integers, i.e. constraints that speeds up the solving or narrows solution space, BEE works well. However, when the side-channel information is modeled as integers, noise should be considered, that is to say, each integer should be defined with an interval or a set rather than a specific value in order to trade robustness for informativeness.

3   Algebraic Side-Channel Attacks Under the Hamming Weight Leakage Model

In this section we explain the efficiency of our method through algebraic side-channel attacks against some popular implementations where the Hamming weight (distance) leakage model can be built. Our examples are PRESENT-80 [7], AES-128 [11] and SIMON-32 [3] (in Appendix B). In these examples we assume that the noisy Hamming weight or Hamming distance information during the encryption is obtained (no leakage during the key schedule of the cipher), and we focus on solving the corresponding equation system with our new method.

To begin with, we introduce the notion of *offset*, standing for the offset of the measured Hamming weight (or Hamming distance) from the correct one. For simplicity, we only consider three typical cases with offset 0, ± 1 and ± 2, and denote them as offset = 0, offset = 1 and offset = 2. More general offsets can also be analyzed. Obviously, larger offsets tolerate greater noise, so the offset is determined by the error model of the template.

3.1   PRESENT-80

PRESENT is a cipher with substitution-permutation network and with a block size of 64 bits [7]. The recommended size for the key is 80 bits, while 128-bit keys are also suggested. In this paper we just analyze PRESENT-80, the version with 80-bit keys.

The encryption of PRESENT-80 is composed of 31 rounds, each of which consists of an XOR operation to introduce a round key K_i for $1 \leq i \leq 31$, a linear bitwise permutation and a nonlinear substitution layer which parallelly applies a 4-bit S-box 16 times. An additional round key K_{32} is used for post-whitening.

Both the encryption and key schedule of PRESENT-80 are simple with respect to algebraic representations. In our attack, each S-box is described with four equations as shown in Appendix A. Since the algebraic representations of the S-boxes are the most complex part of the equation system, we introduce new variables for the input and output bits of each S-box to get low degree polynomial equations. In this way we get a system of 4276 equations in 4292 variables.

For an implementation of PRESENT-80 in a PIC 16F877 8-bit RISC-based microcontroller, a measurement setup described in [28] can be exploited to extract a power consumption that strongly correlates with the Hamming weight of the data manipulated. This is also the model used in [25] where the Hamming weight of the data commuting on the bus is indicated to be recovered with a probability of 0.986. In this implementation, the whole encryption of a single plaintext leaks the Hamming weight information corresponding to the computation of $2 \times 8 \times 31$ bytes.

Let us first consider the case that the accurate Hamming weight information can be recovered, and then move on to other cases of inaccurate Hamming weight information. All of our experiments are conducted with MiniSat as the underlying solver of BEE on a PC with 3.4 GHz CPU (only one core is used) and 4 GB Memory. All solving times are given in seconds and are averaged over on 50 random instances.

For accurate Hamming weight information, it can be added to the equation system as constraints in the way described in Sect. 2 with $i = j = 0$. Following [25], we consider four different attack scenarios according to known/unknown plaintext-ciphertext pairs and consecutive/random Hamming weight leakages. Table 1 lists the solving times using one trace compared with [25] when a 100 % success rate is reached, where "#rounds" means the number of rounds which are observed in the side-channel information, and the leakage rate means the ratio between the number of leaked bytes and the number of all bytes in the measured rounds. Thus, 50 % indicates random leakages and 100 % infers to consecutive leakages.

According to Table 1, our attack requires less leakages than [25]. However, under the unknown plaintext and ciphertext scenario with random leakages, our attack fails and the experiments ran overtime.

Next, we consider the cases where the Hamming weight leakages are noisy with offset = 1 and offset = 2. Table 2 exhibits the experimental results under known plaintext/ciphertext scenario. If the leakages are consecutive, two traces are enough to retrieve the cipher key within an hour even when the offset is ± 2. For the case that offset = 2 and the leakage rate is 0.7, three traces are required. For unknown plaintext/ciphertext scenario, it takes a very long time to return a solution.

3.2   AES-128

The block cipher AES-128 [11] accepts 128-bit blocks and 128-bit keys and iterates 10 rounds. Each round, except the last one, consists of four operations— AddRoundKey, SubByte, ShiftRow and MixColumn. The last round omits the

Table 1. Experimental results of PRESENT-80 with a single trace when offset = 0. Experiments in [25] were performed on an Intel-based server with a Xeon E5420 processor cadenced at 2.5 GHz running a linux 32-bit 2.6 Kernel.

Scenario	leakage rate	[25]		this paper	
		#rounds	time (s)	#rounds	time(s)
known P/C	100 %	8	79.69	2.5	0.21
known P/C	50 %	18	117.10	5	104.31
unknown P/C	100 %	8	45.59	4.5	92.55
unknown P/C	50 %	26	214.12	> 8	> 3600

Table 2. Experimental results of PRESENT-80 when offset = 1,2

Scenarios	offset	leakage rate	#rounds	#traces	time (s)
known P/C	1	100 %	4	2	6.86
known P/C	1	50 %	4	2	39.40
known P/C	2	100 %	5	2	3084.39
known P/C	2	70 %	4	3	33.27

MixColumn operation. The SubByte operation applies an 8-bit S-box 16 times in parallel and is the only nonlinear operation in AES.

In order to represent AES as a system of low degree Boolean polynomial equations, we introduce new variables for both the input bits and output bits of SubByte and apply the technique proposed in [10] to describe the S-box with 23 quadratic equations. Then the key schedule algorithm and the encryption of a plaintext can be represented with a system of 6296 equations in 3168 variables.

For an 8-bit PIC microcontroller implementation of AES, there are 84 Hamming weight leakages in each round corresponding to 16 weights in AddRoundKey, 16 weights in SubBytes and $4 \cdot 13$ weights in MixColumn [21,23,26,30]. The work in [26] is the first algebraic side-channel attack against AES, which showed how the keys can be recovered from a single measurement trace, provided that the attacker can identify the correct Hamming weight leakages of several intermediate computations during the encryption process. Later, Zhao el al. proposed an enhanced method named MDASCA to deal with the noise in measurement using a set rather than a single value to describe the Hamming weight [30]. More elaborate techniques in a framework similar to MDASCA were discussed in [21]. Recently, a novel method that models the cipher and the template as a graph and finds the most possible key with a decoding algorithm from low-density parity check codes was proposed in [32].

Following the notations in the previous subsections, we give our experimental results on AES comparing with two latest works [21,30]. The experiments are carried out with CryptoMiniSat as the underlying solver of BEE on a PC with 3.4 GHz CPU (only one core is used) and 4 GB Memory. The results are summarized in Table 3. It shows the method in [30] outperforms that of [21],

Table 3. Experimental results of AES-128. The symbol "-" indicates that no related information was provided. The experiments of [30] were ran on an AMD Athlon 64 Dual core 3600+ processor clocked at 2.0 GHz. All solving times are given in seconds.

Scenario	offset	leakage rate	[25] #rounds	time	[30] #rounds	time	this paper #rounds	time
known P/C	0	100 %	2	-	1	10	1	2.74
known P/C	0	50 %	10	-	5	120	3	118.00
unknown P/C	0	100 %	5	-	2	10	2	6.75
unknown P/C	0	50 %	not clear	-	6	100	6	69.17
known P/C	1	100 %	-	-	2(2 traces)	120	2(2 traces)	37.11
							3	974.67
known P/C	2	100 %	-	-	-	-	1(3 traces)	33.29

while our attacks push the results of [30] further. Specifically, for offset = 1 our method can recover the secret key of AES using a single trace, less than what is needed in [30]. For a greater offset, offset = 2, only three traces are needed. Note that method in [32] also provides good results. In [32], the noise level is parameterized with signal-to-noise ratio, which makes it difficult to compare our results with that of [32].

4   Cold Boot Attacks and Other Applications

In general, we can feed into BEE any problem instance that can be solved by a SAT solver. In fact, BEE was designed for problems that are characterized by certain constraints, for example algebraic side-channel attacks under the Hamming weight leakage model. Besides this, BEE can also be applied in other algebraic attacks like cold boot attacks [15].

4.1   Cold Boot Attacks Against AES-128

Cold boot attacks were first proposed in [15]. In a cold boot attack, an attacker tries to recover the cryptographic key from DRAM based on the fact that the data may persist in memory for several minutes after removal of power by reducing the temperature of memory. For block ciphers, a cold boot attack is to recover the secret key from an observed set of the round keys in memory, which are disturbed by errors due to memory bit decay. From the point of view of algebraic analysis, the cold boot problem can be modeled as solving a polynomial system $\{f_1, f_2, \cdots, f_m\}$ with noise.

There are different methods proposed to tackle the cold boot problem [1,16]. In [1] a system of equations derived from the cold boot attack is solved with a mixed integer programming solver SCIP [5]. Specifically, for each f_i a new Boolean variable e_i is added, and then the system is converted to a mixed integer programming problem with Σe_i as the objective function. Hence, the cold boot problem turns to be a maximum satisfiability problem, which may also be solved with another method named ISBS [16]. The basic idea of ISBS is to solve the polynomial system $\{f_1 + e_1, f_2 + e_2, \cdots, f_m + e_m\}$ with the characteristic set method [29] by searching all $\{e_1, e_2, \cdots, e_m\}$. The solution with $\{e_1, e_2, \cdots, e_m\}$ achieving the smallest Hamming weight is the target solution.

Following the ideas of [1,16], BEE can be used instead in the following way. First, represent the polynomial system $\{f_1 + e_1, f_2 + e_2, \cdots, f_m + e_m\}$ with the BEE syntax, and introduce a new integer variable, say w, to describe the Hamming weight of $\{e_1, e_2, \cdots, e_m\}$, and then solve the problem with the BEE functional sentence as *solve minimize w*.

Before experimentally verifying the efficiency of BEE for solving cold boot problems, the bit decay model should be illuminated first. According to [15], bit decay in DRAM is usually asymmetric: bit flips $0 \to 1$ and $1 \to 0$ occur with different probabilities, depending on the ground state. Consider an efficiently computable vectorial Boolean function $\mathcal{KS} : \mathbb{F}_2^n \to \mathbb{F}_2^N$ where $N > n$, and two real numbers $0 \le \delta_0, \delta_1 \le 1$. Let $K = \mathcal{KS}(k)$ be the image for some $k \in \mathbb{F}_2^n$, and K_i be the i-th bit of K. Given K, we compute $K' = (K'_0, K'_1, \cdots, K'_{N-1}) \in \mathbb{F}_2^N$ according to the following probability distribution:

$$Pr[K'_i = 0 | K_i = 0] = 1 - \delta_1, Pr[K'_i = 1 | K_i = 0] = \delta_1,$$
$$Pr[K'_i = 1 | K_i = 1] = 1 - \delta_0, Pr[K'_i = 0 | K_i = 1] = \delta_0.$$

Therefore, K' can be considered as a noisy version of $K = \mathcal{KS}(k)$ for some unknown $k \in \mathbb{F}_2^n$, where the probability of a bit 1 in K flipping to 0 is δ_0 and the probability of a bit 0 in K flipping to 1 is δ_1.

In our experiments, the target is the key schedule of AES-128 and the same algebraic representation of the key schedule is used as in Subsect. 3.2. We set δ_1 to be 0.001 to generate the K' as in [1,16,31] and assume $\delta_1 = 0$ for solving the cold boot problem. Figure 2 shows the experimental success rate of key recovery of AES for different δ_0, compared with methods from [1,16] denoted as SCIP and ISBS respectively. It is manifest that BEE provides an increase over 25 % in success rate. The details of running time can be found in Appendix C which shows that BEE solves the problem in several seconds even when δ_0 increases to 0.5. This may be explained by the low nonlinearity of the key schedule of AES-128 and the optimization of BEE. The experiments also include the case where BEE simply takes the cold boot problem as a satisfiability problem denoted as "BEE satisfiability". If we use information of all rounds of the key schedule, this method almost corresponds to the method in [31] and the key can be recovered in 1.3 hours even when $\delta_0 = 0.8$.

4.2 Side-Channel Cube Attacks

Cube attacks were proposed by Dinur and Shamir at Eurocrypt 2009 [12]. It is a type of generic key recovery attacks applicable to any cryptosystem whose ciphertext bit can be represented by a low degree multivariate polynomial in the secret and public variables. The aim of a cube attack is to derive a system of

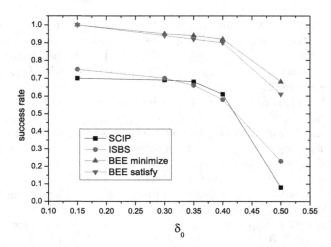

Fig. 2. Success rate of key recovery considering 4 rounds of key schedule output

linear or quadratic equations with the secret key bits as unknowns which can be solved easily. However, block ciphers tend to resist against cube attacks, since they iteratively apply a nonlinear round function a large number of times such that it is unlikely to obtain a low degree polynomial to represent any cipher-text bit.

Fortunately, in a side-channel attack where some intermediate variables leak, cube attacks are still useful [19]. Due to the side-channel noise, the derived equation system may contain errors, which resembles the situation in a cold boot attack. As a consequence, it is likely that our method can also be applied efficiently in side-channel cube attacks against block ciphers.

5   Discussion

We have introduced a new method of algebraic side-channel attacks that considers the noisy leakage as an integer restricted to an interval and finds secret information with the help of BEE, a compiler in constraint programming. We exemplified the efficiency of our method by analyzing some popular implementations of three block ciphers—PRESENT, AES and SIMON under the Hamming weight or Hamming distance leakage model. In addition we applied our method to cold boot attacks against AES.

As a new compiler for SAT problems, BEE can be added to the tool set for side-channel attacks. In the literature, SAT solvers usually outperform MIP solvers in cryptanalysis. For instance, an MIP solver determines the initial state of Bivium B [24] in $2^{63.7}$ seconds [8] while the MiniSat takes only $2^{42.7}$ seconds. For side-channel attacks in the presence of errors as mentioned above, the SAT-based BEE works better than the methods based on MIP solvers. It is likely that BEE has its own advantages for certain algebraic attacks. The feathers of our BEE-based method are summarized below.

- With the side-channel information modeled as constraints, BEE shows a widespread use in algebraic side-channel attacks, for example, side-channel attacks under Hamming weight leakage model, cold boot attacks and cube attacks.
- BEE, as a SAT-based tool, may outperform the tools based on MIP solvers in many classes of algebraic attacks.
- It is natural for use, and BEE can simplify constraints and optimizes the resulted CNF automatically.
- Algebraic side-channel attacks are more efficient than classical side-channel attacks like differential power attack (DPA) in respect of the number of traces needed.

6   Conclusion

In this paper we introduced a new method of algebraic side-channel attacks that treats the noisy leakage as an integer restricted to an interval and finds secret information with the help of BEE. We showed that this method is efficient and flexible.

We analyzed some popular implementations of PRESENT, AES and SIMON under the Hamming weight or Hamming distance leakage model to illustrate the efficiency of constraint programming in cryptanalysis. The results on AES are better than previous ones under the same error model and we provided the first analytical results on PRESENT and SIMON under the Hamming weight and Hamming distance leakage model respectively in the presence of errors.

To further show the flexibility of BEE in algebraic side-channel attacks, we extended its use in cold boot attacks. In the cold boot attacks against AES, our method provides an increase over 25 % in success rate and all of our attack experiments were done within seconds. It is also likely to apply our method in cube attacks and it is a future work to verify its efficiency experimentally in new applications.

Acknowledgement. The authors would like to thank Amit Metodi and Michael Codish for helping us in using BEE, and thank the anonymous reviewers for their valuable comments and suggestions. The work of this paper was supported by the National Key Basic Research Program of China (2013CB834203), the National Natural Science Foundation of China (Grants 61472417, 61472415, 61402469 and 61272477), the Strategic Priority Research Program of Chinese Academy of Sciences under Grant XDA06010702, and the State Key Laboratory of Information Security, Chinese Academy of Sciences.

Appendix

A   Equations of the S-Box in PRESENT

Suppose the input nibble of the 4-bit S-box in PRESENT is $X = x_3x_2x_1x_0$ and the output nibble is $Y = y_3y_2y_1y_0$. Then four Boolean polynomial equations on x_is and y_js are as follows.

$$x_0 + x_2 + x_1 x_2 + x_3 + y_0 = 0,$$
$$x_1 + x_0 x_1 x_2 + x_3 + x_1 x_3 + x_0 x_1 x_3 + x_2 x_3 + x_0 x_2 x_3 + y_1 = 0,$$
$$1 + x_0 x_1 + x_2 + x_3 + x_0 x_3 + x_1 x_3 + x_0 x_1 x_3 + x_0 x_2 x_3 + y_2 = 0,$$
$$1 + x_0 + x_1 + x_1 x_2 + x_0 x_1 x_2 + x_3 + x_0 x_1 x_3 + x_0 x_2 x_3 + y_3 = 0.$$

B   Algebraic Side-Channel Attack of SIMON-32 Under Hamming Distance Leakage Model

SIMON is a family of lightweight block ciphers designed by researchers from the National Security Agency (NSA) of the USA to provide an optimal hardware implementation performance [3]. SIMON comes in a variety of block sizes and key sizes. In this section we analyze its smallest version, SIMON-32, which accepts 64-bit keys and 32-bit blocks and iterates 32 rounds.

The design of SIMON follows a classical Feistel structure, operating on two n-bit halves in each round. For SIMON-32, n is 16. The round function makes use of three n-bit operations: XOR ($\oplus$), AND ($\&$) and circular shift ($\lll$), and given a round key k it is defined on two inputs x and y as

$$R_k(x, y) = (y \oplus f(x) \oplus k, x),$$

where $f(x) = ((x \lll 1) \& (x \lll 8)) \oplus (x \lll 2)$. The key schedule algorithm of SIMON is a linear transformation.

The algebraic representation of SIMON is intuitive due to the simplicity of the round function. We introduce new variables for the intermediate state after each round operation in both the encryption and key schedule algorithm. Consequently, a system of 960 equations in 992 variables is built from the encryption of a single plaintext and the key scheduling.

A typical implementation of SIMON is based on ASIC [3] which leaks the Hamming distance between the input and the output of the round function. The Hamming distance varies from 0 to 16. Following the attacks on PRESENT and AES, we consider the measured Hamming distance, compared with the correct one, to be with a small offset offset = 0,1,2.

Table 4 exhibits our results of experiments running on a PC with 2.83 GHz CPU (only one core is used) and 3.25 GB Memory with CryptoMiniSat as the underlying solver of BEE, where all solving times are given in seconds and are averaged over 50 random instances. Our attacks are performed under the known plaintext or known ciphertext scenario and there is no difference between them. For offset=0, the BEE works seriously overtime with only one trace and 5 traces are advisable to recover the key within a proper time. For offset=2, as many as 13 traces are required. It is observed that the Hamming distances leaked near the known plaintext or ciphertext is more useful than the ones in the middle for solving the system in a reasonable time. Note that more traces are required for attacking SIMON-32 than for AES or PRESENT. This is because the Hamming distance leakages on 16-bit states provide less information than that on 8-bit states.

Table 4. Experimental results of SIMON-32

offset	#traces	#rounds	time (s)
0	5	6	36.32
1	11	7	386.34
2	13	8	320.11

C   Running Time of Cold Boot Attack against AES-128

In this appendix the running time of the cold boot attack against AES-128 is shown in Table 5, where "SCIP" stands for the method in [1]; "ISBS" represents the method in [16]; "BEE min." and "BEE sat." are methods in this paper and short for "BEE minimize" and "BEE satisfiability" respectively. Our experiments are carried out with CryptoMiniSat as the underlying solver of BEE on a PC with 3.4 GHz CPU (only one core is used) and 4 GB Memory. Experiments of "SCIP" and "ISBS" are conducted on PCs with 2.6 Ghz and 2.8 Ghz respectively.

Table 5. The running time of key recovery considering 4 rounds of key schedule output of AES-128 (in seconds)

δ_0	Method	limit t	min t	avg. t	max t
0.15	SCIP	60	1.78	11.77	59.16
	ISBS	60	0.002	0.07	0.15
	BEE min.	60	1.29	2.02	2.36
	BEE sat.	60	1.25	1.94	2.33
0.30	SCIP	3600	4.86	117.68	719.99
	ISBS	3600	0.002	0.14	2.38
	BEE min.	60	1.34	2.15	2.64
	BEE sat.	60	1.34	2.27	2.55
0.35	SCIP	3600	4.45	207.07	1639.55
	ISBS	3600	0.002	0.27	7.87
	BEE min.	60	1.41	2.10	2.76
	BEE sat.	60	1.42	2.34	2.59
0.40	SCIP	3600	4.97	481.99	3600
	ISBS	3600	0.002	0.84	20.30
	BEE min.	60	1.48	2.44	3.34
	BEE sat.	60	1.44	2.43	3.11
0.50	SCIP	3600	6.57	3074.36	3600
	ISBS	3600	0.002	772.02	3600
	BEE min.	60	1.47	1.94	4.18
	BEE sat.	60	1.62	2.82	3.94

References

1. Albrecht, M., Cid, C.: Cold boot key recovery by solving polynomial systems with noise. In: Lopez, J., Tsudik, G. (eds.) ACNS 2011. LNCS, vol. 6715, pp. 57–72. Springer, Heidelberg (2011)
2. Bard, G., Courtois, N., Jefferson, C.: Efficient methods for conversion and solution of sparse systems of low-degree multivariate polynomial over GF(2) via SAT-solvers. In: IACR Cryptology ePrint Archive, no. 024 (2007)
3. Beaulieu, R., Shors, D., Smith, J., Treatman-Clark, S., Weeks, B., Wingers, L.: The SIMON and SPECK Families of Lightweight Block Ciphers. Cryptology ePrint Archive, Report 2013/404 (2013). http://eprint.iacr.org/
4. BEE. http://amit.metodi.me/research/bee/
5. Berthold, T., Heinz, S., Pfetsch, M.E., Winkler, M.: SCIP C solving constraint integer programs. In: SAT 2009 Competitive Events Booklet (2009)
6. Biryukov, A., De Cannière, C.: Block ciphers and systems of quadratic equations. In: Johansson, T. (ed.) FSE 2003. LNCS, vol. 2887, pp. 274–289. Springer, Heidelberg (2003)
7. Bogdanov, A.A., Knudsen, L.R., Leander, G., Paar, C., Poschmann, A., Robshaw, M., Seurin, Y., Vikkelsoe, C.: PRESENT: an ultra-lightweight block cipher. In: Paillier, P., Verbauwhede, I. (eds.) CHES 2007. LNCS, vol. 4727, pp. 450–466. Springer, Heidelberg (2007)
8. Borghoff, J., Knudsen, L.R., Stolpe, M.: Bivium as a mixed-integer linear programming problem. In: Parker, M.G. (ed.) Cryptography and Coding 2009. LNCS, vol. 5921, pp. 133–152. Springer, Heidelberg (2009)
9. Chari, S., Rao, J.R., Rohatgi, P.: Template attacks. In: Kaliski Jr., B.S., Koç, Ç.K., Paar, C. (eds.) Cryptographic Hardware and Embedded Systems - CHES 2002, vol. 2523, pp. 13–28. Springer, Heidelberg (2003)
10. Courtois, N.T., Pieprzyk, J.: Cryptanalysis of block ciphers with overdefined systems of equations. In: Zheng, Y. (ed.) ASIACRYPT 2002. LNCS, vol. 2501, pp. 267–287. Springer, Heidelberg (2002)
11. Daemen, J., Rijmen, V.: AES Proposal: Rijndael (1998)
12. Dinur, I., Shamir, A.: Cube attacks on tweakable black box polynomials. In: Joux, A. (ed.) EUROCRYPT 2009. LNCS, vol. 5479, pp. 278–299. Springer, Heidelberg (2009)
13. Een, N., Sorensson, N.: MiniSat v1.13 - A SAT Solver with Conflict-Clause Minimization(2005). http://minisatsePapers.html
14. Ganesh, V., Dill, D.L.: A decision procedure for bit-vectors and arrays. In: Damm, W., Hermanns, H. (eds.) CAV 2007. LNCS, vol. 4590, pp. 524–536. Springer, Heidelberg (2007)
15. Halderman, J.A., Schoen, S.D., Heninger, N., Clarkson, W., Paul, W., Calandrino, J.A., Feldman, A.J., Appelbaum, J., Felten, E.W.: Lest we remember: lest we remember: cold boot attacks on encryption keys. In: USENIX Security Symposium, pp. 45–60. USENIX Association (2009)
16. Huang, Z., Lin, D.: A new method for solving polynomial systems with noise over $\mathbb{F}_2$ and its applications in cold boot key recovery. In: Knudsen, L.R., Wu, H. (eds.) SAC 2012. LNCS, vol. 7707, pp. 16–33. Springer, Heidelberg (2013)
17. Karnaugh, M.: The map method for synthesis of combinational logic circuits. AIEE Trans. Commun. Electron. **72**(9), 593–599 (1953)
18. Knudsen, L.R., Miolane, C.V.: Counting equations in algebraic attacks on block ciphers. Int. J. Inf. Secur. **9**(2), 127–135 (2010)

19. Li, Z., Zhang, B., Fan, J., Verbauwhede, I.: A new model for error-tolerant side-channel cube attacks. In: Bertoni, G., Coron, J.-S. (eds.) CHES 2013. LNCS, vol. 8086, pp. 453–470. Springer, Heidelberg (2013)
20. Metodi, A., Codish, M.: Compiling finite domain constraints to SAT with BEE. TPLP **12**(4–5), 465–483 (2012)
21. Mohamed, M.S.E., Bulygin, S., Zohner, M., Heuser, A., Walter, M., Buchmann, J.: Improved algebraic side-channel attack on AES. In: IEEE HOST 2012, pp. 146–151 (2012)
22. Mouha, N., Preneel, B.: Towards finding optimal differential characteristics for ARX: application to salsa20. In: IACR Cryptology ePrint Archive, no. 328 (2013)
23. Oren, Y., Kirschbaum, M., Popp, T., Wool, A.: Algebraic side-channel analysis in the presence of errors. In: Mangard, S., Standaert, F.-X. (eds.) CHES 2010. LNCS, vol. 6225, pp. 428–442. Springer, Heidelberg (2010)
24. Raddum, H.: Cryptanalytic results on Trivium. eSTREAM report 2006/039 (2006). http://www.ecrypt.eu.org/stream/triviump3.html
25. Renauld, M., Standaert, F.-X.: Algebraic side-channel attacks. In: Bao, F., Yung, M., Lin, D., Jing, J. (eds.) Inscrypt 2009. LNCS, vol. 6151, pp. 393–410. Springer, Heidelberg (2010)
26. Renauld, M., Standaert, F.-X., Veyrat-Charvillon, N.: Algebraic side-channel attacks on the AES: why time also matters in DPA. In: Clavier, C., Gaj, K. (eds.) CHES 2009. LNCS, vol. 5747, pp. 97–111. Springer, Heidelberg (2009)
27. Soos, M., Nohl, K., Castelluccia, C.: Extending SAT solvers to cryptographic problems. In: Kullmann, O. (ed.) SAT 2009. LNCS, vol. 5584, pp. 244–257. Springer, Heidelberg (2009)
28. Standaert, F.-X., Archambeau, C.: Using subspace-based template attacks to compare and combine power and electromagnetic information leakages. In: Oswald, E., Rohatgi, P. (eds.) CHES 2008. LNCS, vol. 5154, pp. 411–425. Springer, Heidelberg (2008)
29. Wu, W.T.: Basic principles of mechanical theorem-proving in elementary geometries. J. Autom. Reasoning **2**, 221–252 (1986)
30. Zhao, X., Zhang, F., Guo, S., Wang, T., Shi, Z., Liu, H., Ji, K.: MDASCA: an enhanced algebraic side-channel attack for error tolerance and new leakage model exploitation. In: Schindler, W., Huss, S.A. (eds.) COSADE 2012. LNCS, vol. 7275, pp. 231–248. Springer, Heidelberg (2012)
31. Kamal, A.A., Youssef, A.M.: Applications of SAT solvers to AES key recovery from decayed key schedule images. In: Proceedings of the Fourth International Conference on Emerging Security Information, Systems and Technologies, SECURWARE 2010, Venice/Mestre, Italy, July 18–25 (2010)
32. Veyrat-Charvilon, N., Gérard, B., Standaert, F.-X.: Soft Analytical Side-Channel Attacks. Cryptology ePrint Archive, Report 2014/410 (2014). http://eprint.iacr.org/

SEDB: Building Secure Database Services
for Sensitive Data

Quanwei Cai[1,2,3], Jingqiang Lin[1,2(✉)], Fengjun Li[4], and Qiongxiao Wang[1,2]

[1] State Key Laboratory of Information Security, Institute of Information
Engineering, Chinese Academy of Sciences, Beijing 100093, China
{qwcai,linjq,qxwang}@is.ac.cn
[2] Data Assurance and Communication Security Research Center,
Chinese Academy of Sciences, Beijing 100093, China
[3] University of Chinese Academy of Sciences, Beijing 100049, China
[4] The University of Kansas, Lawrence, KS 66045, USA
fli@ku.edu

Abstract. Database outsourcing reduces the cost of data management;
however, the confidentiality of the outsourced data is a main challenge.
Existing solutions [9,13,16,17] either adopt multiple encryption schemes
for data confidentiality that only support limited operations, or focus
on providing efficient retrieval with problematic update support. In this
paper, we propose a secure database outsourcing scheme (SEDB) based
on Shamir's threshold secret sharing for practical confidentiality against
honest-but-curious database servers. SEDB supports a set of commonly
used operations, such as addition, subtraction, and comparison, and is
among the first to support multiplication, division, and modulus. We
implement a prototype of SEDB, and the experiment results demonstrate
a reasonable processing overhead.

Keywords: Database · Outsourcing · Confidentiality · Secret sharing

1 Introduction

In the cloud computing environment, database outsourcing can lower costs [4],
thus enables organizations to focus on their core businesses. However, outsouring
sensitive data to the third parties increases the risk of unauthorized disclosure,
as curious administrators can snoop on sensitive data, and attackers can access
all the outsourced data once it compromises the data servers.

There are two approaches to provide confidentiality in database outsouring.
One is based on client-side encryption, where the clients (or proxies) encrypt
the data before uploading it to database servers so that the servers perform the
requested operations over the encrypted data. Fully homomorphic encryption [6]
allows the servers to execute arbitrary functions over one encryption of the data.
However, fully homomorphic encryption is still prohibitive impractical [7], which
requires slowdowns on the order of $10^9 \times$. CryptDB [13] and MONOMI [17]
implement multiple cryptosystems, each of which supports a class of SQL queries,

© Springer International Publishing Switzerland 2015
L.C.K. Hui et al. (Eds.): ICICS 2014, LNCS 8958, pp. 16–30, 2015.
DOI: 10.1007/978-3-319-21966-0_2

such as AES with a variant of the CMC mode [10] for equality comparison, order-preserving encryption [3] for range query, Paillier cryptosystem [12] for summation, and the efficient retrieval protocol [15] for word search. As a result, they have to maintain multiple copies of a same sensitive data. Moreover, these schemes do not support the update operation well. For instance, when the data is updated by summation, only the copy encrypted with Paillier cryptosystem will be updated while the other copies remain stale, which harms the execution of other queries. Last but not least, these schemes cannot support operations such as multiplication, division, and modulus.

The other solutions are based on threshold secret sharing [14] in which the clients split the sensitive data into shares and store them in independent servers. Solutions of this category require more servers than the encryption-based ones do. However, with the advances in virtualization, the hardware cost has been decreased remarkably. It is believed that the implementation cost should not be the main obstacle to the adoption of these solutions. Several schemes are proposed to achieve efficient retrieval. For example, AS5 [9] preserves the order of the data in the shares by choosing appropriate coefficients of the polynomial for secret sharing, and a B^+ index tree is built to improve the query processing in [16]. With a focus on efficient retrieval, these solutions not only require a priori knowledge about the data, but also support the update operations poorly.

In this paper, we proposed a secure database outsourcing scheme (SEDB) based on Shamir's threshold secret sharing. SEDB employs three independent database servers to store shares of each sensitive data item, and coordinates the three servers to complete the clients' requested operations cooperatively. In summary, SEDB achieves the following properties:

- It supports a wider set of operations including multiplication, division and modulus in addition to addition, subtraction and comparison. To the best of our knowledge, it is the first practical solution that supports these operations.
- SEDB is easy to deploy as it is an out-of-the-box solution. SEDB doesn't needs any modification on the database management system (DBMS) or the applications of database services. Moreover, SEDB doesn't need any priori knowledge of the data for the setup of the database services.
- It provides a continuous database outsourcing service. Existing encryption-based solutions requires costly and problematic coordination to keep multiple copies of data consistent, and the secret sharing based solutions often need to maintain additional information (e.g., the index tree [16], the mapping [1,9]), which may interrupt the database services during data update. Unlike them, SEDB only maintains one share of the data at each database server, and thus ensures a continuous database outsourcing service. We have implemented SEDB on MySQL, which is the first prototype providing continuous database outsourcing services based on secret sharing, to the best of our knowledge.

2   System Overview

As shown in Fig. 1, SEDB consists of three backend database servers, a SEDB coordinator, and a set of SEDB client plug-ins (denoted as SEDB plug-ins), one

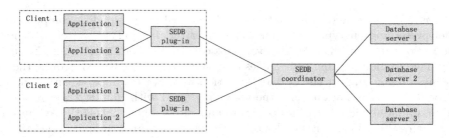

Fig. 1. The architecture of SEDB.

at each client. A client has several applications of the database service. When an application issues an SQL query, the SEDB plug-in rewrites the query according to its operation type and sends it to the SEDB coorinator which generates three SQL queries from it and distributes each to the backend database server. There is an unmodified DBMS and several user-defined functions (UDFs) in each backend database server, which executes the requested operations over the shares of sensitive data. In SEDB, the applications need no modification to execute the functions over sensitive data, they issues the SQL queries through the standard API and library; the SEDB plug-in is responsible for sharing sensitive data and recovering it for the applications; the SEDB coordinator ensures the requets processed at each database server in the same order and makes the backend database servers complete the requested operation through one or two phases of communications with the database servers.

Trust Model. In SEDB, we assume the clients that are authorized to process the sensitive data are trusted. The SEDB plug-in deployed at client side is also trusted and assumed to follow the protocol strictly without leaking any sensitive data. On the contrary, the SEDB coordinator and the backend database servers deployed at different third parties are assumed to be honest-but-curious: on one hand, the honest coordinator/server executes the requested operations without tampering with query content, the execution and results, or the shares in the DBMS; on the other hand, a curious coordinator/server may infer the sensitive data from the submitted queries, the execution results, or the priori knowledge about the outsourced data.

Network Assumption. We assume the messages transmitted between the client (the SEDB plug-in) and the SEDB coordinator, the SEDB coordinator and the database servers can be captured by attackers. Therefore, we employ AES to ensure message confidentiality. Each server shares a secret key with each of the other servers and all clients, e.g., $k_{c,si}$ between the client c and server i. The message m encrypted with the key k is denoted as $[m]_k$. Moreover, we assume the clients have limited bandwidth, while the bandwidth of the SEDB coordinator and the servers are reasonably large enough in the cloud computing environment.

Finally, although we present SEDB with a focus on the process over the integers, it can be extended to support the data of other types (e.g., char, varchar and float), by transforming them into one or more integers. As we adopt Shamir's threshold secret sharing scheme [14] to share sensitive data, we assume that there exists a large prime p such that all the computation results on the sensitive data are in the interval $[-(p-1)/2, \ (p+1)/2]$.

3 The Protocol

In SEDB, the applications, SEDB plug-ins, SEDB coordinators and database servers exchange messages through SQL queries, which ensures no modification of DBMSes and applications. For example, to insert a value v into the table *test* as the attribute *attr*, the application issues "insert into *test(attr)* values(v)". The SEDB plug-in sends "insert into *test(attr)* values(*encshares(v)*)" to the SEDB coordinator, in which $encshares(v) = \{[share_1(v)]_{k_{c,s1}}, [share_2(v)]_{k_{c,s2}},$ $[share_3(v)]_{k_{c,s3}}\}$, where $[share_i(v)]_{k_{c,si}}$ is the encrypted share for server i. The SEDB coordinator splits the received SQL queries and sends "insert into *test(attr)* values(DecShare(*encshares(v)[i]*))" to server i, where DecShare is a UDF to execute decryption. The SQL queries for all the operations are detailed in the Appendix A.

We assume, in each table, there is a unique identifier of each row (i.e., the primary key). SEDB needs a shadow for each table to store the intermediate transformation of the original data. The shadow table is designed for the process of comparison, division and modulus.

3.1 Query Processing

SEDB supports a set of operations including addition, subtraction, comparison, multiplication, division, and modulus. We first describe the detailed process of each single operator and then discuss the process of SQL queries that contain multiple operators in Sect. 3.2.

3.1.1 Insert

The applications use insert operation to insert a confidential value v into the database. An application invokes an insert process by sending the SQL query with v as the parameter to the SEDB plug-in.

The SEDB plug-in parses the SQL query to get the value v, and uses Shamir's (2, 3)-threshold secret sharing scheme [14] to split v into 3 shares, where any 2 or more shares can be used to reconstruct v. To compute the shares of v, the SEDB plug-in produces the polynomial $f(x) = a_1x + a_0$, where $a_0 = v$, and a_1 is a non-zero integer chosen randomly from $[-(p-1)/2, \ (p+1)/2)$. Using the predefined vector $X = \{x_1, \ x_2, \ x_3\}$, where non-zero $x_i \in [-(p-1)/2, \ (p+1)/2)$, the SEDB plug-in calculates $f(x_i)$ as the share for database server i. The large prime p and the vector X are known to all participants. Then, the SEDB plug-in rewrites the query by replacing v with the share vector $\{[f(x_1)]_{k_{c,s1}}, [f(x_2)]_{k_{c,s2}}, [f(x_3)]_{k_{c,s3}}\}$, and sends it to the SEDB coordinator. After that, the SEDB plug-in discards the polynomial. The SEDB coordinator splits the received SQL query into three queries, each with one encrypted share, for three backend database servers. On receiving the query, each database server decrypts the encrypted share, and stores it in the database.

3.1.2   Select

The applications use the select operation to retrieve the values that satisfy a specified condition. The SEDB plug-in forwards the `select` SQL query from the application to the SEDB coordinator directly, which further sends the received query to all three database servers. Then, each server encrypts its shares, and sends them to the SEDB coordinator as responses. On receiving the responses, the SEDB coordinator sorts them by the servers' identifiers, and sends them to the SEDB plug-in. Finally, the SEDB plug-in decrypts the encrypted shares, reconstructs the values and returns the retrieved values to the applications.

3.1.3   Addition and Subtraction

In SEDB, applications can achieve the addition and subtraction of two or more confidential values without recovering them. The process of the subtraction is the same as the addition, except that each server executes the subtraction instead of addition on the shares. So we only present the process for the addition here.

The application may want to perform additions on existing values in the database, or add a constant to an existing value. Without loss of generality, the former case can be expressed as updating v_3 with $v_1 + v_2$. To process it, the SEDB plug-in and SEDB coordinator simply forward the update query to three database servers, where each server updates its share of v_3 with the summation of its local shares of v_1 and v_2. Assume the polynomials for v_1 and v_2 are $f_1(x) = a_1 x + v_1$ and $f_2(x) = b_1 x + v_2$ respectively. Since the Shamir's secret sharing scheme is linear, v_3 is shared using the polynomial $f_3(x) = (a_1 + b_1)x + (v_1 + v_2)$. In the latter case, when the application wants to add a constant *const* to an existing value v_1 in the database, the SEDB plug-in needs to pre-process *const* by splitting it using the (2,3)-threshold secret sharing scheme. The encrypted shares are decrypted at each server and added to the corresponding share, respectively.

3.1.4   Multiplication

Compared to addition, the process of multiplication is more complicated since the multiplication of two shares increases the degree of the generated secret-sharing polynomial. In particular, when updating v_3 with $v_1 * v_2$, the degrees of the polynomials for v_1 and v_2 are 1, while the degree of the generated polynomial for v_3 increases to 2, which means 3 shares are needed to recover the result of the multiplication. To reduce the degree back to 1, we adopt the degree reduction scheme [5] in the process of the multiplication.

To process the multiplication, we introduce three UDFs at database servers: NewMul1, NewMul2, and MulConst. When the SEDB coordinator receives a multiplication query from the SEDB plug-in, it rewrites the query by replacing the operator $*$ with UDF NewMul1 and sends the rewritten query to all three backend database servers. To execute NewMul1, server i multiplies its shares of v_1 and v_2 to compute $mul1_i = v_1 * v_2$, and then splits $mul1_i$ using (2, 3)-threshold secret sharing scheme. The share vector $\{[share_1(mul1_i)]_{k_{s1,si}}, [share_2(mul1_i)]_{k_{s2,si}},$ $[share_3(mul1_i)]_{k_{s3,si}}\}$, with each subshare encrypted by pairwise secret key, is returned to the SEDB coordinator.

The SEDB coordinator combines the share vectors from three servers to generate parameters of UDF NewMul2. In particular, database server i takes parameter $([share_i(mul1_1)]_{k_{s1,si}}, [share_i(mul1_2)]_{k_{s2,si}}, [share_i(mul1_3)]_{k_{s3,si}})$ to compute $mul_i = \sum_{k=1}^{3} \lambda_k * share_i(mul1_k)$ where $\{\lambda_1, \lambda_2, \lambda_3\}$ is the first row of the following matrix in $[-(p-1)/2, (p+1)/2)$, and $\{x_1, x_2, x_3\}$ is the predefined vector for secret sharing. Then, mul_i is server i's share of the multiplication result using (2, 3)-threshold secret sharing scheme.

$$\begin{bmatrix} 1 & x_1 & x_1^2 \\ 1 & x_2 & x_2^2 \\ 1 & x_3 & x_3^2 \end{bmatrix}^{-1} \tag{1}$$

The multiplication with a constant can take two different approaches. The SEDB plug-in can simply invoke a UDF MulConst at three backend database servers to multiply each local share with this constant. In the case where the value of the constant needs protected, the SEDB plug-in needs to take a similar process as presented earlier in this section: it first splits the constant with a (2, 3)-threshold secret sharing scheme, sends the encrypted sub-shares to each backend database server, and executes the multiplication of two shares.

3.1.5   Division and Modulus

In SEDB, we cannot directly perform the division or modulus on the shares in the backend database servers. Certain transformations of the operands are necessary to support the division and modulus operations. In particular, to calculate v_1/v_2 or $v_1 \% v_2$, we propose to generate $v_1' = t_1 * v_1 + t_1 * t_2 * v_2$ and $v_2' = t_1 * v_2$, where t_1 and t_2 are non-zero integers chosen randomly from $[-(p-1)/2, (p+1)/2)$. Then we can represent the division and modulus of v_1 and v_2 as a combination of addition, subtraction and multiplication operations on v_1, v_2, and v_1'/v_2', i.e., $v_1/v_2 = v_1'/v_2' - t_2$, $v_1 \% v_2 = v_1 - v_1'/v_2' * v_2 + t_2 * v_2$. If v_1 or v_2 is a constant, we can create a dummy column firstly, then the computing is the same as the division and modulus on existing values in the database.

Division: The SEDB plug-in and the SEDB coordinator cooperate to generate the random transformations v_1' and v_2' for v_1 and v_2 respectively, and compute the value of v_1/v_2 based on v_1' and v_2'. In particular, the SEDB plug-in first chooses three different polynomials of degree 1 to share t_1, t_2 and $t_1 * t_2$, then sends the encrypted shares to the SEDB coordinator. The SEDB coordinator forwards the shares to corresponding backend database servers and invokes a UDF `Div1` at each database server to calculate its shares of v_1' and v_2'. With $([share_i(t_1)]_{k_{c,si}}, [share_i(t_2)]_{k_{c,si}}, [share_i(t_1 * t_2)]_{k_{c,si}})$, the server i updates the shadow of v_1 with $share_i(v_1) * share_i(t_1) + share_i(v_2) * share_i(t_1 * t_2)$, and the shadow of v_2 with $share_i(v_2) * share_i(t_1)$, encrypts the shadows for the other two servers, and returns the result to the SEDB coordinator. Then the SEDB coordinator forwards the encrypted shadows to the corresponding servers and invokes a UDF `Div2` in each database server to reconstruct v_1' and v_2'. As a result, each server calculates its share of v_1/v_2 as $v_1'/v_2' - share_i(t_2)$.

Modulus: To calculate $v_1 \% v_2$, the SEDB plug-in and the SEDB coordinator take a similar process to prepare the Shamir's $(2, 3)$-threshold shares of t_1, t_2, $t_1 * t_2$, and update the shadows of v_1 and v_2 by invoking a UDF `Mod1` at three database servers. In the execution of `Mod1`, each server invokes `NewMul1` to generate the share vector for $t_2 * v_2$. Then, the SEDB coordinator invokes a UDF `Mod2` at each server, which generates its share of $t_2 * v_2$ by invoking `NewMul2`, recovers v_1' and v_2', and generates its share of $v_1 \% v_2$ by calculating $share_i(v_1) - v_1'/v_2' * share_i(v_2) + share_i(t_2 * v_2)$.

3.1.6 Comparison

As the shares of the confidential values are not order-preserving in SEDB, we perform the comparison by comparing the order-preserving transformations of the values. For example, to compare two values v_1 and v_2, we first compute $v_1' = t_1 * v_1 + t_2$ and $v_2' = t_1 * v_2 + t_2$, where t_1 is randomly chosen from $(0, (p+1)/2)$ and t_2 from $[-(p - 1)/2, (p + 1)/2)$. As a monotonic transformation, the order of v_1' and v_2' determines the order of v_1 and v_2.

To calculate v_1' and v_2', the SEDB plug-in prepares the three shares for t_1 using a polynomial of degree 1 and a polynomial of degree 2 for t_2, and then sends the encrypted shares to the SEDB coordinator, which further forwards $([share_i(t_1)]_{k_{c,si}}, [share_i(t_2)]_{k_{c,si}})$ to server i as the input of a UDF `Compare1`. Each backend database server i executes `Compare1` by computing $share_i(t_1) * share_i(v_1) + share_i(t_2)$ and $share_i(t_1) * share_i(v_2) + share_i(t_2)$, encrypts the results for other two servers, and returns the encrypted results to the SEDB coordinator. After collecting the results from all three backend database servers, the SEDB coordinator invokes a UDF `Compare2` to reconstruct v_1' and v_2' at each server using the $(3, 3)$-threshold secret sharing schemes, for comparison.

To compare a confidential value with a constant $const$, the SEDB plug-in firstly computes $t_1 * const + t_2$, encrypts it, and sends it to each server, which compares it with the same transformations of the confidential value.

3.2 Discussions

SEDB supports complex SQL queries that contain a combination of the above operators. The SEDB plug-in needs to determine the order of operations, and prepares the parameters for all the operators and sends it in one SQL query to the SEDB coordinator. The SEDB coordinator parses the received query, extracts the parameters for each UDF, and then invokes multiple UDFs at the backend database servers in order.

SEDB supports aggregation queries. SEDB processes the count() function similarly as in the original DBMS. To calculate the sum() of data in a particular column, the SEDB coordinator asks all servers to return the summation of their shares for all the data in that column, and returns the result to the SEDB plug-in for recovering the summation of that column. From the results of sum() and count(), the SEDB plug-in can calculate the average of a particular column. To process the min(), max(), group by, or order by operations on a column, the SEDB coordinator invokes UDFs Compare1 and Compare2 to update the shadow of that column using its order-preserving transformation, and executes the min(), max(), group by and order by functions on the shadow column.

SEDB supports the join of columns as well. The process of join is similar to the comparison, that is, we process the join on the shadow columns, which is the same order-preserving transformations of the selected columns.

Since many SQL operators process NULL differently from the execution on non-NULL values, SEDB stores the NULL values in plaintext. Finally, SEDB is limited in supporting certain DBMS mechanisms such as the transactions and indexing in its current version for the complexity in multi-round processing between the SEDB coordinator and the backend database servers.

4 Security Analysis

In this section, we analyze the security of SEDB briefly. In SEDB, the sensitive data is split using Shamir's threshold secret sharing scheme. The adversaries and SEDB coordinator can never obtain any plaintext share, as they have no keys to decrypt the transmitted encrypted shares, thus they can never infer the sensitive data. Each database server cannot reconstruct the sensitive data from its local shares, as it owns only one share for each data. Moreover, the servers are assumed to be honest, they never collude with each other to acquire enough shares to reconstruct the data. In the following, we show that the database servers cannot infer the sensitive data from the process of the operations, either.

In SEDB, the servers with no priori knowledge of the data and queries, cannot infer any sensitive data during the executions. To process addition, each server summarizes its local shares and gains no information from others. To process multiplication, each server cooperatively completes the degree reduction. As analyzed in [5], the generated polynomial is random, and each server owns only one share of the multiplication. To process division and modulus, each server obtains the transformations of two confidential values v_1 and v_2, such as $t_1 * v_1 + t_1 * t_2 * v_2$ and $t_1 * v_2$. As the randomly chosen t_1 and t_2 are different in different processes and never reconstructed, each server cannot deduce v_1 and v_2 from the transformations. Each server determines the order of two confidential values v_1 and v_2 by the order-preserving transformation $t_1 * v_1 + t_2$ and $t_1 * v_2 + t_2$. As t_1 and t_2 are chosen randomly and differently each time, and never reconstructed, the servers cannot infer v_1 and v_2 or other statical information (e.g., $v_1 - v_2$, v_1/v_2) from the transformations.

SEDB prevents the curious servers inferring the sensitive data from priori knowledge of the data and queries. The server may attempt to gain the sensitive data from some known values (e.g., the minimum and maximum) or keywords in some special queries. As all data are split independently, and the statical relation of the values isn't preserved in their shares, the server cannot deduce unknown values from its local database. In the execution of addition and multiplication, each server only gains its share of the result, no useful information for statical attacks. To execute v_1/v_2 and $v_1 \% v_2$, each server obtains the transformations $v_1' = t_1 * v_1 + t_1 * t_2 * v_2$ and $v_2' = t_2 * v_2$. However, because t_1 (or t_2) is chosen independently in different executions, the adversarial server cannot infer t_1 (or t_2) from multiple executions; in one execution, the adversarial server cannot deduce v_2, t_1 or t_2 even if it knows v_1, v_1' and v_2'; it can either infer v_1, t_1 even if it knows v_2, v_1' and v_2'. Therefore, the server cannot gain any unknown value from the known ones and their transformations in the process of division and modulus.

For comparison, SEDB can be extended to prevent statistical attacks. In the current version, with two known values (e.g. the maximal and minimum values) and their order-preserving transformations, an adversary can deduce the coefficients of the transformation, and thus infers other unknown confidential values in the same column from their transformations. To compare v_1 and v_2, we extend SEDB as follows: (1) we calculate $v_1' = t_1 * v_1 + t_2$ and $v_2' = t_1 * v_2 + t_2'$, where t_2 and t_2' are chosen independently and randomly from $[1, r]$; (2) if $v_1' - v_2' > (r - 1)$ or $v_2' - v_1' > (r - 1)$, the order of v_1 and v_2 is determined by v_1' and v_2', otherwise, the shares of v_1 and v_2 are returned to the SEDB plug-in who recovers v_1 and v_2 for comparison. The value r is specified at the setup of the database, if r is set as the size of that column, all comparison are processed at the SEDB plug-in, which leaks no information at the cost of efficiency. In the extended version, the adversarial server cannot infer any unknown confidential value even it has some priori knowledge about the sensitive data, and knows the transformation of the unknown confidential value and t_1, as it cannot distinguish the exact value from r potential inverses of the transformation.

5　Performance Evaluation

We have implemented the prototype of SEDB, which consists of the SEDB plug-in, SEDB coordinator and backend database servers. The SEDB plug-in and SEDB coordinator each contain a C++ library and a Lua module. The library in the SEDB plug-in rewrites the queries from applications, constructs the results based on the results from the SEDB coordinator, splits and reconstructs the confidential values, encrypts and decrypts the shares. The library in the SEDB coordinator splits the query from the SEDB plug-in for each backend database server, issues the query based on the replies from the servers, and constructs the result for the SEDB plug-in. To provide transparent database service, we adopts MySQL proxy [11] which invokes our Lua module to pass queries and results to and from the C++ library in the SEDB plug-in. MySQL proxy is also deployed in the SEDB coordinator which invokes the Lua module to capture the queries from the SEDB plug-in, and passes them to the C++ library for further process. Each backend database server uses MySQL 5.1 as DBMS, we implement 15 UDFs at each server to complete the computation on the shares. The big prime p is 128 bits, and the X vector is set as $\{1, 2, 3\}$. The secret sharing scheme and AES are implemented using NTL [18].

All experiments ran with three database servers, one trusted client and one SEDB coordinator in an isolated 100 Mbps Ethernet. The database servers and SEDB coordinator ran on identical workstations with an Intel i7-3770 (3.4 GHz) CPU and 4 GB of memory. The application and SEDB plug-in were deployed in one physical machine with an Intel 2640 M (2.8 GHz) CPU and 4 GB of memory. The operating systems of all the nodes are Ubuntu 12.04. Each database server maintains a table $test$, which sets id as the primary key and has two attributes $attr1$ and $attr2$.

We evaluated the processing overhead for ensuring confidentiality of sensitive data in SEDB, by comparing each operation's processing time in SEDB with it in the original MySQL. We measured the average processing time by issuing a SQL query with a single operation 100 times, to operate on $test$ with different numbers of rows (denoted as n). For better comparison, we classify the operations into two classes according to the number of needed communication rounds between the SEDB coordinator and each database server. The operations select, insert, addition and subtraction, need only one round and belong to the first class. The remaining ones need two rounds and are categorized into the second class.

Table 1 lists the ratio of the processing time in SEDB to that in MySQL for the operations in the first class. To evaluate the processing time for insert, select and addition, we use SQL queries "insert into $test(attr1, attr2)$ values (u_1, u_2)" (u_1 and u_2 are random values), "select * from $test$" and "update $test$ set $attr1 = attr1 + attr2$" respectively. As illustrated in Table 1, the overhead for operations in the first class is modest. For insert and addition, the processing overhead is independent of n, and is at most 3.6× and 2.31× respectively when $n \leq 10000$. The main sources of SEDB's overhead for insert and addition is the message transmitting, as the critical communication path is 3 in SEDB and 1 in MySQL.

The processing overhead for select increases slightly as n increases, from 3.35× when $n = 1$ to 7.33× when $n = 10000$. The overhead is increasing mainly because the size of messages for the clients increases quicker in SEDB than in MySQL, as the SEDB plug-in has to receive three shares instead of the original data.

Table 2 illustrates the processing overhead for operations in the second class. We evaluate the processing time for multiplication, division, modulus and comparison, using SQL queries "update $test$ set $attr1 = attr1 * attr2$", "update $test$ set $attr1 = attr1/attr2$", "update $test$ set $attr1 = attr1 \% attr2$" and "update $test$ set $attr1 = attr1$ where $attr1 > attr2$" respectively. As among the existing solutions, only the ones based on fully homomorphic encryption can execute the multiplication at the servers, which introduces a overhead of $10^9 \times$ [17], SEDB is a more practical solution, whose overhead for multiplication is at most 168.41× when $n \leq 5000$. For the operations in the second class, the processing overhead

Table 1. The average response time for operations in the first class (in ms).

Num of rows		1	2	10	40	100	400	1000	3000	5000	10000
Insert	SEDB	5.00	5.01	5.34	5.37	5.06	4.99	5.47	5.70	5.73	5.86
	MySQL	1.45	1.65	2.28	1.82	1.34	1.72	1.19	1.24	1.11	1.29
	Ratio	3.45	3.04	2.34	2.95	3.78	2.91	4.62	4.60	5.18	4.56
Select	SEDB	3.23	3.19	3.72	5.38	8.33	23.11	46.97	129.95	200.17	364.87
	MySQL	0.74	0.85	0.91	1.31	1.52	3.47	6.53	14.72	28.33	43.80
	Ratio	4.35	3.75	4.07	4.10	5.49	6.66	7.19	8.83	7.07	8.33
Add	SEDB	4.65	4.55	4.79	5.11	5.82	8.81	15.56	32.60	51.44	93.79
	MySQL	1.47	1.46	1.59	1.54	2.16	3.73	6.08	12.08	18.45	35.47
	Ratio	3.17	3.11	3.00	3.31	2.69	2.36	2.56	2.70	2.79	2.64

Table 2. The average response time for operations in the second class (in ms).

Num of rows		1	2	10	40	100	400	1000	3000	5000
Mul	SEDB	9.01	10.82	18.14	41.24	87.53	273.35	742.00	1910.84	3185.17
	MySQL	1.77	1.73	1.78	1.96	2.43	3.85	5.68	12.47	18.80
	Ratio	5.09	6.27	10.17	21.00	36.03	70.92	130.73	153.19	169.41
Div	SEDB	9.10	14.36	24.95	75.50	149.92	451.35	1336.40	6918.89	15391.94
	MySQL	1.81	1.67	1.45	2.03	2.18	3.60	6.00	12.66	19.00
	Ratio	5.02	8.62	17.18	37.28	68.63	125.30	222.88	546.64	809.93
Mod	SEDB	10.94	16.05	45.31	135.35	296.01	1283.04	2417.34	6132.38	14270.56
	MySQL	1.73	1.80	1.33	1.94	2.00	4.05	6.84	15.00	27.33
	Ratio	6.31	8.92	33.94	69.65	147.77	316.71	353.22	408.84	522.18
Compare	SEDB	9.73	11.59	21.22	53.72	119.97	304.24	795.89	2545.82	5671.55
	MySQL	0.86	0.85	0.92	1.26	1.35	2.25	4.14	10.59	32.68
	Ratio	11.34	13.69	23.07	42.75	88.72	135.45	192.14	240.36	173.52

in SEDB increases with n, from a rather small one (10.34× for comparison when $n = 1$) to 808.93× for division when $n = 5000$. It's mainly because, with the increase of n: (1) the time for the servers to complete the operations increases quicker in SEDB than in MySQL, as the servers in SEDB have to invoke UDFs n times; (2) the sizes of messages transmitted by the SEDB coordinator increase, the sizes are $9zn$, $15zn$, $24zn$, $12zn$ for multiplication, division, modulus and comparison, where z is the size of the share and is 16 bytes in our evaluation. The overhead can be reduced when the database servers and SEDB coordinator are deployed in the cloud, where the computing resources and bandwidth are increased remarkably.

6   Related Works

Hacigumus et al. [8] firstly proposed to provide the database as a service in 2002. They encrypt the database with a symmetric encryption, and then place it on the untrusted server. Hacigumus partitions the domain of each column into several disjoint subsets and assigns each partition with a unique partition id. When accessing the database service, the trusted client rewrites the query by replacing the confidential value with the index of the partition that the value belongs to. Therefore, the results from the server contains false ones which will require the clients to postprocess it. Moreover, this scheme doesn't support the aggregates well, for example, when the client wants to get summation of some column, it should acquire the entire column firstly, while each database returns the summation of the shares to the client (SEDB plug-in) directly in SEDB.

CryptDB [13] is a more practical solution. It uses different cryptosystems to support different types of queries, and maintains up to four columns for one column in the original database. CryptDB cannot ensure the consistency of the different shadow columns for one original column which makes the result of some queries false. For example, when an addition is executed on the column encrypted using Paillier [12], the data in other columns are stale. In SEDB, there is only one column that stores the shares which ensures the correctness of the results. Moreover, CryptDB cannot support SQL queries involving the multiplication or division as it does not adopt any cryptosystem that can handle multiplications.

MONOMI [17] extends CryptDB to support more SQL queries by splitting client/server execution of complex queries, which executes as much of the query as is practical over encrypted data on the server, and executes the remaining components on trusted clients, who will decrypt the data and process queries further. SEDB provides the transparent database service and doesn't require the modification on the clients. Cipherbase [2] provides secure database outsourcing services with the trusted hardware on the untrusted server. The trusted hardware executes arbitrary computation over the encrypted data.

Threshold secret sharing scheme has also been used to provide secure database outsourcing services. Existing works mainly focus on improving the performance for retrieval. Tian [16] builds a privacy preserving index to accelerate query. Agrawal [1] utilizes hash functions to generate the distribution polynomials to achieve efficient retrieval. AS5 [9] preserves the order of the confidential values in their shares by choosing the appropriate polynomials, to make query execution efficient. However, these schemes need to know the distribution of the data in advance, and doesn't support the update on the data.

7   Conclusion

In this paper, we propose a secure database oursourcing scheme (SEDB) to ensure the confidentiality of the outsourced database. SEDB is based on Shamir's threshold secret sharing scheme, in which the sensitive data is split into three shares and stored in three independent, honest-but-curious servers. In SEDB, the database servers execute functions over the shares without recovering the data. The execution is leaded by a honest-but-curious SEDB coordinator, which makes the servers cooperatively execute the operation. SEDB supports the functions including insert, select, addition, subtraction, multiplication, division, modulus and comparison, and provides continuous database outsourcing services.

Acknowledgments. Quanwei Cai, Jingqiang Lin and Qiongxiao Wang were partially supported by National 973 Program of China under award No. 2014CB 340603 and No. 2013CB338001, and the National Natural Science Foundation of China (Grant No. 61402470). Fengjun Li was partially supported by National Science Foundation under Award No. EPS-0903806 and matching support from the State of Kansas through the Kansas Board of Regents.

A   Appendix

We describe a sample of the message exchanges in SEDB for each operation in Fig. 2. In particular, we assume the application operates on the table *test*, which sets *id* as the primary key, and has three attributes *attr*1, *attr*2 and *attr*3. The table *shadowtest* is the shadow of *test*.

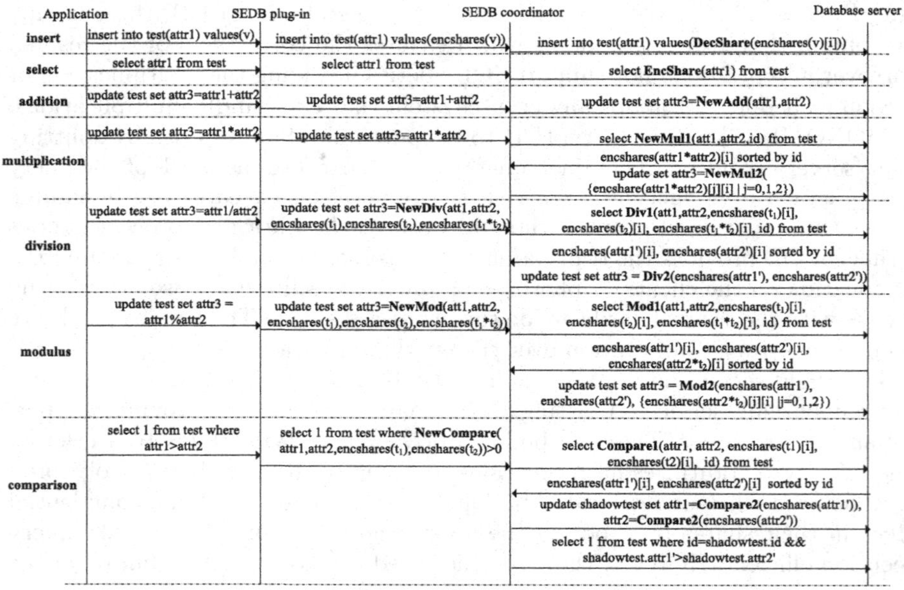

Fig. 2. The message exchange in SEDB.

To execute insert, the SEDB plug-in replaces the confidential value v with its encrypted share vector $encshares(v)$, the SEDB coordinator invokes a UDF DecShare with the corresponding encrypted share $encshares(v)[i]$ at database server i, which decrypts the share and stores it in *test*. For select and addition, the SEDB plug-in doesn't modify the SQL queries, while the SEDB coordinator invokes a UDF EncShare to get the encrypted shares from server i to complete select, and a UDF NewAdd to make server i execute the addition of the columns.

In the process of multiplication, the SQL query is transmitted to the SEDB coordinator without modification, who firstly invokes a UDF NewMul1 at each server i. Server i sorts the rows in $test$ by id, generates the share vector for the multiplication of its local shares of values in columns $attr1$ and $attr2$ in order, then returns the encrypted share vectors $encshares(attr1*attr2)[i]$. On receiving the replies from three database server, the SEDB coordinator constructs the parameter for a UDF $NewMul2$ as in Sect. 3.1.4, and invokes it to complete the degree reduction.

To execute division and modulus, the SEDB plug-in firstly chooses t_1 and t_2 for each row in $test$ and generates the encrypted share vectors for each t_1, t_2 and $t_1 * t_2$, then it invokes $NewDiv$ and $NewMod$ at the SEDB coordinator. To process the $NewDiv$, the SEDB coordinator firstly invokes a UDF $Div1$ to get the encrypted shares of v_1' and v_2' ($encshares(attr1')[i]$ and $encshares(attr2')[i]$) of all rows ordered by id in $test$ from server i; then the SEDB coordinator combines them to generate $encshares(attr2')$ and $encshares(attr2')$, and invokes $Div2$ to complete the division at each server. For $NewMod$, by invoking a UDF $Mod1$, the SEDB coordinator gains $encshares(attr1')[i]$ and $encshares(attr2')[i]$ as in the process of $Div1$, together with the encrypted share vector ($encshare$ $(attr2 * t_2)[i]$) of the multiplication of the corresponding local shares of $attr2$ with the share of t_2 from server i, where $encshare(attr2 * t_2)[i]$ is also ordered by id. Then, the SEDB coordinator recombines the $encshare(attr2 * t_2)[i]$ as in Sect. 3.1.4, and invokes a UDF $Mod2$. To execute $Mod2$, each database server firstly complete the degree reduction as in $NewMul2$ to get its share of $attr2 * t_2$, then calculates its share of the modulus as described in Sect. 3.1.5.

To compare two columns in $test$, the SEDB plug-in invokes the $NewCompare$ with the encrypted share vector of t_1 and t_2 at the SEDB coordinator. The coordinator firstly invokes a UDF $Compare1$ at each server i, to get the encrypted shares of t_1' and t_2' of all rows ordered by id in $test$ from server i, then combines them to update the $shadowtest$ through a UDF $Compare2$, finally the coordinator sends a query to make each server complete the comparison on the $shadowtest$.

References

1. Agrawal, D., El Abbadi, A., Emekci, F., Metwally, A., Wang, S.: Secure Data Management Service on Cloud Computing Infrastructures. In: Agrawal, D., Candan, K.S., Li, W.-S. (eds.) Information and Software as Services. LNBIP, vol. 74, pp. 57–80. Springer, Heidelberg (2011)
2. Arasu, A., Blanas, S., Eguro, K., et al.: Secure database-as-a-service with Cipherbase. In: Proceedings of the 2013 international conference on Management of data, pp. 1033–1036. ACM (2013)
3. Boldyreva, A., Chenette, N., Lee, Y., O'Neill, A.: Order-preserving symmetric encryption. In: Joux, A. (ed.) EUROCRYPT 2009. LNCS, vol. 5479, pp. 224–241. Springer, Heidelberg (2009)
4. Elmore, A.J., Das, S., Agrawal, D., El Abbadi, A.: Zephyr: Live migration in shared nothing databases for elastic cloud platforms. In: Proceedings of SIGMOD, pp. 301–312. ACM (2011)

5. Gennaro, R., Rabin, M.O., Rabin, T.: Simplified VSS and fast-track multiparty computations with applications to threshold cryptography. In: Proceedings of the Annual ACM Symposium on Principles of Distributed Computing, pp. 101–111. ACM (1998)
6. Gentry, C.: Fully homomorphic encryption using ideal lattices. In: Proceedings of the 41st Annual ACM Symposium on Symposium on Theory of Computing (STOC), pp. 169–169. ACM Press (2009)
7. Gentry, C., Halevi, S., Smart, N.P.: Homomorphic evaluation of the AES circuit. In: Safavi-Naini, R., Canetti, R. (eds.) CRYPTO 2012. LNCS, vol. 7417, pp. 850–867. Springer, Heidelberg (2012)
8. Hacigümüş, H., Iyer, B., Li, C., et al.: Executing SQL over encrypted data in the database-service-provider model. In: Proceedings of SIGMOD, pp. 216–227. ACM (2002)
9. Hadavi, M.A., Damiani, E., Jalili, R., Cimato, S., Ganjei, Z.: AS5: a secure searchable secret sharing scheme for privacy preserving database outsourcing. In: Di Pietro, R., Herranz, J., Damiani, E., State, R. (eds.) DPM 2012 and SETOP 2012. LNCS, vol. 7731, pp. 201–216. Springer, Heidelberg (2013)
10. Halevi, S., Rogaway, P.: A tweakable enciphering mode. In: Boneh, D. (ed.) CRYPTO 2003. LNCS, vol. 2729, pp. 482–499. Springer, Heidelberg (2003)
11. Taylor, M.: MySQL proxy. https://launchpad.net/mysql-proxy
12. Paillier, P.: Public-key cryptosystems based on composite degree residuosity classes. In: Stern, J. (ed.) EUROCRYPT 1999. LNCS, vol. 1592, pp. 223–238. Springer, Heidelberg (1999)
13. Popa, R.A., Redfield, C., Zeldovich, N., Balakrishnan, H.: CryptDB: Processing queries on an encrypted database. Commun. ACM 55, 103–111 (2012)
14. Shamir, A.: How to share a secret. Commun. ACM 22, 612–613 (1979)
15. Song, D.X., Wagner, D., Perrig, A.: Practical techniques for searches on encrypted data. In: Proceedings of IEEE S&P, pp. 44–55. IEEE (2000)
16. Tian, X.X., Sha, C.F., Wang, X.L., Zhou, A.Y.: Privacy preserving query processing on secret share based data storage. In: Yu, J.X., Kim, M.H., Unland, R. (eds.) DASFAA 2011, Part I. LNCS, vol. 6587, pp. 108–122. Springer, Heidelberg (2011)
17. Tu, S., Kaashoek, M.F., Madden, S., Zeldovich, N.: Processing analytical queries over encrypted data. In: Proceedings of the VLDB Endowment, vol. 6, pp. 289–300. VLDB Endowment (2013)
18. Shoup, V.: NTL: A library for doing number theory. http://www.shoup.net/ntl/

Mdaak: A Flexible and Efficient Framework for Direct Anonymous Attestation on Mobile Devices

Qianying Zhang(✉), Shijun Zhao, Li Xi, Wei Feng, and Dengguo Feng

Trusted Computing and Information Assurance Laboratory, Institute of Software,
Chinese Academy of Sciences, Beijing, China
zsjzqy@gmail.com,
{zhaosj,xili,fengwei,feng}@tca.iscas.ac.cn

Abstract. In this paper, we investigate how to implement Direct Anonymous Attestation (DAA) on mobile devices, whose processing and storage capabilities are limited. We propose a generic framework providing a secure and efficient DAA functionality based on ARM TrustZone. Our framework is flexible enough to support multiple DAA schemes, and is efficient by leveraging the powerful ARM processor in secure mode to perform computations originally delegated to the Trusted Platform Module (TPM). Besides, our framework uses an SRAM PUF commonly available in the On-Chip Memory (OCM) of mobile devices for secure storage of user signing keys, which achieves a low-cost design. We present a prototype system that supports four DAA schemes on real TrustZone hardware, and give evaluations on its code size and performance together with comparisons of the four schemes with different curve parameters. The evaluation results indicate that our solution is feasible, efficient, and well-suited for mobile devices.

Keywords: Direct anonymous attestation · Mobile devices · ARM TrustZone · Physical unclonable functions · Performance evaluation

1 Introduction

Modern mobile devices provide lots of compelling capacities allowing the realization of various applications such as mobile payment and mobile ticketing, which bring many benefits to users. However, the widespread use of mobile applications poses a serious threat to user privacy. In particular, authentication is a prerequisite for proper access control to many services, but it often leads to the identification of users. This issue can be resolved by anonymous credential systems [15,16], which allow anonymous yet authenticated and accountable transactions between users and service providers. In an anonymous credential system, users can authenticate themselves by proving the possession of credentials without revealing any other information. However, without additional countermeasures, an adversary could share a legitimate user's credential by just copying all necessary authentication data, such that he can gain unauthorized access to services without being detected.

© Springer International Publishing Switzerland 2015
L.C.K. Hui et al. (Eds.): ICICS 2014, LNCS 8958, pp. 31–48, 2015.
DOI: 10.1007/978-3-319-21966-0_3

To some extent, this problem can be effectively solved by Direct Anonymous Attestation (DAA), which uses hardware security features to protect authentication secrets. DAA was first proposed by Brickell, Camenisch, and Chen [11] for remote anonymous authentication of the Trusted Platform Module (TPM), and it is an anonymous credential system designed specifically to encapsulate security-critical operations in the TPM. In a DAA scheme, a signer proves possession of his credential to a verifier by providing a DAA signature, and the TPM is responsible for protecting the secret signing key, such that other entities even the host the TPM embedded in are prevented from learning it and hence from producing a valid signature without interaction with the TPM. The original DAA scheme [11], which we call BCC04, is based on the strong-RSA assumption, and to achieve better efficiency, researchers have constructed DAA schemes with elliptic curves and pairings [12–14,17,19,20], which we call ECC-DAA in this paper. To date, DAA has gained lots of favor with standard bodies [2,4,18,40,41] and industry, which makes it have better prospects for practical applications than other anonymous credential systems.

Although DAA is attractive for mobile anonymous authentication, realizing DAA on mobile devices with reasonable efficiency and cost while preserving security is a non-trivial task. The major challenge is that DAA requires complex cryptographic computations, making its use on mobile devices which have limited power and processing capabilities rather difficult. The problem is exacerbated by the sheer number of different DAA schemes that have been proposed, since real-world applications involve plenty of service providers adopting various DAA schemes, which should all be supported by the user's device. Furthermore, demanding computations originally performed by the TPM put high requirements on the security of the execution environment of the signer's device. In addition, DAA requires secure storage on the device for protection of signing keys that must not be copied and moved to a different device, while mobile devices typically do not provide sufficient secure persistent storage.

In this paper, we investigate how to implement DAA on mobile devices with sufficient security, high efficiency and minimum overhead, and present the Mobile Direct Anonymous Attestation frameworK (Mdaak), a generic framework that allows multiple DAA schemes to be integrated into it. Mdaak is carefully crafted to provide an efficient and low-cost implementation of DAA schemes without the expense of security. It leverages the Trusted Execution Environment (TEE) provided by ARM TrustZone which is available on many mobile devices to perform security-critical computations, and uses a secret extracted from the on-chip SRAM PUF (Physical Unclonable Function) as the root of trust for storage of the device key and user signing keys.

1.1 Our Contributions

The contributions of this paper are summarized as follows:

- We propose a framework that allows implementation of DAA on mobile devices with a perspective focusing on generality and performance. The framework is flexible enough to support variant DAA schemes and enables elastic

DAA scheme selections and updates. It leverages the TEE provided by Trust-Zone to obtain the full power of the processor for security-critical operations, which leads to a simpler and more efficient DAA implementation and obviates the need for any additional security hardware, e.g., smart cards or the TPM.

- We propose a cost-effective approach for secure storage of user signing keys. We extract a secret from the on-chip SRAM PUF, which is commonly available on current System-on-Chips (SoCs), and securely store user signing keys using the secret. The physical unclonable property of the SRAM PUF can prevent copying of user signing keys, and this approach requires no additional secure non-volatile memory, which decreases the cost of devices.
- We implement a prototype of Mdaak on real TrustZone hardware. The proto-type realizes four typical ECC-DAA schemes. To the best of our knowledge, this is the first practical implementation of multiple variants of ECC-DAA on TrustZone-enabled platforms.
- We perform a thorough performance evaluation on the four ECC-DAA schemes with different security levels, and the results show that our proto-type is efficient. Based on the results, we give our suggestions on how to select DAA schemes and curve parameters for real-world application scenarios.

1.2 Outline

The remainder of this paper is organized as follows. We provide background information in Sect. 2. The objectives and thread model of our framework is described in Sect. 3. We describe the design of our framework in Sect. 4. Our implementation and evaluation are described in Sects. 5 and 6, respectively. Finally, we explore related work in Sect. 7 and conclude our work in Sect. 8.

2 Background

In this section, we present the background technologies and concepts used in this paper.

2.1 ARM TrustZone

TrustZone [7] is a hardware security technology incorporated into ARM proces-sors, which consists of security extensions to an ARM SoC covering the proces-sor, memory, and peripherals. TrustZone enables a single physical processor to execute code in one of two possible operating modes: the normal world and the secure world, which have independent memory address spaces and different privileges. TrustZone-aware processors propagate the security state into AMBA AXI bus to achieve Broad SoC security, which ensures that normal world com-ponents cannot access secure world resources and constructs a strong perimeter boundary between the worlds. Security-critical processor core status bits and System Control Coprocessor registers are either totally inaccessible to the nor-mal world or access permissions are strictly under the control of the secure world.

For the purpose of switching worlds, a special monitor mode exists in the secure world, and the secure monitor acts as a virtual gatekeeper controlling migration between the worlds. The monitor generally saves the state of the current world and restores the state of the world at the location to which it switches. It then restarts processing in the restored world by performing a return-from-exception. To summarize, a TrustZone processor can be seen as two virtual processors with different privileges and a strictly controlled communication interface.

2.2   Physical Unclonable Functions and Fuzzy Extractors

Physical Unclonable Functions [35] are functions where the relationship between input (or challenge) and output (or response) is defined via a physical system, which has the additional properties of being random and unclonable. The system's unclonability originates from random variations in a device's manufacturing process, which cannot be controlled even by the manufacturer. A PUF takes a challenge as its input and generates a unique but noisy response as its output. The uniqueness property of PUFs can be used to store a secret key [42], but the noise in responses should be eliminated first. Algorithms known as fuzzy extractors [24] can solve this issue, which leverage non-secret helper data to work around the noisy nature of responses. A fuzzy extractor consists of a pair of procedures: generate (Gen) and reproduce (Rep). The Gen procedure extracts a key k from the PUF's response r and generates a helper data H, which is not sensitive. The Rep procedure reproduces k from a noisy response r' under the help of H.

PUFs provide significantly higher physical security by extracting keys from complex physical systems rather than storing them in non-volatile memory. Additionally, PUFs are cost-effective, since they are the results of a preexisting manufacturing process and do not require any additions, such as a special manufacturing process or programming and testing steps. In this paper, we focus on SRAM PUFs [27], which take an SRAM cell's address as the challenge and return its power up value as the response.

3   Objectives and Threat Model

In this section, we formulate objectives of Mdaak and discuss the threat model.

3.1   Objectives

Mdaak is designed to meet the following three objectives:

- **Security.** The main object of Mdaak is to prevent the adversary from being able to impersonate a legitimate user. While attacks against the authentication procedure are prevented by DAA protocol designs, Mdaak must protect user signing keys from being accessible or forged by the adversary. More specifically, the framework has to ensure that: (1) the adversary cannot access signing keys stored on mobile devices; (2) he cannot exploit or modify the security-critical code that processes signing keys (the key-processing code). Therefore, Mdaak should possess secure storage only accessible by the key-processing code, isolate the key-processing code from other code and preserve its integrity.

– **Practicability.** Mdaak should be based on widely used hardware components and compatible with software environments on mobile platforms. Its implementation cost must be low and suitable for embedded devices, and the requirements for additional hardware components should be as little as possible. The imposed performance of Mdaak must be feasible for mobile devices, and users should not notice significant delay while they authenticate to service providers.

– **Flexibility.** To meet various requirements from service providers and users, Mdaak should support different DAA schemes and allow configurations and updates of DAA schemes and curve parameters.

3.2   Threat Model

We assume that there is secure anonymous communication between a mobile device and other entities, such as issuers, service providers, and other mobile devices. Mdaak protects the DAA functionality against the following adversary:

– The adversary can perform software attacks. He can compromise the mobile OS or existing applications and access Mdaak interfaces, which are provided through specific TrustZone mechanisms.

– The adversary can obtain physical access to user devices. He can reboot the mobile platform and gain access to data residing on persistent storage. However, he is not able to tamper with the TrustZone hardware or mount successful side-channel attacks [34].

4   Design

To build an efficient and economical DAA framework that guarantees the security of signing keys, we propose to implement the DAA functionality in a software-only way, run the software on the TrustZone-enabled hardware, and adopt the on-chip SRAM PUF to extract a secret as the root of trust for storage of signing keys. The framework runs security-critical operations in the TEE provided by TrustZone, which makes it can leverage the full power of the processor to obtain great performance. Furthermore, protected by the secret extracted from the SRAM PUF, signing keys can be stored in the insecure non-volatile memory such as flash and SD cards, which eliminates the need for secure persistent storage and makes our design inexpensive. Additionally, as the DAA functionality of the framework is implemented by software, it is flexible and extensible.

Figure 1 shows the detailed design of the Mdaak architecture and an overview of how components interact with each other. The framework contains three major components: a small security-sensitive component **DAA Trustlet** and a larger

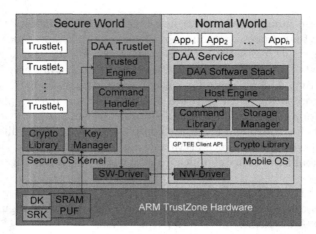

Fig. 1. Mdaak architecture.

untrusted component DAA Service, which together provide the DAA function-ality, and a key management component Key Manager. DAA Service runs in the normal world, while DAA Trustlet and Key Manager run in the secure world and are isolated via TrustZone from all code running in the normal world.

In the remainder of this section, after a brief introduction to the basic prim-itives of Mdaak, we describe the components of Mdaak and our secure storage for signing keys, and then discuss the security of our design.

4.1 Mdaak Primitives

We use $KDF_k(m)$ to denote a Key Derivation Function (KDF), which derives new keys from a string m using a key k.

1. **Root of Trust.** Mdaak extracts a unique secret s from start-up values of the on-chip SRAM PUF using a fuzzy extractor. s serves as the root of trust for storage, since it derives the device key and the storage root key, which securely stores user signing keys.
2. **Device Key (DK).** It is a device-specific key pair $dk = (dsk, dpk)$ derived from s and computed as follows: $dk = KDF_s(\text{'identity'})$, where 'identity' is a value used to differentiate the uses of the KDF. The private part dsk is available only inside the TEE. The public part dpk should be certified by a trusted authority. Typically, the device manufacturer will perform the cer-tification at the time of the device manufacturing process: it signs dpk and issues the device certificate dcert, which is used for platform authentication to promise that dpk belongs to a device supporting Mdaak.
3. **Storage Root Key (SRK).** It is a symmetric key srk derived from s, i.e., $srk = KDF_s(\text{'storage'})$, where 'storage' is also a value used to differen-tiate the uses of the KDF. The SRK is the root key for secure storage and used to generate other storage keys.

4. **Storage Key.** It is a program-specific symmetric key derived from the SRK using the program identifier, which is a digest of the program's code. More specifically, for DAA Trustlet, its storage key sk is computed as follows: sk = KDF_{srk}(H(DAA Trustlet)), where H(DAA Trustlet) is the digest of DAA Trustlet's code.

4.2 Mdaak Components

As shown in Fig. 1, Mdaak is split into the normal world and the secure world of TrustZone: the normal world hosts DAA Service and the mobile OS containing NW-Driver, while the secure world hosts DAA Trustlet, Key Manager and the secure OS kernel containing SW-Driver. DAA Service and DAA Trustlet are components providing the DAA functionality, and DAA Service invokes DAA Trustlet through the GP TEE Client API [26], which leverages NW-Driver to communicate with the secure world. Key Manager is a component used for controlling the usage of keys. Crypto Library in both worlds provide cryptographic algorithms for other components. The SRAM PUF is used to extract the unique secret s, which is the seed for deriving the DK and SRK. In the following, we present a more detailed description.

1. **Key Manager.** It generates the primitives described in Sect. 4.1 and provides the seal and unseal functions to protect signing keys for DAA Trustlet. The technical details of the seal and unseal functions will be described in Sect. 4.3.
2. **DAA Service.** It is the central component running all DAA protocols and offering the DAA functionality for mobile applications. This service executes the computations of DAA protocols on the host side and manages the storage of DAA public keys, credentials, and sealed signing keys. It consists of the following four components:
   - DAA Software Stack: provides mobile applications with DAA interfaces. It receives a DAA request from a mobile application and transfers the request to Host Engine, which processes the request. Then, it returns the result to the mobile application.
   - Host Engine: executes the computations of DAA protocols on the host side. It includes different engines each of which is responsible for executing one specific DAA scheme. It invokes Storage Manager to access DAA public keys and credentials, and sends requests to Command Library for security-critical computations.
   - Storage Manager: controls the storage and access of DAA public keys, credentials, and sealed signing keys, which are stored in the insecure persistent memory of the mobile device.
   - Command Library: provides interfaces that enable Host Engine to interact with DAA Trustlet. It takes a request from Host Engine, invokes DAA Trustlet through the GP TEE Client API, and returns the result from DAA Trustlet to Host Engine.
3. **DAA Trustlet.** It is the core component that operates on user signing keys. Specifically, it performs computations originally delegated to the TPM,

i.e., the computations of DAA protocols on the TPM side, and contains the following two components:

- Command Handler: receives a request from SW-Driver and transfers it to Trusted Engine, which processes the request. Then, it forwards the result returned by Trusted Engine to SW-Driver.
- Trusted Engine: executes the computations of DAA protocols on the TPM side. Similarly to Host Engine, it supports different engines each of which is responsible for executing one specific DAA scheme. It invokes Key Manager to seal/unseal signing keys.

4.3 Storage Support

Key Manager is used to protect signing keys of DAA Trustlet from being obtained by adversaries from the normal world and other trustlets running in the secure world. We achieve this goal by letting Key Manager: first derive a storage key by leveraging a fuzzy extractor, which takes as input the SRAM PUF initial data, and then provide seal and unseal functions, which use the storage key to protect signing keys. The unclonable property of the SRAM PUF prevents signing keys from being copied and shared. As the storage key is generated during runtime, it does not require specific secure non-volatile memory. In this section, we describe how to extract a unique, persistent, device-specific secret s from the SRAM PUF initial data and the seal and unseal functions.

Secret Extraction. The secret s is associated with the device by the manufacturer when the device is in the production facility. The Gen procedure of the fuzzy extractor takes as input the on-chip SRAM initial data r and a randomly selected large value s, and then performs the following steps:

1. Encode s with the BCH error correction code to obtain a code $C = BCH_{Enc}(s)$.
2. Create the helper data $H = C \oplus r$.
3. Use s as the seed to derive the device key $dk = KDF_s(\text{'identity'})$, and issue the device certificate dcert by signing the device public key dpk.
4. Store H and dcert in the device's insecure non-volatile memory.

After the manufacturer associates the device with the secret s, Key Manager can re-generate s by running the Rep procedure of the fuzzy extractor. The Rep procedure proceeds as follows: it takes as input the on-chip SRAM start-up values r', which is a noisy variant of the initial SRAM start-up values r, generates a noisy BCH code $C' = r' \oplus H$ using r' and the helper data H, and transfers code C' to the BCH decoder, which eliminates noise and generates the same s that the manufacturer selects during the Gen procedure. Finally, the DK and SRK are derived from s by $dk = KDF_s(\text{'identity'})$ and $srk = KDF_s(\text{'storage'})$, respectively.

Key Sealing and Unsealing. The seal function binds data to some trustlet by encrypting the data with the storage key derived from the identifier of the trustlet, while the unseal function yields the data contained in the sealed envelope. In the following, we describe how DAA Trustlet protects signing keys using the seal and unseal functions.

As described in Sect. 4.1, sk, which is derived from the SRK and the digest of the DAA Trustlet's code, is used to seal user signing keys. To seal signing keys, the seal function generates two symmetric keys ck and ik from sk. ck is a confidentiality key used for encrypting signing keys, and ik is an integrity key used for computing an integrity check on the encrypted signing keys to protect their integrity. Unsealing is the reverse: using the digest of DAA Trustlet to derive sk from the SRK, computing ck and ik, using ik to check the integrity of the encrypted signing keys, and finally decrypting signing keys using ck. Since sk is device-specific and program-specific, signing keys are inherently bound to DAA Trustlet of the specific device, thereby being kept privy to other trustlets on the device and prevented from being copied to other devices.

4.4 Security Analysis

In this section, we revisit the security objectives of Mdaak identified in Sect. 3.1 and informally reason how Mdaak achieves those objectives.

Secure storage of user signing keys. We achieve this by sealing signing keys before storing them in the insecure non-volatile memory. The integrity and confidentiality of signing keys are protected by an integrity check and an encryption, respectively. The sealing key is derived from the SRK using the identifier of DAA Trustlet, and the SRK is extracted from the SRAM PUF initial data, which is only available in the secure world (as after the initial data of the SRAM is obtained by the secure world, it is erased). Therefore, signing keys will never be disclosed to any entity other than DAA Trustlet and cannot be copied and moved to other devices.

Protection of the key-processing code. The key-processing code contains two components: Key Manager and DAA Trustlet. The integrity of these components can be verified by the BootROM during the system booting: this is done by measuring the image of the secure OS kernel and comparing the result with a hash value signed by the manufacture. It's common for the BootROM to provide the verification ability in devices supporting secure boot, such as the Zynq-7000 SoC [37] and iOS platforms [6]. The runtime protection of the key-processing code is guaranteed by the memory isolation provided by TrustZone, which ensures that the key-processing code executing within TEE cannot be affected by code running in the normal world.

5   Implementation

We prototyped Mdaak on real TrustZone hardware and leveraged existing open source software.

5.1   Hardware Testbed

We choose a development board Zynq-7000 AP SoC Evaluation Kit [44]. It is TrustZone-enabled and equipped with dual ARM Cortex-A9 MPCore, 1GB of DDR3 Memory, and an On-Chip Memory (OCM) module consisting of 256 KB of SRAM and 128 KB of ROM (BootROM). Although Zynq-7000 AP SoC has 256 KB of on-chip SRAM, it is initialized by the BootROM once the board is powered on, preventing us from reading its initial data. We then use an SRAM chip that is of the type IS61LV6416-10TL [29] to serve as our SRAM PUF. This SRAM chip is equipped in a board [5] whose core is the ALTERA Cyclone II EP2C5T144 chip. In our implementation, the SRAM initial data is transferred to the Zynq development board by an FPGA implementation of Universal Asynchronous Receiver/Transmitter (UART) in Verilog hardware description language. A UART receiver in the Zynq board receives the SRAM data via a General Purpose I/O pin and stores the data in a RAM cache. Then the CPU can fetch the SRAM data in the RAM cache via the AXI bus.

5.2   Software Implementation

There are two types of ECC-DAA variants: LRSW-DAA whose security is based on the LRSW assumption [31] and SDH-DAA whose security is based on the q-SDH assumption [10]. We implemented four typical ECC-DAA schemes, including two LRSW-DAA schemes (BCL08 [12], CPS10 [19]) and two SDH-DAA schemes (CF08 [20], BL10 [14]). To achieve maximum efficiency, the prototype code is developed in the C language. Communication between the secure and normal worlds is through the GP TEE Client API. Furthermore, we use the Pairing-Based Cryptography (PBC) library [30] as Crypto Library of the two worlds for elliptic curve arithmetic and pairing computation.

Secure World. The secure world runs the Open Virtualization SierraTEE, which provides a basic secure OS in the secure world of TrustZone and is compliant with the GP's TEE Specifications [25].

For Key Manager, the fuzzy extractor is based on an open source BCH code [32], which can build BCH codes with different parameters. We customize a [1020,43,439]-BCH code based on [32] and optimize the source code to make it require less than 40KB memory. The [1020,43,439]-BCH code can decode a noisy 1020 bits message whose errors are less than $\lfloor 493/2 \rfloor = 219$ bits, and obtain 43 "error-free" bits. As the secret s is of length 256 bits, we require at least $\lceil 256/43 \rceil * 1020 = 6120$ bits SRAM initial data and need to run the BCH code $\lceil 256/43 \rceil = 6$ times. In addition, we implement the KDF of asymmetric keys using the RSAREF library [36], and use the KDF from SP800-108 [33] for the generation of symmetric keys. We use AES and HMAC-SHA1 to implement the seal and unseal functions, and use SHA1 to compute the identifier of DAA Trustlet.

To build DAA Trustlet, we leverage an open-source project TPM Emulator [39]. The project provides the implementation of a software-based TPM emulator, which contains the DAA functionality of BCC04 [11] but does not provide any ECC-DAA functionality. To implement DAA Trustlet with a small size of code, we remove unnecessary command processing code from the emulator and only keep the necessary code, such as command handling and parsing code and DAA command processing code. We then develop four ECC-DAA trusted engines, which provide the cryptographic operations for the four ECC-DAA schemes on the TPM side. Finally, we change the DAA command processing code in the emulator to interact with the new ECC-DAA engines.

Normal World. In the normal world, we run a Linux OS with kernel version 3.8. NW-Driver and the GP TEE Client API are provided by the SierraTEE project. We now briefly describe the realization of two components: DAA Service and an application DAA Tester, which is used to evaluate DAA Service.

We leverage the libtpm library [28] to implement DAA Service, which provides a low level API to TPM command ordinals. We add DAA function code to libtpm and borrow the TPM utility function code (tpmutil) of libtpm to interface to DAA Trustlet. Specifically, we (1) develop four ECC-DAA host engines performing the computations of the four ECC-DAA schemes on the host side, (2) add command processing code to interact with the engines, (3) change the I/O interface to invoke the GP TEE Client API to interact with DAA Trustlet, and (4) add Storage Manager to control the storage of DAA public keys, credentials, and sealed signing keys.

To allow an evaluation that does not take the network latency and throughput into account, we implemented an application DAA Tester in the normal world, which serves the issuer functionality as well as the verifier functionality. In particularly, DAA Tester can

1. run as an issuer: generate its secret key and DAA public key, and invoke DAA Service to execute the Join protocol.
2. run as a verifier: generate a basename, a message, and a nonce, invoke DAA Service to generate a DAA signature, and verify the signature received from DAA Service.

6   Evaluation

In this section, we first give a description of the elliptic curve choices in our evaluation. Afterwards, we present the code size of the prototype and perform a performance evaluation. Finally, we give our suggestions on the selection of DAA schemes and curve parameters on TrustZone-enabled platforms.

6.1   Curve Parameters

The selection of elliptic curve parameters impacts both the credential and signature sizes and the computational efficiency. For the evaluation, we use eight different elliptic curves offering varied levels of security. Table 1 presents the

Table 1. Description of the elliptic curve parameters used in our evaluation

Curve	k	$\mathcal{R}(G_1)$ (bits)	$\mathcal{R}(G_T)$ (bits)	$\mathcal{S}$ (bits)
SS512	2	512	1024	80
SS768	2	768	1536	96
MNT160	6	160	960	80
MNT224	6	224	1344	96
BN160	12	160	1920	80
BN192	12	192	2304	96
BN224	12	224	2688	112
BN256	12	256	3072	128

curve choices along with relevant details. Let k denote the embedding degree, $\mathcal{R}(G_i)$ $(i = 1, T)$ denote the approximate number of bits to optimally represent an element of the group G_i, and $\mathcal{S}$ denote an estimate of the security level, which is the number of operation required to break a cryptographic algorithm. For symmetric pairings, we choose two supersingular (SS) curves over a prime finite field with $k = 2$ according to [1]. For asymmetric pairings, based on [3], we consider two MNT curves with $k = 6$ and four BN curves with $k = 12$.

6.2 Code Size

We use the metric of *lines of code* (LOC) to measure the code size of our implementation, and the result is shown in Table 2. For DAA Trustlet, DAA Service, and DAA Tester, column *Main* refers to the main function's code size, the following four columns respectively denote the code size of a specific engine, and column *Total* refers to the whole code size of the component. For other components, we only measure their total code size and label '-' in other columns. In addition, row *Secure World* and *Normal World* show the overall code size for the secure and normal worlds, respectively. The total size of our prototype is about 71.6 KLOC: the secure world components comprise 35.9 KLOC, and the normal world components comprise 35.7 KLOC. Generally, the code size of our implementation is small enough to be run on mobile devices. Note that in both worlds, more than 83 % of the overall size is consumed by PBC library. As we have made no effort to strip unused content from PBC library, significant reductions in code size are readily attainable.

6.3 Performance

This section presents a performance evaluation of Mdaak. We evaluate Mdaak through a series of experiments on the four DAA schemes with different curve parameters listed in Sect. 6.1. In total, we conduct 20 experiments: two for BCL08 (using SS512 and SS768 respectively), six for each of the rest three schemes CPS10, CF08, and BL10 (using MNT160, BN160, MNT224, BN192, BN224,

Table 2. Code size of our implementation (in LOC)

Component	Main	BCL08	CPS10	CF08	BL10	Total
PBC library	-	-	-	-	-	29.9K
Key Manager	-	-	-	-	-	3.9K
DAA Trustlet	887	344	269	301	272	2.1K
Secure World	-	-	-	-	-	35.9K
PBC library	-	-	-	-	-	29.9K
DAA Service	971	489	347	400	408	2.6K
DAA Tester	45	783	787	811	751	3.2K
Normal World	-	-	-	-	-	35.7K

and BN256 respectively). The security levels of the DAA schemes in our experiments range from 80 bits to 128 bits. For each security level, we measure the performance of the individual scheme using the specified curve and compare the results with each other. The obtained performance results for each security level of the DAA schemes are analyzed in the following.

80-bit security level. Figure 2 plots the evaluation results of seven experiments for 80-bit security level, showing the execution time of all entities. For the Sign process, we measure the performance results of each world. The *SW Signing* refers to the execution time in the secure world, while the *NW Signing* denotes the execution time in the normal world. The *Verification* refers to the performance of the Verify process, which is represented by the vertical axis on the right. The results show that for the Sign process, the CPS10 scheme using MNT160 outperforms others and takes 60.7 ms, while for the Verify process, the BL10 scheme using MNT160 is most efficient and costs 142.2 ms.

96-bit security level. Figure 3 shows the performance results of seven experiments for 96-bit security level. It clearly demonstrates the performance advantages of CPS10 using BN192 in Sign and BL10 using MNT224 in Verify, and they take on average 104.7 ms and 254.3 ms, respectively. For CPS10, the signing

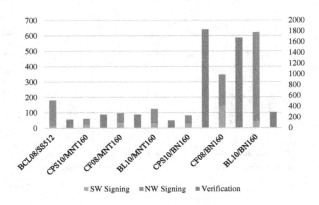

Fig. 2. Execution time of DAA schemes with 80-bit security level (in ms).

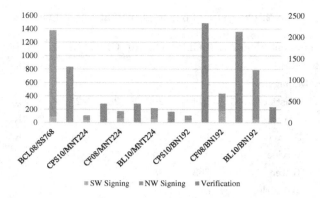

Fig. 3. Execution time of DAA schemes with 96-bit security level (in ms).

performance using MNT224 is only slightly slower than the signing performance using BN192. However, it requires about 445.4 ms to complete a verification using MNT224 but about 2322.7 ms using BN192. Therefore, for this scheme, using MNT224 at 96-bit security level is more competitive than using BN192.

Higher security level. Figure 4 presents a detailed overview of execution times of experiments with two higher security level: (1) 112-bit and (2) 128-bit. From the figure, it is apparent that the signing performance of CPS10 is always much higher than CF08 and BL10. For 112-bit and 128-bit security level, its signing time is about 105.5 ms and 133.9 ms, respectively. Moreover, the verification efficiency of BL10 exceeds the other two schemes for both security levels. With 112-bit security level it requires 360.1 ms for a verification, and with 128-bit security level it requires 450.8 ms for a verification.

As can be concluded from the results presented in Figs. 2, 3, and 4, execution time varies with the DAA scheme and the curve parameter. Depending on the scheme and curve, signing lasts about 60.7 ms−1377.9 ms, and verification is done within 142.2 ms−2835.5 ms. Six of the 20 experiments require more than 2 s to verify a signature, which may seem like a long time for realistic use, while note that verification is a less critical factor regarding mobile device performance, as

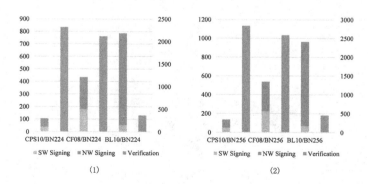

Fig. 4. Execution time of DAA schemes with 112-bit and 128-bit security level (in ms).

it is generally performed on powerful server machines. Overall, the results of our practical evaluation show that the implementation of our framework provides promising performance, and all the four DAA schemes are competitive in terms of performance, even for the Verify process. It is obvious that DAA can be implemented efficiently enough on mobile devices, and our framework is feasible and well suitable for mobile environment.

6.4 Suggestions

Through above measurement results, we find that the choice of DAA schemes and curve parameters has a big effect on the performance. As efficiency is an important factor when deploying DAA in practice, we give our suggestions on the selection of DAA schemes and elliptic curves for different application scenarios in the following.

- For the most common application scenarios, where users authenticate themselves to a powerful server through low-power computing devices, the signing efficiency of DAA schemes is crucial, as users will hardly accept a long waiting time. Then CPS10 will be the best choice.
- In some applications, authentication servers may have low performance or there may be a large number of verification requests to an authentication server. Then verification becomes a performance bottleneck. BL10 is well suitable for this type of applications, as it achieves high performance on verification.
- For applications with low security requirements, where security level less than 96-bit is enough, MNT curve is more practical, as it is more efficient than BN curve at low security levels up to 96-bit.
- BN curve is recommended for high-security applications. When security level at least 112-bit is needed, above two recommended schemes show better performance using BN curve than using MNT curve.

7 Related Work

There are various publications [8,9,22,38] discussing how to employ DAA on mobile devices based on smart cards. Bichsel et al. [9] implemented a variant of BCC04 [11] using a standard JavaCard, which executes the entire computations, even the host computations in a smart card. As a result, computing a signature takes about 7.4 s for a 1280-bit modulus, and up to 16.5 s for a 1984-bit modulus. To increase efficiency, in [38], the computation of a signature is divided between a smart card and a host, and the on-card execution time for a signature using a 1024-bit modulus is about 4.2 s. However, this approach requires partial trust on the host. Balasch [8] implemented BCC04 [11] on an AVR micro controller, and the signing time of his approach is about 133.5 s on an 8 bit micro-controller for a 1024-bit modulus. Dietrich [22] proposes to implement BCC04 [11] using an on-board smart card. This approach takes about 4.8 s for computing a signature using a 2048-bit modulus on card, and it is still a heavy load for an authentication process.

Some following publications propose to implement DAA on mobile devices without using additional hardware. Dietrich [21] presents an implementation of BCC04 [11] in Java on off-the-shelf mobile phones. The protection of his approach can only be guaranteed by the security properties of the Java virtual machine and the mobile operating system. To improve security, in [23], Dietrich et al. implemented above approach on a TrustZone-based device, and the protection is achieved by the TrustZone processor extensions. However, these approaches both realize the RSA-based DAA scheme which is less efficient, and their implementations use Java which in general is much slower then C. Hence, Wachsmann et al. [43] propose a design of anonymous authentication for mobile devices by modifying an ECC-DAA scheme [19] and present their prototype, which is implemented in C and based on TrustZone. Their scheme "requires a hardware-protected environment that ensures confidentiality of the secret key", but they did not specify how to achieve it in the paper.

8   Conclusion

In this paper, we propose Mdaak, a generic framework that enables cost-effective deployment of DAA on mobile devices, while ensures the security of user signing keys and the efficiency of authentication by using ARM TrustZone. The framework is flexible enough to support various DAA schemes and achieves high performance by performing security-critical computations on the powerful ARM processor in secure mode. Furthermore, our framework leverages an SRAM PUF available in OCM of mobile devices as the root of trust for secure storage to prevent copying and sharing of signing keys. We present a full implementation of Mdaak on real TrustZone hardware and give detailed performance measurements of four typical ECC-DAA schemes using different curve parameters. The experiments provide strong evidence that our framework is highly efficient for practical deployment of DAA on the current generation of mobile hardware. In conclusion, we are confident that our solution is a practical approach to realize DAA in mobile environment.

Acknowledgement. This work was supported by the National Natural Science Foundation of China (91118006 and 61202414), and the National Basic Research Program of China (2013CB338003).

References

1. IEEE P1636.3/D1: Draft standard for identity-based public-key cryptographyusing pairings (2008)
2. ISO/IEC 11889: 2009 Information technology-Security techniques-Trusted Platform (2009)
3. ISO/IEC 15946-5: 2009 Information technology-Security techniques-Cryptographic techniques based on elliptic curves-Part 5: Elliptic curve generation (2009)

4. ISO/IEC 20008-2: 2013 Information technology-Security techniques-Anonymous digital signatures-Part 2: Mechanisms using a group public key (2013)
5. Anne's fashion shoes: ALTERA EP2C8F256 Core Board (2014)
6. Apple: iOS Security. http://images.apple.com/ipad/business/docs/iOS_Security_Feb14.pdf
7. ARM: ARM TrustZone. http://www.arm.com/products/processors/technologies/trustzone
8. Balasch, J.: Smart card implementation of anonymous credentials. Master's thesis, K.U. Leuven (2008)
9. Bichsel, P., Camenisch, J., Groß, T., Shoup, V.: Anonymous credentials on a standard java card. In: Proceedings of the 16th ACM Conference on Computer and Communications Security, pp. 600–610. ACM (2009)
10. Boneh, D., Boyen, X.: Short signatures without random oracles. In: Cachin, C., Camenisch, J.L. (eds.) EUROCRYPT 2004. LNCS, vol. 3027, pp. 56–73. Springer, Heidelberg (2004)
11. Brickell, E., Camenisch, J., Chen, L.: Direct anonymous attestation. In: Proceedings of the 11th ACM Conference on Computer and Communications Security, pp. 132–145. ACM (2004)
12. Brickell, E., Chen, L., Li, J.: A new direct anonymous attestation scheme from bilinear maps. In: Lipp, P., Sadeghi, A.-R., Koch, K.-M. (eds.) Trust 2008. LNCS, vol. 4968, pp. 166–178. Springer, Heidelberg (2008)
13. Brickell, E., Li, J.: Enhanced privacy ID from bilinear pairing. IACR Cryptology ePrint Archive (2009)
14. Brickell, E., Li, J.: A pairing-based DAA scheme further reducing TPM resources. In: Acquisti, A., Smith, S.W., Sadeghi, A.-R. (eds.) TRUST 2010. LNCS, vol. 6101, pp. 181–195. Springer, Heidelberg (2010)
15. Chaum, D.: Security without identification: transaction systems to make big brother obsolete. Commun. ACM **28**(10), 1030–1044 (1985)
16. Chaum, D., Evertse, J.-H.: A secure and privacy-protecting protocol for transmitting personal information between organizations. In: Odlyzko, A.M. (ed.) CRYPTO 1986. LNCS, vol. 263, pp. 118–167. Springer, Heidelberg (1987)
17. Chen, L.: A DAA scheme requiring less TPM resources. In: Bao, F., Yung, M., Lin, D., Jing, J. (eds.) Inscrypt 2009. LNCS, vol. 6151, pp. 350–365. Springer, Heidelberg (2010)
18. Chen, L., Li, J.: Flexible and scalable digital signatures in TPM 2.0. In: Proceedings of the 20th ACM Conference on Computer and Communications Security, pp. 37–48. ACM (2013)
19. Chen, L., Page, D., Smart, N.P.: On the design and implementation of an efficient DAA scheme. In: Gollmann, D., Lanet, J.-L., Iguchi-Cartigny, J. (eds.) CARDIS 2010. LNCS, vol. 6035, pp. 223–237. Springer, Heidelberg (2010)
20. Chen, X., Feng, D.: Direct anonymous attestation for next generation TPM. J. Comput. **3**(12), 43–50 (2008)
21. Dietrich, K.: Anonymous credentials for java enabled platforms: a performance evaluation. In: Chen, L., Yung, M. (eds.) INTRUST 2009. LNCS, vol. 6163, pp. 88–103. Springer, Heidelberg (2010)
22. Dietrich, K.: Anonymous RFID authentication using trusted computing technologies. In: Ors Yalcin, S.B. (ed.) RFIDSec 2010. LNCS, vol. 6370, pp. 91–102. Springer, Heidelberg (2010)

23. Dietrich, K., Winter, J., Luzhnica, G., Podesser, S.: Implementation aspects of anonymous credential systems for mobile trusted platforms. In: De Decker, B., Lapon, J., Naessens, V., Uhl, A. (eds.) CMS 2011. LNCS, vol. 7025, pp. 45–58. Springer, Heidelberg (2011)

24. Dodis, Y., Reyzin, L., Smith, A.: Fuzzy extractors: how to generate strong keys from biometrics and other noisy data. In: Cachin, C., Camenisch, J.L. (eds.) EUROCRYPT 2004. LNCS, vol. 3027, pp. 523–540. Springer, Heidelberg (2004)

25. GlobalPlatform: GlobalPlatform Device Specifications. http://www.globalplatform.org

26. GlobalPlatform: TEE client API specification version 1.0 (2010)

27. Guajardo, J., Kumar, S.S., Schrijen, G.-J., Tuyls, P.: FPGA intrinsic PUFs and their use for IP protection. In: Paillier, P., Verbauwhede, I. (eds.) CHES 2007. LNCS, vol. 4727, pp. 63–80. Springer, Heidelberg (2007)

28. IBM: libtpm. http://ibmswtpm.sourceforge.net/#libtpm

29. Integrated Silicon Solution Inc: IS61LV6416-10TL. http://www.alldatasheet.com/datasheet-pdf/pdf/505020/ISSI/IS61LV6416-10TL.html

30. Lynn, B.: PBC Library - The Pairing-Based Cryptography Library. http://crypto.stanford.edu/pbc/

31. Lysyanskaya, A., Rivest, R.L., Sahai, A., Wolf, S.: Pseudonym systems (Extended Abstract). In: Heys, H.M., Adams, C.M. (eds.) SAC 1999. LNCS, vol. 1758, pp. 184–199. Springer, Heidelberg (2000)

32. Morelos-Zaragoza, R.: Encoder/decoder for binary BCH codes in C (Version 3.1) (1994)

33. NIST: Recommendation for Key Derivation Using Pseudorandom Functions (2009)

34. Oren, Y., Sadeghi, A.-R., Wachsmann, C.: On the effectiveness of the remanence decay side-channel to clone memory-based PUFs. In: Bertoni, G., Coron, J.-S. (eds.) CHES 2013. LNCS, vol. 8086, pp. 107–125. Springer, Heidelberg (2013)

35. Pappu, R., Recht, B., Taylor, J., Gershenfeld, N.: Physical one-way functions. Science **297**(5589), 2026–2030 (2002)

36. RSA Laboratories: RSAREF(TM): A Cryptographic Toolkit Library Reference Manual (1994)

37. Sanders, L.: Secure Boot of Zynq-7000 All Programmable SoC (2013)

38. Sterckx, M., Gierlichs, B., Preneel, B., Verbauwhede, I.: Efficient implementation of anonymous credentials on Java Card smart cards. In: Proceedings of the 1st IEEE International Workshop on Information Forensics and Security, pp. 106–110. IEEE (2009)

39. Strasser, M.: TPM Emulator. http://tpm-emulator.berlios.de/

40. TCG: TPM Main Specification Level 2 Version 1.2, Revision 116 (2011)

41. TCG: Trusted Platform Module Library Specification Family "2.0" Level 00, Revision 01.07 (2013)

42. Tuyls, P., Schrijen, G.-J., Škorić, B., van Geloven, J., Verhaegh, N., Wolters, R.: Read-proof hardware from protective coatings. In: Goubin, L., Matsui, M. (eds.) CHES 2006. LNCS, vol. 4249, pp. 369–383. Springer, Heidelberg (2006)

43. Wachsmann, C., Chen, L., Dietrich, K., Löhr, H., Sadeghi, A.-R., Winter, J.: Lightweight anonymous authentication with TLS and DAA for embedded mobile devices. In: Burmester, M., Tsudik, G., Magliveras, S., Ilić, I. (eds.) ISC 2010. LNCS, vol. 6531, pp. 84–98. Springer, Heidelberg (2011)

44. Xilinx: Zynq-7000 All Programmable SoC ZC702 Evaluation Kit. http://www.xilinx.com/products/boards-and-kits/EK-Z7-ZC702-G.htm

Protecting Elliptic Curve Cryptography Against Memory Disclosure Attacks

Yang Yang[1,2,3], Zhi Guan[1,2,3]([⊠]), Zhe Liu[4], and Zhong Chen[1,2,3]

[1] Institute of Software, School of EECS,, Peking University, Beijing, China
{yangyang,guanzhi,chen}@infosec.pku.edu.cn
[2] MoE Key Lab of High Confidence Software Technologies (PKU), Beijing, China
[3] MoE Key Lab of Network and Software Security Assurance (PKU), Beijing, China
[4] Laboratory of Algorithmics, Cryptology and Security, University of Luxembourg,
Walferdange, Luxembourg
zhe.liu@uni.lu

Abstract. In recent years, memory disclosure attacks, such as cold boot attack and DMA attack, have posed huge threats to cryptographic applications in real world. In this paper, we present a CPU-bounded memory disclosure attacks resistant yet efficient software implementation of elliptic curves cryptography on general purpose processors. Our implementation performs scalar multiplication using CPU registers only in kernel level atomically to prevent the secret key and intermediate data from leaking into memory. Debug registers are used to hold the private key, and kernel is patched to restrict access to debug registers. We take full advantage of the AVX and CLMUL instruction sets to speed up the implementation. When evaluating the proposed implementation on an Intel i7-2600 processor (at a frequency of 3.4 GHz), a full scalar multiplication over binary fields for key length of 163 bits only requires 129 μs, which outperforms the unprotected implementation in the well known OpenSSL library by a factor of 78.0 %. Furthermore, our work is also flexible for typical Linux applications. To the best of our knowledge, this is the first practical ECC implementation which is resistant against memory disclosure attacks so far.

Keywords: Elliptic curve cryptography · Efficient implementation · Memory disclosure attack · Cold boot attack · AVX · CLMUL

1 Introduction

Main memory has long been commonly used to store private keys at runtime for various cryptosystems because of the assumption that memory space isolation mechanism of operating system and volatility of dynamic RAM (DRAM) prevent access from adversaries both logically and physically. However, the presence of *cold boot attack* [5] shows acquiring memory contents is much easier than most people thought. Cold boot attack leverages the data remanence property which is a fundamental physical property of DRAM chips, because of which DRAM

© Springer International Publishing Switzerland 2015
L.C.K. Hui et al. (Eds.): ICICS 2014, LNCS 8958, pp. 49–60, 2015.
DOI: 10.1007/978-3-319-21966-0_4

contents take a significant time to fade away gradually. This property exists in all DRAM chips and it determines how DRAM chips works: holding memory contents by refreshing the state of each memory unit periodly. The problem is that the time before memory contents fading away after the moment at which memory chips lost power can be significant extended at a low temperature, and memory contents stop fading away and become readable again once memory chips power on, so memory contents may survive across boots. As a result, for a running target machine physically accessible to adversaries, adversaries are able to transplant the memory chips from the machine to a well prepared attack machine after cooling down the memory chips, and cold boot the attack machine with a customized boot loader to bypass all defence mechanisms of the target machine and dump the memory contents to some persistent storage to get a snapshot of the memory contents.

Cold boot attack is not the only attack can be used to acquire the memory contents. DMA attack is another powerful attack which uses direct memory access through ports like Firewire, IEEE1394 to access physical memory space of the target machine. And the recently exposed vulnerable of OpenSSL called "HeartBleed"[1] which leaks memory contents onto network can also be used for memory acquisition. These attacks are called **memory disclosure attacks** in general, since they disclose contents in memory partially or entirely to adversaries while adversaries are unable to actively change the contents in the memory. Not only PCs and laptops, smart phones have also been demonstrated to be vulnerable to these attacks [11]. These attacks pose huge and prevalent threats to the implementation of both public-key and symmetric-key cryptosystems which hold secret keys in memory at runtime, and adversaries are able to reconstruct the key efficiently when only a part of the key or key schedule is acquired [5,7]. Compared to symmetric-key cryptosystems, these attacks may cause more damage on public-key cryptosystems, since revoking a compromised private key is very expensive, sometimes even impossible: private keys often have a long life cycle such as several years, leakage of high sensitive private keys leads to serious consequences.

Memory disclosure attacks have become a research hotspot since the presence of cold boot attack [5]. Akavia et al. proposed a new security model to formally describe memory disclosure attacks [1], in which the total amount of key leakage is bounded while "only computation leaks information" in traditional model of side channel attacks. Based on this model, several schemes have been proposed to resist memory disclosure attacks theoretically [1,2,15]. These solutions are not practical and cannot be used to protect existing cryptographic primitives, such as AES, RSA, etc.

Several solutions based on CPU-bounded encryption have been proposed to protect existing cryptographic primitives. The underlying idea of which is to avoid DRAM usage completely by storing the secret key and sensitive inner state in CPU registers, since there has been no known attacks can be used to acquire contents of CPU registers. AESSE [13] from Müller et al. implemented an AES cryptosystem using X86 SSE registers as the key storage. The performance of AESSE is

---

[1] http://heartbleed.com.

about 6 times slower than a standard implementation. As a successor of AESSE, TRESOR [14] utilizes the new X86 AES-NI instructions for AES encryption to provide a better performance and a better compatibility with Linux distributions. Loop-Amnesia [16] stores a master key inside Machine Specific Registers (MSRs), and supports multiple AES keys securely inside RAM by scrambling them with the master key. TreVisor [12] builds TRESOR into the hypervisor layer to yield an OS-independent disk encryption solution.

On the other hand, resisting memory disclosure attacks for public key cryptosystem is more challenging. Garmany et al. [4] have proposed a memory disclosure attacks resistant RSA implementation based on CPU-bounded encryption. They achieved 21 ms per operation for modular exponentiation, which is about ten times slower than off-the-shelf cryptographic libraries. And the TLS server based on their implementation achieved a significant higher latency under high load in the benchmark.

An important reason for the unsatisfied performance in PRIME is the extreme large key size of RSA for CPU registers. On the other hand, elliptic curve cryptography (ECC) [8,10] provides the same level of security as RSA with a much smaller key size, and thus, requires less memory storage. In this case, efficient implementation of ECC which resists against memory disclosure attacks is still a challenging work. Our work presented in this paper is going to make up for the gap.

1.1 Contributions

In this paper, we propose an efficient elliptic curve cryptography (ECC) implementation that also resists memory disclosure attacks by keeping the private key and sensitive intermediate state out of the memory. In detail, our major contributions are listed as follows:

- We proposed an efficient and memory disclosure attack resistant CPU-bounded elliptic curve cryptography cryptosystem using new features on modern X86-64 CPUs. The cryptosystem keeps the private key and sensitive intermediate data within CPU registers after the private key is loaded so that attackers have no chance to retrieve the key or key schedule from the memory.
- The cryptosystem makes full use of AVX and CLMUL instruction sets of X86-64 CPU architecture to speed up the computation. The performance evaluation of our solution on an Intel i7-2600 processor found our implementation achieves a performance of 129 μs for a scalar multiplication operation over binary fields for key length of 163 bits. This result outperforms the unprotected fashion of OpenSSL by a factor of 78.0 %.
- To the best of our knowledge, this work provides the first memory disclosure attacks resistant ECC implementation, and the first public-key cryptographic implementation that resists these attacks, and provides a better performance than off-the-shelf cryptographic libraries at the same time.

The rest of this paper is organized as follows. A brief introduction of elliptic curve cryptography is given in Sect. 2 together with architecture we focus on.

Next we describe how we design and implement the solution in Sect. 3. Then the evaluation on security and performance is given in Sect. 4. Finally, we conclude this paper in Sect. 5.

2   Preliminaries

In this section, we first recap the basic knowledge of elliptic curve cryptography and then give a brief description of the CPU architecture and key instruction sets we used for our implementation.

2.1   Elliptic Curve Cryptography

Elliptic curve cryptography (ECC) can be considered as an approach of public-key cryptography based on the algebraic structure of elliptic curves over finite fields [8,10]. An elliptic curve over a field K is defined by Eq. 1.

$$E : y^2 + a_1 xy + a_3 y = x^3 + a_2 x^2 + a_4 x + a_6 \tag{1}$$

The equation can be simplified for the characteristic of K is 2, 3, or greater than 3, respectively. The points satisfying the equation and a distinguished point at infinity which is the identity element forms a set, together with group operations of the elliptic group theory form an Abelian group. The group is used in the construction of elliptic curve cryptographic system.

There are two basic group operations in ECC: a point addition adds two different points together and a point doubling operation doubles a single point. Point addition and point doubling are computed according to a *chord-and-tangent* rule. *Scalar multiplication* computes $k \cdot P$ where k is a scalar and P is a point on an elliptic curve, that is adding P together k times. A scalar multiplication is computed as a serious of point additions and point doublings. Like the integer exponentiation in RSA cryptosystem, scalar multiplication is the basic cryptographic operation of various ECC schemes.

Domain parameters define the field and the curve of an ECC system, including the field order f, the curve constants a and b, the base point(subgroup generator) G, the order of the base point n and the cofactor h. The generation of domain parameters is time consuming, therefore several standard bodies published domain parameters for several common field sizes, which are commonly known as "standard curves" or "named curves". Domain parameters must be agreed on by all parties before use.

Each party must also generate a public-private key pair before use. The private key d is a randomly selected scalar. The public key Q is computed as $Q = d \cdot G$, where G is the base point. The security of an ECC cryptosystem relies on the assumption that finding the discrete logarithm of a random elliptic curve point with respect to a public known base point is infeasible.

Elliptic Curve Diffie-Hellman(ECDH) is an anonymous key agreement protocol that allows two parties to establish a shared secret over an insecure channel.

It is a variant of the Diffie-Hellman protocol using elliptic curve cryptography. Denote two parties **A** and **B**, the key pairs of them are (d_A, Q_A) and (d_B, Q_B), then they can compute $d_A Q_B$ and $d_B Q_A$ respectively to get a shared secret, as $(x_k, y_k) = d_A Q_B = d_A d_B G = d_B Q_A$ where x_k is the shared secret. A symmetric key can be derived from the shared secret to encrypt subsequent communications. The key exchange protocol is one of the most important applications for public key cryptography.

2.2 The X86-64 CPU Architecture

x86-64 is the 64-bit version of x86 instruction set. It supports larger memory address space and register files. X86-64 is supported by mainstream operating systems and widely used in modern desktop and laptop computers. Besides the base instruction set, we mainly use its two extensions: CLMUL and AVX.

Carry-Less Multiplication. The Carry-Less Multiplication(CLMUL)[2] instruction set is an X86 extension that can be used to compute a polynomial multiplication, which is the product of two operands without the generation or propagation of carry values. Carry-less multiplication is an essential processing component of several cryptographic systems and standards, including of the Galois Counter Mode(GCM) and elliptic curve cryptography over binary fields. Software implementations of carry-less multiplication are often inefficient and suffer from potential side channel attacks, while CLMUL instruction set provides an convenient and efficient way to calculate carry-less multiplications.

Advanced Vector Extensions. The Advanced Vector Extensions (AVX/ AVX2/AVX–512)[3] are X86 SIMD extensions proposed by Intel. AVX and AVX2 are supported by recent processors, while AVX–512 will be supported in 2015. AVX/AVX2 doubles the amount of SIMD registers from 8 to 16, which are named as YMM0–YMM15 respectively, and extends the width of each register from 128 bits to 256 bits. AVX–512 doubles the amount and width of SIM registers again to 32 and 512 bits resprectively. AVX introduces a non-destructive three-operand SIMD instruction format. Mixed usage of AVX and legacy SSE instructions should be avoided to prevent AVX-SSE transition penalties. For any legacy SSE instruction, there is an equivalent VEX encoded instruction which should be used instead to avoid the penalty.

3   System Design and Implementation

3.1   System Overview

We hold the private key and intermediate data in CPU registers to avoid the leakage of secret data. We implement the ECC scalar multiplication using assembly language to control the usage of registers precisely to ensure no secret data

---

[2] http://en.wikipedia.org/wiki/CLMUL_instruction_set.
[3] http://en.wikipedia.org/wiki/Advanced_Vector_Extensions.

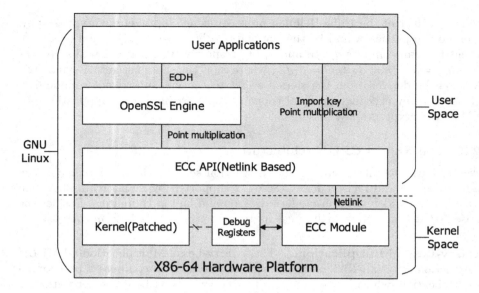

Fig. 1. The architecture of the proposed ECC cryptosystem.

leaks into memory explicitly. To avoid the implicit leakage of secret data by context switch mechanism, we deploy the ECC implementation in kernel level in a loadable kernel module(LKM) and make the computation atomically by disabling the interruption and kernel preemption during the computation. Netlink based interfaces are provided for user level applications. We also implement an OpenSSL engine to provide an interface based on our implementation for ECDH operations to demonstrate the possibility of integrating our implementation with existed applications. A private key is imported into the cryptosystem before use. The imported key is stored in debug registers and loaded into YMM registers before each scalar multiplication. The kernel of the operating system is patched to restrict access to debug registers. The architecture of the system is shown in Fig. 1.

3.2   Implementation of Secure Scalar Multiplication in ECC

Field Operations. For domain parameters "sect163k1", there are two sizes of polynomial involved in field operations: 163-bit and 325-bit. The former is the size of polynomials over the field $\mathbb{F}_{2^{163}}$, while the latter is the size of the product of two polynomial and will be further reduced to 163 bits. As we implement field operations mainly with AVX instructions and YMM registers, we use one YMM register for a 163-bit polynomial and two YMM registers for a 325-bit polynomial.

Operations over binary field are carry-less operations, which means the operation is performed without the generation or propagation of any carry values.

In this case, for any polynomial a and b over the binary field, the following equation holds:

$$a + b = a - b = a \oplus b$$

Namely that an addition and a subtraction over binary field can be simply calculated by XORing two operands.

The presence of CLMUL instruction set makes it much easier to implement carry-less multiplication efficiently and securely. Denote the 163-bit input operands A and B by $[A_2 : A_1 : A_0]$ and $[B_2 : B_1 : B_0]$, where $A_i, B_j, 0 \leq i, j \leq 2$ is a 64-bit quad-word. The carry-less multiplication between A_i and B_j can be simply calculated with a VPCLMULQDQ instruction:

$$C_{ij} = A_i \cdot B_j = \text{VPCLMULQDQ}(A_i, B_j), 0 \leq i, j \leq 2$$

Then the product C of A and B can be calculated as:

$$C = A \cdot B = [C_{22} : C_{21} \oplus C_{12} : C_{20} \oplus C_{11} \oplus C_{02} : C_{10} \oplus C_{01} : C_{00}]$$

Therefore we can implement a carry-less multiplication of two 163-bit operands with only 9 PCLMULQDQ instructions for partial products, 4 bitwise XOR instructions to combine partial products together, and several register manipulation instructions to put the partial products into right place in the result. A squaring operation can be implemented similarly as multiplicate the operand with itself.

The result of a multiplication or a squaring is a 325-bit polynomial, therefore it has to be reduced to 163 bits before further use. We use the NIST fast reduction algorithm and modulo $f(z) = z^{163} + z^7 + z^6 + z^3 + z^1$ defined in FIPS 186-2 [3] for reduction.

The inversion operation is to find a polynomial $g = a^{-1} \bmod f$ over F_{2^m} for the polynomial a satisfying $ag \equiv 1 (\bmod f)$. The inverse can be efficiently calculated by the extended Euclidean algorithm for polynomials. In our solution, we use the "modified almost inverse algorithm for inversion in $\mathbb{F}_{2^m}$" algorithm [6] to calculate the inversion of a polynomial in $\mathbb{F}_{2^{163}}$. An inversion operation takes much longer time than other basic field operations, therefore the group operation algorithm must be carefully selected to reduce the number of inversion operations.

Group Operations. We employ Montgomery ladder for elliptic curves over binary fields to compute a scalar multiplication [9]. One advantage of this algorithm is that it does not have any extra storage requirements, which is suitable for our CPU-bounded ECC cryptosystem since the storage space we can use is limited. It is also efficient enough and has been used in mainstream cryptographic libraries, such as OpenSSL. We use the projective version of the algorithm in order to reduce field inversions, as described by López and Dahab [9].

In this algorithm, each iteration j between line 4–13 performs an addition (line 7 and 10) and a doubling (line 8 and 11) to compute the x-coordinates only of $T_j = [lp, (l + 1)p]$, where l is the integer represented by the jth left most bit of k. After the final iteration, x-coordinates of kP and $(k+1)P$ have been computed, and line 14 and 15 are used to compute the affine coordinates of kP. Using temporary variables for intermediate result, one addition requires 4 field multiplications and one squaring, and one doubling requires 2 field multiplications and 4 squarings. The number of temporary variables used by an addition and a doubling is 2 and 1 respectively. The operation used to convert kP and $(k+1)P$ back to affine coordinates requires 3 temporary variables, 10 field multiplications, 1 field squaring and 1 field inversion.

We allocate the YMM registers as follows. One YMM register for storing a dimension of a point on elliptic curve over $\mathbb{F}_{2^{163}}$, and thus, two YMM registers are sufficient for a point represented in affine coordinates. Following the equations listed above, we implement addition and doubling with field operation in MACROs. Consequently, a doubling operation requires five YMM registers and an addition requires eight YMM registers, as well as the scalar multiplication algorithm (i.e. doubling-and-addition) requires 12 YMM registers. At the end, the ECC private key is a polynomial over the field and can be stored into one YMM register.

3.3   Deployment of ECC Cryptosystem in the Operating System

The implementation of ECC scalar multiplication should be carefully deployed in the operating system to make it be secure and accessible to user space applications. As described above, we implement the ECC cryptosystem as a loadable kernel module(LKM) to make it run atomically and patched the kernel to protect the private key. We demonstrate the modification and deployment successfully on Ubuntu 14.04, the kernel version is 3.13.0-34.

Atomicity.   The private key and sensitive intermediate data is kept in YMM registers during cryptographic computations, so we have to make the computation atomic to prevent sensitive intermediate data being swapped into the memory. This can be achieved by disabling the interruption and the kernel preemption by `preempt_disable()`, `local_irq_save()` and `local_irq_disable()`, before the computation, and enable the interruption and the kernel preemption again after the computation by `local_irq_enable()`, `local_irq_restore()` and `preempt_enable()` to make the system run normally.

User Space Interface.   We provide two interfaces based on netlink mechanism, which is widely used for communications between kernel and user space processes of the same host:

private_key_import Import the private key into the debug registers. The input is the plain text of the private key, which is a 163-bit big number.

private_key_operation Calculate the product of the point multiplication between the private key and a given point. The input is a point which is represented by two big numbers.

Each interface is implemented as a request-response round trip, namely the user space process send the request consisting of the function name and input values into the kernel then block until a response is received.

Private Key Protection. Access to debug registers should be prevented from either user space or kernel space other than the code of our system to prevent key damage and loss of secret data. Debug registers can only be accessed with ring 0 privilege directly. Access to debug registers in user space and kernel space are finally delegated to kernel functions `ptrace_set_debugreg`, `ptrace_get_debugreg`, `native_set_debugreg` and `native_get_debugreg`. We modified these functions to discard any change to debug registers and inform the caller there is no debug registers available. We searched the source of the kernel we are using thoroughly and found no other accesses to debug registers besides in these functions, which means only our module has access to debug registers in our patched system in both user space and kernel space.

Debug registers are per-core registers, therefore we have to copy the key into debug registers on all CPUs to prevent logical errors. We implement this procedure with the help of the kernel function `smp_call_function` which runs a certain function on all other CPUs.

4   Evaluation and Discussion

4.1   Security Verification

We assume the procedure of loading the key from a secure storage to the registers is safe and the memory trace of the key is erased immediately. This assumption is reasonable, because this procedure is transient and the user of the system has to physically access the computer to load the key, which also prevent the physical access from attackers. Therefore our system focus on the life cycle since the private key has been loaded into the registers.

We implement ECC in a way that no private key or sensitive intermediate data leaks into memory once the private key has been loaded into debug registers. Considering about the threats posed by memory disclosure attacks, our approach resists these attacks since adversaries cannot get the private key or any private key related data which can be used for key recovery with these attacks from our cryptosystem. In this section, we analyze and evaluate the approach to verify its security under the threats of these attacks.

Since we have already patched kernel functions which are used to access debug registers, and Müller et al. have verified debug registers are reset to zero after both cold and warm reboot, there is no way for the key to be moved into memory from debug registers or be accessed with cold boot attack.

For intermediate data and the private key in YMM registers, they will not appear in memory unless we write them to memory explicitly or be swapped into memory due to interruptions during the execution. We reviewed our code

Table 1. Performance comparison of scalar multiplication between OpenSSL and this work. $\star$: unprotected version. $\dagger$: protected version

Implementation	Operations Per Second
OpenSSL	4346*
This work	7734†
Improvements	78.0 %

thoroughly and made sure only the final result is written into memory. As preemption and interruption are disabled during the computation, our system is theoretically not vulnerable to memory disclosure attacks.

We also verified the correctness of the system on the test machine. Since we have already known the private key, we do this by acquire a series of snapshots of the memory contents after the key is loaded and search for the private key in them. If our system works correctly, there will be no match in snapshots. Performing a memory disclosure attack such as cold boot attack actually is time consuming, and these attacks get no more than memory contents, so we used a tool called **fmem**[4] to acquire the whole range of memory contents instead. We also performed this test on a system running a process using OpenSSL ECC library with the same private key as a comparison. The result shows there is a match of the private key on the system using OpenSSL while there is no significant match on the system using our approach.

As should be noted that the security of cryptographic application in real world is not trivial, single countermeasure can not mitigate different attacks. But our method is compatible with other countermeasures such as software based power analysis defeat method and can be used together.

4.2 Performance

Our benchmark is running on a desktop with an Intel Core i7-2600 processor set to be constantly running at 3.4 GHz. The operating system is Ubuntu Linux 13.10 64-bit with our modified kernel at version 3.11.0. We implemented an OpenSSL ECDH engine using scalar multiplication in our approach, and compared the performance of ECDH operation on curve SECT163K1 in our implementation with the same operation provided by OpenSSL[5] at version 1.0.1e. The evaluation shows the performance improvements precisely and practically, since ECDH is widely used and each operation comprises mainly a single scalar multiplication. The performance is measured by operations per second with the OpenSSL built-in speed tool. the result is shown in Table 1.

As shown in the table, an ECDH operation, namely a scalar multiplication in our solution is faster than that in OpenSSL by a factor of 78.0 %. The result of performance evaluation is encouraging, since our implementation is memory disclosure attacks resistant and that in OpenSSL is not, ours is also much more

---

[4] http://hysteria.sk/~niekt0/fmem/.

[5] https://www.openssl.org/.

Table 2. Performance comparison of field arithmetic operations between OpenSSL and this work (in μs per operation)

Implementation	Modular Add.	Modular Mul.	Modular Sqr.	Inversion
OpenSSL	0.013	0.160	0.117	3.670
This work	0.004	0.084	0.083	3.133
Improvements	225 %	90.1 %	41.0 %	17.1 %

efficient. We also compared the performance of running scalar multiplications directly and running with the APIs exposed into user space, and found communications between user space and kernel brings 2 %–5 % overheads, which are acceptable.

We also compared the performance improvements of each field operations, the result is shown in Table 2. The performance of field addition, modular multiplication and modular squaring in our solution is faster than that in OpenSSL by a factor of 225 %, 90.1 % and 41.0 % respectively. The performance of inversion in our solution is faster than that in OpenSSL by a factor of 17 %. The performance improvements due to the reduction of branches, unrolled loops and the power of CLMUL and AVX instruction sets, etc.

5 Conclusion and Future Work

Memory disclosure attacks such as cold boot attack have become a threat that must be considered by designers and developers of cryptographic libraries and applications. To mitigate such threats, we present a systematic solution on protecting public key cryptography based on the idea that restricts the private key and the intermediate states during the cryptographic operations inside CPU. Our solution is implemented as a Linux kernel patch with interfaces in the user space to provide secure elliptic curve scalar multiplications, and various secure ECC schemes can be constructed based on it. Evaluation shows our approach leaks none of the information that can be exploited by attackers to the memory, therefore it resists the cold boot attack and other memory disclosure attacks effectively. An ECC scalar multiplication over binary fields for key length of 163 bits in our solution is about 78.0 % faster than that in OpenSSL. To the best of our knowledge, our solution is the first efficient ECC implementation that is memory disclosure attacks resistant.

One of our future work is to support multiple private keys in our cryptosystem so that it supports multiple applications at the same time. After the release of processors supporting AVX-512, we will provide support of larger key size since AVX-512 has 4 times more register space than AVX/AVX2.

Acknowledgments. This work is supported by National High Technology Research and Development Program of China under Grant No. 2014AA123001.

References

1. Akavia, A., Goldwasser, S., Vaikuntanathan, V.: Simultaneous hardcore bits and cryptography against memory attacks. In: Reingold, O. (ed.) TCC 2009. LNCS, vol. 5444, pp. 474–495. Springer, Heidelberg (2009)
2. Dodis, Y., Haralambiev, K., López-Alt, A., Wichs, D.: Efficient public-key cryptography in the presence of key leakage. In: Abe, M. (ed.) ASIACRYPT 2010. LNCS, vol. 6477, pp. 613–631. Springer, Heidelberg (2010)
3. PUB FIPS. 186–2. digital signature standard (DSS). National Institute of Standards and Technology (NIST) (2000)
4. Garmany, B., Mller, T.: PRIME: private RSA infrastructure for memory-less encryption. In: Proceedings of the 29th Annual Computer Security Applications Conference, ACSAC 2013, pp. 149–158. ACM
5. Halderman, J.A., Schoen, S.D., Heninger, N., Clarkson, W., Paul, W., Calandrino, J.A., Feldman, A.J., Appelbaum, J., Felten, E.W.: Lest we remember: cold boot attacks on encryption keys. In: USENIX Security Symposium, pp. 45–60 (2008)
6. Hankerson, D., Hernandez, J.L., Menezes, A.: Software implementation of elliptic curve cryptography over binary fields. In: Paar, C., Koç, Ç.K. (eds.) CHES 2000. LNCS, vol. 1965, pp. 1–24. Springer, Heidelberg (2000)
7. Heninger, N., Shacham, H.: Reconstructing RSA private keys from random key bits. In: Halevi, S. (ed.) CRYPTO 2009. LNCS, vol. 5677, pp. 1–17. Springer, Heidelberg (2009)
8. Koblitz, N.: Elliptic curve cryptosystems. Math. Comp. 48(177), 203–209
9. López, J., Dahab, R.: Fast multiplication on elliptic curves over $GF(2_m)$ without precomputation. In: Koç, Ç.K., Paar, C. (eds.) CHES 1999. LNCS, vol. 1717, p. 316. Springer, Heidelberg (1999)
10. Miller, V.S.: Use of elliptic curves in cryptography. In: Williams, H.C. (ed.) CRYPTO 1985. LNCS, vol. 218, pp. 417–426. Springer, Heidelberg (1986)
11. Müller, T., Spreitzenbarth, M.: FROST. In: Jacobson, M., Locasto, M., Mohassel, P., Safavi-Naini, R. (eds.) ACNS 2013. LNCS, vol. 7954, pp. 373–388. Springer, Heidelberg (2013)
12. Müller, T., Taubmann, B., Freiling, F.C.: TreVisor. In: Bao, F., Samarati, P., Zhou, J. (eds.) ACNS 2012. LNCS, vol. 7341, pp. 66–83. Springer, Heidelberg (2012)
13. Müller, T., Dewald, A., Freiling, F.C.: AESSE: a cold-boot resistant implementation of AES. In: Proceedings of the Third European Workshop on System Security, EUROSEC 2010, pp. 42–47. ACM, New York, NY, USA (2010)
14. Müller, T., Freiling, F.C., Dewald, A.: TRESOR runs encryption securely outside RAM. In: Proceedings of the 20th USENIX Conference on Security, SEC 2011, p. 17. USENIX Association, Berkeley, CA, USA (2011)
15. Naor, M., Segev, G.: Public-key cryptosystems resilient to key leakage. 41(4), 772–814
16. Simmons, P.: Security through amnesia: a software-based solution to the cold boot attack on disk encryption. In: ACSAC, pp. 73–82 (2011)

4P_VES: A Collusion-Resistant Accountable Virtual Economy System

Hong Zhang[1], Xiaolei Dong[2](✉), Zhenfu Cao[2](✉), and Jiachen Shen[1]

[1] Department of Computer Science and Engineering, Shanghai Jiao Tong University,
Shanghai 200240, China
{zefan,jiachenshen}@sjtu.edu.cn
[2] Shanghai Key Lab for Trustworthy Computing, East China Normal University,
Shanghai 200062, China
{dongxiaolei,zfcao}@sei.ecnu.edu.cn

Abstract. Virtual economy develops rapidly and accounts for quite a large proportion in the entire economy. Markets of virtual goods, such as games, apps and cloud services, are quite active and contribute a lot to the revenue of platforms and providers. The existing virtual economy systems mainly rely on the trustworthiness of the platforms who maintain the accounts of all participants, which is short of transparency. Another concern is how to maintain the market order when conspiracy between participants happens. In this paper, we extend the Verito scheme (NDSS 2013) and introduce a new participant Payment to obtain our 4P_VES scheme, in which collusion between two parties can be detected while satisfying required properties of transparency and accountability at the same time. We also analyze the properties and prove the security of our scheme. Finally, we evaluate the additional cost compared with Verito and find that our scheme is a cost affordable and practical one which enhances the system's independency and security.

Keywords: Virtual economy · E-coin · Homomorphic commitment · Dynamic accumulator

1 Introduction

With the rapid development of Internet, network economy expands to nearly all kinds of market segments and accounts for a large proportion in the entire economy. The recent years have seen the boom of transactions of virtual goods and services, including online games, apps and cloud services. According to Face book annual report 2013, payments revenue, generated almost exclusively from game applications, in the fourth quarter is $241 million. It is the largest source of revenue after advertising [1]. For cloud services, it is estimated that the Amazon Web Service hits $3.8 billion revenue in 2013. In China, Ten cent, one of the leading providers of internet value-added services, declares that the revenue of virtual goods and services, mainly contributed by online games, reached 11,972 million Yuan, or about 2 billion dollars, in the fourth quarter of 2013, accounting for 70 percent in the total revenue [2].

© Springer International Publishing Switzerland 2015
L.C.K. Hui et al. (Eds.): ICICS 2014, LNCS 8958, pp. 61–73, 2015.
DOI: 10.1007/978-3-319-21966-0_5

Usually these virtual economies are carried out on platforms using virtual currencies rather than real ones. Due to the high frequency and small-valued size of virtual transactions, it is inconvenient for both sides to use a real currency. Thus the platforms issue virtual currencies, which can be sold in bulk, to perform the function of circulation. There are a number of virtual currencies now, including Face book credits, Q-coins (issued by Ten cent), U-coins (issued by Sina, a top portal in China), etc. Due to the lack of strong supervision and effective regulation in virtual economy, platforms are able to issue virtual currency without any limit. This makes the exchange rate from virtual coins to real currency unpredictable. Additionally, the virtual economy is globally oriented, making the issue more complicated. Because of the very divergent pricing policies and floating exchange rates from region to region, the possibility of arbitrage should also be taken into consideration.

Raghav Bhaskar *et al.* proposed a solution Verito [8] in NDSS 2013 which provides four properties viz., transparency, fairness, non-repudiation and scalability to address the issue mentioned above. The main idea of their scheme is to make a commitment which binds a virtual coin with a price in real currency. [8] assumes that no two of the three parties (i.e. Platform, Merchant and User) will collude to compromise the third. However, according to the property of fairness they mentioned, the merchants cannot distinguish between any two coins even if they are of different real values, so the User does not have incentive to check the coin's real value. This leaves room to the conspiracy between Platform and User. Thus it is a necessity to propose an anti-collusion scheme.

Our Contribution: We modify the Verito to obtain our own solution, in which collusion can be detected while supporting the essential properties at the same time. As the majority of transactions take place online and third-party payments such as Paypal, Alipay are widely adopted, we introduce the third-party payment into our system to defend against collusion. We propose 4P_VES, a virtual economy system composed of four parties (Platform, Provider, Player and Payment) which provides transparency and accountability even allowing the existence of collusion. We also analyze the security as well as the feasibility in our paper.

In summary, this paper makes three main contributions:

- First, we identify the possibility of collusion between Platform and Player in virtual economy system as a realistic threat;
- Second, we modify Verito to obtain an anti-collusion system 4P_VES with the combination of cryptographic primitives: commitment and accumulator.
- Finally, we discuss the properties of our system and the security under concrete assumptions.

The rest of the paper is organized as follows: We describe the system and define the model in Sect. 2. Section 3 gives the preliminaries including cryptographic primitives and assumptions. Section 4 presents the concrete construction of our scheme. Properties and security are analyzed in Sect. 5. We evaluate its performance and compare it with different schemes in Sect. 6. We review related work in Sect. 7 and finally conclude in Sect. 8.

2   System Model

4P_VES consists of four parties: Platform, Provider, Payment and Player. (4P refers to these four parties whose names all start with P). The Platform (Face book, Ten cent etc.) provides an ecosystem for the transaction. It maintains the resources of system and deals with both the Provider and the Player. The Provider is the company or individual who is registered with Platform and provides virtual goods or services. Online games and application vendors are examples of the Provider, such as King, Wooga (registered in Face book). Players are the customers who buy virtual goods and services with virtual currency. And Payment (Paypal, Alipay, etc.) is the third party in charge of pay and encashment.

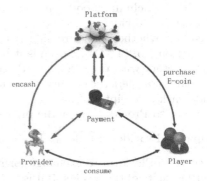

Fig. 1. Participants and interactions

Virtual currency, referred as e-coin in this paper, is adopted during the transaction. Platform issues e-coins and maintains the virtual accounts of both Provider and Player. Player purchases e-coins in bulk from Platform and pay with real currency through Payment. Player spends e-coins to buy virtual goods and services, such as apps and in-game props supplied by Provider. And Provider offers virtual goods or services in exchange for e-coins which can be encashed in bulk from Platform through Payment later. Payment plays a vital role in our system and is responsible for payment and encashment. The additional duty of Payment is to supervise the behavior of Platform and Player, checking whether there is conspiracy. It is reasonable to introduce the Payment party in our scheme. First, third party payment such as Paypal and Alipay are widely adopted in real world. Second, Payment is much more reliable than common users. Considering the large number of users registered, it is infeasible to verify and regulate all the users' behavior. Third party payment is under the public and government's supervision and is much easier for regulation. Furthermore, third party payment reduces the computation burden of clients, which makes the system more practical since the clients tend to use terminals with limited computational capacity. Therefore, the party, Payment, is introduced in our system.

The main interactions of the virtual economy (Fig. 1) are listed as follows.

(1) Purchase e-coins (Participants: Player, Platform, Payment):

- Player chooses the quantity and type of e-coins to buy from Platform.
- Platform generates the e-coins requested by Player.
- Payment verifies whether the real value bound to the e-coins is equal to the posted price. If the verification succeeds, Payment authenticates the e-coins by a signature scheme and transfers real currency from Player's account to Platform's. Otherwise, it rejects the Purchase action.
- Player receives e-coins together with the signature of Payment.

(2) Consume (Participants: Player, Provider, Platform):

- Player chooses the products (including goods and services) to buy and sends the e-coins as posted price to Provider.
- Provider checks the e-coins whether they are signed by Payment. Provider then generates a Transaction No. (TNO) and sends it back to Player.
- Player sends the TNO together with the e-coins to Platform.
- Platform verifies the e-coins, transfers the e-coins from Player's virtual account to Provider's and sends back a receipt to Player.
- Player forwards the receipt to Provider to get the products.

(3) Encash (Participants: Provider, Platform, Payment):

- Provider sends the e-coins to Platform to exchange for real currency.
- Platform checks the authenticity of the e-coins. If it is valid, Platform produces a proof that convinces the Provider that the aggregate value of the cashed e-coins is v without revealing the value of any individual e-coin.
- Provider reviews the proof.
- Platform removes the e-coins from Provider's virtual account.
- Payment transfers real currency from Platform's account to the Provider's.

3   Preliminaries

As our scheme follows [8] closely, the same modern cryptographic primitives, commitment and dynamic accumulator, are employed. In addition, to obtain a collusion-free system, we adopt another much more familiar primitive, digital signature, which is omitted here to save space.

3.1   Commitment

A commitment scheme includes two main phases: committing and revealing. Vividly, it can be thought of as analogous to an envelope. When a user Alice wants to form a commitment to a certain value, she puts the value into the envelope and seals it. The envelope is sealed in a special way that no one except Alice can open it. Then the envelope can be sent as a commitment to another user Bob. When it is time to reveal the value, Alice opens the envelope. There are two properties of commitment: hiding and binding. The hiding property: As the value is sealed in the envelope, Bob cannot learn any information about the value before Alice reveals it. The binding property: Because the envelope is sealed, Alice cannot change the value in the envelope without Bob's notice. We denote the commitment of value m as $c = Com(m)$ and the revealing phase as $OpenCom(c, r, m)$, r is the randomness used to form the commitment.

One more property required in our commitment scheme is additive homomorphism, i.e. $Com(m_1 + m_2) = Com(m_1) \odot Com(m_2)$. There are several homomorphic commitment schemes such as [3, 12, 14, 15]. To best suit our purpose, we adopt the Pedersen commitment [15], which relies on the security of the Discrete Logorithm assumption. Following is the main construction of [15].

$ComSetup()$: generate large primes p and q such that $q|(p - 1)$. Let $\mathbb{G}_q \preceq \mathbb{Z}_p^*$, $|\mathbb{G}_q| = q$. Randomly choose a generator $g \in \mathbb{G}_q$ and an element $h \in \mathbb{G}_q$ such that $log_g h$ is unknown.

$Com(m)$: to commit an element $m \in \mathbb{Z}_q$, choose $r \in \mathbb{Z}_q$ at random and compute $c = g^m h^r$.

$OpenCom(c, r, m)$: output 1 if $g^m h^r \equiv c$, otherwise 0.

3.2 Dynamic Accumulator

An accumulator scheme, introduced by Benaloh and de Mare [7], allows aggregation of a large set of values into one constant size value. Camenisch and Lysyanskaya extended the accumulator to dynamic accumulator (DA), where the cost of adding or deleting elements from the accumulator and witness updating do not depend on the size of the accumulated set [5, 10]. Here is the construction of [4, 10] adopted in our implementation.

$\mathcal{F}_k$ is a family of functions that correspond to exponentiating modulo safe-prime products with length k. $f_n \in \mathcal{F}_k$, $f_n(u, x) = u^x \mod n$, $n = pq$, $p = 2p' + 1$, $q = 2q' + 1$, where p, p', q, q' are all prime, $x \in \mathbb{X} = \{a \mid a \text{ is prime}, a \neq p', q'\}$.

The accumulator value will be updated when an element is added or deleted. Adding an element $\tilde{x} \in \mathbb{X}$ to the accumulator v:

$$v' = AccAdd(v, \tilde{x}) = f_n(v, \tilde{x}) = v^{\tilde{x}} \mod n;$$

Deleting an element $\tilde{x}$ from the accumulator v:

$$v' = AccDel(v, \tilde{x}) = D((p, q), v, \tilde{x}) = v^{\tilde{x}^{-1} \mod (p-1)(q-1)} \mod n.$$

For each element x accumulated in v, there is a corresponding witness w such that $w^x \equiv v$.

$$AccVerify(v, x) = 1, \; iff \; w^x \equiv v \mod n.$$

Updating the witness w of x after $\tilde{x}$ has been added:

$$w' = f_n(w, \tilde{x}) = w^{\tilde{x}} \mod n;$$

Updating the witness w of x after $\tilde{x}(\tilde{x} \neq x)$ has been deleted:

$$w' = w^b v'^a \mod n, \ ax + b\tilde{x} = 1.$$

And multi-elements can be added or deleted at once. Let π_a be the product of elements to be added while π_d be the product of ones to be deleted. Then

$$v' = v^{\pi_a \pi_d^{-1} \mod (p-1)(q-1)} \mod n;$$

$$w' = (w^{\pi_a})^b v'^a \mod n, \ ax + b\pi_d = 1.$$

3.3 Cryptographic Assumptions

The construction of our scheme is based on the following assumptions.

Discrete Logarithm (DL) Assumption: given a group $\mathbb{G}$ with generator g, $|\mathbb{G}| = p$, for all non-uniform probabilistic polynomial-time (PPT) algorithms $\mathcal{A}$,

$$\Pr_{h \leftarrow \mathbb{G}}[\mathcal{A}(h) = \log_g h] \text{ is negligible}$$

As the Pohlig-Hellman algorithm can solve the DL problem efficiently in the case when $p - 1$ is a product of small primes, usually p is required to be a safe prime ($p = 2q + 1$, q is prime).

Strong RSA Assumption: given a modulus n of unknown factorization and a ciphertext c, it is infeasible to find a pair (m, e) such that $c = m^e \mod n$.

4   Scheme Construction

This section details the key parts of our system using the cryptographic primitives mentioned above. Other familiar primitives such as symmetric encryption and signature are also used. To best adapt our scheme, we adopt DES as $E_k(r, m)$ while RSA signature is used in function $sign()$.

(1) Setup
Platform sets the system parameters, generates a signing $keypair(vk, sk)$ and a symmetric key k to encrypt the commitment's open key which should be hidden from the Provider. It also runs the $ComSetup()$ to set the parameters used in commitment: p, q, g, h and $Accgen()$ to initiate the registered Players' and Providers' accumulator values.
(2) E-coin construction
There is a list mapping the e-coin's nominal value to its real value (including the currency type and amount) published by the Platform (Shown in Table 1). $E\text{-}coin = (Com(m), E_k(r, m))$ where $Com(m) = g^m h^r$, and r is chosen randomly from $\mathbb{Z}_q$.
(3) Purchase e-coins
Player chooses the type and quantity of e-coins to buy. Platform searches the corresponding Identity Number m_i of the chosen e-coin type and calls the

Table 1. Example of E-coins list

ID NO	E-coin Type	Real Price
m_1	Type1	\$0.1
m_2	Type2	£0.6
m_3	Type3	¥10
...	...	...

Table 2. Number of rounds of interactions

rounds \ schemes phases	Verito	4P_VES	Variant
Purchase	2	4	3
Consume	5	7	6
Encash	2	4	3

construction function to generate the required e-coins. Then the e-coins are sent together with the open keys to Payment. Payment opens the commitments (using the homomorphic property here) to check the commited value and sends them to Player after signing. It also transfers corresponding amount of real currency from Player's account to Platform's. The Platform updates the accumulator of the Player's e-coins by *AccAdd* and sends the accumulator value to Player. Player updates all of his e-coins' witness, signs the accumulator value and sends back the signed value to Platform as a receipt. The detail is showed in Algorithm 1.

Algorithm 1. Purchase e-coins

Require: The type $type_i$ and number $\#num$ of e-coins to buy.
   Platform
1: $m_i \leftarrow search(type_i)$ // search the ID of the $type_i$ e-coin
2: $ECOINS \leftarrow \emptyset$
3: **for** $k = 1$; $k <= \#num$; $k + +$ **do**
4:     $Com(m_i) = g^{m_i} h^{r_i}$;
5:     $E_k(m_i, r_i)$;
6:     $coin_k \leftarrow (Com(m_i), E_k(m_i, r_i))$
7:     $\sigma(coin_k) = sign_{sk}(coin_k)$
8:     $ECOINS = ECOINS \cup \{coin_k\}$
9: **end for**
10: $C = \prod_{i=1}^{\#num} Com(m_i)$
11: $Openkey = \sum_{i=1}^{\#num} r_i$
12: $v_{id} = AccAdd(v_{id}, C)$ //v_{id} is the accumulator value of $Player'_{id}s$ e-coins
   Payment
13: $M = \sum m_i$
14: **if** $OpenCom(C, Openkey, M) == 1$ **then**
15:     **for** $k = 1$; $k <= \#numn$; $k + +$ **do**
16:         $\sigma(coin_k) = sign_{psk}(coin_k)$ //psk is the private key of Payment
17:     **end for**
18:     transfer() // transfer money from real cash account
19: **end if**
   Player
20: **for** each $coin_i$ accumulated in v_{id} **do**
21:     $wit_i = WitUpdate(wit_i, C) = f_n(wit_i, C)$.
22: **end for**
23: $\sigma(v_{id}) = sign_{psk_{id}}(v_{id})$ //psk_{id} is the private key of $Player_{id}$

---

(4) Consume
Player initiates a transaction by sending the e-coins as posted price to the Provider to purchase virtual products. The Provider verifies the received e-coins by checking the signatures of Payment. If the verification succeeds, it accepts the

transaction and sends back a Transaction No. (TNO) to the Player. Then the Player sends e-coins to Platform together with the TNO and witnesses. Platform checks whether these e-coins are in the whitelist of the Player by $AccVerify$. If it is valid, it removes the e-coins from the Player's accumulator by $AccDel$ and adds them to the Provider's by $AccAdd$. It sends back the updated accumulator values of the Player and the Provider to the Player. The Player updates the remaining e-coins' witnesses and forwards the Provider's accumulator value to the Provider. The Provider updates its e-coins' witnesses and provides the Player with the chosen products. At last, the Player and Provider sign their accumulator values and send back to the Platform. Algorithm 2 shows the detail.

Algorithm 2. Consume

Require: The products to buy and the required $\{ecoin_i\}$, $ecoin_i = (Com(m_i), E_k(r_i, m_i))$
  Provider(prid)
 1: **for** each $ecoin_i \in \{ecoin_i\}$ **do**
 2: $VerifySign_{pvk}(ecoin_i)//pvk$ is the public key of Payment
 3: **end for**
 4: $TNO \leftarrow TransactionNO.$
  Platform
 5: **for** each $ecoin_i \in \{ecoin_i\}$ **do**
 6: $AccVerify(v_{id}, Com(m_i))//$check the $ecoin_i$ is in the Player's accumulated value v_{id}
 7: **end for**
 8: $v_{id} = AccDel(v_{id}, \prod Com(m_i))//v_{id}$ is the accumulator of $Player_{id}$
 9: $v_{prid} = AccAdd(v_{prid}, \prod Com(m_i))//v_{prid}$ is the accumulator of $Provider_{id}$
  Player(id)
 10: **for** each $ecoin_i$ accumulated in v_{id} **do**
 11: $wit_i = WitUpdate(wit_i, \prod Com(m_i))$
 12: **end for**
 13: $\sigma(v_{id}) = sign_{psk_{id}}(v_{id})$ //psk_{id} is the private key of $Player_{id}$
  Provider(prid)
 14: **for** each $ecoin_i$ accumulated in v_{prid} **do**
 15: $wit_i = WitUpdate(wit_i, \prod Com(m_i))$
 16: **end for**
 17: $\sigma(v_{prid}) = sign_{prsk_{id}}(v_{prid})$ //$prsk_{id}$ is the private key of $Provider_{id}$
 18: provide products

---

(5) Encash

Provider sends a batch of e-coins to the Platform in exchange for real currency. The Platform verifies the e-coins and checks whether they are accumulated in the Provider's whitelist. If the verification succeeds, it computes the total value of the e-coins, decrypts the keys and computes the $Openkey$ to open the product of commitments $\pi_{commitments}$ according to the homomorphism. The Provider opens $\pi_{commitments}$ with $Openkey$ and checks whether the sum of money equals to the one Platform announced. The Platform also removes the e-coins from the Provider's accumulator by $AccDel$ and sends back the updated accumulator value. The Provider updates the remaining e-coins' witnesses, signs the accumulator value and sends back to the Platform. At last, the Payment transfers the money (after deducting the Platform's profit) from Platform's real currency account to the Provider's. See the detail in Algorithm 3.

Algorithm 3. Encash

Require: The set of e-coins to cash $\{ecoin_i\}$, $ecoin_i = (Com(m_i), E_k(r_i, m_i))$
     Platform
1: **for** each $ecoin_i \in \{ecoin_i\}$ **do**
2:    $AccVerify(v_{prid}, Com(m_i))$//check the $ecoin_i$ is in the Provider's accumulated value v_{prid}
3: **end for**
4: $C = \prod Com(m_i)$
5: $Openkey = \sum r_i$
6: $M = \sum m_i$
7: $v_{prid} = AccDel(v_{prid}, \prod Com(m_i))$//$v_{prid}$ is the accumulator of $Provider_{id}$
     Provider(prid)
8: **if** $OpenCom(C, Openkey, M) == 1$ **then**
9:    **for** each $ecoin_i$ remained in v_{prid} **do**
10:        $wit_i = WitUpdate(wit_i, C)$
11:    **end for**
12:    $\sigma(v_{prid}) = sign_{prsk_{id}}(v_{prid})$ //$prsk_{id}$ is the private key of $Provider_{id}$
13: **end if**
     Payment
14: $transfer()$

5 Property Analysis

The properties of e-coin and virtual economy are given in this section. We define the properties formally as well as the attack model. We also analyze the security and discuss the cryptographic assumptions on which it is based.

Consistency: Once an e-coin is generated, the Platform should not be able to change its real value. The adversary is the Platform in this game.

- The adversary generates an e-coin with real value m;
- The adversary changes the value m to m' without other party's notice.

Formally, the adversary wins if it can find $m' \neq m$ that $Com(m') = Com(m)$. Analysis:

$$Pr[Adv\ wins] = Pr[Com(m') = Com(m) \wedge m' \neq m] = Pr[g^{m'}h^{r'} = g^m h^r \wedge m' \neq m].$$

$r' = (m - m')(log_g h)^{-1} + r$, according to the DL Assumption, it is with negligible probability to compute r'.

Indistinguishability: The Provider cannot distinguish between different e-coins with the same nominal value. This is a necessity to ensure the fairness of the virtual market as the Provider cannot give priority to the Player whose e-coins with higher real value. In this attack game, the adversary is the Provider and the challenger is the Player. The model is:

- Challenger randomly picks $t \in \{0, 1\}$ and sends $ecoin_t$ to adversary. $ecoin_0$ and $ecoin_1$ are two coins with the same face value but different real values.
- The adversary responds $t' \in \{0, 1\}$

The adversary wins if it guess $t' = t$ with probability $1/2 + \epsilon$, ϵ is non negligible.
    Analysis: $c_0 = g^{m_0}h^{r_0} \mod p$, $c_1 = g^{m_1}h^{r_1} \mod p$. c_0 and c_1 are information-theoretically indistinguishable since the randomness of r and r'.

Unreusability: The Player cannot re-spend an e-coin and the Provider should not be able to encash an e-coin more than once.

In this game, the challenger is the Platform. The adversary is the Player in re-spending and the Provider in re-encashment.

- The adversary generates two sets of e-coins: S_1, S_2, $S_1 \cap S_2 \neq \emptyset$.
- The challenger removes the e-coins $\in S_1$ from the adversary's accumulator.
- The challenger verifies the e-coins $\in S_2$.

The adversary wins if the verification succeeds.

Analysis: When S_1 is removed from S(accumulator value v), v is updated to v', v' is the accumulator of $S'(S' = S - S_1)$. If the verification in the third step succeeds, for each e-coin $\in S_2$, it needs to generate a valid witness. Let $x \in S_1 \cap S_2$, then $x \notin S'$, we need to find the witness w' of x such that $w'^x = v' = w^{\prod \{x_i | x_i \in S'\}}$, according to [10], it can be reduced to the strong RSA problem.

Transparency: All the real cash inflow should be accountable without relying on the assumption of the Platform's honesty. Let $EcoinS$ denote the set of e-coins that have been sold. Let $Cashed$ and $Uncashed$ denote the sets of all e-coins which have been encashed and not cashed respectively. $Value(S)$ denotes the function computing the aggregate real value of the e-coins set S. Then $Value(Ecoins) = Value(Cashed) + Value(Uncashed)$ holds;

In this game the challenger is the Provider and the adversary is the Platform.

- The challenger sends the e-coins set $\{(Com(m_i), E_k(r_i, m_i))\}$ to the Platform together with the witnesses.
- The adversary responds to the challenger with the $Openkey$ to reveal the aggregated commitment $\pi_{Com(m_i)}$ as a proof of the e-coins' total value M.
- The challenger opens the $\pi_{Com(m_i)}$ with $Openkey$ to check the value M.

The adversary wins if $M = Open(\pi_{Com(m_i)}, Openkey)$ while $M \neq \sum m_i$.

Analysis: $Pr[Adv\ wins] = Pr[\pi_{Com(m_i)} = g^M h^{Openkey} \wedge M \neq \sum m_i]$

$$= Pr[g^{\sum m_i} h^{\sum r_i} = g^M h^{Openkey} \wedge M \neq \sum m_i] = Pr[h^{Openkey} = g^{\sum m_i - M} h^{\sum r_i}].$$

$Openkey = (\sum m_i - M)(log_g h)^{-1} + \sum r_i$, finding such an $Openkey$ can be reduced to the DL problem.

Collusion-Resistance: As discussed in the previous sections, it is possible for the Platform to collude with the Player. The Platform creates an e-coin with committed value m while selling it at a price m'. $4P\_VES$ introduces Payment to defend this conspiracy. The Payment will open the commitment before signing the e-coins. Provider will verify the Payment's signature whenever it receives an e-coin. As no one can forge the signature of Payment, there is no possibility of collusion between Platform and Player without the Provider's notice.

6   Performance Evaluation

In this section, we evaluate the performance of 4P_VES and compare it with Verito. As a new party Payment is introduced, additional cost of computation

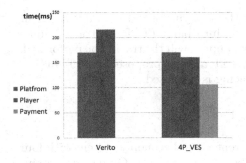

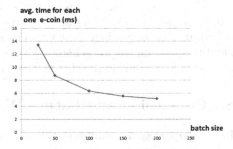

Fig. 2. Each party's cost in Purchase

Fig. 3. Avg. cost of Purchase with diff. sizes

and communication is inevitable. We will show the extra cost is acceptable. We also try to optimize the performance by proposing a variant of 4P_VES.

During the purchase phase, as the commitment is opened by the Payment rather by the Player in Verito to detect conspiracy in our solution, the cost of this step is transferred from the Player to the Payment. And the Payment is also in charge of signing the e-coins which brings about extra cost. Figure 2 describes the cost of each party in purchase phase. As the cost of generating e-coins depends on the number of e-coins, we assume the Player buys a batch of 50 e-coins in our evaluation. The total time cost of Player and Payment is about 23 % higher than the cost of Player in Verito.

As the commitment is homomorphic and the accumulator is dynamic, the cost of opening commitment and updating accumulator can be amortized. Therefore the more e-coins in a batch, the less average cost it takes. Figure 3 shows the performance of purchase phase with different batch sizes.

Our solution adds interactions between the participants to make the system less rely on the Platform's honesty. Every time when the accumulator value changes, the Platform needs to require the corresponding signature. Table 2 compares the interaction rounds of different solutions. The variant version of 4P_VES is a tradeoff between security and communication efficiency. In the variant, the Player or Provider sends the accumulator value's signature together with the transaction request messages which will save one interaction. The expense is that the Platform merely holds the last accumulator value rather than the current one's signature which leaves a little room for the Platform's trick.

As evaluated above, although extra cost and delay are introduced in our solution, it is still within acceptable tolerance. That is to say, our solution is practical that enhances the Verito with little overhead.

7   Related Work

Our work is closely related to [8] in which the possibility of collusion between participants is not considered and the account's consistency relies on the honesty of platform. Our work is based on [8] and tries to avoid some of its shortcomings.

Other electronic cash systems focus on the anonymous and traceable payment [16]. Schemes [11,17] introduce the trusted third party (TTP) to trace double-spending. And only when some vital crime happens will the tracing be performed. Double-spending tracing schemes without TTP are also proposed in [6,9]. In [13], a provably secure E-cash scheme with tracing is proposed.

8   Conclusion and Future Work

In this paper, an accountable and transparent virtual economy system with four participant parties is proposed based on the scheme of Verito. Our system retains the properties of Verito while further study the anti-collusion problem. We introduce a new participant Payment to detect possible collusion. Our solution also enhances the security and reduces the dependency on Platform's honesty.

Although our solution solves the problem of collusion, it introduces extra cost. How to reduce computation and communication overhead and make the system more efficient and feasible is an interesting problem. In future, we will also extend our scheme to other application situations.

Acknowledgement. This work is supported in part by the National Natural Science Foundation of China under Grant 61321064, Grant 61371083, Grant 61373154, and Grant 61411146001, and in part by the Specialized Research Fund for the Doctoral Program of Higher Education of China through the Prioritized Development Projects under Grant 20130073130004.

References

1. Face book annual report (2013). http://investor.fb.com/annuals.cfm
2. Ten cent financial reports (2013). http://tencent.com/en-us/content/ir/rp/2013/attachments/201302.pdf
3. Abe, M., Cramer, R., Fehr, S.: Non-interactive distributed-verifier proofs and proving relations among commitments. In: Zheng, Y. (ed.) ASIACRYPT 2002. LNCS, vol. 2501, pp. 206–223. Springer, Heidelberg (2002)
4. Au, M.H., Tsang, P.P., Susilo, W., Mu, Y.: Dynamic universal accumulators for DDH groups and their application to attribute-based anonymous credential systems. In: Fischlin, M. (ed.) CT-RSA 2009. LNCS, vol. 5473, pp. 295–308. Springer, Heidelberg (2009)
5. Barić, N., Pfitzmann, B.: Collision-free accumulators and fail-stop signature schemes without trees. In: Fumy, W. (ed.) EUROCRYPT 1997. LNCS, vol. 1233, pp. 480–494. Springer, Heidelberg (1997)
6. Belenkiy, M., Chase, M., Kohlweiss, M., Lysyanskaya, A.: Compact E-cash and simulatable VRFs revisited. In: Shacham, H., Waters, B. (eds.) Pairing 2009. LNCS, vol. 5671, pp. 114–131. Springer, Heidelberg (2009)
7. Benaloh, J.C., de Mare, M.: One-way accumulators: a decentralized alternative to digital signatures. In: Helleseth, T. (ed.) EUROCRYPT 1993. LNCS, vol. 765, pp. 274–285. Springer, Heidelberg (1994)
8. Bhaskar, R., Guha, S., Laxman, S., Naldurg, P.: Verito: A practical system for transparency and accountability in virtual economies. In: NDSS (2013)

9. Camenisch, J.L., Hohenberger, S., Lysyanskaya, A.: Compact E-cash. In: Cramer, R. (ed.) EUROCRYPT 2005. LNCS, vol. 3494, pp. 302–321. Springer, Heidelberg (2005)
10. Camenisch, J.L., Lysyanskaya, A.: Dynamic accumulators and application to efficient revocation of anonymous credentials. In: Yung, M. (ed.) CRYPTO 2002. LNCS, vol. 2442, p. 61. Springer, Heidelberg (2002)
11. Canard, S., Delerablée, C., Gouget, A., Hufschmitt, E., Laguillaumie, F., Sibert, H., Traoré, J., Vergnaud, D.: Fair E-cash: be compact, spend faster. In: Samarati, P., Yung, M., Martinelli, F., Ardagna, C.A. (eds.) ISC 2009. LNCS, vol. 5735, pp. 294–309. Springer, Heidelberg (2009)
12. Groth, J.: A verifiable secret shuffle of homomorphic encryptions. J. Cryptology **23**(4), 546–579 (2010)
13. Lian, B., Chen, G., Li, J.: Provably secure e-cash system with practical and efficient complete tracing. Int. J. Inf. Secur. **13**(3), 271–289 (2014)
14. Lipmaa, H.: Verifiable homomorphic oblivious transfer and private equality test. In: Laih, C.-S. (ed.) ASIACRYPT 2003. LNCS, vol. 2894, pp. 416–433. Springer, Heidelberg (2003)
15. Pedersen, T.P.: Non-interactive and information-theoretic secure verifiable secret sharing. In: Feigenbaum, J. (ed.) CRYPTO 1991. LNCS, vol. 576, pp. 129–140. Springer, Heidelberg (1992)
16. Stadler, M.A., Piveteau, J.-M., Camenisch, J.L.: Fair blind signatures. In: Guillou, L.C., Quisquater, J.-J. (eds.) EUROCRYPT 1995. LNCS, vol. 921, pp. 209–219. Springer, Heidelberg (1995)
17. Zhang, J., Ma, L., Wang, Y.: Fair e-cash system without trustees for multiple banks. In: International Conference on Computational Intelligence and Security Workshops, CISW 2007, pp. 585–587. IEEE (2007)

Privacy-Preserving Distance-Bounding Proof-of-Knowledge

Ahmad Ahmadi[(✉)] and Reihaneh Safavi-Naini

University of Calgary, Calgary, Canada
ahmadi@ucalgary.ca

Abstract. In distance-bounding protocols a prover wants to prove that it is located within a distance bound $\mathbb{D}$ from a verifier. Distance-bounding (DB) protocols have numerous applications including authentication and proximity checking. The privacy problem in DB protocols was limited to privacy against *MiM* adversaries. Gambs *et al.* [11] extended this limitation and proposed a protocol that provides *strong* privacy when the verifier is malicious, or *honest-but-curious* registration authority. The protocol however does not provide resistance against terrorist-fraud.

In this paper we consider private DB protocols that provide the strongest level of security against all known DB attacks, in particular terrorist-fraud, and provide anonymity of the prover and unlinkability of its sessions against *malicious* verifiers and assuming an *honest-but-curious* registration authority. We define private distance-bounding as a special ZKPoK in which a prover presents a commitment on its long-term private-key, and later proves in zero-knowledge that; (i) she knows the committed value, (ii) she knows a signature of the authority on the committed value (registration proof), and (iii) she is located within a pre-defined distance to the verifier. The prover stays anonymous and its sessions will be unlinkable. We propose a protocol PDB with these properties that resists against all known attacks including terrorist-fraud. PDB is based on Bussard-Bagga [5] (DBPK-Log). PDB also fixes the vulnerability of the protocol pointed out by Bay *et al.* [2] resulting in a secure public-key DB protocol, hence answering the open question of constructing a secure public-key DB protocol.

1 Introduction

In DB protocols, there are two types of entities; provers and verifiers. In concurrent execution of DB protocols, multiple protocol instances are run at the same time. Provers and verifiers are usually connected to a back-end server, which only takes care of the registration phase and is silent otherwise.

Secure DB protocols provide two functionalities: (1) authentication of a registered prover to a verifier, and (2) bounding the prover's distance to the verifier. The bounding is commonly by measuring the round trip time in a *fast-exchange* phase between the prover and the verifier, during which the verifier presents challenges to the prover and verifies if the prover's responses are correct. The round-trip times of correct challenge and responses are used to estimate the

© Springer International Publishing Switzerland 2015
L.C.K. Hui et al. (Eds.): ICICS 2014, LNCS 8958, pp. 74–88, 2015.
DOI: 10.1007/978-3-319-21966-0_6

distance between prover and verifier, and then compare it against a specified distance bound $\mathbb{D}$.

Privacy is a necessary property in many location-based services. One approach for providing privacy in location-privacy, is to modify the geometric data, for example loose accuracy of location data, to achieve privacy [15, 21]. In distance-bounding however, the location accuracy is a requirement. To achieve both privacy and location accuracy, one can unlink the location data from provers' authentication information. This problem has been well studied in the context of RFID systems [13, 22]. In these systems the location of provers are known by the verifiers, but provers hide their identity in their interactions. In RFID systems however, verifiers are assumed trusted, and the privacy is only against Man-In-the-Middle (MiM) adversaries. The assumption of trusted verifier is not acceptable in many distance-based location services in which the verifiers can get exploited, and so it is important to consider stronger privacy models, in particular consider untrusted verifiers.

In a symmetric-key DB protocol, there is a shared-key between prover and registration authority and so privacy is not achievable against an adversary who can access the internal state of the authority. One can always achieve prover privacy by using the same key for all provers. This however is unacceptable because of the threat it exposes to the whole system. There are three famous public-key based DB protocols in the literature: (a) The seminal Brands-Chaum protocol [4], which uses commitments and signatures. The protocol is not secure against Terrorist-Fraud Attack (TFA). (b) Bussard-Bagga [5] protocol (DBPK-Log), which uses bit commitment and was designed to provide TFA resistance, but it was recently broken [2]. And, (c) the recent Hermans *et al.* [14] protocol, which uses elliptic curve cryptography and does not provide TFA resistance. It also does not allow the privacy adversary to access the internal state of the registration authority. Therefore, there is no DB protocol, which is both public-key based and is secure against terrorist-fraud adversary.

The following questions have been open in the literature. (i) Design a public-key based DB protocol that is, secure against terrorist-fraud adversary; and (ii) design a secure privacy preserving DB protocol that provides privacy for provers against a privacy adversary who controls the verifier, and has access to the internal state of registration authority.

In this paper we answer to these open problems. Our contributions is three-fold; first we propose a privacy model which we refer to it as *extensive-privacy*, and show that it is stronger than the *wide-privacy* notion of [22], and the privacy model of Gambs *et al.* [11], with respect to the adversary's access to the state of the *non-prover* entities. Second, we fix the security flaw of DBPK-Log protocol, and achieve the first public-key based distance-bounding protocol, which is secure against TFA adversary (called DBPK-log$^+$ protocol). Finally, we propose the protocol PDB, as an extension of DBPK-log$^+$, which is secure in the proposed privacy model.

2   Background

In DB systems, since the seminal paper [4], the implicit assumption about all secure DB protocols is the presence of a secure function which generates and distributes the private-keys of the entities. In some cases this function can be executed by a verifier. A distance-bounding protocol allows a registered *prover* to prove that she is within a distance bound to *verifier*, and in possession of the secret-key which is used for user authentication information.

In order to have a *privacy-preserving distance-bounding* system, we need to consider three properties; *Authentication, Distance-Bounding* and *Privacy*. By having *authentication* property, the verifiers determines whether an approaching entity is indeed a legitimate prover or not. *Distance-Bounding* property guarantees that the prover is located within a pre-defined distance. And *privacy* property provides assurance to provers that their interactions in the system is not traceable.

Authentication is obtained by a protocol between *prover* and *verifier*. The prover must prove that she knows a secret value which is registered to the system. The protocol must satisfy two properties; *correctness* and *soundness*. The *correctness* holds when the honest verifier accepts, if an honest prover, who knows the secret value is involved. The *soundness* holds when no adversary who doesn't have access to the secret value of a registered prover, can convince the honest verifier to accept in the authentication. Gambs *et al.* [11] consider these two properties, but make two assumptions: (1) the *server* revokes all corrupted provers upon corruption, and (2) dishonest *provers* cannot yield their private-key to the adversary, unless they get un-registered. Implementing these assumptions are major challenges, and so one of the goals of our work is to weaken these assumptions.

Distance-Bounding protocols run a *fast-exchange* phase, which guarantees presence of the owner of the secret-key within distance bound $\mathbb{D}$. By assuming that no prover is willing to disclose her secret-key to others, five attacking scenarios have been studied in *DB* protocols: *Distance-Fraud Attack (DFA)* [4]; a dishonest prover $\mathcal{P}^*$, which is not located within distance $\mathbb{D}$ to verifier $\mathcal{V}$, tries to convince $\mathcal{V}$ that she is located within distance $\mathbb{D}$ to $\mathcal{V}$. *Mafia-Fraud Attack (MFA)* [8]; an adversary $\mathcal{A}$, which is located within distance $\mathbb{D}$ to $\mathcal{V}$ (between $\mathcal{V}$ and far away honest prover $\mathcal{P}$), convinces $\mathcal{V}$ that $\mathcal{P}$ is close-by. *Terrorist-Fraud Attack (TFA)* [8]; an adversary $\mathcal{A}$ (located within distance $\mathbb{D}$ to $\mathcal{V}$) co-operates with a dishonest prover $\mathcal{P}^*$ (far away) to convince $\mathcal{V}$ that $\mathcal{P}^*$ is located within distance $\mathbb{D}$ to $\mathcal{V}$. *Distance-Hijacking* [7]; a dishonest prover $\mathcal{P}^*$, which is not located within the distance $\mathbb{D}$ to a verifier $\mathcal{V}$, exploits some honest provers $\mathcal{P}_1, \ldots, \mathcal{P}_n$ to mislead $\mathcal{V}$ about the actual distance between $\mathcal{P}^*$ and $\mathcal{V}$. *Impersonation-Attack* [1]; a dishonest prover $\mathcal{P}^*$ purports to be another prover in her interaction with $\mathcal{V}$.

Vaudenay *et al.* [23] proposed a general attack model, which captures all these attacks;

- **Distance-Fraud** is defined to capture the classic DFA and *Distance-Hijacking*.
- **MiM** attack captures MFA and *Impersonation-Attack*.
- **Collusion-Fraud** is a different game-based definition about TFA. Based on this definition, if there is any PPT adversary who can win the TFA game with probability γ, then there exist a weaker MiM adversary who can succeed in a specific MiM game with probability γ'.

Authentication and *Distance-Bounding* have been studied in DB protocols. Recently, a considerable amount of focus have been on proposing formal definitions and provably secure of symmetric DB protocols [3,9,10]. In Dürholz *et al.* [9], the strong simulation-based terrorist-fraud for "single prover, single verifier" setting have been defined. Fischlin-Onete [10] have extended [9] and defined even stronger simulation-based model and proposed a protocol with security proof. On the other hand, Boureanu *et al.* [3] showed that the definition of Dürholz *et al.* is too strong, and proposed a general and practical game-based terrorist-fraud model for "multiple prover, multiple verifier" setting (same model as [23]). Boureanu *et al.* proposed the *SKI* protocol, which is claimed to be secure against the defined *distance-fraud*, *MiM* and *collusion-fraud*. By the way, this protocol is not proven to be secure under the defined *collusion-fraud* adversary, despite their claim. The provided proof is just for deterministic PPT adversaries in the TFA game, rather than any PPT adversary in this game.

Privacy is considered as un-traceablility of different sessions of a single prover. This notion of *privacy* have been well studied in the RFID framework against MiM adversaries, which mostly use symmetric setting and assume trusted verifier and registration authority [13,22]. In Hermans *et al.* [13] model, privacy is defined as a game between an *adversary* and a *challenger*. The adversary has oracle access to the following functionalities; create honest provers (CreateProver), launch a session of a pre-defined protocol (Launch), ask the *challenger* to choose one of the given two provers and return an anonymous handle (DrawProver), send message to an anonymous prover (SendProver), free the anonymous handle of a prover (Free), send message to the verifier in a protocol session (SendVerifier), see output of the verifier in a session of protocol (Result), and finally get the non-volatile internal state of an honest prover (Corrupt). The adversary wins the privacy game if she can find out the chosen bit of challenger in DrawProver oracle. Peeters-Hermans [19] added a new oracle to the above list by which, the adversary can create insider prover and have control on it (CreateInsider).

Vaudenay [22] have classified the adversaries, based on their access to the above oracles. A *wide* adversary has access to Result oracle, otherwise it will be a *narrow* adversary. In parallel, the adversary can be *weak* (no access to Corrupt oracle), *forward* (Corrupt queries can only be followed by other Corrupt queries), *destructive* (Corrupt queries destroys the access to the corrupted prover), and *strong* (unlimited access to Corrupt oracle). Paise-Vaudenay [17] showed that *destructive* and *strong* privacy is not achievable in symmetric-key systems.

Gambs *et al.* [11] built of the work of Hermans *et al.* [14] to define public-key DB protocols that are privacy-preserving and constructed the first protocol, which is secure against three separate adversaries: (1) MiM adversary, (2) a MiM adversary who has access to the internal state of the verifier, and (3) an honest-but-curious adversary who knows the internal state of the verifier and the registration server. We extend this model and introduce a stronger adversary who has access to the internal state of verifiers and registration server (*extensive*[1] adversary). Therefore, the following order in the new classification holds; $NARROW \subseteq WIDE \subseteq$ Gambs *et al.* $\subseteq EXTENSIVE$ based on having access to the state of *verifiers* and *registration authority*, as well as $WEAK \subseteq FORWARD \subseteq DESTRUCTIVE \subseteq STRONG$ based on having access to the state of *provers*.

In this paper we propose a new protocol, which provides *authentication*, *distance-bounding* (*distance-fraud*, *MiM* and *terrorist-fraud* resistance) and *privacy* (against *extensive-weak* adversary).

2.1 Distance-Bounding Proof-of-Knowledge (DBPK-Log)

Bussard-Bagga [5] proposed the only public-key DB protocol which was designed to be secure against TFA adversary. This protocol combines a *fast-exchange* DB protocol, Pedersen commitment scheme [18] and *zero-knowledge proof-of-knowledge* [20]. In this protocol, a prover chooses a key pair and registers the public-key with a trusted server. The verifiers are trusted and have access to the public-key of provers. The system parameters are set by a trusted authority, and uses a cyclic group whose order is a strong prime. These parameters are shared and used by all the participants. This protocol was designed to be secure against DFA, MFA and TFA adversaries, while the information leakage about the private-key of provers is minimal.

The protocol combines the bitwise operation, used for *fast-exchange* phase, and modular operations that are required for commitment schemes. This results in some security loss of the secret-keys, while maintaining indistinguishability of the secret-keys.

Bay *et al.* [2] showed TFA and DFA attacks on this protocol, which takes advantage of poor auditing of un-used elements in the Commitment Opening phase (i.e. half of the bit commitments won't get opened).

2.2 BBS$^+$ Signature Scheme [6]

This signature scheme uses bilinear mapping and supports signing of committed message block[2] $M = \{m_1, \ldots, m_L\}$, without knowing about the actual message. Two entities are invloved in this scheme; a trusted signer (S) who holds the signing key, and a client (C) who knows a message block.

This signature scheme, follows the standard operations [12] of all signature schemes BBS$^+$ = (KeyGen, Sign, Verify):

---

[1] Extensive privacy will be defined in Definition 5.

[2] A single message that is represented as string of integers.

- $(sk_S, pk_S = h_0^{sk_S}) \leftarrow \texttt{KeyGen}(1^\lambda)$; S creates a key pair and publishes the public-key.
- $\texttt{Sign}[\texttt{C}(M, pk_S; \sigma = sign_S(M)) \leftrightarrow \texttt{S}(sk_S; partial(\sigma), cmt(M))]$, s.t. $M = \{m_1, \ldots, m_L\}$, $\sigma = (A, e, s)$, $partial(\sigma) = (A, e)$, $cmt(M) = (\{C_i = g_1^{m_i} g_2^{r_i}\}$, $C_M = g_1^{s'} g_2^{m_1} \ldots g_{L+1}^{m_L})$, and $A = (g_0 g_1^s g_2^{m_1} \ldots g_{L+1}^{m_L})^{\frac{1}{e+sk_S}}$ for random values of $\{r_i\}, s, s', e$; C and S get involved in a protocol for signing a committed message block (M). In this protocol, first C calculates the commitment $cmt(M) = (\{C_i\}, C_M)$ as mentioned above, and sends it to S, then they run $PoK\{(\{m_i, r_i\}, s') : C_M \bigwedge \{C_i\}\}$ to verify the possession and integrity of the values in the commitment. Then S creates the signature as $A = (g_0 g_1^{s''} C_M)^{\frac{1}{e+sk_S}}$ for random e and s'' and sends $\{A, e, s''\}$ to C. And finally C calculates $s = s' + s''$, checks the validity of $\sigma = \{A, e, s\}$ and keeps σ as the signature of S on M.
- $\texttt{Verify}[\texttt{C}(M, \sigma; \emptyset) \leftrightarrow \texttt{E}(pk_S; Out_P, \{C_i'\})]$, s.t. $C_i' = g_1^{m_i} g_2^{r_i'}$ for random r_i'; C and any entity(E) with access to the public parameters of system, get involved in a protocol for proving the possession of a signature on a committed message block. First C creates new commitments on each element of the message block $\{C_i'\}$ and sends it to E. Then they run a *signature proof-of-knowledge* $SPK\{(A, e, s, m_1, \ldots, m_L) : A = (g_0 g_1^s g_2^{m_1} \ldots g_{L+1}^{m_L})^{\frac{1}{e+sk_S}}\}$ to prove possession of a valid signature on M, which is committed by $\{C_i'\}$. S returns $Out_P = 1$ if no error happens.

This signature scheme provides two extra properties, beside the standard properties of signature schemes (*authenticity, integrity* and *non-repudiation*), as follows:

- *blind-sign*: $\texttt{Sign}$ protocol allows a client to obtain the signature of signer on a message, which is committed as $cmt = Commit(M)$ using Pedersen commitment. The client uses $ZKPoK$ to prove that the committed values are correctly calculated from message. The protocol perfectly hides the message from the signer. The signature is secure under LRSW assumption [16].
- *blind-verify*: In $\texttt{Verify}$ protocol, the client computes a *non-interactive honest-verifier zero-knowledge proof-of-knowledge (SPK)* protocol in order to prove to any verifier that she knows a message block (M) and a signature on it, where the commitment of the message is presented. The proof does not leak any information about the message and the signature.

3 Model

There are three types of entities; a set of untrusted *provers* $\mathcal{P} = \{\mathcal{P}_1, \ldots, \mathcal{P}_n\}$, a set of untrusted *verifiers* $\mathcal{V} = \{\mathcal{V}_1, \ldots, \mathcal{V}_m\}$, and a honest-but-curious *registration authority* $(\mathcal{RA})$ with a key-pair $(pk_{\mathcal{RA}}/sk_{\mathcal{RA}})$. We assume $\mathcal{RA}$ can generate her key pair. Each registered prover $\mathcal{P}_i$ has a secret key sk_i, and a certificate of $\mathcal{RA}$ for it $(\sigma_i = Sign_{\mathcal{RA}}(sk_i))$. The communication channels are public. We assume there exists a public and secure board which keeps the public parameters of the system, including the public-key of *registration authority* and every entity has secure read access to the board.

There are three operational phases in this model; (1) $\mathcal{RA}$ makes a key pair by executing "KeyGen" phase and puts the public-key on the public board. (2) In "Registration" phase, a new prover $(\mathcal{P}_i)$ with a chosen secret-key (sk_i), and $\mathcal{RA}$ interact, resulting in $\mathcal{P}_i$ obtaining a registeration certificate (sk_i, σ_i). (3) In "DB" phase, a registered prover $\mathcal{P}_i$ interacts with a verifier $\mathcal{V}_j$, that has read access to the public board. At the end of this phase, $\mathcal{P}_i$ proves that she knows a secret key (sk_i), she has a signature of $\mathcal{RA}$ on sk_i, and is located within a distance bound $\mathbb{D}$ to $\mathcal{V}_j$. The verifier returns a single bit $Out_{\mathcal{V}}$ as the output of protocol ($Out_{\mathcal{V}} = 1$ for accept and $Out_{\mathcal{V}} = 0$ for reject).

Definition 1. Correctness: *for any pair of honest prover and honest verifier, with mutual distance of at most $\mathbb{D}$, the "DB" protocol should always return $Out_{\mathcal{V}} = 1$.*

The protocol's **soundness** is against two types of adversaries: distance-bounding adversary $(\mathcal{A}_{DB})$ and privacy adversary $(\mathcal{A}_P)$. The distance-bounding adversary $\mathcal{A}_{DB}$ can, (1) read the public board, and (2) control the corrupted provers. The aim of $\mathcal{A}_{DB}$ is to convice an honest verifier to return $Out_{\mathcal{V}} = 1$ as the output of DB operation. The privacy adversary $\mathcal{A}_P$ can, (1) read the public board, and (2) read the internal state of $\mathcal{RA}$, and (3) control all verifiers and corrupted provers. The aim of $\mathcal{A}_P$ is to distinguish between two honest provers based on their interactions with the system.

We define three general *DB* attacks. The definition of *distance-fraud* and *MiM* attacks are in-line with Vaudenay *et al.*'s [23] approach, but the proposed *terrorist-fraud* attack is following the classic definition. First, a simple two-party attack is considered, where a dishonest prover is far away from the verifier, but wants to convince the verifier that she is within the distance.

Definition 2. α-resistance Distance-Fraud: *For any PPT adversary $\mathcal{A}$, which is not located within the distance $\mathbb{D}$ to an honest verifier $\mathcal{V}_j$, and is able to run a Registration session with $\mathcal{RA}$, the probability of returning $Out_{\mathcal{V}} = 1$ in an interaction with $\mathcal{V}_j$ is not more than α.*

This definition captures *Distance-Hijacking*, in which a dishonest far-away prover $\mathcal{P}^*$ may mis-use some honest provers to successfully authenticate to $\mathcal{V}_j$. In this attack, the adversary is allowed to mis-behave in the Registration session, which results in a more powerful adversary in comparison to the *distance-fraud* adversary of Vaudenay *et al.* [23]. The second DB attack is a three-party attack in which an honest *prover* $\mathcal{P}$ is far-away from honest *verifier* $(\mathcal{V})$, but a malicious adversary $\mathcal{A}_2$ which is located within the distance $\mathbb{D}$, wants to convince $\mathcal{V}$ about the distance bound of $\mathcal{P}$.

Definition 3. β-resistance MiM: *For any PPT adversary $\mathcal{A}$, which can*

(i) *initiate Registration or DB session of an honest prover $(\mathcal{P}_i)$,*
(ii) *listen/block/change the communications of a Registration session between an honest prover $(\mathcal{P}_i)$ and $\mathcal{RA}$,*

(iii) listen the communications of polynomially bounded instances of DB *sessions between any honest verifier* $\mathcal{V}_j$ *and* $\mathcal{P}_i$, *when she is located within distance* $\mathbb{D}$ *to* $\mathcal{V}_j$ *(learning phase),*

(iv) listen/block/change the communications of polynomially bounded instances of DB *sessions between any honest verifier* $\mathcal{V}_k$ *and* $\mathcal{P}_i$, *when she is not located within distance* $\mathbb{D}$ *to* $\mathcal{V}_k$,

(v) run any polynomially bounded instances of algorithms with independent inputs from above,

the probability of returning $Out_\mathcal{V} = 1$ *in any of* DB *sessions with* $\mathcal{V}_k$ *is not more than* β.

Impersonation-Attack is an special case of this attack, in which there is no learning phase and no honest prover. If a protocol is secure against *MiM* adversary, then it is secure against *impersonation-attack* with at least the same probability. With the same argument as before (i.e. more freedom in **Registration** phase), this definition is stronger than the *MiM* adversary of Vaudenay *et al.* [23].

In the third attack, three parties are involved; a dishonest *prover* ($\mathcal{P}^*$) which is far away from the honest *verifier* ($\mathcal{V}_j$), and an *adversary* which is located within the distance to $\mathcal{V}_j$ and helps $\mathcal{P}^*$ to convince $\mathcal{V}_j$ about the distance bound of $\mathcal{P}^*$.

Definition 4. γ-**resistance Terrorist-Fraud:** *For any pair of PPT adversary* $\mathcal{A}^{TF}$ *and dishonest prover* ($\mathcal{P}_i^*$), *which is not located within distance* $\mathbb{D}$ *to an honest verifier* ($\mathcal{V}_j$), *when they have the following abilities;*

(i) $\mathcal{P}_i^*$ *is able to run a* **Registration** *session with* $\mathcal{RA}$

(ii) $\mathcal{P}_i^*$ *can communicate with* $\mathcal{A}^{TF}$ *outside the* DB *protocol, but is not willing to leak any information about her own secret key,*

(iii) $\mathcal{A}^{TF}$ *can listen/block/change the communications of a* DB *session between any honest verifier* $\mathcal{V}_j$ *and* $\mathcal{P}_i^*$, *and*

then the probability of convincing $\mathcal{V}_j$ *to return* $Out_\mathcal{V} = 1$ *in the* DB *session is not more than* γ.

We define **privacy** in terms of the distinguishability advantage of an adversary in a game with a challenger. The adversary chooses two provers $\mathcal{P}_0$ and $\mathcal{P}_1$, and gives them to the challenger. The challenger chooses a random bit $b \in_R \{0, 1\}$ and returns the anonymous handle of $\mathcal{P}_b$, to the adversary. The adversary can have access the orcales listed below, for any polynomial number of times, and then outputs a bit b'. Success probability of adversary is in terms of $\Pr(b = b')$. The formal definition is as follows:

Definition 5. $\rho-$**Extensive Privacy:** *Consider the following game between a challenger and adversary* $\mathcal{A}_P$ *who can make query to the following oracles:*

– ($\mathcal{P}_i$) $\leftarrow$ CreateProver(); *creates a prover with a unique identifier* $\mathcal{P}_i$. *This oracle creates the internal keys and certificates of a new prover and returns* $\mathcal{P}_i$.

- $(\mathcal{P}_i, stt_\mathcal{P}) \leftarrow$ CreateInsider(); *This oracle is same as* CreateProver, *but it also returns the internal state of the prover.*
- $(\pi, m) \leftarrow$ Launch(); *this oracle runs a pre-defined protocol on verifier and returns the session identifier π and the message sent by the verifier.*
- $(vtag) \leftarrow$ DrawProver($\mathcal{P}_i, \mathcal{P}_j$); *on input of two provers, this oracle returns a unique virtual fresh identifier to either $\mathcal{P}_i$ for $b = 0$, or $\mathcal{P}_j$ for $b = 1$. It first checks if any of them is an insider or already drawn, and terminates if so. Then asks from challenger to choose one bit $b \in_R \{0, 1\}$. Based on this bit, creates an anonymous handle vtag for the chosen prover and returns it. Note that in this step, there a private table $\mathcal{T}$, which stores the tuple $(vtag, \mathcal{P}_i, \mathcal{P}_j, b)$.*
- $(m') \leftarrow$ SendProver($vtag, m$); *on input of anonymous handle of a prover and a message m, this oracle sends the message m to the prover, and returns prover's reply message (m').*
- $() \leftarrow$ Free($vtag$); *on input of anonymous handle of a prover, this oracle removes the handle, which eliminates any access to the prover through this handle. And by using the recorded tuple in the database, the related prover will get reset (i.e. erase volatile memory).*
- $(m') \leftarrow$ SendVerifier(π, m); *on input of a protocol session (π) and a message m, this oracle sends the message m to the verifier in the session π, and returns verifier's reply message (m').*
- $(stt_\mathcal{V}) \leftarrow$ StateVerifier(); *this oracle returns the internal state of the verifier. This oracle includes the functionality of the* Result *oracle in [22], which just returns the final output of session π.*
- $(stt_{\mathcal{R}\mathcal{A}}) \leftarrow$ StateRA(); *this oracle returns the internal state of $\mathcal{R}\mathcal{A}$.*

$\mathcal{A}_P$ *wins if she can find the choice of challenger in* DrawProver *oracle. A protocol is ρ-extensive private, if and only if there is no PPT adversary $\mathcal{A}_P$ who can win the game with advantage of more than ρ.*

Note 1. Extensive-privacy is stronger than *wide-privacy* [22] and the privacy model of Gambs *et al.* [11], in regards to the view of adversary about all *non-prover* entities. That's because the adversary has access to two more oracles StateVerifier and StateRA at the same time. This classification is about the view of adversary about all *non-prover* entities. The view of adversary about the provers have been considered independently based on her access to Corrupt oracle, which is not in the scope of this privacy model.

Finally, we define the security of PDB:

Definition 6. $(\alpha, \beta, \gamma, \rho)$−**secure Privacy-Preserving Distance-Bounding:** *A PDB protocol is defined by a tuple (KeyGen, reg$_\mathcal{P}$, reg$_{\mathcal{R}\mathcal{A}}$, db$_\mathcal{P}$, db$_\mathcal{V}$, $\mathbb{D}$), as follows:*

1. $(pk_{\mathcal{R}\mathcal{A}}, sk_{\mathcal{R}\mathcal{A}}) \leftarrow$ KeyGen(1^λ): *A randomized algorithm such that on the input of the security parameter λ, returns a key pair to $\mathcal{R}\mathcal{A}$.*
2. reg$_\mathcal{P}(pk_{\mathcal{R}\mathcal{A}}; sk_i, \sigma_i) \leftrightarrow$ reg$_{\mathcal{R}\mathcal{A}}(sk_{\mathcal{R}\mathcal{A}}; \emptyset)$: *An interactive protocol between two PPT ITMs;* reg$_\mathcal{P}$ *returns a secret-key and signature of $\mathcal{R}\mathcal{A}$ on it ($sk_i, \sigma_i = Sign_{\mathcal{R}\mathcal{A}}(sk_i)$) by taking $pk_{\mathcal{R}\mathcal{A}}$ as input, while* reg$_{\mathcal{R}\mathcal{A}}$ *takes $sk_{\mathcal{R}\mathcal{A}}$ as input.*

3. $\mathsf{db}_{\mathcal{P}}(sk_i, \sigma_i; \emptyset) \leftrightarrow \mathsf{db}_{\mathcal{V}}(pk_{\mathcal{RA}}; Out_{\mathcal{V}})$: *An interactive protocol between two PPT ITMs;* $\mathsf{db}_{\mathcal{V}}$ *returns a single bit* $Out_{\mathcal{V}}$, *by taking* $pk_{\mathcal{RA}}$ *as input, while* $\mathsf{db}_{\mathcal{P}}$ *takes prover's secret-key and* $\mathcal{RA}$*'s signature* $(sk_i, \sigma_i = Sign_{\mathcal{RA}}(sk_i))$ *as input.* $\mathsf{db}_{\mathcal{P}}$ *provides a commitment on* sk_i, *and then provides three proofs about the commitment; (i) proves that she knows the committed value* (sk_i), *(ii) proves that she knows a valid signature of* $\mathcal{RA}$ *on the committed value* (σ_i), *and (iii) proves that she (owner of* sk_i*) is located within the distance* $\mathbb{D}$. $\mathsf{db}_{\mathcal{V}}$ *returns* $Out_{\mathcal{V}} = 1$ *if the three proofs are correct, otherwise* $Out_{\mathcal{V}} = 0$.
4. $\mathbb{D}$ *is an integer indicating the distance bound.*

The protocol is secure, if the following properties hold; **Correctness** *(Definition 1),* α-**distance-fraud** *(Definition 2),* β-**MiM** *(Definition 3),* γ-**terrorist-fraud** *(Definition 4),* ρ-**extensive-privacy** *(Definition 5).*

4   PDB Construction

In this section we introduce our protocol, as an extension of DBPK-Log [5], by using *Pedersen commitment* [18], *zero-knowledge proof-of-knowledge protocols* [20] and *signature proof-of-knowledge protocols* [12]. The overview of the protocol is as follows:

1. **Setup**: $\mathcal{RA}$ creates a key-pair for signing secret-key of new *provers*. This operation is an instance of "BBS$^+$.KeyGen" function.
2. **Registration**: A new *prover* $(\mathcal{P}_i)$ gets registered by $\mathcal{RA}$. $\mathcal{P}_i$ chooses a random secret-key (sk_i), and gets the signature of $\mathcal{RA}$ for it $(\sigma_i = Sign_{\mathcal{RA}}(sk_i))$ in a blind form. This operation is an instance of "BBS$^+$.Sign" interactive protocol.
3. **Distance-Bounding**: A registered *prover* $(\mathcal{P}_i)$ provides distance-bounding proof to a *verifier* $(\mathcal{V}_j)$. $\mathcal{P}_i$ sends a Pedersen commitment $C = commit(sk_i)$ to $\mathcal{V}$, and then provides three proofs about the commitment; (i) proves that she knows the committed value (sk_i), (ii) proves that she knows a valid signature of $\mathcal{RA}$ on the committed value, by using "BBS$^+$.Verify" non-interactive protocol, and (iii) proves that she is located within the distance bound $\mathbb{D}$. This proof is based on **fast-exchange** bitwise operation of every single bit of sk_i.

Global Common Parameters. By considering λ as the security parameter, let's define $(\mathbb{G}_1, \mathbb{G}_2)$ as a bilinear group pair with computable isomorphism ψ such that $|\mathbb{G}_1| = |\mathbb{G}_2| = p$ for a λ-bit strong prime p, such that $p = 2q + 1$ for a large prime number q. $\mathbb{G}_p$ is a group of order p, and the bilinearity mapping is $\hat{e} : \mathbb{G}_1 \times \mathbb{G}_2 \to \mathbb{G}_p$. $H : \{0,1\}^* \to \mathbb{Z}_p$ and $H_{evt} : \{0,1\}^* \to \mathbb{G}_p$ are hash functions. Let g_0, g_1, g_2 be generators of $\mathbb{G}_1$, h_0, h_1, h_2 be generators of $\mathbb{G}_2$ such that $\psi(h_i) = g_i$, and u_0, u_1, u_2 be generators of $\mathbb{G}_p$ such that the discrete logarithm of the generators are unknown. The generation of these parameters can be done by a trusted general manager, which is present just once at the begining. We use BBS$^+$ signature scheme [6] with a block message of size one $(M = \{sk_i\})$, so obviously the parameters of BBS$^+$ is included in these parameters. These values are public and considered as the input of all operations (omitted for simplicity).

The steps of the protocol are as follows:

1. Setup: $(sk_{RA}, pk_{RA} = h_0^{sk_{RA}}) \leftarrow$ BBS$^+$.KeyGen(1^λ)

2. Registration: $\mathcal{P}_i(pk_{RA}; sk_i, Sign_{RA}(sk_i)) \leftrightarrow RA(sk_{RA}; \emptyset)$. They do the following steps:

– $\mathcal{P}_i$ randomly chooses an odd number $sk_i \in_R \mathbb{Z}_p \setminus \{q\}$.
– They execute BBS$^+$.Sign$\big[\mathcal{P}_i(sk_i, pk_{RA}; \sigma_i = Sign_{RA}(sk_i)) \leftrightarrow RA(sk_{RA}; .)\big]$

3. Distance-Bounding: $\mathcal{P}_i(sk_i, Sign_{RA}(sk_i);) \leftrightarrow \mathcal{V}_j(pk_{RA}; Out_\mathcal{V})$. There are

five steps in this phase; (i) BBS$^+$.Verify, (ii) Bit Commitments, (iii) Fast-Exchange, (iv) Commitment Opening and (v) Proof-of-Knowledge. At any step of this phase, $\mathcal{V}$ terminates with $Out_\mathcal{V} = 0$, if any failure happens, otherwise if it reaches the end, it returns $Out_\mathcal{V} = 1$ as the output.

(i) BBS$^+$.Verify$\big[\mathcal{P}_i(sk_i, \sigma_i = Sign_{RA}(sk_i); .) \leftrightarrow \mathcal{V}_j(pk_{RA}; Out, C = g_1^{sk_i} . g_2^r)\big]$. If $Out = 1$, then $\mathcal{V}_j$ continues to the next step and keeps the value of C.

(ii) In Bit Commitment step, the process of Fig. 1 gets executed. At the end of this phase, $\mathcal{V}_j$ is able to compute:

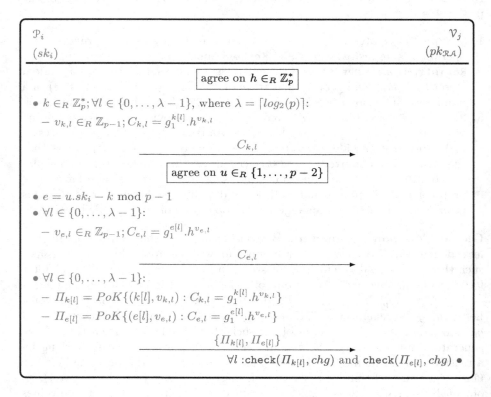

Fig. 1. PDB: Bit Commitment step

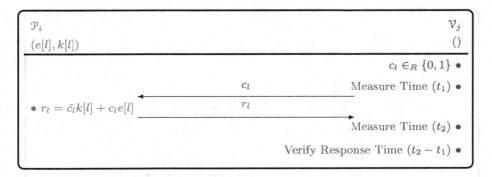

Fig. 2. PDB: Fast-Exchange step

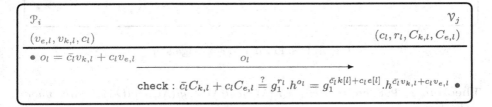

Fig. 3. PDB: Commitment Opening step

$$z = \prod_{l=0}^{\lambda-1} (C_{k,l} C_{e,l})^{2^l} = g_1^{\sum_{l=0}^{\lambda-1}(2^l.k[l]+2^l.k[l])}.h^{\sum_{l=0}^{\lambda-1}(2^l.(v_{k,l}+v_{e,l}))} = g_1^{k+e}.h^v =$$
$$g_1^{u.sk_i}.h^v \bmod p$$

such that: $k = \sum_{l=0}^{\lambda-1}(2^l.k[l]) \bmod p - 1$, $e = \sum_{l=0}^{\lambda-1}(2^l.e[l]) \bmod p - 1$, $e = \sum_{l=0}^{\lambda-1}(2^l.e[l]) \bmod p - 1$, $v = \sum_{l=0}^{\lambda-1}(2^l.(v_{k,l}+v_{e,l})) \bmod p - 1$.

(iii) In **Fast-Exchange** step, process of Fig. 2 runs for $\forall l \in \{0, \dots, \lambda-1\}$.

(iv) In **Commitment Opening** step, the process of Fig. 3 runs for $\forall l \in \{0, \dots, \lambda-1\}$.

(v) Finally in **Proof-of-Knowledge** step, and interactive instance of $PoK[(sk_i, v, r) : z = g_1^{u.sk_i}.h^v \wedge C = g_1^{sk_i}.g_2^r]$ takes place to make sure that the summation of the secret values k and e is equal to randomized form of the committed secret-key ($u.sk_i$). One possible way of doing the PoK is repeating the process of Fig. 4 for t times. The process continues, unless occurance of failure.

If all t times verifications succeed, then $\mathcal{V}_j$ returns $Out_V = 1$. Note that if we replace the secret-key commitments ($C = g_1^{sk_i}.g_2^r$) with public-keys of the prover ($pk_i = g_1^{sk_i}$), and remove the **BBS$^+$** signature scheme, then we would have a secure public-key distance-bounding protocol (**DBPoK-log$^+$**), which fixes the vulnerabilities of **DBPK-Log** [5]. Now we provide our claim about the security of **PDB** protocol.

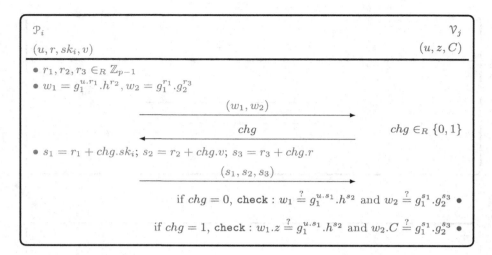

Fig. 4. PDB: `Proof-of-Knowledge` step

Theorem 1. PDB *protocol is* $(negl(\lambda), negl(\lambda), negl(\lambda), negl(\lambda))$-*secure, under Definition 6.*

The security proof of this theorem will be provided in the full version paper.

5 Conclusion

In this paper we solved the open problem of having a public-key DB protocol, which is secure against all DB adversaries by proposing a new protocol (DBPoK-log$^+$). This protocol is based on DBPoK-Log protocol which has shown to be vulnerable against DFA and TFA. We achieved security by adding some PoK operations. The computational cost of this achievement is equivalent to about $4.\lambda$ exponentiations in a prime order cyclic group per each DB instance.

Moreover we proposed a new privacy model for the provers against *dishonest* verifiers and *honest-but-curious* registration authority. And finally extended DBPoK-log$^+$ protocol to build a privacy-preserving DB protocol (PDB) in the new privacy model. This protocol, inherits *distance-bounding* properties from DBPoK-log$^+$ protocol. We replaced the public-key setting of provers, with Pedersen commitments and adopted BBS$^+$ signature scheme to provide *privacy* and *authentication* at the same time. As a result, PDB provides all three properties together; *distance-bounding, privacy* and *authentication*. The computational cost of this achievement, is about 25 extra exponentiations per each DB instance, in comparison with DBPoK-log$^+$.

There are still two open problems in this field; (1) having a DB protocol secure against all DB adversaries, which supports *extensive* privacy against an adversary who has access to `corrupt` oracle. And (2) having the same DB protocol in the presence of dishonest registration authority.

References

1. Avoine, G., Bingöl, M.A., Kardaş, S., Lauradoux, C., Martin, B.: A framework for analyzing RFID distance bounding protocols. J. Comput. Secur. **19**, 289–317 (2011)
2. Bay, A., Boureanu, I., Mitrokotsa, A., Spulber, I., Vaudenay, S.: The bussard-bagga and other distance-bounding protocols under attacks. In: Kutyłowski, M., Yung, M. (eds.) Inscrypt 2012. LNCS, vol. 7763, pp. 371–391. Springer, Heidelberg (2013)
3. Boureanu, I., Mitrokotsa, A., Vaudenay, S.: Secure & lightweight distance-bounding. In: Second International Workshop on Lightweight Cryptography for Security and Privacy (2013)
4. Brands, S., Chaum, D.: Distance bounding protocols. In: Helleseth, T. (ed.) EURO-CRYPT 1993. LNCS, vol. 765, pp. 344–359. Springer, Heidelberg (1994)
5. Bussard, L., Bagga, W.: Distance-bounding proof of knowledge protocols to avoid terrorist fraud attacks. Technical report, Institut Eurecom, France (2004)
6. Camenisch, J.L., Lysyanskaya, A.: Signature schemes and anonymous credentials from bilinear maps. In: Franklin, M. (ed.) CRYPTO 2004. LNCS, vol. 3152, pp. 56–72. Springer, Heidelberg (2004)
7. Cremers, C., Rasmussen, K.B., Schmidt, B., Capkun, S.: Distance hijacking attacks on distance bounding protocols. In: Security and Privacy, pp. 113–127 (2012)
8. Desmedt, Y.: Major security problems with the "unforgeable" (feige-)fiat-shamir proofs of identity and how to overcome them. In: Congress on Computer and Communication Security and Protection Securicom 1988, pp. 147–159 (1988)
9. Dürholz, U., Fischlin, M., Kasper, M., Onete, C.: A formal approach to distance-bounding rfid protocols. In: Lai, X., Zhou, J., Li, H. (eds.) ISC 2011. LNCS, vol. 7001, pp. 47–62. Springer, Heidelberg (2011)
10. Fischlin, M., Onete, C.: Terrorism in distance bounding: modeling terrorist-fraud resistance. In: Jacobson, M., Locasto, M., Mohassel, P., Safavi-Naini, R. (eds.) ACNS 2013. LNCS, vol. 7954, pp. 414–431. Springer, Heidelberg (2013)
11. Gambs, S., Onete, C., Robert, J.M.: Prover anonymous and deniable distance-bounding authentication. In: Proceedings of the 9th ACM Symposium on Information, Computer and Communications Security, pp. 501–506 (2014)
12. Goldwasser, S., Micali, S., Rivest, R.L.: A digital signature scheme secure against adaptive chosen-message attacks. SIAM J. Comput. **17**, 281–308 (1988)
13. Hermans, J., Pashalidis, A., Vercauteren, F., Preneel, B.: A new RFID privacy model. In: Atluri, V., Diaz, C. (eds.) ESORICS 2011. LNCS, vol. 6879, pp. 568–587. Springer, Heidelberg (2011)
14. Hermans, J., Peeters, R., Onete, C.: Efficient, secure, private distance bounding without key updates. In: Proceedings of the sixth ACM conference on Security and privacy in wireless and mobile networks, pp. 207–218. ACM (2013)
15. Krumm, J.: A survey of computational location privacy. Pers. Ubiquitous Comput. **13**, 391–399 (2009)
16. Lysyanskaya, A., Rivest, R.L., Sahai, A., Wolf, S.: Pseudonym systems (extended abstract). In: Heys, H.M., Adams, C.M. (eds.) SAC 1999. LNCS, vol. 1758, p. 184. Springer, Heidelberg (2000)
17. Paise, R.I., Vaudenay, S.: Mutual authentication in RFID: security and privacy. In: Proceedings of the 2008 ACM Symposium on Information, Computer and Communications Security. pp. 292–299 (2008)
18. Pedersen, T.P.: Non-interactive and information-theoretic secure verifiable secret sharing. In: Feigenbaum, J. (ed.) CRYPTO 1991. LNCS, vol. 576, pp. 129–140. Springer, Heidelberg (1992)

19. Peeters, R., Hermans, J.: Wide strong private RFID identification based on zero-knowledge. IACR Cryptol. ePrint Arch. **2012**, 389 (2012)
20. Pieprzyk, J., Hardjono, T., Seberry, J.: Fundamentals of Computer Security. Springer, Heidelberg (2003)
21. Shokri, R., Theodorakopoulos, G., Le Boudec, J.Y., Hubaux, J.P.: Quantifying location privacy. In: 2011 IEEE Symposium on Security and Privacy (SP), pp. 247–262 (2011)
22. Vaudenay, S.: On privacy models for RFID. In: Kurosawa, K. (ed.) ASIACRYPT 2007. LNCS, vol. 4833, pp. 68–87. Springer, Heidelberg (2007)
23. Vaudenay, S., Boureanu, I., Mitrokotsa, A., et al.: Practical & provably secure distance-bounding. In: The 16th Information Security Conference (2013)

Distance Lower Bounding

Xifan Zheng[(✉)], Reihaneh Safavi-Naini, and Hadi Ahmadi

University of Calgary, Calgary, AB, Canada
{xzheng,rei,hahmadi}@ucalgary.ca

Abstract. Distance (upper)-bounding (DUB) allows a verifier to know whether a proving party is located within a certain distance bound. DUB protocols have many applications in secure authentication and location based services. We consider the dual problem of distance lower bounding (DLB), where the prover proves it is outside a distance bound to the verifier. We motivate this problem through a number of application scenarios, and model security against distance fraud (DF), Man-in-the-Middle (MiM), and collusion fraud (CF) attacks. We prove impossibility of security against these attacks without making physical assumptions. We propose approaches to the construction of secure protocols under reasonable assumptions, and give detailed design of our DLB protocol and prove its security using the above model. This is the first treatment of the DLB problem in the untrusted prover setting, with a number of applications and raising new research questions. We discuss our results and propose directions for future research.

1 Introduction

Distance (upper) bounding (DUB) protocols have been widely studied in recent years: a *verifier* V interacts with a *prover* P to obtain assurance that the prover is at a distance at most B from the verifier. A DUB protocol was first proposed in [3] to thwart relay attacks in authentication protocols, by using the location as an unforgeable attribute of the prover. DUB protocols have been widely used for proximity based authentication (e.g., passive keyless entry and start system in modern cars [8]), proximity based control (e.g., implantable medical device [15]), and Radio-Frequency Identification (RFID) authentication [1,18].

Secure DUB protocols estimate distance by measuring the round-trip time between a challenge and its response, which are transmitted as light-speed electromagnetic (EM) signals. We refer to protocols that use this method for distance estimation, as class $\mathcal{EF}$ (i.e., EM fast-exchange). In this paper, we consider the dual problem of *distance lower bounding* (DLB), where a prover P wants to prove its distance from a verifier V is higher than a bound B. DLB problem naturally arises in application scenarios where privileges are given based on the distance of the requester to a verifier. For example a company offering unrestricted Internet access to games and entertainment software to employees, when they are outside of main office area of the company campus (e.g., Google campus), and restricted access when employees are within the main office area. Here the requirement is

© Springer International Publishing Switzerland 2015
L.C.K. Hui et al. (Eds.): ICICS 2014, LNCS 8958, pp. 89–104, 2015.
DOI: 10.1007/978-3-319-21966-0_7

for employees to prove they are outside the main working area. A second scenario is when the parking lot is divided into zones and parking charge depends on the distance of the car to the main point of interest (e.g. discounted rate will be given if users park their car at farer distance from the shopping mall entrance). In both cases once the privilege is granted based on the distance, one needs to use monitoring mechanisms such as continuous authentication to ensure that the user stays within the claimed area. Embedding such authentication in streaming services such as games or music is straightforward. For the latter scenario, one can use random scanning of the area to ensure correct claim. Although determined users may be able to bypass the authentication, but they will be inconvenient (e.g. move the car frequently) and also have to accept the risk of detection and penalty.

Despite the relation between DUB and DLB and the fact that a successful DUB protocol run proves an upper bound on the prover's distance, its failure does not say anything about the distance of the prover. None of the DUB protocols protect against distance enlargement attack [6], where the malicious prover enlarges the distance by delaying the response. Other applications of DUB protocol, such as using DUB protocols with multiple verifiers for secure positioning [6], will also be vulnerable to distance enlargement attack. A second approach would be to use Global Positioning System (GPS)[11] to determine the location of the user. However one needs to trust the GPS measurements, which is known to be vulnerable to attacks, such as GPS spoofing attack [21] where fake satellite signals are used to modify the GPS location data. This solution also results in privacy loss and so one needs to consider privacy enhancing GPS solutions that require extra infrastructure.

Attacks on DLB protocols depend on the application scenario. In Sect. 2.1 we formalize attacks that are applicable in the above application scenarios, and show that they are parallel to attacks on DUB protocols. DUB protocols have been analyzed against three broad classes of attacks [20]: *distance fraud (DF)* where the prover is malicious and wants to shorten its distance to the verifier; *collusion fraud (CF)* where the prover is malicious and has a helper that would assist them to shorten its distance to the verifier; and finally *Man-in-the-middle (MiM) attack* where the prover is honest and is the victim of an external attacker, who aims to shorten the distance between the honest prover and the verifier. These classes include attacks such as impersonation, Mafia fraud and Terrorist fraud, that are traditionally considered for DUB. We show that all above attacks are directly applicable to our DLB scenario above and capture important DLB attacks.

The solution to DLB problem depends on the trust assumption. DLB problem in a setting that *both the prover and the verifier are trusted*, has been considered in [19]. In this paper, we consider a setting where *the prover is untrusted* and the verifier is trusted.

Here we unravel the main difference between DUB and DLB protocols: DUB protocols have been primarily designed in the setting that an untrusted prover interacts with a trusted verifier. However in Sect. 2.2, we prove that it is impossible to have secure DLB protocol if provers are fully untrusted (have full control of the device hardware and software), which allows them to deviate arbitrarily from the protocol. One however can have secure protocols by making assumptions on the malicious prover's access to the device and/or communication channel. Table 1 summarizes trust assumptions in the two problems.

Table 1. Impossibility result of DB protocols with different trust assumptions

Trust	DLB problem	DUB problem
Trusted prover	Possible (e.g., secure ranging [19])	Possible ^{a} (c.f., DB [2])
Fully untrusted prover^b	Impossible (Sect. 2.2)	
Partially trusted prover^c	Possible (Sect. 3, Π_{DLB-BM})	

  ^{a} DUB protocols with fully untrusted prover are secure in other trust settings.
  ^{b} Malicious prover with unrestricted control of the prover device hardware/software.
  ^{c} Restricted Malicious prover who can run malicious software on the prover device.

Our Contribution. First, we initiate the study of distance lower bounding (DLB) problem in a setting where the prover is untrusted using motivating application scenarios. Second, we construct security model for DLB problem and define three broad classes of attacks: distance fraud (DF), Man-in-the-middle attack (MiM) and collusion fraud (CF). Third, we prove that security against any of these attacks without making *physical assumptions*[1] is impossible. In particular, a fully malicious prover can *always* succeed in the DF attack, and an external attacker (without the cryptographic credentials) can always jam-and-delay the signal between the verifier and the prover, and succeed in the MIM attack. This also implies that a malicious prover that has a helper (CF) will always succeed. Fourth, we construct a secure DLB protocols under reasonable assumptions, and prove its security against DF, MiM and CF attacks. Finally, we estimate time, memory and energy requirements of our protocol and conclude with open questions and directions for future research.

Related Work. There is a large body of research on secure positioning and distance estimation, including distance bounding protocols [2,3,10], positioning techniques [6,11] and secure ranging protocols [19]. As we argued earlier, these approaches are not directly applicable to the DLB problem in the setting that the prover is not trusted. GPS systems use a set of satellites signals to determine the location and are designed for non-adversarial setting, and so GPS systems are vulnerable to signal spoofing attacks [21]; DUB protocols protect against malicious provers trying to shorten the distance, but are in general vulnerable to the distance enlargement attack [6]; secure positioning systems use a DUB protocol with multiple verifiers to triangulate the prover's location, but is also vulnerable to distance enlargement attack, making positioning an insecure approach for DLB; and secure ranging systems only consider non-adversarial setting as well.

---

[1] Including limited access to the device hardware, and/or the communication channel.

To our knowledge, this is the first paper to study DLB in a setting where the prover is not trusted. Our approach to defining attacks, distance estimation, and design of the protocol is inspired by the large body of literature on DUB, in particular, [20] for formalization of attacks, and [2,10] for the design of the protocol. The use of bounded-memory assumption for the prover's device in the context of secure code update had been considered in [13]. We refer to [22]. for a complete review of relevant works.

2   DLB - Model and Impossibilities

We consider a multi-party system where a party U is modeled by a polynomially bounded interactive Turing machine (ITM) with a certain location loc_U, and some pre-shared key. A party can be a *prover* or a *verifier*. A *prover* P engages in a two-party protocol with a *verifier* V, to prove the claim that its distance to the verifier satisfies certain bound. Honest parties run predefined algorithms for their side of the interaction. The verifier V is always honest. The prover however may be malicious, in which case it is denoted by P^*. A protocol instance defines an experiment denoted by $exp = (P(x; r_P) \leftrightarrow \mathcal{A}(r_A) \leftrightarrow V(y; r_V))$. At the end of a protocol instance, V has an output Out_V, which is 1 or 0, showing acceptance or rejection of the DLB, respectively. The prover does not have an output. A participant in an experiment has a *view* consisting of all its inputs, coins, and messages that it can see. The external attacker $\mathcal{A}$ may interact with multiple Ps and Vs, and its view will include all these interactions.

Definition 1 (DLB Protocol). *A Distance Lower Bounding (DLB) protocol is a tuple (Gen, P, V, B), where $(x, y) \leftarrow Gen(1^s, r_k)$ is a randomized key-generation algorithm that takes security parameter s and randomness r_k and outputs keys x and y; $P(x; r_P)$ is the prover's ppt ITM that takes secret-key] x and randomness r_P; $V(y; r_V)$ is the verifier's ppt ITM taking secret-key y and randomness r_V , and B is a distance-bound. It satisfies two properties:*

- *Termination: $(\forall s)(\forall R)(\forall r_k; r_V)(\forall loc_V)$ if $(.; y) \leftarrow Gen(1^s; r_k)$ and $(R \leftrightarrow V(y; r_V))$ is an execution of the protocol between the verifier and any (unbounded) prover algorithm, V halts in $Poly(s)$ computational steps;*
- *p-Completeness: $(\forall s)(\forall loc_V; loc_P$ such that $d(loc_V; loc_P) \geq B)$ we have*

$$Pr_{r_k; r_P; r_V} \left[Out_v = 1 : \begin{array}{c} (x; y) \leftarrow Gen(1^s; r_k)) \\ P(x; r_P) \leftrightarrow V(y; r_V) \end{array} \right] \geq p$$

2.1   Attacks on DLB Protocols

We consider three classes of attacks: distance fraud (DF), man-in-the-middle (MiM) attack, and collusion fraud (CF). In DF, P^*, with $d(P^*, V) < B$ wants to convince V that its distance is at least B. In MiM attack, an external attacker who does not have the secret key, interacts with multiple Ps and Vs, and finally succeeds in taking the role of a prover in a protocol instance (See Fig. 1a). In

Fig. 1. MiM and CF attack in DLB

CF, P^* colludes with a helper to claim a longer distance to V (See Fig. 1b). The collusion should not leak the prover's secret key to the helper. The formal definitions of the attacks are below.

Definition 2 (DF-resistance). *A DLB protocol Π is α-resistant to distance fraud if $(\forall s)(\forall P^*)(\forall loc_v$ such that $d(loc_v, loc_{p*}) \leq B)(\forall r_k)$, we have*

$$Pr_{r_v}\left[Out_v = 1 : \begin{array}{l} (x,y) \leftarrow Gen(1^s; r_k) \\ P^*(x) \leftrightarrow V(y; r_v) \end{array}\right] \leq \alpha$$

where P^* is any dishonest prover. Because of the concurrent setting we effectively allow polynomially bounded number of $P(x')$ and $V(y')$ close to $V(y)$ with independent (x', y').

Distance hijacking Definition 2 captures *distance hijacking attack* [7] against DLB protocols. In this attack, P^* who is at distance $< B$, uses DLB communications of unaware honest provers at a distance $\geq B$, to claim a distance $\geq B$.

Definition 3 (MiM-resistance). *A DLB protocol Π is β-resistant to MiM attack if $(\forall s)$, $(\forall m, \ell, z)$ are polynomially bounded, $(\forall A_1, A_2)$ polynomially bounded, for all locations such that $d(loc_{P_j}, loc_V) < B$, where $j \in \{m+1, \cdots, \ell\}$, we have*

$$Pr_{r_v}\left[Out_v = 1 : \begin{array}{l} (x,y) \leftarrow Gen(1^s) \\ P_1(x)...P_m(x) \leftrightarrow A_1 \leftrightarrow V_1(y)...V_z(y) \\ P_{m+1}(x)...P_\ell(x) \leftrightarrow A_2(View_{A_1}) \leftrightarrow V(y) \end{array}\right] \leq \beta$$

Here probability is over all random coins of the protocol, and $View_{A1}$ is the final view of A_1. The definition effectively allows polynomially bounded number of $P(x')$, $P^*(x')$, and $V(y')$ with independent (x', y'), anywhere.

Mafia fraud and impersonation attack. Definition 3 covers Mafia fraud and impersonation attack as special cases. In Mafia fraud, there is no learning phase. The attacker interacts with an honest prover and makes the verifier to output accept. That is, $m = z = 0$ and, $\ell = 1$ in the attack phase. In impersonation attack the attacker uses multiple possibly concurrent interactions with the verifier to make the verifier output 1. This attack is captured by letting $\ell = m$.

Definition 4 (CF-resistance). *A DLB protocol Π is (γ, η) resistant to collusion fraud if $(\forall s)(\forall P^*)(\forall loc_{v_0}$ such that $d(loc_{v_0}, loc_{P*}) < D)$, $(\forall A^{CF} ppt.)$:*

$$Pr_{r_v}\left[Out_{v_0} = 1 : \begin{array}{c} (x,y) \leftarrow Gen(1^s) \\ P^*(x) \leftrightarrow A^{CF} \leftrightarrow V_0(y) \end{array}\right] > \gamma$$

implies existence of an extended[2] MiM attack with $m, \ell, z, A_1, A_2, P_i,$
P_j, V_i that uses interaction with P and P^* both, and V in learning and satisfies

$$Pr\left[Out_v = 1 : \begin{array}{c} (x,y) \leftarrow Gen(1^s) \\ P_1^{(*)}(x)...P_m^{(*)}(x) \leftrightarrow A_1 \leftrightarrow V_1(y)...V_z(y) \\ P_{m+1}(x)...P_\ell(x) \leftrightarrow A_2(View_{A1}) \leftrightarrow V(y) \end{array}\right] > \eta$$

*Here, prover $P^{(*)}$ is either P or P^* and we have $d(loc_{P_j}, loc_V) < B$, for $j \in$
$\{m + 1 \cdots \ell\}$. We implicitly allow a polynomial number of $P(x')$, $P^*(x')$, and
$V(y')$ with independent (x', y') anywhere but honest participants are close to V_0.*

Terrorist fraud. In Terrorist fraud, P^*, with $d(P^*, V) < B$, gets aid from a
helper who does not have the secret key. Definition 4 captures terrorist fraud as
a special case by letting $m = z = \ell = 1$, by simply allowing A_1 to run A^{CF} and
succeed in impersonation and making V to accept.

2.2   Impossibility Results

We consider protocols in $\mathcal{EF}$. Let C denote speed of light, t_c and t_r denote the
verifier's clock readings, when the challenge is sent and the response is received,
respectively. If the received response is correct, the verifier calculates $T_\Delta = t_r - t_c$
to estimate the distance of the prover. Let T_{proc} denote the *processing time* of
the prover. The verifier estimates the prover's distance D as

$$D = \frac{(T_\Delta - T_{proc})C}{2}. \tag{1}$$

Theorem 1. *1. Any DLB protocol in $\mathcal{EF}$ is vulnerable to DF if P^* has full
(hardware and software) control over the prover's device.*
  *2. No DLB protocols in $\mathcal{EF}$ can provide β-resistance with $\beta < 1$ to MiM attack
by an external attacker who can jam and delay messages to/from the prover.*
  *3. For any DLB protocol in $\mathcal{EF}$, P^* can succeed in CF with probability 1 and
negligible key leakage to the helper, if the helper has full access to the communication channels with P^*, and P^* has full control over the prover's device.
The result holds even if communication is only allowed in one direction
between the prover and the helper.*

The proof sketch of Theorem 1 can be found in Appendix A.

2.3   Restricted DF, MiM, and CF

To remove the above impossibility results, we must use reasonable assumptions
(restrictions) on the adversary's control of the device and/or the communication
channel. We refer to attacks under these conditions as restricted DF, MiM and
CF (rDF, rMiM and rCF), to emphasize extra assumptions are needed.

---

[2] Because learning phase allows interaction with P^*.

Table 2. DLB security against the three attacks in different settings.

Attacks	Assumptions			
	No Assumption	Prover's device [BM]	Communication [$\overline{OC}$]	Combined [$BM + \overline{OC}$]
DF-security	×	✓	×	✓
MiM-security	×	×	✓	✓
CF-security	×	×	×	✓

Notations. We use PD to denote the prover's device, and rX$^{[Y]}$ to denote restricted version of attack X, where $X \in \{DF, MiM, CF\}$ and restrictions are stated in Y. For example, rDF$^{[BM]}$ refers to the restricted DF attack, under the restriction that PD has bounded memory.

Table 2 summarizes our impossibility results and shows assumptions used in our construction in Sect. 3. The assumptions that we use for security against rDF are, (i) P^* cannot access (read or write) the PD 's read-only memory (ROM), and (ii) PD has *bounded memory (BM)*. Note that the first assumption still allows P^* to inject malicious codes into the device writable memory (RAM), and modify correct execution of the protocol. The bounded memory assumption is a well-established model in cryptography [4], and has been used in the design of security systems [13]. To achieve the security against rMiM and rCF, in addition to the above assumptions, we require the helper to have no *On-line Communication (OC)* with the prover during the fast-exchange phase. In Sect. 3, we present a DLB protocol that provides security against rDF, rMiM and rCF under the above assumptions. Note that one may achieve rDF, rMiM and rCF resistance using other assumptions that restrict the prover and the helper. For example instead of assuming a root of trust on the PD, one may establish a dynamic root of trust using software attestation. We give a software attestation-based DLB protocol in full version [22]. This protocol also requires no online-communication assumption for security against all attacks. We also provide an overview of security analysis and implementation challenges of the protocol.

3 DLB Protocol Constructions

Assumptions and Attack Model. We assume the PD is a bounded memory device with a protected memory (ROM), and a writable memory (RAM) of (fixed) L bit size. We consider RAM as an array indexed from 1 to L. The DLB protocol code is stored partly in ROM, denoted by DLB_{ROM}, and partly in RAM, denoted by DLB_{RAM}. We assume V has a shared key with the PD, and holds the same DLB code. The secret key of PD is stored in ROM and is accessible only to the code in ROM. We assume communication channel is noise free, although our results are extendable to noisy communication by applying similar methods as [17]. The adversary may store and run arbitrary malicious code on the RAM of the PD, but is not able to tamper the hardware of the device.

Approach. Using Eq. 1, P^* at distance D can always delay the response by $2D'/C$ second(s) to claim a longer distance $D + D'$. Let T_{max} denote the maximum expected response generation (processing) time by the verifier. (This can be estimated for example, by measuring the processing time of a set of functional devices, and choosing T_{max} larger than all the measured times.) Knowing that $0 \leq T_{proc} \leq T_{max}$, the verifier uses the round-trip time T_Δ to obtain the following distance bounds.

$$D \geq D_{lower} = \frac{(T_\Delta - T_{max})C}{2} \tag{2}$$

We propose a protocol that assumes *bounded memory for* PDand enables V *to force an upper bound on the delay introduced by P^*.*

3.1 The Protocol Π_{DLB-BM}

The secret key consists of two binary strings, x, and $\hat{x}$ in $\{0,1\}^\ell$ respectively. When clear from context, we refer to each string as *key* also. The protocol uses a secure Pseudo Random Function (PRF) $f_x : \{0,1\}^{2k} \rightarrow \{0,1\}^{2n}, x \in \{0,1\}^\ell$, and a secure keyed-hash function $(H_{\hat{x}})_{\hat{x} \in \{0,1\}^\ell} : \{0,1\}^* \rightarrow \{0,1\}^b$. Figure 2 shows the messages communicated in the three phases of the protocol.

Phase 1: Initialization Phase. The prover generates a k-bit nonce N_p and sends it to the verifier. The verifier selects a k-bit nonce N_v and a $2n$-bit random string A, calculates $M = A \oplus f_x(N_p, N_v)$, and sends (M, N_v) to the prover. With this information, the prover decrypts M to retrieve $A = M \oplus f_x(N_p, N_v)$ and stores it in memory. A is the *response table* that will be used by the prover to respond to challenges in Phase 2. Considering $A = (a_{(1,j)}, a_{(2,j)})$, where $j = 1 \cdots n$, as a sequence of n bit pairs, we define a third string $a_{(3,j)} = a_{(1,j)} \oplus a_{(2,j)} \oplus x$. $a_{(3,j)}$ is computed at run time from the response table and so is not stored in memory.

Phase 2: Fast-exchange Phase. This phase proceeds in n consecutive challenge-response rounds. In each round $1 \leq i \leq n$, the verifier chooses a random challenge $c_i \in \{1, 2, 3\}$ and sends it to the prover, immediately followed by a random erasing sequence RS_i of length z_i. In Sect. 3.2, we will discuss how z_i is determined. The role of RS_i is to prevent P from delaying the response to extend its distance. On receiving the challenge c_i, the prover will retrieve the response $r_i = a_{(c_i,i)}$. When $z_i - 1$ bits of RS_i are received, the prover must send r_i to avoid it being overwritten by the final bit of RS_i. The prover must also send the response to the erasing sequence (also referred to as proof of erasure h_i). By correctly designing the computation of the hash, the correct proof of erasure will "prove" that the prover has received and stored the full RS_i and also has kept the code DLB_{RAM} intact (see Sect. 3.2 for details). In addition, the verifier records the time difference $T_{\Delta,i}$ between sending c_i and receiving r_i.

Phase 3: Verification Phase. The verifier checks the correctness of response r_i and proof of erasure h_i for all rounds, $i = 1 \cdots n$. It also verifies whether all response

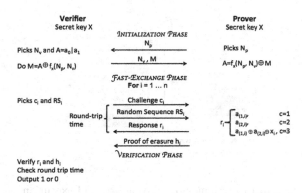

Fig. 2. Distance lower bounding protocol Π_{DLB-BM}

times are higher than a threshold θ, determined as follows. Let B denote the distance-bound, and $T(z_i - 1)$ denote the time interval required by the prover to receive $z_i - 1$ bits. The acceptable round-trip time in round i must satisfy $T_{\Delta,i} \geq \theta = \frac{2B}{C} + T(z_i - 1)$, where $C = 3 * 10^8$ is the speed of light (see Eq. 2). The verifier outputs $Out_v = 1$, if and only if all verifications and time checks succeed. For simplicity, we assumed the communication channel is noiseless; thus, a successful protocol requires all challenges to be correctly responded.

3.2 The Design of Erasure Sequence and Its Response

In fast-exchange round i, an erasure sequence RS_i is sent to the P, and a correct response is required. RS_i is used to guarantee all the device memory is erased, except DLB code and the part of the memory that is required for future response. The length of the erasing sequence RS_i must be chosen as follows.

Sequence Length. Let the sizes of the RAM and DLB_{RAM}, be L and λ, respectively. After the initialization phase, the $2n$-bit random table A is stored in the prover's device memory. In Round 1, the erasing sequence RS_1 must erase $L - \lambda - 2n$ unused memory, together with $(a_{(1,1)}, a_{(2,1)})$, the two response bits associated with round 1. In each subsequent challenge-response round i, two additional bits $(a_{(1,i)}, a_{(2,i)})$ of A will be used and so the length of the erasing sequence must be increased by two bits. By induction, the random sequence RS_i in round $1 \leq i \leq n$ must have length $L - \lambda - 2(n - i)$. Figure 3 shows the state of the prover's memory during protocol execution.

Response to the Erasure Sequence. The response in round i, denoted by h_i, must guarantee that the PD's memory, contains the sequence RS_i and DLB code DLB_{RAM} in full, and prove that the rest of the memory is erased. We refer to this response as *proof of erasure*, as it is inspired by [13]. An efficient approach is to send the cryptographic hash of RS_i. To prevent the prover from calculating the hash value in real-time without storing the whole RS_i, we require

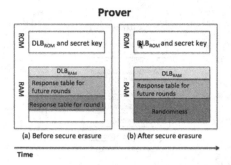

Fig. 3. Prover's memory during protocol execution

the hash function to be applied to the received sequence in the reverse order of arrival. That is, assuming $RS_i = (u_1 \cdots u_{z_i})$, the hash will be applied to $\bar{RS}_i = (u_{z_i} \cdots u_1)$. This leaves the prover no choice other than waiting for the last bit to arrive, before starting the calculation. To prevent P^* to simply store the required hash value of the code, we use $h_i = H_{\hat{x}}(\bar{RS}_i \parallel DLB_{RAM})$. In this construction, $\bar{RS}_i$ serves as a random nonce, and rules out the possibility of P^* successfully passing the verification without storing the full DLB_{RAM}. The response calculation must be such that it cannot be delegated to a helper. This requirement is for achieving security against rCF (Sect. 4). We thus use a *keyed-hash message authentication code,* that requires the prover's secret key. The keyed-hash message authentication code uses a suitable cryptographic hash function in a specific structure (e.g. HMAC), to construct a secure MAC, which ensures the keyed-hash value cannot be forged.

4   Security Analysis of Π_{DLB-BM}

Π_{DLB-BM} protocol uses a PRF and HMAC, and we analyse its security against a computationally bounded adversary. We note that it is possible to construct an information theoretically secure version of this protocol, by replacing the PRF and HMAC with appropriate primitives.

rDF$^{[BM]}$ resistance. In DF, a malicious prover P^* with $d(loc_v, loc_{P^*}) \leq B$, wants to prove, its distance is higher than the bound. To achieve this goal, P^* must send the correct response bit r_i, and the correct proof of erasure h_i, both with sufficient delay, in all rounds $1 \leq i \leq n$, of the fast-exchange phase. Theorem 2 proves that the DF resistance of the DLB protocol Π_{DLB}, assuming that a malicious code of length at least g bits is required.

Theorem 2. Π_{DLB-BM} *is ϵ-resistant to rDF$^{[BM]}$, with $\epsilon = \max\left(2^{-(\frac{g}{2})^2},\right.$ $\left. 2^{-n(n+1)}\right)$, against any rDF$^{[BM]}$ attack that requires at least g-bit malicious code, assuming $H_x()$ is HMAC with a suitable cryptographic hash function.*

The proof is given in Appendix B. The theorem implies that attacks with longer codes directly reduce the success probability of P^*. This substantially limits designing malicious codes. Note that for a 1-byte malicious code ($g = 8$) leads to a success chance of $\epsilon < 10^{-6}$, for protocols with at least 4 rounds, $n \geq 4$.

rMiM$^{[\overline{OC}]}$ resistance. In rMiM$^{[\overline{OC}]}$, the adversary cannot send or receive signal to, or from the prover during the fast-exchange phase of the target instance. It however has full communication power during other phases. We do allow the adversary to jam communications between the verifier and provers in all phases of the protocol (including fast exchange phase). The proof outline of the following Theorem 3 is given in full version [22].

Theorem 3. *The DLB protocol* Π_{DLB-BM} *is β-resistant to rMiM$^{[\overline{OC}]}$ attack with $\beta = 2^{-l}$, by choosing $b > \frac{l}{n} - 1$.*

rCF$^{[BM,\ \overline{OC}]}$ resistance. Providing rCF security requires security against rDF and rMiM, and so their associated assumptions. We consider rCF$^{[BM,\ \overline{OC}]}$, and show (i) this is a stronger attack than rDF$^{[BM]}$, and (ii) Π_{DLB-BM} is secure against this attack (see Theorem 4 and its formal proof is given in [22]).

Theorem 4. *The protocol* Π_{DLB} *is (γ, η)-resistant to rCF$^{[BM,\ \overline{OC}]}$, with $\eta = 2^{-l}$ and $\gamma \leq \max\{2^{-\frac{g+0.5}{2}\frac{g+1}{2}}, 2^{-(n+0.25)(n+1)}\}$, assuming malicious code length $\geq g$.*

5   Practical Consideration

The computation during the initialization and challenge-response is similar to DUB protocols and so the excellent works [14] on the implementation of DUB protocols can be used for performance estimates. However using erasing sequence is unique to Π_{DLB-BM}. We estimate memory, time, and energy consumption of Π_{DLB-BM} on a MicaZ sensor [12] using TinyOS. We assume the following parameters: $n = 10$ rounds and $k = 192$ bits of nonces. We use HMAC-SHA1, denoted by $HMAC(.;.)$, for the PRF, f_x, and generation of response for RS_i, $H_{\hat{x}}$. That is, $f_x(N_p, N_v)$ equals the first $2n = 20$ bits of $HMAC(x; N_p||N_v)$ and $H_{\hat{x}}(\bar{RS}_i||DLB_{RAM})$ equals $HMAC(\hat{x}; \bar{RS}_i||DLB_{RAM})$ of length $b = 160$ bits.

MicaZ Sensor Specifications. The device is supplied by two AA batteries and includes an ATMEGA128 microcontroller and a TI-CC2420 radio transceiver. The micro-controller provides 4 KB of writable memory (SRAM), with 4 KB of EEPROM and 640 KB of write-protected flash memory. The radio transceiver chip works for an RF band of 2.4–2.48 GHz and has 250 Kbps data rate.

Memory Consumption. HMAC-SHA1 takes code size of 4650 bytes [13] for implementation on ROM, and around 124 bytes of RAM to load data structures and stack. Considering $l = 128$ of secret key x, we have a reasonable estimation of code size to be 10 KB. Although the EEPROM is only 4 KB large, the

ATMEGA128 architecture allows for ROM extension via the use of mask ROM, locked flash memory, and fuse bits. Using these extension methods, one can build read-only memory of size 10 KB or more. Note that in order to obtain maximum energy consumption, we assume the size of DLB_{RAM} to be 0.

Energy and Time Consumption. The writable memory in ATMEGA128 (when flash memory is write-protected) is the 4KB SRAM. For a $n = 10$ rounds DLB protocol, the erasing sequence has length 32758 bits on average.

Communication Costs. The protocol requires the prover to receive N_v, M in initialization phase and c_i, RS_i in each fast-exchange round, which gives a total of $l_{rx} = len(N_v) + len(M) + 2n + n \times len(RS_i) = 326912$ bits. There is also requirement for sending N_p, r_i's, and h_i's which sums to $l_{tx} = len(N_p) + n + n \times len(h_i) = 1802$ transmission bits. Sending (resp. receiving) a single bit requires $E_{rx} = 2.34\mu J/b$ (resp. $E_{tx} = 4.6\mu J/b$) by the radio transceiver with typical power adjustments [5]. The total communication energy is thus $E_{comm} = l_{tx}E_{tx} + l_{rx}E_{rx} = 773mJ$.

Computation Costs. The cost is highly due to computing h_i. The rest is negligible. Extrapolating memory erasure phase figures in [13] to our 4KB-memory device, we require less than 600 milliseconds time for computing proof of erasure, which is quite practical. As for energy consumption, each HMAC-SHA1 computation uses $3.5\mu J$ per memory byte. Considering the memory size and the number of rounds, the required computation energy is obtained as $E_{comp} = 3.5 \times 10^{-6} \times 4 \times 2^{10} \times 10 = 140mJ$. Each AA battery is capable of delivering 1.2 Amperes under an average voltage of 1.2 Volts for one hour [5], implying the power supply of $10,368J$ via the two batteries. This means the proving device can be used for approximately $\frac{10,368}{(773+140)10^{-3}} > 11,000$ runs of DLB protocol before the batteries die. This is quite a reasonable turn out for power consumption. Although we should consider idle/sleep mode energy consumption for more accurate analysis, this consideration will not cause a drastic change on the above result.

6   Concluding Remarks

We motivated the novel security problem of DLB in the setting that the prover is not trusted using a number of application scenarios, and gave formal definition of security against three general classes of attacks (DF, MiM and CF). We proved that it is impossible to provide security against any of these attacks without making physical assumptions. Our results show that an adversary, even if it is computationally bounded, will *always succeed* in DF if it has unrestricted access to the prover's device (fully untrusted prover), and will succeed in MiM attacks, if it has unrestricted access to the communication channel. And security against CF requires restrictions on both types of accesses. These results show a fundamental difference between DLB and DUB problems. The only physical assumption in DUB protocols, is that the speed of EM signals is constant. In DLB protocols however, in addition to this assumption, one must assume other restrictions on the physical access of the adversary.

Our protocol provides security against $rDF^{[BM]}$, $rMiM^{[\overline{OC}]}$, and $rCF^{[BM, \overline{OC}]}$, using reasonable assumptions that have been used in theoretical cryptography as well as security systems in practice, including systems for secure code update [13]. Enforcing assumptions in practice would need special technologies such as targeted jamming [9]. One can replace the above assumptions with other reasonable assumptions. For example, instead of assuming bounded memory, one can use a software-based *externally verifiable code execution (EVCE)* system such as Pioneer [16], to guarantee that the *target executable* code associated with the distance measurement, is executed without modification by a malicious code that may reside on the device. a trusted network to eliminate proxy attacks allowing the construction to provide security against $rMiM^{[\overline{OC}]}$ and $rCF^{[SA, \overline{OC}]}$. The important point to note is that *one must restrict the adversary's physical access to the environment to achieve any DLB security.*

Our primary application scenarios of DLB in this paper were examples of proximity-based access control. Other application scenarios in DLB may have different security requirements. Examining these requirements will be an important step in modelling security and designing secure protocols. Another interesting question is to efficiently incorporate DLB in DUB protocol to provide security against distance enlargement.

A   Proof Sketch of Theorem 1

For (1), assume a malicious prover (who can calculate correct responses to the verifier challenges) at $D < B$. To claim a longer distance $D + D'$, the prover modifies the execution to add appropriate delay by tampering with the hardware/software and responds after $2D'/C$ second(s). The attack succeeds with probability 1. For (2), A MiM attacker can use the following strategy: upon receiving a message from one party, the adversary jams the signal to prevent it from being received by the other, and later forwards it with appropriate delay. For (3), note that CF resistance requires both DF resistance and MiM resistance: A CF attacker can simply simulate a successful DF attacker by simply ignoring the helper. It can also simulate a successful MiM attacker, by allowing P^* in the CF attack to run the algorithm of P, and the helper in CF to run the algorithm of the MiM adversary, A^{MiM}.

B   Proof of Theorem 2

A dishonest prover P^* succeeds if it passes verification in all rounds. A P^*'s strategy σ, is defined by a sequence of actions that it will take over the n rounds. P^* needs a malicious code of size at least g to implement its strategy. The code must be stored in the PD's RAM. In each round, P^* must dedicate g bits of RAM for the malicious code MC, by either over-writing the response table $A^{[i]}$, or RS_i, or DLB_{RAM}, or part of each, Here $A^{[i]}$ is the un-used part of A at the start of round i. It is important to note that success probability of P^* in each round, depends on the action taken in the current round, and all actions taken in all the previous rounds. For example if P^* has overwritten $(a_{(1,i)}, a_{(2,i)})$, during an earlier round j, where $j < i$, then the success probability of producing the correct response to c_i, will be at most $1/2$.

Let $\Pr(Succ_{DF}^\sigma)$ denote the prover's success probability for a strategy σ (n-round strategy, possibly adaptive) used by P^*. Let S_i denote the event associated with the success in round i, $1 \le i \le n$. We have the following:

$$Pr(Succ_{DF}^\sigma) = \Pr(\bigwedge_{i=1}^{n} S_i) = \prod_{i=1}^{n} \Pr(S_i | S_{i-1}, \ldots, S_1).$$

The properties of probability imply: $\forall i$, $\Pr(S_i | S_{i-1}, \ldots, S_1) \le 1$. In round i, P^*'s device receives a challenge symbol c_i, followed by $L - \lambda - 2(n - i)$ bits of RS_i. The response consists of r_i, and $h_i = H_{\hat{x}}(\bar{RS_i} || DLB_{RAM})$. Because of the unforgeability of HMAC, to calculate h_i, the string RS_i must be fully stored, and DLB_{RAM} must remain intact. If some of these bits, say ℓ, are overwritten, to generate the correct response, the ℓ missing bits can be guessed., with success probability $2^{-\ell}$.

Let g be even and smaller than the response table original size, $g \le 2n$. In each round, 2 bits of the table are used and the erasing sequence is lengthened by 2 bits. The reduction in the size of the table in each round finally reaches a round $n_0 \overset{\triangle}{=} n - \frac{g}{2}$, after which the size of $A^{[i]}$, $i > n_0$, is less than the malicious code. That is, $2(n - i) < g$ and the length of RS_i satisfies $L - 2(n - i) > L - g$. From round $i > n_0$, to keep the g bit malicious code, some bits from RS_i must be overwritten and this number equals,

$$g - 2(n - i) = g - 2(n_0 + \frac{g}{2} - i) = 2(i - n_0).$$

This leads to a success chance of $2^{-(2(i-n_0)+1)}$ in calculating h_i in round i. The overall success chance is given by,

$$\Pr(Succ_{DF}^\sigma) \le \prod_{1 \le i \le n_0} 1 \times \prod_{n_0+1 \le i \le n} 2^{-(2(i-n_0))}$$
$$= 2^{-\left(\sum_{i=n_0+1}^{n} 2(i-n_0)\right)} = 2^{-\left(\sum_{i'=1}^{n-n_0} 2i'\right)} = 2^{-(\frac{g}{2})(\frac{g}{2}+1)} < 2^{-(\frac{g}{2})^2}.$$

If g is odd: A similar argument can show that the prover needs to drop $2(i-n_0)-1$ bits in rounds $i > n_0 \overset{\triangle}{=} n - \frac{g+1}{2}$. The success probability equals

$$\Pr(Succ_{DF}^\sigma) \le 2^{-\left(\sum_{i=n_0+1}^{n} 2(i-n_0)-1\right)} = 2^{-\left(\sum_{i'=1}^{n-n_0} 2i'-1\right)}$$
$$= 2^{-(\frac{g+1}{2})(\frac{g+1}{2}+1)} \cdot 2^{\frac{g+1}{2}} = 2^{-(\frac{g+1}{2})^2} < 2^{-(\frac{g}{2})^2}.$$

If $g \geq 2n$. Here, the prover needs to drop some bits of the erasing string RS_i in all rounds $1 \leq i \leq n$; in other words, $n_0 = 0$ and the prover's success chance is,

$$\Pr(Succ^\sigma_{DF}) \leq \prod_{1 \leq i \leq n} 2^{-(2i)} = 2^{-\left(\sum_{i=1}^n 2i\right)} = 2^{-n(n+1)}.$$

This means that the success probability of P^* in *any strategy* is bounded, and the proof is complete.

References

1. Avoine, G., Tchamkerten, A.: An efficient distance bounding RFID authentication protocol: balancing false-acceptance rate and memory requirement. In: Samarati, P., Yung, M., Martinelli, F., Ardagna, C.A. (eds.) ISC 2009. LNCS, vol. 5735, pp. 250–261. Springer, Heidelberg (2009)
2. Boureanu, I., Mitrokotsa, A., Vaudenay, S.: Secure and lightweight distance-bounding. In: Avoine, G., Kara, O. (eds.) LightSec 2013. LNCS, vol. 8162, pp. 97–113. Springer, Heidelberg (2013)
3. Brands, S., Chaum, D.: Distance bounding protocols. In: Helleseth, T. (ed.) EURO-CRYPT 1993. LNCS, vol. 765, pp. 344–359. Springer, Heidelberg (1994)
4. Cachin, C., Maurer, U.M.: Unconditional security against memory-bounded adversaries. In: Kaliski Jr., B.S. (ed.) CRYPTO 1997. LNCS, vol. 1294, pp. 292–306. Springer, Heidelberg (1997)
5. Calle, M., Kabara, J.: Measuring energy consumption in wireless sensor networks using GSP. In: Personal, Indoor and Mobile Radio Communications (2006)
6. Capkun, S., Hubaux, J.-P.: Secure positioning in wireless networks. IEEE J. Sel. Areas Commun. **24**(2), 221–232 (2006)
7. Cremers, C., Rasmussen, K.B., Schmidt, B., Capkun, S.: Distance hijacking attacks on distance bounding protocols. In: S&P, pp. 113–127 (2012)
8. Francillon, A., Danev, B., Capkun, S.: Relay attacks on passive keyless entry and start systems in modern cars. In: NDSS (2011)
9. Gollakota, S., Hassanieh, H., Ransford, B., Katabi, D., Fu, K.: They can hear your heartbeats: non-invasive security for implantable medical devices. In: ACM SIGCOMM, pp. 2–13 (2011)
10. Hancke, G.P., Kuhn, M.G.: An rfid distance bounding protocol. In: SecureComm, pp. 67–73 (2005)
11. Hofmann-Wellenhof, B., Lichtenegger, H., Collins, J.: Global Positioning System Theory and Practice. Springer, Wien (1993)
12. C. T. Inc., Micaz datasheet
13. Perito, D., Tsudik, G.: Secure code update for embedded devices via proofs of secure erasure. In: Gritzalis, D., Preneel, B., Theoharidou, M. (eds.) ESORICS 2010. LNCS, vol. 6345, pp. 643–662. Springer, Heidelberg (2010)
14. Rasmussen, K.B., Capkun, S.: Realization of rf distance bounding. In: USENIX Security Symposium, pp. 389–402 (2010)
15. Rasmussen, K.B., Castelluccia, C., Heydt-Benjamin, T.S., Capkun, S.: Proximity-based access control for implantable medical devices. In: Computer and Communications Security, pp. 410–419 (2009)
16. Seshadri, A., Luk, M., Perrig, A., Doorn, L.v., Khosla, P.: Externally verifiable code execution. Commun. ACM **49**(9), 45–49 (2006)

17. Singelée, D., Preneel, B.: Distance bounding in noisy environments. In: Stajano, F., Meadows, C., Capkun, S., Moore, T. (eds.) ESAS 2007. LNCS, vol. 4572, pp. 101–115. Springer, Heidelberg (2007)
18. Song, B., Mitchell, C.J.: RFID authentication protocol for low-cost tags. In: Wireless Network Security (2008)
19. Tippenhauer, N.O., Rasmussen, K.B., Capkun, S.: Secure ranging with message temporal integrity. IACR Cryptology ePrint Archive (2009)
20. Vaudenay, S., Boureanu, I., Mitrokotsa, A. et al.: Practical & provably secure distance-bounding. In: the 16th Information Security Conference (2013)
21. Warner, J.S., Johnston, R.G.: A simple demonstration that the global positioning system (gps) is vulnerable to spoofing. J. Secur. Adm. **25**(2), 19–27 (2002)
22. X. Zheng, R. Safavi-Naini, and H. Ahmadi. Distance lower bounding. Cryptology ePrint Archive, Report 2014/xxx (2014). http://eprint.iacr.org/

Efficient Adaptive Oblivious Transfer Without q-type Assumptions in UC Framework

Vandana Guleria$^{(\boxtimes)}$ and Ratna Dutta

Department of Mathematics, Indian Institute
of Technology Kharagpur, Kharagpur 721302, India
vandana.math@gmail.com, ratna@maths.iitkgp.ernet.in

Abstract. Oblivious transfer is one of the basic building blocks of cryptography. Due to its importance as a building block in the construction of secure multiparty computation protocols, the efficiency and security are two big issues in its design. In this paper, we present an efficient, *universal composable* (UC) secure adaptive oblivious transfer without *q-type assumptions*. The proposed protocol is UC secure under Decision Linear (DLIN), Decision Bilinear Diffie-Hellman (DBDH) and Square Decision Bilinear Diffie-Hellman (SqDBDH) assumptions in the presence of malicious adversary in static corruption model. The proposed protocol exhibits low computation and communication overheads as compared to the existing similar schemes.

Keywords: Oblivious transfer · Universally composable security · Non-interactive zero-knowledge proofs

1 Introduction

Adaptive Oblivious Transfer ($\mathsf{OT}^N_{k \times 1}$) is a two-party protocol, where a sender with messages $m_1, m_2, \ldots, m_N$ interacts with a receiver with indices $\sigma_1, \sigma_2, \ldots,$ $\sigma_k \in [N]$ in such a way that at the end the receiver obtains $m_{\sigma_1}, m_{\sigma_2}, \ldots, m_{\sigma_k}$ without learning anything about the remaining $N - k$ messages and the sender does not learn anything about the indices $\sigma_1, \sigma_2, \ldots, \sigma_k$. The receiver may obtain $m_{\sigma_{i-1}}$ before deciding on σ_i. The $\mathsf{OT}^N_{k \times 1}$ protocol consists of a *initialization phase* and k *transfer phases*. In initialization phase, the sender encrypts the messages $m_1, m_2, \ldots, m_N$ using some encryption scheme and publishes the encrypted database. In each transfer phase, the receiver interacts with the sender to decrypt the ciphertext of its choice in order to recover the desired message. The $\mathsf{OT}^N_{k \times 1}$ is an interesting primitive. It is a basic building block for secure multiparty computation and adaptive oblivious search of large database such as medical, financial, patent etc.

Naor and Pinkas [18] introduced the *first* $\mathsf{OT}^N_{k \times 1}$ protocol in half-simulataion model in which the security of one party follows real/ideal world paradigm while the security of other party is supported by heuristic argument only. The *first* fully-simulatable $\mathsf{OT}^N_{k \times 1}$ in which security of both the parties follow real/ideal

© Springer International Publishing Switzerland 2015
L.C.K. Hui et al. (Eds.): ICICS 2014, LNCS 8958, pp. 105–119, 2015.
DOI: 10.1007/978-3-319-21966-0_8

world paradigm is proposed by Camenisch *et al.* [7]. Afterwards, there are quite a number of $OT_{k \times 1}^N$ protocols [1, 12–15, 17, 20, 22]. Peikert *et al.* [19] introduced the *universal composabe* (UC) secure oblivious transfer protocols. The security of $OT_{k \times 1}^N$ protocols [1, 14, 17, 20] are also proven in UC framework [8, 9]. The UC secure $OT_{k \times 1}^N$ protocols retain their security even when composed with arbitrary protocols during concurrent execution. The aforementioned $OT_{k \times 1}^N$ protocols are based on *q-type assumptions* except [1, 15]. The q-type assumptions state that given q solutions of the underlying problem, it is not possible to come up with a new solution. During simulation, these q solutions are used by the simulator to answer the queries by an adversary and then convert the adversary's forgery into a new solution of the problem. Abe *et al.* [1] introduced $OT_{k \times 1}^N$ without q-type assumptions in UC framework.

Our Contribution. Adaptive Oblivious Transfer ($OT_{k \times 1}^N$) is an extensively used primitive in cryptography. Designing an efficient $OT_{k \times 1}^N$ is not a trivial task. In this paper, we provide an efficient $OT_{k \times 1}^N$ protocol without q-type assumptions which is provable secure in UC framework. Our scheme assumes a common reference string CRS similar to existing works as UC secure $OT_{k \times 1}^N$ protocol cannot be constructed without any trusted setup assumptions. The proposed $OT_{k \times 1}^N$ protocol couples Water's signature [21] with non-interactive Groth-Sahai [16] proofs and is secure under Decision Linear (DLIN), Decision Bilinear Diffie-Hellman (DBDH) and Square Decision Bilinear Diffie-Hellman (SqDBDH) assumptions. The Water's signature [21] and non-interactive Groth-Sahai [16] proofs are used to create some checks during protocol construction to control the malicious activities of the parties. If the receiver or sender deviates from the protocol constructions, it will get detected with these checks.

Security is proven in static corruption model in which corrupted parties are pre-decided by the adversary. Throughout the protocol execution, corrupted parties remain corrupted and honest parties remain honest. The security of the proposed $OT_{k \times 1}^N$ protocol is proved by proving the sender and receiver's security separately in the trusted setup assumptions. The sender's (receiver's) security requires the existence of an efficient simulator such that no distinguisher can distinguish *real world* (where an honest sender (receiver) is interacting with an adversary) from *ideal world* (where the simulator is given access to ideal functionality).

The proposed $OT_{k \times 1}^N$ protocol is efficient as compared to the existing similar schemes [1, 14, 17, 20]. The efficiency includes number of rounds, computation complexity and communication complexity. The computation complexity is measured by counting the number of pairings and exponentiations which are performed during initialization and transfer phases. The communication complexity includes number of rounds, storage and group elements transformation from the sender to the receiver and vice-versa.

2   Preliminaries

Throughout, we use ρ as the security parameter, $x \xleftarrow{\$} A$ means sample an element x uniformly at random from the set A, $y \leftarrow B$ indicates y is the output of algorithm B, $X \overset{c}{\approx} Y$ means X is computationally indistinguishable from Y, $[\ell]$ denotes $\{1, 2, \ldots, \ell\}$ and $\mathbb{N}$ the set of natural numbers. A function $f(n)$ is *negligible* if $f = o(n^{-c})$ for every fixed positive constant c.

2.1   Bilinear Pairing and Mathematical Assumptions

Definition 1 *(Bilinear Pairing). Let* $\mathbb{G}_1, \mathbb{G}_2$ *and* $\mathbb{G}_T$ *be three multiplicative cyclic groups of prime order* p *and* g_1, g_2 *be generators of groups* $\mathbb{G}_1$ *and* $\mathbb{G}_2$ *respectively. Then the map* $e : \mathbb{G}_1 \times \mathbb{G}_2 \rightarrow \mathbb{G}_T$ *is bilinear if it satisfies the following conditions. (i) Bilinear –* $e(x^a, y^b) = e(x, y)^{ab} \; \forall \; x \in \mathbb{G}_1, y \in \mathbb{G}_2, a, b \in \mathbb{Z}_p$. *(ii) Non-Degenerate –* $e(x, y)$ *generates* $\mathbb{G}_T$, $\forall \; x \in \mathbb{G}_1, y \in \mathbb{G}_2, x \neq 1, y \neq 1$. *(iii) Computable – the pairing* $e(x, y)$ *is computable efficiently* $\forall \; x \in \mathbb{G}_1, y \in \mathbb{G}_2$.

If $\mathbb{G}_1 = \mathbb{G}_2$, then e is *symmetric* bilinear pairing. Otherwise, e is *asymmetric* bilinear pairing. Throughout the paper, we use symmetric bilinear pairing.

BilinearSetup: The BilinearSetup is an algorithm which on input security parameter ρ generates params $= (p, \mathbb{G}, \mathbb{G}_T, e, g)$, where $e : \mathbb{G} \times \mathbb{G} \rightarrow \mathbb{G}_T$ is a symmetric bilinear pairing, g is a generator of group $\mathbb{G}$ and p, the order of the groups $\mathbb{G}$ and $\mathbb{G}_T$, is prime, i.e. params $\leftarrow$ BilinearSetup(1^ρ).

Definition 2 *(DBDH [21]). The Decision Bilinear Diffie-Hellman (DBDH) assumption in* $(\mathbb{G}, \mathbb{G}_T)$ *states that for all PPT algorithm* $\mathcal{A}$, *with running time in* ρ, *the advantage* $\mathsf{Adv}_{\mathbb{G}, \mathbb{G}_T}^{DBDH}(\mathcal{A}) = \Pr[\mathcal{A}(g, g^a, g^b, g^c, e(g, g)^{abc})] - \Pr[\mathcal{A}(g, g^a, g^b, g^c, Z)]$ *is negligible in* ρ, *where* $g \xleftarrow{\$} \mathbb{G}, Z \xleftarrow{\$} \mathbb{G}_T, a, b, c \in \mathbb{Z}_p$.

Definition 3 *(SqDBDH [10]). The Square Decision Bilinear Diffie-Hellman assumption in* $(\mathbb{G}, \mathbb{G}_T)$ *states that for all PPT algorithm* $\mathcal{A}$, *with running time in* ρ, *the advantage* $\mathsf{Adv}_{\mathbb{G}, \mathbb{G}_T}^{SqDBDH}(\mathcal{A}) = \Pr[\mathcal{A}(g, g^a, g^b, e(g, g)^{a^2 b})] - \Pr[\mathcal{A}(g, g^a, g^b, Z)]$ *is negligible in* ρ, *where* $g \xleftarrow{\$} \mathbb{G}, Z \xleftarrow{\$} \mathbb{G}_T, a, b \in \mathbb{Z}_p$.

Definition 4 *(DLIN [5]). The Decision Linear (DLIN) assumption in* $\mathbb{G}$ *states that for all PPT algorithm* $\mathcal{A}$, *with running time in* ρ, *the advantage* $\mathsf{Adv}_{\mathbb{G}}^{DLIN}(\mathcal{A})$ $= \Pr[\mathcal{A}(g, g^a, g^b, g^{ra}, g^{sb}, g^{r+s})] - \Pr[\mathcal{A}(g, g^a, g^b, g^{ra}, g^{sb}, t)]$ *is negligible in* ρ, *where* $g \xleftarrow{\$} \mathbb{G}, t \xleftarrow{\$} \mathbb{G}, a, b, r, s \in \mathbb{Z}_p$.

2.2   Non-Interactive Verification of Pairing Product Equation [16]

The Groth-Sahai proofs are two party protocols between a prover and a verifier for non-interactive verification of a pairing product equation

$$\prod_{q=1}^{Q} e(a_q \prod_{i=1}^{n} x_i^{\alpha_{q,i}}, b_q \prod_{i=1}^{n} y_i^{\beta_{q,i}}) = t_T, \tag{1}$$

where $a_{q=1,2,...,Q} \in \mathbb{G}, b_{q=1,2,...,Q} \in \mathbb{G}, \{\alpha_{q,i}, \beta_{q,i}\}_{q=1,2,...,Q,i=1,2,...,n} \in \mathbb{Z}_p$ and $t_T \in \mathbb{G}_T$ are the coefficients of the pairing product Eq. 1 which are given to the verifier. The prover knows secret values $x_{i=1,2,...,n}, y_{i=1,2,...,n} \in \mathbb{G}$ also called witnesses that satisfy the Eq. 1. The prover wants to convince the verifier in a non-interactive way that he knows x_i and y_i without revealing anything about x_i and y_i to the verifier. Let $\mathcal{W} = \{x_{i=1,2,...,n}, y_{i=1,2,...,n}\}$ be the set of all secret values in the pairing product Eq. 1. The set $\mathcal{W}$ is referred as witnesses of the pairing product equation. The product of two vectors is defined component wise, i.e., $(a_1, a_2, a_3)(b_1, b_2, b_3) = (a_1 b_1, a_2 b_2, a_3 b_3)$ for $(a_1, a_2, a_3), (b_1, b_2, b_3) \in \mathbb{G}^3$ for a finite order group $\mathbb{G}$.

For non-interactive verification of the pairing product Eq. 1, a trusted party upon input a security parameter ρ generates common reference string $\mathsf{GS} = (\mathsf{params}, u_1, u_2, u_3, \mu, \mu_T)$, where $\mathsf{params} = (p, \mathbb{G}, \mathbb{G}_T, e, g) \leftarrow \mathsf{BilinearSetup}(1^\rho)$, $u_1 = (g^a, 1, g) \in \mathbb{G}^3, u_2 = (1, g^b, g) \in \mathbb{G}^3, u_3 = u_1^{\xi_1} u_2^{\xi_2} = (g^{a\xi_1}, g^{b\xi_2}, g^{\xi_1+\xi_2}) \in \mathbb{G}^3, \xi_1, \xi_2 \overset{\$}{\leftarrow} \mathbb{Z}_p, a, b \overset{\$}{\leftarrow} \mathbb{Z}_p$ and $\mu : \mathbb{G} \to \mathbb{G}^3, \mu_T : \mathbb{G}_T \to \mathbb{G}_T^9$ are two efficiently computable embeddings such that

$$\mu(g) = (1, 1, g) \text{ and } \mu_T(t_T) = \begin{pmatrix} 1 & 1 & 1 \\ 1 & 1 & 1 \\ 1 & 1 & t_T \end{pmatrix} \forall g \in \mathbb{G}, t_T \in \mathbb{G}_T.$$

Note that $\mu_T(t_T)$ is an element of $\mathbb{G}_T^9$. For convenience, it has been written in matrix form. The product of two elements of $\mathbb{G}_T^9$ is also component wise. The trusted party publishes GS to both the parties. The prover generates commitment to all the witnesses $x_{i=1,2,...,n}$ and $y_{i=1,2,...,n}$ using GS. To commit $x_i \in \mathbb{G}$ and $y_i \in \mathbb{G}$, the prover picks $r_{1i}, r_{2i}, r_{3i} \overset{\$}{\leftarrow} \mathbb{Z}_p$ and $s_{1i}, s_{2i}, s_{3i} \overset{\$}{\leftarrow} \mathbb{Z}_p$, sets

$$c_i = \mathsf{Com}(x_i) = \mu(x_i) u_1^{r_{1i}} u_2^{r_{2i}} u_3^{r_{3i}}, d_i = \mathsf{Com}(y_i) = \mu(y_i) u_1^{s_{1i}} u_2^{s_{2i}} u_3^{s_{3i}}.$$

The prover generates the proof components

$$P_j = \prod_{q=1}^{Q} \left(\mu(a_q) \prod_{i=1}^{n} \mu(x_i)^{\alpha_{q,i}} \right)^{\sum_{i=1}^{n} \beta_{q,i} s_{ji}} \left(\widehat{d_q} \right)^{\sum_{i=1}^{n} \alpha_{q,i} r_{ji}},$$

using random values r_{ji}, s_{ji}, which were used for generating commitments to $x_{i=1,2,...,n}, y_{i=1,2,...,n}$, and gives proof $\pi = (c_1, c_2, \ldots, c_n, d_1, d_2, \ldots, d_n, P_1, P_2, P_3)$ to the verifier, where $\widehat{d_q} = \mu(b_q) \prod_{i=1}^{n} d_i^{\beta_{q,i}}, i = 1, 2, \ldots, n, j = 1, 2, 3$. The verifier computes

$$\widehat{c_q} = \mu(a_q) \prod_{i=1}^{n} c_i^{\alpha_{q,i}}, \widehat{d_q} = \mu(b_q) \prod_{i=1}^{n} d_i^{\beta_{q,i}},$$

using c_i, d_i, coefficients $\alpha_{q,i}, \beta_{q,i}$ and outputs VALID if the following equation holds

$$\prod_{q=1}^{Q} F(\widehat{c_q}, \widehat{d_q}) = \mu_T(t_T) \prod_{j=1}^{3} F(u_j, P_j), \tag{2}$$

where $F : \mathbb{G}^3 \times \mathbb{G}^3 \to \mathbb{G}_T^9$ is defined as

$$F((x_1, x_2, x_3), (y_1, y_2, y_3)) = \begin{pmatrix} e(x_1, y_1) & e(x_1, y_2) & e(x_1, y_3) \\ e(x_2, y_1) & e(x_2, y_2) & e(x_2, y_3) \\ e(x_3, y_1) & e(x_3, y_2) & e(x_3, y_3) \end{pmatrix}.$$

Note that the function F is also symmetric bilinear and $F((x_1, x_2, x_3), (y_1, y_2, y_3))$ is an element of $\mathbb{G}_T^9$. The product of two elements of $\mathbb{G}_T^9$ is component wise. For convenience, it has been written in matrix form.

The Eq. 2 holds if and only if Eq. 1 holds. The Eq. 1 is non-linear. If in Eq. 1 only $y_{i=1,2,\dots,n}$ are secrets, then it is a linear equation. For a linear equation, the verifier has to verify the following equation

$$\prod_{q=1}^{Q} F\left(\mu(a_q) \prod_{i=1}^{n} \mu(x_i)^{\alpha_{q,i}}, \widehat{d_q}\right) = \mu_T(t_T) \prod_{j=1}^{3} F(u_j, P_j), \qquad (3)$$

$$\text{where} \quad P_j = \prod_{q=1}^{Q} \left(\mu(a_q) \prod_{i=1}^{n} \mu(x_i)^{\alpha_{q,i}} \right)^{\sum_{i=1}^{n} \beta_{q,i} s_{ji}}, j = 1, 2, 3. \qquad (4)$$

Note that there are two types of settings in Groth-Sahai proofs - *perfectly sound* setting and *witness indistinguishability* setting. The common reference string $\mathsf{GS} = (u_1, u_2, u_3)$ discussed above is in perfectly sound setting, where $u_1 = (g^a, 1, g)$, $u_2 = (1, g^b, g)$, $u_3 = (g^{a\xi_1}, g^{b\xi_2}, g^{\xi_1 + \xi_2})$. One who knows the *extractable trapdoor* $\mathsf{t_{ext}} = (a, b, \xi_1, \xi_2)$, can extract the secret values from their commitments. In witness indistinguishability setting, $\mathsf{GS'} = (u_1, u_2, u_3)$, where $u_1 = (g^a, 1, g)$, $u_2 = (1, g^b, g)$, $u_3 = (g^{a\xi_1}, g^{b\xi_2}, g^{\xi_1 + \xi_2 + 1})$. One who knows the *simulation trapdoor* $\mathsf{t_{sim}} = (a, b, \xi_1, \xi_2)$, may open the commitment differently in a pairing product equation as shown in an example given below.

Example 1. Let $\mathsf{Com}(x) = \mu(x) u_1^{\theta_1} u_2^{\theta_2} u_3^{\theta_3}$ in witness indistinguishability setting, where $\theta_1, \theta_2, \theta_3 \overset{\$}{\leftarrow} \mathbb{Z}_p$. Opening values to $\mathsf{Com}(x)$ are $(D_1 = g^{\theta_1}, D_2 = g^{\theta_2}, D_3 = g^{\theta_3})$. The simulator knowing witness x opens $\mathsf{Com}(x)$ to any value x' using $\mathsf{t_{sim}} = (a, b, \xi_1, \xi_2)$ and D_1, D_2, D_3 as follows. The simulator sets $D_1' = D_1(\frac{x'}{x})^{\xi_1}, D_2' = D_2(\frac{x'}{x})^{\xi_2}, D_3' = D_3\frac{x}{x'})$ and opens the $\mathsf{Com}(x)$ to x' by computing $\frac{x g^{\theta_1 + \theta_2 + \theta_3(\xi_1 + \xi_2 + 1)}}{D_1' D_2' (D_3')^{\xi_1 + \xi_2 + 1}}$.

In GS, $g^a, g^b, g, g^{a\xi_1}, g^{b\xi_2}, g^{\xi_1 + \xi_2}$ forms a DLIN tuple, whereas in $\mathsf{GS'}$, $g^a, g^b, g, g^{a\xi_1}, g^{b\xi_2}, g^{\xi_1 + \xi_2 + 1}$ is not a DLIN tuple. The commitments in both the setting are computationally indistinguishable by the following theorem.

Theorem 1 *[16]. The common reference string in perfectly sound setting is computationally indistinguishable from the common reference string in witness indistinguishability setting under DLIN assumption.*

Definition 5 *(NIWI). The non-interactive witness-indistinguishable (NIWI) proof states that for all PPT algorithm $\mathcal{A}$, with running time in ρ, the advantage*

$$\mathsf{Adv}_{\mathbb{G}, \mathbb{G}_T}^{\mathsf{NIWI}}(\mathcal{A}) = \mathsf{Pr}\left[\mathcal{A}(\mathsf{GS}, \mathcal{S}, \mathcal{W}_0) = \pi\right] - \mathsf{Pr}\left[\mathcal{A}(\mathsf{GS}, \mathcal{S}, \mathcal{W}_1) = \pi\right]$$

is negligible in ρ under DLIN assumption, where GS *is the common reference string in perfectly sound setting,* S *is a pairing product equation,* $\mathcal{W}_0, \mathcal{W}_1$ *are two distinct set of witnesses satisfying* S *and* π *is the proof for* S.

Definition 6 *(NIZK)*. *The non-interactive zero-knowledge (*NIZK*) proof states that for all PPT algorithm* $\mathcal{A}$, *with running time in* ρ, *the advantage*

$$\mathsf{Adv}^{\mathsf{NIZK}}_{\mathbb{G},\mathbb{G}_T}(\mathcal{A}) = \Pr[\mathcal{A}(\mathsf{GS}', S, \mathcal{W}) = \pi_0] - \Pr[\mathcal{A}(\mathsf{GS}', S, \mathsf{t_{sim}}) = \pi_1]$$

is negligible in ρ *under DLIN assumption, where* GS' *is the common reference string in witness indistinguishability setting,* S *is a pairing product equation,* $\mathcal{W}$ *is a set of witnesses satisfying* S, π_0 *is the proof for* S *and* π_1 *is the simulated proof for* S.

The notations $\mathsf{NIWI}\left\{(\{x_i, y_i\}_{1\leq i\leq n})|\prod_{q=1}^{Q} e(a_q \prod_{i=1}^{n} x_i^{\alpha_{q,i}}, b_q \prod_{i=1}^{n} y_i^{\beta_{q,i}}) = t_T\right\}$ and $\mathsf{NIZK}\left\{(\{x_i, y_i\}_{1\leq i\leq n})|\prod_{q=1}^{Q} e(a_q \prod_{i=1}^{n} x_i^{\alpha_{q,i}}, b_q \prod_{i=1}^{n} y_i^{\beta_{q,i}}) = t_T\right\}$, for NIWI and NIZK proof are followed respectively in our construction. The convention is that the quantities in the parenthesis denote elements the knowledge of which are being proved to the verifier by the prover while all other parameters are known to the verifier. We have the following theorem.

Theorem 2 *[16]*. *The Groth-Sahai proofs are composable* NIWI *and* NIZK *for satisfiability of a set of pairing product equation over a bilinear group under DLIN assumption.*

3   Security Model of $\mathsf{OT}^N_{k\times 1}$

UC Framework: The security of the proposed $\mathsf{OT}^N_{k\times 1}$ is done in universal composable (UC) model assuming static corruption. The UC framework consists of two worlds, one is a *real world* and other is an *ideal world*. In the real world, a sender, a receiver and a real world adversary $\mathcal{A}$, who has the ability of corrupting the parties (sender and receiver), interact with each other according to $\mathsf{OT}^N_{k\times 1}$ protocol Ψ. In the ideal world, there are dummy parties (sender and receiver), an ideal world adversary $\mathcal{A}'$ and a trusted party called ideal functionality $\mathcal{F}^{N\times 1}_{\mathsf{OT}}$. The parties are dummy in the sense that they submit their inputs to $\mathcal{F}^{N\times 1}_{\mathsf{OT}}$ and receive respective outputs from $\mathcal{F}^{N\times 1}_{\mathsf{OT}}$ instead of performing any computation by themselves. A protocol is said to be secure in UC framework if no interactive distinguisher, called *environment machine* $\mathcal{Z}$, can distinguish the execution of the protocol Ψ in the *real world* from the execution of the protocol in the *ideal world*.

Let us now describe ideal functionality $\mathcal{F}^{\mathcal{D}}_{\mathsf{CRS}}$ for the generation of common reference string (CRS) parameterized by some specific distribution $\mathcal{D}$ and ideal functionality $\mathcal{F}^{N\times 1}_{\mathsf{OT}}$ for $\mathsf{OT}^N_{k\times 1}$ protocol following [9].

$\mathcal{F}^{\mathcal{D}}_{\mathsf{CRS}}$ **Hybrid Model**– Upon receiving a message (sid, P, CRS), from a party P (either S or R), $\mathcal{F}^{\mathcal{D}}_{\mathsf{CRS}}$ first checks if there is a recorded value crs. If there is no recorded value, $\mathcal{F}_{\mathsf{CRS}}^{\mathcal{D}}$ generates crs $\xleftarrow{\$} \mathcal{D}(1^{\rho})$ and records it. Finally, $\mathcal{F}_{\mathsf{CRS}}^{\mathcal{D}}$ sends $(\mathsf{sid}, P, \mathsf{crs})$ to the party P and $\mathcal{A}'$, where sid is the session identity. In the proposed construction $\mathcal{D}$ is CRSSetup algorithm, i.e., crs $\leftarrow$ CRSSetup(1^{ρ})

In the ideal world, the parties just forward their inputs to the $\mathcal{F}_{\mathsf{OT}}^{N \times 1}$ and get back their respective outputs. The functionality $\mathcal{F}_{\mathsf{OT}}^{N \times 1}$ is as follows:

DBInit – The $\mathcal{F}_{\mathsf{OT}}^{N \times 1}$ upon receiving a message $(\mathsf{sid}, S, \mathsf{dbsetup}, \mathsf{DB})$ from S, stores DB, where $\mathsf{DB} = (m_1, m_2, \ldots, m_N)$, $m_i \in \mathbb{G}_T$, $i = 1, 2, \ldots, N$.
Transfer – Upon receiving the message $(\mathsf{sid}, R, \mathsf{transfer}, \sigma)$ from R, $\mathcal{F}_{\mathsf{OT}}^{N \times 1}$ sends $(\mathsf{sid}, \mathsf{request})$ to S and receives (sid, S, b) in response from S. If $b = 1$, then $\mathcal{F}_{\mathsf{OT}}^{N \times 1}$ returns m_{σ} to R. Otherwise, $\mathcal{F}_{\mathsf{OT}}^{N \times 1}$ returns $\perp$ to R.

Definition 7. *A protocol Ψ securely realizes the ideal functionality $\mathcal{F}_{\mathsf{OT}}^{N \times 1}$ if for any real world adversary $\mathcal{A}$, there exists an ideal world adversary $\mathcal{A}'$ such that for any environment machine $\mathcal{Z}$, $\mathsf{REAL}_{\Psi, \mathcal{A}, \mathcal{Z}} \overset{c}{\approx} \mathsf{IDEAL}_{\mathcal{F}_{\mathsf{OT}}^{N \times 1}, \mathcal{A}', \mathcal{Z}}$, where $\mathsf{REAL}_{\Psi, \mathcal{A}, \mathcal{Z}}$ is the output of $\mathcal{Z}$ after interacting with $\mathcal{A}$ and the parties running the protocol Ψ in the real world and $\mathsf{IDEAL}_{\mathcal{F}_{\mathsf{OT}}^{N \times 1}, \mathcal{A}', \mathcal{Z}}$ is the output of $\mathcal{Z}$ after interacting with $\mathcal{A}'$ and dummy parties interacting with $\mathcal{F}_{\mathsf{OT}}^{N \times 1}$ in the ideal world.*

4   The Protocol

A high level description of our adaptive oblivious transfer $(\mathsf{OT}_{k \times 1}^{N})$ is given in Fig. 1. Formally our $\mathsf{OT}_{k \times 1}^{N}$ protocol is a tuple of the following PPT algorithms: $\mathsf{OT}_{k \times 1}^{N} =$ (CRSSetup, DBInit = (DBSetup, DBVerify), Transfer = (RequestTra, ResponseTra, CompleteTra)).

- CRSSetup(1^{ρ}): This randomized algorithm on input security parameter ρ generates common reference string crs as follows. It first generates params $\leftarrow$ BilinearSetup(1^{ρ}), where params $= (p, \mathbb{G}, \mathbb{G}_T, e, g)$. The algorithm chooses $a, b, \xi_1, \xi_2, \widetilde{a}, \widetilde{b}, \widetilde{\xi_1}, \widetilde{\xi_2} \xleftarrow{\$} \mathbb{Z}_p^*$ and sets $g_1 = g^a, g_2 = g^b, \widetilde{g_1} = g^{\widetilde{a}}, \widetilde{g_2} = g^{\widetilde{b}}, u_1 = (g_1, 1, g), u_2 = (1, g_2, g), u_3 = u_1^{\xi_1} u_2^{\xi_2} = (g_1^{\xi_1}, g_2^{\xi_2}, g^{\xi_1 + \xi_2}), \widetilde{u_1} = (\widetilde{g_1}, 1, g), \widetilde{u_2} = (1, \widetilde{g_2}, g), \widetilde{u_3} = \widetilde{u_1}^{\widetilde{\xi_1}} \widetilde{u_2}^{\widetilde{\xi_2}} = (\widetilde{g_1}^{\widetilde{\xi_1}}, \widetilde{g_2}^{\widetilde{\xi_2}}, g^{\widetilde{\xi_1} + \widetilde{\xi_2}}), \mathsf{GS}_R = (u_1, u_2, u_3), \mathsf{GS}_S = (\widetilde{u_1}, \widetilde{u_2}, \widetilde{u_3}), \mathsf{crs} = (\mathsf{params}, \mathsf{GS}_R, \mathsf{GS}_R)$. GS_R is used for creating non-interactive witness indistinguishable (NIWI) proof by a receiver and GS_S for generating non-interactive zero-knowledge (NIZK) proof by a sender.
- DBSetup(crs): This randomized algorithm upon input crs $= (\mathsf{params}, \mathsf{GS}_R, \mathsf{GS}_S)$ from the sender S, generates database public key pk, database secret key sk, proof ψ and ciphertext database cDB, where params $= (p, \mathbb{G}, \mathbb{G}_T, e, g)$, $\mathsf{GS}_R = (u_1, u_2, u_3)$, $\mathsf{GS}_S = (\widetilde{u_1}, \widetilde{u_2}, \widetilde{u_3})$. It chooses $\alpha \xleftarrow{\$} \mathbb{Z}_p^*, \widehat{g_2}, f', f_1, f_2, \ldots, f_n \xleftarrow{\$} \mathbb{G}$, sets $\widehat{g_1} = g^{\alpha}$. The algorithm sets

$$\mathsf{pk} = (\widehat{g_1}, \widehat{g_2}, f', f_1, f_2, \ldots, f_n), \mathsf{sk} = (\alpha, \widehat{g_2}^{\alpha}).$$

$$\text{crs} = (\text{params}, \text{GS}_S, \text{GS}_R)$$
$$\text{params} = (p, \mathbb{G}, \mathbb{G}_T, e, g)$$

Sender S $\hspace{8cm}$ Receiver R

Initialization Phase

$(\text{pk}, \text{sk}, \psi, \text{cDB}) \leftarrow \text{DBSetup}$
$\text{pk} = (\widehat{g}_1, \widehat{g}_2, f', f_1, f_2, \ldots, f_n)$
$\text{sk} = (\alpha, \widehat{g}_2{}^{\alpha})$
$\psi = \text{NIZK}\{(\widehat{g}_2{}^{\alpha}, g') \mid e(g, \widehat{g}_2{}^{\alpha})e(g', \widehat{g}_2{}^{-1}) = 1 \wedge$
$\qquad e(g', \widehat{g}_2) = e(\widehat{g}_1, \widehat{g}_2)\}$
$\text{cDB} = (\Phi_1, \Phi_2, \ldots, \Phi_N)$

$\xrightarrow{(\text{sid}, S, \text{pk}, \psi, \text{cDB})}$

$\hspace{8cm}$ ACCEPT $\leftarrow$ DBVerify

Transfer Phase

$\hspace{8cm} \sigma_j \in \{1, 2, \ldots, n\}$
$\hspace{8cm} (\text{Req}_{\sigma_j}, \text{Pri}_{\sigma_j}) \leftarrow \text{RequestTra}$
$\hspace{8cm} \text{Req}_{\sigma_j} = (d_{1,\sigma_j}, \pi_{\sigma_j})$
$\hspace{8cm} \text{Pri}_{\sigma_j} = t_{\sigma_j}$

$\xleftarrow{(\text{sid}, R, \text{Req}_{\sigma_j})}$

$(\text{Res}_{\sigma_j}, \delta_{\sigma_j}) \leftarrow \text{ResponseTra}$
$\text{Res}_{\sigma_j} = e(d_{1,\sigma_j}, \widehat{g}_2{}^{\alpha})$

$\xrightarrow{(\text{sid}, S, \text{Res}_{\sigma_j}, \delta_{\sigma_j})}$

$\hspace{8cm} m_{\sigma_j} \leftarrow \text{CompleteTra}$

Fig. 1. Communication flow of our $\text{OT}^N_{k \times 1}$ for the jth transfer phase, $j = 1, 2, \ldots, k$.

The algorithm generates NIZK proof ψ using $\text{GS}_S = (\widetilde{u_1}, \widetilde{u_2}, \widetilde{u_3})$ as

$$\psi = \text{NIZK}\{(\widehat{g}_2{}^{\alpha}, g') \mid e(g, \widehat{g}_2{}^{\alpha})e(g', \widehat{g}_2{}^{-1}) = 1 \wedge e(g', \widehat{g}_2) = e(\widehat{g}_1, \widehat{g}_2)\}.$$

The $\text{Com}(\widehat{g}_2{}^{\alpha}) = \mu(\widehat{g}_2{}^{\alpha})\widetilde{u_1}^{s_1}\widetilde{u_2}^{s_2}\widetilde{u_3}^{s_3}$, $\text{Com}(g') = \mu(g')\widetilde{u_1}^{\ell_1}\widetilde{u_2}^{\ell_2}\widetilde{u_3}^{\ell_3}$ and proof components for the equations $e(g, \widehat{g}_2{}^{\alpha})e(g', \widehat{g}_2{}^{-1}) = 1 \wedge e(g', \widehat{g}_2) = e(\widehat{g}_1, \widehat{g}_2)$ are embedded in proof ψ as in Sect. 2.2, where $s_1, s_2, s_3, \ell_1, \ell_2, \ell_3 \xleftarrow{\$} \mathbb{Z}_p^*$. For $i = 1$ to N, the algorithm generates $\Phi_i = (c_i^{(1)}, c_i^{(2)}, c_i^{(3)})$ as follows.

1. Pick $r_i \xleftarrow{\$} \mathbb{Z}_p^*$, set $c_i^{(1)} = g^{r_i}$.
2. Let $\mathcal{I}_i = i_1 i_2 \ldots i_n$ be the n bit representation of i, i_ℓ be the ℓ-th bit of i and $\mathcal{M}_i \subseteq \{1, 2, \ldots, n\}$ be the set of all ℓ for which i_ℓ is 1. The algorithm

   sets $c_i^{(2)} = \widehat{g}_2{}^{\alpha} \left(f' \prod_{\ell \in \mathcal{M}_i} f_\ell \right)^{r_i}$.

3. Set $c_i^{(3)} = m_i \cdot e(\widehat{g}_1, \widehat{g}_2)^{r_i}$.

The ciphertext database is set to be $\text{cDB} = (\Phi_1, \Phi_2, \ldots, \Phi_N)$. The algorithm outputs $(\text{pk}, \text{sk}, \psi, \text{cDB})$ to the sender S. The sender S publishes $\text{pk}, \psi, \text{cDB}$ to all parties and keeps sk secret to itself. The computation cost involved in this algorithm is $3N + 25$ exponentiations and 1 pairing.

- DBVerify$(\text{pk}, \psi, \text{cDB}, \text{crs})$: The receiver R upon receiving $\text{pk}, \psi, \text{cDB}$ from S runs this randomized algorithm to verify the correctness of proof ψ and ciphertext database cDB as follows. The validity of proof ψ is checked by verifying the pairing product equation as in Sect. 2.2. The ciphertext database is verified for each $\Phi_i = (c_i^{(1)}, c_i^{(2)}, c_i^{(3)})$, by verifying the following equation

$$e\left(c_i^{(2)}, g\right) = e(\widehat{g}_1, \widehat{g}_2)e\left(f'\prod_{\ell \in \mathcal{M}_i} f_\ell, c_i^{(1)}\right),\ i = 1, 2, \ldots, N, \tag{5}$$

where $c_i^{(1)} = g^{r_i}, c_i^{(2)} = \widehat{g}_2^{\ \alpha}\left(f'\prod_{\ell \in \mathcal{M}_i} f_\ell\right)^{r_i}, \mathcal{M}_i \subseteq \{1, 2, \ldots, n\}$ be the set of all ℓ for which i_ℓ is 1, i_ℓ be the ℓ-th bit of i. If the the proof ψ and Eq. 5 hold, the algorithm outputs VALID, otherwise, INVALID. This algorithm has to perform $2N + 23$ pairings.

- RequestTra$(\mathsf{crs}, \mathsf{pk}, \sigma_j, \Phi_{\sigma_j})$: The receiver R runs this randomized algorithm to generate request Req_{σ_j} as follows.

1. Pick $v_{\sigma_j} \xleftarrow{\$} \mathbb{Z}_p^*$, set $d_{1,\sigma_j} = c_{\sigma_j}^{(1)} \cdot g^{v_{\sigma_j}} = g^{r_{\sigma_j} + v_{\sigma_j}}$,
2. $d_{2,\sigma_j} = c_{\sigma_j}^{(2)} \cdot (f'\prod_{\ell \in \mathcal{M}_{\sigma_j}} f_\ell)^{v_{\sigma_j}} = \widehat{g}_2^{\ \alpha}(f'\prod_{\ell \in \mathcal{M}_{\sigma_j}} f_\ell)^{r_{\sigma_j} + v_{\sigma_j}}, t_{\sigma_j} = \widehat{g}_2^{\ v_{\sigma_j}}$.
3. Generate NIWI proof $\pi_{\sigma_j} = \mathsf{NIWI}\{(c_{\sigma_j}^{(1)}, c_{\sigma_j}^{(2)}, f'\prod_{\ell \in \mathcal{M}_{\sigma_j}} f_\ell, t_{\sigma_j}, d_{2,\sigma_j})\ |$

$$e(c_{\sigma_j}^{(1)}, \widehat{g}_2)e(t_{\sigma_j}, g) = e(d_{1,\sigma_j}, \widehat{g}_2) \wedge$$

$$e(c_{\sigma_j}^{(2)}, \widehat{g}_2)e(f'\prod_{\ell \in \mathcal{M}_{\sigma_j}} f_\ell, t_{\sigma_j}) = e(d_{2,\sigma_j}, \widehat{g}_2) \wedge$$

$$e(d_{1,\sigma_j}, f'\prod_{\ell \in \mathcal{M}_{\sigma_j}} f_\ell)e(\widehat{g}_1, \widehat{g}_2) = e(d_{2,\sigma_j}, g)\}$$

using $\mathsf{GS}_R = (u_1, u_2, u_3)$. The proof π_{σ_j} consists of commitments to $c_{\sigma_j}^{(1)}, c_{\sigma_j}^{(2)}, f'\prod_{\ell \in \mathcal{M}_{\sigma_j}} f_\ell, t_{\sigma_j}, d_{2,\sigma_j}$, and proof components for three equations. As each commitment takes 3 group elements, proof component of a linear equation takes 3 group elements and of a nonlinear equation takes 9 group elements, so, the size of π_{σ_j} is 30 group elements. The computation cost involved in generating π_{σ_j} is 68 exponentiations and 1 pairing.

4. Set $\mathsf{Req}_{\sigma_j} = (d_{1,\sigma_j}, \pi_{\sigma_j})$, $\mathsf{Pri}_{\sigma_j} = t_{\sigma_j}$.

- ResponseTra$(\mathsf{crs}, \mathsf{pk}, \mathsf{sk}, \mathsf{Req}_{\sigma_j})$: The sender S upon receiving Req_{σ_j} from R runs this randomized algorithm to generate Res_{σ_j} as follows.

1. The algorithm verifies the proof π_{σ_j} by verifying each pairing product equation in π_{σ_j} as in Sect. 2.2. The verification of π_{σ_j} takes 62 pairings. If fails, it aborts the execution.
2. Otherwise, the algorithm generates $\mathsf{Res}_{\sigma_j} = e(d_{1,\sigma_j}, \widehat{g}_2^{\ \alpha}) = e(d_{1,\sigma_j}^\alpha, \widehat{g}_2)$ using secret α and $\widehat{g}_2^{\ \alpha}$.
3. Generate NIZK proof δ_{σ_j} using $\mathsf{GS}_S = (\widetilde{u_1}, \widetilde{u_2}, \widetilde{u_3})$ as

$$\delta_{\sigma_j} = \mathsf{NIZK}\{(a_{1,\sigma_j}, a_{2,\sigma_j}, a_{3,\sigma_j})\ |\ e(d_{1,\sigma_j}, a_{2,\sigma_j})e(a_{3,\sigma_j}, \widehat{g}_2^{\ -1}) = 1$$

$$\wedge\ e(a_{1,\sigma_j}, \widehat{g}_2^{\ -1})e(g, a_{2,\sigma_j}) = 1 \wedge e(a_{1,\sigma_j}, \widehat{g}_2) = e(\widehat{g}_1, \widehat{g}_2)\}$$

The proof δ_{σ_j} consists of commitments to $a_{1,\sigma_j} = \widehat{g_1}, a_{2,\sigma_j} = \widehat{g_2}^{\alpha}, a_{3,\sigma_j} = d_{1,\sigma_j}^{\alpha}$ and proof components of three pairing product equations. The size of proof δ_{σ_j} is 18 group elements and computation cost in generating δ_{σ_j} is 36 exponentiations.

The algorithm outputs $(\mathsf{Res}_{\sigma_j}, \delta_{\sigma_j})$. The sender S sends $(\mathsf{Res}_{\sigma_j}, \delta_{\sigma_j})$ to R.

- CompleteTra$(\mathsf{crs}, \mathsf{Res}_{\sigma_j}, \delta_{\sigma_j}, \mathsf{Pri}_{\sigma_j}, \varPhi_{\sigma_j})$: The receiver R with input $(\mathsf{crs}, \mathsf{Res}_{\sigma_j}, \delta_{\sigma_j}, \mathsf{Pri}_{\sigma_j}, \varPhi_{\sigma_j})$ runs this deterministic algorithm to recover m_{σ_j} as follows.
  1. The algorithm verifies the proof δ_{σ_j} by verifying each pairing product equation in δ_{σ_j} as discussed in the Sect. 2.2. The verification of δ_{σ_j} takes 36 pairings. If fails, it aborts the execution.
  2. Otherwise, it computes

$$\frac{c_{\sigma_j}^{(3)} \cdot e(\widehat{g_1}, t_{\sigma_j})}{\mathsf{Res}_{\sigma_j}} = m_{\sigma_j} \tag{6}$$

Correctness of Eq. 6:

$$\frac{c_{\sigma_j}^{(3)} \cdot e(\widehat{g_1}, t_{\sigma_j})}{\mathsf{Res}_{\sigma_j}} = \frac{m_{\sigma_j} \cdot e(\widehat{g_1}, \widehat{g_2})^{r_{\sigma_j}} e(\widehat{g_1}, \widehat{g_2}^{v_{\sigma_j}})}{e(g^{r_{\sigma_j}+v_{\sigma_j}}, \widehat{g_2}^{\alpha})} = \frac{m_{\sigma_j} e(\widehat{g_1}, \widehat{g_2})^{r_{\sigma_j}+v_{\sigma_j}}}{e(\widehat{g_1}, \widehat{g_2})^{r_{\sigma_j}+v_{\sigma_j}}} = m_{\sigma_j},$$

as $\widehat{g_1} = g^{\alpha}$, $t_{\sigma_j} = \widehat{g_2}^{v_{\sigma_j}}$, $c_{\sigma_j}^{(3)} = m_{\sigma_j} \cdot e(\widehat{g_1}, \widehat{g_2})^{r_{\sigma_j}}$.

5 Security Analysis

Theorem 3. *The* $\mathsf{OT}_{k\times1}^{N}$ *presented in Sect. 4 securely realizes the ideal functionality* $\mathcal{F}_{\mathsf{OT}}^{N\times1}$ *in the* $\mathcal{F}_{\mathsf{CRS}}^{\mathcal{D}}$*-hybrid model described in Sect. 3 under the DLIN, DBDH and SqDBDH assumptions.*

Proof. Let $\mathcal{A}$ be a static adversary interacting with the protocol $\varPsi$ in the real world. Our task is to construct an ideal world adversary $\mathcal{A}'$ in the ideal world interacting with the ideal functionality $\mathcal{F}_{\mathsf{OT}}^{N\times1}$ such that no environment machine $\mathcal{Z}$ can distinguish its interaction with the protocol $\varPsi$ and $\mathcal{A}$ in the real world from its interactions with $\mathcal{F}_{\mathsf{OT}}^{N\times1}$ and $\mathcal{A}'$ in the ideal world. We will show $\mathsf{IDEAL}_{\mathcal{F}_{\mathsf{OT}}^{N\times1}, \mathcal{A}', \mathcal{Z}} \stackrel{c}{\approx} \mathsf{REAL}_{\varPsi, \mathcal{A}, \mathcal{Z}}$ in each of the cases: (a) simulation when the receiver R is corrupted and the sender S is honest, (b) simulation when the sender S is corrupted and the receiver R is honest. When both the parties (the sender S and the receiver R) are honest or both the parties are corrupt are not discussed as these are trivial cases.

The security proof is presented using sequence of hybrid games. Let $\Pr[\mathsf{Game}\ i]$ be the probability that $\mathcal{Z}$ distinguishes the transcript of Game i from that in the real execution.

(a) Simulation when the receiver R is corrupted and the sender S is honest. In this case, the receiver R is controlled by $\mathcal{A}$ and $\mathcal{A}'$ simulates the honest sender S without knowing the database DB.

Game 0: This game is same as the real world protocol in which R interacts with honest S having database $\mathsf{DB} = (m_1, m_2, \ldots, m_N)$. So, $\Pr[\mathsf{Game\ 0}] = 0$.

Game 1: This game is exactly the same as Game 0 except that $\mathcal{A}'$ simulates the common reference string crs. The adversary $\mathcal{A}'$ first generates $\mathsf{params} = (p, \mathbb{G}, \mathbb{G}_T, e, g) \leftarrow \mathsf{BilinearSetup}(1^\rho)$, picks $a, b, \xi_1, \xi_2, \tilde{a}, \tilde{b}, \tilde{\xi}_1, \tilde{\xi}_2 \xleftarrow{\$} \mathbb{Z}_p^*$ and sets $g_1 = g^a, g_2 = g^b, \tilde{g}_1 = g^{\tilde{a}}, \tilde{g}_2 = g^{\tilde{b}}, u_1 = (g_1, 1, g), u_2 = (1, g_2, g), u_3 = u_1^{\xi_1} u_2^{\xi_2} = (g_1^{\xi_1}, g_2^{\xi_2}, g^{\xi_1 + \xi_2}), \widetilde{u_1} = (\tilde{g}_1, 1, g), \widetilde{u_2} = (1, \tilde{g}_2, g), \widetilde{u_3} = \widetilde{u_1}^{\tilde{\xi}_1} \widetilde{u_2}^{\tilde{\xi}_2} (1, 1, g) = (\tilde{g}_1^{\tilde{\xi}_1}, \tilde{g}_2^{\tilde{\xi}_2}, g^{\tilde{\xi}_1 + \tilde{\xi}_2 + 1}), \mathsf{GS}_R = (u_1, u_2, u_3), \mathsf{GS}_S = (\widetilde{u_1}, \widetilde{u_2}, \widetilde{u_3}),$ $\mathsf{crs} = (\mathsf{params}, \mathsf{GS}_R, \mathsf{GS}_S)$, trapdoors $\mathsf{t}_{\mathsf{ext}} = (a, b, \xi_1, \xi_2)$, $\widetilde{\mathsf{t}_{\mathsf{sim}}} = (\tilde{a}, \tilde{b}, \tilde{\xi}_1, \tilde{\xi}_2)$. The GS_R is generated in perfectly sound setting and GS_S in witness-indistinguishability setting. When the parties query $(\mathsf{sid}, \mathsf{CRS})$, $\mathcal{A}'$ returns $(\mathsf{sid}, \mathsf{CRS}, \mathsf{crs})$. The trapdoors $\mathsf{t}_{\mathsf{ext}}$ and $\widetilde{\mathsf{t}_{\mathsf{sim}}}$ are kept secret by $\mathcal{A}'$. The crs generated by $\mathcal{A}'$ in Game 1 and that by algorithm CRSSetup in actual protocol run are computationally indistinguishable by Theorem 1. Therefore, there exists a negligible function $\epsilon_1(\rho)$ such that $|\Pr[\mathsf{Game\ 1}] - \Pr[\mathsf{Game\ 0}]| \leq \epsilon_1(\rho)$.

Game 2: This game is exactly the same as Game 1 except that $\mathcal{A}'$ extracts the index σ_j for each request by $\mathcal{A}$ as follows in each transfer phase $j = 1, 2, \ldots, k$. The adversary $\mathcal{A}'$ parses Req_{σ_j} as $(d_{1,\sigma_j}, \pi_{\sigma_j})$ and checks the correctness of π_{σ_j}. If fails, $\mathcal{A}'$ aborts the execution, otherwise, $\mathcal{A}'$ extracts the witnesses and index from proof π_{σ_j} as follows. The proof π_{σ_j} consists of commitments to $c_{\sigma_j}^{(1)}, c_{\sigma_j}^{(2)}, f' \prod_{\ell \in \mathcal{M}_{\sigma_j}} f_\ell, t_{\sigma_j}, d_{2,\sigma_j}$, and proof components of the pairing product equations

$$e(c_{\sigma_j}^{(1)}, \widehat{g_2}) e(t_{\sigma_j}, g) = e(d_{1,\sigma_j}, \widehat{g_2}) \wedge e(c_{\sigma_j}^{(2)}, \widehat{g_2}) e(f' \prod_{\ell \in \mathcal{M}_{\sigma_j}} f_\ell, t_{\sigma_j}) = e(d_{2,\sigma_j}, \widehat{g_2}) \wedge$$

$$e(d_{1,\sigma_j}, f' \prod_{\ell \in \mathcal{M}_{\sigma_j}} f_\ell) e(\widehat{g_1}, \widehat{g_2}) = e(d_{2,\sigma_j}, g).$$

- The adversary $\mathcal{A}'$ extracts first witness wit_1 from $\mathsf{Com}(c_{\sigma_j}^{(1)}) = \mu(c_{\sigma_j}^{(1)}) u_1^{\tilde{r}_1} u_2^{\tilde{r}_2} u_3^{\tilde{r}_3}$ $= (g_1^{\tilde{r}_1 + \tilde{r}_3 \xi_1}, g_2^{\tilde{r}_2 + \tilde{r}_3 \xi_2}, c_{\sigma_j}^{(1)} g^{\tilde{r}_1 + \tilde{r}_2 + \tilde{r}_3 (\xi_1 + \xi_2)})$ as $\dfrac{c_{\sigma_j}^{(1)} g^{\tilde{r}_1 + \tilde{r}_2 + \tilde{r}_3 (\xi_1 + \xi_2)}}{(g_1^{\tilde{r}_1 + \tilde{r}_3 \xi_1})^{\frac{1}{a}} (g_2^{\tilde{r}_2 + \tilde{r}_3 \xi_2})^{\frac{1}{b}}} = c_{\sigma_j}^{(1)} = $ wit_1 using $\mathsf{t}_{\mathsf{ext}} = (a, b, \xi_1, \xi_2)$, where $\tilde{r}_1, \tilde{r}_2, \tilde{r}_3$ are random values which were used for generating $\mathsf{Com}(c_{\sigma_j}^{(1)})$. Similarly, $\mathcal{A}'$ extracts $\mathsf{wit}_2 = c_{\sigma_j}^{(2)}$, $\mathsf{wit}_3 = f' \prod_{\ell \in \mathcal{M}_{\sigma_j}} f_\ell$, $\mathsf{wit}_4 = t_{\sigma_j}$, $\mathsf{wit}_5 = d_{2,\sigma_j}$ from their respective commitments.

- The adversary $\mathcal{A}'$ checks whether $\mathsf{wit}_1 = c_\zeta^{(1)}$ and $\mathsf{wit}_2 = c_\zeta^{(2)}$, $\zeta = 1, 2, \ldots, N$. Suppose no matching index found, i.e., $\sigma_j \notin \{1, 2, \ldots, N\}$ and a valid proof π_{σ_j} is constructed by $\mathcal{A}$ for the ciphertext $\Phi_{\sigma_j} \notin \mathsf{cDB} = (\Phi_1, \Phi_2, \ldots, \Phi_N)$ in order to generate Req_{σ_j}. The validity of the proof π_{σ_j} generated by $\mathcal{A}$ for Φ_{σ_j} indicates that the ciphertext Φ_{σ_j} must be a correct ciphertext. This eventually means that $\mathcal{A}$ generates a valid Water's signature on index σ_j and outputs $c_{\sigma_j}^{(1)}, c_{\sigma_j}^{(2)}$ as a forgery contradicting the fact that the Water's signature is existentially unforgeable under the hardness of DBDH problem [21]. Let σ_j

be the matching index and $\mathcal{I}_{\sigma_j} = \sigma_{j_1}\sigma_{j_2}\ldots\sigma_{j_n}$ be the n bit representation of σ_j. The adversary $\mathcal{A}'$ checks whether $\mathsf{wit}_3 = f'\prod_{\ell\in\mathcal{M}_{\sigma_j}} f_\ell$, where $\mathcal{M}_{\sigma_j}$ be the set of all $\ell \in [n]$ for which σ_{j_ℓ} is 1. If fails, aborts the execution.

- Otherwise, $\mathcal{A}'$ queries $\mathcal{F}_{\mathsf{OT}}^{N\times 1}$ with the message $(\mathsf{sid}, \mathsf{transfer}, \sigma_j)$. The $\mathcal{F}_{\mathsf{OT}}^{N\times 1}$ gives m_{σ_j} to $\mathcal{A}'$.

The difference between Game 3 and Game 2 is negligible provided that DBDH assumptions hold. Therefore, there exists a negligible function $\epsilon_3(\rho)$ such that $|\Pr[\mathsf{Game\ 3}] - \Pr[\mathsf{Game\ 2}]| \le \epsilon_3(\rho)$.

Game 3: This game is the same as Game 2 except that the response Res_{σ_j} and proof δ_{σ_j} are simulated by $\mathcal{A}'$ for each transfer phase j, where $j = 1, 2, \ldots, k$. The ciphertext $\Phi_{\sigma_j} = (c_{\sigma_j}^{(1)} = g^{r_{\sigma_j}}, c_{\sigma_j}^{(2)} = \widehat{g_2}^\alpha(f'\prod_{\ell\in\mathcal{M}_{\sigma_j}} f_\ell)^{r_{\sigma_j}}, c_{\sigma_j}^{(3)})$. The adversary $\mathcal{A}'$ simulates response Res'_{σ_j} and proof δ'_{σ_j} as follows. The simulated response

$$\mathsf{Res}'_{\sigma_j} = \frac{c_{\sigma_j}^{(3)}\cdot e(\widehat{g_1}, \mathsf{wit}_4)}{m_{\sigma_j}} = \frac{c_{\sigma_j}^{(3)}\cdot e(\widehat{g_1}, t_{\sigma_j})}{m_{\sigma_j}} = \frac{m_{\sigma_j}e(\widehat{g_1}, \widehat{g_2})^{r_{\sigma_j}}\cdot e(\widehat{g_1}, \widehat{g_2}^{v_{\sigma_j}})}{m_{\sigma_j}}$$
$$= e(\widehat{g_1}, \widehat{g_2})^{r_{\sigma_j}+v_{\sigma_j}}.$$

The honestly generated response

$$\mathsf{Res}_{\sigma_j} = e(d_{1,\sigma_j}, \widehat{g_2}^\alpha) = e(g^{r_{\sigma_j}+v_{\sigma_j}}, \widehat{g_2}^\alpha) = e(\widehat{g_1}, \widehat{g_2})^{r_{\sigma_j}+v_{\sigma_j}},$$

as $\widehat{g_1} = g^\alpha$. The simulated Res'_{σ_j} has the same distribution as honestly generated response Res_{σ_j} by algorithm ResponseTra discussed in the Sect. 4. The adversary $\mathcal{A}'$ also simulates δ'_{σ_j} to prove that Res'_{σ_j} is correctly framed. The proof

$$\delta_{\sigma_j} = \mathsf{NIZK}\{(a_{1,\sigma_j}, a_{2,\sigma_j}, a_{3,\sigma_j}) \mid e(d_{1,\sigma_j}, a_{2,\sigma_j})e(a_{3,\sigma_j}, \widehat{g_2}^{-1}) = 1\wedge$$

$$e(a_{1,\sigma_j}, \widehat{g_2}^{-1})e(g, a_{2,\sigma_j}) = 1 \wedge e(a_{1,\sigma_j}, \widehat{g_2}) = e(\widehat{g_1}, \widehat{g_2})\}$$

consists of commitments to secret values $a_{1,\sigma_j} = \widehat{g_1}, a_{2,\sigma_j} = \widehat{g_2}^\alpha, a_{3,\sigma_j} = d_{1,\sigma_j}^\alpha$ and proof components to 3 pairing product equations. For simulation, $\mathcal{A}'$ sets $a_{1,\sigma_j} = a_{2,\sigma_j} = a_{3,\sigma_j} = 1$ and generate commitments to $a_{1,\sigma_j}, a_{2,\sigma_j}, a_{3,\sigma_j}$ using GS_S. The adversary $\mathcal{A}'$ also generates opening value of commitment a_{1,σ_j}. With the help of trapdoor $\widetilde{\mathsf{t}_{\mathsf{sim}}}$ and opening value, $\mathcal{A}'$ can open the commitment of a_{1,σ_j} to 1 in second equation and a_{1,σ_j} to $\widehat{g_1}$ in third equation as discussed in Example 1 in Sect. 2.2. As Groth-Sahai proofs are composable NIZK by Theorem 2, the simulated proof δ'_{σ_j} is computationally indistinguishable from the honestly generated proof δ_{σ_j} under the DLIN assumption. Therefore, there exists a negligible function $\epsilon_4(\rho)$ such that $|\Pr[\mathsf{Game\ 4}] - \Pr[\mathsf{Game\ 3}]| \le \epsilon_4(\rho)$.

Game 4: This game is the same as Game 3 except that the S's database $\mathsf{DB} = (m_1, m_2, \ldots, m_N)$ is replaced by random database $\widehat{\mathsf{DB}} = (\widehat{m_1}, \widehat{m_2}, \ldots, \widehat{m_N})$, thereby, $\mathcal{A}'$ replaces S's first message $(\mathsf{sid}, S, \mathsf{pk}, \psi, \mathsf{cDB})$ by $(\mathsf{sid}, S, \mathsf{pk}', \psi', \mathsf{cDB}')$, where $(\mathsf{pk}', \psi', \mathsf{cDB}')$ are simulated by $\mathcal{A}'$ with a database $\mathsf{DB}' = (\widehat{m_1}, \widehat{m_2}, \ldots, \widehat{m_n})$, where $\widehat{m_1}, \widehat{m_2}, \ldots, \widehat{m_N} \xleftarrow{\$} \mathbb{G}_T$. In each transfer phase, the response $(\mathrm{sid}, S, \mathsf{Res}_{\sigma_j}, \delta_{\sigma_j})$ is replaced by the simulated response $(\mathrm{sid}, S, \mathsf{Res}'_{\sigma_j}, \delta'_{\sigma_j})$ as in above game, but here the simulated response is computed on invalid statement. The only difference between Game 4 and Game 3 is in the generation of ciphertexts. In Game 4, cDB' is the encryption of random messages $\widehat{m}_1, \widehat{m}_2, \ldots, \widehat{m}_n$, whereas cDB in Game 3 is that of perfect messages $m_1, m_2, \ldots, m_N$. By the Lemma 1 given below, Game 3 is computationally indistinguishable from Game 4. Therefore, $|\Pr[\text{Game 4}] - \Pr[\text{Game 3}]| \leq \epsilon_4(\rho)$, where $\epsilon_4(\rho)$ is a negligible function.

Lemma 1. *Let* $\mathsf{DB} = (m_1, m_2, \ldots, m_N)$ *be any database and* $\widehat{\mathsf{DB}} = (\widehat{m}_1, \widehat{m}_2, \ldots, \widehat{m}_N)$ *be a set of random messages. Under the hardness of SqDBDH, no distinguisher* $\mathcal{Z}$ *can distinguish the transcript of* Game 3 *from the transcript of* Game 4.

Thus Game 4 is the ideal world interaction whereas Game 0 is the real world interaction. Now $|\Pr[\text{Game 4}] - [\text{Game 0}]| \leq |\Pr[\text{Game 4}] - [\text{Game 3}]| + |\Pr[\text{Game 3}] - [\text{Game 2}]| + |\Pr[\text{Game 2}] - [\text{Game 1}]| + |\Pr[\text{Game 1}] - [\text{Game 0}]| \leq \epsilon_5(\rho)$, where $\epsilon_5(\rho) = \epsilon_4(\rho) + \epsilon_3(\rho) + \epsilon_2(\rho) + \epsilon_1(\rho)$ is a negligible function. Hence, $\mathsf{IDEAL}_{\mathcal{F}_{\mathsf{OT}}^{N \times 1}, \mathcal{A}', \mathcal{Z}} \stackrel{c}{\approx} \mathsf{REAL}_{\Psi, \mathcal{A}, \mathcal{Z}}$.

(b) Simulation when the sender S is corrupted and the receiver R is honest. Due to lack of space, proof of Lemma 1 and simulation of Case (b) will be given in full version.

6 Comparison

In this section, we compare our $\mathsf{OT}_{k \times 1}^{N}$ with the existing similar schemes [1,14,17,20]. Green and Hohenberger' [14] scheme employes Boneh, Boyen and Shacham (BBS) [5] encryption, Camenisch-Lysyanskaya (CL) signature [6], Boneh-Boyen signature [3], non-interactive Groth-Sahai proofs [16] and is secure under symmetric external Diffie-Hellman (SXDH), DLIN, q-hidden

Table 1. Comparison summary (PO stands for number of pairing operations, EXP for number of exponentiation operations, IP for initialization phase, TP for transfer phase, cDB for a ciphertext database, pk for public key, $\alpha X + \beta Y$ for α elements from the group X and β elements from the group Y, N is database size, n bit length of each index).

UC secure $\mathsf{OT}_{k \times 1}^{N}$	Pairing PO		Exponentiation EXP			Communication		Storage		q-type assum.
	TP	IP	TP	IP	crs	Request	Response	crs	(cDB + pk)	
[14]	$\geq 207k$	$24N+1$	$249k$	$20N+13$	18	$(68\mathrm{G}_1 + 38\mathrm{G}_2)k$	$(20\mathrm{G}_1 + 18\mathrm{G}_2)k$	$7\mathrm{G}_1 + 7\mathrm{G}_2$	$(15N+5)\mathrm{G}_1 + (3N+6)\mathrm{G}_2$	✓
[20]	$> 450k$	$15N+1$	$223k$	$12N+9$	15	$(65\mathrm{G})k$	$(28\mathrm{G})k$	$23\mathrm{G}$	$(12N+7)\mathrm{G}$	✓
[17]	$147k$	$5N+1$	$150k$	$17N+5$	18	$(47\mathrm{G})k$	$(28\mathrm{G})k$	$16\mathrm{G}$	$(12N+5)\mathrm{G}$	✓
[1]	$> 142k$	$10N$	$> 74k$	$16N+17$	11	$(73\mathrm{G})k$	$> (1\mathrm{G})k$	$13\mathrm{G}$	$(16N+15)\mathrm{G}$	✗
Ours	$101k$	$2N+24$	$108k$	$3N+25$	10	$(31\mathrm{G})k$	$(18\mathrm{G} + 1\mathrm{G}_T)k$	$11\mathrm{G}$	$(3N+n+15)\mathrm{G}$	✗

Lysyanskaya, Rivest, Sahai and Wolf (LRSW) assumptions. Rial et al.'s [20] UC secure *priced* $\mathsf{OT}_{k\times 1}^{N}$ protocol combines BBS [5] encryption, P-signatures [2], non-interactive Groth-Sahai proofs [16] and achieves security under hidden strong Diffie-Hellman (HSDH), triple Diffie-Hellman (TDH) and DLIN assumptions. Guleria and Dutta's [17] scheme combines BBS [5] encryption, batch Boneh and Boyen (BB) [4] signature with non-interactive Groth-sahai proofs [16], trapdoor commitments of Fischlin *et al.* [11] and is secure under q-SDH, DLIN assumptions.

The schemes [14,17,20] use dynamic q-type assumptions. Abe *et al.* [1] proposed the first adaptive oblivious transfer without q-type assumptions in UC framework. It uses ElGamel encryption, structure preserving signature [1], non-interactive Groth-Sahai proofs [16], interactive zero-knowledge proofs. The construction is proven to be secure under the hardness of SXDH, DLIN and decisional Diffie-Hellman in target group (DDH_T) problems. Some components of the ciphertexts in [1,14,20] are never used in the real protocol. Instead they are included to facilitate simulation of the security proof in UC model. Consequently, nothing can prevent a cheating sender to replace these components with garbage values without affecting the security and correctness of these protocols. However from efficiency point of view, we feel that these type of redundancies are not desirable in practice. It will be better if we can design a protocol in which all the components of the ciphertext are used in real protocol execution retaining the same security level.

Motivated by [1], our scheme also does not use q-type assumptions. We use Water's signature [21], non-interactive Groth-sahai proofs [16], and our scheme is secure under DLIN and DBDH assumptions. Our proposed construction takes 2 rounds in each transfer phase while [1] takes 3 rounds in each transfer phase. As illustrated in Table 1, our $\mathsf{OT}_{k\times 1}^{N}$ outperforms the best known schemes [1,14, 17,20], which are to best of our knowledge, the only existing basic UC secure adaptive oblivious transfer protocols so far.

References

1. Abe, M., Camenisch, J., Dubovitskaya, M., Nishimaki, R.: Universally composable adaptive oblivious transfer (with access control) from standard assumptions. In: ACM Workshop on Digital Identity Management, pp. 1–12. ACM (2013)
2. Belenkiy, M., Chase, M., Kohlweiss, M., Lysyanskaya, A.: P-signatures and noninteractive anonymous credentials. In: Canetti, R. (ed.) TCC 2008. LNCS, vol. 4948, pp. 356–374. Springer, Heidelberg (2008)
3. Boneh, D., Boyen, X.: Efficient selective-ID secure identity-based encryption without random oracles. In: Cachin, C., Camenisch, J.L. (eds.) EUROCRYPT 2004. LNCS, vol. 3027, pp. 223–238. Springer, Heidelberg (2004)
4. Boneh, D., Boyen, X.: Short signatures without random oracles. In: Cachin, C., Camenisch, J.L. (eds.) EUROCRYPT 2004. LNCS, vol. 3027, pp. 56–73. Springer, Heidelberg (2004)
5. Boneh, D., Boyen, X., Shacham, H.: Short group signatures. In: Franklin, M. (ed.) CRYPTO 2004. LNCS, vol. 3152, pp. 41–55. Springer, Heidelberg (2004)

6. Camenisch, J.L., Lysyanskaya, A.: Signature schemes and anonymous credentials from bilinear maps. In: Franklin, M. (ed.) CRYPTO 2004. LNCS, vol. 3152, pp. 56–72. Springer, Heidelberg (2004)
7. Camenisch, J.L., Neven, G., Shelat, A.: Simulatable adaptive oblivious transfer. In: Naor, M. (ed.) EUROCRYPT 2007. LNCS, vol. 4515, pp. 573–590. Springer, Heidelberg (2007)
8. Canetti, R.: Universally composable security: a new paradigm for cryptographic protocols. In: FOCS-2001, pp. 136–145. IEEE (2001)
9. Canetti, R., Lindell, Y., Ostrovsky, R., Sahai, A.: Universally composable two-party and multi-party secure computation. In: ACM 2002, pp. 494–503. ACM (2002)
10. Datta, P., Dutta, R., Mukhopadhyay, S.: Universally composable efficient priced oblivious transfer from a flexible membership encryption. In: Susilo, W., Mu, Y. (eds.) ACISP 2014. LNCS, vol. 8544, pp. 98–114. Springer, Heidelberg (2014)
11. Fischlin, M., Libert, B., Manulis, M.: Non-interactive and re-usable universally composable string commitments with adaptive security. In: Lee, D.H., Wang, X. (eds.) ASIACRYPT 2011. LNCS, vol. 7073, pp. 468–485. Springer, Heidelberg (2011)
12. Garay, J.A., Wichs, D., Zhou, H.-S.: Somewhat non-committing encryption and efficient adaptively secure oblivious transfer. In: Halevi, S. (ed.) CRYPTO 2009. LNCS, vol. 5677, pp. 505–523. Springer, Heidelberg (2009)
13. Green, M., Hohenberger, S.: Blind identity-based encryption and simulatable oblivious transfer. In: Kurosawa, K. (ed.) ASIACRYPT 2007. LNCS, vol. 4833, pp. 265–282. Springer, Heidelberg (2007)
14. Green, M., Hohenberger, S.: Universally composable adaptive oblivious transfer. In: Pieprzyk, J. (ed.) ASIACRYPT 2008. LNCS, vol. 5350, pp. 179–197. Springer, Heidelberg (2008)
15. Green, M., Hohenberger, S.: Practical adaptive oblivious transfer from simple assumptions. In: Ishai, Y. (ed.) TCC 2011. LNCS, vol. 6597, pp. 347–363. Springer, Heidelberg (2011)
16. Groth, J., Sahai, A.: Efficient non-interactive proof systems for bilinear groups. In: Smart, N.P. (ed.) EUROCRYPT 2008. LNCS, vol. 4965, pp. 415–432. Springer, Heidelberg (2008)
17. Guleria, V., Dutta, R.: Efficient adaptive oblivious transfer in UC framework. In: Huang, X., Zhou, J. (eds.) ISPEC 2014. LNCS, vol. 8434, pp. 271–286. Springer, Heidelberg (2014)
18. Naor, M., Pinkas, B.: Oblivious transfer with adaptive queries. In: Wiener, M. (ed.) CRYPTO 1999. LNCS, vol. 1666, pp. 573–590. Springer, Heidelberg (1999)
19. Peikert, C., Vaikuntanathan, V., Waters, B.: A framework for efficient and composable oblivious transfer. In: Wagner, D. (ed.) CRYPTO 2008. LNCS, vol. 5157, pp. 554–571. Springer, Heidelberg (2008)
20. Rial, A., Kohlweiss, M., Preneel, B.: Universally composable adaptive priced oblivious transfer. In: Shacham, H., Waters, B. (eds.) Pairing 2009. LNCS, vol. 5671, pp. 231–247. Springer, Heidelberg (2009)
21. Waters, B.: Efficient identity-based encryption without random oracles. In: Cramer, R. (ed.) EUROCRYPT 2005. LNCS, vol. 3494, pp. 114–127. Springer, Heidelberg (2005)
22. Zhang, B.: Simulatable adaptive oblivious transfer with statistical receiver's privacy. In: Boyen, X., Chen, X. (eds.) ProvSec 2011. LNCS, vol. 6980, pp. 52–67. Springer, Heidelberg (2011)

TagDroid: Hybrid SSL Certificate
Verification in Android

Hui Liu[✉], Yuanyuan Zhang, Hui Wang, Wenbo Yang,
Juanru Li, and Dawu Gu

Department of Computer Science and Engineering,
Shanghai Jiao Tong University, Shanghai, China
yyjess@sjtu.edu.cn

Abstract. SSL/TLS protocol is designed to protect the end-to-end
communication by cryptographic means. However, the widely applied
SSL/TLS protocol is facing many inadequacies on current mobile platform. Applications may suffer from MITM (Man-In-The-Middle) attacks
when the certificate is not appropriately validated or local truststore
is contaminated. In this paper, we present a hybrid certificate validation approach combining basic certificate validation against a predefined
norm truststore with ways by virtue of aid from online social network
friends. We conduct an analysis of official and third-party ROMs. The
results show that some third-party ROMs add their own certificates in
the truststore, while some do not remove compromised CA certificates
from the truststore, which makes defining a norm truststore necessary.
And the intuition to leverage social network friends to validate certificate is out of the distributed and "always online" feature of mobile social
network. We implemented a prototype on Android, named TAGDROID.
A thorough set of experiments assesses the validity of our approach in
protecting SSL communication of mobile devices without introducing
significant overhead.

Keywords: MITM attacks · SSL certificate verification · Mobile SNS

1 Introduction

SSL is widely used to secure communications over the Internet. To authenticate
the identity of communication entity, X.509 certificates and hence Public Key
Infrastructure (PKI) are used. In PKI system, an X.509 certificate binds a public key with a particular distinguished name, and it certifies this relationship
by means of signatures signed by the Certificate Authority (CA). Therefore, to
establish a secure connection between client and server, i.e. to prevent MITM

Supported by the National Science and Technology Major Projects
(2012ZX03002011-002), National Key Technology Research and Development
Program of the Ministry of Science and Technology of China (2012BAH46B02) and
the National Natural Science Foundation of China (No.61103040).

L.C.K. Hui et al. (Eds.): ICICS 2014, LNCS 8958, pp. 120–131, 2015.
DOI: 10.1007/978-3-319-21966-0_9

attacks, a client must verify the certificate received from the server to guarantee the following two critical points: (1) the received certificate is issued for the server (distinguished name matches the hostname); (2) the CA who signed the certificate is in the predefined set of trusted root CAs, which is known as *truststore*.

While in traditional desktop environment, SSL is mostly used in Web browsers and its implementation is taken good care of by several large corporations, it is noticeable that, with the proliferation of Android devices and thereby prominent emergence of Android apps in recent years, SSL is used more and more to secure communications in varieties of apps developed by millions of developers. However, out of different reasons ranging from wanting to use self-signed certificates during development to being unaware of security implication of accepting any certificate [9], the developers fail to correctly implement the certificate verification when using SSL, which gives rise to the insecure communication.

Besides, there still exists issues even if the certificate verification is correctly carried out. On one hand, the truststore is a critical part. For Android, the truststore that comes along with the system can be manipulated, which is a potential threat. If a malicious root CA is trusted, all the certificates it issued will be accepted. On the other hand, there might be some severs that provide certificates signed by untrusted root CAs. It's been found that SSL/TLS communications without a valid certificate (e.g., self-signed certificate provided by the server) are quite common. A study in [5] found that the false warning ratio is 1.54 % when examining 3.9 billion TLS connections, which is an unacceptably high rate since benign scenarios are orders of magnitude more common than attacks. And for users, when faced with a self-signed certificate, they hardly have a clue to tell whether it is from the legitimate server or it is replaced by a MITM attacker.

Existing approaches to dealing with these problems are introduced in Sect. 6 and their limitations are depicted. While at the same time, we notice that the "always online" feature of smart mobile device is becoming the most popular vector of social network service (SNS). Emerging works leverage the distributed nature of SNS in file sharing [6,10], poll/e-voting and other scenarios.

In this paper, we attempt to deal with the server authentication issue in Android through a way that combines the basic certificate validation with ways by virtue of online social network friends helping verify the certificate. It is carried out in three steps. Firstly, we aim to secure communications even if the apps are not correctly developed, since a large number of apps that fail to validate certificate correctly have already been installed on massive number of devices. Thus, we perform as a friendly proxy that takes care of all the SSL connections, and for every connection, we perform a strict certificate validation. Secondly, to prevent truststore from being manipulated, we define a *norm truststore*. The strict certificate validation is carried out against the norm truststore such that only the certificates issued by CAs in the norm truststore are accepted. Lastly, for the certificates that fail to pass the strict check or are not issued by CAs in the norm truststore, we launch a collaborative certificate verification to seek for extra information to decide whether it is really presented by server or it is a malicious certificate. We consult to social network friends for help, asking them to fetch certificates from the same server and provide a credibility indicator about the certificate.

We implement a prototype named TagDroid and conduct experiments to evaluate the effectiveness and overhead. The results indicate that this scheme is effective in defeating MITM attack and dealing with self-signed certificates without significant overhead.

2   Background

2.1   Android and SSL Certificate Verification

When authenticating a server, two key parts must be guaranteed: the certificate is signed by a trusted source, and the server talking to presents the right certificate. The Android framework takes care of verifying certificates and hostnames and checking the trust chain against the system truststore. By simply including the two lines below, a client can launch a secure connection.

```
URL url = new URL("https://example.org");
URLConnection Conn = url.openConnection()
```

If a certificate is not issued by CA in truststore, e.g. a self-signed certificate, or the DN does not match hostname, an exception will be thrown out.

However, prior work [8] indicates that 8.0 % apps are not correctly implemented and thus vulnerable to MITM attacks, and a deep analysis shows that these apps use "customized" SSL implementations that either accept all certificates or accepts all hostnames.

2.2   Android and TrustStore

The Android framework validates certificates against the system truststore by default. In pre-ICS (Ice Cream Sandwich, Android 4.0), the truststore is a single file stored in /system/etc/security/cacerts.bks, and is hard-wired into the firmware. User has no control over it, but if the device is rooted, a keytool can be used to repackage the file and replace the original one. This kind of operation may not be possible for attackers or malicious apps to leverage. However, the truststore comes along with the firmware, and now many third-party ROMs are available and widely installed. We conduct a detail analysis on truststores from both third-party and official ROMs, which is described in Sect. 4.2. The results indicate that a third-party ROM that has been downloaded more than 2,000,000 times is found to have added 3 extra certificates compared with the official one of same version. According to the result, we can reasonably assume a malicious third-party ROM maker could deliberately add a root CA into the truststore, via which he could launch MITM attacks successfully. And devices having installed this malicious ROM would have no chance to find out something is going wrong.

Since Android 4.0, user can add and remove trusted certificates, which gives user more power in controlling the truststore. Users are provided with an option "Settings > Security > Install From Storage" to add root certificates, with no root permission required but needing pin lockscreen on. The other way of changing truststore is to directly copy the certificate to the directory /etc/security/cacerts with root permission. The truststore is under threat as well. Apart from the factor of third-party ROMs, an application with root permission granted can successfully add a certificate to the cacerts directory without any prompt coming out.

Furthermore, as Android version evolves, some root certificates are removed for some reason (for example, a compromised CA). But devices with old version installed still trust those certificates and therefore ones signed by them. Attackers can make use of this weakness with little effort.

An effective approach for apps to defeat attacks mentioned above is to initialize a TrustManagerFactory with their own keystore file that contains the server's certificate or the issuing certificate, which is called pinning [11]. However, this is only suitable for those who do not need to connect to practically every possible host in the Internet. By using pinning, no matter what happens to system truststore, there will be no effect on these apps.

Another issue concerning validating certificate against truststore is that when a user connects to a server whose certificate is issued by private CAs, a warning is prompted asking whether to proceed. But the user will see the same warning when the received certificate is signed by the MITM attacker who fails to manipulate user's truststore. Therefore, under this condition, there is no extra information to help the user make further decision.

3   Attack Scenario

In this section, we present the type of attacks we aim to tackle with. We only consider the local MITM attacks. As shown in Fig. 1. The attacker (Mallory) is located near the client (Alice) and replaces the certificate (CertB) sent by server (Bob) with its own certificate (CertM). If Alice accepts CertM, all messages exchanged between Alice and Bob will be plaintext to Mallory. According to the certificate Mallory presents to Alice, we define the following two attack scenarios.

3.1   Self-signed Certificate

Mallory simply uses a self-signed certificate with the property that either DN does not match hostname or it is not issued by CAs trusted by Alice. This is the easiest kind of attack to carry out, and apps having correctly implemented the verification using standard APIs will not be vulnerable to this attack.

However, as mentioned in Sect. 2.1, lots of apps using customized implementation are not able to take care of this verification. We tested some of the most popular apps in China, using BurpSuite to replace the certificate sent from the server with a self-signed certificate, and find out there indeed are apps that don't validate the certificate and all the traffic can be decrypted.

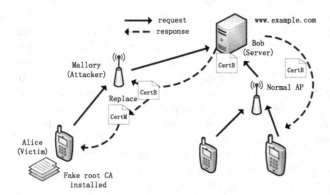

Fig. 1. Attack scenario. Local attacker Mallory between Alice and Bob replaces certB sent from Bob with certM. Alice may have installed a fake root CA such that Mallory can decrypt most of Alice's secure communication even if correct certificate verification is carried out.

3.2   Installed Malicious Root CA-signed Certificate

In this scenario, Mallory manages to have root CA installed in client's truststore, so certificates signed by this pre-installed root CA are trusted by apps validating certificates in the default way. This attack is much more difficult since Mallory needs a certificate installed in user's truststore in advance. However, third-party ROMs pave the way for this kind of attacks (see Sect. 4.2).

As mentioned in Sect. 2.2, this kind of attack can be avoided by using certificate pinning if apps only need to connect to a limited number of servers. Pinning performs good but seems to be not widely adopted yet since lots of apps are found vulnerable.

We conduct the experiment by installing the root CA of BurpSuite in the truststore that signs all the certificates. Some apps related to banking and payments are found to be vulnerable to this kind of MITM attacks.

4   TagDroid

To correctly authenticate a server, there are three aspects to meet:

– guarantee all the certificates to be accepted are for the right server from a trusted source. This security can be provided by the framework, either the Android framework or the web/application framework when implementing correctly.
– constrain the trusted source to a definite set, which will assure the truststore is not contaminated.
– able to tell whether it is from the server or a malicious MITM attacker when a self-signed certificate or a private CA issued certificate is received.

Out of these three reasons, we propose our TagDroid, which aims to protect all apps involving secure communication from MITM attacks. In this section, we will take an overview of TagDroid, and elaborate on the two modules which respectively take care of validating certificates against the norm truststore correctly and keeping everything going when exceptions happen.

4.1   Overview

TagDroid takes care of the secure communication traffics in and out of the system, and its first module, named ValMod, validates the received certificate against local truststore by checking (1) whether it is issued for the right server the app want to talk to and (2) it is issued by a trusted source.

The first check is completed by using the standard API that Android framework supplies, while the norm truststore is what we constructed by comparing all the certificates included in different versions of Android and different ROMs widely used. The second module comes into effect when the received certificate fails to pass ValMod. This can happen considering that we have constrained the truststore and there are servers using self-signed certificate. We consult to social network friends for help at this point by asking what the certificate is from their perspectives, and this procedure is called PeerVerify. The high level overview of TagDroid is shown in Fig. 2.

4.2   ValMod

The main task for ValMod is to perform a strict certificate validation against the norm truststore for each received certificate.

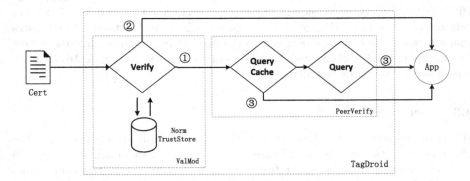

Fig. 2. Architecture of TagDroid. All certificates received are passed through TagDroid first. (1) Cert fails to pass the ValMod validation against norm truststore, so it is passed to PeerVerify for further verification. (2) Cert succeeds to pass ValMod so that it is directly send to apps. (3) If Cert fails to pass PeerVerify, it is discarded and the corresponding app is alerted; Otherwise, it is directly send to apps.

Table 1. The number of certificates in official and third-party ROMs.

Version	2.3.5	2.3.7	3.2.4	4.0.3	4.0.4	4.1.2	4.2.2	4.3.1	4.4.2
Official	128	127	132	134	134	139	140	146	150
HTC	128	128	-	164	170	139	-	-	150
SONY	127	105	-	137	134	142	-	-	150

To decide which root CA certificate to be included in the norm truststore, we conduct an analysis of truststores from different versions of official [2] and third-party ROMs. The result is shown in Table 1.

For official ROMs, we can see that the number increases as version evolves. Each change has some certificates removed and others added [3]. It is worth to mention that from 2.3.5 to 2.3.7, the certificate removed is DigiNotar, who confirmed to have a security breach in March, 2011, which resulted in the fraudulent issuing of certificates. For third-party ROMs, HTC 2.3.7 did not remove DigiNotar. This ROM has been downloaded 270,000 times by far and this data is only from one website. While in version 4.0.3 and 4.0.4, HTC added lots of certificates. On the other hand, SONY added its own certificates in 4.0.3 and 4.1.2, and removed 23 certificate in 2.3.7.

We have no idea why these certificates are added or removed. But this is persuasive to make clear that third-party ROMs can add or remove certificates as they want. This condition makes it necessary for us to define a norm truststore when we enforce our own validation. What's more, the update of ROM poses a problem on lots of devices. With old version ROM installed, passing the certificate verification against system truststore is not enough to guarantee secure connection.

Therefore, we define the norm truststore as all the certificates included in the official ROM of newest version (for now, it is version 4.4.2), and ValMod takes care of correctly validating certificate against this norm truststore. Certificates that succeed to pass the validation is guaranteed to be genuine, while those fails to pass are not definitely forged since there are servers using certificates that are self-signed or issued by untrusted CA.

4.3   PeerVerify

When certificates are not trusted by ValMod, there still are chances that the client receives the genuine certificates. So we need extra information to help confirm these certificates and refuse malicious certificates at the same time. We consult to social network friends by sending them the website address and asking which certificates they receive. If most of the responses contain the very certificate that we receive, we can make the positive decision. Otherwise, we believe the certifiate we receive is not trustworthy. We assume friends will report honestly and communications among friends are secured by the social network application, for example Gtalk. We turn to social network friends for help out of the following reasons: (1) on mobile platform, friends are much more likely to be online and the online status can be stable for a long time. (2) instead of consulting a dedicated server, we believe seeking help from friends can defeat denial of service attacks. Besides, in terms of privacy, we observe that a dedicated server could raise a large number of requests ("bigdata") which may be used to dig deeper information, while the number of requests sent to each friend are quite small since the scheme described below can make the requests evenly distributed on average.

PeerVerify can flexibly handle how many friends to ask and whom to ask. The workflow consists of three phases: *initialization, chained querying* and *feedback analysis*. To make things clear, we define some terms here. A *session* indicates the whole process which starts from the time when a user makes a query and ends at the time when the user gets corresponding responses. A user who starts a session is called an *initiator*, and we call each involved friend as a *peer*. During initialization phase, the initiator picks a number called *expectation* to indicate how many friends it wants to consult. And the message that peer sends back contains a value called *reputation* indicating the confidence of the result.

An example shown in Fig. 3 shows how PeerVerify works. In the initialization phase, initiator picks expectation 10, chooses 3 peers with the assigned expectation 4, 4 and 2 respectively and sends the request message. In the chained querying phase, those chosen peers who receive the message do the same thing as if they are an initiator who picks 3, 3 and 1. A peer who receives request with expectation 1 does not query his friends and just sends the result back. When peers receive response message, they make some analysis and send upward until the real initiator gets the response, and this is the feedback phase.

We give further details in the rest of this part.

Initialization. The main task of initialization is to decide how many peers to ask and whom to ask. Then sends the request message containing a url and *expectation* n to chosen peers. Geographically distant peers are chosen with high priority and are assigned with larger expectation, which could largely avoid peers being in the same attack area and thus providing useless information. The choice of n relies on the number of online friends, the network distance, the quality of the network connection etc. And users can impact on the choice of n by setting security option to different levels, with each level standing for a value range within which n is picked.

Chained Querying. The basic chained query idea is to recursively pass down the query from one to another. For a peer who are assigned the expectation of n_b, he expects aids from $n_b - 1$ peers in total, so he split $n_b - 1$ into $n_{b1} + n_{b2} + \cdots + n_{bi} + \cdots + n_{bx}$, in which x indicates the number of peers he chooses and n_{bi} indicates the expectation assigned to each peer.

Feedback Analysis. After the recursive query procedures, peers send back the feedbacks according to the query message they've received. By collecting and comparing the received feedbacks, peer starts a **reputation calculation**

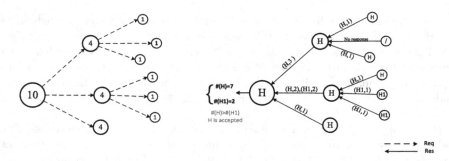

Fig. 3. An example that illustrates how PeerVerify works. (Left) Chained querying phase that recursively pass down the expectation. (Right) Feedback analysis phase that peers collect and process responses, and initiator correspondingly makes decision.

process. For example, initiator Alice receives the responses from peer Bob (set $\{(H_1, r_{b1}), (H_2, r_{b2})\}$) and Charlie ($set\{(H_1, r_{c1})\}$), and Alice herself gets the hash H_1. H stands for the certificate hash and r stands for the reputation. Alice calculates the set union $set\{(H_1, r_{b1}), (H_2, r_{b2})\} \cup set\{(H_1, r_{c1})\} \cup set\{(H_1, 1)\} = set\{(H_1, r_{b1} + r_{c1} + 1), (H_2, r_{b2})\}$. If she is initiator, she compares the value of $r_{b1} + r_{c1} + 1$ with r_{b2} to decide accept H_1 or H_2. If not, she just sends the calculated set upwards.

In all, after PeerVerify, initiator can get a certificate hash H that trusted by most peers. If the hash of the certificate that initiator receives equals H, TagDroid will accept the certificate. Otherwise, it considers the certificate as malicious and terminates the connection.

5   Evaluation

We implemented a TAGDROID prototype on Android platform, and its Peer-Verify module piggybacks on the popular IM application Google Talk. Smack, an Open Source XMPP (Jabber) client library [4], is used to build the customized Google Talk client. The customized client also records how many query it has launched, to evaluate the performance of ValMod's norm truststore.

We built a *virtual social network* environment which simulates the chained querying and feedback, to evaluate the time latency and communication overhead brought by PeerVerify. This environment is set up by creating a $Watts-Strogatz$ [14] small world graph in Python, which is generated with parameter (N, k, p), meaning N nodes forming a ring and each node connects with its k nearest neighbors. For each edge u-v, it has a probability of p to be replaced with a new edge u-w, and w is randomly chosen from the existing nodes. Each node stands for a single user, and the edge connecting node (u, v) stands for the friend relationship. Each node is assigned the ability to divide expectation in a way that, for a initiator who has f *long-distance peers* and chooses expectation n, it randomly divides n into x parts with x randomly chosen from $[1, f]$. Then it distributes these x parts to x long-distance peers. For a node with ordinal i, long-distance peers are defined as nodes with ordinal j that $|i - j| > k/2$.

5.1 Effectiveness

Since untrusted CA issued certificates will definitely fail to pass ValMod, these questionable certificates are all sent to PeerVerify. We conduct our experiment with TagDroid installed on SamSung Note 3 under an attack environment that replaces all the certificates with ones that issued by an untrusted CA. When TagDroid does not take effect, apps that are vulnerable to self-signed attack accept the forged certificate and others will reject since they validate certificates against system truststore. When having the untrusted CA installed in system, only a few reject the forged certificates because of pinning. While with TagDroid taking effect, these forged certificates are all rejected.

5.2 Performance

Communication Overhead. All the extra communications are brought by PeerVerify. And the total communication overhead increases proportionally with the expectation n chosen by the initiator. The payload $S_{payload}$ generated by a complete query session can be approximately calculated as $S_{payload} = n * S^{ij}_{payload}$. $S^{ij}_{payload}$ stands for the payload generated by a *smallest session* that peer j helps peer i validate the certificate with peer j asking no more peer for help. $S^{ij}_{payload}$ contains two part: the Google Talk traffic that generated by communication of peer i and j, and the SSL traffic that j generated when communicating with the server to get the certificate. By running the TagDroid client installed on two devices that connect to the same monitored hotspot, we can capture the whole traffic. By adding these traffic up, $S^{ij}_{payload}$ amounts to about 8470 bytes. This data may vary since the length of content field in query and response message is different for different URL and expectation n.

Latency. The time period of a complete and successful PeerVerify session is regarded as the latency in our evaluation. It begins from the initiator sends out the query, and ends in that the trust decision has been made. The *latency* of a complete session can be calculated by the longest hops h and latency $latency_{ij}$ generated by a smallest session with $latency = h * latency_{ij}$. By conducting a smallest session on TagDroid client, we can see the $latency_{ij}$ is about 1s. Therefore, *latency* varies with h. h is related with expectation n and the decision of each peer about how to divide and distribute n. To get a general idea of h, we conduct an experiment in simulation environment. The results show that, given network size, h is related with *expectation* n and the number of friends k in the list. With the increasing of expectation, the latency (max hops h) increases as well. However, the larger k is, the slower latency increases, and when k is large enough($k > 20$) and expectation is less than 30, latency will not decrease with growing k. Besides, peer only waits for response for a limited time t, so the total time will not be larger than $h * t$.

6   Related Work

The existing approaches to enhancing CA-based certificate authentication can be classified into two categories, either by relying on existing architectures such as DNS or PGP, or by introducing notary [1,12,15] to provide reference information. But they all have their limitations. For DNS based approach, widely deployment is challenging. Others have issues such as limited number of notaries, requiring server cooperation, etc. For proposals that aim to fix implementation issues in Android applications, they either provide developers with easy-to-use APIs [9], or reference extra information provided by a specific server [7]. The former scheme requires system modification, which may have deployment issue. The latter consults to a fixed server, making the security of the whole scheme rely on the security of a specific server, and having only one entity to reference may fail to provide enough information to help user make the right decision. For approaches to dealing with certificate verification problems in general, [13] proposes a social P2P notary network, which uses advanced techniques (such as secret sharing, ring signatures and distributed hash table) to tackle privacy, availability and scalability issues. But this scheme is too much to apply on Android platform, since most Android applications only talk to a few specialized server.

7   Conclusion

Due to the lack of proper certificate verification and untrusted CAs installed in system truststore, some Android applications that use SSL protocol to secure the communication are vulnerable to the MITM attacks. TagDroid is proposed to tackle this problem. It is a hybrid verification system combining correct certificate validation against a norm truststore with a collaborative way that relies on the social friends to help notarize questioned certificates. TagDroid is capable of detecting illegitimate certificates which defeats MITM attack to a large extent. We implement a prototype called TagDroid and easily install it on the genuine Android system. It does not require any modification on the system, and just has little effect on system performance such that users can barely notice its existence. To define the norm truststore, we carry out a thorough analysis of ROMs both from official and third party. To evaluate the performance impact of TagDroid as a network system, TagDroid is deployed on a Samsung Note 3 and a simulation is carried out in a large scaled social network with 10,000 peers. The performance analysis results show that TagDroid brings low latency and communication overhead.

References

1. Perspectives project. http://perspectives-project.org/
2. Android source. https://android.googlesource.com/platform/libcore/
3. Android Source Diff. https://android.googlesource.com/platform/libcore/log/android-2.3.4_r0.9/luni/src/main/files/cacerts

4. Smack api. http://www.igniterealtime.org/projects/smack/
5. Akhawe, D., Amann, B., Vallentin, M., Sommer, R.: Here's my cert, so trust me, maybe? Understanding TLS errors on the web. In: Proceedings of the 22nd International Conference on World Wide Web, International World Wide Web Conferences Steering Committee, pp. 59–70 (2013)
6. Chen, K., Shen, H., Sapra, K., Liu, G.: A social network integrated reputation system for cooperative P2P file sharing. In: 2013 22nd International Conference on Computer Communications and Networks (ICCCN), pp. 1–7. IEEE (2013)
7. Conti, M., Dragoni, N., Gottardo, S.: MITHYS: mind the hand you shake - protecting mobile devices from SSL usage vulnerabilities. In: Accorsi, R., Ranise, S. (eds.) STM 2013. LNCS, vol. 8203, pp. 65–81. Springer, Heidelberg (2013)
8. Fahl, S., Harbach, M., Muders, T., Smith, M., Baumgärtner, L., Freisleben, B.: Why eve and mallory love android: an analysis of android SSL (in) security. In: Proceedings of the 2012 ACM Conference on Computer and Communications Security, pp. 50–61. ACM (2012)
9. Fahl, S., Harbach, M., Perl, H., Koetter, M., Smith, M.: Rethinking SSL development in an appified world. In: Proceedings of the 2013 ACM SIGSAC Conference on Computer and Communications Security, pp. 49–60. ACM (2013)
10. Kamvar, S.D., Schlosser, M.T., Garcia-Molina, H.: The eigentrust algorithm for reputation management in P2P networks. In Proceedings of the 12th International Conference on World Wide Web, pp. 640–651. ACM (2003)
11. Langley: Public key pinning. https://www.imperialviolet.org/2011/05/04/pinning.html
12. Marlinspike, M.: Convergence. http://convergence.io/index.html
13. Micheloni, A., Fuchs, K.-P., Herrmann, D., Federrath, H.: Laribus: privacy-preserving detection of fake SSL certificates with a social P2P notary network. In: 2013 Eighth International Conference on Availability, Reliability and Security (ARES), pp. 1–10. IEEE (2013)
14. Watts, D.J., Strogatz, S.H.: Collective dynamics of networks. Nature **393**(6684), 440–442 (1998)
15. Wendlandt, D., Andersen, D.G., Perrig, A.: Perspectives: improving SSH-style host authentication with multi-path probing. In: USENIX Annual Technical Conference, pp. 321–334 (2008)

A Guess-Then-Algebraic Attack on LFSR-Based Stream Ciphers with Nonlinear Filter

Xiao Zhong[1,2]($\boxtimes$), Mingsheng Wang[3], Bin Zhang[1,4], and Shengbao Wu[1,2]

[1] Trusted Computing and Information Assurance Laboratory, Institute of Software, Chinese Academy of Sciences, Beijing, China
zhongxiao456@163.com,
{zhangbin,wushengbao}@tca.iscas.ac.cn
[2] Graduate School of Chinese Academy of Sciences, Beijing, China
[3] State Key Laboratory of Information Security, Institute of Information Engineering, Chinese Academy of Sciences, Beijing, China
mingsheng_wang@aliyun.com
[4] State Key Laboratory of Computer Science, Institute of Software, Chinese Academy of Sciences, Beijing, China

Abstract. This paper introduces a new parameter called 1-st minimum algebraic immunity $AI_{min}(f)$, along with some theoretical properties of $AI_{min}(f)$. Based on our results, we propose a guess-then-algebraic attack on LFSR-based stream ciphers with nonlinear filter Boolean function f. Our method takes some particular guessing strategy by taking advantage of the properties of $AI_{min}(f)$, and makes full use of each guessed bit to generate as many equations of degree $AI_{min}(f)$ as possible. The cost of time and data is less than that of the traditional algebraic attack under some condition. Our attack suggests that $AI_{min}(f)$ should not be too small, which is a new design criterion for the filter Boolean function f. We apply our method to a 80-stage keystream generator with a MAI Boolean function f as its filter, while $AI_{min}(f)$ is very small, which disobeys our criterion. The time and data complexities of the traditional algebraic attack are $O(2^{73.56})$ and $O(2^{24.52})$ respectively, with a memory cost of $O(2^{49})$. The time and data complexity of our method are $O(2^{56.86})$ and $O(2^{5.36})$ respectively, and the memory cost is $O(2^{10.72})$.

Keywords: Algebraic attack · Algebraic immunity · Guess-then-algebraic attack · LFSR-based stream ciphers · 1-st minimum algebraic immunity

1 Introduction

The research of the LFSR-based stream ciphers with nonlinear filter generators or combination generators has spawned many analytical methods and theoretical research. A most important cryptanalytic tool is algebraic attack.

Courtois, N.T. and Meier, W. proposed algebraic attack on stream ciphers with linear feedback in 2003 [3], which is a classical and efficient analytical method towards LFSR-based stream ciphers. The basic idea of the algebraic attack is divided into three steps:

© Springer International Publishing Switzerland 2015
L.C.K. Hui et al. (Eds.): ICICS 2014, LNCS 8958, pp. 132–142, 2015.
DOI: 10.1007/978-3-319-21966-0_10

Step 1: Construct a nonlinear equation system $\mathcal{A}$ with the secret key bits or initial vector values as its variables by using the keystream bits.

Step 2: Multiply a nonzero function g of low degree to each equation of the system, resulted to an equation system $\mathcal{B}$ with degree lower than that of $\mathcal{A}$.

Step 3: Solve the equation system $\mathcal{B}$.

Since algebraic attack was proposed, there have emerged many research issues related to it. Scholars try to explore the properties of the nonzero function g in Step 2, resulting to the research areas of algebraic immunity and annihilators for the Boolean functions [1, 2, 4, 6, 8, 10, 12, 13, 15, 16]. Denote $AN(f) = \{g \in B_n | f \cdot g = 0\}$. Any function $g \in AN(f)$ is called an annihilator of f. The algebraic immunity of f, named $AI(f)$, is the minimum algebraic degree of nonzero annihilators of f or $f + 1$ [11], which measures the ability of the Boolean functions against algebraic attack. The maximum algebraic immunity for n-variable Boolean functions is $\lceil \frac{n}{2} \rceil$ [3], and a Boolean function with maximum algebraic immunity is called MAI Boolean function.

In this paper, for a Boolean function $f \in B_n$ (where B_n is the n-variable Boolean ring), we introduce a parameter called 1-st minimum algebraic immunity $AI_{min}(f)$. We prove that when $AI(f)$ is optimum, $AI_{min}(f) \leq AI(f)$, particularly, when n is odd, $AI_{min}(f) < AI(f)$. A simple algorithm is given to compute $AI_{min}(f)$.

When the filter of a LFSR-based stream cipher is a MAI Boolean function f, it can resist the algebraic attack to the greatest extent. Based on our theoretical results related to $AI_{min}(f)$, we propose a guess-then-algebraic attack on such kind of LFSR-based stream ciphers. The strategy of guessing is very important in the guess and determine attack. Our method takes some particular guessing strategy by taking advantage of the properties of $AI_{min}(f)$. First, we guess some initial state bits, the locations of which are determined by the specific structure of the LFSR and the properties of $AI_{min}(f)$. After guessing enough LFSR state bits, we derive equations of degree $AI_{min}(f)$ as many as possible by taking advantage of the specific structure of the LFSR and the filter taps, and then we solve the resulted equation system.

Our method has three special merits. (a) It makes full use of each guessed bit to derive equations of degree $AI_{min}(f)$ as many as possible. In fact, $AI_{min}(f)$ is strictly less than $AI(f)$ in most cases. (b) It utilizes not only the properties of f but also the tap positions, which helps to derive as much information as possible. The cost of time and data is less than that of the traditional algebraic attack given in [3] under some condition. (c) Our attack suggests that $AI_{min}(f)$ should not be too small, which is a new design criterion for the filter Boolean function f.

Moreover, we apply our method on a 80-stage keystream generator. Its filter generator is a 9-variable MAI Boolean function f, while $AI_{min}(f)$ is very small, which disobeys our design criterion. This model can resist the traditional algebraic attack given in [3] to the greatest extent. The time and data complexities of the traditional algebraic attack are $O(2^{73.56})$ and $O(2^{24.52})$ respectively, with a memory cost of $O(2^{49})$. While the time and data complexity of our method are $O(2^{56.86})$ and $O(2^{5.36})$ respectively, and the memory cost is $O(2^{10.72})$.

Notice that Debraize, B. and Goubin, L. proposed a guess-and-determine algebraic attack on the self-shrinking generator (SSG) with low Hamming weight feedback polynomial in [7]. It mainly aims to analyze the self-shrinking generators, while our method targets to the LFSR-based stream ciphers with filter Boolean functions of optimum algebraic immunity. They guess some information first, then write a system of polynomial equations and solve the system with SAT solver algorithm MiniSAT. While our method pays attention to the locations of the guessed bits by taking advantage of the theoretical properties of $AI_{min}(f)$, which is a new parameter in the academic sector of the stream cipher. Moreover, the degree of the equations derived after guessing some state bits is $AI_{min}(f)$, which is the most different character between our method and the guess-and-determine algebraic attack proposed in [7].

This paper is organized as follows: Sect. 2 introduces some basic knowledge related to our work. In Sect. 3, we introduce a new parameter called 1-st minimum algebraic immunity $AI_{min}(f)$, along with some theoretical analysis. We also give a simple algorithm to compute $AI_{min}(f)$. In Sect. 4, for LFSR-based keystream generators with nonlinear filter Boolean function, we propose a guess-then-algebraic attack by taking advantage of $AI_{min}(f)$ and give some design criterion of the LFSR-based keystream generators. In Sect. 5, we apply our method to a keystream generator which does not obey our criterion. Section 6 concludes this paper.

2   Preliminaries

Courtois, N.T. and Meier, W. proposed the algebraic attack on stream ciphers with linear feedback [3]. They mainly focused on the LFSR-based keystream generators with nonlinear filter Boolean function. Figure 1 shows the general model.

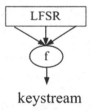

keystream

Fig. 1. LFSR-based keystream generator with nonlinear filter

First, we give a brief description for this model. Let the length of the linear feedback shift register be l. L is the "connection function" of the LFSR, and it is linear. Let the initial state of the LFSR be $s^0 = (s_0, s_1, ..., s_{l-1})$, then it generates a m-sequence $s_0, s_1, s_2....$ For sake of narrative convenience, we call this m-sequence as LFSR sequence. The state of the LFSR at time t is

$$s^t = (s_t, s_{t+1}, ..., s_{t+l-1}) = L^t(s_0, s_1, ..., s_{l-1}),$$

Table 1. Complexity of AA for the model in Fig. 1

Data	Memory	Complexity
$O(M)$	$O(M^2)$	$O(M^\omega)$

which is filtered by a balanced nonlinear Boolean function $f \in B_n$. The generator outputs one bit c_t at time t. For each c_t, we can construct an equation involving some key bits and initial value as its variables. Denote the output of the filter generator by $c_0, c_1, c_2, ...$, where $c_i \in F_2$, then we can get the following equation system:

$$\begin{cases} c_0 = f \quad (s_0, s_1, ..., s_{l-1}) \\ c_1 = f(L\,(s_0, s_1, ..., s_{l-1})) \\ c_2 = f(L^2(s_0, s_1, ..., s_{l-1})) \\ \vdots \end{cases} \qquad (1)$$

The problem of recovering the l initial state bits of the LFSR is reduced to solving the equation system (1).

Table 1 shows the complexity of the traditional algebraic attack (AA) in [3] on the model given in Fig. 1, where $M = \binom{l}{AI(f)}$, and ω is the parameter of the Gaussian elimination and in theory $\omega \leq 2.376$ [5].

While as the authors of [3] declare, the (neglected) constant factor in that algorithm is expected to be very big and they regard Strassen's algorithm [14] as the fastest practical algorithm. Then they evaluate the complexity of the Gaussian reduction to be $7 \cdot M^{log_2^7}/64$ CPU clocks. For convenience, scholars usually use $\omega = 3$ in Table 1 to estimate the time and data complexity of the traditional algebraic attack.

We can get that the complexity of the traditional algebraic attack on the model given in Fig. 1 is determined by l and $AI(f)$. When using the traditional algebraic attack given in [3], for each keystream bit, the lowest degree of equations that the analysts can obtain is $AI(f)$. In the next section, we try to find a way to see if we can decrease the time and data complexity by further exploring the properties of the nonlinear filter function and the structure of the filter tap positions.

3   1-st Minimum Algebraic Immunity $AI_{min}(f)$

In this section, for a Boolean function $f \in B_n$, we give a new definition called 1-st minimum algebraic immunity $AI_{min}(f)$. To begin with, we give the following definition.

Definition 1. *Given a Boolean function* $f(x_1, x_2, ..., x_n) \in B_n$, *for some fixed* i, $i \in [1, n]$, *define*

$$AI(f|_{x_i=0}) = AI(f(x_1, x_2, ..., x_{i-1}, 0, x_{i+1}, ..., x_n)).$$

$$AI(f|_{x_i=1}) = AI(f(x_1, x_2, ..., x_{i-1}, 1, x_{i+1}, ..., x_n)).$$

Definition 2. *Given a Boolean function* $f(x_1, x_2, ..., x_n) \in B_n$, *for some fixed* i, $i \in [1, n]$, *define*

$$AI_i(f) = max\{AI(f|_{x_i=0}), AI(f|_{x_i=1})\}.$$

Definition 3. *For a Boolean function* $f(x_1, x_2, ..., x_n) \in B_n$, *define the 1-st minimum algebraic immunity of* f *as*

$$AI_{min}(f) = min\{AI_i(f) : i \in [1, n]\}.$$

Also define

$$N_{AI_{min}}(f) = \sharp\{i | AI_i(f) = AI_{min}(f) : i \in [1, n]\},$$

where "$\sharp$" denote the number of the elements in a set.
Let $G = \{g \in AN(f|_{x_i=c}) | deg(g) = AI_{min}(f)\}$, *and also denote* $n_{i,c} = \sharp G$, *where* $c \in \{0, 1\}$.

Based on the above definitions, we derive Theorem 1:

Theorem 1. *For a Boolean function* $f(x_1, x_2, ..., x_n) \in B_n$, *if its algebraic immunity is optimum, then*

$$AI_{min}(f) \leq AI(f).$$

Particularly, if n *is odd, then*

$$AI_{min}(f) < AI(f).$$

Proof. Given $f(x_1, x_2, ..., x_n) \in B_n$, it can be expressed as:

$$f(x_1, x_2, ..., x_n) = x_i f_1(x_1, ..., x_{i-1}, x_{i+1}, ..., x_n) + f_2(x_1, ..., x_{i-1}, x_{i+1}, ..., x_n).$$

When x_i is fixed, there are only $n - 1$ variables left, then from Definitions 1–3, we can get that

$$AI_{min}(f) \leq AI_i(f) \leq \lceil \frac{n-1}{2} \rceil \leq AI(f).$$

Particularly, if n is odd, then

$$AI_{min}(f) \leq AI_i(f) \leq \lceil \frac{n-1}{2} \rceil < \lceil \frac{n}{2} \rceil = AI(f).$$

The following example verifies Theorem 1.

Example 1. The Boolean function $f = x_1x_2x_3x_5 + x_1x_2x_5 + x_1x_2 + x_1x_3x_4x_5 + x_1x_3x_4 + x_1x_3x_5 + x_1x_4x_5 + x_1x_4 + x_2x_3 + x_2x_4x_5 + x_2x_5 + x_3x_4 + x_4x_5 + 1$ is a 5-variable Carlet-Feng Boolean function. We can get that $AI(f) = 3$, which is optimum. The $AI_i(f), i \in [1, 5]$ of f are listed in Table 2.

We can see that $AI_{min}(f) = AI_i(f) = 2 < AI(f) = 3$, $N_{AI_{min}}(f) = 5 > 1$.

In fact, for a Boolean function $h \in B_n$, although $AI(h)$ is not maximum, it is possible that $AI_{min}(h)$ is strictly less than $AI(h)$. For instance, for the filter function f_d adopted by the stream cipher LILI-128 [9], $AI_{min}(f_d) = 3 < AI(f_d) = 4$, $N_{AI_{min}}(f_d) = 4$.

Table 2. Compute the $AI_i(f)$ of f

x_i	x_1	x_2	x_3	x_4	x_5
$AI_i(f)$	2	2	2	2	2

Algorithm 1 shows how to compute $AI_{min}(f)$ and $N_{AI_{min}}(f)$ for a Boolean function f.

Algorithm 1. Compute $AI_{min}(f)$ and $N_{AI_{min}}(f)$

Input: $I = \{1, 2, ..., n\}$, Boolean function $f \in B_n$.
Set $F = \emptyset$, $E = \emptyset$, $c \in \{0, 1\}$.
for $i \in I$ **do**
 Compute all the $AI_i(f)$ defined in Definition 2 and the corresponding $n_{i,c}$
 defined in Definition 3;
 if $AI_i(f) \leq AI(f)$ **then**
  $F = F \cup \{(x_i, AI_i(f), n_{i,0}, n_{i,1})\}$;

Denote the minimum $AI_i(f)$ in F as $AI_{min}(f)$;
$E = E \cup \{(x_i, AI_i(f), n_{i,0}, n_{i,1}) \in D | AI_i(f) = AI_{min}(f), i \in I\}$;
$N_{AI_{min}}(f) = \sharp E$;
Output E, $N_{AI_{min}}(f)$.

---

4   A Guess-Then-Algebraic Attack on LFSR-Based Stream Ciphers via Our Theoretical Results

Designers often choose a MAI Boolean function as the filter of the LFSR-based keystream generators, which helps to resist the traditional algebraic attack to the greatest extent. Section 3 shows that for a Boolean function f of optimum algebraic immunity, $AI_{min}(f) \leq AI(f)$. Even if $AI(f)$ is not maximum, it is possible that $AI_{min}(f) < AI(f)$. We consider to take advantage of the properties of $AI_{min}(f)$ to recover the initial state of the LFSR.

The strategy of guessing is very important in the guess and determine attack. In this section, we would like to give a guess-then-algebraic attack, which takes some particular guessing strategy by taking advantage of the properties of $AI_{min}(f)$ proposed in Sect. 4. First we choose to guess some (initial) internal state bits of the LFSR, resulted to equations of degree $AI_{min}(f)$. Here we make use of each guessed bit to the greatest extent, that is, we would use each guessed bit to construct as many low-degree equations as possible. The positions of the guessed internal state bits of the LFSR should obey some rules according to the detailed structure of the LFSR, the properties of the filter Boolean function, and the filter tap positions. After guessing a suitable number of (initial) internal state bits, we can get an equation system of degree $AI_{min}(f)$.

In the following, we propose an attack by using our theoretical results in Sect. 3. We focus on the LFSR-based keystream generator with nonlinear filter shown in Fig. 1. With the same description in Sect. 2, we target to recover the initial state bits $s^0 = (s_0, s_1, ..., s_{l-1})$ by solving the following equation system:

$$\begin{cases} c_0 = f(s_0^1, s_0^2, ..., s_0^n) \\ c_1 = f(s_1^1, s_1^2, ..., s_1^n) \\ c_2 = f(s_2^1, s_2^2, ..., s_2^n) \\ \vdots \end{cases} \tag{2}$$

where $s_t^i, i = 1, 2, ..., n$ are the n LFSR state bits tapped as the input of the filter Boolean function $f(x_1, x_2, ..., x_n)$ at time t.

Guess-then-algebraic Attack:
Assume that the LFSR shifts right and it is regularly clocked.
Step I: For $f(x_1, x_2, ..., x_n) \in B_n$, compute $AI_{min}(f)$, E and $N_{AI_{min}}(f)$ via Algorithm 1. Suppose we get $E = \{(x_{i_1}, AI_{min}(f), n_{i_1,0}, n_{i_1,1}), ..., (x_{i_m}, AI_{min}(f),$ $n_{i_m,0}, n_{i_m,1}) : 1 \leq i_1 < i_2 < \cdots < i_m \leq n\}$, $N_{AI_{min}}(f) = m$, $AI_{min}(f) = k$.
Step II: With the parameters derived from Step I, we do the following operation:
  (1) At time t, denote the inputs of the filter function as $s_t^1, ..., s_t^n$, find the LFSR state bit corresponding to x_{i_1} in set E, and denote it as $s_t^{i_1}$.
  (2) Guess $s_t^{i_1} = a$, where $a \in \{0, 1\}$, then we can derive an equation

$$f_t(s_t^1, s_t^2, ..., s_t^{i_1-1}, a, s_t^{i_1+1}, ..., s_t^n) = c_t.$$

From Algorithm 1 we get that $AI(f_t) = AI_{min}(f) = k$.
  (3) For each clock, denote the distance of the locations for the LFSR state bits corresponding to the variables x_i and x_j of f as $d_{i,j}$.
  Notice that $E = \{(x_{i_1}, AI_{min}(f), n_{i_1,0}, n_{i_1,1}), ..., (x_{i_m}, AI_{min}(f), n_{i_m,0}, n_{i_m,1}) :$ $1 \leq i_1 < i_2 < \cdots < i_m \leq n\}$, then we clock the stream cipher d_{i_1,i_2} clocks from time t. Find the LFSR state bit corresponding to x_{i_2} in the set E at time $t+d_{i_1,i_2}$, and denote it as $s_{t+d_{i_1,i_2}}^{i_2}$. With the keystream bit $c_{t+d_{i_1,i_2}}$ and the guessed value of $s_t^{i_1} = a$, we get another equation at time $t + d_{i_1,i_2}$ by substitute $s_{t+d_{i_1,i_2}}^{i_2}$ by a.

$$f_{t+d_{i_1,i_2}}(s_{t+d_{i_1,i_2}}^1, s_{t+d_{i_1,i_2}}^2, ..., s_{t+d_{i_1,i_2}}^{i_2-1}, a, s_{t+d_{i_1,i_2}}^{i_2+1}, ..., s_t^n) = c_{t+d_{i_1,i_2}}.$$

In the same way, we can get a group of m equations, and the algebraic immunity of the functions $f_t, f_{t+d_{i_1,i_2}}, ..., f_{t+d_{i_1,i_m}}$ is $AI_{min}(f) = k$.

$$\begin{cases} f_t(s_t^1, ..., s_t^{i_1-1}, a, s_t^{i_1+1}, ..., s_t^n) = c_t \\ f_{t+d_{i_1,i_2}}(s_{t+d_{i_1,i_2}}^1, ..., s_{t+d_{i_1,i_2}}^{i_2-1}, a, s_{t+d_{i_1,i_2}}^{i_2+1}, ..., s_{t+d_{i_1,i_2}}^n) = c_{t+d_{i_1,i_2}} \\ \vdots \\ f_{t+d_{i_1,i_m}}(s_{t+d_{i_1,i_m}}^1, ..., s_{t+d_{i_1,i_m}}^{i_m-1}, a, s_{t+d_{i_1,i_m}}^{i_m+1}, ..., s_{t+d_{i_1,i_m}}^n) = c_{t+d_{i_1,i_m}} \end{cases} \tag{3}$$

Until now, we get m equations by guessing one LFSR state bit. For each equation, we can derive $n_{i_j,c_{t+d_{i_j,i_k}}}$ (or $n_{i_j,c_{t+d_{i_j,i_k}}}+1$ when $c_{t+d_{i_j,i_k}} = 0$) equations of degree $AI_{min}(f)$, where $n_{i_j,c_{t+d_{i_j,i_k}}}$ is the number of annihilators defined in

Definition 3. We guess another LFSR state bit which is appropriately chosen, and get another group of equations, and so on.

We hope that the guessed bits are all the initial state bits of the LFSR, which can make the analysis much easier. If the guessed bits are not all the initial state bits, more careful analysis is needed.

Usually, we choose the parameter $t = 0$, for it can make the number of the guessed initial bits among all the guessed LFSR state bits as large as possible, which can make the analysis much easier.

Here we analyze the situation that the guessed bits are all the initial state bits of the LFSR. Suppose we guess r initial LFSR state bits, then we can get $r \cdot \sum_{1 \leq j < k \leq m} n_{i_j, c_{t+d_{i_j}, i_k}}$ equations with the initial LFSR state bits as the variables by using the linear feedback recursion of the LFSR. Then we use the same method to analyze the complexity with the method mentioned in [3].

After guessing r LFSR initial state bits, we reduce the problem of solving the l initial LFSR state bits with a filter Boolean function f of algebraic immunity $AI(f)$ to solving $l - r$ unknown initial bits with a filter Boolean function of algebraic immunity $AI_{min}(f)$.

When the condition

$$r \cdot \sum_{1 \leq j < k \leq m} n_{i_j, c_{t+d_{i_j}, i_k}} \geq \binom{l - r}{AI_{min}(f)} \tag{4}$$

is satisfied, the time complexity to solve the equation system derived from Step II is

$$T_1 = N^\omega,$$

where $N = \binom{l-r}{AI_{min}(f)}$, and ω is the parameter of the Gaussian elimination, and we adopt $\omega = 3$ in this paper. The complexity to recover the initial state of the LFSR is

$$T = 2^r N^\omega.$$

The data that we need is

$$D = max(rm, \binom{l - r}{AI_{min}(f)}).$$

The key condition is that the inequality (4) is satisfied. In fact, when $AI_{min}(f)$ is small enough (especially when $AI_{min}(f) = 1$), the condition can be satisfied in most cases. Under this situation, we can directly see that the data complexity is better than that of the algebraic attack in [3]. While the improvement of the time complexity is not determined. It can be derived that the time complexity of our attack is less than that of the conventional algebraic attack given in [3] when r satisfies the following inequality:

$$\frac{r}{w} < log_2 \binom{l}{d} - log_2 \binom{l - r}{k}, \tag{5}$$

where r is the number of the guessed initial state bits, $d = AI(f)$, $k = AI_{min}(f)$, and ω is the parameter of the Gaussian elimination.

In fact, the number of the equations that can be derived by guessing r-bit initial state can be more than $r \cdot \sum_{1 \leq j < k \leq m} n_{i_j, c_{t+d_{i_j}, i_k}}$ if we can make full use of the annihilators for $f|_{x_i=c}$. Let $G = \{g \in AN(f|_{x_i=c}) | deg(g) = AI_{min}(f)\}$, for an element $g \in G$, multiply monomials of degree less than $AI_{min}(f)$ to g, and we may get new polynomials that can be used to construct equations.

Our method suggests a new design criterion for the filter Boolean function f adopted by the LFSR-based stream ciphers, that is, the parameters of the keystream generator should not satisfy the inequality (4) and inequality (5) in the same time, which means that designers should pay attention that their keystream generator should satisfy that:

(a)$AI_{min}(f)$ should be large enough to resist our guess-then-algebraic attack.
(b)The number of variables corresponding to $AI_{min}(f)$ should not be too large.

Notice that our method can be applied to all kinds of LFSR-based stream ciphers with nonlinear filter. If the target stream cipher satisfies the inequalities (4) and (5), then we can decrease the time and data complexity.

5   Application of Our Method on a LFSR-Based Stream Cipher Overlooking Our Criterion

In this section, we would like to give an example to show that the $AI_{min}(f)$ should not be too small for the nonlinear filter Boolean function.

The target model is the same with the one shown in Fig. 1. The length of the LFSR is 80, and its initial state bits are $(s_0, s_1, ..., s_{79})$. The linear feedback polynomial is primitive. The filter Boolean function is a 9-variable Boolean function $f = f(x_1, x_2, ..., x_9)$, $AI(f)$ is optimum. Suppose the LFSR shifts left and it is regularly clocked. The 9 inputs to f are taken from LFSR according to this full positive difference set: (0,1,3,7,12,20,30,44,65).

From the above description we can get that this model can resist the traditional algebraic attack given in [3] to the greatest extent. In the following, we would show that although $AI(f)$ is optimum, our method works if the model disobeys our criterion mentioned in Sect. 4.

Suppose $AI_{min}(f) = 1$, and the corresponding variable is x_7, that is, $AI(f|_{x_7=0}) = AI(f|_{x_7=1}) = 1$, which means that this model disobeys our criterion.

According to the guess-then-algebraic attack given in Sect. 4, we can guess $r = 41$ initial state bits $(s_{38}, s_{31}, ..., s_{79})$. Then we can get at least 41 linear equations, which satisfy the inequality (4), that is $r \geq \binom{80-r}{AI_{min}(f)} = 39$. The time complexity of our attack is

$$T = 2^r \binom{80-r}{1}^\omega = 2^{56.86},$$

where m is the number of variables for f corresponding to $AI_{min}(f)$. The data complexity is

$$D = max(r, \binom{80-r}{1}) = 2^{5.36}.$$

The memory complexity is
$$M = 2^{10.72}.$$

Table 3 shows the comparison between our method (GA) and the traditional attack (AA) given in [3] on this model.

Table 3. Comparison between GA and AA in [3]

	T	D	M
Our method	$O(2^{56.86})$	$O(2^{5.36})$	$O(2^{10.72})$
Algebraic attack	$O(2^{73.56})$	$O(2^{24.52})$	$O(2^{49})$

Remark 1. This example verifies that although the target model obsesses a filter Boolean function of optimum algebraic immunity, if it disobeys our criterion, analysts can still use our guess-then-algebraic attack to recover the initial state with time and data complexities less than that of the traditional algebraic attack given in [3].

6 Conclusion

This paper introduces a new parameter called 1-st minimum algebraic immunity $AI_{min}(f)$ for the Boolean function f, along with some theoretical properties of $AI_{min}(f)$. Based on our results, we propose a guess-then-algebraic attack on the LFSR-based stream cipher with nonlinear filter Boolean function f by guessing some state bits in advance and then applying algebraic attack on it. Our method makes full use of each guessed bit to generate as many equations of degree less than or equal to $AI(f)$ as possible. The cost of time and data is less than that of the traditional algebraic attack in [3] under some condition. Our method suggests a new design criterion for the LFSR-based keystream generators with nonlinear filter. We apply our method to a 80-stage keystream generator with a MAI Boolean function f as its filter, while $AI_{min}(f)$ is very small, which disobeys our criterion. The time, memory and data complexities of our method are less than that of the traditional algebraic attack.

Acknowledgements. We are grateful to the anonymous reviewers for their valuable comments on this paper. This work was supported by the National Basic Research Program of China (Grant No. 2013CB834203, Grant No. 2013CB338002) and the National Natural Science Foundation of China (Grant No. 61379142, Grant No. 11171323, Grant No. 60833008, Grant No. 60603018, Grant No. 61173134, Grant No. 91118006, Grant No. 61272476), the Strategic Priority Research Program of the Chinese Academy of Sciences (Grant No. XDA06010701).

References

1. Armknecht, F., Carlet, C., Gaborit, P., Künzli, S., Meier, W., Ruatta, O.: Efficient computation of algebraic immunity for algebraic and fast algebraic attacks. In: Vaudenay, S. (ed.) EUROCRYPT 2006. LNCS, vol. 4004, pp. 147–164. Springer, Heidelberg (2006)
2. Carlet, C., Feng, K.: An infinite class of balanced functions with optimal algebraic immunity, good immunity to fast algebraic attacks and good nonlinearity. In: Pieprzyk, J. (ed.) ASIACRYPT 2008. LNCS, vol. 5350, pp. 425–440. Springer, Heidelberg (2008)
3. Courtois, N.T., Meier, W.: Algebraic attacks on stream ciphers with linear feedback. In: Biham, E. (ed.) EUROCRYPT 2003. LNCS, vol. 2656, pp. 345–359. Springer, Heidelberg (2003)
4. Carlet, C., Zeng, X.Y., Li, C.L., Hu, L.: Further properties of several classes of Boolean functions with optimum algebraic immunity. Des. Codes Crypt. (DCC) 52(3), 303–338 (2009)
5. Coppersmith, D., Winograd, S.: Matrix multiplication via arithmetic progressions. J. Symb. Comput. 9, 251–280 (1990)
6. Tang, D., Carlet, C., Tang, X.H.: Highly nonlinear boolean functions with optimal algebraic immunity and good behavior against fast algebraic attacks. IEEE Trans. Inf. Theor. (TIT) 59(1), 653–664 (2013)
7. Debraize, B., Goubin, L.: Guess-and-determine algebraic attack on the self-shrinking generator. In: Nyberg, K. (ed.) FSE 2008. LNCS, vol. 5086, pp. 235–252. Springer, Heidelberg (2008)
8. Dalai, D.K., Maitra, S., Sarkar, S.: Basic theory in construction of Boolean functions with maximum possible annihilator immunity. Des. Codes Crypt. 40(1), 41–58 (2006)
9. Dawson, E., Golić, J.D., Millan, W., Simpson, L.: The LILI-II keystream generator. In: Batten, L., Seberry, J. (eds.) ACISP 2002. LNCS, vol. 2384, pp. 25–39. Springer, Heidelberg (2002)
10. Limniotis, K., Kolokotronis, N., Kalouptsidis, N.: Secondary constructions of Boolean functions with maximum algebraic immunity. Crypt. Commun. (CCDS) 5(3), 179–199 (2013)
11. Meier, W., Pasalic, E., Carlet, C.: Algebraic attacks and decomposition of Boolean functions. In: Cachin, C., Camenisch, J.L. (eds.) EUROCRYPT 2004. LNCS, vol. 3027, pp. 474–491. Springer, Heidelberg (2004)
12. Peng, J., Wu, Q.S., Kan, H.B.: On symmetric Boolean functions with high algebraic immunity on even number of variables. IEEE Trans. Inf. Theor. 57(10), 7205–7220 (2011)
13. Rizomiliotis, P.: On the security of the Feng-Liao-Yang Boolean functions with optimal algebraic immunity against fast algebraic attacks. Des. Codes Crypt. (DCC) 57(3), 283–292 (2010)
14. Strassen, V.: Gaussian elimination is not optimal. Numer. Math. 13, 354–356 (1969)
15. Zeng, X., Carlet, C., Shan, J., Hu, L.: More balanced Boolean functions with optimal algebraic immunity and good nonlinearity and resistance to fast algebraic attacks. IEEE Trans. Inf. Theor. 57(9), 6310–6320 (2011)
16. Chen, Y.D., Lu, P.Z.: Two classes of symmetric Boolean functions with optimum algebraic immunity: construction and analysis. IEEE Trans. Inf. Theor. 57(4), 2522–2538 (2011)

A Private Lookup Protocol with Low Online Complexity for Secure Multiparty Computation

Peeter Laud[(⊠)]

Cybernetica AS, Tartu, Estonia
peeter.laud@cyber.ee

Abstract. We present a secure multiparty computation (SMC) protocol for obliviously reading an element of an array, achieving constant *online* communication complexity. While the total complexity of the protocol is linear in the size of the array, the bulk of it is pushed into the offline precomputation phase, which is independent of the array and the index of the element.

Although private lookup is less general than oblivious RAM (ORAM), it allows us to give new and/or more efficient SMC protocols for a number of important computational tasks. In this paper, we present protocols for executing deterministic finite automata (DFA), and for finding shortest distances in sparse graphs.

All our protocols are given in the arithmetic black box model, which allows them to be freely composed and used in larger applications.

Keywords: Secure multiparty computation · Arithmetic black box · Private lookup

1 Introduction

In Secure Multiparty Computation (SMC), p parties compute $(y_1, \ldots, y_p) = f(x_1, \ldots, x_p)$, with the party P_i providing the input x_i and learning no more than the output y_i. For any functionality f, there exists a SMC protocol for it [19,36]. While the general construction is inefficient in practice, several SMC frameworks have appeared [3,6,12,21,29] and certain classes of algorithms can be executed with reasonable efficiency on top of them. In particular, these algorithms should have control flow and data access patterns that depend only or mostly on public data.

Private information retrieval (PIR) and oblivious RAM (ORAM) are among techniques for hiding the patterns of data access. They both posit a client-server setting, where the client queries the elements in server's memory without the server learning which elements are accessed. For a n-element vector, the asymptotic complexity of both PIR (which allows only reading) and ORAM techniques (which also allow writing) is $\tilde{O}(\log^2 n)$. To adapt these techniques to the SMC setting, at least the client's computations have to be performed through SMC protocols. This brings further complications.

© Springer International Publishing Switzerland 2015
L.C.K. Hui et al. (Eds.): ICICS 2014, LNCS 8958, pp. 143–157, 2015.
DOI: 10.1007/978-3-319-21966-0_11

We provide an alternative mechanism for reading an element of a vector according to a private index (private writing is not considered in this paper). We give a private lookup protocol, the operations of which can be partitioned into the offline part — these that can be done without knowing the actual inputs —, and the online part — these that require the inputs. In case of private lookup, it makes sense to consider even three phases — offline, vector-only (where the actual vector, either public or private, is available) and online (where the private index is also available). In our protocols, the online phase requires only a constant number of costly SMC operations, while the bulk of the work is done in the offline and, depending on the protocol and the secrecy of the vector elements, in the vector-only phases. In cases where the main cost of SMC operations is communication between parties, the offline (and vector-only) computations could be performed using dedicated high-bandwidth high-latency channels.

Our private lookup protocols are universally composable, they may be freely used as components in protocols for more complex privacy-preserving applications. In this paper we demonstrate their use in two applications that need oblivious read access to data, but where the pattern for write accesses is public. We have implemented SMC protocols for executing deterministic finite automata (DFA), and for finding the single-source shortest distances (SSSD) in sparse graphs. The latter protocol is based on the well-known Bellman-Ford algorithm. In both protocols, the processed objects (automaton, input string, the graph) are private, except for their sizes.

Our protocols inherit the security guarantees of the underlying SMC implementation. If the SMC implementation provides security against passive resp. also active adversaries, then so do our protocols. If the security provided by the SMC implementation is information-theoretical resp. only computational, then this also applies to our protocols. Perhaps surprisingly, the protocols in this paper are the first *information-theoretically* secure protocols for DFA execution, if an information-theoretically secure protocol set for SMC is used. All previous protocols have used cryptographic constructions (encryption) that rely on computational hardness assumptions for security.

Structure of the Paper. We review work related to privacy-preserving data access, and to our example applications in Sect. 2. In Sect. 3 we describe the framework in which our protocols are defined and their security and performance properties stated. Sect. 4 presents the private lookup and discusses its security and performance. In Sects. 5 and 6 we describe our implementations of privacy-preserving DFA execution and SSSD, and discuss their performance. Finally, we draw the conclusions in Sect. 7.

2   Related Work

Secure multiparty computation (SMC) protocol sets can be based on a variety of different techniques, including garbled circuits [36], secret sharing [4,17,32] or homomorphic encryption [9]. A highly suitable abstraction of SMC is the universally composable Arithmetic Black Box (ABB) [14], the use of which allows very simple security proofs for higher-level SMC applications. Using the ABB to derive efficient privacy-preserving implementations for various computational tasks is an ongoing field of research [1,8,11,27], also containing this paper.

Conceptually, our protocols are most similar to private information retrieval (PIR) [24], for which there exist protocols with $O(\log^2 n)$ communication and $O(n/\log n)$ public-key operations [26]. We know of no attempts to implement these techniques on top of SMC, though.

Oblivious RAM (ORAM) [20] is a more versatile technique with similar communication complexity [33] (but higher round complexity and client's memory requirements). The integration of ORAM with SMC has been studied [13,18,22,28]. In general, such systems require at least $O(\log^3 n)$ overhead for oblivious data access. We also note that the "trivial" way of expanding the private index into its characteristic vector and computing its scalar product with the array brings $O(n)$ overhead, but may be more efficient in practice due to smaller constants hidden in the O-notation [22,25].

In this paper, we present protocols for DFA execution, and for SSSD in sparse graphs. In [15,30], garbled circuits have been adapted for DFA execution, where one party knows the DFA and the other one the input string. This approach, which is not universally composable, works well if the automaton and alphabet are small (but the input string may be long). In [2,16,34,35], DFA execution protocols based on homomorphic encryption are given, some of them resembling PIR protocols. Privacy-preserving graph algorithms have been studied in [5] in a non-composable manner. Composable SSSD protocols for dense graphs have been studied in [1]. Recently, ORAM-with-SMC techniques have been used to implement Dijkstra's algorithm for sparse graphs [22].

3 Preliminaries

Universal composability (UC) [7] is a framework for stating security properties of systems. It considers an ideal functionality $\mathcal{F}$ and its implementation π with identical interfaces to the intended users. The latter is *at least as secure as* the former, if for any attacker $\mathcal{A}$ there exists an attacker $\mathcal{A}_S$, such that $\pi\|\mathcal{A}$ and $\mathcal{F}\|\mathcal{A}_S$ are indistinguishable to any potential user of $\pi/\mathcal{F}$. The value of the framework lies in the composability theorem: if π is at least secure as $\mathcal{F}$, then ξ^π is at least as secure as $\xi^\mathcal{F}$ for any system ξ that uses $\pi/\mathcal{F}$. We say that such ξ is implemented *in the $\mathcal{F}$-hybrid model*. When arguing about the security of such ξ, we may assume that it uses the ideal functionality $\mathcal{F}$ as a subroutine. All derived conclusions will be valid also for ξ^π.

The *arithmetic black box* is an ideal functionality $\mathcal{F}_{\mathsf{ABB}}$. It allows its users (a fixed number p of parties) to securely store and retrieve values, and to perform computations with them. When a party sends the command store(v) to $\mathcal{F}_{\mathsf{ABB}}$, where v is some value, the functionality assigns a new *handle* h (sequentially taken integers) to it by storing the pair (h,v) and sending h to all parties. If a sufficient number (depending on implementation details) of parties send the command retrieve(h) to $\mathcal{F}_{\mathsf{ABB}}$, it looks up (h,v) among the stored pairs and responds with v to all parties. When a sufficient number of parties send the command compute($op; h_1, \ldots, h_k; params$) to $\mathcal{F}_{\mathsf{ABB}}$, it looks up the values $v_1, \ldots, v_k$ corresponding to the handles $h_1, \ldots, h_k$, performs the operation op (parametrized with $params$) on them, stores the result v together with a new handle h, and sends h to all parties. In this way, the parties can perform computations without revealing anything about the intermediate values or results, unless a sufficiently large coalition wants a value to be revealed.

The existing implementations of ABB are protocol sets π_{ABB} based on either secret sharing [3,6,12] or threshold homomorphic encryption [14,21]. Depending on the implementation, the ABB offers protection against a honest-but-curious, or a malicious party, or a number of parties (up to a certain limit). E.g. the implementation of the ABB by SHAREMIND [3] consists of three parties, providing protection against one honest-but-curious party.

In this paper, the protocols are given and their security (and correctness) argued in the $\mathcal{F}_{\mathsf{ABB}}$-hybrid model. The arguments remain valid if $\mathcal{F}_{\mathsf{ABB}}$ is replaced with a secure implementation π_{ABB}.

Typically, the ABB performs computations with values v from some ring $\mathbb{R}$. The set of operations definitely includes addition/subtraction, multiplication of a stored value with a public value (this operation motivates the $params$ in the compute-command), and multiplication. Even though all algorithms can be expressed using just these operations, most ABB implementations provide more operations (as primitive protocols) for greater efficiency of the implementations of algorithms on top of the ABB. In all ABB implementations, addition, and multiplication with a public value occur negligible costs; hence they're not counted when analyzing the complexity of protocols using the ABB. Other operations may require a variable amount of communication (in one or several rounds) between parties, and/or expensive computation. The ABB can execute several operations in parallel; the *round complexity* of a protocol is the number of communication rounds all operations of the protocol require, when parallelized as much as possible.

It is common to use $[\![v]\!]$ to denote the value v stored in the ABB. The notation $[\![v_1]\!]$ op $[\![v_2]\!]$ denotes the computation of v_1 op v_2 by the ABB (translated to a protocol in the implementation π_{ABB}).

In the next section, we give a protocol for private lookup. Formally, we are presenting a secure implementation for the functionality $\mathcal{F}_{\mathsf{ABB+LU}}$ that accepts the same commands as $\mathcal{F}_{\mathsf{ABB}}$, answering them in the same manner. Additionally, it accepts the command lookup($h_1, \ldots, h_n, h_{\mathsf{idx}}$). When a sufficient number of parties has sent such command to $\mathcal{F}_{\mathsf{ABB+LU}}$, it looks up the value v_{idx} corresponding to h_{idx} and the value v' corresponding to $h_{v_{\mathsf{idx}}}$. It stores v' together with a new handle h' and sends h' to all parties.

The implementation $\pi_{\mathsf{ABB+LU}}$ is given in the $\mathcal{F}_{\mathsf{ABB}}$-hybrid model. It simply invokes $\mathcal{F}_{\mathsf{ABB}}$ for all $\mathcal{F}_{\mathsf{ABB}}$ commands. The implementation of the lookup-command is given below.

Algorithm 1. Private look-up protocol

Data: Vector of indices $i_1, \ldots, i_m \in \mathbb{F}\backslash\{0\}$
Data: Vector of values $(\llbracket v_{i_1} \rrbracket, \ldots, \llbracket v_{i_m} \rrbracket)$ with $v_{i_1}, \ldots, v_{i_m} \in \mathbb{F}$.
Data: Index $\llbracket j \rrbracket$ to be looked up, with $j \in \{i_1, \ldots, i_m\}$.
Result: The looked up value $\llbracket w \rrbracket = \llbracket v_j \rrbracket$.
Offline phase

1 $(\llbracket r \rrbracket, \llbracket r^{-1} \rrbracket) \xleftarrow{\$} \mathbb{F}^*$
2 **for** $k = 2$ **to** $m - 1$ **do** $\llbracket r^j \rrbracket \leftarrow \llbracket r \rrbracket \cdot \llbracket r^{j-1} \rrbracket$;
3 Compute the coefficients $\lambda_{j,k}^{\mathbf{I}}$ from $i_1, \ldots, i_m$.
  Vector-only phase
4 **foreach** $k \in \{0, \ldots, m-1\}$ **do** $\llbracket c_k \rrbracket \leftarrow \sum_{l=1}^{m} \lambda_{k,l}^{\mathbf{I}} \llbracket v_l \rrbracket$;
5 **foreach** $k \in \{0, \ldots, m-1\}$ **do** $\llbracket y_k \rrbracket \leftarrow \llbracket c_k \rrbracket \cdot \llbracket r^k \rrbracket$;
  Online phase
6 $z \leftarrow \mathsf{retrieve}(\llbracket j \rrbracket \cdot \llbracket r^{-1} \rrbracket)$
7 $\llbracket w \rrbracket = \sum_{k=0}^{m-1} z^k \llbracket y_k \rrbracket$

---

4   Protocol for Private Lookup

Our protocol, depicted in Algorithm 1, takes the handles to elements $v_{i_1}, \ldots, v_{i_m}$ (with arbitrary non-zero, mutually different indices) and the handle to the index j stored inside the ABB, and returns a handle to the element v_j. It represents the elements as a polynomial V over a suitable field $\mathbb{F}$, satisfying $V(i_j) = v_{i_j}$ for all $j \in \{1, \ldots, m\}$ (with $i_1, \ldots, i_m$ also belonging to $\mathbb{F}$). The lookup then amounts to the evaluation of the polynomial in a point. Similar ideas have appeared in [35] (for DFAs). We will then combine these ideas with a method to move offline most of the computations for the polynomial evaluation [27]. Both the idea and the method have been slightly improved and expanded in this paper.

Let our ABB work with the values from the field $\mathbb{F}$, where $|\mathbb{F}| \geq m + 1$. There exist protocols for generating a uniformly random element of $\mathbb{F}$ inside the ABB (denote: $\llbracket r \rrbracket \xleftarrow{\$} \mathbb{F}$), and for generating a uniformly random non-zero element of $\mathbb{F}$ together with its inverse (denote: $(\llbracket r \rrbracket, \llbracket r^{-1} \rrbracket) \xleftarrow{\$} \mathbb{F}^*$). These protocols require a small constant number of multiplications on average for any ABB [11].

There exist Lagrange interpolation coefficients $\lambda_{j,k}^{\mathbf{I}}$ depending only on the set $\mathbf{I} = \{i_1, \ldots, i_m\}$, such that $V(x) = \sum_{j=0}^{m-1} c_j x^j$, where $c_j = \sum_{k=1}^{m} \lambda_{j,k}^{\mathbf{I}} v_{i_k}$. These coefficients are public and computed in the offline phase of Algorithm 1.

Correctness. The definition of c_k gives $\sum_{k=0}^{m-1} c_k l^k = v_l$ for all $l \in \{i_1, \ldots, j_m\}$. We can now verify that $w = \sum_{k=0}^{m-1} y_k z^k = \sum_{k=0}^{m-1} c_k r^k j^k r^{-k} = v_j$.

Security and Privacy. To discuss the security properties of a protocol in the $\mathcal{F}_{\mathsf{ABB}}$-hybrid model, we only have to consider which extra information the adversary may be able to obtain from the retrieve-commands, and how it can affect the run of the protocol through the values it store-s (the latter is significant only if the adversary is active). There are no store-commands in Algorithm 1.

The results of the retrieve-commands are uniformly randomly distributed elements of $\mathbb{F}^*$, independent of everything else the adversary sees. These can be simulated without any access to $v_{i_1}, \ldots, v_{i_m}$ and j. Hence Algorithm 1 is secure and private against the same kinds of adversaries that the used implementation π_{ABB} of $\mathcal{F}_{\text{ABB}}$ can tolerate.

Complexity. In the offline stage, we perform $m - 2$ multiplications. We also generate one random invertible element together with its inverse, this generation costs the same as a couple of multiplications [11]. The round complexity of this computation, as presented in Algorithm 1 is also $O(m)$, which would be bad for online computations. For offline computations, the acceptability of such round complexity mainly depends on the latency of the used communication channels. The offline phase could be performed in $O(1)$ rounds [11] at the cost of increasing the number of multiplications a couple of times. In the vector-only phase, the computation of the values $[\![c_k]\!]$ is free, while the computation of the values $[\![y_k]\!]$ requires $m - 1$ multiplications (the computation of $[\![y_0]\!]$ is free). All these multiplications can be performed in parallel. If the vector v were public then the computation of $[\![y_k]\!]$ would have been free, too. The only costly operations in the online phase is a single multiplication and a single retrieve-operation; these have similar complexities in existing ABB implementations.

4.1   Speeding Up the Offline Phase

The preceding complexity analysis is valid for any implementation of the ABB. Some implementations contain additional efficient operations that speed up certain phases of Algorithm 1. If we use the additive secret sharing based implementation, as used in SHAREMIND [4], and a binary field $\mathbb{F}$, then we can bring down the complexity of the offline phase to $O(\sqrt{m})$ as shown in the following.

The SHAREMIND ABB is realized by three parties, offering protection against passive attacks by one of the parties. The ABB stores elements of some ring $\mathbb{R}$; a value $v \in \mathbb{R}$ is represented by π_{ABB} as $[\![v]\!] = ([\![v]\!]_1, [\![v]\!]_2, [\![v]\!]_3) \in \mathbb{R}^3$ satisfying $[\![v]\!]_1 + [\![v]\!]_2 + [\![v]\!]_3 = v$, where the *share* $[\![v]\!]_i$ is kept by the i-th party P_i. Messages depending on these shares are sent among the parties, hence it is important to rerandomize $[\![v]\!]$ before each use. The *resharing* protocol [4, Algorithm 1] (repeated here as Algorithm 2; all indices of the parties are *modulo* 3) is used for this rerandomization. We note that in this algorithm, the generation and distribution of random elements can take place offline. Even better, only random seeds can be distributed ahead of the computation and new elements of $\mathbb{R}$ generated from them as needed. Hence we consider the resharing protocol to involve only local operations and have the cost 0 in our complexity analysis.

If the ring $\mathbb{R}$ is a binary field $\mathbb{F}$, then the additive sharing is actually bit-wise secret sharing: $[\![v]\!] = [\![v]\!]_1 \oplus [\![v]\!]_2 \oplus [\![v]\!]_3$, where $\oplus$ denotes bit-wise exclusive or. For such sharings, the usual arithmetic operations with shared values in $\mathbb{Z}_{2^n}$ are more costly, compared to additive sharings over $\mathbb{Z}_{2^n}$, but equality checks and comparisons are cheaper [4]. As most operations with array indices are expected to be comparisons, bit-wise secret sharing may be a good choice for them.

Algorithm 2. Resharing protocol $[\![w]\!] \leftarrow \mathsf{Reshare}([\![u]\!])$ in SHAREMIND [4]

Data: Value $[\![u]\!]$
Result: Value $[\![w]\!]$ such that $w = u$ and the components of $[\![w]\!]$ are independent of everything else
Party P_i generates $r_i \stackrel{\$}{\leftarrow} \mathbb{R}$, sends it to party P_{i+1}
Party P_i computes $[\![w]\!]_i \leftarrow [\![u]\!]_i + r_i - r_{i-1}$

Algorithm 3. Multiplication protocol in the ABB of SHAREMIND [4]

Data: Values $[\![u]\!]$ and $[\![v]\!]$
Result: Value $[\![w]\!]$, such that $w = uv$
1 $[\![u']\!] \leftarrow \mathsf{Reshare}([\![u]\!])$
2 Party P_i sends $[\![u']\!]_i$ to party P_{i+1}
3 $[\![v']\!] \leftarrow \mathsf{Reshare}([\![v]\!])$
4 Party P_i sends $[\![v']\!]_i$ to party P_{i+1}
5 Party P_i computes $[\![w']\!]_i \leftarrow [\![u']\!]_i \cdot [\![v']\!]_i + [\![u']\!]_i \cdot [\![v']\!]_{i-1} + [\![u']\!]_{i-1} \cdot [\![v']\!]_i$
6 $[\![w]\!] \leftarrow \mathsf{Reshare}([\![w']\!])$

SHAREMIND's multiplication protocol [4, Algorithm 2] (repeated as Algorithm 3) is based on the equality $([\![u]\!]_1 + [\![u]\!]_2 + [\![u]\!]_3)([\![v]\!]_1 + [\![v]\!]_2 + [\![v]\!]_3) = \sum_{i,j=1}^{3} [\![u]\!]_i [\![v]\!]_j$. After the party P_i has sent $[\![u]\!]_i$ and $[\![v]\!]_i$ to party P_{i+1} (here and subsequently, all party indices are *modulo* 3), each of these nine components of the sum can be computed by one of the parties. The multiplication protocol is secure against one honest-but-curious party [4, Theorem 2]. Indeed, as the sending of $[\![u]\!]_i$ from P_i to P_{i+1} takes place after resharing $[\![u]\!]$, the value $[\![u]\!]_i$ is a uniformly random number independent of all other values P_{i+1} sees. Hence the simulator for P_{i+1}'s view could itself generate this value. The same consideration also underlies the security proof of the specialized offline phase protocol given in Algorithm 4, the properties of which we discuss below.

Privacy. We have to show that the view of a single party P_i can be simulated without access to the shares held by other parties. Party P_i receives messages only in lines 4 and 9 of Algorithm 4. In both cases, it receives a share of a freshly reshared value. Hence this message can be simulated by a uniformly random number, as discussed above.

Complexity. We consider local computation and resharings to be free, hence we have to count the number of messages sent by the parties. It is easy to see that a party sends at most $\sqrt{m+1}$ elements of the field $\mathbb{F}$ in lines 4 and 9 of Algorithm 4. This is also the round complexity of Algorithm 4. But by tracking the data dependencies in the first loop, we see that its iterations no. $2^{k-1}, \ldots, 2^k - 1$ could be done in parallel for each $k \in \{1, \ldots, q-1\}$. Hence Algorithm 4 could be executed in $O(\log m)$ rounds.

Correctness. We can use Algorithm 4 only if $\mathbb{F}$ is a binary field. In this case squaring a shared value $[\![u]\!]$ is a local operation: $([\![u]\!]_1 + [\![u]\!]_2 + [\![u]\!]_3)^2 = [\![u]\!]_1^2 +$

Algorithm 4. Computing $(\llbracket v^2 \rrbracket, \ldots, \llbracket v^m \rrbracket)$ from $\llbracket v \rrbracket$ in SHAREMIND

Data: $m \in \mathbb{N}$ and the value $\llbracket v \rrbracket$, where $v \in \mathbb{F}$, char $\mathbb{F} = 2$
Result: Values $\llbracket u_0 \rrbracket, \ldots, \llbracket u_m \rrbracket$, where $u_j = v^j$

1 $q \leftarrow \lceil \log \sqrt{m+1} \rceil$
2 $\llbracket u_0 \rrbracket \leftarrow (1, 0, 0)$
3 $\llbracket u_1 \rrbracket \leftarrow \mathsf{Reshare}(\llbracket v \rrbracket)$
4 Party P_i sends $\llbracket u_1 \rrbracket_i$ to party P_{i+1}
5 **for** $j = 1$ **to** $2^{q-1} - 1$ **do**
6 $\quad$ P_i computes $\llbracket u_{2j} \rrbracket_i \leftarrow \llbracket u_j \rrbracket_i^2$ and $\llbracket u_{2j} \rrbracket_{i-1} \leftarrow \llbracket u_j \rrbracket_{i-1}^2$
7 $\quad$ P_i computes $\llbracket t \rrbracket_i \leftarrow \llbracket u_j \rrbracket_i \cdot \llbracket u_{j+1} \rrbracket_i + \llbracket u_j \rrbracket_i \cdot \llbracket u_{j+1} \rrbracket_{i-1} + \llbracket u_j \rrbracket_{i-1} \cdot \llbracket u_{j+1} \rrbracket_i$
8 $\quad$ $\llbracket u_{2j+1} \rrbracket \leftarrow \mathsf{Reshare}(\llbracket t \rrbracket)$
9 $\quad$ Party P_i sends $\llbracket u_{2j+1} \rrbracket_i$ to party P_{i+1}
10 **foreach** $j \in \{2^q, \ldots, m\}$ **do**
11 $\quad$ Let $(r, s) \in \{0, \ldots, 2^q - 1\}$, such that $2^q r + s = j$
12 $\quad$ Party P_i computes $\llbracket t \rrbracket_i \leftarrow \llbracket u_r \rrbracket_i^{2^q} \cdot \llbracket u_s \rrbracket_i + \llbracket u_r \rrbracket_i^{2^q} \cdot \llbracket u_s \rrbracket_{i-1} + \llbracket u_r \rrbracket_{i-1}^{2^q} \cdot \llbracket u_s \rrbracket_i$
13 $\quad$ $\llbracket u_j \rrbracket \leftarrow \mathsf{Reshare}(\llbracket t_j \rrbracket)$

$\llbracket u \rrbracket_2^2 + \llbracket u \rrbracket_3^2$ and the computation of $\llbracket u^2 \rrbracket_i = \llbracket u \rrbracket_i^2$ only requires the knowledge of $\llbracket u \rrbracket_i$. Regarding Algorithm 4, note that its first loop satisfies the invariant that in the beginning of each iteration, each party P_i knows the values $\llbracket v^0 \rrbracket_i, \ldots, \llbracket v^{2j-1} \rrbracket_i$ and also $\llbracket v^0 \rrbracket_{i-1}, \ldots, \llbracket v^{2j-1} \rrbracket_{i-1}$. With these values, it can compute $\llbracket v^{2j} \rrbracket_i$ and $\llbracket v^{2j+1} \rrbracket_i$ (effectively, we are computing $v^{2j} = (v^j)^2$ and $v^{2j+1} = v^j \cdot v^{j+1}$). Party P_i can also compute $\llbracket v^{2j} \rrbracket_{i-1}$. It receives $\llbracket v^{2j+1} \rrbracket_{i-1}$ from P_{i-1}. In the second loop, we compute $v^j = (v^r)^{2^q} \cdot v^s$ for $j = 2^q \cdot r + s$. Again, $\llbracket (v^r)^{2^q} \rrbracket_i$ is locally computed from $\llbracket v^r \rrbracket_i$ by squaring it q times.

4.2 Speeding Up the Vector-Only Phase

A different kind of optimization is available if the ABB implementation is based on Shamir's secret sharing [32], using Gennaro et al.'s multiplication protocol [17] (examples are VIFF [12] and SEPIA [6]). Such ABB impelementations (for p parties), secure against t parties can be given if $2t + 1 \leq p$ (for passive security) or $3t + 1 \leq p$ (for active security). In such implementation, a value $v \in \mathbb{F}$ for a field $\mathbb{F}$ of size at least $p + 1$ is stored in the ABB as $\llbracket v \rrbracket = (\llbracket v \rrbracket_1, \ldots, \llbracket v \rrbracket_p)$, such that there exists a polynomial f over $\mathbb{F}$ with degree at most t and satisfying $f(0) = v$ and $f(c_i) = v_i$ for all $i \in \{1, \ldots, p\}$, where $\mathbf{C} = \{c_1, \ldots, c_p\}$ is a set of mutually different, public, fixed, nonzero elements of $\mathbb{F}$. The *share* v_i is kept by the i-th party P_i.

Our optimization relies on the computation of a scalar product $\llbracket \sum_{i=1}^{k} u_i v_i \rrbracket$ from the values $\llbracket u_1 \rrbracket, \ldots, \llbracket u_k \rrbracket$ and $\llbracket v_1 \rrbracket, \ldots \llbracket v_k \rrbracket$ stored inside the ABB having the same cost as performing a single multiplication of stored values. For reference, Algorithm 5 presents the scalar product protocol in the SSS-based ABB providing passive security (thus $2t + 1 \leq p$) [17]. The multiplication protocol can be obtained from it simply by letting the length of the vectors to be 1.

Algorithm 5. Scalar product protocol in an SSS-based ABB [17]

Data: Vectors $(\llbracket u_1 \rrbracket, \ldots, \llbracket u_n \rrbracket)$ and $(\llbracket v_1 \rrbracket, \ldots, \llbracket v_n \rrbracket)$
Result: Value $\llbracket w \rrbracket$, such that $w = \sum_{j=1}^{n} u_j v_j$
Party P_i computes $d_i \leftarrow \sum_{j=1}^{n} \llbracket u_j \rrbracket_i \llbracket v_j \rrbracket_i$
Party P_i picks a random polynomial f_i of degree at most t, such that $f_i(0) = d_i$.
Party P_i sends $f_i(c_j)$ to P_j
Party P_i computes $\llbracket w \rrbracket_i \leftarrow \sum_{j=1}^{p} \lambda_j^C f_j(c_i)$.

Algorithm 6. Improved vector-only and online phases of the private lookup protocol

---

Data: Lagrange interpolation coefficients $\lambda_{j,k}^I$
Data: Random non-zero $\llbracket r \rrbracket$ and its powers $\llbracket r^{-1} \rrbracket, \llbracket r^2 \rrbracket, \ldots, \llbracket r^{m-1} \rrbracket$.
Data: Vector of values $(\llbracket v_{i_1} \rrbracket, \ldots, \llbracket v_{i_m} \rrbracket)$ with $v_{i_1}, \ldots, v_{i_m} \in \mathbb{F}$.
Data: Index $\llbracket j \rrbracket$ to be looked up, with $j \in \{i_1, \ldots, i_m\}$.
Result: The looked up value $\llbracket w \rrbracket = \llbracket v_j \rrbracket$.
Vector-only phase
1 **foreach** $k \in \{0, \ldots, m-1\}$ **do** $\llbracket c_k \rrbracket \leftarrow \sum_{l=1}^{m} \lambda_{k,l}^I \llbracket v_l \rrbracket$;
Online phase
2 $z \leftarrow \mathsf{retrieve}(\llbracket j \rrbracket \cdot \llbracket r^{-1} \rrbracket)$
3 **foreach** $j \in \{0, \ldots, m-1\}$ **do** $\llbracket \zeta_j \rrbracket \leftarrow z^j \llbracket r^j \rrbracket$;
4 $\llbracket w \rrbracket = (\llbracket c_0 \rrbracket, \ldots, \llbracket c_{m-1} \rrbracket) \cdot (\llbracket \zeta_0 \rrbracket, \ldots, \llbracket \zeta_{m-1} \rrbracket)$

In this protocol, the values λ_i^C are the Lagrange interpolation coefficients satisfying $f(0) = \sum_{i=1}^{p} \lambda_i^C f(c_i)$ for any polynomial f over $\mathbb{F}$ of degree at most $2t$. The protocols providing active security are much more complex [10], but similarly have equal costs for multiplication and scalar product.

Our optimization consists of a reordering of the operations of the vector-only and online phases of the private lookup protocol, as depicted in Algorithm 6. We see that compared to Algorithm 1, we have moved the entire computation of the products $z^j \llbracket c_j \rrbracket \llbracket r^j \rrbracket$ to the online phase, thereby reducing the vector-only phase to the computation of certain linear combinations. The online phase becomes more complex, but only

Table 1. Communication costs (in elements of $\mathbb{F}$) of different private lookup protocols

Sharing	offline	vec-only	online
additive	$3\sqrt{m}$	$6m$	12
(public v)	$3\sqrt{m}$	0	12
Shamir's	$6m$	0	15
(public v)	$6m$	0	9

by a single scalar product, which costs the same as a single multiplication. The correctness and privacy arguments for Algorithm 6 are the same as for Algorithm 1.

Unfortunately, we cannot use the optimizations of both Sects. 4.1 and 4.2 at the same time, as the cost of converting from one representation to the other would cancel any efficiency gains. If we have three parties and seek passive security against one of them, then our choices are given in Table 1. Recall that multiplication in both representations and retrieval in the additive representation requires the communication of 6 field elements in total. Retrieval in Shamir's secret sharing based representation requires 3 field elements to be sent.

5   Protocol for DFA Execution

A DFA is a tuple $A = (Q, \Sigma, \delta, q_0, F)$, where Q is a set of states, Σ is the alphabet (a set of characters), $q_0 \in Q$ is the initial state, $F \subseteq Q$ is the set of final states and $\delta : Q \times \Sigma \to Q$ is the transition function. To *execute* a string $w = w_1 \cdots w_\ell \in \Sigma^*$ on A means to find the states $q_1, \ldots, q_\ell$, such that $q_i = \delta(q_{i-1}, w_i)$ for all $i \in \{1, \ldots, \ell\}$ and check whether $q_\ell \in F$.

In our implementation, the size of the problem — the numbers $|Q| = m$, $|\Sigma| = n$ and $|w| = \ell$ — is public, but δ and F are private. We need private lookup to implement δ. It is represented as a table of $|Q| \cdot |\Sigma|$ private values. We compute the private index from $[\![q_{i-1}]\!]$ and $[\![w_i]\!]$ and use it to find $[\![q_i]\!]$ from this table, seen as a vector of length $N = mn$. We have implemented DFA execution using both additive sharing and Shamir's sharing, in fields $GF(p)$ for $p = 2^{32} - 5$ and $GF(2^{32})$. We have measured the performance of Algorithm 1 in all cases, as well as the optimizations of Algorithm 4 and 6 in appropriate cases. Our tests were performed on three computing nodes, each of which was deployed on a separate machine. The computers in the cluster were connected by an Ethernet local area network with link speed of 1 Gbps. Each computer in the cluster had 48 GB of RAM and a 12-core 3 GHz CPU with Hyper Threading.

Our implementation is sub-optimal in the round complexity (which is $O(\ell)$), as it faithfully implements the definition of the DFA execution. Hence the running time of the online phase is currently dominated by the latency of the network. On the other hand, this also implies that many instances of DFA execution run in parallel would have almost the same runtime (for online phase) as the single instance. It is well-known that the DFA execution could be implemented in parallel fashion, using $O(\log \ell)$ time (or SMC rounds). This, however, increases the total work performed by the algorithm by a factor of $O(m)$.

We see that for the vector-only phase of the private lookup, we need the description of δ, but not yet the string w. This corresponds very well to certain envisioned cloud services, in particular to privacy-preserving spam filtering, where the spamminess is detected with regular expressions.

Table 2 presents the actual running times of our DFA execution implementation. All running times are in milliseconds, given with 2–3 significant digits. We have measured the running time for different automaton sizes m and alphabet sizes n, with $N = mn$ being between 6 and 30000. The length of the input string was always 2000 — the work performed by the algorithm, as well as its timing behavior is perfectly linear in this length.

We see that the running time of the online phase is indeed only slightly dependent on N: it is $\approx 286 + 0.042N$ μs per character of the input string when using the field $GF(p)$ (for $GF(2^{32})$, it is around $290 + 0.105N$). This slight dependence on N is caused by the local computations, the amount of

Table 2. DFA execution benchmarks (times in milliseconds, $\ell = 2000$)

$(m, n) =$		$(3, 2)$	$(15, 10)$	$(100, 30)$	$(1000, 30)$
Using only Algorithm 1 for lookup					
$GF(p)$, additive	offline	7	120	2260	23000
	vector-only	4	75	1440	22000
	online	560	590	830	3100
$GF(2^{32})$, additive	offline	11	160	3000	30000
	vector-only	5	110	2200	49000
	online	563	620	1230	6800
$GF(p)$, Shamir	offline	7	120	2600	27000
	vector-only	4	86	1520	23000
	online	580	580	810	3100
$GF(2^{32})$, Shamir	offline	12	200	3900	38000
	vector-only	6	128	2400	53000
	online	570	620	1190	6800
With optimizations of Algorithm 4 or Algorithm 6					
$GF(2^{32})$, additive	offline	12	72	1140	10600
$GF(p)$, Shamir	vector-only	0	1	89	8100
	online	900	900	1230	4300
$GF(2^{32})$, Shamir	vector-only	0	2	310	32000
	online	900	940	1900	13000

which depends on N. Its effect would be even lower if the network latency were higher. Other phases depend much more on N: offline phase requires $0.4N$ μs and vector-only phase $0.23N + 4.7 \cdot 10^{-6} N^2$ μs per character for $GF(p)$.

Among related work, running times of their algorithm implementations have been presented in [15, 30]. Our implementation is significantly more efficient than [15]. They report the running time of 8 s for processing a string of length $\ell = 10$ on an automaton with $mn = 40000$. Compare this number with our reported running time of ≈ 3 s for the online phase or even with ≈ 40 s for all three phases of processing a 2000-character string on an automaton with $mn = 30000$.

Our running times do not seem that impressive when compared to [30], where, with a more optimized implementation inspired by garbled circuits, running times as low as 12 s are reported for $n = 2$ and $\{m, \ell\} = \{20, 150000\}$. But even then, if we consider $mn\ell$ to be a valid measure of the size of the problem, our implementation is a couple of times faster (and the online phase requires only 10 % of that time). Also, they are solving a narrower problem, with one of the parties knowing the automaton and the other knowing the input string, while our protocols are universally composable. On the other hand, their implementation is secure against malicious adversaries, while we have tested our protocols only on ABB implementations secure against passive attacks only.

6   Protocol for SSSD

Let $G = (V, E)$ be a directed graph with $s, t : E \rightarrow V$ giving the source and target, and $w : E \rightarrow \mathbb{N}$ giving the length of each edge. Let $v_0 \in V$. Bellman-Ford (BF) algorithm for SSSD starts by defining $d_0[v] = 0$, if $v = v_0$, and $d_0[v] = \infty$ for $v \in V \backslash \{v_0\}$. It will then compute $d_{i+1}[v] = \min(d_i[v], \min_{e \in t^{-1}(v)} d_i[s(e)] + w(e))$ for all $v \in V$ and $i \in \{0, \ldots, |V| - 2\}$. The vector $d_{|V|-1}$ is the result of the algorithm.

We have implemented the BF algorithm on top of the SHAREMIND platform, hiding the structure of the graph, as well as the lengths of edges. In our implementation, the numbers $n = |V|$ and $m = |E|$ are public, and so are the in-degrees of vertices (obviously, these could be hidden by using suitable paddings). In effect, the mapping t in the definition of the graph is public, while the mappings s and w are private. During the execution, we use private lookup to find $d_i[s(e)]$. As the vectors d_i have to be computed one after another, but the elements of the same vector can be computed in parallel, our implementation has $O(n)$ rounds in the online phase.

As the vector d_i is not yet available at the start of computation, we use the optimized vector-only phase to avoid an $O(n)$ factor during the execution of the BF algorithm. Hence we use Shamir's secret sharing based ABB implementation. We have to perform arithmetic and comparisons with secret values, hence we must use a prime field as the field $\mathbb{F}$ (we use $GF(p)$ with $p = 2^{32} - 5$).

Table 3 presents the actual running times of our implementation of the Bellman-Ford algorithm on sparse graphs. All running times are in seconds, given with 2–3 significant digits. We have measured the running time for different graphs with n vertices (where $100 \le n \le 2000$) and m edges, also matching the problem sizes in related work. Hence we have included cycle graphs (where $m = n$), as well as the complete directed graph on 100 vertices (with $m = 9900$). We also believe that in applications, the used graphs are often planar. Thus we have selected the parameters of certain graphs to match planar graphs, where most faces are triangles and edges are bidirectional ($m \approx 6n$).

Table 3. SSSD execution benchmarks (times in seconds)

n	100	100	100	100	300	300	300	600	600	600	1000	1000	2000
m	100	600	1000	9900	300	1800	3000	600	3600	6000	1000	6000	2000
offline	0.3	1.3	1.9	19	5.2	31	52	41	240	400	190	1100	1540
online	6.0	7.9	9.2	68	10.4	49	72	39	190	310	110	580	550

We see that in our tests, the offline phase requires around $4.74n^2 + 1.28mn + 0.181mn^2$ μs, and the online phase around $14.7n^2 + 67.3mn + 0.0257mn^2$ μs. The asymptotic running time of the BF algorithm is $O(mn)$. Hence we see that the online phase depends much less on the mn^2 term than the offline phase.

The running times reported in related work are much higher. The protocols of [1] are implemented on VIFF [12], running with three parties on a single machine, and requiring 5622 s for SSSD in 128-vertex complete graph. Compare this with our running time of 87 s (offline + online) for the 100-vertex complete graph. We require $(550 + 1540)$ s (online + offline) for a graph with $m = n = 2000$. In [22], the same graph requires around 10000 s with implementation based on SPDZ [23] (hence their time probably does not include SPDZ precomputations).

7 Conclusions

In this paper, we have shown that arithmetic black boxes support fast lookups from private tables according to a private index. We have used this operation to obtain very efficient algorithms for certain tasks. Our results show that for private lookups in an ABB, complex techniques based on Oblivious RAMs [13] are not necessary. Beside the DFA execution or the Bellman-Ford algorithms, we expect our techniques to have wide applicability in making algorithms with sensitive data reading patterns privacy preserving.

References

1. Aly, A., Cuvelier, E., Mawet, S., Pereira, O., Van Vyve, M.: Securely solving simple combinatorial graph problems. In: Sadeghi, A.-R. (ed.) FC 2013. LNCS, vol. 7859, pp. 239–257. Springer, Heidelberg (2013)
2. Blanton, M., Aliasgari, M.: Secure outsourcing of DNA searching via finite automata. In: Foresti, S., Jajodia, S. (eds.) Data and Applications Security and Privacy XXIV. LNCS, vol. 6166, pp. 49–64. Springer, Heidelberg (2010)
3. Bogdanov, D., Laur, S., Willemson, J.: Sharemind: a framework for fast privacy-preserving computations. In: Jajodia, S., Lopez, J. (eds.) ESORICS 2008. LNCS, vol. 5283, pp. 192–206. Springer, Heidelberg (2008)
4. Bogdanov, D., Niitsoo, M., Toft, T., Willemson, J.: High-performance secure multi-party computation for data mining applications. Int. J. Inf. Sec. 11(6), 403–418 (2012)
5. Brickell, J., Shmatikov, V.: Privacy-preserving graph algorithms in the semi-honest model. In: Roy, B. (ed.) ASIACRYPT 2005. LNCS, vol. 3788, pp. 236–252. Springer, Heidelberg (2005)
6. Burkhart, M., Strasser, M., Many, D., Dimitropoulos, X.: SEPIA: Privacy-preserving aggregation of multi-domain network events and statistics. In: USENIX Security Symposium. pp. 223–239. Washington, D.C., USA (2010)
7. Canetti, R.: Universally composable security: a new paradigm for cryptographic protocols. In: FOCS, pp. 136–145. IEEE Computer Society (2001)
8. Catrina, O., Saxena, A.: Secure computation with fixed-point numbers. In: Sion, R. (ed.) FC 2010. LNCS, vol. 6052, pp. 35–50. Springer, Heidelberg (2010)
9. Cramer, R., Damgård, I.B., Nielsen, J.B.: Multiparty computation from threshold homomorphic encryption. In: Pfitzmann, B. (ed.) EUROCRYPT 2001. LNCS, vol. 2045, pp. 280–299. Springer, Heidelberg (2001)

10. Cramer, R., Damgård, I.: Multiparty computation, an introduction. In: Catalano, D., Cramer, R., Di Crescenzo, G., Pointcheval, D., Takagi, T., Damgård, I. (eds.) Contemporary Cryptology, Advanced Courses in Mathematics - CRM Barcelona, pp. 41–87. Birkhuser, Basel (2005). http://dx.doi.org/10.1007/3-7643-7394-6_2

11. Damgård, I.B., Fitzi, M., Kiltz, E., Nielsen, J.B., Toft, T.: Unconditionally secure constant-rounds multi-party computation for equality, comparison, bits and exponentiation. In: Halevi, S., Rabin, T. (eds.) TCC 2006. LNCS, vol. 3876, pp. 285–304. Springer, Heidelberg (2006)

12. Damgård, I., Geisler, M., Krøigaard, M., Nielsen, J.B.: Asynchronous Multiparty computation: theory and implementation. In: Jarecki, S., Tsudik, G. (eds.) PKC 2009. LNCS, vol. 5443, pp. 160–179. Springer, Heidelberg (2009)

13. Damgård, I., Meldgaard, S., Nielsen, J.B.: Perfectly Secure oblivious RAM without random oracles. In: Ishai, Y. (ed.) TCC 2011. LNCS, vol. 6597, pp. 144–163. Springer, Heidelberg (2011)

14. Damgård, I.B., Nielsen, J.B.: Universally composable efficient multiparty computation from threshold homomorphic encryption. In: Boneh, D. (ed.) CRYPTO 2003. LNCS, vol. 2729, pp. 247–264. Springer, Heidelberg (2003)

15. Frikken, K.B.: Practical private DNA string searching and matching through efficient oblivious automata evaluation. In: Gudes, E., Vaidya, J. (eds.) Data and Applications Security XXIII. LNCS, vol. 5645, pp. 81–94. Springer, Heidelberg (2009)

16. Gennaro, R., Hazay, C., Sorensen, J.S.: Text search protocols with simulation based security. In: Nguyen, P.Q., Pointcheval, D. (eds.) PKC 2010. LNCS, vol. 6056, pp. 332–350. Springer, Heidelberg (2010)

17. Gennaro, R., Rabin, M.O., Rabin, T.: Simplified VSS and fact-track multiparty computations with applications to threshold cryptography. In: PODC, pp. 101–111 (1998)

18. Gentry, C., Goldman, K.A., Halevi, S., Julta, C., Raykova, M., Wichs, D.: Optimizing ORAM and using it efficiently for secure computation. In: De Cristofaro, E., Wright, M. (eds.) PETS 2013. LNCS, vol. 7981, pp. 1–18. Springer, Heidelberg (2013)

19. Goldreich, O., Micali, S., Wigderson, A.: How to play any mental game or a completeness theorem for protocols with honest majority. In: STOC, pp. 218–229. ACM (1987)

20. Goldreich, O., Ostrovsky, R.: Software protection and simulation on oblivious RAMs. J. ACM **43**(3), 431–473 (1996)

21. Henecka, W., Kögl, S., Sadeghi, A.R., Schneider, T., Wehrenberg, I.: TASTY: tool for automating secure two-party computations. In: CCS 2010: Proceedings of the 17th ACM Conference on Computer and Communications Security, pp. 451–462. ACM, New York (2010)

22. Keller, M., Scholl, P.: Efficient, Oblivious Data Structures for MPC. Cryptology ePrint Archive, Report 2014/137 (2014). http://eprint.iacr.org/

23. Keller, M., Scholl, P., Smart, N.P.: An architecture for practical actively secure MPC with dishonest majority. In: Sadeghi et al. [31], pp. 549–560

24. Kushilevitz, E., Ostrovsky, R.: Replication is not needed: single database, computationally-private information retrieval. In: FOCS, pp. 364–373. IEEE Computer Society (1997)

25. Launchbury, J., Diatchki, I.S., DuBuisson, T., Adams-Moran, A.: Efficient lookup-table protocol in secure multiparty computation. In: Thiemann, P., Findler, R.B. (eds.) ICFP, pp. 189–200. ACM (2012)

26. Lipmaa, H.: First CPIR protocol with data-dependent computation. In: Lee, D., Hong, S. (eds.) ICISC 2009. LNCS, vol. 5984, pp. 193–210. Springer, Heidelberg (2010)

27. Lipmaa, H., Toft, T.: Secure equality and greater-than tests with sublinear online complexity. In: Fomin, F.V., Freivalds, R., Kwiatkowska, M., Peleg, D. (eds.) ICALP 2013, Part II. LNCS, vol. 7966, pp. 645–656. Springer, Heidelberg (2013)

28. Liu, C., Huang, Y., Shi, E., Katz, J., Hicks, M.: Automating efficient RAM-model secure computation. In: Proceedings of 2014 IEEE Symposium on Security and Privacy. IEEE (2014)

29. Malka, L., Katz, J.: Vmcrypt - modular software architecture for scalable secure computation. Cryptology ePrint Archive, Report 2010/584 (2010). http://eprint.iacr.org

30. Mohassel, P., Niksefat, S., Sadeghian, S., Sadeghiyan, B.: An efficient protocol for oblivious DFA evaluation and applications. In: Dunkelman, O. (ed.) CT-RSA 2012. LNCS, vol. 7178, pp. 398–415. Springer, Heidelberg (2012)

31. Sadeghi, A.R., Gligor, V.D., Yung, M. (eds.): 2013 ACM SIGSAC Conference on Computer and Communications Security, CCS 2013, pp.4–8, ACM, Berlin, November 2013

32. Shamir, A.: How to share a secret. Commun. ACM **22**(11), 612–613 (1979)

33. Stefanov, E., van Dijk, M., Shi, E., Fletcher, C.W., Ren, L., Yu, X., Devadas, S.: Path ORAM: an extremely simple oblivious RAM protocol. In: Sadeghi et al. [31], pp. 299–310

34. Troncoso-Pastoriza, J.R., Katzenbeisser, S., Celik, M.U.: Privacy preserving error resilient DNA searching through oblivious automata. In: Ning, P., di Vimercati, S.D.C., Syverson, P.F. (eds.) ACM Conference on Computer and Communications Security, pp. 519–528. ACM (2007)

35. Wei, L., Reiter, M.K.: Third-party private DFA evaluation on encrypted files in the cloud. In: Foresti, S., Yung, M., Martinelli, F. (eds.) ESORICS 2012. LNCS, vol. 7459, pp. 523–540. Springer, Heidelberg (2012)

36. Yao, A.C.C.: Protocols for secure computations (extended abstract). In: FOCS, pp. 160–164. IEEE (1982)

Reverse Product-Scanning Multiplication and Squaring on 8-Bit AVR Processors

Zhe Liu[1][✉], Hwajeong Seo[2], Johann Großschädl[1], and Howon Kim[2]

[1] Laboratory of Algorithmics, Cryptology and Security (LACS),
University of Luxembourg, 6, rue Richard Coudenhove-Kalergi, 1359
Luxembourg, Luxembourg
{zhe.liu,johann.groszschaedl}@uni.lu
[2] School of Computer Science and Engineering, Pusan National University, San-30,
Jangjeon-Dong, Geumjeong-Gu, Busan 609–735, Republic of Korea
{hwajeong,howonkim}@pusan.ac.kr

Abstract. High performance, small code size, and good scalability are important requirements for software implementations of multi-precision arithmetic algorithms to fit resource-limited embedded systems. In this paper, we describe optimization techniques to speed up multi-precision multiplication and squaring on the AVR ATmega series of 8-bit microcontrollers. First, we present a new approach to perform multi-precision multiplication, called *Reverse Product Scanning (RPS)*, that resembles the hybrid technique of Gura et al., but calculates the byte-products in the inner loop in reverse order. The RPS method processes four bytes of the two operands in each iteration of the inner loop and employs two carry-catcher registers to minimize the number of **add** instructions. We also describe an optimized algorithm for multi-precision squaring based on the RPS technique that is, depending on the operand length, up to 44.3 % faster than multiplication. Our AVR Assembly implementations of RPS multiplication and RPS squaring occupy less than 1 kB of code space each and are written in a parameterized fashion so that they can support operands of varying length without recompilation. Despite this high level of flexibility, our RPS multiplication outperforms the looped variant of Hutter et al.'s operand-caching technique and saves between 40 and 51 % of code size. We also combine our RPS multiplication and squaring routines with Karatsuba's method to further reduce execution time. When executed on an ATmega128 processor, the "karatsubarized RPS method" needs only 85 k clock cycles for a 1024-bit multiplication (or 48 k cycles for a squaring). These results show that it is possible to achieve high performance without sacrificing code size or scalability.

1 Introduction

Multi-precision multiplication and squaring are performance-critical operations of a variety of public-key cryptographic algorithms, including RSA [18], elliptic curve schemes [14,17], and pairing-based cryptosystems [4]. In fact, these two operations can easily account for more than 80 % of the overall execution time

© Springer International Publishing Switzerland 2015
L.C.K. Hui et al. (Eds.): ICICS 2014, LNCS 8958, pp. 158–175, 2015.
DOI: 10.1007/978-3-319-21966-0_12

of a modular exponentiation (such as needed for RSA) or scalar multiplication (needed in elliptic curve cryptography [10]). Consequently, any effort spent on optimizing multi-precision multiplication and squaring is well spent. This is in particular the case for multi-precision arithmetic to be executed on embedded or mobile devices as they are often severely restricted in processing power and memory (RAM) capacity. For example, an ordinary smart card or sensor node features just an 8-bit processor clocked with a frequency of between 5 and 10 MHz. The 8-bit AVR architecture is widely used in these application domains and has, therefore, been the target platform numerous research projects in the area of lightweight implementation of cryptographic primitives. A typical 8-bit AVR processor (e.g. ATmega128 [2]) has 4 kB RAM, 128 kB flash memory to store program code, and provides 32 registers. Three register pairs can serve as 16-bit pointer registers and hold the address of operands in RAM [1]. The ATmega128 also comes with a hardware multiplier that needs two clock cycles to compute the 16-bit product of two 8-bit operands held in registers.

In the past ten years, a large body of research has been devoted to improve the performance of multi-precision arithmetic operations on resource-restricted 8-bit platforms such as the ATmega family of processors. At CHES 2004, Gura et al. presented a landmark paper in which they compared ECC with RSA on 8-bit CPUs and introduced the now-classical *hybrid method* for multiplication [9]. The hybrid method exploits the large register file of the AVR platform to store several bytes of the operands in registers and, in this way, combines the advantages of the *product scanning* and *operand scanning* technique [10]. Since the publication of Gura et al.'s work, there have been a number of attempts to further improve hybrid multiplication. An obvious approach for optimization is to completely unroll the loops since loop unrolling eliminates a lot of overhead (e.g. update of a loop counter or execution of a branch instruction) and allows for a specific "tuning" of each iteration (see e.g. [19,23]), which is not possible with "rolled" loops. A second line of research focused on speeding up the inner-loop operation, i.e. Multiply-ACcumulate (MAC) operation, by scheduling the execution of mul instructions in a special way and other low-level optimization techniques (see e.g. [15,16,24] for representative examples).

A recent milestone in the area of fast multi-precision multiplication on the 8-bit AVR platform is the *operand caching method*, introduced by Hutter and Wenger at CHES 2011 [12]. The operand caching method follows a similar idea as hybrid multiplication, but splits the computation of the product into several small(er) parts with the goal of reducing the overall number of ld instructions through a sophisticated caching of operand bytes. Later, fully unrolled versions of the operand caching approach with slightly better results were presented in [20,21] by Seo et al. Very recently, Hutter and Schwabe [11] further improved the speed record for unrolled multi-precision multiplication on AVR processors by a carefully-optimized implementation of Karatsuba's multiplication method [13]. Their results demonstrate that the operand length at which Karatsuba's approach starts to become beneficial is surprisingly low, namely 48 bits.

In this paper, we describe a new approach for multi-precision multiplication and squaring on 8-bit AVR processors and other platforms that feature a large number of general-purpose working registers. Our main contribution is the *Reverse Product Scanning (RPS) method* for multiplication, which resembles the basic loop structure of Gura et al.'s hybrid technique [9], but computes subsets of the partial products in the inner loop in reverse order, i.e. from more to less significant positions. Furthermore, the RPS method uses two so-called "carry-catcher" registers to minimize the number of `adc` instructions executed in the inner loop. The RPS method for AVR processors we present in this paper aims for a practical trade-off between performance, code size and scalability instead of "pure speed" as most other implementations. Achieving such a trade-off is a very challenging task since, for example, high performance and small code size usually contradict each other. Before presenting our contributions in detail, we first explain why fast execution time, small code size, and high scalability are all important requirements for multi-precision arithmetic software.

Requirements

Achieving fast execution time has been a major goal of virtually all implementations of multi-precision arithmetic described in the recent literature, and the present work is no exception. As stated before, the efficiency of multi-precision multiplication and squaring has a clear and direct impact on the performance of higher-level operations like exponentiation or scalar multiplication, which, in turn, determines the overall processing time of key establishment mechanisms and signature schemes. Besides reducing the delay of public-key primitives and protocols, fast multi-precision arithmetic is crucial for another reason, namely energy efficiency. In general, the energy consumption of cryptographic software executed on a microprocessor increases proportionally with the execution time [7]. This, together with the fact that a large portion of embedded systems are battery powered, makes a good case for minimizing execution time, even if the target application does not impose stringent delay constraints on cryptographic primitives. While the importance of high performance is unanimously accepted in the cryptographic community, the situation is not so clear when it comes to code size and scalability since both were often ignored in previous work.

Paying attention to code size is important since the binary executable image of an application (which includes the object file containing the arithmetic functions) needs to fit into the available program ROM or flash memory. Many embedded microcontrollers are quite restricted in code space; for example, the Atmel ATmega128 [2] provides only 128 kB of programmable flash memory to store program code. In light of such constraints, it is often unattractive (and in some cases even impossible) to apply certain code-size-increasing optimization techniques like (full) loop unrolling. The operand-caching method for AVR, as described in [12], serves as a good example to make this more clear. A fully unrolled implementation of operand-caching multiplication for 1024-bit operands has a binary code size of about 150 kB, which exceeds the flash capacity of the ATmega128 by more than 20 kB. But even for smaller operands typically used in ECC (e.g. 256 bits), full loop unrolling can be infeasible since, depending on the code size of the operating system, networking stack, security protocol, and the actual application, only a tiny fraction of the 128 kB flash memory may be available for multiple-precision arithmetic. And, of course, the smaller the code size of the cryptographic primitives and underlying arithmetic operations, the more code space remains for the actual application.

In the context of cryptographic software, the term scalability relates to the ability to process operands of arbitrary size without the need to re-write or re-compile the software. A scalable implementation of multi-precision arithmetic is parameterized, which means that the operands (or, more precisely, pointers to the operands in RAM) are passed as parameters to the arithmetic function along with an additional parameter specifying the length of the operands. The function body executes the arithmetic operation in a "looped" fashion, where-by the operand length determines the number of loop iterations. Virtually all cryptographic libraries of practical relevance contain a scalable implementation of multi-precision arithmetic, and also the multiplication/squaring routines we describe in the following sections are scalable. The importance of scalability is best explained by taking RSA [18] as example. Private-key operations, such as decryption and signature generation, can exploit the Chinese Remainder Theo-rem to perform an n-bit exponentiation through two $(n/2)$-bit exponentiations using the prime decomposition P, Q of the modulus N. On the other hand, all operations involving a public key (e.g. encryption, signature verification) have to be performed on full-length (i.e. n-bit) operands. A scalable implementation of multiple-precision modular arithmetic is able to accommodate both operand lengths, which simplifies the software development process as only one function for multiplication and modular reduction has to be written. Scalability makes it also very easy to adapt an RSA implementation to larger key sizes, e.g. from 1024 to 1536 or 2048 bits.

Contributions

We present the RPS method for multi-precision multiplication and squaring on processors featuring a large number of general-purpose registers. As mentioned before, our RPS approach has the same loop structure as the hybrid technique and, consequently, employs the column-wise strategy (i.e. product scanning) as "outer algorithm." However, the byte-level multiplications in the inner loop are (partly) executed in reverse order, i.e. some more-significant byte-products are calculated before less-significant ones. Furthermore, the RPS method uses two so-called carry-catcher registers to reduce the propagation of carries (which, in turn, reduces the number of adc instructions), similar to the optimized hybrid method of Scott and Szczechowiak [19]. We also describe how to apply the RPS approach for multi-precision squaring and introduce an optimized technique to calculate the byte-level squares in the "main diagonal" that appear only once in the final result. Last but not least, we combine our RPS multiplication and squaring with Karatsuba's algorithm [13] to further reduce the execution time for large operands (i.e. ≥ 512 bits) such as used in RSA.

Table 1. Comparison of AVR implementations of multi-precision multiplication and squaring with respect to code size, scalability, and whether the implementation was evaluated in the original paper for operand lengths used in ECC or RSA (the letters U, L, P indicate whether an implementation is unrolled, looped, or parameterized)

Implementation	Code size	Scalable	RSA	ECC	Speed record
Multi-precision multiplication on 8-bit AVR processors:					
Gura et al. [9]	n/a		✓	✓	
Hutter et al. [11]	3.1–7.6 kB			✓	✓ (U)
Hutter et al. (L) [12]	1.5–1.9 kB		✓	✓	
Hutter et al. (U) [12]	3.7–151 kB			✓	
Liu et al. [16]	n/a		✓		
Scott et al. [19]	n/a			✓	
Seo et al. [21]	3.6–10 kB			✓	
Uhsadel et al. [23]	n/a			✓	
Zhang et al. [24]	n/a	✓		✓	
This work (RPS mul)	914 B	✓	✓	✓	✓ (L,P)
Multi-precision squaring on 8-bit AVR processors:					
Liu et al. [16]	1.5 kB		✓		
Seo et al. [22]	3.2–9.1 kB			✓	✓ (U)
This work (RPS sqr)	844 B	✓	✓	✓	✓ (L,P)

We implemented the proposed RPS multiplication and RPS squaring in Assembly language, and "karatsubarized" versions thereof in portable C using the Assembly functions as sub-routines. Our prototype implementations satisfy the requirements mentioned before; in particular, they are scalable and, thus, able to support operands of (essentially) arbitrary length. Both RPS multiplication and RPS squaring have a code size of less than 1 kB, which is small compared to other implementations described in the literature (see Table 1). Despite its scalability and compact size, our RPS multiplication for AVR is faster than the bulk of previous work, beaten only by the three fully unrolled implementations [11,12,21]. Most notably, the RPS technique we propose outperforms the looped variant[1] of the operand caching approach (see Sect. 4 for details).

2   Multiplication Techniques

In this section, we give a brief overview of standard algorithms and techniques for fast execution of multi-precision multiplication on a w-bit general-purpose processor. We assume that A and B are n-bit operands represented by arrays

---

[1] A looped implementation has "rolled" loops [12], but in contrast to a parameterized implementation, the number of iterations is "hard-coded" and, hence, fixed. Looped implementations are smaller, but also slower, than their unrolled counterparts.

of $s = \lceil n/w \rceil$ single-precision (i.e. w-bit) words a_i and b_i, which means we have $A = (a_{s-1}, \ldots, a_0)$ and $B = (b_{s-1}, \ldots, b_0)$ with $0 \leq a_i, b_i < 2^w$ for $0 \leq i < s$.

2.1   Operand Scanning Method

A simple and easy-to-implement technique for multi-precision multiplication is the operand scanning method [10], also known as schoolbook method [7]. The operand scanning method, as specified in [7, Algorithm 1], has a characteristic nested-loop structure with an outer loop iterates through the s words b_i of the operand B, starting with the least-significant word b_0. In the inner loop, b_i is multiplied with a word a_j of operand A and the $2w$-bit product is added to the intermediate result obtained so far. More precisely, the operation performed in the inner loop is a special Multiply-Accumulate (MAC) operation of the form $(u, v) \leftarrow a \cdot b + c + d$, whereby (u, v) represents a double-precision (i.e. $2w$-bit) quantity and a, b, c, and d are all single-precision words.

When implemented for an 8-bit ATmega128 processor, the MAC operation consists of a `mul`, two `add`, and two `adc` (i.e. add-with-carry) instructions. The operand scanning method is fairly easy to program in a high-level language like C or Java [7], but is generally less efficient than the product scanning method (described below) if both are written in Assembly language. In summary, when multiplying two s-word operands, the operand scanning method has to execute s^2 `mul`, $4s^2$ `add` (resp. `adc`), $2s^2 + s$ `ld` (i.e. load), as well as $s^2 + s$ `st` (store) instructions [7].

2.2   Product Scanning Method

An alternative way of performing multi-precision multiplication is the product scanning method, sometimes credited to Paul Comba [6], who was the first to describe an efficient implementation of this method on an Intel processor. The product scanning method (specified in [7, Algorithm 2]) comprises two nested loops; one computes the lower half of the result and the second contributes the upper half. As the name suggests, the two outer loops of the product scanning method move through the product itself, starting at the least significant word [6,7]. More precisely, the product is obtained one word at a time, whereby the i-th word contains all partial products $a_j \cdot b_k$ with $j + k = i$. A graphical representation of the product scanning method (see e.g. [8, Fig.1]) shows that the partial products are processed in a column-wise fashion, whereas the operand scanning technique outlined above follows a row-wise schedule. The inner loop of the product scanning method executes a simple MAC operation of the form $(t, u, v) \leftarrow (t, u, v) + a \cdot b$, which means two w-bit words are multiplied and the $2w$-bit product is added to a cumulative sum held in three w-bit registers.

An AVR Assembly implementation of the inner-loop operation consists of a `mul`, an `add`, and two `adc` instructions. Hence, the product scanning technique executes one `add` instruction less in the inner loop than the operand scanning method. Furthermore, the product scanning technique performs memory-write (i.e. store) operations exclusively in the outer loop(s), which means the overall number of st instructions grows linearly with s instead of quadratically. When multiplying two s-word operands, the product scanning method has to execute s^2 mul, $3s^2$ add (resp. adc), $2s^2$ ld, and $2s$ st instructions [7].

2.3 Hybrid Method

Both the operand scanning and the product scanning method require (at least) $2s^2$ ld instructions if the two operands consist of s words. The hybrid method aims at reducing the number of ld instructions on processors with a large register file by processing $d \geq 2$ words of A and B at once in each iteration of the inner loop. From an algorithmic point of view, the hybrid method combines the two techniques described in the previous subsections, which means it employs the product scanning approach as "outer algorithm" and the operand scanning approach as "inner algorithm" [9]. In each iteration of the inner loops, d words of A and d words of B are loaded from memory, multiplied together and added to a cumulative sum held in $2d + 1$ general-purpose registers. By doing so, the number of loop iterations and, hence, the number of ld instructions is reduced by a factor of d. The speed-up achievable through the hybrid method depends on d, which, in turn, is determined by the number of available registers.

Most hybrid implementations for AVR processors with 32 working registers use $d = 4$, which means the hybrid method has to execute just a quarter of the ld instructions of the straightforward product scanning method. However, this saving usually comes at the expense of an increased number of add (resp. adc) or mov (resp. movw) instructions.

2.4 Operand Caching Method

The operand caching technique, introduced in [12], is currently the fastest quadratic-complexity multiplication method for 8-bit ATmega processors. Thanks to a sophisticated caching of operand bytes, it held the speed record for looped multi-precision multiplication until now. The operand caching method follows the basic approach of product scanning, but divides the calculation into several row sections. By reordering the execution of inner and outer row sections, the operand caching method can reuse the operands that have already been loaded into working registers to generate the next partial product(s). In this way, the overall number of memory access operations, in particular ld instructions, can be massively reduced. The actual performance of the operand-caching method depends on the size of a row, i.e. the number of words of one operand that can be kept (i.e. "cached") in working registers. In total, the operand caching method performs $3s^2/e + s$ memory access operations, whereby e denotes the row size [12]. Among these memory accesses are $2s^2/e$ loads and $s^2/e + s$ stores.

On an ATmega processor, e can be as high as 10 when the operand caching method is implemented in a completely unrolled fashion, or 9 in the case of a looped implementation. Since $e \gg d$, the operand caching method outperforms the hybrid method by approximately 15 % on average [12].

2.5 Karatsuba Multiplication

The most important multiplication method with sub-quadratic complexity was introduced by Karatsuba in the early 1960s [13]. Karatsuba's approach reduces a multiplication of two operands consisting of s words to three multiplications of $(s/2)$-word operands and a couple of additions. The half-size multiplications can be performed with any multiplication technique, including the conventional operand-scanning and product-scanning method. Alternatively, it is possible to apply Karatsuba's idea recursively until the operands consist of just one single word, in which case the asymptotic complexity becomes $\theta(s^{log_2(3)})$.

There exist two variants of Karatsuba's multiplication technique, namely an additive form and a subtractive form [11]. Both require the s-word operands to be split up into a lower half consisting of the $k = \lceil s/2 \rceil$ least significant words and an upper half comprising the $\lfloor s/2 \rfloor = s - k$ most significant words, i.e. we have $A = A_H \cdot 2^{kw} + A_L$ whereby $A_L = A \bmod 2^{kw}$ and $A_H = A \operatorname{div} 2^{kw}$. The additive variant of Karatsuba's method obtains the product $A \cdot B$ through the following equation.

$$A_H B_H \cdot 2^{2kw} + [(A_H + A_L)(B_H + B_L) - A_H B_H - A_L B_L] \cdot 2^{kw} + A_L B_L \quad (1)$$

On the other hand, the subtractive variant computes $A \cdot B$ as follows.

$$A_H B_H \cdot 2^{2kw} + [A_H B_H + A_L B_L - (A_H - A_L)(B_H - B_L)] \cdot 2^{kw} + A_L B_L \quad (2)$$

Consequently, Karatsuba's method performs a multiplication of size s via three multiplications and eight additions of size $s/2$ (plus a potential carry propagation). In 2009, Bernstein [3] refined Karatsuba's technique to save an addition of size $s/2$, which slightly improves performance. Hutter and Schwabe describe in [11] a carefully optimized AVR implementation of the subtractive Karatsuba technique for operands of up to 256 bits that currently holds the speed record for multi-precision multiplication on an 8-bit processor.

3 Our Implementation

In the next two subsections, we describe the RPS technique for multi-precision multiplication and squaring on 8-bit AVR processors in full detail, whereby we first present the "big picture" (i.e. the algorithm itself) and then concentrate on the inner-loop operation.

3.1 Loop Structure

From an algorithmic point of view, our RPS multiplication method is similar to Gura et al.'s hybrid technique [9] since both resemble the basic loop structure of the classical product-scanning approach [10]. Consequently, the RPS method computes the product $A \cdot B$ through two nested loops one word at a time. The first nested loop produces the s least significant words, while the second nested

---

Algorithm 1. Multiple-precision multiplication

Input: Two s-word operands $A = (A_{s-1}, \ldots, A_1, A_0)$ and $B = (B_{s-1}, \ldots, B_1, B_0)$
Output: $2s$-word product $R = A \times B = (R_{2s-1}, \ldots, R_1, R_0)$
 1: $Z \leftarrow A_0 \times B_0$
 2: $R_0 \leftarrow Z \bmod 2^w$; $Z \leftarrow Z/2^w$
 3: **for** i from 1 by 1 to $s - 1$ **do**
 4:    $k \leftarrow i + 1$
 5:    **for** j from 0 by 1 to i **do**
 6:       $k \leftarrow k - 1$
 7:       $Z \leftarrow Z + A_j \times B_k$
 8:    **end for**
 9:    $R_i \leftarrow Z \bmod 2^w$; $Z \leftarrow Z/2^w$
10: **end for**
11: **for** i from s by 1 to $2s - 3$ **do**
12:    $k \leftarrow s$
13:    **for** j from $i - (s - 1)$ by 1 to $s - 1$ **do**
14:       $k \leftarrow k - 1$
15:       $Z \leftarrow Z + A_j \times B_k$
16:    **end for**
17:    $R_i \leftarrow Z \bmod 2^w$; $Z \leftarrow Z/2^w$
18: **end for**
19: $Z \leftarrow Z + A_{s-1} \times B_{s-1}$
20: $R_{2s-2} \leftarrow Z \bmod 2^w$; $Z \leftarrow Z/2^w$
21: $R_{2s-1} \leftarrow Z \bmod 2^w$
22: **return** $(R_{2s-1}, \ldots, R_1, R_0)$

---

loop yields the upper half of the $2s$-word product. When following the original product-scanning approach (as described in e.g. [7]), the bitlength w of a word is normally chosen to match the native word-size of the processor, which means $w = 8$ in the case of AVR, i.e. each word consists of a byte. However, since we process $d = 4$ bytes at a time, similar to the hybrid technique described in the previous section, our word-size is $w = 32$ (i.e. four bytes) despite the fact that we work on an 8-bit processor. To distinguish between words and bytes, we use from now on indexed capital letters to represent words, and indexed lowercase letters to denote the individual bytes a word is composed of. Consequently, an n-bit integer A consists of $s = \lceil n/32 \rceil$ words $A_i \in [0, 2^{32} - 1]$, each of which, in turn, contains four bytes, i.e. $A_i = (a_{4i+3}, a_{4i+2}, a_{4i+1}, a_{4i})$ for $0 \le i < s$.

Algorithm 1 specifies the RPS multiplication technique using said notation for the w-bit words. The algorithm has the characteristic nested-loop structure of the classical product-scanning method and computes the product $A \times B$ in a column-wise fashion, one word at a time [7]. In each iteration of one of the two inner loops, a conventional Multiply-ACcumulate (MAC) operation of the form $Z \leftarrow Z + A_j \times B_k$ is executed, i.e. a w-bit word A_j of operand A is multiplied by a w-bit word B_k of operand B and the $2w$-bit product $A_j \times B_k$ is added to a cumulative sum Z. In our case, both A_j and B_k contain four bytes, while the sum Z is nine bytes long. Operations of the form $R_i \leftarrow Z \bmod 2^w$ simply write

---

Algorithm 2. Multiple-precision squaring

Input: An s-word operand $A = (A_{s-1}, \ldots, A_1, A_0)$
Output: $2s$-word square $R = A^2 = (R_{2s-1}, \ldots, R_1, R_0)$
1: $Z \leftarrow 0$; $R_0 \leftarrow 0$
2: **for** i from 0 by 1 to $s - 1$ **do**
3:    $k \leftarrow i + 1$
4:    **for** j from 0 by 1 to $k - 2$ **do**
5:      $k \leftarrow k - 1$
6:      $Z \leftarrow Z + A_j \times A_k$
7:    **end for**
8:    $R_i \leftarrow Z \bmod 2^w$; $Z \leftarrow Z / 2^w$
9: **end for**
10: **for** i from s by 1 to $2s - 3$ **do**
11:    $k \leftarrow s$
12:    **for** j from $i - (s - 1)$ by 1 to $k - 2$ **do**
13:      $k \leftarrow k - 1$
14:      $Z \leftarrow Z + A_j \times A_k$
15:    **end for**
16:    $R_i \leftarrow Z \bmod 2^w$; $Z \leftarrow Z / 2^w$
17: **end for**
18: $R_{2s-2} \leftarrow Z \bmod 2^w$; $R_{2s-1} \leftarrow 0$
19: $Z \leftarrow 0$
20: **for** i from 0 by 1 to $s - 1$ **do**
21:    $Z \leftarrow Z + A_i \times A_i + 2(R_{2i+1} \cdot 2^w + R_{2i})$
22:    $R_{2i} \leftarrow Z \bmod 2^w$; $Z \leftarrow Z / 2^w$
23:    $R_{2i+1} \leftarrow Z \bmod 2^w$; $Z \leftarrow Z / 2^w$
24: **end for**
25: **return** $(R_{2s-1}, \ldots, R_1, R_0)$

---

the w least significant bits (i.e. the four least significant bytes if $d = 4$) of Z to the destination R_i. The divisions of Z by 2^w (e.g. in line 2, 9, 17, and 20) are nothing else than simple w-bit (i.e. 4-byte) right shifts of Z. A further common characteristic between our RPS technique and the product-scanning method is that the words A_j of A are loaded in ascending order, starting with the least-significant word A_0, whereas the words B_k of operand B are loaded in opposite order, i.e. from more to less significant words.

Algorithm 1 differs from the straightforward product-scanning approach as described in e.g. [7,10] in a few details. First, we "peeled off" the very first and the very last MAC operation (in which $A_0 \times B_0$ and $A_{s-1} \times B_{s-1}$ are formed) from the nested loops and execute them outside the loop body. In this way, we do not need to initialize the sum Z with 0 and can replace the very first MAC operation by a simple multiplication. Also the last MAC operation allows for a special optimization to reduce execution time. Namely, after the very last MAC operation, we can directly write the eight least significant bytes of S to the two result words R_{2s-2} and R_{2s-1} in one pass without shifting S. Finally, the two loop counters j and k are updated such that one can take full advantage of the automatic pre-decrement and post-increment addressing modes of AVR.

Algorithm 2 shows our implementation of multiple-precision squaring based on the product-scanning method. It is well known that the square $R = A^2$ of a long integer A can be computed much more efficiently than the product of two distinct integers due to the "symmetry" of partial products [10]. Namely, when a normal multiplication algorithm is used for squaring (e.g. Algorithm 1 if we set $B = A$), then all partial products of the form $A_j \times A_k$ with $j \neq k$ are computed twice because $A_j \times A_k = A_k \times A_j$. Dedicated squaring algorithms avoid such unnecessary overheads by calculating these partial products only once and then doubling them through a left-shift. Also the partial products in the "main diagonal" (i.e. the partial products of the form $A_i \times A_i$) appear exactly once in the final result and have to be treated separately. Algorithm 2 is based on this approach; it first computes the partial products $A_j \times A_k$ with $j \neq k$ and sums them up in a similar way as in product-scanning multiplication. Thereafter, the result obtained so far is doubled and the main diagonal containing the partial products of the form $A_i \times A_i$ is added.

The two nested loops of Algorithm 2 (i.e. line 2 to 17) compute the partial products $A_j \times A_k$ to be doubled and have a very similar structure as the loops of Algorithm 1. In fact, there are only two minor differences, namely that the very first and the last partial product are not peeled off from the nested loops anymore (since they form now part of the third loop) and that the inner loops are iterated fewer times. For example, the first inner loop (starting at line 4) is iterated while the condition $j \leq k - 2$ is true; in C-like programming languages this for-loop would be written as follows.

$$\text{for } (\mathsf{j} = 0; \mathsf{j} <= \mathsf{k} - 2; \mathsf{j} + +)$$

As j is incremented and k decremented in each iteration of the inner loop, the overall number of loop iterations in roughly halved compared to the inner loop of the RPS multiplication in Algorithm 1. This is also the case with the second inner loop starting at line 12. Because of these modifications of the loop-termination conditions, the total number of ($w \times w$)-bit multiplications (resp. MAC operations) performed by the two loops is reduced from $s^2 - 2$ (Algorithm 1) to $(s^2 - s)/2$. In the third loop (line 20), the intermediate result produced by the two nested loops is doubled and the s partial products of the form $A_i \times A_i$ are added. Putting all three loops together, Algorithm 2 executes $(s^2 + s)/2$ MAC operations to obtain the square of an s-word integer, which is almost 50 % less compared to the s^2 MAC operations (or multiplications) of Algorithm 1.

3.2   Inner-Loop Operation

The two nested loops of both Algorithms 1 and 2 execute basic MAC operations of the form $Z \leftarrow Z + A_j \times B_k$ in their inner loops. As mentioned in the previous subsection, the two w-bit words A_j and B_k consist of $d = 4$ bytes each. Consequently, in each iteration of the inner loop(s), four bytes of operand A

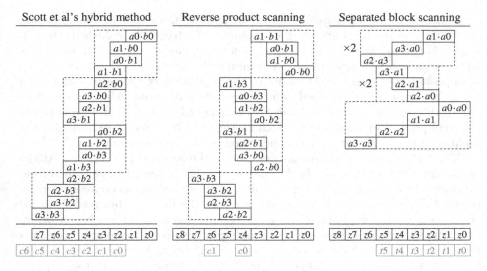

Fig. 1. Inner-loop operation based on Scott et al.'s carry-catcher method (left, taken from [19, Fig.1(ii)]), our RPS method using two carry-catcher registers (middle), and our SBS technique for computing the square of a 4-byte word (right)

are multiplied by four bytes of operand B and the 8-byte product is added to a cumulative sum Z consisting of nine bytes. The (4×4)-byte multiplication can be carried out in various different ways; for example, Gura et al. used the operand-scanning technique in their seminal paper [9]. Alternatively, it is also possible to apply the product-scanning method; Scott et al.'s implementation from [19] (depicted on the left side of Fig. 1) serves as a good example for this approach. If $d = 4$, a total of 16 byte-products needs to be computed, which is done from top to bottom, i.e. $a_0 \cdot b_0$ is generated first and $a_3 \cdot b_3$ is the last one to be processed. A particular issue when using the product-scanning technique in the inner loop is the propagation of carries; for example, the addition of the byte-product $a_0 \cdot b_0$ to the two least significant bytes (z_1, z_0) of the cumulative sum Z can produce a carry, which, in the worst case, may propagate up to the most significant byte of Z. To limit such carry propagation, Scott et al. introduced so-called *carry-catcher registers*, shown in red in Fig. 1. For $d = 4$, there are eight registers for the cumulative sum Z (which we denote as accu registers z_0 to z_7) and seven carry-catcher registers (c_0 to c_6). A carry generated by the addition of e.g. $a_0 \cdot b_0$ to (z_1, z_0) is not propagated along the z_i registers (up to z_7 in the worst case), but simply added to c_0. In this way, only an **add** and two **adc** instructions need to be performed to accumulate a byte-product. After the last iteration of the inner loop, the six carry-catcher registers are added to the accu registers to yield the correct Z, and then they are cleared.

Our approach of implementing the inner-loop operation is also based on the product-scanning technique and depicted in the middle of Fig. 1. In contrast to Scott et al., we have nine accu registers (z_0 to z_8), but only two carry catchers

(c_0 and c_1). To aid the explanation of our approach, we split the computation of the 16 byte-products up into four groups, indicated by four dashed boxes in Fig. 1. For example, the first group consists of $a_1 \cdot b_1$, $a_0 \cdot b_1$, $a_1 \cdot b_0$, as well as $a_0 \cdot b_0$. Compared to Scott et al., we compute the byte-products within a group in opposite order (see Fig. 1), and also the processing of the second and third group is reversed. The reversed-order computation of byte-products inspired us to call this approach *Reverse Product Scanning (RPS)*. Our main idea is to use the byte-products themselves to catch carries, which allows us to minimize the number of carry-catcher registers and speed up the computation.

The RPS method performs an iteration of the inner loop as follows. At the beginning, the four bytes b_3, b_2, b_1, and b_0 of a 32-bit word B_k are loaded from memory into four registers using the automatic pre-decrement addressing mode of the AVR architecture. Furthermore, we load the first two bytes of the word A_j, namely a_0 and a_1, taking advantage of post-increment addressing. Now, we multiply a_1 by b_1 and copy the 16-bit byte-product to two temporary registers t_0 and t_1 with help of the `movw` instruction. Register t_0 holds the "lower" byte of the product and t_1 the "upper" byte. Next, we form the product $a_0 \cdot b_1$ and add the product to accu register z_1 and the temporary register t_0. A potential carry from this addition can be safely added to the temporary register t_1 without overflowing it. Thereafter, we multiply a_1 by b_0, add the product $a_1 \cdot b_0$ to z_1 and t_0, and propagate the carry from the last addition to t_1. As before, it is not possible to overflow t_1, not even in the most extreme case where the bytes a_0, b_0, a_1, b_1, as well as the involved accu byte z_1, have the maximum possible of 255. After computation of the last byte-product of the first block (which is $a_0 \cdot b_0$), we add it together with the content of the temporary registers t_0, t_1 to the four accu registers z_0, z_1, z_2, z_3, and, finally, propagate the carry bit from the last addition to the carry-catcher register c_0. Overall, the processing of the first dashed block in the middle of Fig. 1 takes four `mul`, one `movw`, and a total of 11 `add` or `adc` instructions, respectively.

The second and third block are processed in essentially the same way as the first one; the only difference is the loading of the remaining two operand bytes of A_j, i.e. a_2 and a_3. Again, we use a carry-catcher register, namely c_1, to deal with the carry that may be generated when adding the last byte-product along with the content of the temporary registers t_0 and t_1 to the four accu registers z_2, z_3, z_4, and z_5. The two operand bytes a_2 and a_3 are loaded right after the computation of the second block, since a_0 and a_1 are not needed anymore. We load a_2 into the register holding a_0 and a_3 into the register of a_1, thereby overwriting a_0 and a_1. In summary, the second and third block execute exactly the same number of instructions as the first block. The fourth block, in which the final four byte-products are generated and added to the accu registers, differs slightly from the former three because no carry-catcher register is needed. Once a_2 has been multiplied by b_2, we add the concatenation of $a_2 \cdot b_2$ with the temporary registers t_0, t_1 to the four accu registers z_4, z_5, z_6, and z_7. However, the carry from the last addition is directly propagated to the most significant accu register z_8. Consequently, the fourth block of byte-products executes the same number of add/adc instructions as the first three blocks, namely 11.

Putting all blocks together, the MAC operation for $d = 4$ comprises a total of eight ld (i.e. load), four movw, 16 mul, and 44 add or adc instructions. On an ATmega128 processor, these instruction counts translate to an execution time of exactly 96 clock cycles [2]. The overall execution time of one iteration of the inner loop (including incrementation of a loop counter and branch instruction) amounts to 99 clock cycles.

The first two nested loops of our RPS squaring technique (Algorithm 2) are very similar to that of RPS multiplication (Algorithm 1), only the termination conditions of the inner loops differ. In particular, the MAC operation executed in the two inner loops is exactly the same and can be implemented in the same way as discussed before. The third loop (line 20 to 24 in Algorithm 2) is unique in the sense that it is only needed for squaring. It is a simple (i.e. "un-nested") loop and squares a w-bit (i.e. 4-byte) word A_i in each iteration. Furthermore, a $2w$-bit quantity of the form $R_{2i+1} \cdot 2^w + R_{2i}$ is doubled and then added to the $2w$-bit square $A_i \times A_i$. The $2w$-bit quantity $R_{2i+1} \cdot 2^w + R_{2i}$ is made up of two w-bit words that form part of the intermediate result of the first two loops; in our case it is simply a 64-bit word of which R_{2i+1} is the upper half and R_{2i} the lower half. Since we have $d = 4$, any w-bit (i.e. 4-byte) word A_i can be squared by computing $(d^2 + d)/2 = 10$ byte-products; six of these have to be doubled and the remaining four not. Therefore, it makes sense to split the computation of $A_i \times A_i$ up into blocks and separate the computation of the byte-products to be doubled from the ones that are not doubled. This technique, which we call *Separated Block Scanning (SBS)*, is illustrated on the right of Fig. 1.

When using the SBS approach for the third loop, the computation of byte-products for a square $A_i \cdot A_i$ is organized in three blocks, indicated by dashed boxes in Fig. 1. At the beginning of an iteration, the four bytes of word A_i and eight bytes of the intermediate result R are loaded from RAM into 12 registers labeled with a_0 to a_3 and z_0 to z_7, respectively. Next, the register z_8 is copied to carry-catcher register c_0 and then cleared. After multiplication of the bytes a_1 and a_0, the product $a_1 \cdot a_0$ is moved to the temporary registers t_0 and t_1. In the next step, the byte-product $a_3 \cdot a_0$ is computed and moved to t_2, t_3. Once $a_2 \cdot a_3$ has been produced, we add all three byte-products to the accu registers z_1 to z_6 and propagate the carry generated by the last addition up to z_8. The second block starts with the multiplication of a_3 by a_0 and a movw instruction to copy the upper byte of $a_3 \cdot a_0$ to t_1 and the lower byte to t_0. Thereafter, we multiply a_2 by a_1, add the byte-product to the accu register pair (z_4, z_3), and propagate the carry into t_1. Finally, the byte-product $a_2 \cdot a_0$ is computed and added along with the content of (t_1, t_0) to the four accu registers z_2 to z_5. The carry from the last addition is again propagated up to z_8, which concludes the second block. Now, the nine accu registers z_0 to z_8 are doubled by executing an add and eight adc instructions. The third block contains all the byte-products that are not doubled, namely $a_l \cdot a_l$ for $0 \leq l \leq 3$. First, we compute the byte-product $a_0 \cdot a_0$, add the carry-catcher c_0 to it, and move the result to the two

Table 2. Execution time (in clock cycles) and code size (in bytes) of different multi-precision multiplication and squaring implementations for operands ranging from 160 to 512 bits on an ATmega128 (the letters U, L, P indicate whether an implementation is unrolled, looped, or parameterized; results marked with * are estimated results)

Implementation	Metric	160 bit	192 bit	224 bit	256 bit	384 bit	512 bit
AVR implementations of multi-precision multiplication:							
Hutter et al. (U) [11]	Time	2030	2987	n/a	4961	n/a	n/a
	Size	3106	4492	n/a	7616	n/a	n/a
Hutter et al. (U) [12]	Time	2396	3470	4694	6124	13702	24318
	Size	3778	5436	7340	9558	21350	37884
Seo et al. (U) [21]	Time	2346	3437	n/a	6128*	n/a	24205*
	Size	3662	n/a	n/a	n/a	n/a	n/a
Hutter et al. (L) [12]	Time	2693	3861	5267	6871	15457	27503
	Size	1562	1866	1538	1766	1614	1544
Liu et al. (P) [15]	Time	2778	4004	5398	7000	15488	27304
	Size	940	940	940	940	940	940
RPS Mul. (P)	Time	2690	3831	5170	6707	14835	26131
	Size	918	918	918	918	918	918
AVR implementations of multi-precision squaring:							
Seo et al. (U) [22]	Time	1456	2014	n/a	n/a	n/a	n/a
	Size	3204	5678	n/a	n/a	n/a	n/a
Liu et al. (L) [16]	Time	2375	3270	4305	5480	11580	19920
	Size	n/a	n/a	n/a	1542	n/a	n/a
RPS Sqr. (P)	time	1795	2457	3218	4078	8508	14522
	size	844	844	844	844	844	844

temporary registers t_0, t_1. Thereafter, the byte-products $a_1 \cdot a_1$ and $a_2 \cdot a_2$ are moved to t_2, t_3 and t_4, t_5, respectively. Finally, we compute $a_3 \cdot a_3$ and add all four byte-products in one pass to the eight accu registers z_0 to z_7, whereby the carry from the last addition is propagated into z_8.

The operation performed in the body of the third loop has a total execution time of 116 clock cycles (excluding counter update and branch instruction).

4   Performance Evaluation and Comparison

In this section, we report implementation results of the proposed RPS method for multiple-precision multiplication and squaring, including execution time (in clock cycles) and code size (in bytes). All timings were obtained by simulation with AVR studio version 4.19 using the ATmega128 [2] as target device.

Table 2 summarizes our results for different operand lengths (ranging from 160 to 512 bits) and compares them with execution time and code size figures of related work. The first three rows show the best previous results for unrolled implementations of multiplication [11,12,21], while the fourth and fifth row in Table 2 contain the fastest looped [12] and parameterized [15] version, respectively. Thereafter, the results of our parameterized RPS method are given. The main conclusion that can be drawn from these results is that the RPS method is slightly faster (and much smaller) than the looped variant of Hutter et al.'s operand caching method [12]. While the difference is merely three clock cycles for 160-bit operands, it increases to about 5 % when the operands are 512 bits long. Our RPS technique sets new records for "not-fully-unrolled" (i.e. looped or parameterized) implementations of multiple-precision multiplication, beaten only by the fully unrolled implementations [11,12,21] at the cost of very large code size. For example, the unrolled operand caching technique for 512 bits has a code size of roughly 37.9 kB, which is almost 30 % of the flash memory of the ATmega128 processor [2]. For comparison, our parameterized implementation of RPS multiplication and squaring occupies less than 1 kB in flash each. RPS squaring is between 33.3 % (160-bit operands) and 44.3 % (512 bits) faster than RPS multiplication. In accordance with common practice, the timings given in Table 2 do not include the function-call overhead and the push/pop of "callee-saved" registers to/from the stack. Both together amounts to 89 clock cycles in the case of RPS multiplication and 85 cycles for RPS squaring.

We combined our RPS multiplication/squaring with Karatsuba's algorithm to further improve performance. More precisely, we implemented a subtractive Karatsuba variant as described in [11, Sect.3] to get a regular execution profile and constant execution time. Part of this effort was to implement a "constant-time conditional negation," which we did as proposed in [11]. However, unlike [11], we decided to not merge all sub-operations of a Karatsuba multiplication

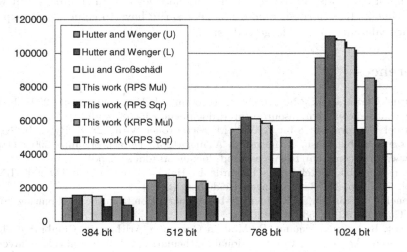

Fig. 2. Execution time (in clock cycles) of different implementations of multiplication and squaring for "large" operand sizes ranging from 384 to 1024 bits

into a single function, but execute them by calling low-level functions (such as subtraction, RPS multiplication, negation) to minimize code size. A graphical comparison of the execution times of our "karatsubarized" RPS multiplication (KRPS multiplication in short) and squaring (i.e. KRPS squaring) is shown in Fig. 2. Since the KRPS multiplication calls 12 low-level functions (which introduces a total function-call overhead of several 100 cycles), Karatsuba's method starts to become beneficial only for relatively large operands, namely 384 bits for multiplication and 640 bits in the case of squaring. When the operands have a length of 512 bits or more, our KRPS variant even outperforms the unrolled operand-caching approach. To give two concrete results, a KRPS multiplication needs 85 k cycles for 1024-bit operands, while a squaring takes 48 k cycles.

5   Conclusions

In this paper we advanced the state-of-the-art in multiple-precision multiplication and squaring on 8-bit AVR processors. We first presented some arguments in favor of parameterized implementations of multiple-precision arithmetic and pointed out that, besides execution time, also scalability and code size deserve consideration. Our main contribution is the RPS technique multiplication and squaring, which follows the basic approach of Gura et al.'s hybrid method from CHES 2004, but optimizes the execution of MAC operations in the inner loops by reversing the order of the byte multiplications. Experimental results show a clear advantage of our RPS technique over a looped realization of the operand caching approach; we are not only faster, but also smaller in terms of code size (e.g. 51 % for 192-bit operands). Combining our RPS method with Karatsuba's idea allowed us to achieve record-setting execution times for multiplication and squaring of operands of a length of 512 bits and beyond. In summary, our work shows that high performance does not necessarily have to come at the expense of poor scalability and/or large code size.

References

1. Atmel Corporation: 8-bit ARV® Instruction Set. User Guide, July 2008. http://www.atmel.com/dyn/resources/prod_documents/doc0856.pdf
2. Atmel Corporation: 8-bit ARV® Microcontroller with 128 K Bytes In-System Programmable Flash: ATmega128, ATmega128L. Datasheet, June 2008. http://www.atmel.com/dyn/resources/prod_documents/doc2467.pdf
3. Bernstein, D.J.: Batch binary Edwards. In: Halevi, S. (ed.) CRYPTO 2009. LNCS, vol. 5677, pp. 317–336. Springer, Heidelberg (2009)
4. Boneh, D., Franklin, M.K.: Identity-based encryption from the Weil pairing. SIAM J. Comput. **32**(3), 586–615 (2003)
5. Brent, R.P., Zimmermann, P.: Modern Computer Arithmetic, Cambridge Monographs on Applied and Computational Mathematics, vol. 18. Cambridge University Press, Cambridge (2010)
6. Comba, P.G.: Exponentiation cryptosystems on the IBM PC. IBM Syst. J. **29**(4), 526–538 (1990)

7. Großschädl, J., Avanzi, R.M., Savaş, E., Tillich, S.: Energy-efficient software implementation of long integer modular arithmetic. In: Rao, J.R., Sunar, B. (eds.) CHES 2005. LNCS, vol. 3659, pp. 75–90. Springer, Heidelberg (2005)
8. Großschädl, J., Savaş, E.: Instruction set extensions for fast arithmetic in finite fields GF(p) and GF(2^m). In: Joye, M., Quisquater, J.-J. (eds.) CHES 2004. LNCS, vol. 3156, pp. 133–147. Springer, Heidelberg (2004)
9. Gura, N., Patel, A., Wander, A., Eberle, H., Shantz, S.C.: Comparing elliptic curve cryptography and RSA on 8-bit CPUs. In: Joye, M., Quisquater, J.-J. (eds.) CHES 2004. LNCS, vol. 3156, pp. 119–132. Springer, Heidelberg (2004)
10. Hankerson, D.R., Menezes, A.J., Vanstone, S.A.: Guide to Elliptic Curve Cryptography. Springer Verlag, New York (2004)
11. Hutter, M., Schwabe, P.: Multiprecision multiplication on AVR revisited. Cryptology ePrint Archive, Report 2014/592 (2014). http://eprint.iacr.org/
12. Hutter, M., Wenger, E.: Fast multi-precision multiplication for public-key cryptography on embedded microprocessors. In: Preneel, B., Takagi, T. (eds.) CHES 2011. LNCS, vol. 6917, pp. 459–474. Springer, Heidelberg (2011)
13. Karatsuba, A.A., Ofman, Y.P.: Multiplication of multidigit numbers on automata. Soviet Physics - Doklady **7**(7), 595–596 (1963)
14. Koblitz, N.I.: Elliptic curve cryptosystems. Math. Comput. **48**(177), 203–209 (1987)
15. Liu, Z., Großschädl, J.: New speed records for montgomery modular multiplication on 8-Bit AVR microcontrollers. In: Pointcheval, D., Vergnaud, D. (eds.) AFRICACRYPT. LNCS, vol. 8469, pp. 215–234. Springer, Heidelberg (2014)
16. Liu, Z., Großschädl, J., Kizhvatov, I.: Efficient and side-channel resistant RSA implementation for 8-bit AVR microcontrollers. In: Proceedings of the 1st International Workshop on the Security of the Internet of Things (SECIOT 2010) (2010)
17. Miller, V.S.: Use of elliptic curves in cryptography. In: Williams, H.C. (ed.) CRYPTO 1985. LNCS, vol. 218, pp. 417–426. Springer, Heidelberg (1986)
18. Rivest, R.L., Shamir, A., Adleman, L.M.: A method for obtaining digital signatures and public key cryptosystems. Commun. ACM **21**(2), 120–126 (1978)
19. Scott, M., Szczechowiak, P.: Optimizing multiprecision multiplication for public key cryptography. Cryptology ePrint Archive, Report 2007/299 (2007). http://eprint.iacr.org
20. Seo, H., Kim, H.: Multi-precision multiplication for public-key cryptography on embedded microprocessors. In: Lee, D.H., Yung, M. (eds.) WISA 2012. LNCS, vol. 7690, pp. 55–67. Springer, Heidelberg (2012)
21. Seo, H., Kim, H.: Optimized multi-precision multiplication for public-key cryptography on embedded microprocessors. Int. J. Comput. Commun. Eng. **2**(3), 255–259 (2013)
22. Seo, H., Liu, Z., Choi, J., Kim, H.: Multi-precision squaring for public-key cryptography on embedded microprocessors. In: Paul, G., Vaudenay, S. (eds.) INDOCRYPT 2013. LNCS, vol. 8250, pp. 227–243. Springer, Heidelberg (2013)
23. Uhsadel, L., Poschmann, A., Paar, C.: Enabling full-size public-key algorithms on 8-bit sensor nodes. In: Stajano, F., Meadows, C., Capkun, S., Moore, T. (eds.) ESAS 2007. LNCS, vol. 4572, pp. 73–86. Springer, Heidelberg (2007)
24. Zhang, Y., Großschädl, J.: Efficient prime-field arithmetic for elliptic curve cryptography on wireless sensor nodes. In: Proceedings of the 1st International Conference on Computer Science and Network Technology (ICCSNT 2011), vol. 1, pp. 459–466. IEEE (2011)

New Security Proof for the Boneh-Boyen IBE: Tight Reduction in Unbounded Multi-challenge Security

Nuttapong Attrapadung, Goichiro Hanaoka, and Shota Yamada[✉]

National Institute of Advanced Industrial Science and Technology (AIST),
Chiyoda-ku, Tokyo, Japan
{n.attrapadung,hanaoka-goichiro,yamada-shota}@aist.go.jp

Abstract. Identity-based encryption (IBE) is an advanced form of public key encryption and one of the most important cryptographic primitives. Of the many constructions of IBE schemes, the one proposed by Boneh and Boyen (in Eurocrypt 2004) is quite important from both practical and theoretical points of view. The scheme was standardized as IEEE P1363.3 and is the basis for many subsequent constructions. In this paper, we investigate its multi-challenge security, which means that an adversary is allowed to query challenge ciphertexts multiple times rather than only once. Since single-challenge security implies multi-challenge security, and since Boneh and Boyen provided a security proof for the scheme in the single-challenge setting, the scheme is also secure in the multi-challenge setting. However, this reduction results in a large security loss. Instead, we give *tight* security reduction for the scheme in the multi-challenge setting. Our reduction is tight even if the number of challenge queries is not fixed in advance (that is, the queries are *unbounded*). Unfortunately, we are only able to prove the security in a selective setting and rely on a non-standard parameterized assumption. Nevertheless, we believe that our new security proof is of interest and provides new insight into the security of the Boneh-Boyen IBE scheme.

1 Introduction

1.1 Background

Identity-Based Encryption. Identity-based encryption (IBE) is an advanced form of public key encryption. It differs in that it enables one to encrypt a message for any string (or identity). A user possessing a private key corresponding to the string can decrypt the ciphertext.

The notion of IBE was first proposed by Shamir [37]. The first realization of a concrete IBE scheme was proposed in [10] (and independently in [36]). This scheme uses a bilinear map on elliptic curves. The notion of hierarchical IBE (HIBE), in which hierarchical key generation is possible, was first proposed

N. Attrapadung—supported by a JSPS Research Fellowship for Young Scientists.

© Springer International Publishing Switzerland 2015
L.C.K. Hui et al. (Eds.): ICICS 2014, LNCS 8958, pp. 176–190, 2015.
DOI: 10.1007/978-3-319-21966-0_13

in [29]. Later, the first HIBE scheme was proposed in [25]. The IBE scheme proposed by Boneh and Franklin [10] as well as the one proposed in [25] have been proven secure under the random oracle model. However, there are several criticisms of the security proof under the random oracle model [13]. Thus, a construction proven secure without the random oracle model (i.e., the standard model) is desirable. The first construction of an (H)IBE scheme proven secure under the standard model was proposed in [14]. Later, a more efficient construction was given in [7]. While they were proven secure without using the random oracle model, they were only proven selectively secure. Subsequently, (H)IBE schemes with adaptive security in the standard model were proposed in [8, 22, 23, 32, 38, 39].

Importance of Tight Security Reduction. When proving the security for a cryptographic scheme, we often have to rely on a number theoretic assumption. In the security proof, first, an adversary who can break the security of the scheme with probability ϵ is assumed, and then an algorithm that has access to the adversary $\mathcal{A}$ and breaks the assumption with probability ϵ' is constructed.[1] If ϵ' is only polynomially smaller than ϵ, ϵ' is negligible assuming ϵ is negligible. The latter is true as long as the number theoretic assumption holds. If it is, we can claim that the scheme is secure. However, this claim is somewhat conditional. Even though the scheme is secure in an *asymptotic* sense, the scheme instantiated with specific security parameters would be broken in the real world. This is because it is possible that ϵ is very small while ϵ' is not very small. We only have that ϵ' is polynomially larger than ϵ, and this polynomial could be very large (e.g., $\epsilon = 2^{-\lambda} = 2^{-128}$, $\epsilon' = \lambda^{15}2^{-\lambda} = 2^{-23}$ and $\lambda = 128$). Thus, a tight security proof, in which $\epsilon' \approx \epsilon$, is desirable.

Previous Works on Tightly Secure IBE. In the case of IBE, security loss caused by a reduction is measured using two parameters: the number of challenge queries to the encryption oracle ($= q_c$) and the number of key generation queries issued by an adversary in a security game ($= q_k$). Since it is shown by the standard hybrid argument that single-challenge security ($q_c = 1$) implies security for the general case, only single-challenge security was considered in most of the previous work. However, this reduction incurs a security loss of $O(q_c)$. Multi-challenge security captures security against an adversary in the real world who chooses weak ciphertext as the target to attack from a large number of ciphertexts. Since q_c could be very large, this would lead to significant security degradation in the real world, as shown by example in [5]. It is thus desirable to construct an IBE scheme with tight reduction in terms of q_c (and of course in terms of q_k).

Constructing an IBE scheme for which the reduction cost of the security proof does not depend on q_c and q_k is an important remaining challenge. Several IBE schemes with tight reduction in terms of q_k have been proposed and thus provide partial solutions to the problem. Attrapadung et al. [4] proposed an IBE scheme with tight reduction in terms of q_k in the random oracle model. Gentry [22] showed such construction in the standard model, but he relied on a less standard parameterized (or q-type) assumption. Chen and Wee [17] recently proposed an

---

[1] Here, we ignore running time of the adversary and algorithm for simplicity.

IBE scheme that is almost tightly secure. The reduction cost in their security proof is a small polynomial in the security parameter and does not depend on q_k. Very recently, Attrapadung [3] showed a security proof for a variant of the Boneh-Boyen IBE scheme implemented on a composite order pairing group. Its reduction cost depends only on the number of key extraction queries before the (single) challenge query. Since all of this previous work considered only single-challenge security, reductions to fully-fuledged multi-challenge security incurs q_c security loss.

1.2   Our Contribution

In this paper, we give a new security proof for the Boneh-Boyen IBE scheme [7] rather than constructing a new IBE scheme. The reduction cost is *tight* and does not depend on q_c. The reason we choose the Boneh-Boyen IBE scheme is that it is important both from practical and theoretical points of view. First, it is one of the most practical IBE schemes and has been standardized as IEEE P1363.3. Second, it is theoretically interesting. The scheme is very simple and is a base for many IBE scheme with adaptive security [30, 32, 38] and schemes based on lattice assumptions [1]. Our new security proof provides new insights into the security of the Boneh-Boyen IBE scheme and is thus potentially useful.

Unfortunately, we are only able to prove the security in the selective model in which the adversary outputs a set of challenge identities $S^\star = \{\mathsf{ID}_1^\star, \ldots, \mathsf{ID}_q^\star\}$ at the outset of the security game. This is very difficult to avoid since a proof for adaptive security of the Boneh-Boyen IBE scheme is not known even under a loose reduction. Even in the selective model, providing a security proof for which the reduction cost does not depend on the number of challenge identities $|S^\star| = q$ is not straightforward. In particular, the original security proof in [9] for the Boneh-Boyen IBE scheme under the decisional bilinear Diffie-Hellman (DBDH) assumption does not work without change. The technique used in the original security proof depends heavily on the "all but one" simulation paradigm in which information about the challenge identity $\mathsf{ID}^\star$ is embedded in the public parameter so that a simulator can generate a private key for any $\mathsf{ID} \neq \mathsf{ID}^\star$. Furthermore, a simulator can generate the challenge ciphertext only for $\mathsf{ID}^\star$. For our setting, we should extend the technique to "all but q". One possible way to achieve this is to use a (selective) $(q, 1)$-programmable hash function, which has been used in previous work [16, 27, 28]. However, this requires changing the construction of the IBE. We would like to prove the security without changing the scheme. Furthermore, such schemes are tightly secure only for an attacker who outputs $S^\star$ such that $|S^\star| \leq q$, where q is *fixed* at the set up of the public parameter. We want to prove tight security for an *unbounded* q.[2]

---

[2] This could be achieved by using a $(\mathsf{poly}, 1)$-programmable hash function, which is a $(q, 1)$-programmable hash function for any polynomial q. However, the known construction of the $(\mathsf{poly}, 1)$-programmable hash function [20] uses a multi-linear map and is thus impractical. Furthermore, there is an impossibility result for construction of $(\mathsf{poly}, 1)$-programmable hash function for prime order groups with a bilinear map [26].

To prove tight security for an unbounded q, we use an "individual randomness technique", which has been used to prove the security of unbounded attribute-based encryption and revocation schemes [3, 31, 33, 35, 40–42], instead of using the $(q, 1)$-programmable hash approach. The use of this technique requires a non-standard number theoretic assumption. We introduce a parameterized assumption that we call the truncated q-RW assumption to prove the security. The assumption is a weaker variant of the q-2 assumption introduced by Rouse-lakis and Waters (RW) [35] to prove the security of an unbounded key-policy attribute-based encryption scheme. In our proof, we also require a certain kind of random self reducibility of the truncated q-RW assumption. We show this following an argument similar to that of [34], who proved random self-reducibility of the DDH assumption.

To make our proof more modular and clearer, we divide it into two steps. In the first step, we introduce a new assumption that we call the oracle truncated q-RW assumption and show that this assumption is tightly reduced to the (seemingly weaker) truncated q-RW assumption. This step essentially shows random self reducibility of the truncated q-RW assumption. In the second step, we show that the multi-challenge security of the Boneh-Boyen IBE scheme is tightly reduced to the truncated q-RW assumption. Combining these results, we obtain a tight security proof for the Boneh-Boyen IBE scheme from the truncated q-RW assumption.

2 Definition of Identity-Based Encryption

2.1 Syntax

Let $\mathcal{ID}$ be the ID space of the scheme. If a collision resistant hash function $H : \{0, 1\}^* \to \mathcal{ID}$ is available, then one can use an arbitrary string as an identity. An IBE scheme is defined by the following four algorithms.

Setup$(\lambda) \to$ (mpk, msk): The setup algorithm takes as input a security parameter λ and outputs a master public key mpk and a master secret key msk.

KeyGen(msk, mpk, ID) $\to$ sk$_{\mathsf{ID}}$: The key generation algorithm takes as input the master secret key msk, the master public key mpk, and an identity ID $\in \mathcal{ID}$. It outputs a private key sk$_{\mathsf{ID}}$. We assume that ID is implicitly included in sk$_{\mathsf{ID}}$.

Encrypt(mpk, M, ID) $\to C$: The encryption algorithm takes as input a master public key mpk, the message M, and a ciphertext attribute ID $\in \mathcal{ID}$. It outputs a ciphertext C. We assume that ID is implicitly included in C.

Decrypt(mpk, C, sk$_{\mathsf{ID}}$) $\to$ M or $\perp$: We assume that the decryption algorithm is deterministic. The decryption algorithm takes as input the master public key mpk, a ciphertext C, and a private key sk$_{\mathsf{ID}}$. It outputs the message M or $\perp$ which means that the ciphertext is not in a valid form.

We require correctness of decryption: that is, for all λ, all (mpk, msk) produced by Setup(λ), all ID $\in \mathcal{ID}$, and all sk$_{\mathsf{ID}}$ returned by KeyGen(msk, mpk, ID), Decrypt(mpk, Encrypt(mpk, M, ID), ID, sk$_{\mathsf{ID}}$) = M holds.

2.2   Security

We now define the security for an IBE scheme Π. This security notion is defined by the following game between a challenger and an adversary $\mathcal{A}$.

Setup. At the outset of the game, $\mathcal{A}$ outputs a set of identities $S^\star = \{\mathsf{ID}_1^\star, \ldots, \mathsf{ID}_q^\star\} \subseteq \mathcal{ID}$. The challenger flips a random coin $\mathsf{coin} \xleftarrow{\$} \{0,1\}$. The challenger also runs the setup algorithm and gives mpk to $\mathcal{A}$.

Then, $\mathcal{A}$ may adaptively make following two types of queries in arbitrary order and arbitrary many times.

- **Key Extraction Queries.** $\mathcal{A}$ may adaptively make key-extraction queries. If $\mathcal{A}$ submits $\mathsf{ID} \notin S^\star$ to the challenger, the challenger returns $\mathsf{sk}_{\mathsf{ID}} \leftarrow \mathsf{KeyGen}(\mathsf{msk}, \mathsf{mpk}, \mathsf{ID})$.
- **Challenge Queries.** $\mathcal{A}$ may also make challenge queries. If $\mathcal{A}$ outputs two equal length messages $(\mathsf{M}_0, \mathsf{M}_1)$ and an identity $\mathsf{ID}^\star \in S^\star$, the challenger runs $\mathsf{Encrypt}(\mathsf{mpk}, \mathsf{M}_{\mathsf{coin}}, \mathsf{ID}^\star) \to C^\star$ and gives challenge ciphertext $C^\star$ to $\mathcal{A}$.

Guess. Finally, $\mathcal{A}$ outputs guess $\widehat{\mathsf{coin}}$ for coin. We say that $\mathcal{A}$ succeeds if $\widehat{\mathsf{coin}} = \mathsf{coin}$ and denote the probability of this event by $\Pr_{\mathcal{A},\Pi}$. The advantage of $\mathcal{A}$ is defined as $Adv_{\mathcal{A},\Pi}^{PE} = |\Pr_{\mathcal{A},\Pi} - \frac{1}{2}|$. We say that adversary $\mathcal{A}$ $(t, q, q_k, q_c, \epsilon)$-breaks Π if it runs in time t, outputs $S^\star$ with a size that is at most q, makes at most q_k key extraction and q_c challenge queries, and has advantage ϵ. We say that Π is secure if ϵ is negligible for any probabilistic polynomial time $\mathcal{A}$.

We call this security game the *(selective) multi-challenge security game* to distinguish it from the ordinary selective security game [7,14]. The ordinary game is captured as a special case of the selective game in that the adversary obtains only one challenge ciphertext, and the size of $S^\star$ is restricted to $|S^\star| = 1$. We call this security notion single-challenge ciphertext security.

RELATION TO SINGLE-CHALLENGE SECURITY. Note that multi-challenge security is implied by single-challenge security, as shown by the standard hybrid argument. However, this incurs a security loss of $O(q_c)$. See Appendix A for a sketch of the proof.

3   Number Theoretic Assumptions

In this section, we define number theoretic assumptions that will be used in our security proof for the Boneh-Boyen IBE scheme. We introduce two assumptions named the truncated q-RW assumption and the oracle truncated q-RW assumption. The former assumption holds in the generic group model and is weaker than the q-2 assumption introduced by Rouselakis and Waters [35] although it is parameterized and a non-standard assumption. The latter assumption is more complicated, but we will see in Sect. 3.2 that it is implied by the simpler former assumption. In the next section, we show the (multi-challenge ciphertext) security of the Boneh-Boyen IBE scheme using the latter assumption. These results together imply that the scheme is secure under the first assumption. The reason we introduce the latter assumption is that it makes our proof clearer and more modular.

3.1 Definition of Assumptions

Truncated q-RW Assumption. Let $x, y, z, b_1, \ldots, b_q \xleftarrow{\$} \mathbb{Z}_p$ and $g \xleftarrow{\$} \mathbb{G}^*$. We define Ψ as

$$
\Psi = \begin{pmatrix}
g & & \\
g^{xzb_i}, \; g^{y/b_i^2}, \; g^{b_i} & & \forall i \in [q] \\
g^{xyzb_i/b_j^2}, \; g^{yb_i/b_j^2} & \forall (i,j) \in [q] \times [q], \; i \neq j
\end{pmatrix}
$$

We say that an algorithm $\mathcal{A}$ (t, ϵ)-breaks the truncated q-RW assumption on $(\mathbb{G}, \mathbb{G}_T)$ if it runs in time t and $\frac{1}{2}|\Pr[\mathcal{A}(\Psi, T = e(g,g)^{xyz}) \to 0] - \Pr[\mathcal{A}(\Psi, T = R) \to 0]| \geq \epsilon$ where $R \xleftarrow{\$} \mathbb{G}_T$. We say that the truncated q-RW assumption holds if there exists no algorithm that (t, ϵ)-breaks the truncated q-RW assumption with polynomial t and non-negligible ϵ.

COMPARISON TO PREVIOUS ASSUMPTIONS. This assumption is weaker than the q-2 assumption introduced and used by Rouselakis and Waters [35] to prove the security of an unbounded key-policy attribute-based encryption scheme. In the q-2 assumption, compared with the truncated q-RW assumption defined above, algorithm $\mathcal{A}$ can obtain extra group elements in addition to Ψ. This is the basis for name of the truncated q-RW assumption. Since the q-2 assumption holds in the generic group model, the truncated q-RW assumption also holds in the generic group model. In Appendix B, we give a direct proof. If $q = 1$, this assumption corresponds to the standard decisional bilinear Diffie-Hellman (DBDH) assumption, which roughly states that, given $g^\alpha, g^\beta, and \; g^\gamma$, it is infeasible to distinguish $e(g,g)^{\alpha\beta\gamma}$ from a random group element of $\mathbb{G}_T$, where $\alpha, \beta, \gamma \xleftarrow{\$} \mathbb{Z}_p$. This can be seen by observing that $(g^{xzb_1}, g^{y/b_1^2}, g^{b_1})$ is distributed uniformly randomly over $\mathbb{G}_p^3$ and $xyz = (xzb_1) \cdot (y/b_1^2) \cdot b_1$.

Next we define the other new assumption used in our security proof. We show that the assumption is equivalent to the truncated q-RW assumption in Sect. 3.2.

Oracle Truncated q-RW Assumption. Let $y, b_1, \ldots, b_q \xleftarrow{\$} \mathbb{Z}_p$ and $g \xleftarrow{\$} \mathbb{G}^*$. We define Ψ' as

$$
\Psi' = \begin{pmatrix}
g & & \\
g^{y/b_i^2}, \; g^{b_i} & & \forall i \in [q] \\
g^{yb_i/b_j^2} & \forall (i,j) \in [q] \times [q], \; i \neq j
\end{pmatrix}
$$

We say that algorithm $\mathcal{A}$ $(t, \bar{q}, \epsilon)$-breaks the oracle truncated q-RW assumption on $(\mathbb{G}, \mathbb{G}_T)$ if it runs in time t, $\frac{1}{2}|\Pr[\mathcal{A}(\Psi')^{\mathcal{O}_0(\cdot)} \to 0] - \Pr[\mathcal{A}(\Psi')^{\mathcal{O}_1(\cdot)} \to 0]| \geq \epsilon$, and $\mathcal{A}$ queries the oracle at most $\bar{q}$ times. Here, oracle $\mathcal{O}_\beta(\cdot)$ for $\beta \in \{0,1\}$ is an oracle that takes index $\tau \in [q]$ as input and returns

$$
\left(g^s, \quad g^{sy/b_j^2} \; \forall j \in [q]\backslash\{\tau\}, \quad T' = R'_\beta \right)
$$

to $\mathcal{A}$. Here, $s \xleftarrow{\$} \mathbb{Z}_p$, $R'_0 = e(g,g)^{sy/b_\tau}$, and $R'_1 \xleftarrow{\$} \mathbb{G}_T$. We emphasize that s and R'_1 are *freshly chosen* every time $\mathcal{A}$ accesses the oracle. We say that the oracle truncated q-RW assumption holds if there exists no algorithm that $(t, \bar{q}, \epsilon)$-breaks the assumption with polynomials t and $\bar{q}$ and non-negligible ϵ.

3.2   Relationship Between Assumptions

Here we show that the oracle truncated q-RW assumption can be *tightly* reduced to the truncated q-RW assumption. Essentially, we prove that the truncated q-RW assumption has random self-reducibility in some sense. The proof is similar to the one used in [34], where random self-reducibility of the DDH assumption was proved.

Theorem 1. *If there exists $\mathcal{A}$ that $(t, \bar{q}, \epsilon)$-breaks the oracle truncated q-RW assumption, there exists $\mathcal{B}$ that (t', ϵ')-breaks the truncated q-RW assumption where $t' = t + O(q\bar{q}t_{\mathsf{exp},\mathbb{G}}) + O(\bar{q}(t_{\mathsf{exp},\mathbb{G}_T} + t_{\mathsf{pair}})$ and $\epsilon' = \epsilon - 1/p$. Here, $t_{\mathsf{exp},\mathbb{G}}$, $t_{\mathsf{exp},\mathbb{G}_T}$, and t_{pair} are the times needed for one exponentiation in $\mathbb{G}$ and $\mathbb{G}_T$ and for pairing computation, respectively.*

Proof. We construct $\mathcal{B}$ that breaks the truncated q-RW assumption with advantage ϵ' using an adversary $\mathcal{A}$ that breaks the oracle truncated q-RW assumption with advantage ϵ. $\mathcal{B}$ is given problem instance of truncated q-RW assumption (Ψ, T) where $T = e(g,g)^{xyz+\delta}$. Here, $\delta = 0$ or $\delta \xleftarrow{\$} \mathbb{Z}_p$ and $\mathcal{B}$ should guess which is the case. Then, $\mathcal{B}$ gives part of the problem instance $\Psi' := \{g, g^{y/b_i^2}, g^{b_i} \, \forall i \in [q], g^{yb_i/b_j^2} \, \forall(i,j) \in [q] \times [q], i \neq j\}$ to $\mathcal{A}$. As k-th query, $\mathcal{A}$ would outputs $\tau \in [q]$. To answer the query, $\mathcal{B}$ first picks $c^{(k)}, d^{(k)} \xleftarrow{\$} \mathbb{Z}_p$ and computes

$$g^{s^{(k)}} := (g^{xzb_\tau})^{c^{(k)}} \cdot g^{d^{(k)}},$$
$$g^{s^{(k)}y/b_j^2} := (g^{xyzb_\tau/b_j^2})^{c^{(k)}} \cdot (g^{y/b_j^2})^{d^{(k)}} \quad \forall j \in [q] \backslash \{\tau\},$$
$$T'^{(k)} := T^{c^{(k)}} \cdot e(g^{y/b_\tau^2}, g^{b_\tau})^{d^{(k)}}.$$

These terms can be efficiently computed from Ψ. $\mathcal{B}$ gives these group elements to $\mathcal{A}$. Here, $\mathcal{B}$ implicitly sets $s^{(k)} = c^{(k)}xzb_\tau + d^{(k)}$. At last, $\mathcal{A}$ outputs a bit. $\mathcal{B}$ outputs the same bit.

Next, we analyze the view of $\mathcal{A}$. We first observe that Ψ' is correctly distributed. We also observe that $s^{(k)} = c^{(k)}xzb_\tau + d^{(k)}$ is uniformly distributed over $\mathbb{Z}_p$ due to $d^{(k)}$ for all $k \in [\bar{q}]$. We remark that $(c^{(k)}, d^{(k)})$ is uniformly distributed over $\mathbb{Z}_p^2$ under the constraint that $s^{(k)} = c^{(k)}xzb_\tau + d^{(k)}$. In particular, all $c^{(k)}$ is information theoretically hidden from $\mathcal{A}$ and uniformly distributed over $\mathbb{Z}_p$. More subtle part of the proof is analysis of the distribution of $T'^{(k)}$. We have that

$$T'^{(k)} = (e(g,g)^{xyz+\delta})^{c^{(k)}} \cdot (e(g,g)^{y/b_\tau})^{d^{(k)}}$$
$$= e(g,g)^{y/b_\tau(xzb_\tau c^{(k)}+d^{(k)})} \cdot e(g,g)^{\delta c^{(k)}}$$
$$= e(g,g)^{s^{(k)}y/b_\tau} \cdot e(g,g)^{c^{(k)}\delta}$$

for all $k \in [\bar{q}]$. If $\delta = 0$, we have $T'^{(k)} = e(g,g)^{s^{(k)}y/b_\tau}$ for $\tau \in [\bar{q}]$ and the response of $\mathcal{B}$ for $\mathcal{A}$'s queries corresponds to that of $\mathcal{O}_0$. On the other hand, in the case of $\delta \neq 0$ (which is the case with probability $1 - 1/p$ if $\delta \xleftarrow{\$} \mathbb{Z}_p$), $T'^{(k)}$ is uniformly distributed over $\mathbb{G}_T$ and independent from anything. This is because $c^{(k)}$ is information theoretically hidden from $\mathcal{A}$. To sum up, in the case of $\delta = 0$, the distribution of $\mathcal{B}$'s response to the queries made by $\mathcal{A}$ corresponds to that of $\mathcal{O}_0$ while it corresponds to $\mathcal{O}_1$ if $\delta \neq 0$. Thus, we have that

$$
\begin{aligned}
\epsilon' &= \frac{1}{2} |\Pr[\mathcal{B}(\Psi, T = e(g,g)^{xyz}) \to 0] - \Pr[\mathcal{B}(\Psi, T \leftarrow \mathbb{G}_T) \to 0]| \\
&= \frac{1}{2} |\Pr[\mathcal{A}^{\mathcal{O}_0(\cdot)}(\Psi') \to 0] - \Pr[\mathcal{B}(\Psi, T \xleftarrow{\$} \mathbb{G}_T) \to 0|\delta \neq 0] \Pr[\delta \neq 0] \\
&\quad - \Pr[\mathcal{B}(\Psi, T \xleftarrow{\$} \mathbb{G}_T) \to 0|\delta = 0] \Pr[\delta = 0]| \\
&= \frac{1}{2} |\Pr[\mathcal{A}^{\mathcal{O}_0(\cdot)}(\Psi') \to 0] - \Pr[\mathcal{A}(\Psi')^{\mathcal{O}_1(\cdot)} \to 0](1 - 1/p) \\
&\quad - \Pr[\mathcal{B}(\Psi, T \xleftarrow{\$} \mathbb{G}_T) \to 0|\delta = 0]/p| \\
&\geq \frac{1}{2} |\Pr[\mathcal{A}^{\mathcal{O}_0(\cdot)}(\Psi') \to 0] - \Pr[\mathcal{A}(\Psi')^{\mathcal{O}_1(\cdot)} \to 0]| - 1/p = \epsilon - 1/p
\end{aligned}
$$

as desired.

4   New Security Proof for the Boneh-Boyen IBE Scheme

In this section, we show a tight security proof for the multi-challenge ciphertext security of the Boneh-Boyen IBE scheme under the truncated q-RW assumption (or equivalently, oracle truncated q-RW assumption). We first review the description of the Boneh-Boyen IBE scheme [7].

Setup(λ): It chooses bilinear groups $(\mathbb{G}, \mathbb{G}_T)$ of prime order $p > 2^\lambda$ with $g \xleftarrow{\$} \mathbb{G}^*$. It also picks $u, v \xleftarrow{\$} \mathbb{G}$ and $\alpha \xleftarrow{\$} \mathbb{Z}_p$. It finally outputs the master public key $\mathsf{mpk} = (g, u, v, e(g,g)^\alpha)$ and the master secret key $\mathsf{msk} = \alpha$.

KeyGen($\mathsf{msk}, \mathsf{mpk}, \mathsf{ID}$): To generate a private key for ID, it chooses $r \xleftarrow{\$} \mathbb{Z}_p$ and outputs $\mathsf{sk_{ID}} = (K_1 = g^\alpha \cdot (u^{\mathsf{ID}}v)^r, K_2 = g^r)$.

Encrypt($\mathsf{mpk}, \mathsf{ID}, \mathsf{M}$): To encrypt a message M for ID, it chooses $s \xleftarrow{\$} \mathbb{Z}_p$ and outputs a ciphertext $C = (C_0 = e(g,g)^{s\alpha} \cdot \mathsf{M}, C_1 = g^s, C_2 = (u^{\mathsf{ID}}v)^s)$.

Decrypt($\mathsf{sk_{ID}}, C$): To decrypt a ciphertext, it first computes $e(C_1, K_1)/e(C_2, K_2) = e(g,g)^{s\alpha}$ and outputs $C_0/e(g,g)^{s\alpha} = \mathsf{M}$.

The following theorem establishes the multi-challenge ciphertext security of the Boneh-Boyen IBE scheme under the oracle truncated q-RW assumption.

Theorem 2. *If there is $\mathcal{A}$ that $(t, q, q_k, q_c, \epsilon)$-breaks the Boneh-Boyen IBE scheme, there is $\mathcal{B}$ that $(t', q_c, \epsilon/2)$-breaks the oracle truncated q-RW assumption where $t' = t + O(q^2 q_k t_{\mathsf{exp},\mathbb{G}}) + O(qq_c(t_{\mathsf{exp},\mathbb{G}} + t_{\mathsf{exp},\mathbb{G}_T} + t_{\mathsf{pair}}))$. Here, $t_{\mathsf{exp},\mathbb{G}}$, $t_{\mathsf{exp},\mathbb{G}_T}$, and t_{pair} are the times needed for one exponentiation in $\mathbb{G}$ and $\mathbb{G}_T$ and for pairing computation, respectively.*

Proof. We construct an algorithm $\mathcal{B}$ that breaks the oracle truncated q-RW assumption using an adversary $\mathcal{A}$ against the Boneh-Boyen IBE scheme. $\mathcal{B}$ is given problem instance Ψ' and has oracle access for $\mathcal{O}_\beta$.

Setup. At the outset of the game, the adversary $\mathcal{A}$ declares a set of challenge identities $S^\star = (\mathsf{ID}_1^\star, \ldots, \mathsf{ID}_q^\star)$. $\mathcal{B}$ then picks $\tilde{u}, \tilde{v}, \tilde{\alpha} \xleftarrow{\$} \mathbb{Z}_p$ and computes

$$u = g^{\tilde{u}} \cdot \prod_{i \in [q]} g^{y/b_i^2}, \quad v = g^{\tilde{v}} \cdot \prod_{i \in [q]} (g^{y/b_i^2})^{-\mathsf{ID}_i^\star}, \quad e(g,g)^\alpha = e(g,g)^{\tilde{\alpha}} \cdot \prod_{i \in [q]} e(g^{b_i}, g^{y/b_i^2})$$

Note that $\mathcal{B}$ implicitly sets $\alpha = \tilde{\alpha} + \sum_{i \in [q]} y/b_i$. Then $\mathcal{B}$ gives master public key $\mathsf{mpk} = (g, u, v, e(g,g)^\alpha)$ to $\mathcal{A}$. $\mathcal{B}$ also flips random coin $\mathsf{coin} \xleftarrow{\$} \{0, 1\}$.

Key Extraction Queries. During the game, $\mathcal{A}$ makes key extraction queries for ID such that $\mathsf{ID} \notin \{\mathsf{ID}_1^\star, \ldots, \mathsf{ID}_q^\star\}$. Then, $\mathcal{B}$ picks $\tilde{r} \xleftarrow{\$} \mathbb{Z}_p$ and implicitly sets

$$r = \tilde{r} - \sum_{i \in [q]} \frac{b_i}{\mathsf{ID} - \mathsf{ID}_i^\star}.$$

Since $\mathsf{ID} \notin \{\mathsf{ID}_1^\star, \ldots, \mathsf{ID}_q^\star\}$, the denominators $\mathsf{ID} - \mathsf{ID}_i^\star$ are non zero and thus r is well defined. Notice that r is properly distributed because $\tilde{r}$ is uniformly distributed over $\mathbb{Z}_p$. Then, $\mathcal{B}$ can computes

$$K_2 = g^r = g^{\tilde{r}} \cdot \prod_{i \in [q]} (g^{b_i})^{-1/(\mathsf{ID} - \mathsf{ID}_i^\star)}$$

and

$$
\begin{aligned}
K_1 &= g^\alpha \cdot (u^{\mathsf{ID}} v)^r \\
&= g^{\tilde{\alpha}} \cdot \prod_{i \in [q]} g^{y/b_i} \cdot \Big(g^{\tilde{u}\mathsf{ID}+\tilde{v}} \cdot \prod_{i \in [q]} (g^{y/b_i^2})^{\mathsf{ID}-\mathsf{ID}_i^\star}\Big)^r \\
&= g^{\tilde{\alpha}} \cdot K_2^{\tilde{u}\mathsf{ID}+\tilde{v}} \cdot \prod_{i \in [q]} g^{y/b_i} \cdot \Big(\prod_{i \in [q]} (g^{y/b_i^2})^{\mathsf{ID}-\mathsf{ID}_i^\star}\Big)^r \\
&= \underbrace{g^{\tilde{\alpha}} \cdot K_2^{\tilde{u}\mathsf{ID}+\tilde{v}} \cdot \prod_{i \in [q]} (g^{y/b_i^2})^{\tilde{r}(\mathsf{ID}-\mathsf{ID}_i^\star)} \cdot \prod_{i \in [q]} g^{y/b_i}}_{=\Phi} \\
&\qquad \cdot \Big(\prod_{i \in [q]} (g^{y/b_i^2})^{\mathsf{ID}-\mathsf{ID}_i^\star}\Big)^{-\sum_{j \in [q]} b_j/(\mathsf{ID}-\mathsf{ID}_j^\star)} \\
&= \Phi \cdot \prod_{i \in [q]} g^{y/b_i} \cdot \prod_{(i,j) \in [q] \times [q]} (g^{yb_j/b_i^2})^{-(\mathsf{ID}-\mathsf{ID}_i^\star)/(\mathsf{ID}-\mathsf{ID}_j^\star)} \\
&= \Phi \cdot \prod_{i \in [q]} g^{y/b_i} \cdot \prod_{i \in [q]} (g^{y/b_i})^{-(\mathsf{ID}-\mathsf{ID}_i^\star)/(\mathsf{ID}-\mathsf{ID}_i^\star)} \\
&\qquad \cdot \prod_{\substack{(i,j) \in [q] \times [q] \\ i \neq j}} (g^{yb_j/b_i^2})^{-(\mathsf{ID}-\mathsf{ID}_i^\star)/(\mathsf{ID}-\mathsf{ID}_j^\star)}
\end{aligned}
$$

$$= \Phi \cdot \prod_{\substack{(i,j)\in[q]\times[q] \\ i\neq j}} (g^{yb_j/b_i^2})^{-(\mathsf{ID}-\mathsf{ID}_i^\star)/(\mathsf{ID}-\mathsf{ID}_j^\star)}$$

where $\Phi = g^{\tilde\alpha} \cdot K_2^{\tilde u \mathsf{ID}+\tilde v} \cdot \prod_{i\in[q]}(g^{y/b_i^2})^{\tilde r(\mathsf{ID}-\mathsf{ID}_i^\star)}$. In the last equation above, problematic terms g^{y/b_i} for $i \in [q]$ are cancelled out. It is possible to verify that $\mathcal{B}$ can compute K_1 efficiently from the given terms. Finally, $\mathcal{B}$ gives $\mathsf{sk}_{\mathsf{ID}} = (K_1, K_2)$ to $\mathcal{A}$.

Challenge Queries. During the game, $\mathcal{A}$ outputs a pair of messages $\mathsf{M}_0, \mathsf{M}_1$ and an identity $\mathsf{ID}_\tau^\star \in S^\star$. $\mathcal{B}$ computes challenge ciphertext for $\mathsf{ID}_\tau^\star$ as follows. $\mathcal{B}$ first sends τ to its oracle $\mathcal{O}_\beta$ to obtain group elements $\{g^s, g^{sy/b_j^2} \; \forall j \in [q]\backslash\{\tau\}, T' = R_\beta'\}$. Then $\mathcal{B}$ sets $C_1 = g^s$ and computes

$$
\begin{aligned}
C_2 &= (u^{\mathsf{ID}_\tau^\star}v)^s \\
&= \Big(g^{\tilde u \mathsf{ID}_\tau^\star+\tilde v} \cdot \prod_{i\in[q]}(g^{y/b_i^2})^{\mathsf{ID}_\tau^\star-\mathsf{ID}_i^\star}\Big)^s \\
&= C_1^{\tilde u \mathsf{ID}_\tau^\star+\tilde v} \cdot \prod_{i\in[q]\backslash\{\tau\}}(g^{sy/b_i^2})^{\mathsf{ID}_\tau^\star-\mathsf{ID}_i^\star}.
\end{aligned}
$$

The problematic term g^{sy/b_τ^2} above is cancelled out. Thus, $\mathcal{B}$ can compute C_2 efficiently. $\mathcal{B}$ then computes C_0 as

$$C_0 = e(g^s,g)^{\tilde\alpha} \cdot \prod_{i\in[q]\backslash\{\tau\}} e(g^{b_i}, g^{sy/b_i^2}) \cdot T' \cdot \mathsf{M}_{\mathsf{coin}}$$

and gives (C_0, C_1, C_2) to $\mathcal{A}$. If $T' = e(g,g)^{sy/b_\tau}$, it can be seen that the distribution of (C_0, C_1, C_2) corresponds to correctly generated ciphertext since

$$
\begin{aligned}
C_0 &= e(g^s,g)^{\tilde\alpha} \cdot \prod_{i\in[q]\backslash\{\tau\}} e(g^{b_i}, g^{sy/b_i^2}) \cdot T' \cdot \mathsf{M}_{\mathsf{coin}} \\
&= e(g,g)^{s\cdot\tilde\alpha} \cdot \prod_{i\in[q]\backslash\{\tau\}} e(g^{y/b_i}, g^s) \cdot e(g,g)^{sy/b_\tau} \cdot \mathsf{M}_{\mathsf{coin}} \\
&= e(g,g)^{s\cdot(\tilde\alpha + \prod_{i\in[q]\backslash\{\tau\}} y/b_i)} \cdot e(g,g)^{sy/b_\tau} \cdot \mathsf{M}_{\mathsf{coin}} \\
&= e(g,g)^{s\cdot(\tilde\alpha + \prod_{i\in[q]} y/b_i)} \cdot \mathsf{M}_{\mathsf{coin}} \\
&= e(g,g)^{s\alpha} \cdot \mathsf{M}_{\mathsf{coin}}.
\end{aligned}
$$

On the other hand, if $T' \xleftarrow{\$} \mathbb{G}_T$, C_2 is uniformly distributed over $\mathbb{G}_T$ and the distribution of (C_0, C_1, C_2) is independent of coin.

Guess. Finally, $\mathcal{A}$ outputs $\widehat{\mathsf{coin}}$ as its guess for coin. $\mathcal{B}$ outputs 0 if $\mathsf{coin} = \widehat{\mathsf{coin}}$ and 1 if $\mathsf{coin} \neq \widehat{\mathsf{coin}}$. Then, we analyze the advantage of $\mathcal{B}$. We observe that $\mathcal{B}$ perfectly simulates security game of IBE for $\mathcal{A}$ if the oracle is $\mathcal{O}_0$. On the other hand, $\mathcal{A}$'s view is perfectly independent of coin if the oracle is $\mathcal{O}_1$. Thus we have

$$\frac{1}{2}|\Pr[\mathcal{B}^{\mathcal{O}_0(\cdot)}(\Psi') \to 0] - \Pr[\mathcal{B}^{\mathcal{O}_1(\cdot)}(\Psi') \to 0]| = \frac{1}{2}|\Pr[\mathcal{A} \text{ outputs coin}] - 1/2| = \frac{\epsilon}{2}$$

as desired. This completes the proof of Theorem 2.

Combining Theorems 1 and 2, we get the following theorem, which states that the security of the Boneh-Boyen IBE scheme is *tightly* reduced to the truncated q-RW assumption.

Theorem 3. *If there is $\mathcal{A}$ that $(t, q, q_k, q_c, \epsilon)$-breaks the Boneh-Boyen IBE scheme, then there is $\mathcal{B}$ that $(t', q_c, \epsilon/2)$-breaks truncated q-RW assumption where $t' = t + O(q^2 q_k t_{\mathsf{exp},\mathbb{G}}) + O(q q_c(t_{\mathsf{exp},\mathbb{G}} + t_{\mathsf{exp},\mathbb{G}_T} + t_{\mathsf{pair}}))$. Here, $t_{\mathsf{exp},\mathbb{G}}$, $t_{\mathsf{exp},\mathbb{G}_T}$, and t_{pair} are necessary time for one exponentiation in $\mathbb{G}$, $\mathbb{G}_T$, and for pairing computation, respectively.*

REMARK. The above proof corresponds to the original security proof for the Boneh-Boyen IBE scheme given in [7] when $q = 1$. Recall that the truncated q-RW assumption (as well as the oracle truncated q-RW assumption, by Theorem 1) corresponds to the DBDH assumption when $q = 1$.

5   Discussion

Tightness of Our Reduction. Here, we validate our claim that our proof is tight. First, we recall a measure called work factor, which was introduced by Galindo [21] and used in [6]. For an adversary running in time t with advantage ϵ, the work factor is defined as t/ϵ. This quantity can be defined naturally for IBE and number theoretic assumptions. The work factor can be used to compare the tightness of reductions. We can say that a reduction is tight if the increase in the work factor in the security reduction is small.

Theorem 3 says that we can convert an adversary having work factor t/ϵ against the Boneh-Boyen IBE scheme into an adversary against the truncated q-RW assumption that has work factor $2\big(t + O(q^2 q_k t_{\mathsf{exp},\mathbb{G}}) + O(q q_c(t_{\mathsf{exp},\mathbb{G}} + t_{\mathsf{exp},\mathbb{G}_T} + t_{\mathsf{pair}}))\big)/\epsilon$. If q, q_c, and q_k are much smaller than t, which would be the case in the real world since these quantities are related to the number of on-line queries that the adversary makes, we have $t' = t + O(q^2 q_k t_{\mathsf{exp},\mathbb{G}}) + O(q q_c(t_{\mathsf{exp},\mathbb{G}} + t_{\mathsf{exp},\mathbb{G}_T} + t_{\mathsf{pair}})) \approx ct$ for some small constant c. (For example, for $t = 2^{100}$, $q = q_c = q_k = 2^{30}$, $t' \approx 2^{100} + 2^{90} < 2^{101}$). Thus, the increase in the work factor would typically be very small and could be considered a small constant.[3]

As mentioned in Sect. 2, single-challenge security implies multi-challenge security by the standard hybrid argument. Roughly speaking, this reduction converts an adversary against the Boneh-Boyen IBE scheme with work factor t/ϵ into an adversary against the DBDH assumption with work factor $t' q_c/\epsilon$. Typically, $t' \approx t$, so the increase in the work factor is about q_c, which can be very large. (In the example above, $q_c = 2^{30}$).

Implications of Our Result. While our result gives tight security reduction for the Boneh-Boyen IBE scheme, we rely on a non-standard parameterized assumption. It is unclear whether tight reduction from a non-standard assumption such

---

[3] While additive factor $O(q^2 q_k t_{\mathsf{exp},\mathbb{G}})$ in t' is rather large, t' could be much larger than t for certain parameter choices. However, we believe that our reduction is tight for most parameters meaningful in the real world.

as the truncated q-RW assumption is better than loose reduction from a standard assumption such as the DBDH assumption. It is if the truncated q-RW assumption is as hard as the DBDH assumption. Otherwise, it is not. A similar discussion can be found in [22], where the author compares his IBE scheme, which can be tightly reduced to a parameterized assumption, with IBE schemes such as that in [38], which can be proven secure under a standard assumption (such as the DBDH assumption). There are two differences from his setting. First, we have two types of security proof for *the same scheme* rather than two different schemes. Second, while the security assumption used in [22] (decisional augmented bilinear Diffie-Hellman exponent assumption) is vulnerable to Cheon's attack [18], it seems that the attack does not break our assumption, at least without non-trivial modification. Our result is complementary to the original security proof given by Boneh and Boyen and would lead to increased confidence in the security of the scheme.

A   Single-Challenge Security Implies Multi-challenge Security

We briefly show that multi-challenge security is implied by the single-challenge security. We consider a sequence of games. Let $S^\star = \{\mathsf{ID}_1^\star, \ldots, \mathsf{ID}_q^\star\}$. We define $q_c^{(i)}$ as the number of challenge queries for $\mathsf{ID}_i^\star$. Thus, we have $q_c^{(1)} + q_c^{(2)} + \cdots + q_c^{(q)} = q_c$. $\mathsf{Game}_{(i,j)}$ for $i \in [q]$ and $j \in \{0, 1, \ldots, q_c^{(i)}\}$ is defined as a multi-challenge ciphertext security game in which an challenge query for $\mathsf{ID}_\tau^\star$ such that $\tau \in [i-1]$ is answered with a ciphertext that is an encryption of M_0 while an query for $\tau \geq i + 1$ is answered with a ciphertext that is an encryption of M_1. For a ν-th challenge query for $\mathsf{ID}_\tau^\star$ such that $\tau = i$, the challenger returns a ciphertext that is an encryption of M_0 if $1 \leq \nu \leq j$ and M_1 if $j + 1 \leq \nu$. A challenge query is always answered with an encryption of M_1 in $\mathsf{Game}_{(1,0)}$ and with M_0 in $\mathsf{Game}_{(q,q_c^{(q)})}$. We want to show that $\Pr[\mathcal{A} \rightarrow 0 \text{ in } \mathsf{Game}_{(1,0)}] - \Pr[\mathcal{A} \rightarrow 0 \text{ in } \mathsf{Game}_{(q,q_c^{(q)})}]$ is negligible for any $\mathcal{A}$. This implies security for multi-challenge security. Initially, we have $\Pr[\mathcal{A} \rightarrow 0 \text{ in } \mathsf{Game}_{(i-1,q_c)}] - \Pr[\mathcal{A} \rightarrow 0 \text{ in } \mathsf{Game}_{(i,0)}] = 0$ since $\mathsf{Game}_{(i-1,q_c)}$ and $\mathsf{Game}_{(i,0)}$ are the same. Thus, it suffices to show that $\Pr[\mathcal{A} \rightarrow 0 \text{ in } \mathsf{Game}_{(i,j)}] - \Pr[\mathcal{A} \rightarrow 0 \text{ in } \mathsf{Game}_{(i,j+1)}]$ for all (i,j) is bounded by the advantage of another attacker $\mathcal{B}$ against single challenge security of the IBE scheme. Here, we briefly describe $\mathcal{B}$. $\mathcal{B}$ outputs $\mathsf{ID}_i^\star$ as its challenge identity and queries challenge ciphertext for $(\mathsf{M}_0, \mathsf{M}_1)$ to its challenger upon receiving the j-th challenge query for $\mathsf{ID}_i^\star$ made by $\mathcal{A}$. $\mathcal{B}$ can handle key extraction queries made by $\mathcal{A}$ by simply querying the same key for the challenger. Since $\mathcal{A}$ makes only key extraction query for ID such that $\mathsf{ID} \notin S^\star$, we have $\mathsf{ID} \neq \mathsf{ID}_i^\star$. This means that $\mathcal{B}$ does not make a prohibited key extraction query. Since there are $O(q_c)$ hybrid games, if $\mathcal{A}$'s advantage is ϵ, $\mathcal{B}$'s advantage is $O(\epsilon/q_c)$.

B   Justification of the Truncated q-RW Assumption

Here, we briefly show that the truncated q-RW assumption holds in the generic group model. The truncated q-RW assumption is an instance of the $\mathbb{G}_T$-monomial assumption defined in [35]. The authors of [35] showed that, to prove that the $\mathbb{G}_T$-monomial assumption holds in the generic group model, it suffices to show that the pairing result of any two group elements in Ψ does not (symbolically) give rise to the target element T (Corollary D.4 of [35]). To check this condition, we have to show that there is no $X, Y \in \Phi$ such that $e(X, Y) = e(g, g)^{xyz}$. Since the only terms that have z in an exponent are $\{g^{xzb_i}\}$ and $\{g^{xyzb_i/b_j^2}\}$, $X \in \{g^{xzb_i}\} \cup \{g^{xyzb_i/b_j^2}\}$ or $Y \in \{g^{xzb_i}\} \cup \{g^{xyzb_i/b_j^2}\}$ holds. We assume that the former holds without loss of generality. Since there is no such term as g^{y/b_i} or $g^{b_j^2/b_i}$ for $i \neq j$ in Ψ, we can conclude that it is not possible to obtain $e(g, g)^{xyz}$. Thus, the assumption holds in the generic group model.

References

1. Agrawal, S., Boneh, D., Boyen, X.: Efficient lattice (H)IBE in the standard model. In: Gilbert, H. (ed.) EUROCRYPT 2010. LNCS, vol. 6110, pp. 553–572. Springer, Heidelberg (2010)
2. Agrawal, S., Boneh, D., Boyen, X.: Lattice basis delegation in fixed dimension and shorter-ciphertext hierarchical IBE. In: Rabin, T. (ed.) CRYPTO 2010. LNCS, vol. 6223, pp. 98–115. Springer, Heidelberg (2010)
3. Attrapadung, N.: Dual system encryption via doubly selective security: framework, fully secure functional encryption for regular languages, and more. In: Nguyen, P.Q., Oswald, E. (eds.) EUROCRYPT 2014. LNCS, vol. 8441, pp. 557–577. Springer, Heidelberg (2014)
4. Attrapadung, N., Furukawa, J., Gomi, T., Hanaoka, G., Imai, H., Zhang, R.: Efficient identity-based encryption with tight security reduction. In: Pointcheval, D., Mu, Y., Chen, K. (eds.) CANS 2006. LNCS, vol. 4301, pp. 19–36. Springer, Heidelberg (2006)
5. Bellare, M., Desai, A., Jokipii, E., Rogaway, P.: A concrete security treatment of symmetric encryption. In: FOCS, pp. 394–403 (1997)
6. Bellare, M., Ristenpart, T.: Simulation without the artificial abort: simplified proof and improved concrete security for waters' IBE scheme. In: Joux, A. (ed.) EUROCRYPT 2009. LNCS, vol. 5479, pp. 407–424. Springer, Heidelberg (2009)
7. Boneh, D., Boyen, X.: Efficient selective-ID secure identity-based encryption without random oracles. In: Cachin, C., Camenisch, J.L. (eds.) EUROCRYPT 2004. LNCS, vol. 3027, pp. 223–238. Springer, Heidelberg (2004)
8. Boneh, D., Boyen, X.: Secure identity based encryption without random oracles. In: Franklin, M. (ed.) CRYPTO 2004. LNCS, vol. 3152, pp. 443–459. Springer, Heidelberg (2004)
9. Boneh, D., Boyen, X.: Short signatures without random oracles. In: Cachin, C., Camenisch, J.L. (eds.) EUROCRYPT 2004. LNCS, vol. 3027, pp. 56–73. Springer, Heidelberg (2004)
10. Boneh, D., Franklin, M.: Identity-based encryption from the Weil pairing. In: Kilian, J. (ed.) CRYPTO 2001. LNCS, vol. 2139, pp. 213–229. Springer, Heidelberg (2001)

11. Boneh, D., Gentry, C., Hamburg, M.: Space-efficient identity based encryption without pairings. In: FOCS, pp. 647–657 (2007)
12. Boyen, X.: Lattice mixing and vanishing trapdoors: a framework for fully secure short signatures and more. In: Nguyen, P.Q., Pointcheval, D. (eds.) PKC 2010. LNCS, vol. 6056, pp. 499–517. Springer, Heidelberg (2010)
13. Canetti, R., Goldreich, O., Halevi, S.: The random oracle methodology, revisited. J. ACM **51**(4), 557–594 (2004)
14. Canetti, R., Halevi, S., Katz, J.: A forward-secure public-key encryption scheme. In: Biham, E. (ed.) EUROCRYPT 2003. LNCS, vol. 2656, pp. 255–271. Springer, Heidelberg (2003)
15. Cash, D., Hofheinz, D., Kiltz, E., Peikert, C.: Bonsai trees, or how to delegate a lattice basis. In: Gilbert, H. (ed.) EUROCRYPT 2010. LNCS, vol. 6110, pp. 523–552. Springer, Heidelberg (2010)
16. Chatterjee, S., Sarkar, P.: Generalization of the selective-ID security model for HIBE protocols. In: Yung, M., Dodis, Y., Kiayias, A., Malkin, T. (eds.) PKC 2006. LNCS, vol. 3958, pp. 241–256. Springer, Heidelberg (2006)
17. Chen, J., Wee, H.: Fully, (Almost) tightly secure IBE and dual system groups. In: Canetti, R., Garay, J.A. (eds.) CRYPTO 2013, Part II. LNCS, vol. 8043, pp. 435–460. Springer, Heidelberg (2013)
18. Cheon, J.H.: Security analysis of the strong Diffie-Hellman problem. In: Vaudenay, S. (ed.) EUROCRYPT 2006. LNCS, vol. 4004, pp. 1–11. Springer, Heidelberg (2006)
19. Cocks, C.: An identity based encryption scheme based on quadratic residues. In: Honary, B. (ed.) Cryptography and Coding 2001. LNCS, vol. 2260, pp. 360–363. Springer, Heidelberg (2001)
20. Freire, E.S.V., Hofheinz, D., Paterson, K.G., Striecks, C.: Programmable hash functions in the multilinear setting. In: Canetti, R., Garay, J.A. (eds.) CRYPTO 2013, Part I. LNCS, vol. 8042, pp. 513–530. Springer, Heidelberg (2013)
21. Galindo, D.: The exact security of pairing based encryption and signature schemes based on a talk at workshop on provable security, INRIA, Paris (2004). http://www.dgalindo.es/galindoEcrypt.pdf
22. Gentry, C.: Practical identity-based encryption without random oracles. In: Vaudenay, S. (ed.) EUROCRYPT 2006. LNCS, vol. 4004, pp. 445–464. Springer, Heidelberg (2006)
23. Gentry, C., Halevi, S.: Hierarchical identity based encryption with polynomially many levels. In: Reingold, O. (ed.) TCC 2009. LNCS, vol. 5444, pp. 437–456. Springer, Heidelberg (2009)
24. Gentry, C., Peikert, C., Vaikuntanathan, V.: Trapdoors for hard lattices and new cryptographic constructions. In: STOC, pp. 197–206 (2008)
25. Gentry, C., Silverberg, A.: Hierarchical ID-based cryptography. In: Zheng, Y. (ed.) ASIACRYPT 2002. LNCS, vol. 2501, pp. 548–566. Springer, Heidelberg (2002)
26. Hanaoka, G., Matsuda, T., Schuldt, J.C.N.: On the impossibility of constructing efficient key encapsulation and programmable hash functions in prime order groups. In: Safavi-Naini, R., Canetti, R. (eds.) CRYPTO 2012. LNCS, vol. 7417, pp. 812–831. Springer, Heidelberg (2012)
27. Hemenway, B., Libert, B., Ostrovsky, R., Vergnaud, D.: Lossy encryption: constructions from general assumptions and efficient selective opening chosen ciphertext security. In: Lee, D.H., Wang, X. (eds.) ASIACRYPT 2011. LNCS, vol. 7073, pp. 70–88. Springer, Heidelberg (2011)

28. Hofheinz, D., Jager, T., Kiltz, E.: Short signatures from weaker assumptions. In: Lee, D.H., Wang, X. (eds.) ASIACRYPT 2011. LNCS, vol. 7073, pp. 647–666. Springer, Heidelberg (2011)

29. Horwitz, J., Lynn, B.: Toward hierarchical identity-based encryption. In: Knudsen, L.R. (ed.) EUROCRYPT 2002. LNCS, vol. 2332, pp. 466–481. Springer, Heidelberg (2002)

30. Lewko, A.: Tools for simulating features of composite order bilinear groups in the prime order setting. In: Pointcheval, D., Johansson, T. (eds.) EUROCRYPT 2012. LNCS, vol. 7237, pp. 318–335. Springer, Heidelberg (2012)

31. Lewko, A.B., Sahai, A., Waters, B.: Revocation systems with very small private keys. In: IEEE Symposium on Security and Privacy, pp. 273–285 (2010)

32. Lewko, A., Waters, B.: New techniques for dual system encryption and fully secure HIBE with short ciphertexts. In: Micciancio, D. (ed.) TCC 2010. LNCS, vol. 5978, pp. 455–479. Springer, Heidelberg (2010)

33. Lewko, A., Waters, B.: New proof methods for attribute-based encryption: achieving full security through selective techniques. In: Safavi-Naini, R., Canetti, R. (eds.) CRYPTO 2012. LNCS, vol. 7417, pp. 180–198. Springer, Heidelberg (2012)

34. Naor, M., Reingold, O.: Number-theoretic constructions of efficient pseudo-random functions. J. ACM **51**(2), 231–262 (2004)

35. Rouselakis, Y., Waters, B.: New constructions and proof methods for large universe attribute-based encryption. In: ACM Conference on Computer and Communications Security, vol. 2013, p. 583 (2013)

36. Sakai, R., Ohgishi, K., Kasahara, M.: Cryptosystems based on pairing over elliptic curve. In: The 2001 Symposium on Cryptography and Information Security (2001). (in Japanese)

37. Shamir, A.: Identity-based cryptosystems and signature Schemes. In: Blakely, G.R., Chaum, D. (eds.) CRYPTO 1984. LNCS, vol. 196, pp. 47–53. Springer, Heidelberg (1985)

38. Waters, B.: Efficient identity-based encryption without random oracles. In: Cramer, R. (ed.) EUROCRYPT 2005. LNCS, vol. 3494, pp. 114–127. Springer, Heidelberg (2005)

39. Waters, B.: Dual system encryption: realizing fully secure IBE and HIBE under simple assumptions. In: Halevi, S. (ed.) CRYPTO 2009. LNCS, vol. 5677, pp. 619–636. Springer, Heidelberg (2009)

40. Waters, B.: Ciphertext-policy attribute-based encryption: an expressive, efficient, and provably secure realization. In: Catalano, D., Fazio, N., Gennaro, R., Nicolosi, A. (eds.) PKC 2011. LNCS, vol. 6571, pp. 53–70. Springer, Heidelberg (2011)

41. Waters, B.: Functional encryption for regular languages. In: Safavi-Naini, R., Canetti, R. (eds.) CRYPTO 2012. LNCS, vol. 7417, pp. 218–235. Springer, Heidelberg (2012)

42. Yamada, S., Attrapadung, N., Hanaoka, G., Kunihiro, N.: A framework and compact constructions for non-monotonic attribute-based encryption. In: Krawczyk, H. (ed.) PKC 2014. LNCS, vol. 8383, pp. 275–292. Springer, Heidelberg (2014)

Method for Determining Whether or not Text Information Is Leaked from Computer Display Through Electromagnetic Radiation

De-gang Sun[1], Jun Shi[1,2(✉)], Dong Wei[1], Meng Zhang[1], and Wei-qing Huang[1]

[1] Institute of Information Engineering, Chinese Academy of Sciences, Beijing, China
{sundegang,shijun,weidong,zhangmeng, huangweiqing}@iie.ac.cn
[2] University of Chinese Academy of Sciences, Beijing, China

Abstract. Confidential information might be leaked through electro-magnetic radiation from a computer display. To detect the electromagnetic radiation that contains text information, this paper proposed an evaluation method without reconstructing the displayed image. In this method, sparse decomposition in wavelet is used to describe the characteristics of electromagnetic radiation signals contain text information. By using this method, it is easy to detect text information leakage in electromagnetic radiation from a computer display.

Keywords: Information security · Electromagnetic radiation · Text information · Wavelet transform · Sparse decomposition

1 Introduction

A wide variety of information technology equipment (ITE) is involved in our daily activities. Most of ITE devices radiate electromagnetic disturbance unintentionally. If someone intercepts these electromagnetic waves and reconstructs the information, confidential information might be leaked [1, 2]. Electromagnetic radiation was mentioned in some papers as a computer security risk [3–5]. These topic leads to the concept of TEMPEST, which is the technology of electromagnetic leaking research. Electromagnetic radiation from a computer display can be categorized into two types: radiation that contains text information and radiation that does not. TEMPEST focus more on text information leaking because most confidential information is text. The text information has higher risk of secret data leakage than non-text. Thus, it is important to efficiently and accurately distinguish the two types whether for an attacker or a protector.

The current researches on electromagnetic radiation detection mostly based on the harmonic characteristics of electromagnetic radiation signal spectrum, but these methods can't distinguish the radiation that contains text information and radiation that does not [6, 7]. As a direct method, we can reconstruct the display image by using a special receiver, but not all test houses or manufacturers have such specialized

L.C.K. Hui et al. (Eds.): ICICS 2014, LNCS 8958, pp. 191–199, 2015.
DOI: 10.1007/978-3-319-21966-0_14

receivers. Furthermore, to correctly reconstruct the electromagnetic radiation signal, the synchronizing information that including the horizontal synchronizing frequency and vertical synchronizing frequency is essential. However, the computer's synchronization information is un-known in the practical non-cooperative attack scenario.

For these reasons, this paper proposed an evaluation method to determine whether or not text information is contained in electromagnetic radiation without knowing the synchronization information and reconstructing the display image. First, we found the "text - space – text" characteristic for electro-magnetic radiation signal containing text information. Then, we proposed a new method which used sparse decomposition in wavelet to describe this characteristic. By using this method, we can accurately and efficiently detect the text information leakage in electromagnetic radiation from a computer display.

2   Analyzing Display Electromagnetic Radiation Signal Properties

Video signal produce depend on the combined action of horizontal synchronizing signal and vertical synchronizing signal [8]. Video signal can be represented as summation of digital pulses with different amplitude:

$$S_p(t) = \sum_{n=-\infty}^{+\infty} a_n g_T(t - nT_p) \tag{1}$$

where, $g_T(t)$ is code pattern of video pulse, and the symbol cycle is T_p.

For images that contain text information, there are both information signal and horizontal synchronizing signal in the received electromagnetic radiation signal as shown in Fig. 1. At the same time, a text image containing text line and there is a space between every two lines, so there would be "text - space – text" characteristics of the text. The characteristics would also reflect in the electromagnetic radiation signal in

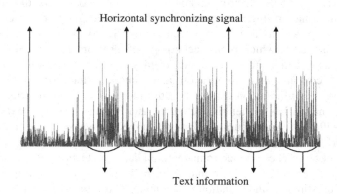

Fig. 1. Electromagnetic radiation signal with text information of computer display in time domain

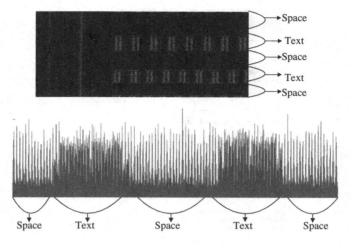

Fig. 2. The "text - space – text" characteristics in image and electromagnetic radiation signal

time domain as shown in Fig. 2. This paper provides a way to describe this characteristics of the text to realize text information detection.

3   Evalution Algorithm

In this paper, sparse knowledge is introduced to describe the characteristics of electromagnetic radiation signals contain text information. The implementation procedures are shown in a flow chart (Fig. 3).

Firstly, make a sparse decomposition in wavelet domain. The sparse decomposition procedures can be represented as [9]

$$X \overset{DWT}{\rightarrow} \{a_L, d_j\} \overset{Threshold}{\rightarrow} \{\tilde{\tilde{a}}_L, \tilde{d}_j\} \overset{IDWT}{\rightarrow} \tilde{X} \tag{2}$$

where X is the initial electromagnetic radiation signal. Decompose X by wavelet and get the wavelet coefficient $\{a_L, d_j\}$. Set a threshold and then get the effective coefficient $\{\tilde{\tilde{a}}_L, \tilde{d}_j\}$. $\tilde{X}$ is sparse signal through wavelet inverse transformation. The threshold is used in hard thresh method.

$$\{\tilde{\tilde{a}}_L, \tilde{d}_j\} = \begin{cases} 0, & |\{a_L, d_j\}| < Thr \\ \{a_L, d_j\}, & |\{a_L, d_j\}| > Thr \end{cases} \tag{3}$$

where,

$$Thr = \sigma\sqrt{2\ln N} \tag{4}$$

where, N is the data length. σ is the standard deviation of noise.

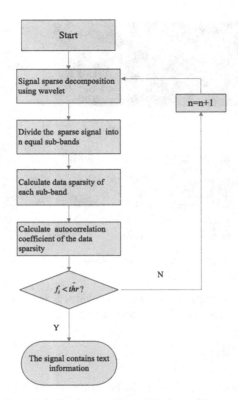

Fig. 3. Flow chart of the implementation procedure of the proposed algorithm

$$\hat{\sigma} = median|Det1|/0.6745 \tag{5}$$

where, $Det1$ represents the most detailed wavelet coefficient.

Secondly, divide the sparse signal $\tilde{X}$ into n equal sub-bands. The length of each sub-band is m.

$$\tilde{X} = [x_1 x_2 x_3 \ldots \ldots x_{n-1} x_n] \tag{6}$$

Thirdly, calculate the sparsity of each sub-band. Sparsity is here defined as the number of non-zero components in the data. Sparsity of sparse signal $\tilde{X}$ is not uniform. The text part is thick and the other part is thin, so the "text - space – text" characteristic in image becomes to "thick-thin-thick" characteristic in the sparse signal $\tilde{X}$. This structure can be described by Block Sparse [10]. Thus, the $\tilde{X}$ can be redescribed as,

$$\tilde{X} = [\underbrace{x_1 \ldots x_{d_1}}_{x[1]} \underbrace{x_{d_1+1} \ldots x_{d_1+d_2-1}}_{x[2]} \cdots \underbrace{x_{n-d_N+1} \ldots x_n}_{x[N]}] \tag{7}$$

where, $n = \sum_{j=1}^{N} d_j$. $x[j]$ is the jth block and its length is $d_j \in Z^+$. Each block has different sparsity. Corresponding sparsity $\tilde{Y}$ is

$$\tilde{Y} = [\underbrace{y_1 \cdots y_{d_1}}_{y[1]} \underbrace{y_{d_1+1} \cdots y_{d_1+d_2-1}}_{y[2]} \cdots \underbrace{y_{n-d_N+1} \cdots y_n}_{y[N]}] \tag{8}$$

Thus, if there is text information in the electromagnetic radiation signal, "text - space – text" characteristic would make the $\tilde{Y}$ present periodic variation. There are many ways to describe periodic signal, correlation is here used.

Finally, calculate correlation of $\tilde{Y}$, and the side lobe peak p_i nearest the zero in the correlation is the period of "text - space – text" characteristic. Thus, the frequency f_i of "text - space – text" characteristic is $f_i = 1/p_i$. The correlation $\hat{r}(k)$ is given as,

$$\hat{r}(k) = \frac{1}{N} \sum_{n=0}^{N-1} y_N(n) y_N(n+k) \tag{9}$$

Considering period would increase with the increase of word size, we set the threshold $\widetilde{thr}$ is the frequency when the word size is 5. Thus, when $f_i < \widetilde{thr}$, it can be concluded that the signal contain text information. For the condition that there is no side lobe peak in correlation of $\tilde{Y}$, the p_i means zero, $f_i \gg \widetilde{thr}$. Thus, it can be concluded that the signal does not contain text information.

4   Experimental Results

In this section, the proposed algorithm is applied to experimental data and the results and analysis are given.

The measurement setup is shown in Fig. 4. The resolution of the computer display was 1024 × 768. A log-periodic antenna was located at 1 m from the front surface of

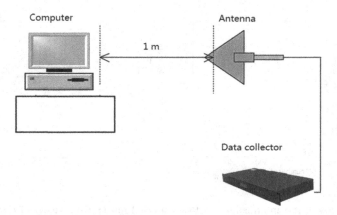

Fig. 4. Measurement setup for data collection

the computer, and its height was the same as the height of the computer display center. An antenna is connected to a data collector, which can be data acquisition card, digital oscilloscope and spectrum analyzer. Digital oscilloscope was here used.

To prove the feasibility of the proposed algorithm, image with text information, image without text information and blank image are tested respectively. The sub-band length m is set to 1000. Through experiment, we got the $\widetilde{thr}$ is equal to 5 Khz.

Firstly, for an image with text information, results are shown in Fig. 5. Figure 5(a) shows the reconstructed image with text information. As can be seen from Fig. 5(b), the sparsity of signal presents the periodic structure "text-space-text" obviously. The correlation of sparsity is shown in Fig. 5(c). It can be seen that the peak nearest the zero is 0.0009081, so $f_i = 1/0.0009081 = 1.1012\ Khz < \widetilde{thr}$. Thus, the experimental result is that the signal contains text information.

Secondly, for a blank image, results are shown in Fig. 6. As can be seen from Fig. 6 (a), the distribution of sparsity is chaotic. Figure 6(b) shows the correlation of sparsity. It can be seen that there is no side lobe peak in correlation of $\tilde{Y}$. Thus, the experimental result is that the signal dose not contain text information.

Thirdly, for an image without text information, results are shown in Fig. 7. Figure 7 (a) shows the original image with text information. Its sparsity of signal is shown in

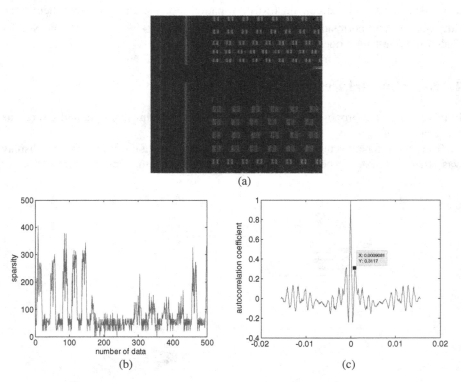

(a)

(b)   (c)

Fig. 5. Image with text information. (a) Reconstructed image. (b) Sparsity of electromagnetic radiation signal. (c) Correlation of sparsity for image with text information.

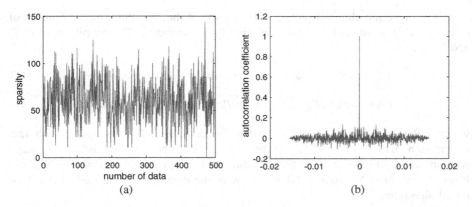

Fig. 6. Blank image. (a) Sparsity of electromagnetic radiation signal. (b) Correlation of sparsity.

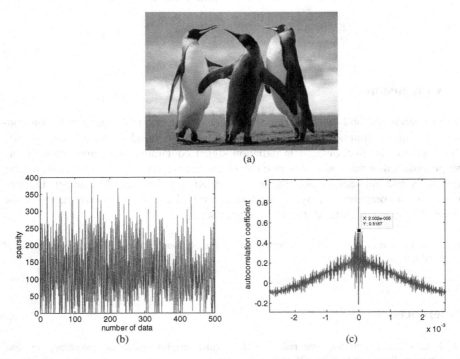

Fig. 7. Non-blank image without text information. (a) Original image. (b) Sparsity of electromagnetic radiation signal (c) Correlation of sparsity

Fig. 7(b). It can be seen that the distribution of sparsity is chaotic. In Fig. 7(c), the correlation of sparsity is shown. The peak nearest the zero is $2.004e^{-5}$, so $f_i = 1/2.004e^{-5} = 49.9\ Khz > \widetilde{thr}$. Thus, the experimental result is that the signal dose not contain text information.

To evaluate the clutter detection performance of the algorithm, the probability of detection (POD) and the false alarm rate (FAR) are computed. The definitions of POD and FAR are:

$$POD = TruePositives/(TruePositives + FalseNegatives) \tag{10}$$

$$FAR = FalsePositives/(FalsePositives + TrueNegatives) \tag{11}$$

where, "Positive" labels the location that the detector judges as image with text information, and "Negative" labels the location that the detector judges as image without text information; In Table 1, True Positive (TP),False Negative (FN),False Positive (FP),True Negative (TN) and FAR of the data are summarized for the proposed algorithm.

Table 1. Performance of algorithm based on data

TP	FN	FP	TN	POD	FAR
195	6	5	194	92.4 %	2.5 %

5   Conclusion

An evaluation method that determines whether or not electromagnetic radiation contains text information is proposed in this paper. First, we found the "text - space – text" characteristic for electromagnetic radiation signal containing text information. Then, we propose a new method to describe this characteristic. By using this method, we can accurately and efficiently detect the text information leakage in electromagnetic radiation from a computer display. In the future, we will analyze the performance of the proposed algorithm under different parameter setting.

Acknowledgment. This work was supported by the National Natural Science Foundation of China (Grant No. 61401460)

References

1. Eck, W.V.: Electromagnetic radiation from video display units: an eavesdropping risk? Comput. Secur. **4**(4), 269–286 (1985)
2. Kuhn, M.G.: Compromising emanations: eavesdropping risks of computer displays. In: Technical Report (2003)
3. Kuhn, M.G.: Eavesdropping attacks on computer displays. In: Information Security Summit, pp, 24–25(2006)
4. Elibol, F., Sarac, U.and Erer, I. : Realistic eavesdropping attacks on computer displays with low-cost and mobile receiver system. In: Proceedings of the 20th European Signal Processing Conference (EUSIPCO), 2012, pp.1767–1771 (2012)

5. Vuagnoux, M., Pasini, S.: An improved technique to discover compromising electromagnetic emanations. In: Electromagnetic Compatibility (EMC), 2010 IEEE International Symposium on Digital Object Identifier, pp. 121–126 (2010)
6. Yamanaka, Y., Fukunaga, K.: Method for determining whether or not information is contained in electromagnetic disturbance radiated from a PC display. IEEE Trans. Electromagn. Compat. **53**(2), 318–324 (2011)
7. Kuhn, M.G.: Compromising emanations of LCD TV sets. Electromagn. Compat. **55**(3), 564–570 (2013)
8. Wiesner, A.: Evaluating the information content of the computer monitor radio frequency radiation using a simple technique. In: International Conference on Network and Service Security, pp. 1–5 (2009)
9. Lo, S.-C.B.: Radiology Department, Georgetown University Medical Center: optimization of wavelet decomposition for image compression and feature preservation. IEEE Trans. Med. Imaging **22**(9), 1141–1151 (2003)
10. Barik, S.: Sparsity-aware sphere decoding: algorithms and complexity analysis. IEEE Trans. Signal Process. **62**(9), 2212–2225 (2014)

How to Compare Selections of Points of Interest for Side-Channel Distinguishers in Practice?

Yingxian Zheng[1], Yongbin Zhou[1(✉)], Zhenmei Yu[2], Chengyu Hu[3], and Hailong Zhang[1]

[1] State Key Laboratory of Information Security,
Institute of Information Engineering, Chinese Academy of Sciences,
89-A, Mingzhuang Rd, Beijing 100093, People's Republic of China
{zhengyingxian,zhouyongbin,zhanghailong}@iie.ac.cn
[2] Shandong Womens University, 45, Yuhan Rd,
Jinan 250002, People's Republic of China
yuzhenmei@gmail.com
[3] Shandong University, 27, Shanda South Rd,
Jinan 250100, People's Republic of China
hcy@sdu.edu.cn

Abstract. Side-channel distinguishers aim to reveal the secrets used in crypto devices by utilizing the subtle dependence between some sensitive intermediate values and physical leakages produced during its executions. For this purpose, one or more points of interest (POIs) corresponding to manipulations of one sensitive intermediate value are usually selected and then fed into distinguishers. However, it turns out in practice that POIs selected, even they are from the same leakage traces, will have significant impacts on the key recovery efficacy of distinguishers. Therefore, it makes a very practical sense to investigate the concrete impacts of POIs selections on side-channel distinguishers, and then pick out from those POIs selections available the most appropriate one for a certain distinguisher. In order to address these problems, we propose an evaluation framework for the analysis of POIs selections for side-channel distinguishers. Basically, our framework consists of two stages: the first stage captures the validity of points selected, while the second one reflects their quality with respect to a certain distinguisher. Specifically, on the one hand, in order to measure the goodness of one POIs selection, we introduce a quantitative metric of accuracy rate, from a perspective of statistics; on the other hand, we adopt the widely accepted security metric of success rate proposed by Standaert et al. at EUROCRYPT 2009 to reflect the quality of the points selected. Eventually, taking five typical POIs selections and three popular side-channel distinguishers as concrete study cases, we perform simulated attacks and practical attacks as well, the results of which not only fully justify our proposed methods but also reveal some interesting observations.

Keywords: Accuracy rate · Evaluation framework · Distinguisher · Selection of points of interest · Side-channel analysis

© Springer International Publishing Switzerland 2015
L.C.K. Hui et al. (Eds.): ICICS 2014, LNCS 8958, pp. 200–214, 2015.
DOI: 10.1007/978-3-319-21966-0_15

1 Introduction

Side-channel attacks aim at revealing the secret information embedded in a cryptographic device from its physical leakages, including execution time [1], power consumption [2], and electromagnetic emanation [3]. Among them, power analysis attack which makes use of instantaneous power consumptions of a cryptographic device is one of the most widely researched side-channel attacks. Therefore, for ease and simplicity of presentation, we concentrate on power analysis attack ONLY for illustrative purposes in this paper.

Side-channel distinguisher plays a crucial role in recovering reveal the secrets in side-channel attacks. It refers to the process during which the adversary uses some statistical tools to exploit the subtle dependence between one sensitive intermediate value and its corresponding power consumptions of cryptographic device. For real-world crypto implementations, one side-channel leakage trace usually contains multiple samples corresponding to manipulations of one sensitive intermediate value. This is quite natural because the manipulations of the sensitive intermediate value targeted usually takes more than one instruction cycle. In addition, according to Nyquist−Shannon sampling theorem, the acquisition rate of the signal acquisition device is always set to be several times faster than the working frequency of the targeted cryptography device. Those samples that exactly correspond to the manipulations of one sensitive intermediate value targeted in one leakage trace are referred to points of interest (POIs).

Based on analysis of values and of distributions, side-channel distinguishers can be divided into two categories. Distinguishers based on values include differential power analysis (DPA) [2], correlation power analysis (CPA) [4], differential cluster analysis (DCA) [5], template attack [6], stochastic method [7], and etc. Mangard et al. showed in [8] that denoted as standard univariate DPA, a number of these type of distinguishers are in fact asymptotically equivalent, given that they are provided with the same a priori information about the leakages. Therefore, in this paper, we choose CPA to be the representative of those distinguishers based on values. Distinguishers based on distributions consist of mutual information analysis (MIA) [9], KS-test based analysis (KSA) [17], MPC-KSA [10], and etc. Considering their popularity, we choose MIA and KSA to be the representatives of those distinguishers based on distributions.

Currently, there are several POIs selections available. In principle, side-channel attacks themselves could serve as the tools for POIs selection, as is already done in the field of side-channel attacks. For example, CPA, MIA and KSA all can be used to select the POIs. In addition, there are also non-attack based POIs selections. Two of them are the Sum Of Squared Pairwise Differences (sosd) [9] and the Sum Of Squared Pairwise T-Differences (sost) [11]. An important observation is that applying different POIs selections onto the same leakage traces could lead to distinct points selected, even if it is explicitly required that all POIs selected must correspond to one sensitive intermediate value targeted, which will have significant impacts on the key recovery efficacy of distinguishers. Therefore, it makes a very practical sense to investigate the concrete impacts of POIs selections on side-channel distinguishers, and then pick out from those POIs selections available the most appropriate one for a certain distinguisher.

For comparison of distinguishers, some well-known frameworks were already proposed. The first one in [13] by Standaert et al. suggests to use a leakage metric to qualify the maximal chance that an optimal attacker would have to extract the secrets. For the comparison of different distinguishers, [13] suggests metrics like o^{th}-order success rate or guessing entropy. In another framework of [14], the distance to the nearest rival is suggested. In [15], Maghrebi et al. proposed a methodology to compare two side-channel distinguishers based on simulations. In [16], some analyses showed pitfalls in the evaluation methodologies for distinguisher, including estimation bias, estimation algorithm, success rate error, and sample errors. To the best of our knowledge, all frameworks known so far concern distinguishers alone; and none of them take POIs selections themselves into serious consideration, let alone any comprehensive evaluation work about concrete impacts of POIs selections over distinguishers in practice.

1.1 Contributions

The contributions of this paper are threefold. First, we propose an two-stage evaluation framework for the analysis of POIs selections for side-channel distinguishers. Second, in order to measure the goodness of the POIs selection, we introduce the notion of accuracy rate. Third, taking five POIs selections commonly used and three typical distinguishers as concrete study cases, we perform simulated attacks and practical attacks. The experimental results not only fully justify our proposed methods, but also reveal some interesting observations.

The rest of this paper is organized as follows. Sect. 2 briefly recalls three typical distinguishers and five POIs selections commonly used; Sect. 3 introduces our proposed two-stage framework; Sect. 4 presents details and results of simulated and practical attacks, together with some useful discussions and interesting observations; Sect. 5 concludes the whole paper.

2 Preliminaries

This section will briefly recall CPA, MIA, and KSA distinguishers. These three distinguishers can also be used for selecting POIs. Besides, we will also briefly introduce sosd and sost POIs selections.

2.1 CPA

CPA identifies the correct key by calculating the Pearson correlation coefficient between real power traces and hypothetical power consumptions. The adversary chooses a sensitive intermediate value $v_i^* = g(x_i, k^*)$, where x_i is the ith plaintext (totally NT traces), k^* is a key guess. For every key guess k^*, the adversary predicates the hypothetical power consumption by $h_i^{k^*} = f(v_i^*)$, where f is a hypothetical leakage function. H^{k^*} denotes a vector of hypothetical power consumptions. L denotes a vector of real power traces. The adversary computes the Pearson correlation coefficient between H^{k^*} and L as

$$\rho(H^{k^*}, L) = \frac{\sum\limits_{i=1}^{NT} (H_i^{k^*} - \overline{H^{k^*}})(L_i - \overline{L})}{\sqrt{\sum\limits_{i=1}^{NT} \left(H_i^{k^*} - \overline{H^{k^*}}\right)^2 \cdot \sum\limits_{i=1}^{NT} \left(L_i - \overline{L}\right)^2}} \tag{1}$$

where $\overline{H^{k^*}}$ and $\overline{L}$ are the mean of H^{k^*} and that of L. Maximal correlation coefficient indicates the most likely candidate key guess as $k = \arg\max\limits_{k^*} \rho(H^{k^*}, L)$.

In practice, CPA can also be used for selecting POIs. The maximal correlation coefficient indicates the location of POIs as $[k, t] = \arg\max\limits_{k^*, t'} \rho(H^{k^*}, T(t'))$. Where $T(t')$ is point t' column of traces matrix T. In order to avoid confusion, hereafter throughout the whole paper, we use CPA-P to stand for CPA for the purpose of selecting POIs. MIA-P and KSA-P have the same meaning.

2.2 MIA

In MIA, one can compute the mutual information (MI) between the real power traces L and a hypothetical power consumption H^{k^*} as

$$I(L; H^{k^*}) = H(L) - H(L|H^{k^*}) = H(L) - \mathop{E}\limits_{h \in H^{k^*}} [H(L|H^{k^*} = h)] \tag{2}$$

In this paper, for the estimation of the probability density function, we will use histogram method [9]. The largest MI indicated the most likely key guess as $k = \arg\max\limits_{k^*} I(L; H^{k^*})$.

Similarly, as is shown in [9], MIA distinguisher can also be used for selecting POIs (MIA-P) as $[k, t] = \arg\max\limits_{k^*, t'} I(T(t'); H^{k^*})$.

2.3 KSA

The KS test quantifies a distance between the empirical cumulative distribution function of two samples to determine the similarity of them. The central idea of KSA distinguisher proposed in [17] is to measure the maximum distance between the global trace distribution L and the conditional trace distribution $L|H^{k^*}$ as

$$D_{KS}(k^*) = E[KS(L||(L|H^{k^*}))] = \mathop{E}\limits_{h \in H^{k^*}} [KS(L||(L|H^{k^*} = h))] \tag{3}$$

The largest distance indicates the most likely key guess as $k = \arg\max\limits_{k^*} D_{KS}(k^*)$.

Similarly, KSA distinguisher can also be used for selecting POIs (KSA-P) as $[k, t] = \arg\max\limits_{k^*, t'} D_{KS}(k^*) = E[KS(T(t')||(T(t')|H^{k^*}))]$

2.4   Sosd and Sost

Denote hypothesis power consumption by $h_i^{k*} = f(v_i^*)$. In Hamming weight model, $h_i^{k*} \in [0, 8]$. We partition all traces T according to h_i^{k*}, $G_j = \{T_i | h_i^{k*} = j\}$, $(j = 0, 1, 2, ..., 8)$. We calculate the mean m_j and the standard deviation σ_j of every partition G_j. For the sosd, we sum up their squared pairwise differences, $sosd = \sum_{i,j=0}^{8} (m_i - m_j)^2$. The sost is based on the T-Test. n_j is the number of traces in partition G_j. The location of POI is where the sosd or sost is biggest.

$$sost = \sum_{i,j=0}^{8} \left(\frac{m_i - m_j}{\sqrt{\frac{\sigma_i^2}{n_i} + \frac{\sigma_j^2}{n_j}}} \right)^2 \tag{4}$$

3   Evaluation Framework

In this section, we will present our framework for analysis of POIs selections for univariate side-channel distinguishers.

We argue that a real-word side-channel attack consists of two essential procedures, namely point extraction and key recovery. Unlike in those works of theoretical analysis, POIs selection really matters in real-world practices and distinguishers are sensitive to the POIs selected. In univariate case, this means once a "bad" point is fed into a certain distinguisher, key recovery efficiency of the attack will lower down, or sometimes even a wrong key guess will be made. Therefore, it is of great help if there is a method for picking out from those POIs selections available the most appropriate one for a certain distinguisher. In order to do this task, we need to measure the quality of the POIs selected. Fortunately, we could use security metric like success rate proposed in [13] to reflect the quality of POIs selected, with respect to a certain distinguisher. Yet, we have to notice that in some cases a successful attack using a certain POIs selected might also be falsity. For example, take for example a CPA attack against an unprotected AES software implementation. In this case, we choose the output of Sbox of the first round of AES encryption to the sensitive intermediate value. The outcome of performing a CPA attack will be the same as that against 4 bytes (i.e. 1st, 5th, 9th, and 13th byte) of outputs of ShiftRow operation. If only partial success rate is considered, this could lead to misleading results. As what we really need in real-world practices are those POIs selected that exactly correspond to the sensitive intermediate value targeted, which could be viewed to be a necessary requirement for a sound POIs selection. This means that success rate really makes sense only when this requirement holds.

For this requirement, we define the validity of a point with respect to a certain sensitive intermediate value. One point is said to be "valid" if it fall into the set of all points corresponding to the manipulations of the sensitive intermediate value; otherwise, it is said to be "invalid". Under the condition that two points are both valid, we say that one point is to have a "better" quality than another point, if the success rate of a key recovery attack using this point is higher than that of using another point, with respect to a certain distinguisher. Now, we can think of how to measure the goodness of one POIs selection. For this purpose, we introduce the notion of accuracy rate, from the perspective of statistics. Intuitively, the accuracy rate is to capture how well one POIs selection method is capable of extracting from side-channel leakage traces those points that exactly correspond to manipulations of one sensitive intermediate value targeted. The formal definition of accuracy rate will presented in Sect. 3.1.

Put above-mentioned ideas together, we put forward our evaluation framework. Basically, our framework contains of two stages. In the first stage, we measure the goodness of POIs selections through capturing the validity of points selected. The second stage reflects the quality of points selected, with respect to a certain distinguisher.

One feature of our framework is that it provides both designers and evaluators a more fine-grained way of examining two essential procedures (i.e. point extraction and key recovery) of real-world side-channel attacks. Another feature of our framework is that it could be jointly used in a very natural way with other well-known frameworks in the field for comparison of distinguishers themselves, including those of Standaert et al. [13] and Whitnall et al. [14,16]. With the help of this powerful framework, we can objectively and fairly compare different POIs selections, and then find the most suitable one for a certain distinguisher afterwards.

3.1 Metrics

We will provide the formal definition of accuracy rate of POIs selection, and then briefly discuss success rate.

Accuracy Rate (AR) of POIs Selection. The accuracy rate of one POIs selection is a expected probability of event S, if the points selected are in the POIs set corresponding to the manipulations of the sensitive intermediate value, we say event S occurs. It is straightforward that if the points are not in the POIs set, they are not pertinent to the chosen sensitive intermediate value, and they are not points we need even though distinguishers can recover the key using them in some cases. We can use this metric to measure the goodness of POIs selections. This is independent of key recovery of distinguishers.

Obviously, there is an important prerequisite, i.e. we need to know the POIs set. The example scenarios include that one performs POIs selection in simulated scenarios where he can control the generation of traces; or one knows all details about the cryptographic algorithm and cryptographic device, then he can calculate the positions or range of POIs by clock frequency of device and sampling frequency of oscilloscope. This metric is designed to be used in evaluation scenarios, because in adversarial scenarios, once we know the POIs set, we need not perform POIs selection any more.

We define a POIs selection adversary as an algorithm $A_{E_K,L}$ with time complexity τ, memory complexity m and q queries to the target physical computer.

The real POIs set tc is determined by the definition of a function β, i.e. $tc = \beta(k)$. In order to select the POIs, we assume that the output of the adversary $A_{E_K,L}$ is a sorted points vector $tg = [tg_1, tg_2, ..., tg_{|W|}]$, where W is the number of points in one whole trace. According to the selection result: the most likely POI being tg_1. Finally, we define a POIs selection of order o with the experiment:

$$ExpA_{A_{E_K,L}}^{ps-ar-o}[tg \leftarrow A_{E_K,L}; tc = \beta(k); k \overset{R}{\leftarrow} \kappa;]$$

$$if \ (tg_1, tg_2, ..., tg_o) \in tc \ then \ return \ 1 \quad else \ return \ 0 \tag{5}$$

The oth-order accuracy rate of $A_{E_K,L}$ against known POIs set is defined as:

$$AR_{A_{E_K,L}}^{ps-ar-o}(\tau, m, q) = \Pr[ExpA_{A_{E_K,L}}^{ps-ar-o} = 1] \tag{6}$$

Success Rate (SR) of Key Recovery [13]. Let $E_K = \{E_k(.)\}_{k \in \kappa}$ be a family of cryptographic abstract computers indexed by a variable key K. Let (E_K, L) be the physical computers corresponding to the association of E_K with a leakage function L. In general, the attack defines a function $\gamma : \kappa \rightarrow S$ which maps each key k onto an equivalent key class $s = \gamma(k)$, such that $|S| << |\kappa|$. We define a side-channel key recovery adversary as an algorithm $A_{E_K,L}$. Its goal is to guess a key class $s = \gamma(k)$ with non negligible probability. For this purpose, we assume that the output of the adversary $A_{E_K,L}$ is a guess vector $g = [g_1, g_2, ..., g_{|S|}]$ with the different key candidates sorted according to the attack result: the most likely candidate being g_1. Finally, we define a side-channel key recovery of order o with the experiment:

$$ExpB_{A_{E_K,L}}^{sc-kr-o}[g \leftarrow A_{E_K,L}; s = \gamma(k); k \overset{R}{\leftarrow} \kappa;]$$

$$if \ s \in [g_1, ..., g_o] \ then \ return \ 1 \quad else \ return \ 0 \tag{7}$$

The oth-order success rate of $A_{E_K,L}$ against a key class is defined as:

$$SR_{A_{E_K,L}}^{sc-kr-o}(\tau, m, q) = \Pr[ExpB_{A_{E_K,L}}^{sc-kr-o} = 1] \tag{8}$$

In this paper, we only consider the 1st-order AR and 1st-order SR.

3.2 Factors

In practice, there are some other factors to affect the key recovery of distinguishers.

Noise Level. Generally, the higher noise level increases, the worse POIs selections perform. POIs selections have different ability to adapt various noise level. We assume that the noise follow the Gaussian distribution with mean 0, and noise level is measured by standard deviation.

Leakage Type and Hypothetical Model. Leakage type refers to leakage model of crypto device. In this paper, we considered four types, i.e. Hamming Weight (HW) leakage, Hamming Distance (HD) leakage, Unevenly Weighted Sum of the Bits (UWSB) leakage and Highly Non-Linear (HNL) leakage [12].

In terms of hypothetical model, in this paper, we consider two kind of adversaries with different characterization ability to the leakage model of crypto device. An adversary with strong ability uses hypothetical leakage model (denoted by HL) as same as real leakage type (denoted by RL) to calculate the hypothetical power consumption, while an adversary with limited ability uses Hamming weight as hypothetical leakage model. We define a tuple <RL,HL> to represent a specific analysis or evaluation scenarios.

4 Experimental Evaluation

In this section, we will conduct comprehensive empirical evaluation. Our experiments will carry out in simulated scenarios and practical scenarios.

4.1 Simulated Experiments

In simulated scenarios, we choose the output of the first Sbox of the first round unprotected AES operation as the target intermediate value. In these scenarios, we know all details about the cryptographic algorithm and cryptographic device, and we control the generation of traces. Therefore, we can use the accuracy rate to evaluate the goodness of five popular POIs selections, i.e. CPA-P, sosd, sost, MIA-P, KSA-P. Three typical leakage types are adopted, i.e. HW leakage[1], UWSB leakage and HNL leakage.

The simulated traces are composed of the signal part and noise part. Firstly, we generate the signal part of 10,000 traces which contain five points corresponding to every intermediate value and five independent points. The intermediate values contains the plaintext, plaintext xor key, the output of Sbox and the result of Shift-Row. The plaintexts are random, and the key is fixed. Secondly, we add Gaussian noise varying in standard deviation to the signal part.

Our experiments are carefully divided into two stages in order to justify our proposed framework. Specifically, stage one, in each of the noise level, five POIs selections run 500 times using 1,000 and 5,000 random selected traces, and count the ARs according to definition of it respectively. Stage two, three distinguishers run 500 times using the points selected by five POIs selections, and count the SRs according to definition of it respectively.

Hamming Weight Leakage. In this scenario, the tuple is <HW,HW>. The ARs of five POIs selections are shown in Fig. 1. The quality of points selected with respect to three distinguishers are shown in Fig. 2. Specifically, we divide

---

[1] HD is another usual leakage types, but it is a linear leakage like Hamming weight. In simulated scenarios, we took Hamming weight as a typical leakage example.

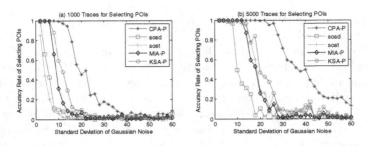

Fig. 1. ARs of five POIs selections in HW leakage simulated scenario

the results of three distinguishers into three groups according to the standard deviation of Guassian noise, and denote these groups by A, B and C, respectively. The standard deviation in Group A, B, C is 4, 8, 16, respectively.

Figure 1 shows the ARs of five POIs selections decrease rapidly with the increase of noise level. When noise level increases highly, all selections fail. However, the ARs of CPA-P is obviously higher than those of other four selections. This implies that CPA-P is the relatively strongest capacity to tolerate noise, while sosd and sost are the poorest. Compared with (a) in Fig. 1, (b) shows that the ability to tolerate noise of all selections improves.

Figure 2 shows the results of stage two in our framework. In Group A, points selected by five POIs selections are all "*valid*" to recover the key, but the SRs using points selected by five POIs selections for a certain distinguisher have subtle differences. When standard deviation of Gaussian noise is 8, points selected are still "*valid*", but the points selected by CPA-P is much better than those selected by other four selections. When standard deviation is 16, the point selected by sosd and sost are "*invalid*", CPA-P is still the best one, followed by KSA-P and MIA-P. The observations above suggest that different points in POIs set could make different key recovery efficiency.

An Unevenly Weighted Sum of the Bits Leakage. In this scenario, the least significant bit dominates in the leakage function with a relative weight of 10 and other bits with a relative weight of 1. An adversary with limited ability to describe the leakage type of device (i.e. the scenario tuple is <UWSB,HW>) and another adversary with strong ability (i.e. the scenario tuple is <UWSB,UWSB>) can get the ARs of five POIs selections. Our experiments show that the curves of ARs have exactly the same trend as those in Fig. 1.

Highly Non-Linear Leakage. In this scenario, the leakage function of cryptographic device is a highly non-linear function. Without loss of generality, S-box is used in this leakage scenario [12,20]. An adversary with limited ability to describe the leakage type of device (i.e. the scenario tuple is <HNL,HW>) can get the goodness evaluation results of POIs selections. Our experiments show that five POIs selections all fail.

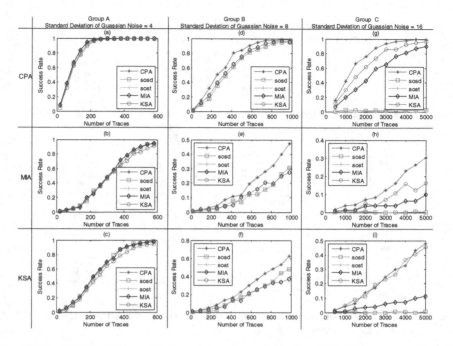

Fig. 2. SRs of CPA, MIA, and KSA using points selected by CPA-P, sosd, sost, MIA-P, KSA-P in HW leakage simulated scenarios

4.2   Practical Experiments.

In practical scenarios, we perform attacks against AES-256 RSM [18] implemented in software on an Atmel ATMega-163 smart card (Case 1) and unprotected AES implemented in hardware on Xilinx Vertex-5 FPGA (Case 2), and we use traces from DPA Contest v4 and DPA Contest v2, respectively. Especially, we ONLY focus on the POIs selection and key recovery against unprotected implementation in this paper. In Case 1, we converted the traces of protected implementation into traces of unprotected implementation using the known masks.

In the view of an adversary, we will choose hypothetical model according to priori knowledge. Specifically, we will use HW model in Case 1, and HD model in Case 2. In these practical scenarios, we cannot obtain the locations or range of POIs, the ARs cannot be computed. However, we can follow the second stage of framework, and utilize the SRs to evaluate the quality of points selected by five methods. For three distinguishers, we respectively perform key recovery attacks 300 times using every points selected by five POIs selections and count the SRs.

Case 1: Attacks Against an Unprotected AES Software Implementation. In this scenario, the output of the first S-box of the first round of AES operation is chosen as the target. The noise level of the traces from software implementation on the Atmel ATMega-163 smart card is very low. In order to

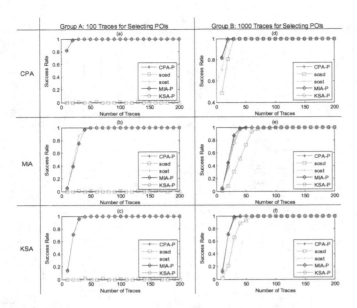

Fig. 3. SRs of CPA, MIA, and KSA using POIs selected by CPA-P, sosd, sost, MIA-P, KSA-P using original traces in Case 1

study the influence of noise level on POIs selections and distinguishers, we use additional Gaussian noise. Particularly, we employed five standard deviations of additional Gaussian noise, i.e. 0, 4, 8, 16, 32, where 0 denotes the original traces.

According to the results on DPA Contest website [19], the number of traces needed to recover the key in non-profiling attacks is at most 130. In order to study the influence of the number of traces on POIs selections, we set up two scenarios i.e. limited (100 traces) scenarios and sufficient (1,000 traces) scenarios.

Using original traces with limited number (100), five POIs selections get three points. Group A of Fig. 3 shows that, CPA, MIA, KSA can achieve 100 % SRs using the points selected by CPA-P, sost, MIA-P, KSA-P. Three distinguishers all fail using point selected by sosd. When the number of traces increases to 1,000, Group B shows that, the quality of points selected by all POIs selections are "good" enough to help three distinguishers achieve 100 % SRs.

When standard deviation of additional Gaussian noise is 4, using 100 traces, our experiments show that the most obvious change compared with Group A of Fig. 3 is that sosd and sost both fail to select a "good" point. When standard deviation 8 (Fig. 4) and 16, MIA-P fails, too. However, when 1,000 traces are used, MIA-P will be "good". We argue that this is because 100 traces are not sufficient to get satisfying probability density function, while 1000 traces do.

When standard deviation of additional Gaussian noise is 32, using limited traces, all POIs selections fail. It is because the noise level is too high and traces is too little. Using 1,000 traces, MIA-P fails. Possibly, it is because the noise

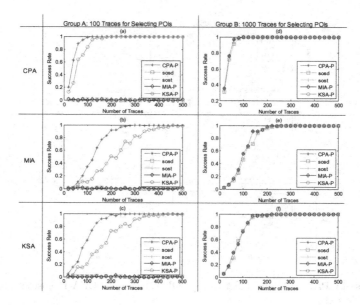

Fig. 4. SRs of CPA, MIA, and KSA using POIs selected by CPA-P, sosd, sost, MIA-P, KSA-P using traces with additional Gaussian noise of standard deviation 8 in Case 1

level is too high to get correct probability density function. This implies that MIA-P has weaker ability to tolerate noise than CPA-P and KSA-P.

Comprehensive analysing the experimental observations above, the quality of points selected by five POIs selections becomes worse with the increase of noise level. In the overall trend, sosd never has selected an "good" POI, sost affected by the noise level mostly, followed by MIA-P. The points selected by CPA-P and KSA-P are relatively more excellent. Moreover, comparing Group A with Group B, an important observation is that the negative impact of noise level could be decreased through increasing the number of traces. In addition, CPA distinguisher needs the least traces to achieve 100 % SR.

Case 2: Attacks Against an Unprotected AES FPGA Implementation. In this scenario, the input of the first S-box of the last round of AES operation is chosen as the target. As we known, the noise level of the traces from hardware implementation on Xilinx Vertex-5 FPGA is relatively high. That can factually represent a kind of common scenarios, so we will not use additional noise.

According to the results on DPA Contest website [19], the numbers of traces needed to achieve 80 % SR in non-profiling attacks range from 5,000 to 16,000. We set up two scenarios, i.e. limited (5,000) traces and sufficient (20,000) traces for selecting POIs. In this case, the SRs of three distinguishers using points selected by five POIs selections are presented in Fig. 5.

Group A of Fig. 5 shows that, using 5,000 traces, CPA can achieve 80 % SR by feeding point selected by only CPA-P. Other four POIs selections fail. MIA and KSA cannot recover the key using any points selected. Group B shows that,

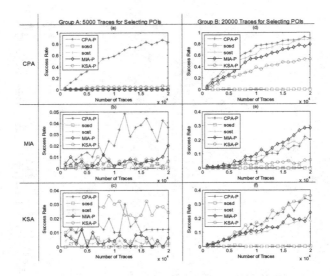

Fig. 5. SRs of CPA, MIA, and KSA using POIs selected by CPA-P, sosd, sost, MIA-P, KSA-P in Case 2

when traces for selecting POIs are sufficient, CPA can achieve 90 % SR using point selected by CPA-P; MIA can achieve 30 % SR using point selected by MIA-P; KSA can achieve 35 % SR using point selected by KSA-P. The SRs in Group B are limited with the trace number provided by DPA Contest v2 official.

4.3   Experimental Observations

According to the results of evaluation experiments in simulated scenarios and practical scenarios, we have the following observations.

1. When evaluations perform in the scenarios RL=HL={HW,UWSB,NL} or <UWSB,HW>,
   - Observation 1: The points selected by five POIs selections are not the same, sometimes differ greatly. The goodness of POIs selections significantly depends on noise level: with the increase of noise level, the goodness of five POIs selections decrease. Specifically, when the number of traces is limited, CPA-P> KSA-P > MIA-P> sosd> sost; when traces are sufficient, CPA-P> KSA-P> sost> MIA-P> sosd ("$A > B$" denotes POIs selection A is better than POIs selection B in a certain scenario).
   - Observation 2: In same noise level, the quality of point selected by CPA-P is the best. Specially, in the scenario <HD,HD>, this conclusion is incorrect.
2. When evaluations perform in the scenarios <NL,HW>,
   - Observation 3: All five POIs selections fail.
   - Observation 4: When in the scenarios <NL,UWSB or HD>, we guess that the conclusions are the same to those of Observation 3.
3. When evaluations perform in the scenario <HD,HD> and noise level is high,
   - Observation 5: We guess that the goodness of five POIs selections are the same to those of Observation 1.

– Observation 6: An interesting pattern is that the quality of points selected depend on certain distinguisher. Specifically, if choosing CPA, the optimal POIs selection is CPA-P; if choosing MIA, the optimal POIs selection is MIA-P; if choosing KSA, the optimal POIs selection is KSA-P.

Some Hints. Generally speaking, the adversary usually does not have powerful enough ability to identify a non-linear leakage. According to the observations above, we suggest that a crypto device with a highly non-linear leakage might be more secure. Some possible ways to implement it contain increasing noise level, making a device with non-linear leakage itself, or some other special methods.

5   Conclusions

In the field of side-channel attacks, POIs selection really matters much more in real-world practices than it is in those of theoretical analysis. In order to investigate the concrete impacts of POIs selections on distinguishers, and then pick out from those selection methods available the most appropriate one for a certain distinguisher, we proposed a two-stage evaluation framework which aims to separate the validity of POIs selected and their quality with respect to a certain distinguisher. This framework equips both designers and evaluators with a powerful tool to examine, in a more fine-grained way, two essential procedures (i.e. point extraction and key recovery). For the goodness of the POIs selection being used, we introduced the accuracy rate. It captures how well one POIs selection is capable of extracting from leakage traces those points that exactly correspond to the manipulations of one sensitive intermediate value targeted. In order to justify our proposed methods, we performed simulated attacks and practical attacks, taking five typical POIs selections and three distinguishers as concrete study cases. The results of these experiments also revealed some interesting observations.

Acknowledgments. This work was supported in part by National Natural Science Foundation of China (Nos. 61472416, 61272478, 61100225 and 61170282), National Key Scientific and Technological Project(No.2014ZX01032401-001), Strategic Priority Research Program of the Chinese Academy of Sciences (No. XDA06010701), One Hundred Talents Project of the Chinese Academy of Sciences, and SKLOIS Research Funding (No.2014-ZD-03).

References

1. Kocher, P.C.: Timing attacks on implementations of diffie-hellman, rsa, dss, and other systems. In: Koblitz, N. (ed.) CRYPTO 1996. LNCS, vol. 1109, pp. 104–113. Springer, Heidelberg (1996)
2. Kocher, P.C., Jaffe, J., Jun, B.: Differential power analysis. In: Wiener, M. (ed.) CRYPTO 1999. LNCS, vol. 1666, p. 388. Springer, Heidelberg (1999)
3. Quisquater, J.-J., Samyde, D.: Electro magnetic analysis (EMA): measures and counter-measures for smart cards. In: Attali, S., Jensen, T. (eds.) E-smart 2001. LNCS, vol. 2140, p. 200. Springer, Heidelberg (2001)

4. Brier, E., Clavier, C., Olivier, F.: Correlation power analysis with a leakage model. In: Joye, M., Quisquater, J.-J. (eds.) CHES 2004. LNCS, vol. 3156, pp. 16–29. Springer, Heidelberg (2004)

5. Batina, L., Gierlichs, B., Lemke-Rust, K.: Differential cluster analysis. In: Clavier, C., Gaj, K. (eds.) CHES 2009. LNCS, vol. 5747, pp. 112–127. Springer, Heidelberg (2009)

6. Chari, S., Rao, J.R., Rohatgi, P.: Template attacks. In: Kaliski, B.S., Koç, C.K., Paar, C. (eds.) CHES 2002. LNCS, vol. 2523, pp. 13–28. Springer, Heidelberg (2003)

7. Schindler, W., Lemke, K., Paar, C.: A stochastic model for differential side channel cryptanalysis. In: Rao, J.R., Sunar, B. (eds.) CHES 2005. LNCS, vol. 3659, pp. 30–46. Springer, Heidelberg (2005)

8. Mangard, S., Oswald, E., Standaert, F.-X., One for All - All for One: Unifying Standard DPA Attacks. IET, pp. 100–111 (2010). ISSN: 1751–8709. doi:10.1049/iet-ifs.2010.0096

9. Gierlichs, B., Batina, L., Tuyls, P., Preneel, B.: Mutual information analysis. In: Oswald, E., Rohatgi, P. (eds.) CHES 2008. LNCS, vol. 5154, pp. 426–442. Springer, Heidelberg (2008)

10. Zhao, H., Zhou, Y., Standaert, F.-X., Zhang, H.: Systematic construction and comprehensive evaluation of kolmogorov-smirnov test based side-channel distinguishers. In: Deng, R.H., Feng, T. (eds.) ISPEC 2013. LNCS, vol. 7863, pp. 336–352. Springer, Heidelberg (2013)

11. Gierlichs, B., Lemke-Rust, K., Paar, C.: Templates vs. stochastic methods. In: Goubin, L., Matsui, M. (eds.) CHES 2006. LNCS, vol. 4249, pp. 15–29. Springer, Heidelberg (2006)

12. Whitnall, C., Oswald, E.: A fair evaluation framework for comparing side-channel distinguishers. J. Cryptographic Eng. 1(2), 145–160 (2011)

13. Standaert, F.-X., Malkin, T.G., Yung, M.: A unified framework for the analysis of side-channel key recovery attacks. In: Joux, A. (ed.) EUROCRYPT 2009. LNCS, vol. 5479, pp. 443–461. Springer, Heidelberg (2009)

14. Whitnall, C., Oswald, E.: A comprehensive evaluation of mutual information analysis using a fair evaluation framework. In: Rogaway, P. (ed.) CRYPTO 2011. LNCS, vol. 6841, pp. 316–334. Springer, Heidelberg (2011)

15. Maghrebi, H., Rioul, O., Guilley, S., Danger, J.-L.: Comparison between side-channel analysis distinguishers. In: Chim, T.W., Yuen, T.H. (eds.) ICICS 2012. LNCS, vol. 7618, pp. 331–340. Springer, Heidelberg (2012)

16. Whitnall, C., Oswald, E., Mather, L.: An exploration of the kolmogorov-smirnov test as a competitor to mutual information analysis. In: Prouff, E. (ed.) CARDIS 2011. LNCS, vol. 7079, pp. 234–251. Springer, Heidelberg (2011)

17. Veyrat-Charvillon, N., Standaert, F.-X.: Mutual information analysis: how, when and why? In: Clavier, C., Gaj, K. (eds.) CHES 2009. LNCS, vol. 5747, pp. 429–443. Springer, Heidelberg (2009)

18. Nassar, M., Souissi, Y., Guilley, S., Danger, J.-L.: RSM: A small and fast countermeasure for AES, secure against 1st and 2nd-order zero-offset SCAs. In: IEEE DATE 2012, pp. 1173–1178 (2012)

19. DPA Contest Available at http://www.dpacontest.org

20. Reparaz, O., Gierlichs, B., Verbauwhede, I.: Generic DPA attacks: curse or blessing? In: Prouff, E. (ed.) COSADE 2014. LNCS, vol. 8622, pp. 98–111. Springer, Heidelberg (2014)

Attribute Based Key-Insulated Signatures with Message Recovery

Y. Sreenivasa Rao$^{(\boxtimes)}$ and Ratna Dutta

Indian Institute of Technology Kharagpur,
Kharagpur 721302, India
{ysrao,ratna}@maths.iitkgp.ernet.in

Abstract. In order to minimize the impact of secret signing key exposure in attribute based signature scenario, we design two attribute based key-insulated signature (ABKIS) with *message recovery* schemes for *expressive* linear secret-sharing scheme (LSSS)-realizable access structures utilizing only *4 bilinear pairing operations* in verification process and making the *message-signature length constant*. The first scheme deals with small universes of attributes while the second construction supports large universe of attributes. The signing key is computed according to LSSS access structure over signer's attributes, and is later updated at discrete time periods with the help of a physically secure but computationally limited device, called helper, without changing the access structure. A signing key for some time period is used to sign every message during that time period. The original message is not required to be transmitted with the signature, however, it can be recovered during verification procedure. The size of signing key in the proposed schemes is quadratic in number of attributes. The (strong) key-insulated security of our ABKIS primitives is reduced to the classical computational Diffie Hellman Exponent problem in selective attribute set and random oracle model. We also show that both the proposed signature constructions provide signer privacy.

Keywords: Attribute based signature · Key-insulation · Message recovery · Linear secret-sharing scheme · Constant message-signature length

1 Introduction

There exist two types of digital signature designs: (1) signature schemes in which the original message of the signature is required to be transmitted together with the signature, and (2) signature schemes with message recovery in which the message is embedded in a signature and can be recovered from the signature during verification process. The latter approach reduces the total size of the original message and the appended signature, hence interesting for applications where bandwidth is at prime concern. Message recovery signatures are also appropriate for applications in which small messages should be signed.

Attribute Based Signature (ABS) schemes are broadly categorized as (i) *key-policy* ABS [6,12]: the signing key is associated with an access structure and

© Springer International Publishing Switzerland 2015
L.C.K. Hui et al. (Eds.): ICICS 2014, LNCS 8958, pp. 215–229, 2015.
DOI: 10.1007/978-3-319-21966-0_16

a message is signed with an attribute set satisfying the access structure, and (ii) *signature-policy* ABS [10,11]: the signing key is tagged with an attribute set and a message is signed with an access structure (or predicate) satisfied by the attribute set.

Maji *et al.* [10,11] proposed signature-policy ABS schemes with formal security definitions of existential unforgeability and signer privacy. The signature leaks no other attribute information about the original signer except the fact that a single user with some set of attributes satisfying the predicate has generated the signature. A formal definition and security model for threshold key-policy ABS are presented in [6,12] together with schemes that support small as well as large attribute universe. In small universe schemes, the set of attributes used in the system is fixed during system setup. On the contrary, in large universe constructions, the size of the attribute universe can be exponentially large in the security parameter as the attribute parameters are dynamically computed after the system setup. The *signer privacy* for key-policy ABS of [6,12] ensures that the signature of a message for the attribute set W reveals nothing about the access structure $\mathbb{A}$ of the signer except the fact that $\mathbb{A}$ is satisfied by W. Specifically, even a computationally unbounded adversary cannot recognize the access structure or the signing key used to compute the given signature. ABS has found several applications like attribute based messaging, attribute based authentication and trust-negotiation, leaking secrets, etc.

The protection of secret key (*decryption key* in case of encryption whereas *signing key* in case of digital signature) is pivotal to all security guarantees in any cryptosystem. Standard notions of security cannot protect the system once its secret key gets compromised. In practice, we cannot assume the secret keys are kept perfectly secure at all times. For instance, an adversary might learn secret information from a physically compromised device or from a malicious user. A variety of frameworks have been proposed in an attempt to mitigate the potential damages caused by secret key exposure, including forward security [2], key-insulated cryptography [5] and intrusion resilience [7]. We focus here on key-insulation mechanism in the context of digital signature design. In this framework, a physically secure but computationally limited device, called *helper*, is involved. Initially, the key generation authority creates a helper key and initial signing key for every user. The helper key is stored in helper whereas the initial signing key is issued to respective user. The lifetime of the system is divided into several discrete time periods. The user can update his initial signing key at regular time periods with the help of helper without further access to the key generation authority. This greatly reduces unnecessary burden on the authority. The updated signing keys are called temporary signing keys. In every time period, the user can obtain the temporary signing key for the current time period by combining the temporary signing key of the previous time period with the partial key returned by the helper. The partial key is computed using helper key. Note also that any temporary signing key can be updated to either future time periods or past time periods according to user choice. The public key remains same throughout the lifetime. A temporary signing key for some time period is used to sign every message during that time period. The signatures are labeled with the time period during which they were generated. The exposure of signing keys for some time periods do not enable an adversary to create signing keys for non-exposed time periods as long as the helper is not compromised (it is assumed that helper is physically secure). Thus this framework can minimize the damage caused by signing key exposure.

Recently, Chen *et al.* [4] added key-insulation mechanism to the key-policy ABS of [9] and constructed an *attribute based key-insulated signature* (ABKIS) scheme in the key-policy setting. The ordinary ABS schemes are not appropriate for certain applications. For instance, consider a scenario in which Alice, who is a bank manager, wishes to take a vacation and wants to delegate her subordinate Bob to complete her daily business. Clearly, the mere ABS schemes are not enough to meet such requirements. Using ABKIS frame work, Alice can compute the temporary signing keys correspond to the time periods of her vacation and send those keys to Bob. Consequently, Bob can sign on behalf of Alice during the designated time periods.

There are several limitations of [4]: (a) The scheme handles only threshold policies, i.e., the signing key is computed according to threshold policy. The signing and verification attribute sets are essentially the same, i.e., the scheme reveals the attributes that the signer used to generate the signature. This may not desirable for certain applications like secret-leaking environments [11]. However, the scheme preserves signer privacy, a legitimate signer is indistinguishable among all the users whose access structures accepting the attribute set specified in the signature verification. (b) The size of the signature and the number of pairings required in verification are proportional to the number of underlying attributes. Specifically, the signature includes 4 group elements for each involved attribute and verification process requires 4 pairing operations for each required attribute, which could be prohibitively costly. (c) The scheme works for small universes of attributes. We address each of these limitations in this work.

Wang *et al.* [13] proposed a threshold policy ABS scheme with message recovery based on [8] and an identity based message recovery signature [15]. The size of the signature and the number of pairings during verification grow linearly with the number of involved attributes, in [13]. There is no ABKIS with message recovery proposed so far. Note that one can extend the ABKIS of [4] to support message recovery mechanism using the framework of [15], but the above mentioned limitations (a), (b) and (c) remain unchanged. To the best of our knowledge, [4] is the only ABKIS scheme (without message recovery) available in the literature.

1.1   Our Contribution

In this work, we consider designing key-insulated signatures with message recovery in the attribute based setting to achieve the following three main goals (i) *secret key security:* to mitigate the damage caused by the signing key exposure, (ii) *communication efficiency:* to realize constant message-signature size and (iii) *expressive access policies:* to exploit as expressive access structures as possible.

Table 1. Comparative summary of ABKIS schemes.

Scheme	Signature Size	Verification cost		Access structure	Security	Assumption	Attribute Universe
		Exp	Pairings				
[4]	$4 \cdot \delta$	δ	$4 \cdot \delta$	threshold policy	selective	cDH	small
SU-ABKIS	4	-	4	LSSS-realizable	selective	cDHE	small
LU-ABKIS	4	δ	4	LSSS-realizable	selective	cDHE	large

We propose the *first* attribute based key-insulated signature, ABKIS, schemes with *message recovery* for *expressive* linear secret-sharing scheme (LSSS)-realizable access structures in the key-policy framework. Our designs feature constant number of pairing computations for signature verification and constant message-signature length. In these constructions, the signing key is computed according to LSSS-realizable access structure over signer's attributes. We present two variants of these schemes, the first for small attribute universe and the second for large universe setting.

Small Universe Construction. We construct an ABKIS scheme with message recovery for small universes of attributes, referred as SU-ABKIS, by adapting the message recovery technique of [15], in which the whole message is embedded in a signature and it can be recovered by the verification algorithm. The signer can update his signing key to any time period without help of the authority and without changing his access structure by interacting with a helper device (it holds another secret key called helper key which is user specific). The signature consists of 4 group elements and a fixed length string (the string is appeared due to message recovery mechanism), and the signature verification can be done within 4 pairing executions. These measures are independent of the number of required attributes.

Large Universe Construction. We also present another ABKIS scheme with message recovery that can deal with large universe of attributes, referred as LU-ABKIS. The LU-ABKIS preserves the same functionality as that of SU-ABKIS except the size of public parameters is linear to the maximum number of attributes used to sign a message, as opposed to the size of attribute universe in small universe construction. And, verification needs δ exponentiations in addition to 4 pairings, δ is the number of attributes used in signing process. In our LU-ABKIS, the actual attribute set used to sign a message is hidden inside a larger attribute set and the verifier is provided with the latter one to verify the signature. As a result, the verifier cannot recognize the actual set of attributes utilized in the signing process (see *Remark* 6 in Sect. 3.1 for details). In contrast, the ABKIS of [4] needs to reveal the original signing attribute set to verify the signature. This means the signing and verification attribute sets are equal. In sum, our LU-ABKIS construction overcomes all the limitations (a), (b) and (c) of [4] mentioned in the previous section (see Table 1).

Both the proposed signature schemes protect signer privacy in the sense that the distribution of the signature is independent of the signing key used to compute it and hence no one can get any information about the signer's access structure or attributes involved in the generation of a signature. Consequently, a legitimate signer is indistinguishable among all the users whose access structures accepting the attribute set specified in the signature verification. The signing key size in both the proposed constructions is quadratic in number of involved attributes. However, the number of required bilinear pairing evaluations is independent of this size. The key-insulated and strong key-insulated security of our ABKIS schemes are analyzed in selective attribute set and random oracle model under the computational Diffie Hellman Exponent (cDHE) assumption.

Table 1 presents comparative summary of our schemes against ABKIS (without message recovery) scheme [4].

2   Preliminaries

We use the following notations in the rest of the paper.

$x \| y$: concatenation of two strings x and y

$\oplus$: X-OR operation in binary system

$^{\ell}[\![y]\!]$: first ℓ bits from left

$[\![y]\!]^{\ell}$: first ℓ bits from right

$[n]$: $\{1, 2, \ldots, n\}$, for any positive integer n

$s \leftarrow_R S$: operation of picking an element s uniformly at random from the set S

$\vec{a}\vec{b}$: $a_1 b_1 + \cdots + a_j b_j$, if $\vec{a} = (a_1, \ldots, a_j), \vec{b} = (b_1, \ldots, b_j) \in \mathbb{Z}_p^j$

$r\vec{a}$: $(ra_1, ra_2, \ldots, ra_j)$, where $r \in \mathbb{Z}_p$ and $\vec{a} = (a_1, \ldots, a_j)$

Definition 1. We use multiplicative cyclic groups $\mathbb{G}, \mathbb{G}_0$ of prime order p with an efficiently computable mapping $e : \mathbb{G} \times \mathbb{G} \rightarrow \mathbb{G}_0$ such that $e(u^a, v^b) = e(u, v)^{ab}$, $\forall\, u, v \in \mathbb{G}$, $a, b \in \mathbb{Z}_p$ and $e(u, v) \neq 1_{\mathbb{G}_0}$ whenever $u, v \neq 1_{\mathbb{G}}$. Here $1_{\mathbb{G}}$ (or $1_{\mathbb{G}_0}$) is identity element in $\mathbb{G}$ (or $\mathbb{G}_0$). We denote the bilinear group parameters as $\Sigma = (p, \mathbb{G}, \mathbb{G}_0, e)$ in the remainder of the paper. □

Definition 2. Given the instance $(g, g^a, \ldots, g^{a^q}, g^{a^{q+2}}, \ldots, g^{a^{2q}}) \in \mathbb{G}^{2q}$, where $a \leftarrow_R \mathbb{Z}_p$, a random generator $g \leftarrow_R \mathbb{G}$, the computational q-Diffie-Hellman Exponent (q-DHE) problem is to compute $g^{a^{q+1}}$. □

Definition 3. Let U be the universe of attributes and $\mathcal{P}(U) = \{S : S \subset U\}$. Let $\mathcal{P}(U)^* = \mathcal{P}(U) \setminus \{\emptyset\}$. Every non-empty subset $\mathbb{A}$ of $\mathcal{P}(U)^*$ is called an *access structure*. Any access structure $\mathbb{A}$ satisfying the condition $[A \subseteq B$ and $A \in \mathbb{A}$ implies $B \in \mathbb{A}]$ is called a *monotone access structure*. An attribute set C *satisfies* the (monotone) access structure $\mathbb{A}$ (in other words, $\mathbb{A}$ *accepts* C) if and only if $C \in \mathbb{A}$. In this case, C is called an *authorized* set in $\mathbb{A}$. Note that C *does not* satisfy $\mathbb{A}$ if and only if $C \notin \mathbb{A}$. □

Definition 4. Let $\mathbb{A}$ be a monotone access structure. A linear secret sharing scheme (LSSS) for $\mathbb{A}$ over a field $\mathbb{Z}_p$ is an $\ell \times k$ matrix $\mathbb{M}$ with entries in $\mathbb{Z}_p$, along with a row labeling function ρ which associates each row i of $\mathbb{M}$ with an attribute $\rho(i)$ in $\mathbb{A}$, that consists of the following two polynomial time algorithms:

Share $(\mathbb{M}, \rho, \alpha)$ takes as input $\mathbb{M}, \rho$ and a secret $\alpha \in \mathbb{Z}_p$ to be shared. It samples $a_2, a_3, \ldots, a_k \leftarrow_R \mathbb{Z}_p$ and sets $\vec{v} = (\alpha, a_2, a_3, \ldots, a_k) \in \mathbb{Z}_p^k$. It outputs a set $\{\lambda_{\rho(i)} : \lambda_{\rho(i)} = \vec{M_i}\vec{v}\}_{i \in [\ell]}$ of ℓ shares, where $\vec{M_i} \in \mathbb{Z}_p^k$ is ith row of the matrix $\mathbb{M}$. The share $\lambda_{\rho(i)}$ belongs to the attribute $\rho(i)$.

Recover $(\mathbb{M}, \rho, L)$ takes as input $\mathbb{M}, \rho$ and an authorized attribute set $L \in \mathbb{A}$. It outputs a set of constants $\{\omega_i\}_{i \in I} \subset \mathbb{Z}_p$, where $I = \{i \in [\ell] : \rho(i) \in L\}$, satisfying $\sum_{i \in I} \omega_i \vec{M_i} = (1, 0, \ldots, 0)$, i.e., $\sum_{i \in I} \omega_i \lambda_{\rho(i)} = \alpha$.   □

Remark 1. Note that the constants $\{\omega_i\}_{i \in I}$ can be computed in time polynomial in the size of the matrix $\mathbb{M}$ using Gaussian elimination. We denote $\mathbb{A}$ by the LSSS $(\mathbb{M}, \rho)$ and is called LSSS-realizable access structure.   □

2.1   ABKIS with Message Recovery Template

Apart from the Trusted Authority (TA), this model employs another device called *helper* which is physically secure but computationally limited. The TA creates a helper key and initial signing key for every user. The initial signing key is computed according to some access structure over user attributes. An ABKIS with message recovery is a set of the following six algorithms.

Setup(κ). The TA takes as input a security parameter κ and generates the system public parameters params and system master key MK. The public parameters params include a description of the attribute universe U, time period index space T and the message space $\mathcal{M}$. Here params are publicly available to all users and MK is kept secret by TA.

KeyGen(params, MK, $\mathbb{A}$). On input params, MK and an access structure $\mathbb{A}$ over a set of attributes $L_{\mathbb{A}} \subset U$, the TA computes a helper key $HK_{\mathbb{A}}$ and an initial signing key $SK_{\mathbb{A}}^0$ associated with $\mathbb{A}$. The helper key $HK_{\mathbb{A}}$ is stored in the helper and the user holds the initial signing key $SK_{\mathbb{A}}^0$.

HelperUpdate(params, $HK_{\mathbb{A}}, t_1, t_2$). This algorithm is executed by the helper for the user holding an access structure $\mathbb{A}$ with the input params, $HK_{\mathbb{A}}$, time period indices t_1, t_2 and returns an update key $UK_{\mathbb{A}}^{t_1 \to t_2}$ for $\mathbb{A}$ from the time period t_1 to time period t_2.

UserUpdate(params, $SK_{\mathbb{A}}^{t_1}, t_1, t_2, UK_{\mathbb{A}}^{t_1 \to t_2}$). Given public parameters params, temporary signing key $SK_{\mathbb{A}}^{t_1}$ associated with $\mathbb{A}$ for time period t_1, time period indices t_1, t_2 and update key $UK_{\mathbb{A}}^{t_1 \to t_2}$, the user performs this algorithm and obtains the temporary signing key $SK_{\mathbb{A}}^{t_2}$ associated with $\mathbb{A}$ for time period t_2. The user erases the temporary signing key $SK_{\mathbb{A}}^{t_1}$ for the time period t_1.

Sign(params, msg, $t, SK_{\mathbb{A}}^t, W$). To generate a signature on a message msg $\in \mathcal{M}$ with respect to an attribute set $W \in \mathbb{A}$ at time period t, the signer runs this algorithm with the input params, msg, $t, SK_{\mathbb{A}}^t, W$ and outputs a signature $\langle t, \Gamma \rangle$ consisting of the time period t and a signature Γ.

Verify(params, $\langle t, \Gamma \rangle, W$). Given a candidate signature $\langle t, \Gamma \rangle$ and an attribute set W, this algorithm outputs 1 if Γ is a valid signature with respect to the attribute set W in time period t. Otherwise, it returns 0.

Remark 2. In the above ABKIS, one can update the temporary signing key $\mathsf{SK}_{\mathbb{A}}^{t_1}$ to $\mathsf{SK}_{\mathbb{A}}^{t_2}$ in one step for any time periods t_1, t_2. This mechanism is called *random-access key updates*. Neither forward secure systems [2] nor intrusion resilience systems [7] support this functionality.   □

2.2   Security Definitions for ABKIS with Message Recovery

Following [4,14], we formalize here the key-insulated and strong key-insulated security, and signer privacy which are the typical security requirements for ABKIS schemes.

Key-insulated and strong key-insulated security. In key-insulated security notion, the exposure of any of the temporary signing keys for some time periods do not enable an adversary to create a valid signature for the non-exposed time periods as long as the corresponding helper keys are not compromised. On the other hand, in *strong* key-insulated security model, the exposure of helper keys do not enable an adversary to generate a valid signature for any time period as long as none of the temporary signing keys are compromised. These security notions are defined based on existential unforgeability under selective attribute set and time period index, and adaptive chosen message attack framework, in which the adversary needs to submit an attribute set and time period index pair before obtaining the system public parameters and the forgery must be created for that pair on any message. Formally, we define these security notions as follows.

Definition 5. (Key-insulated Security). An ABKIS scheme with message recovery is said to be $(\mathcal{T}, q_{\mathsf{KG}}, q_{\mathsf{TSK}}, q_{\mathsf{Sign}}, \epsilon)$-key-insulated if for any probabilistic polynomial time (PPT) adversary $\mathcal{A}$ running in time at most $\mathcal{T}$ that makes at most q_{KG} key generation queries, q_{TSK} temporary signing key queries and q_{Sign} signature queries, the adversary's advantage $Adv_{\mathcal{A}}^{\mathsf{key\text{-}ins}} = \Pr[\mathcal{A} \text{ wins}] \leq \epsilon$ in the following game (between a challenger $\mathcal{C}$ and the adversary $\mathcal{A}$):

1: First $\mathcal{C}$ selects a security parameter κ, and specifies an attribute universe U and time period index space T. Then $\mathcal{A}$ outputs an attribute set $W^* \subset U$ and a time period index $t^* \in T$.

2: $\mathcal{C}$ performs Setup algorithm and sends params to $\mathcal{A}$.

3: $\mathcal{A}$ is given access to the following three oracles.

- Key generation oracle $\mathcal{O}_{\mathsf{KG}}(\mathbb{A})$: when $\mathcal{A}$ submits an access structure $\mathbb{A}$ with the restriction $W^* \notin \mathbb{A}$, $\mathcal{C}$ runs KeyGen algorithm and returns a helper key, initial signing key pair $(\mathsf{HK}_{\mathbb{A}}, \mathsf{SK}_{\mathbb{A}}^0)$ to $\mathcal{A}$.

- Temporary signing key oracle $\mathcal{O}_{\mathsf{TSK}}(\mathbb{A}, t)$: When $\mathcal{A}$ submits an access structure $\mathbb{A}$ and time period index t with the condition $t \neq t^*$, $\mathcal{C}$ computes the temporary signing key $\mathsf{SK}_{\mathbb{A}}^t$ for the time period t by executing HelperUpdate, UserUpdate algorithms and sends it to $\mathcal{A}$.

- Signature oracle $\mathcal{O}_{\mathsf{Sign}}(\mathsf{msg}, W, t)$: On receiving a message $\mathsf{msg} \in \mathcal{M}$, an attribute set $W \subset U$ and a time period index $t \in T$ from $\mathcal{A}$, $\mathcal{C}$ chooses an access structure $\mathbb{A}$ such that $W \in \mathbb{A}$, computes the temporary signing key $\mathsf{SK}_{\mathbb{A}}^{t}$ and forwards the signature $\langle t, \Gamma \rangle$ to $\mathcal{A}$ that is returned by $\mathsf{Sign}(\mathsf{params}, \mathsf{msg}, t, \mathsf{SK}_{\mathbb{A}}^{t}, W)$.

4: At the end $\mathcal{A}$ outputs $(W^{*}, t^{*}, \mathsf{msg}^{*}, \Gamma^{*})$.

We say that $\mathcal{A}$ succeeds if $\mathsf{Verify}(\mathsf{params}, \langle t^{*}, \Gamma^{*} \rangle, W^{*}) = 1$ and $(\mathsf{msg}^{*}, W^{*}, t^{*})$ was never queried to the signature oracle.   □

Remark 3. In the foregoing definition, the adversary can obtain the helper key and initial signing key for any access structure which is *not* satisfied by the challenged attribute set W^{*} by issuing key generation queries. So, he can further compute temporary signing key of that access structure for any time period of his choice including t^{*}, without accessing temporary signing key oracle because he knows the corresponding helper key.

On the other hand, the temporary signing key oracle is actually meant for the access structures accepting W^{*}. Adversary can get temporary signing key of an access structure accepting W^{*} for any time period except t^{*} by querying the temporary signing key oracle. The helper keys of such access structures are not known to adversary. Wlog, we can assume that adversary issues only temporary signing key queries for the access structures accepting W^{*}.   □

In the strong key-insulated security notion defined below, the adversary is prohibited to request temporary signing keys and hence the challenge time period index t^{*} is not necessary to submit before receiving the system public parameters.

Definition 6. (Strong key-insulated Security). An ABKIS scheme with message recovery is said to be $(\mathcal{T}, q_{\mathsf{KG}}, q_{\mathsf{HK}}, q_{\mathsf{Sign}}, \epsilon)$-strong-key-insulated if for any PPT adversary $\mathcal{A}$ running in time at most $\mathcal{T}$ that makes at most q_{KG} key generation queries, q_{HK} helper key queries and q_{Sign} signature queries, the adversary's advantage $Adv_{\mathcal{A}}^{\mathsf{strong\text{-}key\text{-}ins}} = \Pr[\mathcal{A} \text{ wins}] \leq \epsilon$ in the following game (between a challenger $\mathcal{C}$ and $\mathcal{A}$):

1: First $\mathcal{C}$ selects a security parameter κ, and specifies an attribute universe U. Then $\mathcal{A}$ outputs an attribute set $W^{*} \subset U$.
2: $\mathcal{C}$ performs Setup algorithm and sends params to $\mathcal{A}$.
3: $\mathcal{A}$ is given access to the following three oracles.

- Key generation oracle $\mathcal{O}_{\mathsf{KG}}(\mathbb{A})$: Same as Definition 5.
- Helper key oracle $\mathcal{O}_{\mathsf{HK}}(\mathbb{A})$: when $\mathcal{A}$ submits an access structure $\mathbb{A}$, $\mathcal{C}$ runs KeyGen algorithm, obtains the helper key $\mathsf{HK}_{\mathbb{A}}$ and returns it to $\mathcal{A}$.
- Signature oracle $\mathcal{O}_{\mathsf{Sign}}(\mathsf{msg}, W, t)$: Same as Definition 5.

4: At the end $\mathcal{A}$ outputs $(W^{*}, t^{*}, \mathsf{msg}^{*}, \Gamma^{*})$.

We say that $\mathcal{A}$ succeeds if $\mathsf{Verify}(\mathsf{params}, \langle t^{*}, \Gamma^{*} \rangle, W^{*}) = 1$ and $(\mathsf{msg}^{*}, W^{*}, t^{*})$ was never queried to the signature oracle.   □

Remark 4. In Definition 6, temporary signing key queries are not explicitly provided for the adversary. However, the adversary can derive temporary signing keys for the access structures $\mathbb{A}$ such that $W^* \notin \mathbb{A}$ through key generation oracle $\mathcal{O}_{\mathsf{KG}}(\cdot)$. Hence the adversary can compromise a temporary signing key in any time period for the access structures not accepting the challenged attribute set W^*. On the other hand, he can obtain helper key of any access structure independent of such restriction by querying helper key oracle $\mathcal{O}_{\mathsf{HK}}(\cdot)$.   □

Signer Privacy. This property ensures that the distribution of a signature is independent of the temporary signing key that is used to generate it. This means that one cannot get any information about the access structure $\mathbb{A}$ held by the signer from a signature for the attribute set W in time period t, other than the fact that W satisfies $\mathbb{A}$. Precisely, the actual signer is indistinguishable from all the users whose access structures accepting the attribute set specified in the signature. Formally, this security notion is defined as follows.

Definition 7. An ABKIS scheme is said to provide signer privacy if for any message $\mathsf{msg} \in \mathcal{M}$, all $\langle \mathsf{params}, \mathsf{MK} \rangle \leftarrow \mathsf{Setup}(\kappa)$, all signing access structures $\mathbb{A}$ and $\mathbb{A}'$, all time periods t, all signing temporary signing keys $\mathsf{SK}_{\mathbb{A}}^t$ and $\mathsf{SK}_{\mathbb{A}'}^t$, all attribute sets W such that W satisfies both $\mathbb{A}$ and $\mathbb{A}'$, the distributions of $\mathsf{Sign}(\mathsf{params}, \mathsf{msg}, t, \mathsf{SK}_{\mathbb{A}}^t, W)$ and $\mathsf{Sign}(\mathsf{params}, \mathsf{msg}, t, \mathsf{SK}_{\mathbb{A}'}^t, W)$ are equal.   □

3   Proposed ABKIS with Message Recovery

3.1   ABKIS Scheme with Message Recovery for Small Universe

In this section, we present an ABKIS scheme with message recovery for small universes of attributes, referred as SU-ABKIS, that supports fixed length messages. We adapt the key updating technique used in [3] where the keys are randomized by means of pseudorandom function (PRF). A simple randomness is not adequate because the same attribute might held by several users and a user may derive the random exponents for other time periods from the current time period. Hence the randomness introduced in the key update process must be the time period as well as the attribute specific. To this end, we use a PRF family $\mathcal{F} = \{\mathsf{PRF}_s : s \leftarrow_R \{0,1\}^\kappa\}$, where $\mathsf{PRF}_s : \{0,1\}^{2\kappa} \to \{0,1\}^\kappa$ such that given a κ-bit seed s and 2κ-bit input ip, the PRF PRF_s outputs κ-bit string $\mathsf{PRF}_s(ip)$. We treat each time period index as an element in $\mathbb{Z}_p^*$, i.e., $T = \mathbb{Z}_p^*$ and the message space is $\mathcal{M} = \{0,1\}^{\ell_1}$. Let $U = \{1, 2, \ldots, n\} = [n]$ be the attribute universe. Our SU-ABKIS is composed of the following six algorithms.

$\mathsf{Setup}(\kappa)$: The TA carries out the following steps.

1. Choose $\Sigma = (p, \mathbb{G}, \mathbb{G}_0, e)$ according to the security parameter κ.
2. Select four collision resistant hash functions $H : \{0,1\}^* \to \mathbb{G}$, $H_1 : \{0,1\}^{\ell_1} \to \{0,1\}^{\ell_2}$, $H_2 : \{0,1\}^{\ell_2} \to \{0,1\}^{\ell_1}$ and $H' : \{0,1\}^* \to \{0,1\}^{\ell_1 + \ell_2}$, where $\ell_1, \ell_2 \in \mathbb{N}$, the set of all natural numbers.
3. Sample $\alpha \leftarrow_R \mathbb{Z}_p$, a random generator $g \leftarrow_R \mathbb{G}$ and set $Y = e(g,g)^\alpha$.
4. Pick $w_1, w_2 \leftarrow_R \mathbb{G}$. Define a function $F : \mathbb{Z}_p \to \mathbb{G}$ by $F(t) = w_1 w_2^t$.

5. Select $v \leftarrow_R \mathbb{G}$. For each attribute $k \in U = [n]$, choose $v_k \leftarrow_R \mathbb{G}$.
6. The system master key is $\mathsf{MK} = \alpha$ and the system public parameters are published as $\mathsf{params} = \langle \Sigma, g, Y, v, w_1, w_2, \{v_k\}_{k \in [n]}, H, H_1, H_2, H', F, U = [n], T = \mathbb{Z}_p^*, \mathcal{M} = \{0,1\}^{\ell_1} \rangle$.

$\mathsf{KeyGen}(\mathsf{params}, \mathsf{MK}, (\mathbb{M}, \rho))$: To compute a helper key $\mathsf{HK}_{(\mathbb{M}, \rho)}$ and an initial signing key $\mathsf{SK}^0_{(\mathbb{M}, \rho)}$ associated with an access structure $(\mathbb{M}, \rho)$, the TA performs as follows. Each ith row $\vec{M}_i$ of the LSSS matrix $\mathbb{M}$ of size $\nu \times \tau$ is associated with an attribute $\rho(i) \in [n]$. We assume that the time period index is 0 for initial signing key.

1. Pick $\mathsf{hk}_{(\mathbb{M}, \rho)} \leftarrow_R \{0,1\}^\kappa$ and choose $\mathsf{PRF}_{\mathsf{hk}_{(\mathbb{M}, \rho)}} \in \mathcal{F}$.
2. Sample $z_2, \ldots, z_\tau \leftarrow_R \mathbb{Z}_p$ and set $\vec{v} = (\alpha, z_2, \ldots, z_\tau)$.
3. For each row $i \in [\nu]$,
   - compute $\lambda_{\rho(i)} = \vec{M}_i \vec{v}$ and $\gamma_{i,0} = \mathsf{PRF}_{\mathsf{hk}_{(\mathbb{M}, \rho)}}(0||\rho(i))$
     (if the length of each input string for PRF is less than κ, then we add required number of 0s on the left side of the string to make 2κ-bit long),
   - pick $r_i \leftarrow_R \mathbb{Z}_p$ and set
     $d^0_{i,1} = g^{r_i}, d^0_{i,2} = g^{\gamma_{i,0}}, d^0_{i,3} = g^{\lambda_{\rho(i)}}(vv_{\rho(i)})^{r_i} F(0)^{\gamma_{i,0}}, \ d^0_{i,4} = \{d^0_{i,4,k} = v_k^{r_i}\}_{k \in [n] \setminus \{\rho(i)\}}$.
4. The initial signing key is $\mathsf{SK}^0_{(\mathbb{M}, \rho)} = \langle (\mathbb{M}, \rho), \{d^0_{i,1}, d^0_{i,2}, d^0_{i,3}, d^0_{i,4} : i \in [\nu]\} \rangle$.
5. The helper key is $\mathsf{HK}_{(\mathbb{M}, \rho)} = \langle \rho, \mathsf{hk}_{(\mathbb{M}, \rho)} \rangle$.

$\mathsf{HelperUpdate}(\mathsf{params}, \mathsf{HK}_{(\mathbb{M}, \rho)}, t_1, t_2)$: To construct the update key $\mathsf{UK}^{t_1 \to t_2}_{(\mathbb{M}, \rho)}$ for $(\mathbb{M}, \rho)$ from the time period t_1 to time period t_2, the helper carries out the following steps.

1. For each row $i \in [\nu]$,
   - compute $\gamma_{i,t_1} = \mathsf{PRF}_{\mathsf{hk}_{(\mathbb{M}, \rho)}}(t_1||\rho(i))$, $\gamma_{i,t_2} = \mathsf{PRF}_{\mathsf{hk}_{(\mathbb{M}, \rho)}}(t_2||\rho(i))$,
   - set $\mathsf{UK}^{t_1 \to t_2}_{i,1} = F(t_2)^{\gamma_{i,t_2}} \cdot F(t_1)^{-\gamma_{i,t_1}}$, $\mathsf{UK}^{t_1 \to t_2}_{i,2} = g^{\gamma_{i,t_2}}$.
2. The update key is $\mathsf{UK}^{t_1 \to t_2}_{(\mathbb{M}, \rho)} = \{\mathsf{UK}^{t_1 \to t_2}_{i,1}, \mathsf{UK}^{t_1 \to t_2}_{i,2} : i \in [\nu]\}$.

$\mathsf{UserUpdate}(\mathsf{params}, \mathsf{SK}^{t_1}_{(\mathbb{M}, \rho)}, t_1, t_2, \mathsf{UK}^{t_1 \to t_2}_{(\mathbb{M}, \rho)})$: The user computes the temporary signing key $\mathsf{SK}^{t_2}_{(\mathbb{M}, \rho)}$ for time period t_2 from the temporary signing key $\mathsf{SK}^{t_1}_{(\mathbb{M}, \rho)}$ for time period t_1 by using update key $\mathsf{UK}^{t_1 \to t_2}_{(\mathbb{M}, \rho)}$ as follows.

1. Parse the temporary signing key for $(\mathbb{M}, \rho)$ at time period t_1 as $\mathsf{SK}^{t_1}_{(\mathbb{M}, \rho)} = \langle (\mathbb{M}, \rho), \{d^{t_1}_{i,1}, d^{t_1}_{i,2}, d^{t_1}_{i,3}, d^{t_1}_{i,4} : i \in [\nu]\} \rangle$, where $d^{t_1}_{i,1} = g^{r_i}, d^{t_1}_{i,2} = g^{\gamma_{i,t_1}}, d^{t_1}_{i,3} = g^{\lambda_{\rho(i)}}(vv_{\rho(i)})^{r_i} F(t_1)^{\gamma_{i,t_1}}, d^{t_1}_{i,4} = \{d^{t_1}_{i,4,k} = v_k^{r_i}\}_{k \in [n] \setminus \{\rho(i)\}}$.
2. The update key $\mathsf{UK}^{t_1 \to t_2}_{(\mathbb{M}, \rho)}$ is parsed as $\mathsf{UK}^{t_1 \to t_2}_{(\mathbb{M}, \rho)} = \{\mathsf{UK}^{t_1 \to t_2}_{i,1}, \mathsf{UK}^{t_1 \to t_2}_{i,2} : i \in [\nu]\}$.
3. The user sets the temporary signing key for $(\mathbb{M}, \rho)$ and time period t_2 as $\mathsf{SK}^{t_2}_{(\mathbb{M}, \rho)} = \langle (\mathbb{M}, \rho), \{d^{t_2}_{i,1}, d^{t_2}_{i,2}, d^{t_2}_{i,3}, d^{t_2}_{i,4} : i \in [\nu]\} \rangle$, where $d^{t_2}_{i,1} = d^{t_1}_{i,1}, d^{t_2}_{i,2} = \mathsf{UK}^{t_1 \to t_2}_{i,2}, d^{t_2}_{i,3} = d^{t_1}_{i,3} \cdot \mathsf{UK}^{t_1 \to t_2}_{i,1}$ and $d^{t_2}_{i,4,k} = d^{t_1}_{i,4,k}, \forall k \in [n] \setminus \{\rho(i)\}$.
4. The temporary signing key $\mathsf{SK}^{t_1}_{(\mathbb{M}, \rho)}$ for the time period t_1 will be discarded.

Note: At time period t_2, it can be seen that $d_{i,1}^{t_2} = g^{r_i}, d_{i,2}^{t_2} = g^{\gamma_{i,t_2}}, d_{i,3}^{t_2} = g^{\lambda_{\rho(i)}}(vv_{\rho(i)})^{r_i}F(t_2)^{\gamma_{i,t_2}}, d_{i,4}^{t_2} = \{d_{i,4,k}^{t_2} = v_k^{r_i}\}_{k\in[n]\setminus\{\rho(i)\}}$.

Sign(params, msg, t, $\mathsf{SK}_{(\mathbb{M},\rho)}^t$, W): The signer with a temporary signing key $\mathsf{SK}_{(\mathbb{M},\rho)}^t$ for LSSS access structure $(\mathbb{M}, \rho)$ and time period t generates the signature on a message msg $\in \{0,1\}^{\ell_1}$ for the attribute set W satisfying $(\mathbb{M}, \rho)$ as follows. The temporary signing key $\mathsf{SK}_{(\mathbb{M},\rho)}^t$ for the time period t is parsed as $\mathsf{SK}_{(\mathbb{M},\rho)}^t = \langle(\mathbb{M}, \rho), \{d_{i,1}^t, d_{i,2}^t, d_{i,3}^t, d_{i,4}^t : i \in [\nu]\}\rangle$.

1. Compute $\beta = H'(t\|W\|Y), m = H_1(\mathsf{msg})\|(H_2(H_1(\mathsf{msg})) \oplus \mathsf{msg})$ and $c = \beta \oplus m$.
2. Obtain a set of constants $\{\omega_i \in \mathbb{Z}_p : i \in I\} \leftarrow \mathsf{Recover}(\mathbb{M}, \rho, W)$, where $I = \{i \in [\nu] : \rho(i) \in W\}$, satisfying $\sum_{i\in I}\omega_i \vec{M}_i = (1, 0, \ldots, 0)$. This is possible since W satisfies $(\mathbb{M}, \rho)$.
3. Choose $z_2', \ldots, z_\tau' \leftarrow_R \mathbb{Z}_p$ and define $\vec{z} = (0, z_2', \ldots, z_\tau')$.
4. For each $i \in [\nu]$, pick $r_i', b_{i,t} \leftarrow_R \mathbb{Z}_p$ and compute $\widehat{d}_{i,1}^t = d_{i,1}^t \cdot g^{r_i'}, \widehat{d}_{i,2}^t = d_{i,2}^t \cdot g^{b_{i,t}}, \widehat{d}_{i,3}^t = d_{i,3}^t \cdot g^{\vec{M}_i \vec{z}}(vv_{\rho(i)})^{r_i'}F(t)^{b_{i,t}}, \widehat{d}_{i,4}^t = \{\widehat{d}_{i,4,k}^t = d_{i,4,k}^t \cdot v_k^{r_i'}\}_{k\in[n]\setminus\{\rho(i)\}}$.
5. Sample $\theta, \xi, \zeta \leftarrow_R \mathbb{Z}_p$ and set $\sigma = g^\theta, \sigma_1 = g^\xi \prod_{i\in I} \left(\widehat{d}_{i,1}^t\right)^{\omega_i}, \sigma_2 = g^\zeta \prod_{i\in I} \left(\widehat{d}_{i,2}^t\right)^{\omega_i}$,

$$\sigma_3 = \prod_{i\in I} \left(\widehat{d}_{i,3}^t \prod_{k\in W, k\neq\rho(i)} \widehat{d}_{i,4,k}^t\right)^{\omega_i} \cdot \left(v \prod_{k\in W} v_k\right)^\xi \cdot H(c\|\sigma\|\sigma_1\|\sigma_2\|t\|W)^\theta \cdot F(t)^\zeta.$$

6. The signature is $\Gamma = \langle c, \sigma, \sigma_1, \sigma_2, \sigma_3\rangle$ and finally outputs $\langle t, \Gamma\rangle$.

Verify(params, $\langle t, \Gamma\rangle$, W): Given a signature $\langle t, \Gamma = \langle c, \sigma, \sigma_1, \sigma_2, \sigma_3\rangle\rangle$ and an attribute set W, the verifier performs in the following way.

1. Check validity of the following equation

$$\frac{e(\sigma_3, g)}{e(v\prod_{k\in W}v_k, \sigma_1) \cdot e(H(c\|\sigma\|\sigma_1\|\sigma_2\|t\|W), \sigma) \cdot e(F(t), \sigma_2)} \overset{?}{=} Y. \quad (1)$$

If it is not valid, output 0. Otherwise, proceed as follows.

2. Compute $\beta = H'(t\|W\|Y)$ and $m = c \oplus \beta$.
3. Recover the message $\mathsf{msg} = [m]^{\ell_1} \oplus H_2(^{\ell_2}[m])$.
4. Return 1 if $^{\ell_2}[m] = H_1(\mathsf{msg})$ and accept Γ as a valid signature of the message msg in time period t. In this case, the message msg $\in \{0,1\}^{\ell_1}$ is recovered. Otherwise, output 0.

Remark 5. We can modify the above construction for messages of fixed length ℓ_1 to deal with messages of any length, i.e., msg $\in \{0,1\}^*$. To sign a message of length less than ℓ_1, one can pad spaces after the message until ℓ_1 and can use the foregoing scheme. If message size is larger than ℓ_1, a part of the message of length ℓ_1 is embed in a signature and can be recovered in verification phase and the other message segment is sent together with the signature. Specifically, divide the message msg into two parts as msg $= \mathsf{msg}_1\|\mathsf{msg}_2$ such that size of msg_1 is ℓ_1. In the corresponding scheme, replace msg with msg_1, compute $\beta = H'(t\|W\|Y\|\mathsf{msg}_2)$ instead of $\beta = H'(t\|W\|Y)$ and everything else remains the same. In verification phase, recover msg_1 and pad with the available msg_2 as $\mathsf{msg}_1\|\mathsf{msg}_2$ in order to obtain msg. $\quad\square$

Remark 6. In signing process, W satisfies $(\mathbb{M}, \rho)$ means there exists an attribute set $\widehat{W} \subset W \cap L_{(\mathbb{M},\rho)}$, $L_{(\mathbb{M},\rho)}$ is the set of attributes assigned to the rows of the matrix $\mathbb{M}$, such that the rows of $\mathbb{M}$ corresponding to the attributes of $\widehat{W}$ (the row set I in the construction) spans the vector $(1, 0, \ldots, 0)$. The signer computes the signature using the signing key components corresponding to the attributes appeared in $\widehat{W}$. The set $\widehat{W}$ is completely hidden in the process (i.e., hidden in W) and the verifier is given the attribute set W. In verifier or adversary point of view, the signer can use any subset of W. Consequently, the verifier cannot identify the subset of signer attributes which has originally been used to generate a signature from the set $\mathcal{P}(W)^*$ of all non-empty subsets of W. But, he can verify the signature using the whole attribute set W. In contrast, the signing and verification attribute sets are same in existing ABKIS [4], i.e., the signer needs to expose the attributes used to create a signature.   □

3.2   Large Universe ABKIS Scheme with Message Recovery

We present here an ABKIS scheme with message recovery for large universes of attributes, which we denote as LU-ABKIS. In this construction $U = \mathbb{Z}_p^*$ be the attribute universe. We impose a bound, say N, on the size of attribute set used in signing algorithm. Note that one can extend our small universe ABKIS construction to support large universe by using a collision resistant hash function to compute the attribute values after system setup. However, the signer needs to reveal his attributes used to create a signature as in ABKIS scheme of [4], which is not desirable. To preserve signer attribute anonymity as well as to realize constant-size signature like our small universe ABKIS scheme, we change the signing key generation process using the technique of [1].

Setup(κ): Given a security parameter κ, the TA executes the following steps.
1: Choose suitable $\Sigma = (p, \mathbb{G}, \mathbb{G}_0, e)$ according to κ.
2: Select four collision resistant hash functions $H : \{0,1\}^* \to \mathbb{G}$, $H_1 : \{0,1\}^{\ell_1} \to \{0,1\}^{\ell_2}$, $H_2 : \{0,1\}^{\ell_2} \to \{0,1\}^{\ell_1}$ and $H' : \{0,1\}^* \to \{0,1\}^{\ell_1+\ell_2}$, where $\ell_1, \ell_2 \in \mathbb{N}$.
3: Choose a PRF family $\mathcal{F} = \{\mathsf{PRF}_s : s \leftarrow_R \{0,1\}^\kappa\}$, where $\mathsf{PRF}_s : \{0,1\}^{2\kappa} \to \{0,1\}^\kappa$.
4: Sample $\alpha \leftarrow_R \mathbb{Z}_p$, a random generator $g \leftarrow_R \mathbb{G}$ and set $Y = e(g,g)^\alpha$.
5: Pick $w_1, w_2 \leftarrow_R \mathbb{G}$. Define a function $F : \mathbb{Z}_p \to \mathbb{G}$ by $F(t) = w_1 w_2^t$.
6: Pick $V_0, V_1, \ldots, V_N \leftarrow_R \mathbb{G}$. Where N is a bound on the size of signing attribute set used in signing algorithm below.
7: The system master key is $MK = \alpha$ and the system public parameters are params $= \langle \Sigma, N, g, Y, w_1, w_2, V_0, \{V_k\}_{k \in [N]}, H, H_1, H_2, H', F, U = \mathbb{Z}_p^*, T = \mathbb{Z}_p^*, \mathcal{M} = \{0,1\}^{\ell_1}\rangle$.

KeyGen(params, MK, $(\mathbb{M}, \rho)$): The TA performs as follows. Each ith row $\vec{M}_i$ of the matrix $\mathbb{M}$ of size $\nu \times \tau$ is associated with an attribute $\rho(i) \in \mathbb{Z}_p^*$.
1: Pick $\mathsf{hk}_{(\mathbb{M},\rho)} \leftarrow_R \{0,1\}^\kappa$ and choose $\mathsf{PRF}_{\mathsf{hk}_{(\mathbb{M},\rho)}} \in \mathcal{F}$.
2: Sample $z_2, \ldots, z_\tau \leftarrow_R \mathbb{Z}_p$ and set $\vec{v} = (\alpha, z_2, \ldots, z_\tau)$.

3: For each row $i \in [\nu]$, compute $\lambda_{\rho(i)} = \vec{M}_i \vec{v}$ and $\gamma_{i,0} = \mathsf{PRF}_{\mathsf{hk}_{(\mathbb{M},\rho)}}(0||\rho(i))$. Pick $r_i \leftarrow_R \mathbb{Z}_p$ and set $d^0_{i,1} = g^{r_i}, d^0_{i,2} = g^{\gamma_{i,0}}, d^0_{i,3} = g^{\lambda_{\rho(i)}} V_0^{r_i} F(0)^{\gamma_{i,0}}$, $d^0_{i,4} = \{d^0_{i,4,k} = (V_1^{-\rho(i)^{k-1}} V_k)^{r_i}\}_{k=2}^N$.

4: The initial signing key of $(\mathbb{M}, \rho)$ is $\mathsf{SK}^0_{(\mathbb{M},\rho)} = \langle(\mathbb{M}, \rho), \{d^0_{i,1}, d^0_{i,2}, d^0_{i,3}, d^0_{i,4}\}_{i \in [\nu]}\rangle$.

5: The helper key is $\mathsf{HK}_{(\mathbb{M},\rho)} = \langle\rho, \mathsf{hk}_{(\mathbb{M},\rho)}\rangle$.

HelperUpdate(params, $\mathsf{HK}_{(\mathbb{M},\rho)}, t_1, t_2$): Same as SU-ABKIS construction.

UserUpdate(params, $\mathsf{SK}^{t_1}_{(\mathbb{M},\rho)}, t_1, t_2, \mathsf{UK}^{t_1 \to t_2}_{(\mathbb{M},\rho)}$): Same as SU-ABKIS construction.

Sign(params, msg, $t, \mathsf{SK}^t_{(\mathbb{M},\rho)}, W$): Here msg $\in \{0,1\}^{\ell_1}$ and W satisfies $(\mathbb{M}, \rho)$

The signing key $\mathsf{SK}^t_{(\mathbb{M},\rho)}$ is parsed as $\mathsf{SK}^t_{(\mathbb{M},\rho)} = \langle(\mathbb{M}, \rho), \{d^t_{i,1}, d^t_{i,2}, d^t_{i,3}, d^t_{i,4} : i \in [\nu]\}\rangle$. Note that $|W| < N$.

1: Compute $\beta = H'(t||W||Y), m = H_1(\mathsf{msg})||(H_2(H_1(\mathsf{msg})) \oplus \mathsf{msg})$ and $c = \beta \oplus m$.

2: Choose $z'_2, \ldots, z'_\tau \leftarrow_R \mathbb{Z}_p$ and define $\vec{z} = (0, z'_2, \ldots, z'_\tau)$.

3: For each row $i \in [\nu]$, pick $r'_i, b_{i,t} \leftarrow_R \mathbb{Z}_p$ and compute $\widehat{d^t_{i,1}} = d^t_{i,1} \cdot g^{r'_i}, \widehat{d^t_{i,2}} = d^t_{i,2} \cdot g^{b_{i,t}}, \widehat{d^t_{i,3}} = d^t_{i,3} \cdot g^{\vec{M}_i \vec{z}} V_0^{r'_i} F(t)^{b_{i,t}}, \widehat{d^t_{i,4}} = \{\widehat{d^t_{i,4,k}} = d^t_{i,4,k} \cdot (V_1^{-\rho(i)^{k-1}} V_k)^{r'_i}\}_{k=2}^N$.

4: Obtain a set of constants $\{\omega_i \in \mathbb{Z}_p : i \in I\} \leftarrow \mathsf{Recover}(\mathbb{M}, \rho, W)$, where $I = \{i \in [\nu] : \rho(i) \in W\}$, satisfying $\sum_{i \in I} \omega_i \vec{M}_i = (1, 0, \ldots, 0)$. This is possible because W satisfies $(\mathbb{M}, \rho)$.

5: Compute $(y_1, y_2, \ldots, y_N)$ such that $P_W(X) = \prod_{w \in W}(X - w) = \sum_{j=1}^{|W|+1} y_j \cdot X^{j-1}$. Note that if $|W| + 1 < N$, then set $y_{|W|+2} = \cdots = y_N = 0$. So, $P_W(X) = \sum_{j=1}^N y_j \cdot X^{j-1}$.

6: Sample $\theta, \xi, \zeta \leftarrow_R \mathbb{Z}_p$ and set $\sigma = g^\theta, \sigma_1 = g^\xi \prod_{i \in I} (\widehat{d^t_{i,1}})^{\omega_i}, \sigma_2 = g^\zeta \prod_{i \in I} (\widehat{d^t_{i,2}})^{\omega_i}$,

$$\sigma_3 = \prod_{i \in I} \left(\widehat{d^t_{i,3}} \prod_{k=2}^N (\widehat{d^t_{i,4,k}})^{y_k}\right)^{\omega_i} \cdot \left(V_0 \prod_{k \in [N]} V_k^{y_k}\right)^\xi \cdot H(c||\sigma||\sigma_1||\sigma_2||t||W)^\theta \cdot F(t)^\zeta.$$

7: The signature is $\Gamma = \langle c, \sigma, \sigma_1, \sigma_2, \sigma_3\rangle$ and output $\langle t, \Gamma\rangle$.

Verify(params, $\langle t, \Gamma\rangle, W$): Given a signature $\langle t, \Gamma = \langle c, \sigma, \sigma_1, \sigma_2, \sigma_3\rangle\rangle$ and an attribute set W with $|W| < N$, the verifier executes the following steps.

1: Compute $(y_1, y_2, \ldots, y_N)$ such that $P_W(X) = \prod_{w \in W}(X - w) = \sum_{k \in [N]} y_k \cdot X^{k-1}$ as above.

2: Check validity of the following equation

$$\frac{e(\sigma_3, g)}{e(V_0 \prod_{k \in [N]} V_k^{y_k}, \sigma_1) \cdot e(H(c||\sigma||\sigma_1||\sigma_2||t||W), \sigma) \cdot e(F(t), \sigma_2)} \stackrel{?}{=} Y. \quad (2)$$

If it is not valid, output 0. Otherwise, proceed as in a manner similar to that of our small universe construction SU-ABKIS.

3.3 Security Proof of SU-ABKIS and LU-ABKIS

Theorem 1. *Suppose the attribute universe U has q attributes (resp., $N = q$ is a bound on the size of signing attribute set used in signing phase), the hash function H is modeled as random oracle, the hash functions H_1, H_2, H' are collision resistant and $\mathcal{F} = \{PRF_s : s \leftarrow_R \{0,1\}^\kappa\}$ is PRF family. Assume the computational q-DHE problem is $(\mathcal{T}', \epsilon)$-hard in $\mathbb{G}$. Then, our SU-ABKIS (resp., LU-ABKIS) scheme is $(\mathcal{T}, q_{\mathsf{KG}}, q_{\mathsf{TSK}}, q_{\mathsf{Sign}}, \epsilon)$-key-insulated in the random oracle model, where $\mathcal{T} = \mathcal{T}' - \mathcal{O}\big(q^2(q_{\mathsf{KG}} + q_{\mathsf{TSK}}) + q_{\mathsf{Sign}} + q_{\mathsf{H}}\big)\mathcal{T}_{exp} - 2\mathcal{T}_{pair}$. Here, q_{H} is number of H hash queries allowed during simulation, $\mathcal{T}_{exp}$ is cost of one exponentiation and $\mathcal{T}_{pair}$ is cost of one pairing computation.*

Theorem 2. *Suppose the attribute universe U has q attributes (resp., $N = q$ is a bound on the size of signing attribute set used in signing phase), the hash function H is modeled as random oracle, the hash functions H_1, H_2, H' are collision resistant and $\mathcal{F} = \{PRF_s : s \leftarrow_R \{0,1\}^\kappa\}$ is PRF family. Assume the computational q-DHE problem is $(\mathcal{T}', \epsilon)$-hard in $\mathbb{G}$. Then, our SU-ABKIS (resp., LU-ABKIS) scheme is $(\mathcal{T}, q_{\mathsf{KG}}, q_{\mathsf{HK}}, q_{\mathsf{Sign}}, \epsilon)$-strong-key-insulated in the random oracle model, where $\mathcal{T} = \mathcal{T}' - \mathcal{O}\big(q^2 \cdot q_{\mathsf{KG}} + q_{\mathsf{Sign}} + q_{\mathsf{H}}\big)\mathcal{T}_{exp} - 2\mathcal{T}_{pair}$.*

Theorem 3. *Both the proposed SU-ABKIS and LU-ABKIS schemes provide signer privacy.*

Due to page restriction, the proofs will be given in full version of the paper.

4 Some Possible Extensions

Constructions Without Random Oracles. We can further extend our ABKIS schemes to realize security reduction in standard model as follows. The hash function H is redefined as $H : \{0,1\}^* \rightarrow \{0,1\}^\varrho$. Pick $\varpi_0, \varpi_1, \ldots, \varpi_\varrho \leftarrow_R \mathbb{G}$ and define $\widehat{F} : \{0,1\}^\varrho \rightarrow \mathbb{G}$ by $\widehat{F}(x_1, \ldots, x_\varrho) = \varpi_0 \varpi_1^{x_1} \cdots \varpi_\varrho^{x_\varrho}$. In signature component σ_3, replace $H(c||\sigma||\sigma_1||\sigma_2||t||W)^\theta$ with $\widehat{F}\big(H(c||\sigma_1||\sigma_2||t||W)\big)^\theta$ and change the verification tests accordingly.

Schemes Supporting Negative Attributes. We can extend our constructions to support *negative* attributes by treating the negation of an attribute as a separate attribute. This doubles the total number of attributes used in the system. However, the resulting schemes attains the same efficiency as that of our monotone access structure primitives.

5 Conclusion

We presented the *first* ABKIS schemes with message recovery for expressive LSSS-realizable access structures that feature constant number of pairing computations required for signature verification process and constant message-signature length. The (strong) key-insulated security of ABKIS schemes are reduced to the computational q-DHE problem in selective attribute set and random oracle model. Both the proposed constructions provide signer privacy. The signing key size in our constructions is quadratic in number of involved attributes.

Acknowledgement. The authors would like to thank the anonymous reviewers of this paper for their valuable comments and suggestions.

References

1. Attrapadung, N., Herranz, J., Laguillaumie, F., Libert, B., de Panafieu, E., Rfols, C.: Attribute-based encryption schemes with constant-size ciphertexts. Theo. Comput. Sci. **422**, 15–38 (2012)
2. Canetti, R., Halevi, S., Katz, J.: A forward-secure public-key encryption scheme. In: Biham, E. (ed.) EUROCRYPT 2003. LNCS, vol. 2656, pp. 255–271. Springer, Heidelberg (2003)
3. Chen, J.H., Wang, Y.T., Chen, K.F.: Attribute-based key-insulated encryption. J. Inf. Sci. Eng. **27**(2), 437–449 (2011)
4. Chen, J., Long, Y., Chen, K., Guo, J.: Attribute-based key-insulated signature and its applications. Inf. Sci. **275**, 57–67 (2014)
5. Dodis, Y., Katz, J., Xu, S., Yung, M.: Key-Insulated Public Key Cryptosystems. In: Knudsen, L.R. (ed.) EUROCRYPT 2002. LNCS, vol. 2332, pp. 65–75. Springer, Heidelberg (2002)
6. Gagné, M., Narayan, S., Safavi-Naini, R.: Short pairing-efficient threshold-attribute-based signature. In: Abdalla, M., Lange, T. (eds.) Pairing 2012. LNCS, vol. 7708, pp. 295–313. Springer, Heidelberg (2013)
7. Itkis, G., Reyzin, L.: SiBIR: signer-base intrusion-resilient signatures. In: Yung, M. (ed.) CRYPTO 2002. LNCS, vol. 2442, pp. 499–599. Springer, Heidelberg (2002)
8. Li, J., Au, M.H., Susilo, W., Xie, D., Ren, K.: Attribute-based signature and its applications. In: Proceedings of the 5th ACM Symposium on Information, Computer and Communications Security, ASIACCS 2010, pp. 60–69. ACM (2010)
9. Li, J., Kim, K.: Hidden attribute-based signatures without anonymity revocation. Inf. Sci. **180**(9), 1681–1689 (2010)
10. Maji, H.K., Prabhakaran, M., Rosulek, M.: Attribute-based signatures: achieving attribute-privacy and collusion-resistance. IACR Cryptology ePrint Archive 2008, 328 (2008)
11. Maji, H.K., Prabhakaran, M., Rosulek, M.: Attribute-based signatures. In: Kiayias, A. (ed.) CT-RSA 2011. LNCS, vol. 6558, pp. 376–392. Springer, Heidelberg (2011)
12. Shahandashti, S.F., Safavi-Naini, R.: Threshold attribute-based signatures and their application to anonymous credential systems. In: Preneel, B. (ed.) AFRICACRYPT 2009. LNCS, vol. 5580, pp. 198–216. Springer, Heidelberg (2009)
13. Wang, K., Mu, Y., Susilo, W., Guo, F.: Attribute-based signature with message recovery. In: Huang, X., Zhou, J. (eds.) ISPEC 2014. LNCS, vol. 8434, pp. 433–447. Springer, Heidelberg (2014)
14. Weng, J., Liu, S., Chen, K., Li, X.: Identity-based key-insulated signature with secure key-updates. In: Lipmaa, H., Yung, M., Lin, D. (eds.) Inscrypt 2006. LNCS, vol. 4318, pp. 13–26. Springer, Heidelberg (2006)
15. Zhang, F., Susilo, W., Mu, Y.: Identity-based partial message recovery signatures (or how to shorten id-based signatures). In: S. Patrick, A., Yung, M. (eds.) FC 2005. LNCS, vol. 3570, pp. 45–56. Springer, Heidelberg (2005)

XOR Based Non-monotone t-$(k, n)^*$-Visual Cryptographic Schemes Using Linear Algebra

Sabyasachi Dutta and Avishek Adhikari$^{(\boxtimes)}$

Department of Pure Mathematics, University of Calcutta,
Kolkata 700019, India
{saby.math,avishek.adh}@gmail.com

Abstract. XOR-based visual cryptographic schemes for non-monotonic (k, n)-threshold access structures deviate from the fact that the superset of any collection of $k + 1$ or more participants may not get the secret back while providing their shares together. In this paper, we generalize this access structure to non-monotonic t-$(k, n)^*$-access structure in which t-essential participants along with any other $(k - t)$ participants can reveal the secret, $0 \leq t \leq k$ and $2 \leq k \leq n$. This notion is a generalization of the non-monotonic (k, n)-threshold access structure in the sense that if we take $t = 0$, we get the non-monotonic (k, n)-threshold access structure. Visual cryptographic schemes for t-$(k, n)^*$-threshold access structure based on Boolean "OR" operations are available in the literature. However the contrast of the reconstructed image is very poor, resulting a very bad recovery of the secret image visually. In this paper we study the same scenario for the "XOR" based model which provides much better relative contrast for the reconstructed secret image. We provide an efficient technique, based on simple linear algebra, to construct the basis matrices realizing the XOR-based non-monotone (k, n)-VCS with t many essential parties. The contrast of the scheme is significantly better than the existing OR-based schemes. Finally, for some restricted t-$(k, n)^*$ non-monotonic access structures, we provide a scheme which not only achieves the optimal relative contrast but also achieves the optimal pixel expansion.

Keywords: Non-monotone Threshold Access Structure · Essential participants · Pixel expansion · contrast · Linear algebra

1 Introduction

A Visual Cryptographic Scheme (VCS) for a set of n participants $\mathcal{P} = \{1, 2, \ldots, n\}$ is a variant of secret sharing, that encodes a secret image SI into n shares which are distributed by the dealer among n participants in the form of transparencies on which the shares are photocopied. Such shares have the

Sabyasachi Dutta — Research supported by CSIR PhD Fellowship, Government of India, Grant no.- 09/028(0808)/2010-EMR-I.

Avishek Adhikari — Research supported in part by National Board for Higher Mathematics, Department of Atomic Energy, Government of India (No 2/48(10)/2013/NBHM(R.P.)/R&D II/695).

© Springer International Publishing Switzerland 2015
L.C.K. Hui et al. (Eds.): ICICS 2014, LNCS 8958, pp. 230–242, 2015.
DOI: 10.1007/978-3-319-21966-0_17

property that only "qualified" subsets of participants can visually recover the secret image by carefully stacking the tranparencies. A monotone (k, n)-threshold visual cryptographic scheme consists of two phases:

1. **Sharing Phase:** During this phase, the dealer $\mathcal{D}$ shares the secret among the n participants. In this phase the dealer sends some information, known as *share*, to each participant.
2. **Reconstruction Phase:** In this phase, a set of parties (of size at least k) pool their shares to reconstruct the secret.

In the sharing phase dealer wants to share the secret in such a way that satisfies the following two conditions:

1. **Correctness:** Any set of k or more participants can reconstruct the secret by pooling their shares.
2. **Secrecy:** Any set of $k - 1$ or less participants can not reconstruct the secret. Moreover, for *perfect secrecy*, any set of $k - 1$ or less participants will have no information regarding the secret.

The first threshold VCS was proposed by Naor and Shamir [11]. This concept has been extended in [1,2,4,5] to general access structures. In the literature of (k, n)-threshold VCS most of the constructions are realized by constructing so called basis matrices. In 1996 Droste [8] gave a brilliant algorithm to construct basis matrices of any (k, n)-threshold VCS and used linear program for finding the lower bound of the pixel expansion.

The mathematical operation that lies beneath the physical implementation of the above mentioned schemes is the Boolean operation "OR". However the major problems for any OR-based visual cryptographic scheme are the huge share size (pixel expansion) and very poor contrast of the reconstructed image. Several papers have been published to minimize the pixel expansion and to maximize contrast. One may refer to [6,13] for a quick and detailed survey of these problems.

Arumugam et al. [3] introduced a VCS for a special type of access structure, called a $(k, n)^*$-VCS, to address the scenario where one participant is "essential". Guo et al. [7] generalized this concept of $(k, n)^*$-VCS by considering (k, n)-VCS with t essential participants.

1.1 An Alternative for "OR" Based VCS

As pointed earlier, OR based visual cryptographic schemes suffer from the low quality of the reconstructed image. To improve upon the quality (contrast) of the superimposed image, several attempts were made. Tuyls et al. [14] gave a VCS based on polarization of light where the underlying mathematical operation was the Boolean "XOR" operation. The polarization of light is done by inserting a liquid crystal layer into a liquid crystal display (LCD). The advantange is two-fold. First, the liquid crystal layer can be driven in an LCD. Secondly, since the voltage applied to the liquid crystal layer makes it possible to rotate the polarization of light entering the layer over a certain angle, it facilitates a practical updating mechanism. Thus unlike OR-based schemes where a participant has to carry a number of transcripts to update the shares, in a XOR-based VCS a party has to carry just one dedicated trusted device that has a display. For recovering the secret image the shares i.e., the liquid crystal layers are to be stacked together. Moreover, due to the rapid advancement of technology these devices are getting cheaper. It is a reasonable expectation that polarization based visual cryptographic schemes will be implemented in every light-weight cryptographic situation. In [15] the authors constructed a XOR based (n, n)-VCS and proved that a XOR based $(2, n)$-VCS is equivalent to a binary code. Further research were carried out and several papers have been published. One for further studies, may refer to [9,10,16]. All these papers have the common property that all of them are non-monotonic in nature, i.e., superset of the minimal qualified set may not get the secret back if all of them stack their shares.

1.2   Our Contribution

In this paper, we not only generalize the notion of XOR-based non-monotonic (k, n)-threshold access structure to the XOR-based non-monotonic t-$(k, n)^*$-threshold access structure, but also provide efficient construction of the scheme for the latter one with significantly better relative contrast than the existing OR-based VCS. The rational thinking behind the non-monotonicity is that for most of the practical scenarios, the access structure is generally a public information. That is, the participants have complete knowledge of the qualified sets and forbidden sets. Therefore if a qualified set of participants come together then any minimal qualified subset of it may produce the corresponding shares to reconstruct the secret image. Thus it is sufficient to restrict ourselves to the collection of all minimal qualified sets corresponding to the access structure. Based on this observation, we come up with a new XOR-based VCS for the non-monotone t-$(k, n)^*$-threshold access structure which is a generalization of the non-monotonic (k, n)-threshold access structure in the sense that if we take $t = 0$, we get the non-monotonic (k, n)-threshold access structure. For the sake of better presentation and clarity we will denote the VCS for the above mentioned access structure by t-$(k, n)^*$-NM-XVCS from now onwards. Here, "NM" stands for non-monotone and "X" stands for the operation XOR. We define the entire model for the t-$(k, n)^*$-NM-XVCS in terms of basis matrices. We provide an efficient technique, based on simple linear algebra, to construct the basis matrices realizing the t-$(k, n)^*$-NM-XVCS achieving significantly better relative contrast than the existing OR-based schemes. Finally, for some restricted t-$(k, n)^*$ non-monotonic access structures, we provide a scheme which not only achieves the optimal relative contrast but also the optimal pixel expansion.

2   The Model and Construction for t-$(k, n)^*$-NM-XVCS

We follow standard notations and symbols through out. For the sake of completeness we discuss some of the basic notations and tools needed for this paper. Let

$\mathcal{P} = \{1, 2, 3, \ldots, n\}$ denote a set of participants. Without loss of generality, let the first t participants, namely, $1, 2, \ldots, t$ denote the essential participants whose shares are necessary to reconstruct the secret image. At this point we want to emphasize that we work with all those triplets (t, k, n) which are *meaningful*. For example, if $k = n$ then it does not make much sense to talk about a XOR based t-$(n, n)^*$-VCS. Henceforth, we only consider meaningful triplets (t, k, n). The case $t = 0$ with $n \geq k > 1$ is the XOR based (k, n)-threshold VCS where no participant is essential and any k of them can recover the secret. Let $2^{\mathcal{P}}$ denote the set of all subsets of $\mathcal{P}$. Let $\mathcal{Q} \subset 2^{\mathcal{P}}$ and $\mathcal{F} \subset 2^{\mathcal{P}}$, where $\mathcal{Q} \cap \mathcal{F} = \emptyset$, respectively denote the set of all qualified sets and the set of all forbidden sets. The pair $(\mathcal{Q}, \mathcal{F})$ constitutes an access structure on $\mathcal{P}$. In this paper, we consider $\mathcal{Q} = \mathcal{Q}_{min} = \{X \subset \mathcal{P} : 1, 2, \ldots, t \in X \text{ and } |X| = k\}$, the collection of all minimal qualified sets of participants. The collection of forbidden sets is denoted by $\mathcal{F}$, where $Y \in \mathcal{F}$ if and only if there exists $i \in \{1, 2, \ldots, t\}$ such that $i \notin Y$ or $|Y| \leq k - 1$. Note that in this paper, we do not care about any subset $Y \in 2^{\mathcal{P}}$ such that $X \subset Y$, for some $X \in \mathcal{Q}_{min}$. This makes the access structure non-monotone.

Example 1. If $\mathcal{P} = \{1, 2, 3, 4, 5, 6\}$, $t = 2$ and $k = 4$ then $\mathcal{Q}_{min}$ consists of the following minimal qualified subsets of participants $B_1 = \{1, 2, 3, 4\}$, $B_2 = \{1, 2, 3, 5\}$, $B_3 = \{1, 2, 3, 6\}$, $B_4 = \{1, 2, 4, 5\}$, $B_5 = \{1, 2, 4, 6\}$, $B_6 = \{1, 2, 5, 6\}$. Note that $\{1, 2, 3\}$ and $\{2, 3, 4, 5, 6\}$ are some of the members of $\mathcal{F}$.

Notations: Let S be an $n \times m$ Boolean matrix and let $X \subset \mathcal{P}$. By $S[X]$ we denote the matrix obtained by restricting the rows of S to the indices belonging to X. Further, for any $X \subset \mathcal{P}$ the vector obtained by applying the boolean XOR operation "$+$", to the rows of $S[X]$ is denoted by S_X. The Hamming weight of the row vector which represents the number of ones in the vector S_X is denoted by $w(S_X)$.

We are now in a position to give definition of a t-$(k, n)^*$-NM-XVCS and then the definition of the basis matrices realizing it.

Definition 1. *Let $\mathcal{P} = \{1, 2, 3, \ldots, n\}$ be a set of participants among which the first t participants are essential. A t-$(k, n)^*$-NM-XVCS on $\mathcal{P}$ is a visual cryptographic scheme such that the following two conditions hold:*

1. *Any minimal qualified set of participants can recover the secret.*
2. *Any forbidden set of participants does not have any information about the secret image.*

Definition 2. *(via Basis Matrices) A t-$(k, n)^*$-NM-XVCS is realized using two $n \times m$ binary matrices S^0 and S^1 called basis matrices, if there exist two sets of non-negative real numbers $\{\alpha_X\}_{X \in \mathcal{Q}_{min}}$ and $\{t_X\}_{X \in \mathcal{Q}_{min}}$ such that the following two conditions hold:*

1. *(contrast condition) If $X \in \mathcal{Q}_{min}$, then S_X^0, the "XOR" of the rows indexed by X of S^0, satisfies $w(S_X^0) \leq t_X - \alpha_X \cdot m$; whereas, for S^1 it results in $w(S_X^1) \geq t_X$.*

2. (*security condition*) *If* $Y = \{i_1, i_2, \ldots, i_s\} \in \mathcal{F}$ *then the two* $s \times m$ *matrices* $S^0[Y]$ *and* $S^1[Y]$ *obtained by restricting* S^0 *and* S^1 *respectively to rows* $i_1, i_2, \ldots, i_s$ *are identical up to a column permutation.*

The number m is called the pixel expansion of the scheme. Also α_X and $\alpha_X \cdot m$ respectively denote the relative contrast and contrast of the recovered image reconstructed by the minimal qualified set X.

We now describe an efficient method to construct the basis matrices realizing a t-$(k, n)^*$-NM-XVCS. We maintain the same notations described above.

2.1　The Construction

We associate a Boolean variable x_i to each participant i for all $i = 1, 2, \ldots, n$. If $X \in \mathcal{Q}_{min}$ then X must contain $1, 2, \ldots, t$ and $|X| = k$. Thus $|\mathcal{Q}_{min}| = \binom{n-t}{k-t}$. We arrange the elements of $\mathcal{Q}_{min}$ in lexicographic order, say $B_1, B_2, \ldots, B_r$, where $r = \binom{n-t}{k-t}$. We now pair the consecutive subsets, except for the last subset B_r if r is odd, to form $\lfloor \frac{r}{2} \rfloor$ groups. For odd r, the last group consists of only one set, B_r itself. Hence for any r, we have $\lceil \frac{r}{2} \rceil$ many groups.

The groups for 2-$(4, 6)^*$-NM-XVCS as in Example 1 are as follows:

Group 1: (B_1, B_2);　Group 2: (B_3, B_4);　Group 3: (B_5, B_6).

In general, the i-th group can be described as follows:

$$i\text{th Group} = \begin{cases} (B_{2i-1}, B_{2i}), \text{ for } 1 \leq i \leq \lceil \frac{r-2}{2} \rceil, \text{ and any } n > 2; \\ (B_{r-1}, B_r), \text{ for even } r > 2 \text{ and } i = \frac{r}{2}; \\ (B_r), \text{ for odd } r > 2 \text{ and } i = \lceil \frac{r}{2} \rceil. \end{cases}$$

Let $f_{B_j} = 0$ and $f_{B_j} = 1$ respectively denote the linear equations $\sum_{k \in B_j} x_k = 0$ and $\sum_{k \in B_j} x_k = 1$. For $i = 1, 2, \ldots, r$, let $C_i = \{i_1, i_2, \ldots, i_{t_i}\}$, where

$$C_i = \begin{cases} \mathcal{P} \setminus (B_{2i-1} \cup B_{2i}), \text{ for } 1 \leq i \leq \lceil \frac{r-2}{2} \rceil, \text{ and any } n > 2; \\ \mathcal{P} \setminus (B_{r-1} \cup B_r), \text{ for even } r > 2 \text{ and } i = \frac{r}{2}; \\ \mathcal{P} \setminus B_r, \text{ for odd } r > 2 \text{ and } i = \lceil \frac{r}{2} \rceil. \end{cases}$$

Note that C_i may be empty for some i. Further, let $\mathcal{F}_{C_i} = \mathbf{0}$ denote the following system of linear equations:

$$x_{i_1} = 0, \ x_{i_2} = 0, \ldots, \ x_{i_{t_i}} = 0.$$

We consider the following systems of linear equations over the field $\mathbb{Z}_2$: For $1 \leq i \leq \lceil \frac{r-2}{2} \rceil$ and for any $r \geq 3$,

$$\left. \begin{array}{l} f_{B_{2i-1}} = 0 \\ f_{B_{2i}} = 0 \\ \mathcal{F}_{C_i} = \mathbf{0} \end{array} \right\} \cdots (i) \qquad \text{and} \qquad \left. \begin{array}{l} f_{B_{2i-1}} = 1 \\ f_{B_{2i}} = 1 \\ \mathcal{F}_{C_i} = \mathbf{0} \end{array} \right\} \cdots (i')$$

For $i = \frac{r}{2}$ and for even $r > 3$,

$$\left.\begin{array}{l} f_{B_{r-1}} = 0 \\ f_{B_r} = 0 \\ \mathcal{F}_{C_i} = 0 \end{array}\right\} \cdots \left(\frac{r}{2}\right) \qquad \text{and} \qquad \left.\begin{array}{l} f_{B_{r-1}} = 1 \\ f_{B_r} = 1 \\ \mathcal{F}_{C_i} = 0 \end{array}\right\} \cdots \left(\frac{r'}{2}\right)$$

For $i = \lceil \frac{r}{2} \rceil$ and for odd $r \geq 3$,

$$\left.\begin{array}{l} f_{B_r} = 0 \\ \mathcal{F}_{C_i} = 0 \end{array}\right\} \cdots \left(\lceil\frac{r}{2}\rceil\right) \qquad \text{and} \qquad \left.\begin{array}{l} f_{B_r} = 1 \\ \mathcal{F}_{C_i} = 0 \end{array}\right\} \cdots \left(\lceil\frac{r'}{2}\rceil\right)$$

Let for any $r \geq 3$ and $1 \leq i \leq \lceil \frac{r-2}{2} \rceil$, S_i^0 denote the Boolean matrix whose columns are all possible solutions of the system (i). Also, let S_i^1 denote the Boolean matrix whose columns are all possible solutions of the system (i'). Similarly, for any even (odd) $r \geq 3$, $S_{\frac{r}{2}}^0$ ($S_{\lceil\frac{r}{2}\rceil}^0$) and $S_{\lceil\frac{r}{2}\rceil}^1$ ($S_{\lceil\frac{r}{2}\rceil}^1$) denote the Boolean matrices corresponding to the systems $(\frac{r}{2})$ $((\lceil\frac{r}{2}\rceil))$ and $(\frac{r'}{2})$ $(\lceil\frac{r'}{2}\rceil)$ respectively.

Let (S^0, S^1) denote the pair of Boolean matrices obtained by the concatenations:
$$S^0 = S_1^0 || S_2^0 || \cdots || S_{\lceil\frac{r}{2}\rceil}^0 \text{ and } S^1 = S_1^1 || S_2^1 || \cdots || S_{\lceil\frac{r}{2}\rceil}^1.$$

Fact 1: It is a very well known fact from linear algebra that if we consider two systems of linear equations $Ax = 0$ and $Ax = b$ where $b \neq 0$, then all possible solutions of the second system can be obtained by adding (i.e., addition of solution vectors) one particular solution of the second system to each solution of the first system. For more details one may refer to [12].

Observation 1: The way we have constructed S^0 and S^1 it is now easy to see that each block S_i^1 can be obtained from S_i^0 by adding a particular solution of the system (i') to each column of S_i^0.

Theorem 1. *The pair of matrices (S^0, S^1) obtained by the above algorithm, constitutes basis matrices of the t-$(k, n)^*$-NM-XVCS.*

Proof: Let m denote the number of columns of the matrices S^0 or S^1 (i.e., m denotes the pixel expansion). In light of Definition 2 we need to prove the following:

1. If $X \in \mathcal{Q}_{min}$ then $w(S_X^1) - w(S_X^0) \geq \alpha_X \cdot m$.
2. If $Y \subset \mathcal{P}$ is a forbidden set of participants, i.e., if $Y \in \mathcal{Q}$, then $S^0[Y]$ and $S^1[Y]$ are identical upto column permutation. Let us denote $\lceil \frac{r}{2} \rceil$ by p.

First we prove the second condition viz., the security condition. Let $Y = \{i_1, i_2, \ldots, i_s\}$ be a forbidden set. We want to show that $S^0[Y]$ and $S^1[Y]$ are identical upto a column permutation. Thus it is sufficient to prove that $S_i^0[Y]$ and $S_i^1[Y]$ are identical upto a column permutation, for all $i \in \{1, 2, \ldots, p\}$.

We will prove only for $S_1^0[Y]$ and $S_1^1[Y]$. Rest of them follow in the same manner. Recall that each column of S_1^0 and S_1^1 was a solution of the systems

(1) and (1') respectively such that the variables that are not present in any of the equations are all set zero. Therefore, if we can prove that there exists a particular solution of the system (1'), say $c = (c_1, c_2, \ldots, c_n)$ such that $c_j = 0$ for $j = i_1, i_2, \ldots, i_s$ then by *Observation 1*, the restricted matrices $S^0[Y]$ and $S^1[Y]$ are identical upto a column permutation. Now, since Y is a forbidden set of participants therefore $B_i \not\subseteq Y$ for $i = 1, 2$ because otherwise, Y would contain a minimal qualified set and would itself become a qualified set. Suppose μ and σ be two such indices (that is, participants) such that $\mu \in B_1$ and $\sigma \in B_2$ but $\mu, \sigma \notin Y$. If $\mu = \sigma$ then $c_\mu = 1$ and $c_i = 0$ for all $i \neq \mu$, admits a particular solution to (1'). On the other hand if $\mu \neq \sigma$ then $c_\mu = c_\sigma = 1$ and $c_i = 0$ for all $i \neq \mu, \sigma$ gives rise to a particular solution to (1'). In both cases $c_j = 0$ for $j = i_1, i_2, \ldots, i_s$ and hence the proof follows.

In the same manner we can prove that $S_i^0[Y]$ and $S_i^1[Y]$ are identical upto a column permutation for all $i = 1, 2, \ldots, p$. Hence the matrices $S^0[Y]$ and $S^1[Y]$ are identical upto a column permutation.

To prove the first condition that is, the contrast condition let $X \in \mathcal{Q}_{min}$. Then $X = B_j$ for some $1 \leq j \leq r$, where the symbols have their usual meaning. For $S^0[X]$ let us break it up in $S_1^0[X] \| S_2^0[X] \| \cdots \| S_p^0[X]$ and for $S^1[X]$, in $S_1^1[X] \| S_2^1[X] \| \cdots \| S_p^1[X]$.

Without loss of generality, let $X = B_1 = \{1, 2, 3, \ldots, t, t+1, \ldots, k\}$. Let us now consider $S^0[X]$ and $S^1[X]$ that is, we restrict ourselves on the first k rows of the matrices. It is not hard to see that each restricted column c_X say, $(c_1, c_2, \ldots, c_k)^t$ of $S^0[X]$ is a solution of the system (1) and hence $c_1 + c_2 + \cdots + c_t + c_{t+1} + \cdots + c_k = 0$ where "$+$" denotes addition modulo 2 which is essentially XOR. Thus it follows that $w(S_{1[X]}^0) = 0$ and similarly we can prove that $w(S_{1[X]}^1) = 2^{k-1}$. Now since $X \neq B_j$, $j \neq 1$, therefore we argue in a similar manner as for the *security condition* to get that $S_{j,j \neq 1}^0[X]$ and $S_{j,j \neq 1}^1[X]$ are identical upto column permutation and hence $w(S_{j[X]}^0) - w(S_{j[X]}^1) = 0$ for all $j \neq 1$. Taking $\alpha_X = \frac{2^{k-1}}{m}$ it is not hard to see that $w(S_X^1) - w(S_X^0) \geq \alpha_X \cdot m = 2^{k-1}$. The above technique works for any $X \in \mathcal{Q}_{min}$. This completes the proof of the theorem. $\square$

Remark 1. Note that, the difference value for the above case is 2^{k-1} but it will vary for different X depending upon the number of independent variables present in the corresponding system of equations. It is easy to see that the number of independent variables in each of the system is at least $k - 1$. This is illustrated in Remark 2.

Corollary 1. *Let (t, k, n) be a meaningful triplet. Then there exists a t-$(k, n)^*$-NM-XVCS with contrast at least 2^{k-1}.*

Example 1 (continued..). The basis matrices for the 2-$(4, 6)^*$-XVCS following the above construction rule are given by

$$S^0 = \begin{bmatrix} \leftarrow \text{Col 1 to 8} \rightarrow & \leftarrow \text{Col 9 to 24} \rightarrow & \leftarrow \text{Col 24 to 32} \rightarrow \\ 00001111 & 0000000011111111 & 00001111 \\ 00110011 & 0000111100001111 & 00110011 \\ 01010101 & 0011001100110011 & 00000000 \\ 01101001 & 0101010101010101 & 01101001 \\ 01101001 & 0101101010100101 & 01101001 \\ 00000000 & 0011110011000011 & 01010101 \end{bmatrix} \text{ and}$$

$$S^1 = \begin{bmatrix} \leftarrow \text{Col 1 to 8} \rightarrow & \leftarrow \text{Col 9 to 24} \rightarrow & \leftarrow \text{Col 24 to 32} \rightarrow \\ 11110000 & 1111111100000000 & 11110000 \\ 00110011 & 0000111100001111 & 00110011 \\ 01010101 & 0011001100110011 & 00000000 \\ 01101001 & 0101010101010101 & 01101001 \\ 01101001 & 0101101010100101 & 01101001 \\ 00000000 & 0011110011000011 & 01010101 \end{bmatrix}.$$

Remark 2. The contrast for $X = B_1$ is 2^3, while the contrast for $X = B_3$ is 2^4.

3 On the Contrast of t-(k, n)*-NM-XVCS: Achieving Optimal Relative Contrast

In the last section we have seen that the construction of basis matrices of a t-(k, n)*-NM-XVCS via linear algebraic method admits better contrast, more precisely at least 2^{k-1} times more than the contrast of OR-based t-(k, n)*-VCS as in [3,7]. Like OR-based VCS, the basic aim for XOR-based VCS is also to reduce the pixel expansion and to increase the relative contrast. However, one thing that we must note that the maximum achievable relative contrast for OR-based VCS is $\frac{1}{2}$, while the same for XOR-based VCS is 1 which is the maximum for any VCS. As a result, for XOR-based VCS, the qualified set of participants may get the secret back with maximum possible contrast. Next we put forward two scenarios where such optimal relative contrast is achieved for XOR-based VCS.

3.1 $(k - 1)$-(k, n)*-NM-XVCS

Let us consider a $(k - 1)$-(k, n)*-NM-XVCS having $k - 1$ essential participants. Here the minimal qualified sets are $\{1, \ldots, k-1, k\}$, $\{1, \ldots, k-1, k+1\}$, $\{1, \ldots, k-1, k+2\}, \ldots, \{1, \ldots, k-1, n-1\}$, $\{1, \ldots, k-1, n\}$. In this case we need not restrict ourselves in taking two equations at a time to form groups of linear equations. We may take all the equations at a time forming only one group and the values of the variables x_1, x_2, ... ,x_{k-1} determine the values of the rest of the variables. With an essentially same argument as in Theorem 1 we can prove that the solutions of system of equations admit the basis matrices of the $(k - 1)$-(k, n)*-NM-XVCS. In this case the pixel expansion is 2^{k-1} and the contrast is also 2^{k-1}. Hence we have the following theorem.

Theorem 2. *For a meaningful triplet* $(k-1, k, n)$, *there exists a* $(k-1)$-$(k, n)^*$-*NM-XVCS having pixel expansion* 2^{k-1} *and optimal relative contrast* 1.

Example 2. Let us consider 3-$(4, 6)^*$-NM-XVCS. Here, $Q_{min} = \{\{1, 2, 3, 4\}, \{1, 2, 3, 5\}, \{1, 2, 3, 6\}\}$. To construct the basis matrices of 3-$(4, 6)^*$-XVCS, we consider only the following system of linear equations over the binary field $\mathbb{Z}_2$:

$$\begin{cases} x_1 + x_2 + x_3 + x_4 = 0 \\ x_1 + x_2 + x_3 + x_5 = 0 \\ x_1 + x_2 + x_3 + x_6 = 0 \end{cases} \tag{1}$$

$$\begin{cases} x_1 + x_2 + x_3 + x_4 = 1 \\ x_1 + x_2 + x_3 + x_5 = 1 \\ x_1 + x_2 + x_3 + x_6 = 1 \end{cases} \tag{2}$$

Solutions of the above systems admit the following basis matrices

$$S^0 = \begin{bmatrix} 00001111 \\ 00110011 \\ 01010101 \\ 01101001 \\ 01101001 \\ 01101001 \end{bmatrix} \text{ and } S^1 = \begin{bmatrix} 11110000 \\ 00110011 \\ 01010101 \\ 01101001 \\ 01101001 \\ 01101001 \end{bmatrix}.$$

The pixel expansion is 8 and the relative contrast is 1.

3.2 (n, n)-XVCS

As we have mentioned before that the case when $t = 0$ gives rise to the simple threshold XOR-based VCS. Let us consider the (n, n)-XVCS. Here the only minimal qualified set is $\{1, \ldots, n-1, n\}$. In this case also we may take all the equations at a time forming only one group and the values of the variables x_1, $x_2, \ldots, x_{n-1}$ determine the values of the remaining variable. We can prove that the solutions of system of equations admit the basis matrices of the (n, n)-XVCS. In this case the pixel expansion is 2^{n-1} and the contrast is also 2^{n-1}. Hence we have the following theorem.

Theorem 3. *There exists a* (n, n)-*XVCS having pixel expansion* 2^{n-1} *and relative contrast* 1.

4   Reducing Pixel Expansion

We have already seen that given any meaningful triplet (t, k, n) there exists a t-$(k, n)^*$-NM-XVCS with contrast at least 2^{k-1}. Section 3.1 describes the method of construction for the basis matrices by taking two equations at a time. Observe that there are at least $k - 1$ independent variables in each system of equations and thus the pixel expansion becomes at least $2^{k-1} \cdot \lceil \frac{r}{2} \rceil$ where $r = \binom{n-t}{k-t}$ for a t-$(k,n)^*$-NM-XVCS.

We now describe a method that reduces the pixel expansion. The idea is to take more than two equations at a time whenever it is possible, such that each system of equations has exactly $k-1$ many independent variables. The resulting matrices whose columns are the solutions of the corresponding systems of equations satisfy the conditions for basis matrices realizing the underlying t-$(k,n)^*$-NM-XVCS. Let us consider the following example to illustrate the method.

Example 3. Let us reconsider the 2-$(4,6)^*$-NM-XVCS from Example 1. Then the collection of minimal qualified sets is given by $\mathcal{Q}_{min} = \{B_1, B_2, \ldots, B_6\}$, where B_is are arranged in the lexicographic order with $B_1 = \{1,2,3,4\}$ and $B_6 = \{1,2,5,6\}$. Now we form the groups as follows:
$G_1 = \{B_1, B_2, B_3\}$, $G_2 = \{B_4, B_5\}$, $G_3 = \{B_6\}$. Solving the corresponding systems of equations we get the following as the basis matrices:

$$S^0 = \begin{bmatrix} \leftarrow \text{Col 1 to 8} \rightarrow & \leftarrow \text{Col 9 to 16} \rightarrow & \leftarrow \text{Col 16 to 24} \rightarrow \\ 00001111 & 00001111 & 00001111 \\ 00110011 & 00110011 & 00110011 \\ 01010101 & 00000000 & 00000000 \\ 01101001 & 01010101 & 00000000 \\ 01101001 & 01101001 & 01010101 \\ 01101001 & 01101001 & 01101001 \end{bmatrix} \text{ and}$$

$$S^1 = \begin{bmatrix} \leftarrow \text{Col 1 to 8} \rightarrow & \leftarrow \text{Col 9 to 16} \rightarrow & \leftarrow \text{Col 16 to 24} \rightarrow \\ 11110000 & 11110000 & 11110000 \\ 00110011 & 00110011 & 00110011 \\ 01010101 & 00000000 & 00000000 \\ 01101001 & 01010101 & 00000000 \\ 01101001 & 01101001 & 01010101 \\ 01101001 & 01101001 & 01101001 \end{bmatrix}.$$

Now it is easy to see that the pixel expansion for this scheme is $3 \cdot 2^{4-1}$. If we follow the method described in Sect. 3.1 the pixel expansion is 32 which is strictly bigger. Thus the pixel expansion is significantly reduced.

We further see that the following columns are common to both S^0 and S^1 and they may be deleted to reduce pixel expansion further.

S^0	3	5	10	11	13	16	18	24
S^1	16	10	5	24	18	3	13	11

The resulting matrices, after deleting the common columns, still satisfy the conditions for basis matrices with pixel expansion 16, a significant reduction in pixel expansion.

5 Achieving Optimality for both Pixel Expansion and Relative Contrast

We are now going to describe another XOR-based non monotone VCS model in which we shall put forward some restricted access structure for which our proposed

XOR-based VCS not only achieves the optimal relative contrast, namely 1, but also achieves the optimal pixel expansion, namely 1. As a result, the qualified set of participants will get the exact secret back while putting their shares together which is impossible for any classical OR-based VCS. The method that we have described so far constructs the basis matrices realizing all possible t-$(k,n)^*$-NM-XVCS. For some restricted access structures the pixel expansion can be minimized to its optimum value. In this regard we need to introduce the following definition.

Definition 3. *(via Collection of Matrices) Let* $\mathcal{P} = \{1, 2, 3, \ldots, n\}$ *be a set of participants. Let* $(\mathcal{Q}_{min}, \mathcal{F})$ *be the access structure corresponding to* t-$(k,n)^*$-*NM-XVCS defined on* $\mathcal{P}$. *Let* m *and* $\{h_X\}_{X \in \mathcal{Q}_{min}}$ *be non-negative integers satisfying* $1 \le h_X \le m$. *Two collections of* $n \times m$ *binary matrices* $\mathcal{C}_0$ *and* $\mathcal{C}_1$ *realizes* t-$(k,n)^*$-*NM-XVCS , if there exists* $\{\alpha_X > 0 : X \in \mathcal{Q}_{min}\}$ *such that*

1. *For any* $S \in \mathcal{C}_0$, *the "XOR" operation of the rows of* $S[X]$ *for any minimal qualified set* X *results in a vector* v_0 *satisfying* $w(v_0) \le h_X - \alpha_X \cdot m$.
2. *For any* $T \in \mathcal{C}_1$, *the "XOR" operation of the rows of* $T[X]$ *for any minimal qualified set* X *results in a vector* v_1 *satisfying* $w(v_1) \ge h_X$.
3. *Any forbidden set* $Y \in \mathcal{F}$ *has no information on the shared image. Formally, the two collections of* $|Y| \times m$ *matrices* D_t , *with* $t \in \{0, 1\}$, *obtained by restricting each* $n \times m$ *matrix in* C_t *to rows indexed by* Y *are indistinguishable in the sense that they contain the same matrices with the same frequencies.*

We now describe an algorithm for one black/white pixel that works for both the cases $(k-1)$-$(k,n)^*$-NM-XVCS and (n,n)-XVCS. Let (S^0, S^1) and (T^0, T^1) respectively denote the basis matrices obtained by the method described in Sects. 3.1 and 3.2.

Algorithm of share generation for optimal $(k-1)$-$(k,n)^*$-NM-XVCS:

1. The Dealer constructs the basis matrices (S^0, S^1) as described in Sect. 3.1.
2. If the secret pixel is white then the dealer chooses randomly a column say $\boldsymbol{w}_{n \times 1}$ from S^0 and gives to the i-th participant, the i-th entry of the column $\boldsymbol{w}_{n \times 1}$.
3. If the secret pixel is black then the dealer chooses randomly a column say $\boldsymbol{b}_{n \times 1}$ from S^1 and gives to the i-th participant, the i-th entry of the column $\boldsymbol{b}_{n \times 1}$.

Thus the pixel expansion becomes 1 and it can be proved that the pair $(\boldsymbol{w}_{n \times 1}, \boldsymbol{b}_{n \times 1})$ admits $(k-1)$-$(k,n)^*$-NM-XVCS in the sense of Definition 3.

The algorithm for (n,n)-XVCS is the same as described in the above algorithm. The dealer chooses randomly one column each from T^0 and T^1 and distributes the shares to the participants.
We now have the following theorem.

Theorem 4. *There exists* $(k-1)$-$(k,n)^*$-*NM-XVCS that achieves optimality both in terms of pixel expansion and relative contrast for any* $2 \leq k \leq n$. *Also, there exists* (n,n)-*XVCS achieving optimality both in terms of pixel expansion and relative contrast for any* $n \geq 2$.

6 Conclusion

In this paper we have defined a (Black and White) XOR-based model of the (k,n)-VCS with multiple essential participants and given a construction method based on linear algebraic tools to efficiently compute the basis matrices realizing the XOR-based scheme. The contrast of the XOR-based model is $2^{|Q|-1}$ times larger than that of the existing OR-based schemes for $Q \in \mathcal{Q}_{min}$. We showed that for certain restricted access structures the optimality in terms of both pixel expansion and contrast have been achieved. The method described in Sect. 4 to reduce the pixel expansion can be developed further by deleting the columns which are present in both S^0 and S^1, as shown in Example 3. It is an interesting problem to find the exact value of pixel expansion that can be obtained by this method.

Acknowledgement. The authors would like to thank Angsuman Das, Partha Sarathi Roy and Usnish Sarkar of University of Calcutta, Kolkata for fruitful discussions in the initial phase of the work and the anonymous reviewers of ICICS 2014 for their comments and suggestions.

References

1. Adhikari, A.: Linear algebraic techniques to construct monochrome visual cryptographic schemes for general access structure and its applications to color images. Des. Codes Crypt. **73**(3), 865–895 (2014)
2. Adhikari, A., Dutta, T.K., Roy, B.: A new black and white visual cryptographic scheme for general access structures. In: Canteaut, A., Viswanathan, K. (eds.) INDOCRYPT 2004. LNCS, vol. 3348, pp. 399–413. Springer, Heidelberg (2004)
3. Arumugam, S., Lakshmanan, R., Nagar, A.K.: On (k, n)*-visual cryptography scheme. Des. Codes Crypt. **71**(1), 153–162 (2014)
4. Ateniese, G., Blundo, C., Santis, A.D., Stinson, D.R.: Visual cryptography for general access structures. Inf. Comput. **129**, 86–106 (1996)
5. Ateniese, G., Blundo, C., De Santis, A., Stinson, D.R.: Constructions and bounds for visual cryptography. In: Meyer, F., Monien, B. (eds.) ICALP 1996. LNCS, vol. 1099, pp. 416–428. Springer, Heidelberg (1996)
6. Blundo, C., D'arco, P., De Santis, A., Stinson, D.R.: Contrast optimal threshold visual cryptography. SIAM J. Discrete Math. **16**(2), 224–261 (2003)
7. Guo, T., Liu, F., Wu, C.K., Ren, Y.W., Wang, W.: On (k,n) visual cryptography scheme with t essential parties. In: Padró, C. (ed.) ICITS 2013. LNCS, vol. 8317, pp. 59–73. Springer, Heidelberg (2014)
8. Droste, S.: New results on visual cryptography. In: Koblitz, N. (ed.) CRYPTO 1996. LNCS, vol. 1109, pp. 401–415. Springer, Heidelberg (1996)

9. Liu, F., Wu, C.K., Lin, X.J.: Some extensions on threshold visual cryptography schemes. Comput. J. **53**, 107–119 (2010)
10. Liu, F., Wu, C., Lin, X.: Step construction of visual cryptography schemes. IEEE Trans. Inf. Forensics Secur. **5**, 27–38 (2010)
11. Naor, M., Shamir, A.: Visual cryptography. In: De Santis, A. (ed.) EUROCRYPT 1994. LNCS, vol. 950, pp. 1–12. Springer, Heidelberg (1995)
12. Rao, A.R., Bhimasankaram, P.: Linear Algebra. Tata Mc.Graw-Hill Publishing Company Limited, New Delhi (1992)
13. Shyu, S.J., Chen, M.C.: Optimum pixel expansions for threshold visual secret sharing schemes. IEEE Trans. Inf. Forensics Secur. **6**(3), 960–969 (2011)
14. Tuyls, P., Hollmann, H.D.L., Lint, H.H.V., Tolhuizen, L.: A polarisation based visual crypto system and its secret sharing schemes (2002). http://eprint.iacr.org
15. Tuyls, P., Hollmann, H., Lint, J., Tolhuizen, L.: Xor-based visual cryptography schemes. Des. Codes Cryptogr. **37**, 169–186 (2005)
16. Yang, C.-N., Wang, D.-S.: Property analysis of XOR-based visual cryptography. IEEE Trans. Circuits Syst. Video Technol. **24**(2), 189–197 (2014)

A Visual One-Time Password Authentication Scheme Using Mobile Devices

Yang-Wai Chow[1]($\boxtimes$), Willy Susilo[1], Man Ho Au[2],
and Ari Moesriami Barmawi[3]

[1] Centre for Computer and Information Security Research, School of Computer
Science and Software Engineering, University of Wollongong, Wollongong, Australia
{caseyc,wsusilo}@uow.edu.au
[2] Department of Computing, Hong Kong Polytechnic University, Hong Kong, China
csallen@comp.polyu.edu.hk
[3] School of Computing, Telkom University, Bandung, Indonesia
mbarmawi@melsa.net.id

Abstract. The use of passwords for user authentication has become
ubiquitous in our everyday lives. However, password theft is becoming a
common occurrence due to a variety of security problems associated with
passwords. As such, many organizations are moving towards adopting
alternative solutions like one-time passwords, which are only valid for
a single session. Nevertheless, various one-time password schemes also
suffer from a number of drawbacks in terms of their method of generation or delivery. This paper presents the design of a challenge-response
visual one-time password authentication scheme that is to be used in
conjunction with the camera on a mobile device. The main purpose of
the proposed scheme is to be able to send a challenge over a public
channel for a user to obtain a session key, while safeguarding the user's
long-term secret key. In this paper, we present the authentication protocol, the various design considerations and the advantages provided by
the scheme.

Keywords: Authentication · One-time password · Mobile device ·
Visual cryptography

1 Introduction

In this day and age, passwords are widely used in everyday life for user authentication on the Internet. Despite having been used for many years, text passwords are
still the most dominant form of web authentication due to its convenience and simplicity [26]. However, the use of passwords has been shown to be plagued by various
security problems [2,3]. In addition, over the years many security attacks, such as
spyware and phishing attacks, have been used to extract sensitive information from
computers, emails, fraudulent websites, etc., resulting in password theft becoming
a common occurrence.

© Springer International Publishing Switzerland 2015
L.C.K. Hui et al. (Eds.): ICICS 2014, LNCS 8958, pp. 243–257, 2015.
DOI: 10.1007/978-3-319-21966-0_18

For this reason, many business companies and organizations are moving toward adopting alternative solutions to the traditional static password approach. Static password approaches are particularly vulnerable as these passwords can easily be stolen by an adversary via a variety of means (e.g. keyloggers, phishing attacks, Trojans, etc.), and used without the password owner's knowledge. This has led to the increasing popularity of One-Time Password (OTP) schemes, where a password is only valid for a single session. For example, Google's authentication framework using two-step verification employs an OTP approach [7]. In Google's two-step verification, the first step involves the user using the traditional username and static password authentication. In the second step, the user will be asked for a six-digit verification code (the OTP) which the user can obtain through a number of different means, for example, via a Short Message Service (SMS) text message, a voice call to a preregistered phone number, a list of pre-generated one-time codes, or an offline application pre-installed on the user's smartphone [7].

There are a number of common ways in which OTPs can be generated and distributed. However, it has been contended that a number of these methods suffer from various drawbacks. For instance, it has been observed that sending an OTP via SMS to a user's mobile phone cannot be considered to be secure [18]. For one thing, the security of SMS OTP relies on the confidentiality of the SMS messages and the security of the cellular networks, which cannot be guaranteed as there are already several potential attacks that can be conducted on these services. Furthermore, specialized mobile phone Trojans have been created that compromise the security of SMS OTP approaches [18]. Moreover, this approach can be problematic to use if the user is in a location with poor mobile phone reception.

An approach that is commonly used by banks and financial institutions, is to supply the user with a security token which generates OTPs. One technique to generate OTPs on a security token is to use a time dependent pseudo-random algorithm. This approach relies on accurate time synchronization between the token and the authentication server, as the OTPs generated using this approach are only valid for a short period of time. As such, this approach suffers from synchronization issues and the potential for clock skew [23]. Another approach of generating OTPs on security tokens is to use a one-way function in the form of a hash chain. However, hash chains are known to have storage and computational complexity issues [24].

In this paper, we propose a challenge-response visual OTP authentication scheme that uses the camera on a mobile device to obtain the OTP. The purpose of the scheme is to be able to send a challenge over a public channel for a user to obtain a session key, while safeguarding the user's long-term secret key. Our approach is based on the concept of visual cryptography and as such does not rely on mobile phone network reception, or having to establish a network link between a computer and a mobile phone. This paper presents the authentication protocol along with various practical issues that had to be considered in the design of the visual OTP scheme.

Our Contribution. This paper presents the design of a visual one-time password authentication scheme. The proposed scheme is a challenge-response approach that relies on a camera on a mobile device to receive the challenge and to present the response on the mobile device's display. The advantage of this approach is that it does not suffer from common OTP issues concerning mobile phone reception, hash chain complexities or time synchronization mechanisms. In addition, unlike SMS-based approaches, our approach is not restricted to mobile phones and can be used on any mobile device with a camera and display, including tablet computers. In the proposed scheme, the challenge can even be sent on printed media instead of via electronic means.

2   Related Work

Over the years, researchers have proposed a variety of different authentication approaches. In this section, we review the research in the area of authentication that is relevant to our work.

2.1   Visual Authentication

The notion of using human-computer cryptographic approaches for identification and authentication have been around for many years. These approaches typically rely on a challenge-response mechanism that requires a human user to interact with a computer in some manner in order to perform authentication. For example, Matsumoto [16,17] investigated human-computer cryptographic schemes that presented challenges to users in the form of visual images. The approach that was examined in his study relied on the human ability for memorizing and processing to solve the simple challenges. Since then, other researchers and practitioners have also proposed and developed various graphical password schemes. Graphical passwords attempt to leverage human memory for visual information with the shared secret being related to images [1]. This capitalizes on the natural human ability to remember images, which is believed to exceed memory for text [3]. However, graphical passwords are not immune to security attacks. For example, graphical password schemes may suffer from shoulder surfing attacks where credentials are captured through direct observation of the login process, or by recording the process using a recording device [1].

Other schemes that have been proposed in this area are based on using the human visual system to solve the challenge. Naor and Pinkas [19] proposed an authentication and identification approach that is based on visual cryptography. Visual cryptography was introduced by Naor and Shamir [20] as a means of using images to conceal information. The main idea behind visual cryptography is to divide a secret image into a set of shares, each to be printed on a separate transparency. Individually, the shares look like random black and white pixels that reveal no information about the secret image. When the appropriate number of shares are stacked together, the human visual system averages the black and

Fig. 1. Example of Naor and Shamir's visual cryptography scheme. (a) Secret image; (b) Share 1; (c) Share 2; (d) Result of superimposing shares 1 and 2.

white pixel contributions of the superimposed shares to recover the hidden information. Thus, the concealed information can be decrypted by the human visual system without any need of a computer to perform decryption computations [4]. Figure 1 depicts an example of Naor and Shamir's visual cryptography scheme. The secret image, shown in Fig. 1(a), is divided into two shares, which are shown in Fig. 1(b) and (c) respectively. The secret can be recovered by superimposing the two shares, as shown in Fig. 1(d).

In the scheme proposed by Naor and Pinkas [19], the user is required to carry a small transparency, small enough to be carried in a wallet, and the authentication and identification process simply involves the user overlaying the transparency on the message sent by an informant in order to view the concealed information. However, in their scheme, unless the user carries a stack of transparencies, which would be impractical, a single transparency will have to be used for multiple authentication sessions. It has been highlighted that since basic visual cryptography schemes are equivalent to one-time pads, an observer can eventually learn the user's secret by repeated observation [3]. In addition, Naor and Shamir's visual cryptography scheme suffers from the pixel expansion problem, as illustrated in Fig. 1, where each pixel in the secret image is split into four sub-pixels in the shares and the recovered image. As such, the shares are four time the size of the secret image.

To overcome a number of drawbacks with this scheme, Tuyls et al. [27] proposed a scheme where every user was to be given a small decryption display. Their approach was similarly based on visual cryptography where the small decryption display was used to replace the need for transparencies. The small decryption display required very limited computing power to perform authentication and security and since the user was required to carry his/her own trusted decryption display, it would be impossible to be contaminated by Trojans or viruses. However, this approach requires the user to use a special authentication device.

A commercially available scheme called PassWindow [22] uses a similar approach where a small transparent display is embedded in an ID card or some form of payment card. The pattern on the transparent display changes periodically based on a pre-generated sequence of patterns. To perform authentication, the user has to overlay the transparent display of the card over a patterned image sent from the server and to visually identify the digits that form as a result of superimposing the card's display onto the image. However, it should be noted that an image on screen can potentially appear at different sizes depending on the user's display settings. This approach requires that the size of the image that is displayed on screen be exactly the same as the size of the card's transparent display.

2.2 Authentication Using a Personal Device

A number of other authentication approaches that have been proposed make use of personal devices that a user usually carries around (e.g. a cellphone). In a study on how to provide a user with authenticated communication when using an untrusted computer, Clarke et al. [5] proposed a method of using a trusted personal device equipped with a camera to monitor the screen of the untrusted computer. All communication is then authenticated by a trusted proxy. This approach is quite costly in terms of computational resources required to monitor the communication.

Mannan and Oorschot [15] proposed a protocol that they called MP-Auth (*Mobile Password Auth*entication), which uses a mobile device to protect user passwords from easily being recorded. In their approach, the mobile device is assumed to be free from malware as the user will enter the password into the mobile device rather than into an untrusted computer. In another approach proposed by Jeun et al. [11], the user uses an application to store his encrypted password in his smart phone and that application program is used to send the password from the smart phone itself, instead of requiring the user to enter his password via a computer's keyboard.

Phoolproof is another scheme that uses mobile phones for authentication. Phoolproof is a mutual authentication protocol used to prevent phishing using a trusted mobile phone [21]. To use the system, the user must establish a shared secret with the server using an out-of-band channel. This long-term secret is stored on the mobile phone. In order to use this protocol, the mobile phone must establish a secure Bluetooth connection with the web-browser where mutual authentication occurs between the mobile phone and the website.

2.3 One-Time Passwords

To overcome some of the problems associated with static passwords, OTP approaches are increasingly being used for authentication. There are various techniques for generating and distributing OTPs. In addition, several approaches were devised to use OTPs in conjunction with mobile devices.

Paterson and Stebila [23] examined an approach of using OTPs in conjunction with one-time Password Authentication Key Exchange (PAKE) protocols in order to ensure more secure use of OTPs. In a scheme called oPass proposed by Sun et al. [26], a trusted cellphone is used to communicate with the web server (via SMS) and the web-browser (via Wi-Fi or Bluetooth). The user does not input his password into the web-browser, but rather is required to enter his long-term password into the oPass program which will generate an OTP that will be sent by way of an encrypted SMS to the server.

Mulliner et al. [18] investigated attacks against SMS based OTPs and state that attacks against cellular networks and mobile phones have shown that SMS messages cannot be deemed to be secure. They proposed a virtual dedicated OTP channel inside the mobile phone operating system to secure OTP SMS messages from being intercepted by Trojans by removing these messages from the general delivery process and redirecting them to a special OTP application.

Instead of using a mobile device, Huang et al. [9] proposed a scheme where the OTP is delivered via an instant messaging service. This approach assumes that the website which adopts the OTP authentication method must join an instant messaging network and use the network to communicate with the users.

3   Model and Definition of the Visual One-Time Password Authentication System

In this section, we will first define the visual one-time password authentication system and its scenario, and then we will propose a visual authentication protocol. We extend this definition from the visual authentication scheme proposed by Naor and Pinkas [19].

Visual OTP Authentication Scenario. Without losing generality, we assume that there are three entities involved, namely H (Henry), S (Sandra) and an adversary E (Evan). H is a human and therefore H has human visual capabilities. The purpose of the visual OTP authentication system is to enable Sandra to attest whether Henry is present in the protocol in the presence of Evan. Note that Evan can observe the channel used between Henry and Sandra. The security parameter k is involved, such that storage capacities and computing power of Sandra and Evan are polynomial in k.

There are two main stages in the visual OTP authentication scenario. The first stage is the initialization stage, where Sandra can communicate with Henry in an offline private initialization channel, which is inaccessible to Evan. In the second stage, Sandra communicates with Henry via a public channel, in which Evan can also access.

In the first stage, Sandra issues a long-term secret key, lk, to Henry, where its size is polynomial in the security parameter k. In the second stage, Sandra tests to ensure that Henry has acquired lk by producing a random number r, which is sent via a public channel. Henry will then construct a shared visual secret, which is a function of lk and r. For simplicity, this visual share is denoted as S_1. Subsequently, Sandra produces a short-term secret key, sk, and constructs its visual version, S_{sk}. Then, Sandra will construct another visual share S_2, where $S_2 = S_{sk} - S_1$ (an example of an algorithm that can be used to generate S_1 and S_2 is provided in Algorithm 1 below). Subsequently, S_2 is presented to Henry via a public channel. Evan has access to the public channel, and therefore, he has access to both r and S_2. Nevertheless, Evan does not have access to S_1. Using his visual observation capability, Henry can acquire the short-term key, sk, from S_1 and S_2.

Visual OTP Authentication Protocol. S would like to communicate to H to test whether H can reproduce a short-term secret key, sk, in the presence of an adversary E.

- S chooses a random r.
- S generates the short-term key sk and its visual representation S_{sk}.
- S produces the first share S_1, which is a function of lk and r.
- S computes the second share S_2, which is computed from $S_{sk} - S_1$.
- S sends (r, S_2) to H via a public channel.
- H needs to reproduce S_1 from lk and r.
- H uses his visual capability to acquire S_{sk} from S_1 and S_2, and hence, obtains sk.

We note that the public channel is accesible to E. In addition, only S can generate a valid S_2. E will not be able to generate a valid S_2 without knowledge of lk.

Definition 1. Security. *A visual OTP authentication protocol is called* secure *if E cannot retrieve sk after observing the public channel used by S and H to communicate.*

4   Proposed Visual OTP Scheme

4.1   Design

The overall design of the proposed visual OTP scheme is described as follows.

Initialization Stage. H registers with S, in which S will issue a long-term secret key, lk, which has a polynomial size in the security parameter k. lk will be transmitted to H via a secure and authenticated channel. In practice, S can make use of either a traditional public key cryptography (assuming H is equipped with a public key) or an identity-based encryption (assuming the identity of H is known - in a smart phone scenario, this could be via the phone's International Mobile Station Equipment Identity (IMEI) or phone number).

Challenge-Response Stage. In this stage, S selects a random number r, which has a polynomial size in the security parameter k. Then, S will conduct the following:

- Produce a Quick Response (QR) code that contains r, QR_r.
- Generate a short-term secret key sk, and its visual representation S_{sk}.
- Generate the first share S_1, which is derived from $lk||r$, where $||$ denotes concatenation.
- Generate the second share $S_2 = S_{sk} - S_1$.
- Present QR_r and S_2 to H via a public channel.

Upon receiving the challenge (QR_r, S_2), H conducts the following:

- Scan the QR code to retrieve r.
- Use the long-term secret key, lk and r to produce S_1.
- Use H's visual capability to retrieve sk from S_1 and S_2.
- Output sk.

Note that the value of sk is obtained visually and is never stored anywhere.

Figure 2 depicts an example of a practical scenario where the visual OTP scheme can be implemented for conducting an online transaction. The figure gives an overview of the communication between the different components involved in the overall process. In the scenario, the user must first register his mobile device with the authentication server via a secure private channel. The server will in turn generate lk and send this to the user's mobile device. Registration only happens once for the server and mobile device to establish a long-term secret key. Subsequently, whenever the user initiates an online transaction from a web-browser, the server will generate and send (QR_r, S_2) (i.e. the challenge) which will be displayed on the web-browser. Upon receiving (QR_r, S_2), the user will use the camera on his mobile device to scan QR_r. With the value of lk and r, the user's mobile device will be able to generate S_1. On the mobile device's display, S_1 will be overlaid on S_2 to produce S'_{sk} (i.e. the visual reconstruction of S_{sk} on the mobile device's display), and the user will be able to visually obtain sk (i.e. the response/OTP). Only the server can generate a valid S_2, and only the user can obtain sk using S_1 which is generated on the mobile device.

4.2   Practical Issues

In the proposed scheme, r has to be sent to H over a public channel. While it is not necessary to encode and transmit r within a QR code, we find that this is the most appropriate and convenient method of delivery. The QR code is a two-dimensional code that was invented by the company Denso Wave [6]. These days, QR codes are ubiquitous on the Internet and the information contained within a QR code can easily be scanned by a mobile device with a camera. In addition, QR codes have a inbuilt error detection and correction mechanism that can be used to correctly decode corrupted QR codes, which may contain certain errors. Furthermore, QR codes contain a number of patterns to determine rotational orientation and alignment. Since (QR_r, S_2) is sent to H as a single image, QR_r can be used to facilitate the alignment of S_1 and S_2.

It is well known that traditional visual cryptography suffers from the alignment problem, in that when stacking shares, it is difficult to align the shares [14, 30]. Practical approaches typically suggest the use of some reference frame to align the transparencies [19]. However, unlike traditional approaches that use physical transparencies or tokens, our approach relies on the use of a mobile device like a smart phone or a tablet. As such, using the camera's video stream to capture (QR_r, S_2), this can be used in conjunction with image processing techniques to overlay S_1 over S_2. This is akin to techniques using in augmented

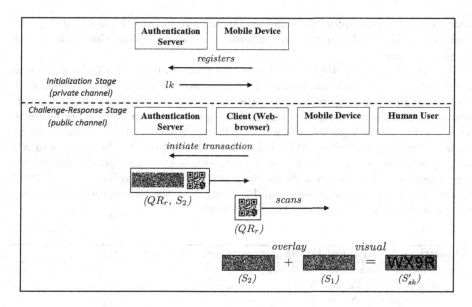

Fig. 2. Overview of the communication between the various components in the visual OTP scheme.

reality to overlay virtual content onto elements of the real world [28]. Adopting this method will allow the mobile device to appropriately scale and rotate S_1 in order for it to align with S_2.

Another problem with traditional visual cryptography when displaying a share on a computer screen and trying to place the corresponding share, which is printed on a transparency, on top of the screen, is that monitors can differ greatly and the computer can be set to different display settings. As such, the image of the share on screen may not be displayed at the same size as the share printed on the transparency. This will prevent the shares from being correctly superimposed, and thus the secret cannot be recovered. In the approach proposed in this paper, we rely on the mobile device to virtually overlay S_1 over S_2. This means that it does not matter what size S_2 is displayed at, as long as the mobile device can accurately capture the image of S_2, because the mobile device can scale S_1 to the appropriate size. To facilitate this, the size of the squares in S_2's image should not be too small.

As previously shown in Fig. 1, traditional visual cryptography suffers from the pixel expansion problem which significantly increases the size of the resulting shares. While there are a number of size invariant visual cryptography schemes like the probabilistic approaches proposed by Ito et al. [10] and Yang [29], these schemes do not produce the ideal visual quality required for the visual OTP. Therefore, for the purpose of generating S_1 and S_2, a random grid visual cryptography approach was deemed to be the most suitable approach. Random grid visual secret sharing was first proposed by Kefri and Keren [12], and over the years a number of random grid approaches have been investigated [8,25]. Using a random grid visual cryptography scheme, it is possible to produce shares with no pixel expansion.

In the proposed visual OTP scheme, the shared image S_1 will be generated from $lk\|r$ and a pseudo-random number generator. Thus, S_1 is a random grid. S_1 can be used in conjunction with the secret image S_{sk} to generate the corresponding challenge image S_2. Algorithm 1 gives an example of a random grid visual secret sharing method that was adapted from Shyu [25], which can be used in the proposed visual OTP scheme. In this approach, black pixels in S_{sk} are reproduced at 100 % in S'_{sk} and white pixels (i.e. transparent pixels) are reproduced at 50 %. Figure 3 shows the results of using Algorithm 1 on a secret image. The secret image, shares 1 and 2, along with the reconstructed image are shown in Fig. 3(a), (b), (c) and (d) respectively.

Algorithm 1. An algorithm for generating S_1 and S_2 from S_{sk}

```
function GENERATESHARES(S_sk, lk, r)
    imgWidth ← S_sk width
    imgHeight ← S_sk height
    for i = 1 to imgWidth do
        for j = 1 to imgHeight do
            /* Generate S_1 as a random grid */
            S_1[i, j] ← randomPixel(lk||r) /* randomPixel() outputs 0 or 1 */
            /* Generate S_2 */
            if S_sk[i, j] = 0 then
                S_2[i, j] ← S_1[i, j]
            else
                S_2[i, j] ← ¬S_1[i, j]
            end if
        end for
    end for
end function
```

Another practical issue to consider when implementing the visual OTP scheme is how clearly the user will be able to perceive the OTP in the visual reconstruction of the secret image. For this we should consider the color of the text and the background. There are two possible variations as depicted in Fig. 4, where Fig. 4(a) shows the reconstructed secret using black text on a white background and Fig. 4(b) shows the reconstructed secret using white text on a black background. It has been argued that using white contents on a black background gives rise to better perceived visual quality in the reconstructed image for images with thin lines [13].

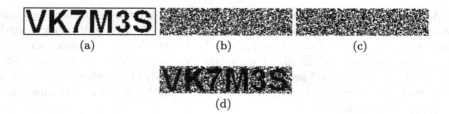
(a)   (b)   (c)

(d)

Fig. 3. Random grid visual cryptography approach. (a) Secret image; (b) Share 1; (c) Share 2; (d) Result of superimposing shares 1 and 2.

Fig. 4. Text and background color. (a) Black text on a white background; (b) White text on a black background.

5   Discussion

5.1   Advantages of the Visual OTP Scheme

The fundamental purpose of the proposed visual OTP scheme is to be able to send a challenge over a public channel for the user to obtain a session key that can be used as an OTP, while safeguarding the user's long-term secret key. In this scheme, the user also does not have to remember any passwords.

As mobile devices are ubiquitous in this day and age, the proposed approach does not require the user to carry around a specialized authentication card or device, or a printed list of OTPs. In addition, unlike authentication schemes like SMS OTP based approaches, authentication in the proposed method does not require any form of communication with a mobile phone network. As such, mobile phone network reception is not an issue. This also means that the visual OTP scheme can be applied to any mobile device which has a camera and is not restricted to only be usable on smart phones. The user simply has to install the visual OTP software and register it with the authentication server.

While the OTP can be used to authenticate the user, another feature provided by the scheme is that the user can also verify that the message containing the challenge was sent by a legitimate party. This is because in the proposed scheme, without knowledge of the long-term secret key an adversary cannot generate a valid challenge. This also prevents an adversary from tampering with the challenge image, as changing QR_r will mean that the mobile device will not be able to generate the correct visual pattern (i.e. S_1) to solve the challenge, and changing S_2 will not produce a valid result when overlaying S_1 over S_2. Furthermore, such an event would raise the suspicion of the user, as it would indicate that the challenge may have been tampered with.

Another advantage of the proposed scheme, is that the challenge does not have to be transmitted via electronic means. For example, if a bank wants to send a letter to an individual who has registered with the bank, the bank can send the person a letter with the challenge printed on paper. The person can verify that the letter was indeed sent from the bank (as only the bank can generate a valid challenge) and also receive the OTP which can be used for authentication purposes with the bank.

In other authentication approaches that involve the user having to overlay a transparency or an authentication token on top of another pattern, the size of the patterns have to perfectly match. Otherwise the user will not be able to recover the secret by superimpose the different sized patterns. This is not an issue in the proposed approach as the mobile device will be responsible for scaling and aligning the patterns. Therefore, the challenge can be displayed in any size as long as it can be captured by the mobile device's camera. The mobile device will then use augmented reality techniques to overlay the virtual pattern onto the image of the challenge pattern.

It should be noted that the OTP is obtained by the human user via the visual channel and the OTP is never stored on any device. This prevents malicious software like keyloggers or even software designed to monitor the user's activities from obtaining the OTP. Furthermore, the one-time password is only valid for a single use. Additionally, the video stream on the mobile device will be used to overlay the visual patterns and present this to the user in real-time. If there is any software designed to monitor the user's activities, this will require a huge amount of information to be streamed to the adversary, which will significantly degrade the system's performance and alert the user of suspicious activity.

In addition, unlike traditional graphical passwords, which may suffer from shoulder surfing attacks, this is not an issue in the proposed visual scheme. Shoulder surfing attacks are where an adversary standing behind the user, and possibly even recording the user's interactions, maybe able to observe and detect some pattern in the image or from the user's interactions, which will compromise the security of the visual password. In the proposed visual OTP scheme, the visual pattern generated on the mobile device to solve a challenge can only be used for that particular challenge. The mobile device will generate different visual patterns for different challenges.

5.2   Limitations

In this section we discuss some of the limitations of the propose visual OTP scheme.

As with all visual challenges or passwords, the proposed scheme relies on the human visual system. This means that it does not cater for the blind or visually impaired, and cannot be used by an individual with a visual disability. Another potential disadvantage is that the challenge image will have to be displayed at a certain size in order for the mobile device's camera to be able to accurately capture the information contained within the challenge image. While this is not seen as a major problem, it may adversely affect the layout or aesthetics of a message, document or webpage.

It should be noted that the proposed scheme does not deal with man-in-the-middle or similar attacks. To handle such attacks, the scheme can be combined with other security protocols that are designed to handle man-in-the-middle attacks. In addition, this approach also does not address the situation where the authentication server is hacked. The server is responsible for its own security and it is assumed that all the necessary security mechanisms are in place.

In the proposed scheme, the mobile device captures the challenge image using its video stream and is responsible for overlaying the virtual image on top of the challenge image. As such, it is assume that the mobile device has the computational capabilities required to process augmented reality techniques in real-time. Additionally, since the mobile device has to be used to visually present the solution to the challenge, a separate means of displaying the challenge has to be employed. In other words, if the user wants to conduct an online transaction via a web-browser, this cannot be done using the mobile device's web-browser as the mobile device itself will have to be used in conjunction with the challenge's display to obtain the OTP. However, this requirement is no different from several other authentication schemes that were previously presented in Sect. 2 of this paper, which also require the use a web-browser and a separate mobile phone to perform authentication.

6 Conclusion

In this paper, we presented the design of a challenge-response visual OTP authentication scheme. Using this scheme, a challenge is sent to a registered individual, this can be via a web-browser or even printed media, and the user can use the camera and display of his mobile device to obtain the solution to the challenge. This approach can be implemented on a variety of mobile devices, such as mobile phones and tablets, with the main requirement being that the device must have a camera. The challenge itself can be transmitted over a public channel without the threat of it being compromised by an adversary, as the adversary can neither correctly generate nor solve the challenge. As such, the scheme does not suffer from the common issues affecting the generation and delivery of OTPs such as mobile phone reception, hash chain complexities or time synchronization mechanisms. In addition, this scheme does not suffer from security issues like shoulder surfing attacks or keyloggers, as the mobile device will generate the specific visual pattern required to solve a particular challenge and will generate a different visual pattern when presented with a different challenge.

References

1. Biddle, R., Chiasson, S., van Oorschot, P.C.: Graphical passwords: Learning from the first twelve years. ACM Comput. Surv. **44**(4), 19 (2012)

2. Bonneau, J., Herley, C., van Oorschot, P.C., Stajano, F.: The quest to replace passwords: A framework for comparative evaluation of web authentication schemes. In: IEEE Symposium on Security and Privacy, pp. 553–567. IEEE Computer Society (2012)

3. Bonneau, J., Herley, C., van Oorschot, P.C., Stajano, F.: The quest to replace passwords: a framework for comparative evaluation of web authentication schemes. Technical report 817, University of Cambridge Computer Laboratory (2012)

4. Chow, Y.-W., Susilo, W., Wong, D.S.: Enhancing the perceived visual quality of a size invariant visual cryptography scheme. In: Chim, T.W., Yuen, T.H. (eds.) ICICS 2012. LNCS, vol. 7618, pp. 10–21. Springer, Heidelberg (2012)

5. Clarke, D.E., Gassend, B., Kotwal, T., Burnside, M., van Dijk, M., Devadas, S., Rivest, R.L.: The untrusted computer problem and camera-based authentication. In: Mattern, F., Naghshineh, M. (eds.) PERVASIVE 2002. LNCS, vol. 2414, pp. 114–124. Springer, Heidelberg (2002)

6. Denso Wave Incorporated. QRcode.com. http://www.qrcode.com/en/

7. Grosse, E., Upadhyay, M.: Authentication at scale. IEEE Secur. Priv. 11(1), 15–22 (2013)

8. Hou, Y.-C., Wei, S.-C., Lin, C.-Y.: Random-grid-based visual cryptography schemes. IEEE Trans. Circuits Syst. Video Techn. 24(5), 733–744 (2014)

9. Huang, C.-Y., Ma, S.-P., Chen, K.-T.: Using one-time passwords to prevent password phishing attacks. J. Netw. Comput. Appl. 34(4), 1292–1301 (2011)

10. Ito, R., Kuwakado, H., Tanaka, H.: Image size invariant visual cryptography. IEICE Trans. Fundam. Electron. Commun. Comput. Sci. 82(10), 2172–2177 (1999)

11. Jeun, I., Kim, M., Won, D.: Enhanced password-based user authentication using smart phone. In: Li, R., Cao, J., Bourgeois, J. (eds.) GPC 2012. LNCS, vol. 7296, pp. 350–360. Springer, Heidelberg (2012)

12. Kafri, O., Keren, E.: Encryption of pictures and shapes by random grids. Opt. Lett. 12(6), 377–379 (1987)

13. Liu, F., Guo, T., Wu, C.K., Qian, L.: Improving the visual quality of size invariant visual cryptography scheme. J. Vis. Commun. Image Represent. 23(2), 331–342 (2012)

14. Liu, F., Wu, C.K., Lin, X.J.: The alignment problem of visual cryptography schemes. Des. Codes Crypt. 50(2), 215–227 (2009)

15. Mannan, M.S., van Oorschot, P.C.: Using a personal device to strengthen password authentication from an untrusted computer. In: Dietrich, S., Dhamija, R. (eds.) FC 2007 and USEC 2007. LNCS, vol. 4886, pp. 88–103. Springer, Heidelberg (2007)

16. Matsumoto, T., Imai, H.: Human identification through insecure channel. In: Davies, D.W. (ed.) EUROCRYPT 1991. LNCS, vol. 547, pp. 409–421. Springer, Heidelberg (1991)

17. Matsumoto, T.: Human-computer cryptography: an attempt. J. Comput. Secur. 6(3), 129–150 (1998)

18. Mulliner, C., Borgaonkar, R., Stewin, P., Seifert, J.-P.: SMS-based one-time passwords: attacks and defense. In: Rieck, K., Stewin, P., Seifert, J.-P. (eds.) DIMVA 2013. LNCS, vol. 7967, pp. 150–159. Springer, Heidelberg (2013)

19. Naor, M., Pinkas, B.: Visual authentication and identification. In: Kaliski Jr., B.S. (ed.) CRYPTO 1997. LNCS, vol. 1294, pp. 322–336. Springer, Heidelberg (1997)

20. Naor, M., Shamir, A.: Visual Cryptography. In: De Santis, A. (ed.) EUROCRYPT 1994. LNCS, vol. 950, pp. 1–12. Springer, Heidelberg (1995)

21. Parno, B., Kuo, C., Perrig, A.: Phoolproof phishing prevention. In: Di Crescenzo, G., Rubin, A. (eds.) FC 2006. LNCS, vol. 4107, pp. 1–19. Springer, Heidelberg (2006)

22. PassWindow. http://www.passwindow.com/
23. Paterson, K.G., Stebila, D.: One-time-password-authenticated key exchange. In: Steinfeld, R., Hawkes, P. (eds.) ACISP 2010. LNCS, vol. 6168, pp. 264–281. Springer, Heidelberg (2010)
24. Sella, Y.: On the computation-storage trade-offs of hash chain traversal. In: Wright, R.N. (ed.) FC 2003. LNCS, vol. 2742, pp. 270–285. Springer, Heidelberg (2003)
25. Shyu, S.J.: Image encryption by random grids. Pattern Recogn. **40**(3), 1014–1031 (2007)
26. Sun, H.-M., Chen, Y.-H., Lin, Y.-H.: opass: a user authentication protocol resistant to password stealing and password reuse attacks. IEEE Trans. Inf. Forensics Secur. **7**(2), 651–663 (2012)
27. Tuyls, P., Kevenaar, T.A.M., Schrijen, G.-J., Staring, T., van Dijk, M.: Visual crypto displaysenabling secure communications. In: Hutter, D., Müller, G., Stephan, W., Ullmann, M. (eds.) Security in Pervasive Computing. LNCS, vol. 2802, pp. 271–284. Springer, Heidelberg (2004)
28. Wagner, D., Schmalstieg, D.: Making augmented reality practical on mobile phones, part 1. IEEE Comput. Graph. Appl. **29**(3), 12–15 (2009)
29. Yang, C.-N.: New visual secret sharing schemes using probabilistic method. Pattern Recogn. Lett. **25**(4), 481–494 (2004)
30. Yang, C.-N., Peng, A.-G., Chen, T.-S.: Mtvss: (m)isalignment (t)olerant (v)isual (s)ecret (s)haring on resolving alignment difficulty. Signal Process. **89**(8), 1602–1624 (2009)

Secure and Efficient Scheme
for Delegation of Signing Rights

Rajeev Anand Sahu and Vishal Saraswat$^{(\boxtimes)}$

C.R.Rao Advanced Institute of Mathematics Statistics and Computer Science,
Hyderabad, India
{rajeevs.crypto,vishal.saraswat}@gmail.com

Abstract. A proxy signature scheme enables a signer to transfer its
signing rights to any other user, called the proxy signer, to produce a
signature on its behalf. Multi-proxy signature is a proxy signature primitive which enables a user to transfer its signing rights to a group of
proxy signers in such a way that every member of the authorized group
must "participate" to sign a document on behalf of the original signer.
We propose an efficient and provably secure identity-based multi-proxy
signature scheme from bilinear map based on the hardness of the computational Diffie-Hellman problem. The proposed scheme is proved secure
against adaptive chosen message and adaptive chosen-ID attack in random oracle model under the computational Diffie-Hellman assumption.
Moreover, we do an efficiency comparison with the existing identity-based
multi-proxy signature schemes and show that our scheme is upto 56 %
more efficient in computation than the existing schemes.

Keywords: Identity-based cryptography · Digital signature · Bilinear
map · Multi-proxy signature · Provably secure · CDHP

1 Introduction

Digital signature is a cryptographic primitive to guarantee data integrity, entity
authentication and signer's non-repudiation. A proxy signature scheme enables
a signer, $\mathcal{O}$, also called the *designator* or *delegator*, to delegate its signing rights
(without transferring the private key) to another user $\mathcal{P}$, called the *proxy signer*,
to produce, on the delegator's behalf, signatures that can be verified by a verifier
V under the delegator $\mathcal{O}$'s public key. Multi-proxy signature is a proxy signature primitive which enables a user to transfer its signing rights to a group of
proxy signers in such a way that every member of the authorized group must
"participate" to sign a document on behalf of the original signer. For example,
the director of a company may authorize a certain group of deputy directors or
heads of various departments to sign certain messages on his behalf during a certain period of his absence. Proxy signatures have widespread applications since
delegation of signing rights by a user (or process) to its proxy (or subprocess(es))
is quite common in many applications including distributed systems [17,22], distributed shared object systems [11], global distribution networks [2], grid computing [7] and e-cash systems [18].

© Springer International Publishing Switzerland 2015
L.C.K. Hui et al. (Eds.): ICICS 2014, LNCS 8958, pp. 258–273, 2015.
DOI: 10.1007/978-3-319-21966-0_19

1.1   Related Work

The notion of proxy signature was introduced by Gasser et al. [8] but it took almost seven years for the first construction of a proxy signature scheme [14] to be proposed. Since then many variants of the proxy signature have been proposed and many extensions of the basic proxy signature primitive have been studied. The formal security model of proxy signatures was first formalized by Boldyreva et al. [3] and later extended by Herranz et al. [9] to analyze fully distributed proxy signatures. Malkin et al. [13] extended the model for hierarchical proxy signatures and Schuldt et al. [21] further strengthened the security model for proxy signatures and also extended it to the identity-based setting.

The primitive of multi-proxy signature was introduced in 2000 [10]. An ID-based multi-proxy signature (IBMPS) scheme was proposed in 2005 [12] but this scheme did not have a security proof. The first provably secure IBMPS scheme was proposed in 2009 [4] and a security model was defined based on the work in [3,23] but the scheme was shown to be insecure [24]. In 2011, an ID-based directed multi-proxy signature scheme [19] was proposed but the scheme is very expensive and cost inefficient. In the same year, an efficient IBMPS scheme based on the k-plus problem was proposed [16] but the proposal lacks a formal proof of security. Recently, an efficient and provably secure IBMPS scheme was proposed [20] which too was shown to be insecure in [1,25]. Reference [1] also observes some security pitfalls in general for any multi-proxy signature scheme.

1.2   Our Contribution

To the best of our knowledge, almost all available IBMPS schemes are either too inefficient to be practical or have not been proved to be secure or whose security is based on non-standard assumptions. In view of the growth and advantages of grid computing, distributed systems, and mobile computing, construction of an efficient and provably secure IBMPS scheme is much desired.

We propose an efficient and provably secure IBMPS scheme from bilinear map based on the hardness of the computational Diffie-Hellman problem (CDHP). The proposed scheme is proved secure against adaptive chosen message and adaptive chosen-ID attack in random oracle model. Moreover, we do an efficiency comparison with existing IBMPS schemes [4,12,19,20] and show that our scheme is upto 56 % more efficient in computation in view of overall operation time than the existing IBMPS schemes.

1.3   Outline of the Paper

The rest of this paper is organized as follows. In Sect. 2, some related mathematical definitions, problems and assumptions are described. In Sect. 3, we present the formal definition of IBMPS scheme and describe the security model for such schemes. Our proposed scheme is presented in Sect. 4. In Sect. 5 we prove the security of our scheme. Section 6 includes efficiency analysis of our scheme.

2   Preliminaries

In this section, we introduce some relevant definitions, mathematical problems and assumptions.

Definition 1 (Bilinear Map). Let G_1 be an additive cyclic group with generator P and G_2 be a multiplicative cyclic group with generator g. Let both the groups are of the same prime order q. Then a map $e : G_1 \times G_1 \to G_2$ satisfying the following properties, is called a *cryptographic bilinear map*:

1. *Bilinearity*: For all $a, b \in \mathbb{Z}_q^*$, $e(aP, bP) = e(P, P)^{ab}$, or equivalently, for all $Q, R, S \in G_1$, $e(Q+R, S) = e(Q, S)e(R, S)$ and $e(Q, R+S) = e(Q, R)e(Q, S)$.
2. *Non-Degeneracy*: There exists $Q, R \in G_1$ such that $e(Q, R) \neq 1$. Note that since G_1 and G_2 are groups of prime order, this condition is equivalent to the condition $e(P, P) \neq 1$, which again is equivalent to the condition that $e(P, P)$ is a generator of G_2.
3. *Computability*: There exists an efficient algorithm to compute $e(Q, R) \in G_2$, for any $Q, R \in G_1$.

Definition 2 (Discrete Log Problem). Let G_1 be a cyclic group with generator P.

1. Given a random element $Q \in G_1$, the *discrete log problem* (DLP) in G_1 is to compute an integer $n \in \mathbb{Z}_q^*$ such that $Q = nP$.
2. The *discrete log assumption* (DLA) on G_1 states that the probability of any polynomial-time algorithm to solve the DL problem in G_1 is negligible.

Definition 3 (Computational Diffie-Hellman Problem). Let G_1 be a cyclic group with generator P.

1. Let $a, b \in \mathbb{Z}_q^*$ be randomly chosen and kept secret. Given $P, aP, bP \in G_1$, the *computational Diffie-Hellman problem* (CDHP) is to compute $abP \in G_1$.
2. The (t, ϵ)-*CDH assumption* holds in G_1 if there is no algorithm which takes at most t running time and can solve CDHP with at least a non-negligible advantage ϵ.

3   IBMPS Scheme and Its Security

In this section, we give the formal definition and the security model for an IBMPS scheme.

3.1   Definition of IBMPS Scheme

In an IBMPS scheme, an original signer delegates its signing rights to a group of proxy agents to make a signature on its behalf, where the public keys of original and proxy signers can be computed from their identities by anyone and their private keys are generated using their corresponding identities by a trusted authority, the private key generator (PKG). Let $\mathcal{O}$ be the original signer with identity $ID_{\mathcal{O}}$ and $\mathcal{P}_i$, $i = 1, \ldots, n$, be the proxy signers with corresponding identities $ID_{\mathcal{P}_i}$. Precisely, an IBMPS scheme consists of the following phases:

1. *Setup*: For a security parameter 1^λ as input, the PKG runs this algorithm and generates the public parameters *params* of the system and a master secret. The PKG publishes *params* and keeps the master secret confidential to itself.
2. *Extraction*: This is a private key generation algorithm. By this algorithm, the PKG outputs private key S_{ID}, for the given identity ID, public parameters *params* and a secret key. Finally, the PKG provides private keys through a secure channel to all the users.
3. *Proxy key generation*: This is a protocol between the original signer and all the proxy signers. All participants input their identities $ID_{\mathcal{O}}, ID_{\mathcal{P}_i}$, private keys $S_{\mathcal{O}}, S_{\mathcal{P}_i}$ (for $1 \leq i \leq n$) and the message warrant (or simply, warrant) w which includes some specific information regarding the message as restrictions on the message; time of delegation, identity of original and proxy signers, period of validity etc. After the successful interaction, each proxy signer $\mathcal{P}_i$ for $1 \leq i \leq n$ outputs its partial proxy signing key say $d_{\mathcal{P}_i}$.
4. *Multi-proxy signature*: This is a randomized algorithm, which takes the proxy signing key of each proxy signer, a message m and a warrant w and outputs an IBMPS say $\sigma_{\mathcal{P}}$.
5. *Multi-proxy verification*: This is a deterministic algorithm. This algorithm takes input the identities $ID_{\mathcal{O}}, ID_{\mathcal{P}_i}$ (for $1 \leq i \leq n$) of all the users, a message m, a warrant w, and the IBMPS $\sigma_{\mathcal{P}}$. The algorithm outputs 1 if the signature $\sigma_{\mathcal{P}}$ is a valid IBMPS on message m by the proxy group on behalf of the original signer, and outputs 0 otherwise.

3.2   Security Model for IBMPS Scheme

In this model an adversary $\mathcal{A}$ tries to forge the multi-proxy signature working against a single user, either against the original signer say $\mathcal{O}$ or against one of the proxy signers $\mathcal{P}_i$. The adversary $\mathcal{A}$ can access polynomial number of hash queries, extraction queries, delegation queries, proxy key generation queries and multi-proxy signature queries. Consider that response to each query is provided to $\mathcal{A}$ using the random oracle. The goal of adversary $\mathcal{A}$ is to produce one of the following forgeries:

1. An IBMPS $\sigma_{\mathcal{P}}$ for a message m on behalf of the original signer, where user 1 is one of the proxy signers, such that either the original signer never designated user 1, or m was not submitted to the multi-proxy signing oracle.
2. An IBMPS $\sigma_{\mathcal{P}}$ for a message m by the proxy signers on behalf of the user 1, where user 1 plays the role of original signer, and the proxy signers were never designated by the user 1.

Definition 4.   An IBMPS scheme is said to be existential unforgeable against adaptive chosen message and adaptive chosen-ID attack if no probabilistic polynomial time adversary $\mathcal{A}$ has a non-negligible advantage against the challenger $\mathcal{C}$ in the following game:

1. *Setup*: The challenger $\mathcal{C}$ runs the setup algorithm and provides the public parameters *params* to the adversary $\mathcal{A}$.

2. *Hash queries*: On hash query of adversary $\mathcal{A}$, challenger $\mathcal{C}$ responds through random oracle and maintains lists say L_{H_1} and L_{H_2} for the hash queries.
3. *Extraction queries*: On key extraction query by $\mathcal{A}$ for an identity ID, $\mathcal{C}$ provides the corresponding private key SK_{ID} to $\mathcal{A}$.
4. *Delegation queries*: $\mathcal{A}$ produces a warrant w' and receives its corresponding delegation value $S'_{\mathcal{O}}$ from $\mathcal{C}$.
5. *Proxy key generation queries*: $\mathcal{A}$ produces a valid warrant w' with respect to an adaptively chosen identity ID and receives its corresponding proxy signing key d_{ID} from $\mathcal{C}$.
6. *Multi-proxy signature queries*: $\mathcal{A}$ produces a message m', a valid warrant w' corresponding to the message m' and identity ID and receives from $\mathcal{C}$ an IBMPS σ'_{ID} on the adaptively chosen message.

After the series of queries, $\mathcal{A}$ outputs a new IBMPS $\sigma^*_{\mathcal{P}}$ on message m^* under a warrant w^* for identities $ID_{\mathcal{O}}$ and $ID_{\mathcal{P}_i}$ for $1 \leq i \leq n$, where – $\mathcal{A}$ has not requested the private key for at least one of the $n+1$ users $ID_{\mathcal{O}}$ and $ID_{\mathcal{P}_i}$, $i = 1, \ldots, n$, in extraction queries; $\mathcal{A}$ did not request a delegation query on warrant w^*; $\mathcal{A}$ did not request a proxy key generation query including warrant w^* and identity $ID_{\mathcal{O}}$; $\mathcal{A}$ never requests a multi-proxy signature query on message m^* with warrant w^* and identities $ID_{\mathcal{P}_i}$. The adversary $\mathcal{A}$ wins the above game if it is able to provide a validity proof of IBMPS $\sigma^*_{\mathcal{P}}$ on message m^* under the warrant w^*.

Definition 5. An adversary $\mathcal{A}$ $(t, q_{H_1}, q_{H_2}, q_E, q_d, q_{pk}, q_{mps}, n+1, \epsilon)$-*breaks* an $(n+1)$-user IBMPS scheme by adaptive chosen message and adaptive chosen-ID attack, if $\mathcal{A}$ wins the above game with probability ϵ within time t and makes at most q_{H_1} H_1 queries, q_{H_2} H_2 queries, q_E extraction queries, q_d delegation queries, q_{pk} proxy key generation queries and q_{mps} multi-proxy signature queries.

Definition 6. An IBMPS scheme is $(t, q_{H_1}, q_{H_2}, q_E, q_d, q_{pk}, q_{mps}, n+1, \epsilon)$-secure against adaptive chosen message and adaptive chosen-ID attack, if no probabilistic polynomial time adversary can $(t, q_{H_1}, q_{H_2}, q_E, q_d, q_{pk}, q_{mps}, n+1, \epsilon)$-break it.

4　Proposed Scheme

In this section, we present our IBMPS scheme and its correctness. Our scheme consists of the following phases: setup, extraction, proxy key generation, multi-proxy signature and multi-proxy verification.

4.1　Setup

In the setup phase, the private key generator (PKG), on input security parameter 1^λ, generates the system's master secret key s and the system's public parameters

$$params = (\lambda, G_1, G_2, q, e, H_1, H_2, P, g, Pub),$$

where G_1 is an additive cyclic group of prime order q with generator P; G_2 is a multiplicative cyclic group of prime order q with generator g; $e : G_1 \times G_1 \to G_2$ is a bilinear map defined as above; $H_1 : \{0,1\}^* \to G_1$ and $H_2 : \{0,1\}^* \times G_1 \to \mathbb{Z}_q^*$ are two hash functions; and $Pub = sP \in G_1$ is system's public key.

4.2 Extraction

Given an identity ID, the PKG computes the hash value $H_{ID} := H_1(ID) \in G_1$ and returns the public and private keys for ID as follows:

public key: $PK_{ID} := e(H_{ID}, Pub) \in G_2$; and
private Key: $SK_{ID} := sH_{ID} \in G_1$.

Thus the original signer $\mathcal{O}$ has his private key $SK_{\mathcal{O}}$ while anyone can compute the corresponding public key $PK_{\mathcal{O}}$. Similarly, for the n proxy signers $\mathcal{P}_i$ (for $1 \le i \le n$), the public keys are $PK_{\mathcal{P}_i}$ and corresponding private keys are $SK_{\mathcal{P}_i}$.

4.3 Proxy Key Generation

Make Warrant: In this phase, the original signer $\mathcal{O}$ delegates its signing capability to the n proxy signers through a signed warrant w. The warrant w includes the identity of original signer $\mathcal{O}$, the identities of the proxy signers $\mathcal{P}_i$, $i = 1, \ldots, n$, the time of delegation, the period of validity, the nature of messages that can be signed etc.

Sub Proxy Generation: The original signer $\mathcal{O}$ randomly chooses $x_{\mathcal{O}} \in \mathbb{Z}_q^*$ and computes

- $U_{\mathcal{O}} = x_{\mathcal{O}} P \in G_1$,
- $V_{\mathcal{O}} = x_{\mathcal{O}} Pub \in G_1$ and appends to the warrant w,
- $h = H_2(w \| V_{\mathcal{O}}, U_{\mathcal{O}}) \in \mathbb{Z}_q^*$, and
- $S_{\mathcal{O}} = \frac{SK_{\mathcal{O}}}{x_{\mathcal{O}} + h}$.

Finally, the original signer $\mathcal{O}$ publishes $\sigma = (w \| V_{\mathcal{O}}, S_{\mathcal{O}}, U_{\mathcal{O}})$ to the group of proxy signers with $S_{\mathcal{O}}$ as a delegation value.

Sub Proxy Verification: Each proxy signer $\mathcal{P}_i$, $i = 1, \ldots, n$, accepts the delegation value $S_{\mathcal{O}}$ on warrant w, if the equality

$$e(S_{\mathcal{O}}, Q_{\mathcal{O}}) = PK_{\mathcal{O}}$$

holds, where $Q_{\mathcal{O}} = U_{\mathcal{O}} + hP$. Otherwise, they ask for a new delegation value or terminate the protocol.

Proxy Key Generation: After receiving the (correct) delegation value, each proxy signer $\mathcal{P}_i$ (for $1 \le i \le n$), generates their proxy private key

$$d_{\mathcal{P}_i} = S_{\mathcal{O}} + SK_{\mathcal{P}_i}.$$

4.4 Multi-proxy Signature

In this phase, one of the proxy signers in the proxy group acts as a clerk. The task of the clerk is to combine all the partial proxy signatures generated by each individual proxy signer and to generate the final multi-proxy signature.

Partial Proxy Signature Generation: In this phase each proxy signer $\mathcal{P}_i$ (for $1 \leq i \leq n$), randomly chooses $x_i \in \mathbb{Z}_q^*$, and computes

- $U_{\mathcal{P}_i} = x_i Q_{\mathcal{O}} \in G_1$,
- $h_i = H_2(m, U_{\mathcal{P}_i}) \in \mathbb{Z}_q^*$, and
- $S_{\mathcal{P}_i} = \frac{d_{\mathcal{P}_i}}{x_i + h_i}$.

The proxy signer $\mathcal{P}_i$ then broadcasts $(m, S_{\mathcal{P}_i}, U_{\mathcal{P}_i})$ to the group of proxy signers with $(S_{\mathcal{P}_i}, U_{\mathcal{P}_i})$ as its partial proxy signature.

Partial Proxy Signature Verification: A proxy signer $\mathcal{P}_i$ accepts a partial proxy signature $(S_{\mathcal{P}_j}, U_{\mathcal{P}_j})$, $j = 1, \ldots, n$, on message m, if the equality

$$e(S_{\mathcal{P}_j}, Q_j) = PK_{\mathcal{O}} \, e(H_{\mathcal{P}_j}, V_{\mathcal{O}} + hPub)$$

holds, where $Q_j = U_{\mathcal{P}_j} + h_j Q_{\mathcal{O}}$ and $H_{\mathcal{P}_j} = H_1(ID_{\mathcal{P}_j})$. Otherwise, $\mathcal{P}_i$ asks $\mathcal{P}_j$ for a new signature or terminates the protocol.

Multi-proxy Signature Generation: Each $\mathcal{P}_i$ then computes $R_{\mathcal{P}_i} = (x_i + h_i) \sum_{j \neq i} S_{\mathcal{P}_j}$ and broadcasts it to the group. The designated clerk, who too is one of the proxy signers, verifies all the partial proxy signatures valid, and finally generates the multi-proxy signature on message m as $\sigma_{\mathcal{P}} = (w \| V_{\mathcal{O}}, h', S_{\mathcal{P}}, R_{\mathcal{P}}, U_{\mathcal{P}})$ where

$$h' = \sum_{i=1}^{n} h_i \text{ and } S_{\mathcal{P}} = \sum_{i=1}^{n} S_{\mathcal{P}_i} \text{ and } R_{\mathcal{P}} = \sum_{i=1}^{n} R_{\mathcal{P}_i} \text{ and } U_{\mathcal{P}} = \sum_{i=1}^{n} U_{\mathcal{P}_i}.$$

4.5   Multi-proxy Verification

Getting a multi-proxy signature $\sigma_{\mathcal{P}} = (w \| V_{\mathcal{O}}, h', S_{\mathcal{P}}, R_{\mathcal{P}}, U_{\mathcal{P}})$ and message m, the verifier proceeds as follows:

1. Checks the validity of message m with respect to the warrant w. Continue, if it is a valid one. Rejects otherwise.
2. Checks the authorization of the n proxy signers by the original signer. Stop the verification, if all or any one of the proxy signers is not authorized by the warrant. Continue otherwise.
3. Finally, accepts the multi-proxy signature if the equality

$$e(S_{\mathcal{P}}, Q_{\mathcal{P}}) = PK_{\mathcal{O}}^n \, e(H_{\mathcal{P}}, V_{\mathcal{O}} + hPub) \, e(R_{\mathcal{P}}, Q_{\mathcal{O}})$$

holds, where $Q_{\mathcal{P}} = U_{\mathcal{P}} + h' Q_{\mathcal{O}}$ and $H_{\mathcal{P}} = \sum_{i=1}^{n} H_{\mathcal{P}_i}$, where $H_{\mathcal{P}_i} = H_1(ID_{\mathcal{P}_i})$.

5   Correctness and Security Proof

5.1   Proof of Correctness of Our IBMPS Scheme

To verify the correctness of our scheme, first note that

$$e(S_{\mathcal{P}}, Q_{\mathcal{P}}) = e(S_{\mathcal{P}}, (\sum_{i=1}^{n} U_{\mathcal{P}_i}) + h' Q_{\mathcal{O}}) = e(S_{\mathcal{P}}, \sum_{i=1}^{n} (U_{\mathcal{P}_i} + h_i Q_{\mathcal{O}}))$$

$$= e(S_\mathcal{P}, \sum_{i=1}^{n}(x_i Q_\mathcal{O} + h_i Q_\mathcal{O})) = e(S_\mathcal{P}, \sum_{i=1}^{n}(x_i Q_\mathcal{O} + h_i Q_\mathcal{O}))$$

$$= e(S_\mathcal{P}, \sum_{i=1}^{n}((x_i + h_i)Q_\mathcal{O})) = \prod_{i=1}^{n} e(S_\mathcal{P}, (x_i + h_i)Q_\mathcal{O})$$

$$= \prod_{i=1}^{n} e(\sum_{j=1}^{n} S_{\mathcal{P}_j}, (x_i + h_i)Q_\mathcal{O}) = \prod_{i=1}^{n} \prod_{j=1}^{n} e(S_{\mathcal{P}_j}, (x_i + h_i)Q_\mathcal{O})$$

$$= \prod_{i=1}^{n} (e(S_{\mathcal{P}_i}, (x_i + h_i)Q_\mathcal{O}) \prod_{i=1}^{n} \prod_{j \neq i} e(S_{\mathcal{P}_j}, (x_i + h_i)Q_\mathcal{O})). \qquad (1)$$

Now,

$$\prod_{i=1}^{n} \prod_{j \neq i} e(S_{\mathcal{P}_j}, (x_i + h_i)Q_\mathcal{O}) = \prod_{i=1}^{n} \prod_{j \neq i} e((x_i + h_i)S_{\mathcal{P}_j}, Q_\mathcal{O})$$

$$= e(\sum_{i=1}^{n} \sum_{j \neq i}(x_i + h_i)S_{\mathcal{P}_j}, Q_\mathcal{O})$$

$$= e(\sum_{i=1}^{n} R_{\mathcal{P}_i}, Q_\mathcal{O}) = e(R_\mathcal{P}, Q_\mathcal{O}), \qquad (2)$$

$$e(S_{\mathcal{P}_i}, (x_i + h_i)Q_\mathcal{O}) = e((x_i + h_i)S_{\mathcal{P}_i}, Q_\mathcal{O}) = e(d_{\mathcal{P}_i}, Q_\mathcal{O})$$
$$= e(S_\mathcal{O} + SK_{\mathcal{P}_i}, Q_\mathcal{O}) = e(S_\mathcal{O}, Q_\mathcal{O})e(SK_{\mathcal{P}_i}, Q_\mathcal{O}), \qquad (3)$$

$$e(SK_{\mathcal{P}_i}, Q_\mathcal{O}) = e(sH_{\mathcal{P}_i}, Q_\mathcal{O}) = e(H_{\mathcal{P}_i}, sQ_\mathcal{O}) = e(H_{\mathcal{P}_i}, sQ_\mathcal{O}) = e(H_{\mathcal{P}_i}, s(U_\mathcal{O} + hP))$$
$$= e(H_{\mathcal{P}_i}, sU_\mathcal{O} + shP) = e(H_{\mathcal{P}_i}, sx_\mathcal{O}P + hsP)$$
$$= e(H_{\mathcal{P}_i}, x_\mathcal{O}Pub + hPub) = e(H_{\mathcal{P}_i}, V_\mathcal{O} + hPub), \qquad (4)$$

and

$$e(S_\mathcal{O}, Q_\mathcal{O}) = e(S_\mathcal{O}, U_\mathcal{O} + hP) = e(\frac{SK_\mathcal{O}}{x_\mathcal{O} + h}, x_\mathcal{O}P + hP) = e(SK_\mathcal{O}, P) =$$
$$= e(sH_\mathcal{O}, P) = e(H_\mathcal{O}, sP) = e(H_\mathcal{O}, Pub) = PK_\mathcal{O}. \qquad (5)$$

Combining (1), (2), (3), (4) and (5), we get

$$e(S_\mathcal{P}, Q_\mathcal{P}) = \prod_{i=1}^{n}(e(S_{\mathcal{P}_i}, (x_i + h_i)Q_\mathcal{O}) \prod_{i=1}^{n} \prod_{j \neq i} e(S_{\mathcal{P}_j}, (x_i + h_i)Q_\mathcal{O}))$$

$$= \prod_{i=1}^{n}(e(S_\mathcal{O}, Q_\mathcal{O})e(SK_{\mathcal{P}_i}, Q_\mathcal{O})) \prod_{i=1}^{n} \prod_{j \neq i} e(S_{\mathcal{P}_j}, (x_i + h_i)Q_\mathcal{O})$$

$$= (\prod_{i=1}^{n}(PK_\mathcal{O}e(H_{\mathcal{P}_i}, V_\mathcal{O} + hPub)))e(R_\mathcal{P}, Q_\mathcal{O})$$

$$= PK_\mathcal{O}^n(\prod_{i=1}^{n} e(H_{\mathcal{P}_i}, V_\mathcal{O} + hPub))e(R_\mathcal{P}, Q_\mathcal{O})$$

$$= PK_\mathcal{O}^n e(\sum_{i=1}^{n} H_{\mathcal{P}_i}, V_\mathcal{O} + hPub)e(R_\mathcal{P}, Q_\mathcal{O})$$

$$= PK_\mathcal{O}^n e(H_\mathcal{P}, V_\mathcal{O} + hPub)e(R_\mathcal{P}, Q_\mathcal{O}) \qquad (6)$$

5.2 Proof of Security of Our IBMPS Scheme

In this section, we prove the security of our scheme against existential forgery on adaptive chosen message and adaptive chosen-ID attack in the random oracle model. We allow the adversary $\mathcal{A}$ to adaptively select the identities and the message on which it wants to forge the multi-proxy signature.

Theorem 1. If there exists an adversary $\mathcal{A}$ which $(t, q_{H_1}, q_{H_2}, q_E, q_d, q_{pk}, q_{mps},$ $n+1, \epsilon)$-breaks the proposed IBMPS scheme in time t with success probability ϵ, then there exists an adversary $\mathcal{B}(t', \epsilon')$ which solves CDHP with success probability at least $\epsilon' \geq \epsilon(1 - 1/q)M/(q_E + q_d + 2q_{pk} + (n+1)q_{mps} + n + 1)$ in time at most $t' \geq t + (q_{H_1} + q_E + 3q_d + 4q_{pk} + (6n+5)q_{mps} + 4)C_{G_1}$ where C_{G_1} denotes the maximum time taken for scalar multiplication in G_1.

Proof: Let, for a security parameter 1^λ, the adversary $\mathcal{B}$ is challenged to solve the CDHP for $\langle q, G_1, P, sP, bP \rangle$ where G_1 is an additive cyclic group of prime order q with generator P and $s, b \in \mathbb{Z}_q^*$. The goal of $\mathcal{B}$ is to solve CDHP by computing $sbP \in G_1$ using $\mathcal{A}$, the adversary who claims to forge our proposed IBMPS scheme. $\mathcal{B}$ simulates the security game with $\mathcal{A}$ as follows:

Setup: $\mathcal{B}$ chooses a multiplicative cyclic group $G_2 = \langle g \rangle$ of prime order q and constructs a bilinear map $e : G_1 \times G_1 \to G_2$ and generates the systems public parameter $params = \langle \lambda, G_1, G_2, q, e, H_1, H_2, P, g, Pub := sP \rangle$ for security parameter 1^λ where the hash functions H_1 and H_2 behave as random oracles and respond to hash queries as below.

H_1-*queries:* When $\mathcal{A}$ makes an H_1 query for an identity $ID \in \{0, 1\}^*$, $\mathcal{B}$ responds as follows:

1. $\mathcal{B}$ maintains a list $L_{H_1} = \langle (ID, h_1, a, c) \rangle$ and if the queried ID already appears on the list L_{H_1} in some tuple (ID, h_1, a, c) then algorithm $\mathcal{B}$ replies with $h_1 = H_1(ID)$.
2. Otherwise $\mathcal{B}$ picks a random integer $a \in \mathbb{Z}_q^*$, generates a random coin $c \in \{0, 1\}$ with probability $\Pr[c = 0] = \eta$ for some η, and
   - If $c = 0$, $\mathcal{B}$ sets $h_1 = a(bP)$.
   - If $c = 1$, $\mathcal{B}$ sets $h_1 = aP$.
3. Algorithm $\mathcal{B}$ adds the tuple (ID, h_1, a, c) to the list L_{H_1} and replies to $\mathcal{A}$ with $H_{ID} := h_1$.

H_2-*queries:* When $\mathcal{A}$ makes an H_2 query for a warrant $w' \in \{0, 1\}^*$ and $U', V' \in G_1$, $\mathcal{B}$ responds as follows:

1. $\mathcal{B}$ maintains a list $L_{H_2} = \langle (w||V, U, h) \rangle$ and if the queried $(w'||V', U')$ already appears on the list L_{H_2} in some tuple $(w||V, U, h)$ then algorithm $\mathcal{B}$ replies to $\mathcal{A}$ with $H_2(w'||V', U') := h'$.
2. Otherwise $\mathcal{B}$ picks a random integer $h' \in \mathbb{Z}_q^*$ and replies to $\mathcal{A}$ with $H_2(w'||V', U') := h'$ and adds the tuple $(w'||V', U', h')$ to the list L_{H_2}.

Similarly when $\mathcal{A}$ makes an H_2 query for a message $m' \in \{0, 1\}^*$ and $U' \in G_1$, $\mathcal{B}$ picks a random integer $h' \in \mathbb{Z}_q^*$ and replies to $\mathcal{A}$ with $H_2(m', U') := h'$ and adds the tuple (m', U', h') to the list L_{H_2}.

Extraction Queries: When $\mathcal{A}$ makes a private key query on identity ID, $\mathcal{B}$ responds as follows:

1. B runs the above algorithm for responding to H_1 query on ID and computes $h_1 = H_1(ID)$.
2. Let (ID, h_1, a, c) be the corresponding tuple on the list L_{H_1}.
   - If $c = 0$, then B outputs 'failure' and terminates.
   - If $c = 1$, then B replies to A with $SK_{ID} := aPub$.

Recall that $H_{ID} = H_1(ID) = h_1 = aP$. So, $aPub = a(sP) = s(aP) = sH_{ID}$ is a valid private key of the user with identity ID. Hence, the probability that B does not terminate is $(1 - \eta)$.

Delegation Queries: When A requests a delegation of a warrant $w' \in \{0, 1\}^*$ by the original signer with identity ID to the proxy signers P_i as in the warrant, B responds as follows:

1. B runs the above algorithm for responding to H_1-queries to obtain $H_{ID} = H_1(ID) = aP \in G_1$. If $c = 0$ in the corresponding tuple (ID, h_1, a, c) on the list L_{H_1}, B outputs 'failure' and terminates. Otherwise it proceeds to next step.
2. B selects randomly $x' \in \mathbb{Z}_q^*$ and sets $U' = x'P$ and $V' = x'Pub$. If U' already appears in some tuple (m, U, h) in the list L_{H_2}, B picks another $x' \in \mathbb{Z}_q^*$ randomly and repeats this step. B then runs the above algorithm for responding to H_2-queries for the input $(w'||V', U')$ and outputs $H_2(w'||V', U') = h'$.
3. B computes $S' := aPub/(x' + h')$ and replies to A with $\sigma' = (w'||V', S', U')$.

Recall that $H_{ID} = H_1(ID) = aP$ and $SK_{ID} := aPub$. So, $e(S', Q') =$

$$e(\frac{aPub}{x' + h'}, U' + h'P) = e(\frac{asP}{x' + h'}, x'P + h'P) = e(aP, sP) = e(H_{ID}, Pub) = PK_{ID}.$$

Thus $\sigma' = (w'||V', S', U')$ is a valid delegation of the warrant w'. Also note that the probability that B does not terminate is $(1 - \eta)$.

Proxy Key Generation Queries: Note that in our scheme, the proxy signing key d_{P_i} of any proxy signer P_i is just the sum of the delegation value $S_{\mathcal{O}}$ of the warrant and the private key $SK_{ID_{P_i}}$ of the proxy signer. So when A queries for a proxy signing key of a proxy signer P_i, B runs the above algorithms for extraction query and delegation query and responds accordingly. Since the probability that B does not halt during each of those queries is $1 - \eta$, the probability that B does not halt in this query is $(1 - \eta)^2$.

Multi-proxy Signature Queries: When the adversary A requests for a multi-proxy signature on a message m' satisfying a warrant w' from an original signer $\mathcal{O} = P_0$ to a group of proxy signers $P_1, \ldots, P_n$, B responds as follows:

1. B runs the above algorithm for responding to H_1 query on P_i, $i = 0, 1, \ldots, n$, and computes $h_{1i} = H_1(P_i)$. Let (P_i, h_{1i}, a_i, c_i) be the corresponding tuples on the list L_{H_1}. If $c_i = 0$, for any $i = 0, 1, \ldots, n$, B outputs 'failure' and terminates. Otherwise it proceeds to next step.

2. $\mathcal{B}$ selects randomly $x'_{\mathcal{O}} \in \mathbb{Z}_q^*$ and sets $U'_{\mathcal{O}} = x'_{\mathcal{O}}P$ and $V'_{\mathcal{O}} = x'_{\mathcal{O}}Pub$. If $U'_{\mathcal{O}}$ already appears in some tuple (m, U, h) in the list L_{H_2}, $\mathcal{B}$ picks another $x'_{\mathcal{O}} \in \mathbb{Z}_q^*$ and repeats this step. $\mathcal{B}$ then runs the above algorithm for responding to H_2-queries for the inputs $(w'||V'_{\mathcal{O}}, U'_{\mathcal{O}})$ and adds the tuple $(w'||V'_{\mathcal{O}}, U'_{\mathcal{O}}, h')$ to the list L_{H_2}.

3. $\mathcal{B}$ computes $S'_{\mathcal{O}} = \frac{SK_{\mathcal{O}}}{x'_{\mathcal{O}}+h'} = \frac{a_0 Pub}{x'_{\mathcal{O}}+h'}$ and sets $d'_{\mathcal{P}_i} = S'_{\mathcal{O}} + SK_{\mathcal{P}_i} = S'_{\mathcal{O}} + a_i Pub$ for $i = 1, \ldots, n$.

4. $\mathcal{B}$ selects randomly $x'_i \in \mathbb{Z}_q^*$ and computes $U'_{\mathcal{P}_i} = x'_i P$. If $U'_{\mathcal{P}_i}$ already appears in some tuple (m, U, h) in the list L_{H_2}, $\mathcal{B}$ picks another $x'_i \in \mathbb{Z}_q^*$ and repeats this step. $\mathcal{B}$ then runs the above algorithm for responding to H_2-queries for the inputs $(m', U'_{\mathcal{P}_i})$ and adds the tuple $(m', U'_{\mathcal{P}_i}, h'_i)$ to the list L_{H_2}.

5. $\mathcal{B}$ computes $S'_{\mathcal{P}_i} = \frac{d'_{\mathcal{P}_i}}{x'_i+h'_i}$ for $i = 1, \ldots, n$, $h'' = \sum_{i=1}^n h'_i$, $U'_{\mathcal{P}} = \sum_{i=1}^n U'_{\mathcal{P}_i}$ and $S'_{\mathcal{P}} = \sum_{i=1}^n S'_{\mathcal{P}_i}$.

6. $\mathcal{B}$ then computes $R'_{\mathcal{P}_i} = (x'_i + h'_i)(S'_{\mathcal{P}} - S'_{\mathcal{P}_i})$ for each $i = 1, \ldots, n$ and sets $R'_{\mathcal{P}} = \sum_{i=1}^n R'_{\mathcal{P}_i}$.

7. Finally $\mathcal{B}$ replies to $\mathcal{A}$ with the IBMPS $\sigma'_{\mathcal{P}} = (w'||V'_{\mathcal{O}}, h'', S'_{\mathcal{P}}, R'_{\mathcal{P}}, U'_{\mathcal{P}})$.

Note that the probability that $\mathcal{B}$ does not halt in this query is $(1 - \eta)^{n+1}$. Also, $\mathcal{B}$ follows all the steps correctly and one can check that replies to $\mathcal{A}$ with a valid delegation and that the verification step equality

$$e(S'_{\mathcal{P}}, Q'_{\mathcal{P}}) = PK_{\mathcal{O}}^n \, e(H_{\mathcal{P}}, V'_{\mathcal{O}} + h'Pub) \, e(R'_{\mathcal{P}}, Q'_{\mathcal{O}})$$

holds, where $Q'_{\mathcal{O}} = U'_{\mathcal{O}} + h'P = (x'_{\mathcal{O}} + h')P$, $Q'_{\mathcal{P}} = U'_{\mathcal{P}} + h''Q'_{\mathcal{O}}$ and $H_{\mathcal{P}} = \sum_{i=1}^n H_{\mathcal{P}_i} = \sum_{i=1}^n a_i P$.

Output: The probability that $\mathcal{B}$ does not abort during the above simulation is

$$(1 - \eta)^{q_E + q_d + 2q_{pk} + (n+1)q_{mps}} \tag{7}$$

and in that case, let $\mathcal{A}$ outputs a valid IBMPS $\sigma^*_{\mathcal{P}} = (w^*||V^*_{\mathcal{O}}, S^*_{\mathcal{P}}, R^*_{\mathcal{P}}, U^*_{\mathcal{P}})$ on message m^* which satisfies

$$e(S^*_{\mathcal{P}}, Q^*_{\mathcal{P}}) = PK_{\mathcal{O}}^n \, e(H_{\mathcal{P}}, V^*_{\mathcal{O}} + h^*Pub) \, e(R^*_{\mathcal{P}}, Q^*_{\mathcal{O}})$$

If $\mathcal{A}$ does not query the three hash functions, $H_1(ID)$, $H_2(w^*||V^*, U^*)$ and $H_2(m^*, U^*)$, then the responses to these hash functions are picked randomly so that the probability that verification equality holds is less that $1/q$. Hence $\mathcal{A}$ outputs a new valid IBMPS $\sigma^*_{\mathcal{P}} = (w^*||V^*_{\mathcal{O}}, S^*_{\mathcal{P}}, R^*_{\mathcal{P}}, U^*_{\mathcal{P}})$ on message m^* with the probability

$$(1 - 1/q)(1 - \eta)^{q_E + q_d + 2q_{pk} + (n+1)q_{mps}}.$$

Case 1. $\mathcal{A}$ interacts with $\mathcal{B}$ as a proxy signer, say $\mathcal{P}_1$. $\mathcal{A}$ did not request the private key of $ID_{\mathcal{P}_1}$, $\mathcal{A}$ did not request a delegation value for warrant w^*, $\mathcal{A}$ did not request the proxy signing key for $S^*_{\mathcal{O}}$ and $\mathcal{A}$ did not request a multi-proxy signature for (m^*, w^*).

Let $H_1(ID_{\mathcal{O}}) = a_{\mathcal{O}}P$, $H_1(ID_{\mathcal{P}_i}) = a_{\mathcal{P}_i}P$ for $2 \leq i \leq n$, and $H_1(ID_{\mathcal{P}_1}) = a_{\mathcal{P}_1}(bP)$, which happens with probability $(1-\eta)(1-\eta)^{n-1}\eta = \eta(1-\eta)^n$.

$\mathcal{B}$ has $V'_{\mathcal{O}} = x'_{\mathcal{O}}Pub$, $h' = H_2(w'\|V'_{\mathcal{O}}, U'_{\mathcal{O}})$ and $S'_{\mathcal{P}} = \sum_{i=1}^{n} S'_{\mathcal{P}_i}$ and proceeds to solve CDHP using the equality:

$$e(S'_{\mathcal{P}}, Q'_{\mathcal{P}}) = PK_{\mathcal{O}}^n e(H_{\mathcal{P}}, V'_{\mathcal{O}} + h'Pub)e(R'_{\mathcal{P}}, Q'_{\mathcal{O}})$$

$$= PK_{\mathcal{O}}^n e(\sum_{i=1}^{n} H_{ID_{\mathcal{P}_i}}, x'_{\mathcal{O}}Pub + h'Pub)e(R'_{\mathcal{P}}, Q'_{\mathcal{O}})$$

$$= e(H_{\mathcal{O}}, Pub)^n e(\sum_{i=1}^{n} H_{ID_{\mathcal{P}_i}}, (x'_{\mathcal{O}} + h')Pub)e(R'_{\mathcal{P}}, Q'_{\mathcal{O}})$$

$$= e(a_{\mathcal{O}}P, nPub)e(\{a_{\mathcal{P}_2} + \cdots + a_{\mathcal{P}_n}\}P, (x'_{\mathcal{O}} + h')Pub)$$
$$e(H_1(ID_{\mathcal{P}_1}), (x'_{\mathcal{O}} + h')Pub)e(R'_{\mathcal{P}}, (x'_{\mathcal{O}} + h')P)$$

$$= e(na_{\mathcal{O}}Pub, P)e(\{a_{\mathcal{P}_2} + \cdots + a_{\mathcal{P}_n}\}(x'_{\mathcal{O}} + h')Pub, P)$$
$$e(H_1(ID_{\mathcal{P}_1}), (x'_{\mathcal{O}} + h')Pub)e((x'_{\mathcal{O}} + h')R'_{\mathcal{P}}, P)$$

$$= e([na_{\mathcal{O}} + \{a_{\mathcal{P}_2} + \cdots + a_{\mathcal{P}_n}\}(x'_{\mathcal{O}} + h')]Pub + (x'_{\mathcal{O}} + h')R'_{\mathcal{P}}, P)$$
$$e(H_1(ID_{\mathcal{P}_1}), (x'_{\mathcal{O}} + h')Pub)$$

We have

$$Q'_{\mathcal{P}} = U'_{\mathcal{P}} + h''Q'_{\mathcal{O}} = \sum_{i=1}^{n} U'_{\mathcal{P}_i} + h''\{U'_{\mathcal{O}} + h'P\} = \sum_{i=1}^{n} x'_iP + h''\{x'_{\mathcal{O}}P + h'P\}$$

$$= \{\sum_{i=1}^{n} x'_i + x'_{\mathcal{O}}h'' + h'h''\}P.$$

Let $Z = [na_{\mathcal{O}} + \{a_{\mathcal{P}_2} + \cdots + a_{\mathcal{P}_n}\}(x'_{\mathcal{O}} + h')]Pub + (x'_{\mathcal{O}} + h')R'_{\mathcal{P}}$. Then by above equality, we have

$$e(S'_{\mathcal{P}}, Q'_{\mathcal{P}}) = e(Z, P)e(H_1(ID_{\mathcal{P}_1}), (x'_{\mathcal{O}} + h')Pub)$$

$$e(S'_{\mathcal{P}}, \{\sum_{i=1}^{n} x'_i + x'_{\mathcal{O}}h'' + h'h''\}P) = e(Z, P)e(a_{\mathcal{P}_1}(bP), (x'_{\mathcal{O}} + h')Pub)$$

$$e(S'_{\mathcal{P}}\{\sum_{i=1}^{n} x'_i + x'_{\mathcal{O}}h'' + h'h''\} - Z, P) = e(a_{\mathcal{P}_1}(bP), (x'_{\mathcal{O}} + h')Pub)$$

Let $S_{\mathcal{P}}^{\#} = S'_{\mathcal{P}}\{\sum_{i=1}^{n} x'_i + x'_{\mathcal{O}}h'' + h'h''\} - Z$. Then,

$$e(S_{\mathcal{P}}^{\#}, P) = e(a_{\mathcal{P}_1}(bP), (x'_{\mathcal{O}} + h')Pub)$$
$$= e(a_{\mathcal{P}_1}(x'_{\mathcal{O}} + h')(bP), Pub)$$
$$= e(C(bP), Pub) \qquad \{\text{where } C = a_{\mathcal{P}_1}(x'_{\mathcal{O}} + h')\}$$
$$= e(C(bsP), P).$$

Hence $S_{\mathcal{P}}^{\#} = C(bsP)$ so that $bsP = C^{-1}S_{\mathcal{P}}^{\#}$. Thus, using algorithm $\mathcal{A}$, $\mathcal{B}$ can solve an instance of CDHP and the probability of success is $\eta(1-\eta)^n$.

Case 2. $\mathcal{A}$ interacts with $\mathcal{B}$ as the original signer $\mathcal{O}$. $\mathcal{A}$ did not request the private key of $ID_{\mathcal{O}}$, $\mathcal{A}$ did not request a delegation value for warrant w^*, $\mathcal{A}$ did not request the proxy signing key for $S_{\tilde{O}}^*$ and $\mathcal{A}$ did not request a multi-proxy signature for (m^*, w^*). As the above case we can show that $\mathcal{B}$ can derive sbP with the same success probability $\eta(1 - \eta)^n$. Hence the success probability ϵ' that $\mathcal{B}$ solves the CDHP in the above attack game is at least:

$$(1 - 1/q)\eta(1 - \eta)^{q_E+q_d+2q_{pk}+(n+1)q_{mps}+n}\epsilon.$$

Now the maximum possible value of the above probability occurs for

$$\eta = \frac{1}{q_E + q_d + 2q_{pk} + (n+1)q_{mps} + n + 1}.$$

Hence the optimal success probability is

$$\frac{(1 - 1/q)M}{q_E + q_d + 2q_{pk} + (n+1)q_{mps} + n + 1}\epsilon$$

so that

$$\epsilon' \geq \frac{(1 - 1/q)M}{q_E + q_d + 2q_{pk} + (n+1)q_{mps} + n + 1}\epsilon$$

where M is the maximum value of

$$(1 - \eta)^{q_E+q_d+2q_{pk}+(n+1)q_{mps}+n}$$

which occurs for

$$\eta = \frac{1}{q_E + q_d + 2q_{pk} + (n+1)q_{mps} + n + 1}.$$

Now taking care of running time, one can observe that running time of algorithm $\mathcal{B}$ is same as that of $\mathcal{A}$ plus time taken to respond to the hash, extraction, delegation, proxy key generation and multi-proxy signature queries i.e. $q_{H_1} + q_{H_2} + q_E + q_d + q_{pk} + q_{mps}$. Hence the maximum running time is given by $t' \geq t + (q_{H_1} + q_E + 3q_d + 4q_{pk} + (6n+5)q_{mps} + 4)C_{G_1}$ where C_{G_1} denotes the maximum time taken for scalar multiplication in G_1, as each H_1 hash query requires one scalar multiplication in G_1, extraction query requires one scalar multiplication in G_1, delegation query requires three scalar multiplications in G_1, proxy key generation query requires four scalar multiplications in G_1, multi-proxy signature query requires $(6n+5)$ scalar multiplications in G_1 and, to output CDH solution from $\mathcal{A}$'s forgery, $\mathcal{B}$ requires at most four scalar multiplications in G_1. Hence $t' \geq t + (q_{H_1} + q_E + 3q_d + 4q_{pk} + (6n+5)q_{mps} + 4)C_{G_1}$.

6 Efficiency Comparison

Here, we compare the efficiency of our IBMPS scheme with that of the existing IBMPS schemes [4,12,19] and [20] and show that our scheme is more efficient in the sense of computation and operation time than those schemes. For the

Table 1. Efficiency Comparision

Proxy key generation:

Scheme	P	H	E	SM	OT (ms)
Li et al. [12]	3	0	1	6	103.71
Cao et al. [4]	3	2	0	3	85.34
Rao et al. [19]	3	2	2	3	95.96
Sahu et al. [20]	2	0	0	5	71.98
Our scheme	1*	0*	0	4	45.56

* $PK_\mathcal{O} = e(H_\mathcal{O}, Pub)$ is a one-time computation and can be pre-computed so does not contribute to the operation time.

Multi-proxy Verification:

Scheme	P	H	E	SM	OT (ms)
Li et al. [12]	3	0	1	2	78.19
Cao et al. [4]	4	2	0	2	99.00
Rao et al. [19]	3	1	2	0	73.78
Sahu et al. [20]	2	0	0	4	65.6
Our scheme	3	1	0*	2	75.92

* The quantity $PK_\mathcal{O}^n$ is a one-time computation and can be pre-computed so does not contribute to the operation time.

Multi-proxy signature generation:

Scheme	P	H	E	SM	OT (ms)
Li et al. [12]	3	0	1	3	84.57
Cao et al. [4]	5	1	1	2	121.31
Rao et al. [19]	4	1	3	4	124.65
Sahu et al. [20]	2	0	0	6	78.36
Our scheme	2	1†	0	5	75.02

Overall Time:

Scheme	P	H	E	SM	OT (ms)
Li et al. [12]	9	0	3	11	266.47
Cao et al. [4]	12	5	1	7	305.65
Rao et al. [19]	10	4	7	7	294.39
Sahu et al. [20]	6	0	0	15	215.94
Our scheme	6	2	0	11	196.50

† We have followed the exact same convention as in [5,6] to count the number of bilinear pairings (P), map-to-point hash functions (H), modular-exponentiations (E), scalar multiplications (SM) and the consequent operation time (OT)

computation of operation time, we refer to [6] where the operation time for various cryptographic operations have been obtained using MIRACL [15], a standard cryptographic library, and the hardware platform is a PIV 3 GHZ processor with 512 M bytes memory and the Windows XP operating system. For the pairing-based scheme, to achieve the 1024-bit RSA level security, Tate pairing defined over the supersingular elliptic curve $E = F_p : y^2 = x^3 + x$ with embedding degree 2 was used, where q is a 160-bit Solinas prime $q = 2^{159} + 2^{17} + 1$ and p a 512-bit prime satisfying $p + 1 = 12\,qr$. We note that the OT for one pairing computation is $20.04\,ms$, for one map-to-point hash function it is $3.04\,ms$, for one modular exponentiation it is $5.31\,ms$, for one scalar multiplication it is $6.38\,ms$ and for one general hash function it is $< 0.001\,ms$. To evaluate the total operation time in the efficiency comparison tables, we use the simple method from [5,6]. In each of the three phases: proxy key generation, multi-proxy signature generation and multi-proxy verification, we compare the total number of bilinear pairings (P), map-to-point hash functions (H), modular exponentiations (E), scalar multiplications (SM) and the consequent operation time (OT) while omitting the operation time due to a general hash function which is negligible compared to the other four operations. Further, across all the compared schemes, in the computation tables, we take into consideration the computations of only one of the n proxy signers following the methodology of [5,6].

For example, during the multi-proxy signature generation phase of our scheme, each proxy signer computes 2 pairings, 1 map-to-point hash, 0 modular exponentiation and 5 scalar multiplications, hence the total operation time can be calculated as: $2 \times 20.04 + 1 \times 3.04 + 0 \times 5.31 + 5 \times 6.38 = 75.02\,ms$. The OT for each phase of all the schemes has been computed similarly.

From the efficiency comparison Table 1, it is clear that our scheme is computationally more efficient and having less operation time than the schemes given in [4,12,19,20]. In particular, our scheme is 56 %, 50 %, 36 % and 10 % more efficient than the schemes given in [4,12,19] and [20] respectively.

Acknowledgement. The authors acknowledge the Cryptology Research Society of India and DST-CMS project SR/S4/MS:516/07 for the financial support towards presentation of this paper at ICICS 2014.

References

1. Asaar, M.R., Salmasizadeh, M., Susilo, W.: Security pitfalls of a provably secure identity-based multi-proxy signature scheme. IACR Cryptology ePrint Archive, 2014:496 (2014)
2. Bakker, A., Van Steen, M., Tanenbaum, A.S.: A law-abiding peer-to-peer network for free-software distribution. In Proceedings of IEEE International Symposium on Network Computing and Applications, pp. 60–67 (2002)
3. Boldyreva, A., Palacio, A., Warinschi, B.: Secure proxy signature schemes for delegation of signing rights. J. Cryptol. **25**(1), 57–115 (2012)
4. Cao, F., Cao, Z.: A secure identity-based multi-proxy signature scheme. Comput. Electr. Eng. **35**(1), 86–95 (2009)
5. Cao, X., Kou, W., Xiaoni, D.: A pairing-free identity-based authenticated key agreement protocol with minimal message exchanges. Inf. Sci. **180**(15), 2895–2903 (2010)
6. Debiao, H., Jianhua, C., Jin, H.: An ID-based proxy signature schemes without bilinear pairings. Ann. Telecommun. **66**(11–12), 657–662 (2011)
7. Foster, L.T., Kesselman, C., Tsudik, G., Tuecke, S.: A security architecture for computational grids. In: ACM Conference on Computer and Communications Security, pp. 83–92 (1998)
8. Gasser, M., Goldstein, A., Kaufman, C., Lampson, B.: The digital distributed system security architecture. In: NCSC 1989, pp. 305–319 (1989)
9. Herranz, J., Sáez, G.: Revisiting fully distributed proxy signature schemes. In: Canteaut, A., Viswanathan, K. (eds.) INDOCRYPT 2004. LNCS, vol. 3348, pp. 356–370. Springer, Heidelberg (2004)
10. Hwang, S.-J., Shi, C.-H.: A simple multi-proxy signature scheme. In: NCIS 2000, **138** (2000)
11. Leiwo, J., Hänle, C., Homburg, P., Tanenbaum, A.S.: Disallowing unauthorized state changes of distributed shared objects. In: SEC, pp. 381–390 (2000)
12. Li, X., Chen, K.: ID-based multi-proxy signature, proxy multi-signature and multi-proxy multi-signature schemes from bilinear pairings. Appl. Math. Comput. **169**(1), 437–450 (2005)
13. Malkin, T., Obana, S., Yung, M.: The hierarchy of key evolving signatures and a characterization of proxy signatures. In: Cachin, C., Camenisch, J.L. (eds.) EURO-CRYPT 2004. LNCS, vol. 3027, pp. 306–322. Springer, Heidelberg (2004)

14. Mambo, M., Usuda, K., Okamoto, E.: Proxy signatures: delegation of the power to sign messages. IEICE Trans. Fundam. Electron. Commun. Comput. Sci. **79**(9), 1338–1354 (1996)
15. MIRACL. Multiprecision integer and rational arithmetic cryptographic library. http://certivox.org/display/EXT/MIRACL
16. Mishra, S., Sahu, R.A., Padhye, S., Yadav, R.S.: Efficient ID-based multi-proxy signature scheme from bilinear pairing based on *k-plus* problem. In: Hruschka Jr., E.R., Watada, J., do Carmo Nicoletti, M. (eds.) INTECH 2011. CCIS, vol. 165, pp. 113–122. Springer, Heidelberg (2011)
17. Neuman, B.C.: Proxy-based authorization and accounting for distributed systems. In: ICDCS, pages 283–291 (1993)
18. Okamoto, T., Tada, M., Okamoto, E.: Extended proxy signatures for smart cards. In: Zheng, Y., Mambo, M. (eds.) ISW 1999. LNCS, vol. 1729, p. 247. Springer, Heidelberg (1999)
19. Rao, B.U., Reddy, P.V.: ID-based directed multi-proxy signature scheme from bilinear pairings. Int. J. Comput. Sci. Secur. (IJCSS) **5**(1), 107 (2011)
20. Sahu, R.A., Padhye, S.: Provable secure identity-based multi-proxy signature scheme. Int. J. Commun. Syst. **28**, 497–512 (2013)
21. Schuldt, J.C.N., Matsuura, K., Paterson, K.G.: Proxy signatures secure against proxy key exposure. In: Cramer, R. (ed.) PKC 2008. LNCS, vol. 4939, pp. 141–161. Springer, Heidelberg (2008)
22. Varadharajan, V., Allen, P., Black, S.: An analysis of the proxy problem in distributed systems. In: IEEE Symposium on Security and Privacy, pp. 255–277 (1991)
23. Wang, Q., Cao, Z., Wang, S.: Formalized security model of multi-proxy signature schemes. In: CIT 2005, pp. 668–672 (2005)
24. Xiong, H., Jianbin, H., Chen, Z., Li, F.: On the security of an identity based multi-proxy signature scheme. Comput. Electr. Eng. **37**(2), 129–135 (2011)
25. Yap, W.-S., Goi, B.-M.: Forgery attacks of an identity-based multi-proxy signature scheme. International Journal of Communication Systems, February 2014

Fully Secure Ciphertext-Policy Attribute Based Encryption with Security Mediator

Yuechen Chen[1,5], Zoe L. Jiang[1], S.M. Yiu[2], Joseph K. Liu[3],
Man Ho Au[4], and Xuan Wang[1,6]([✉])

[1] Harbin Institute of Technology Shenzhen Graduate School, Shenzhen 518055, China
[2] HKSAR, The University of Hong Kong, Hong Kong, China
[3] Institute for Infocomm Research, Singapore, Singapore
[4] University of Wollongong, Wollongong, Australia
[5] Shenzhen Applied Technology Engineering Laboratory for Internet Multimedia
Application, Shenzhen, China
[6] Public Service Platform of Mobile Internet Application Security Industry,
Shenzhen, China
wangxuan@cs.hitsz.edu.cn

Abstract. Attribute-Based Encryption (ABE) offers fine-grained decryption policy such that users can do decryption if their attributes satisfy the policy. Such flexibility enables it applicable in various applications in government and business. However, there are two issues that should be solved first before it is deployed in practice, namely user revocation and decryption outsourcing. In this paper, we adopt the slightly modified Lewko et al.'s fully-CCA-secure Ciphertext-Policy-ABE (CP-ABE) combining with Boneh et al.'s idea of mediated cryptography to propose a CP-ABE with SEcurity Mediator (SEM) supporting immediate user revocation. At the same time, by the introduce of SEM, we intendedly outsource most of the computation workload in decryption to SEM side and leave only one exponentiation and one division at user side for decryption. It is proved fully-RCCA-CCA-secure in random oracle model.

Keywords: CP-ABE · Decryption outsourcing · Dual encryption system · Security mediator · User revocation

1 Introduction

In a traditional Identity-Based Encryption (IBE) system, data is encrypted by a certain identity which can be decrypted by the corresponding secret key. Ciphertext encrypted by the identity can only be decrypted by the secret key. However, in many cases, it is required for any user (with a certain set of attributes) who satisfies a policy can decrypt the corresponding data. For example, the head agent may specify that people satisfying ((PUBLIC CORRUPTION OFFICE

Zoe L. Jiang—Co-corresponding author.

© Springer International Publishing Switzerland 2015
L.C.K. Hui et al. (Eds.): ICICS 2014, LNCS 8958, pp. 274–289, 2015.
DOI: 10.1007/978-3-319-21966-0_20

AND (KNOXVILLE OR SAN FRANCISCO)) OR (MANAGEMENT-LEVEL > 5) OR NAME=CHARLIE) to decrypt documents [4]. We call the encryption scheme achieving the above requirement Attribute-Based Encryption (ABE).

ABE can be divided into Key-Policy ABE (KP-ABE) and Ciphertext-Policy ABE (CP-ABE). In KP-ABE [1,2,6,15], secret key is associated with access policy P. And ciphertext is associated with user's attribute set S. The secret key can decrypt the ciphertext if the attribute set S satisfies the policy P. In CP-ABE, ciphertext is associated with policy P, while secret key is associated with user's attribute set S [4,5,11,13].

ACCESS STRUCTURE. ABE is proposed for fine-grained access control on encrypted data. The simplest access structure is Threshold. The user will wish to encrypt a document to all users that have a certain set of attributes. For example, in a department of computer science, the chairperson might want to encrypt a document to all of its systems faculty on a hiring committee. In this case it would encrypt to the attribute set hiring-committee, faculty, systems. Any user who has these attributes could decrypt the document [1]. Access structure with AND and OR gates can be represented by an access tree using 2 of 2 and 1 of 2 Threshold gates as root nodes, respectively. Recall the head agent case in [4] as an example. Such monotone access structure can be further extended to the non-monotonic structure supporting NOT gate [5,6].

SELECTIVE AND FULLY SECURITY. A security model is called *selective* if the adversary is required to announce the intended target before Setup is executed in the game. This is a limited model as the adversary is not necessary to decide the target at the very beginning of the game. There are a list of ABE schemes achieving selective-attribute security [1,2,4–6,11]. The model can be improved to *fully* secure if such limitation is removed such that the adversary will decide the intended target at any time during the game [13–15].

CPA, CCA AND RCCA. To prove an ABE is Chosen-Plaintext-Attack (CPA) secure, we first construct the security game describing the interaction of an adversary $\mathcal{A}$ and challenger $\mathcal{C}$ (i.e., the attacks $\mathcal{A}$ launches), as well as the goal of $\mathcal{A}$ by successfully guessing b from the challenge ciphertext CT_b. Achieving the goal means $\mathcal{A}$ wins the game. We say an ABE is secure if $\mathcal{A}$ wins the game with negligible probability ϵ. Furthermore, we say an ABE is CPA-secure if $\mathcal{A}$ is not allowed to ask for plaintext of his chosen ciphertext. On the contrary, it is Chosen-Ciphertext-Attack secure(CCA-secure). If $\mathcal{A}$ can launch decryption queries on any chosen ciphertext C except the challenge ciphertext C_b (i.e., $C \neq C_b$).The most recent research on ABE is a fully-CCA-secure CP/KP-ABE with monotonic access structure [13]. Replayable CCA (RCCA) was proposed [24] that allows modification to the ciphertext provided they cannot change the underlying plaintext in a meaningful way. Green et al. [16] proposed to outsource the decryption of ABE which is selective-RCCA secure.

USER REVOCATION. Boldyreva, Goyal and Kumar proposed Identity Based Encryption with Efficient Revocation which supports user revocation in IBE [7] in 2008. Then user revocation has been taken notice in many practical ABE systems. User revocation is an essential mechanism in many group-based applications, including ABE systems, because users may leave their group. Revocation of any single user would affect others who have the same attribute with him. An intuitive way is to append to each of the attributes a date for when the attribute expires [4]. It not only degrades the security in terms of Backward and Forward Secrecy, but also has the scalability problem [18]. Another way is to use ABE that supports NOT gate [6]. Particularly, one can append a NOT gate of the revoked users identity to the previous formula with an AND gate. However, it is very inefficient and does not support immediate revocation. Yu et al. proposed a CP-ABE scheme with attribute immediate revocation [19]. However, it depends on a curious-but-honest proxy server to update secret keys for all unrevoked users. The third method is to re-encrypt the affected ciphertexts, and then updates the decryption keys for unrevoked users. The last method is to introduce a mediator who maintains a real-time RL, which is used in our construction.

As discussed above, user revocation is one of the obstacles for ABE into practice. The other obstacle is the efficiency of ABE. As most of the ABE decryption algorithms involve several paring operations, it is a significant challenge for users using light-weight devices for decryption. Therefore, an ABE scheme supporting decryption outsourcing would be a better solution.

Mediated cryptography was designed by Boneh et al. [20] as a method to allow immediate revocation of public keys. The basic idea when deployed in ABE is to introduce an on-line SEcurity Mediator, SEM, for the check of user validity. Once SEM is notified that a user is to be revoked, it can stop the decryption by the user immediately. To this end, SEM is given a partial decryption key with a real-time revocation list (RL). All encrypted data will be sent to SEM first for checking the validity of the corresponding user in RL. SEM executes SEM-Decrypt if and only if he passes the check, and sends the partially decrypted data to the user for User-Decrypt [21]. Therefore, deploying SEM between the data owner and the data user is a promising solution for ABE. Ibraimi et al. combined this idea with Bethencourt et al.'s selective-CPA-secure CP-ABE [4] to propose a selective-CPA-secure mediated CP-ABE to support immediate user revocation with application in Personal Health Records (PHR) management [25]. In addition, SEM can act as an outsourcing server to do partial decryption [16]. In other words, if we consciously leverage most of the decryption computation to SEM, we can achieve a practical ABE scheme in User-Decrypt. Therefore, the introduction of SEM can solve both the user revocation and decryption outsourcing problems, which directly makes an ABE with SEM to practical applications. However, with the introduction of SEM (a new role in the security game), it changes the original security model. We also need to prove its security although the underlying ABE has been proved fully-CCA secure.

1.1 Our Approach

We are able to obtain a fully-RCCA-CCA-secure CP-ABE with mediator.

Firstly, to achieve immediate user revocation, we adopt the slightly modified Lewko et al.'s fully-CCA-secure CP-ABE [13] as the ABE building block combining with Boneh et al.'s idea of security mediator [20] to propose a CP-ABE with mediator (SEM). In this scheme, SEM is given a partial decryption key (SK_M) and a real-time Revocation List (RL). Any ciphertext for user decryption should be sent to SEM for user revocation check first. Only passed ciphertext will be partially decrypted using SEM's SK_M. The output will be further sent to user for final decryption. If some users are revoked, SEM will not send the partial decryption result, named CT_M, to the revoked users.

Secondly, to achieve decryption outsourcing, we employ Green et al.'s idea by moving most of the decryption from user side to SEM side (Suppose SEM has strong computational power in cloud). Specifically, raise user's each part of secret key by $1/z(z \in_R Z_p^*)$ to get the partial decryption key for SEM (SK_M). Redefine user's secret key as $SK = (SK_M, z)$. SEM-Decrypt executed by SEM using SK_M will include all pairing operations. But SEM cannot finally decrypt it due to the absence of z. At last, user is only required to execute 1 exponentiation and 1 division to get the plaintext.

1.2   Related Work

ATTRIBUTE BASED ENCRYPTION. Sahai and Waters [1] proposed fuzzy identity-based encryption in 2005, which was also called attribute-based encryption when it is applied in the case that an encrypted document can only be decrypted by the user who have a certain set of attributes. In other words, a message encrypted by a set of attribute S can only be decrypted by a private key for another set of attributes S', if and only if $|S \cap S'| \geq d$, a Threshold.

Goyal et al. [2] classified it into key-policy attribute-based encryption (KP-ABE) and cipher-policy attribute-based encryption (CP-ABE), and further proposed a small universe KP-ABE supporting a more general access structure, *monotonic access tree*. Any policy/formula with AND and OR gates can be transformed to such access structure. It is selective-attribute CPA secure without random oracle. They also proposed a large universe KP-ABE which is selective-attribute CPA secure in random oracle. They for the first time proved that it is CCA secure by leveraging the delegation property of their large universe KP-ABE and applying the method in [3]. In 2007, Bethencourt et al. [4] gave the first construction of CP-ABE with monotonic access tree, which is selective-attribute CPA secure with random oracle. They also argued that with delegation property, their scheme is CCA secure. They implemented the ABE scheme using the Pairing Based Cryptography library [17]. In the same year, Cheung and Newport [5] proposed a CP-ABE scheme with access structures of AND gates on both positive and negative attributes. Ostrovsky et al. [6] extended Goyal et al.'s scheme [2] to support non-monotonic access structure, i.e., the Boolean formula involving AND, OR, NOT, and Threshold operations.

In 2011, Waters [11] proposed a selective-attribute CPA secure CP-ABE under DPBDHE assumption with ciphertext size, encryption, and decryption time scales linearly with the complexity of the access formula. Lewko et al. [14] proposed the first fully secure CP-ABE under 3 assumption by adapting Waters' dual system encryption technique in proof model [12]. Okamoto and Takashima [15] proposed a fully secure KP-ABE under DLIN assumption in the same year.

Yamada et al. [13] clearly defined the two properties, delegatability and verifiability in ABE, and argued that any CPA-secure ABE can be transformed to a CCA-secure ABE as long as it has either property above. They also instantiated the variation of Lewko et al.'s CP-ABE, which is fully CCA-secure.

ABE WITH REVOCATION. Bethencourt et al. [4] and Pirretti et al. [26,27] respectively realized *coarse-grained* attribute revocation by revoking attribute itself using timed rekeying mechanism, which was implemented by setting expiration time on each attribute. Attrapadung and Imai proposed ABE with user revocation [8] within similar method as described in [7]. Liang etc. proposed CP-ABE with revocation and it is proved secure under standard model [9]. Qian and Dong proposed Fully Secure Revocable ABE, combined dual encryption and user revocable ABE together to get fully secure ABE with user revocation [10]. However their schemes don't allow immediate revocation. For *fine-grained* user revocation, Ostrovsky et al. [6] proposed to add conjunctively the AND of negation of revoked user attributes. Yu et al. [19] achieved a CP-ABE scheme with immediate attribute revocation which is selective-CCA-secure. Hur and Noh [18] proposed attribute-based access control with efficient revocation without formal security proof. Sahai et al. [28] proposed a fully secure revocable key-policy ABE scheme without concerning Forward Secrecy. Ibraimi et al. combined Bethencourt et al.'s selective-CPA-secure CP-ABE [4] with Boneh et al.'s mediated cryptography [20] to propose a selective-CPA-secure mediated CP-ABE to support immediate user revocation with application [25].

ABE WITH DECRYPTION OUTSOURCING. Green et al. [16] proposed a new paradigm by outsourcing the main decryption computation workload of Waters' CP-ABE [11], and proved it secure in Replayable CCA model, followed by implementing it using PBC library [17].

2   Preliminaries

We review Bilinear maps, decisional $q - parallel$ Bilinear Diffie-Hellman Exponent problem and linear secret sharing scheme.

2.1   Bilinear Maps

We review some facts related to groups with efficiently computable bilinear maps in [11] and then give our number theoretic assumptions. Let $\mathbb{G}$ and $\mathbb{G}_T$ be two multiplicative cyclic groups of prime order p. Let g be a generator of $\mathbb{G}$ and e be a bilinear map, $e : \mathbb{G} \times \mathbb{G} \to \mathbb{G}_T$. The bilinear map e has the following properties:

1. Bilinearity: for all $u, v \in \mathbb{G}$ and $a, b \in \mathbb{Z}_p$, we have $e(u^a, v^b) = e(u, v)^{ab}$.
2. Non-degeneracy: $e(g, g) \neq 1$.

We say that $\mathbb{G}$ is a bilinear group if the group operation in $\mathbb{G}$ and the bilinear map $e : \mathbb{G} \times \mathbb{G} \to \mathbb{G}_T$ are both efficiently computable. Notice that the map e is symmetric since $e(g^a, g^b) = e(g, g)^{ab} = e(g^b, g^a)$.

2.2   Decisional Parallel BDHE Assumption

We review the definition of decisional $q-parallel$ Bilinear Diffie-Hellman Exponent problem in [11] as follows. Choose a group $\mathbb{G}$ of prime order p according to the security parameter λ. Let $a, s, b_1, \ldots, b_q \in \mathbb{Z}_p$ be chosen at random and g be a generator of $\mathbb{G}$. If an adversary is given $\boldsymbol{y} =$

$$g, g^s, g^a, \ldots, g^{a^q}, , g^{a^{q+2}}, \ldots, g^{a^{2q}}$$
$$\forall_{1 \leq j \leq q} g^{s \cdot b_j}, g^{a/b_j}, \ldots, g^{a^q/b_j}, , g^{a^{q+2}/b_j}, \ldots, g^{a^{2q}/b_j}$$
$$\forall_{1 \leq j \leq q, k \neq j} g^{a \cdot s \cdot b_k/b_j}, \ldots, g^{a^q \cdot s \cdot b_k/b_j},$$

it is hard to distinguish $e(g, g)^{a^{q+1}s} \in \mathbb{G}_T$ from a random element R in $\mathbb{G}_T$.

An algorithm $\mathcal{B}$ that outputs $z \in \{0, 1\}$ has advantage ϵ in solving decisional q-parallel BDHE in $\mathbb{G}$ if

$$|Pr[\mathcal{B}(\boldsymbol{y}, T = e(g, g)^{a^{q+1}s}) = 0] - Pr[\mathcal{B}(\boldsymbol{y}, T = R) = 0]| \geq \epsilon$$

Definition 1. *We say that the (decision) q-parallel-BDHE assumption holds if no polynomial time algorithm $\mathcal{B}$ has a non-negligible advantage in solving the decisional q-parallel BDHE problem.*

2.3   Linear Secret Sharing Schemes

We review the definition of linear secret sharing scheme (LSSS) in [11] as follows.

Definition 2. (Linear Secret-Sharing Schemes (LSSS)) *A secret-sharing scheme over a set of parties $\mathcal{P}$ is called linear (over $\mathbb{Z}_p$) if*

1. *The shares for each party form a vector over $\mathbb{Z}_p$.*
2. *There exists a matrix an M with ℓ rows and n columns called the share-generating matrix for Π. For all $i = 1, \ldots, \ell$, the i'th row of M, we let the function ρ defined the party labelling row i as $\rho(i)$. When we consider the column vector $v = (s, r_2, \ldots, r_n)$, where $s \in \mathbb{Z}_p$ is the secret to be shared, and $r_2, \ldots, r_n \in \mathbb{Z}_p$ are randomly chosen, then Mv is the vector of ℓ shares of the secret s according to Π. The share $(Mv)_i$ belongs to party $\rho(i)$.*

It is shown in [11] that every LSSS according to the above definition also enjoys the *linear reconstruction* property, defined as follows: Suppose that Π is an LSSS for the access structure $\mathbb{A}$. Let $S \in \mathbb{A}$ be any authorized set, and let $I \subset \{1, 2, \ldots, \ell\}$ be defined as $I = \{i : \rho(i) \in S\}$. Then, there exist constants $\{\omega_i \in \mathbb{Z}_p\}_{i \in I}$ such that, if $\{\lambda_i\}$ are valid shares of any secret s according to Π, then $\sum_{i \in I} \omega_i \lambda_i = s$. Furthermore, it is shown in [11] that these constants ω_i can be found in time polynomial in the size of the share-generating matrix M.

3   Definition of CP-ABE with SEM

We review the definition of CP-ABE with SEM in [25] here. Let S represent a set of attributes, and $\mathbb{A}$ an access structure. We defines $\mathbb{A}$ and S as the inputs to the encryption and key generation algorithm, and the function $f(S, \mathbb{A})$ outputs 1 iff the attribute set S satisfies the access structure $\mathbb{A}$, respectively.

Definition 3. *CP-ABE with SEM, $CP-ABE_{SEM}$ consists of five algorithms:*

$(PK, MSK) \leftarrow$ Setup(λ, U). This algorithm takes security parameter λ and universe U as input. It outputs public parameters PK and master key MSK.

$CT \leftarrow$ Encrypt$(PK, m, \mathbb{A})$. This algorithm takes as input public parameters PK, a message m and an access structure $\mathbb{A}$. It outputs ciphertext CT.

$(SK_U, SK_M) \leftarrow$ KeyGen(MSK, S). This algorithm takes as input master key MSK and an attribute set S. It outputs secret key SK_U and SEM's key SK_M.

$CT_M \leftarrow$ SEM-Decrypt(SK_M, CT). The mediated decryption algorithm takes as input SEM's key SK_M for S and a ciphertext CT that was encrypted under $\mathbb{A}$. It outputs the partially decrypted ciphertext CT_M if $f(S, \mathbb{A}) = 1$. Otherwise, the error symbol $\perp$ is returned.

$M/\perp \leftarrow$ User-Decrypt(SK_U, CT_M). The decrypt algorithm takes as input SK_U for S and CT_M that was originally encrypted under $\mathbb{A}$. It outputs the message m if $f(S, \mathbb{A}) = 1$ and (SK_U, SK_M) were created together. Otherwise, the error symbol $\perp$ is returned.

Some Terminologies. We define some terminologies and properties related to access structures here. Any monotonic (resp., non-monotonic) access structure $\mathbb{A}$ can be represented by a corresponding Boolean formula (resp., with negation), which we denote by $\phi(\mathbb{A})$, over variables in U. This is naturally defined in the sense that $f(S, \mathbb{A}) = 1$ holds iff the evaluation of $\phi(\mathbb{A})$ with the assignment that sets all variables in S to 1 and other variables outside S to 0 yields the value 1.

Consider the case where $\mathbb{A}$ is a monotonic access structure over U. If we denote a minimal representation of $\mathbb{A}$ by $\min(\mathbb{A}) = \{f(S, \mathbb{A}) = 1|$ there exists no $B \in \mathbb{A}$ such that $f(B, \mathbb{A}) = 1\}$. Then, it is straightforward to see that $\phi(\mathbb{A}) = \vee_{S' \in min(\mathbb{A})}(\wedge_{P \in S'} P)$.

For simplicity, we will use the access structure $\mathbb{A}$ and its corresponding Boolean formula $\phi(\mathbb{A})$ interchangeably when specifying a policy.

3.1   Fully-RCCA-CCA Security Model for CP-ABE with SEM

Consider a multi-party ABE with SEM system, where there are a lot of registered users and a mediator with real-time revocation list. An adversary $\mathcal{A}$ of time complexity of polynomial has the following capabilities.

1. $\mathcal{A}$ can corrupt users as his wish in the system to obtain their user secret keys SK_U and the corresponding SK_M from the mediator.

2. $\mathcal{A}$ can make SEM-Decrypt queries to get partially decrypted ciphertext CT_M.
3. $\mathcal{A}$ can make User-Decrypt queries to get plaintext m.

The goal of the adversary $\mathcal{A}$ is either of the two following outputs.

- A partially decrypted ciphertext CT_M for user key SK_U to decrypt although $\mathcal{A}$ has no knowledge of the corresponding SK_M. In particular, the user with SK_U has been revoked by SEM. So SEM will not help to partially decrypt ciphertext CT_M for the user. $\mathcal{A}$ tries to calculate CT_M without knowing SEM's SK_M. If it is the case, $\mathcal{A}$ can further decrypt CT_M successfully.
- A plaintext m decrypted from a partially decrypted ciphertext CT_M by SK_U. In particular, the user is valid and SEM helps to get CT_M. $\mathcal{A}$ tries to successfully decrypt CT_M to get m without knowing SK_U.

To clearly define $\mathcal{A}$'s capabilities and goal, we formally define two games.

Definition 4 [Security of a CP-ABE with SEM]. Let CP-ABE$_{SEM}$ = (Setup, Encrypt, KeyGen, SEM-Decrypt, User-Decrypt) be a CP-ABE with SEcurity Mediator scheme, $\mathcal{A}$ an adversary, $\lambda \in N$ a security parameter. We associate to CP-ABE$_{SEM}$, $\mathcal{A}$ and λ an experiment $\mathbf{Exp}_{CP-ABE_{SEM}}^{IND-RCCA-CCA}(\lambda)$ including the following two games.

In this definition, "RCCA-CCA" means security against users is RCCA while security against SEM is CCA. Now two Games are defined.

In Game-1, $\mathcal{A}$'s target is user.

Game-1
Setup. The challenger $\mathcal{C}$ runs Setup and gives PK to the adversary $\mathcal{A}$.
Phase 1. $\mathcal{C}$ initializes an empty table T_1, an empty set D_1 and an integer $j = 0$. Proceeding adaptively, $\mathcal{A}$ can repeatedly make any of these queries:

- Create(S). $\mathcal{C}$ sets $j := j + 1$. It runs KeyGen on S to obtain the pair (SK_U, SK_M) and stores in table T_1 the entry (j, S, SK_U, SK_M). It then returns to $\mathcal{A}$ SEM's key SK_M.

Note: Create can be repeatedly queried with the same input.

- Corrupt(i). If there exists an ith entry in table T_1, then $\mathcal{C}$ obtains the entry (i, S, SK_U, SK_M) and sets $D_1 := D_1 \cup \{S\}$. It then returns to $\mathcal{A}$ user's secret key SK_U. If no such entry exists, then it returns $\perp$.

- Decrypt(i, CT_M). If there exists an ith entry in table T_1, then $\mathcal{C}$ obtains the entry (i, S, SK_U, SK_M) and returns to $\mathcal{A}$ the output of the decryption algorithm on input (SK_U, CT_M). If no such entry exists, then it returns $\perp$.

- Challenge. $\mathcal{A}$ submits two equal-length messages m_0 and m_1. In addition, $\mathcal{A}$ gives a value $\mathbb{A}^*$ such that for all $S \in D_1$, $f(S, \mathbb{A}^*) \neq 1$. The challenger flips a random coin b, and encrypts m_b under $\mathbb{A}^*$. CT^* is given to $\mathcal{A}$.

Phase 2. Phase 1 is repeated with the restrictions that $\mathcal{A}$ cannot

- trivially obtain a secret key of user for the challenged ciphertext. That is, it cannot issue a Corrupt query that would result in a value S which satisfies $f(S, \mathbb{A}^*) = 1$ being added to D_1.

- issue a trivial decryption query. That is, Decrypt queries will be answered as in Phase 1, except that if the response would be either m_0 or m_1, then C responds with the special message *test* instead.

Guess. The adversary $\mathcal{A}$ outputs a guess b' of b.

The advantage of $\mathcal{A}$ in this game is Adv $_{\text{Game-1}}(\mathcal{A}) = |Prob(b = b') - 1/2|$.

In Game-2, $\mathcal{A}$'s target is SEM.

Game-2

Setup. The challenger C runs Setup and gives PK to the adversary $\mathcal{A}$.

Phase 1. C initializes an empty table T_2, an empty set D_2 and an integer $j = 0$. Proceeding adaptively, $\mathcal{A}$ can repeatedly make any of these queries:

- Create(S). C sets $j := j + 1$. It runs KeyGen on S to obtain the pair (SK_U, SK_M) and stores in table T_2 the entry (j, S, SK_U, SK_M). It then returns to $\mathcal{A}$ user's secret key SK_U.

Note: Create can be repeatedly queried with the same input.

- Corrupt(i). If there exists an ith entry in table T_2, then C obtains the entry (i, S, SK_U, SK_M) and sets $D_2 := D_2 \cup \{S\}$. It then returns to $\mathcal{A}$ SEM's key SK_M. If no such entry exists, then it returns $\perp$.

Challenge. $\mathcal{A}$ submits two equal-length messages m_0 and m_1. In addition, $\mathcal{A}$ gives a value $\mathbb{A}^*$ such that for all $S \in D_2, f(S, \mathbb{A}) = 1$. The challenger flips a random coin b, encrypts m_b under $\mathbb{A}^*$ and gives ciphertext CT^* to $\mathcal{A}$.

Phase 2. Phase 1 is repeated, except CT^* can not be queried.

Guess. The adversary $\mathcal{A}$ outputs a guess b' of b.

The advantage of $\mathcal{A}$ is defined as $\mathsf{Adv}_{\text{Game-2}}(\mathcal{A}) = |Prob(b = b') - 1/2|$.

The adversary $\mathcal{A}$ wins with advantage $\mathsf{Adv}_{\text{Game-1}}(\mathcal{A}) + \mathsf{Adv}_{\text{Game-2}}(\mathcal{A})$.

A CP-ABE with SEM scheme is RCCA-CCA-secure if Adv $_{\text{Game-1}}(\mathcal{A}) +$ Adv $_{\text{Game-2}}(\mathcal{A}) < \epsilon$, where ϵ is negligible.   □

4   Our Construction of CP-ABE with SEM

We now give our main construction of CP-ABE with SEM. Setup(λ, U). This algorithm takes as input the security parameter λ and the attribute universe description $U = \{0, 1\}^*$. First we need to utilize a set W of dummy attributes, which is disjoint from U. A set of dummy attributes will then be associated to a verification key vk of a one-time signature scheme used in Encrypt algorithm. Set $W = \{P_{1,0}, P_{1,1}, P_{2,0}, P_{2,1}, \ldots, P_{\ell,0}, P_{\ell,1}\}$, where ℓ denotes the number of the rows in the LSSS matrix and $P_{i,j}$ are dummy attributes. Then choose the dummy attribute set $S_{vk} \subset W$ for all $vk \in \{0, 1\}$ by setting $S_{vk} = \{P_{1,vk_1}, P_{2,vk_2}, \ldots, P_{\ell,vk_\ell}\}$. Then the algorithm chooses a bilinear group $\mathbb{G}$ of order $N = p_1 p_2 p_3$ (3 distinct primes). Use $\mathbb{G}_{p_i}$ to denote the subgroup of order p_i in $\mathbb{G}$. Then it chooses random exponents $\alpha, a \in \mathbb{Z}_N$, a random group element $g \in \mathbb{G}_{p_1}$ and two hash functions $H_1 : \{0, 1\}^* \to \mathbb{Z}_p$ and $H_2 : \{0, 1\}^* \to \{0, 1\}^k$. For each attribute $i \in \{U \cup W\}$, it chooses a random value $s_i \in \mathbb{Z}_N$.

The public parameters PK are $N, g, g^a, e(g,g)^\alpha, T_i = g^{s_i} \forall i, H_1, H_2$ and a generator X_3 of $\mathbb{G}_{p_3}$. The master secret key MSK is g^α.

KeyGen(MSK, S, PK). This algorithm takes as input the master secret key MSK, public key PK and an attribute set S, where $S \subset U$. It outputs the user's key SK_U and SEM's key $SK_M^{S'}$ for the attribute set S' where $S' = S \cup W$. The algorithm chooses a random $t' \in \mathbb{Z}_N$, and random elements $R_0, R_0', R_i \in \mathbb{G}_{p_3}$. Let $SK' = (PK, K' = g^\alpha g^{at'} R_0, L' = g^{t'} R_0', \{K_x' = T_i^{t'} R_i\}_{x \in S'})$. Then choose $z \in_R \mathbb{Z}_p^*$ as user's secret key SK_U. Let $t = t'/z$ and set SEM's key as

$$SK_M^{S'} = (PK, K = K'^{1/z} = g^{\alpha/z} g^{at'/z} = g^{\alpha/z} g^{at}, L = L'^{1/z} = g^{t'/z} =$$

$$g^t, \{K_x\}_{x \in S'} = \{K_x'^{1/z}\}_{x \in S'}).$$

Encrypt($PK, \mathbb{A} = (M, \rho), m \in \{0,1\}^k$). It takes as input an LSSS access structure $\mathbb{A} = (M, \rho)$, the public parameters PK and a message m to encrypt, where M is an $\ell \times n$ LSSS matrix and the function ρ associates each row M_i to attribute $\rho(i)$. Let the dummy policy $\mathbb{A}' = \mathbb{A} \wedge (\wedge_{P \in S_{vk}} P)$. The algorithm outputs the ciphertext encrypted under policy $\mathbb{A}' = (M', \rho')$, where M' is an $\ell' \times n'$ LSSS matrix and the function ρ' associates each row $M_n'i$ to attribute $\rho'(i)$. The algorithm chooses a vector $v \in_R \mathbb{Z}_p^{n'}$, denoted $v = (s, v_2, \ldots, v_{n'})$. For each row of M', i.e., the vector M_i', calculate $\lambda_i = v \cdot M_i'$. Then choose $r_i \in_R \mathbb{Z}_p$ for $i = 1, \cdots, \ell'$. Then it selects a random $R \in \mathbb{G}_T$ and computes $s = H_1(R, m)$ and $r = H_2(R)$. An attribute parameter can be derived into an element in the group $\mathbb{G}$ by a function $F : \{0,1\}^* \to \mathbb{G}$. The ciphertext CT is shown as

$$(C = Re(g,g)^{\alpha s}, C' = g^s, C'' = m \oplus r, C_i = g^{a\lambda_i} \cdot F(\rho'(i))^{-r_i}, D_i = g^{r_i} \forall i),$$

and CT implicitly contains the access structure $\mathbb{A}' = (M', \rho')$.

Let $\Sigma = (\mathcal{G}, \mathcal{S}, \mathcal{V})$ be a one-time signature scheme. The algorithm creates a one-time signature key pair by running $\mathcal{G} \to (vk, sk)$. It then runs $\mathcal{S}(sk, CT) \to \sigma$. And the algorithm outputs $CT' = (vk, CT, \sigma)$.

SEM-Decrypt($PK, CT', SK_M^{S'}$). It takes as input a ciphertext CT' for a linear access structure $\mathbb{A}' = (M', \rho')$, PK and SEM's key $SK_M^{S'} = (PK, K, L, \{K_x\}_{x \in S'})$ for a set S', where $S' = S \cup W$. It parses the ciphertext CT' as (vk, CT, σ). If $\mathcal{V}(vk, CT, \sigma) = 0$, then it outputs $\perp$.

Otherwise, the mediator can get $SK_M^{S \cup S_{vk}}$ as $(PK, K^{S \cup S_{vk}}, L^{S \cup S_{vk}}, \{K_x^{S \cup S_{vk}}\}_{x \in S})$ for the set $S \cup S_{vk}$ within the method **Delegate** described in [13] as follows. Since S_{vk} is a subset of W, $S \cup S_{vk}$ is a subset of S'. The algorithm random chooses $u \in \mathbb{Z}_N$ and random elements $R_0, R_0', R_i \in G_{p_3}$, and computes

$$(PK, K^{S \cup S_{vk}} = Kg^{au} R_0, L^{S \cup S_{vk}} = Lg^u R_0', \{K_x^{S \cup S_{vk}}\}_{x \in S} = K_i T_i^u R_i, \forall i \in$$
$$S \cup S_{vk}) \text{ as } SK_M^{S \cup S_{vk}}.$$

Let $I \subset \{1, 2, \cdots, \ell\}$ be defined as $I = \{i : \rho(i) \in S \cup S_{vk}\}$. Then, let $\{\omega_i \in \mathbb{Z}_p\}_{i \in I}$ be a set of constants such that if $\{\lambda_i\}$ are valid shares of any secret s according to M, then $\sum_{i \in I} \omega_i \lambda_i = s$. Then SEM computes

$$e(C', K^{S \cup S_{vk}}) / \left(e(\prod_{i \in I} C_i^{\omega_i}, L^{S \cup S_{vk}}) \cdot \prod_{i \in I} (e(D_i^{\omega_i}, K_{\rho(i)}^{S \cup S_{vk}})) \right)$$

$$= e(g^s, g^{\alpha/z} g^{at} g^{au}) / \left(e(\prod_{i \in I} g^{a\lambda_i \omega_i}, g^t g^u) \cdot \prod_{i \in I} e(T_{\rho(i)}^{-r_i}, g^t g^u) \prod_{i \in I} (e(g^{r_i \omega_i}, T_{\rho(i)}^{tu})) \right)$$

$$= e(g^s, g^{\alpha/z}) e(g^s, g^{at}) e(g^s, g^{au}) / \left(e(g^{as}, g^t g^u) \prod_{i \in I} e(T_{\rho(i)}^{-r_i}, g^t g^u) \prod_{i \in I} e(g^{r_i}, T_{\rho(i)}^{tu}) \right)$$

$$= e(g,g)^{\alpha s/z},$$

and sends the partially decrypted ciphertext $CT_M = (C, C'', e(g,g)^{\alpha s/z})$ to user. User-Decrypt(CT_M, SK_U). It takes as input a partially decrypted ciphertext CT_M for a linear access structure (M, ρ), user's secret key SK_U for a set S. It parses CT_M as (CT_0, CT_1, CT_2), and computes $R = CT_0 / CT_2^z$, $m = CT_1 \oplus H_2(R)$, and $s = H_1(R, m)$. If $CT_0 = R \cdot e(g,g)^{\alpha s}$ and $CT_2 = e(g,g)^{\alpha s/z}$, it outputs m; otherwise, it outputs the error symbol $\perp$.

In our construction, if a user has appropriate attribute set S to match the access structure $\mathbb{A}$ on the ciphertext CT, i.e. $f(S, \mathbb{A}) = 1$, the user can decrypt the partially decrypted ciphertext CT_M correctly and get the plaintext.

User Revocation. In our construction, Security Mediator holds a revocation list (RL), which records the revoked users. The mediator can add a user into the revocation list or delete a user from RL. When execute SEM-Decrypt algorithm, SEM will check the revocation list first. If a user is revoked, Security Mediator won't pass the partially decrypted ciphertext CT_M to the user, and the revoked user cannot finish the User-Decrypt algorithm to get the plaintext.

4.1   Security Proof

Theorem 1. *Let Π be a Waters' scheme in [11] and Σ' is our $CP - ABE_{SEM}$ scheme. If Π is a CPA-secure CP-ABE scheme, then our scheme $CP - ABE_{SEM}$ is fully-RCCA-secure.*

Theorem 2. *Let Π be a Waters' scheme in [11] and Σ is a one-time signature, Σ' is our $CP - ABE_{SEM}$ scheme. If Π is a $(\tau, \epsilon_{ABE}, q)$CPA-secure CP-ABE scheme, Σ is (τ, ϵ_{OTS}) secure, then our scheme $CP - ABE_{SEM}$ is $(\tau - o(\tau), \epsilon_{ABE} + \epsilon_{OTS}, q_D, q_E)$ fully-CCA-secure where $q \geq q_D + q_E$.*

Proof 1. Suppose there exists a polynomial-time adversary $\mathcal{A}$, who can break our scheme in our new fully RCCA-security model with non-negligible advantage ϵ, Then we can build a simulator $\mathcal{B}$ for $\mathcal{A}$ who can break Waters' scheme in [11] in the selective CPA-secure model with advantage ϵ minus a negligible amount. However, in [11], Waters' scheme has been proven secure under the decisional parallel BDHE assumption. That is a contradiction.

Setup. $\mathcal{B}$ obtains the public parameter $PK = (g, e(g,g)^\alpha, g^a, F)$, where F is a hash function from Waters' scheme. $\mathcal{B}$ initializes the empty tables T_1, T_{H_1}, T_{H_2}, an empty set D, and an integer $j = 0$. It sends PK to $\mathcal{A}$ as the public parameter.

Phase 1. $\mathcal{B}$ answers $\mathcal{A}$'s queries as follows.

- Random Oracle Hash $H_1(R, m)$. $\mathcal{B}$ checks the table T_{H_1} first. If there exists an entry (R, m, s) in T_{H_1}, returns s to $\mathcal{A}$. Otherwise, $\mathcal{B}$ chooses $s \in_R \mathbb{Z}_p$, records (R, m, s) in T_{H_1} and returns s to $\mathcal{A}$.
- Random Oracle Hash $H_2(R)$. $\mathcal{B}$ checks the table T_{H_2} first. If there exists an entry (R, r) in T_{H_2}, returns r to $\mathcal{A}$. Otherwise, $\mathcal{B}$ chooses $r \in_R \mathbb{Z}_p$, records (R, r) in T_{H_2} and returns r to $\mathcal{A}$.
- Create(S): $\mathcal{B}$ sets $j := j + 1$ and proceeds one of two ways.

– If S satisfies $\mathbb{A}^* = (M^*, \rho^*)$, i.e., $f(S, \mathbb{A}^*) = 1$, $\mathcal{B}$ chooses a fake key pair (SK_U, SK_M): choose $d \in_R \mathbb{Z}_p$ and run KeyGen(g^d, S, PK) to obtain SK'

$$SK' = (PK, K' = g^d g^{at'}, L' = g^{t'}, \left\{ K'_x = F(x)^{t'} \right\}_{x \in S}).$$

Set $SK_M = SK'$. Let $d = \alpha/z$, replace d by α/z and we have $SK_M =$

$$(PK, g^{\alpha/z} g^{at'}, L' = g^{t'}, \left\{ F(x)^{t'} \right\}_{x \in S}) =$$
$$(PK, K = K'^{1/z} = (g^\alpha g^{at''})^{1/z}, L = L'^{1/z} =$$
$$g^{t''/z}, \left\{ K_x = K'^{1/z}_x = (F(x)^{t''})^{1/z} \right\}_{x \in S}).$$

By the replacement, SK_M is properly distributed.

– Otherwise, $\mathcal{B}$ calls Waters' key generation oracle on S to obtain $SK' = (PK, K', L', \{K'_x\}_{x \in S})$. Then, it chooses $z \in_R \mathbb{Z}_p$ and sets

$$SK_M = (PK, K = K'^{1/z}, L = L'_{1/z}, \left\{ K_x = K'^{1/z}_x \right\}_{x \in S}), SK_U = z.$$

Finally, $\mathcal{B}$ stores (j, S, SK_U, SK_M) in the table T and returns SK_M to $\mathcal{A}$.

- Corrupt(i): If no such entry exists (i.e., $i > j_{max}$), or if S in the ith entry (i, S, SK_U, SK_M) satisfies $\mathbb{A}^*$, $\mathcal{B}$ returns $\perp$. Otherwise, $\mathcal{B}$ returns SK_U to $\mathcal{A}$.
- Decrypt(i, CT_M). Let $CT_M = (CT_0, CT_1, CT_2)$ be associated with an access structure $\mathbb{A} = (M, \rho)$. Let j_{max} denote the currently maximum j of the table T.

If $i > j_{max}$, there is no satisfactory entry (i, S, SK_U, SK_M) exists. Then returns $\perp$. If there exists the ith entry (i, S, SK_U, SK_M) in T while $f(S, \mathbb{A}) \neq 1$, $\mathcal{B}$ returns $\perp$, too. Then $\mathcal{B}$ proceeds one of the following two ways.

– If the ith entry (i, S, SK_U, SK_M) does not satisfy the challenge structure $\mathbb{A}^* = (M^*, \rho^*)$, it proceeds as follows.

1. Compute $R = C_0/C_2^z$.

2. Obtain the records (R, m_x, s_x) from T_{H_1}. If no such record exists, return $\perp$. If there exists indices $x_1 \neq x_2$ such that (R, m_{x_1}, s_{x_1}) and (R, m_{x_2}, s_{x_2}) are in T_{H_1}, and $m_{x_1} \neq m_{x_2}$ while $s_{x_1} = s_{x_2}$, $\mathcal{B}$ aborts. As s_{x_1} and s_{x_2} are randomly chosen in $\mathbb{Z}_p$, the probability $\mathcal{B}$ aborts is $(1 - p!/((p - q_{H_1})! \cdot p^{q_{H_1}}))$.
3. Obtain the records (R, r) from T_{H_2}. If no such record exists, return $\perp$.
4. Test if $CT_0 = R(e(g, g)^\alpha)^{s_x}, CT_1 = m \oplus r, CT_2 = e(g, g)^{\alpha s_i/z}$, for each i in the records (R, m_x, s_x) in step 2.

If there is an x passes the above test, return m_x to $\mathcal{A}$. Otherwise return $\perp$.
- If the ith entry (i, S, SK_U, SK_M) satisfies (M^*, ρ^*), it proceeds as follows.

1. Compute $\beta = C_2^{1/d}$.
2. For each record (R_x, m_x, s_x) in table T_{H_1}, test if $\beta = e(g, g)^{s_x}$.
3. If no match is found, $\mathcal{B}$ returns $\perp$.
4. If more than one match are found, $\mathcal{B}$ aborts the simulation.
5. Otherwise, let (R, m, s) be the sole match. Obtain the record (R, r) in table T_{H_2}. If it does not exist, $\mathcal{B}$ returns $\perp$.
6. Test if $CT_0 = R \cdot e(g, g)^{\alpha s}, CT_1 = m \oplus r$ and $CT_2 = e(g, g)^{ds}$. If all tests pass, output m; else, output $\perp$.

Challenge. $\mathcal{A}$ submits two messages $(m_0^*, m_1^*) \in \{0, 1\}^{2k}$. $\mathcal{B}$ acts as follows.

1. $\mathcal{B}$ chooses random $(R_0, R_1) \in \mathbb{G}_T^2$ and passes them onto Waters' challenger to obtain ciphertext $CT_b = (C, C', \{C_i, D_i\}_{i \in \{1, \cdots, \ell\}})$ under (M^*, ρ^*), $b \in \{0, 1\}$.
2. $\mathcal{B}$ chooses a random value $C'' \in \{0, 1\}^k$.
3. $\mathcal{B}$ sends the ciphertext $CT'' = (C, C', C'', \{C_i, D_i\}_{i \in [1, \cdots, \ell]})$ to $\mathcal{A}$.

Phase 2. $\mathcal{B}$ continues to answer queries as in **Phase 1**, except that if the response to a **Decrypt** query would be either m_0^* or m_1^*, then $\mathcal{B}$ answers **test**.

Guess. Eventually, $\mathcal{A}$ must either output a bit or abort, either way $\mathcal{B}$ ignores it. R_0 and R_1 are never revealed to $\mathcal{A}$ except in the challenge ciphertext. A necessary condition for $\mathcal{A}$ to win is to query the hash of the value it obtained from the challenge ciphertext. Since the advantage for $\mathcal{A}$ to break the scheme is ϵ, the probability for $\mathcal{A}$ to query to either or both R_0 and R_1 should be at least ϵ. (If $\mathcal{A}$ does not make the query, it can only win by random guessing.) Next, $\mathcal{B}$ searches through tables T_{H_1} and T_{H_2} to see if R_0 or R_1 appears as the first value in any entry (i.e., $\mathcal{A}$ once issued a query of the form $H_1(R_b)$ or $H_2(R_b)$.)

$\mathcal{B}$'s advantage in **Game 1** is obviously negligible, and Theorem 1 is RCCA secure within this negligible advantage. The proof of Theorem 1 is complete. $\square$

Proof 2. Assume we are given an adversary $\mathcal{A}$ which breaks CCA-security of our scheme Σ' with running time τ, advantage ϵ, q_E key-extraction queries, and, q_D decryption queries. We use $\mathcal{A}$ to construct another adversary $\mathcal{B}$ which breaks CPA-security of the ABE scheme Σ. Describe the game 2 as follows:

Setup. The challenger runs $\mathsf{Setup}(\lambda, U \cup W) \rightarrow (PK, MSK)$. Then $\mathcal{B}$ is given PK and gives it to $\mathcal{A}$. $\mathcal{B}$ also runs $\mathcal{G}(\lambda) \rightarrow (vk^*, sk^*)$.

Phase 1. $\mathcal{A}$ may adaptively make queries of the following types:

- Key-extraction query. When $\mathcal{A}$ submits S, $\mathcal{B}$ submits $S \cup W$ to the challenger. $\mathcal{B}$ is given $SK^{S \cup W}$ for $S \cup W$ and chooses a random $z \in \mathbb{Z}_N$. $\mathcal{B}$ calculates $SK_M^{S \cup W} = (SK^{S \cup W})^{1/z}$ and $SK_U = z$, then gives them to $\mathcal{A}$.
- Decryption query. When $\mathcal{A}$ submits (CT', S) such that $CT' = (vk, CT, \sigma)$, $\mathcal{B}$ first checks whether $\mathcal{V}(vk, CT, \sigma)$ holds. If it does not hold, then $\mathcal{B}$ returns $\perp$. If it holds and $vk^* = vk$, then $\mathcal{B}$ aborts. Otherwise, $\mathcal{B}$ submits $S \cup S_{vk}$ to the challenger and is given $SK_{S \cup S_{vk}}$. Then $\mathcal{B}$ rerandomizes it by $SK^{S \cup S_{vk}} \leftarrow$ Delegate$(PK, SK^{S \cup S_{vk}}, S \cup S_{vk}, S \cup S_{vk})$ and calculates $SK_M^{S \cup S_{vk}}$ by randomly choose $z \in \mathbb{Z}_N$. It returns output of SEM-Decrypt$(PK, CT, SK_M^{S \cup S_{vk}})$ to $\mathcal{A}$.

Challenge. $\mathcal{A}$ declares two equal length messages m_0^*, m_1^* and $\mathbb{A}^*$. Then $\mathcal{B}$ declares the same messages m_0^*, m_1^* and $\mathbb{A}'^*$ for the challenger, where $\mathbb{A}'^*$ is an access structure such that $\psi(\mathbb{A}'^*) = \psi(\mathbb{A}^*) \wedge (\wedge_{P \in S_{vk}} P)$. The challenger flips a random coin $b \in \{0, 1\}$, runs Encrypt$(PK, M_\beta, \psi(\mathbb{A}'^*)) \to CT^*$ and gives CT^* to $\mathcal{B}$. Then $\mathcal{B}$ runs $\mathcal{S}(sk^*, CT^*) \to \sigma^*$ and gives $CT'^* = (VK^*, CT^*, \sigma^*)$ to $\mathcal{A}$ as challenge ciphertext. $\mathcal{B}$ also choose a random $z \in \mathbb{Z}_N$ as SK_U and gives it to $\mathcal{A}$.

Phase 2. $\mathcal{B}$ answers $\mathcal{A}$'s query where $f(S, \mathbb{A}^*) \neq 1, CT \neq CT^*$ as in Phase 1.

Guess. Finally, $\mathcal{A}$ outputs a guess b' for b. Then $\mathcal{B}$ outputs b' as its guess.

Let Win denote the event that $\mathcal{A}$ guess b correctly, Abort denote the event that $\mathcal{B}$ aborts. If Abort does not occur, $\mathcal{B}$'s simulation is perfect. So, $\mathcal{B}$'s advantage for guessing β is estimated as $Pr[\mathcal{B}$ correctly guess $\beta] - \frac{1}{2} = Pr[\text{Win}|\overline{\text{Abort}}]Pr[\overline{\text{Abort}}] - \frac{1}{2} \geq \epsilon - Pr[\overline{\text{Abort}}]$. Since $Pr[\overline{\text{Abort}}] \leq \epsilon_{OTS}$ holds due to the unforgeability of the one-time-signature, Theorem 2 holds. Thus the proof is completed.   □

According to the proofs of Theorems 1 and 2 above, our scheme $CP - ABE_{SEM}$ is a fully-RCCA-CCA-secure CP-ABE with SEM scheme.

5   Conclusion and Discussion

User revocation and decryption outsourcing are two issues for Attribute-Based Encryption scheme apart from practice. To solve them, we propose a fully-ReplayableCCA-CCA-secure Ciphertext-Policy-ABE with SEcurity Mediator, CP-ABE with SEM for short. It introduces SEM for checking the validity of user immediately with a real-time revocation list, and partially decrypting the ciphertext if the user is unrevoked. One interesting future work is to further reduce the computation overload by using prime-order cyclic group without composite-order one. Another direction is to construct a fully-CCA-secure ABE with SEM.

Acknowledgments. The paper is funded by the National Natural Science Foundation of China under Grants 61402136 and 61240011, Shenzhen Development and Reform Commission [2012]720, Shenzhen Development and Reform Commission [2012]900, Shenzhen Basic Research JC201104210032A and JC201005260112A, and the Seed Funding Programme for Basic Research, HKU 201311159040.

References

1. Sahai, A., Waters, B.: Fuzzy identity-based encryption. In: Cramer, R. (ed.) EURO-CRYPT 2005. LNCS, vol. 3494, pp. 457–473. Springer, Heidelberg (2005)
2. Goyal, V., Pandey, O., Sahai, A., Waters, B.: Attribute-based encryption for fine-grained access control of encrypted data. In: 13th ACM Conference on Computer and Communications Security (CCS 2006), pp. 89–98 (2006)
3. Canetti, R., Halevi, S., Katz, J.: Chosen-ciphertext security from identity-based encryption. In: Cachin, C., Camenisch, J.L. (eds.) EUROCRYPT 2004. LNCS, vol. 3027, pp. 207–222. Springer, Heidelberg (2004)
4. Bethencourt, J., Sahai, A., Waters, B.: Ciphertext-policy attribute-based encryption. In: IEEE Symposium on Security and Privacy (SP 2007), pp. 321–334 (2007)
5. Cheung, L., Newport, C.: Provably secure ciphertext policy ABE. In: 14th ACM conference on Computer and communications security (CCS 2007), pp. 456–465 (2007)
6. Ostrovsky, R., Sahai, A., Waters, B.: Attribute-based encryption with non-monotonic access structures. In: 14th ACM Conference on Computer and Communications Security (CCS 2007), pp. 195–203 (2007)
7. Boldyreva, A., Goyal, V., Kumar, V.: Identity-based Encryption with Efficient Revocation. In: ACM conference on Computer and communications security (2008)
8. Attrapadung, N., Imai, H.: Attribute-based encryption supporting direct/indirect revocation modes. In: Parker, M.G. (ed.) Cryptography and Coding 2009. LNCS, vol. 5921, pp. 278–300. Springer, Heidelberg (2009)
9. Liang, X., Lu, R., Lin, X., Shen, X.: Ciphertext policy attribute-based encryption with efficient revocation. Technical report, University of Waterloo (2010)
10. Qian, J., Dong, X.: Fully secure revocable attribute-based encryption. J. Shanghai Jiaotong Univ. (Sci.) **16**, 490–496 (2011)
11. Waters, B.: Ciphertext-policy attribute-based encryption: an expressive, efficient, and provably secure realization. In: Public Key Cryptography (PKC 2011), pp. 53–70 (2011)
12. Waters, B.: Dual system encryption: realizing fully secure IBE and HIBE under simple assumptions. In: Halevi, S. (ed.) CRYPTO 2009. LNCS, vol. 5677, pp. 619–636. Springer, Heidelberg (2009)
13. Yamada, S., Attrapadung, N., Hanaoka, G., Kunihiro, N.: Generic constructions for chosen-ciphertext secure attribute based encryption. In: Catalano, D., Fazio, N., Gennaro, R., Nicolosi, A. (eds.) PKC 2011. LNCS, vol. 6571, pp. 71–89. Springer, Heidelberg (2011)
14. Lewko, A., Okamoto, T., Sahai, A., Takashima, K., Waters, B.: Fully secure functional encryption: attribute-based encryption and (hierarchical) inner product encryption. In: Gilbert, H. (ed.) EUROCRYPT 2010. LNCS, vol. 6110, pp. 62–91. Springer, Heidelberg (2010)
15. Okamoto, T., Takashima, K.: Fully secure functional encryption with general relations from the decisional linear assumption. In: Rabin, T. (ed.) CRYPTO 2010. LNCS, vol. 6223, pp. 191–208. Springer, Heidelberg (2010)
16. Green, M., Hohenberger, S., Waters, B.: Outsourcing the Decryption of ABE Ciphertexts. In: USENIX Security Symposium (2011)
17. Lynn, B.: The Stanford Pairing Based Crypto Library. http://crypto.stanford.edu/pbc
18. Hur, J., Noh, D.K.: Attribute-based access control with efficient revocation in data outsourcing systems. IEEE Trans. Parallel Distrib. Syst. **22**(7), 1214–1221 (2011)

19. Yu, S., Wang, C., Ren, K., Lou, W.: Attribute based data sharing with attribute revocation. In: Proceedings of the 5th ACM Symposium on Information. Computer and Communications Security (AsiaCCS 2010), pp. 261–270 (2010)
20. Boneh, D., Ding, X., Tsudik, G.: Fine-grained control of security capabilities. ACM Trans. Internet Technol. (TOIT) 4(1), 60–82 (2004)
21. Chow, S.S.M., Boyd, C., González Nieto, J.M.: Security-mediated certificateless cryptography. In: Yung, M., Dodis, Y., Kiayias, A., Malkin, T. (eds.) PKC 2006. LNCS, vol. 3958, pp. 508–524. Springer, Heidelberg (2006)
22. Gennaro, R., Gentry, C., Parno, B.: Non-interactive verifiable computing: outsourcing computation to untrusted workers. In: Rabin, T. (ed.) CRYPTO 2010. LNCS, vol. 6223, pp. 465–482. Springer, Heidelberg (2010)
23. Chung, K.-M., Kalai, Y., Vadhan, S.: Improved delegation of computation using fully homomorphic encryption. In: Rabin, T. (ed.) CRYPTO 2010. LNCS, vol. 6223, pp. 483–501. Springer, Heidelberg (2010)
24. Canetti, R., Krawczyk, H., Nielsen, J.B.: Relaxing chosen-ciphertext security. In: Boneh, D. (ed.) CRYPTO 2003. LNCS, vol. 2729, pp. 565–582. Springer, Heidelberg (2003)
25. Ibraimi, L., Petkovic, M., Nikova, S., Hartel, P., Jonker, W.: Mediated ciphertext-policy attribute-based encryption and its application. In: Youm, H.Y., Yung, M. (eds.) WISA 2009. LNCS, vol. 5932, pp. 309–323. Springer, Heidelberg (2009)
26. Pirretti, M., Traynor, P., McDaniel, P., Waters, B.: Secure attribute-based systems. In: ACM Conference on Computer and Communications Security, pp. 99–112 (2006)
27. Pirretti, M., Traynor, P., McDaniel, P., Waters, B.: Secure attribute-based systems. J. Comput. Secur. 18(5), 799–837 (2010)
28. Sahai, A., Seyalioglu, H., Waters, B.: Dynamic credentials and ciphertext delegation for attribute-based encryption. In: Safavi-Naini, R., Canetti, R. (eds.) CRYPTO 2012. LNCS, vol. 7417, pp. 199–217. Springer, Heidelberg (2012)
29. Yang, K., Jia, X., Ren, K., Huang, L.: Enabling efficient access control with dynamic policy updating for big data in the cloud. In: Proceedings IEEE on INFOCOM 2014, pp. 2013–2021 (2014)

MOVTCHA: A CAPTCHA Based on Human Cognitive and Behavioral Features Analysis

Asadullah Al Galib$^{(\boxtimes)}$ and Reihaneh Safavi-Naini

Department of Computer Science, University of Calgary,
2500 University Drive N.W., Calgary, Alberta T2N 1N4, Canada
{aagalib,rei}@ucalgary.ca

Abstract. We propose a new approach to Captcha which estimates human cognitive ability, in particular visual search ability, to differentiate humans from computers. We refer to this Captcha as Movtcha (**M**atching **O**bjects by **V**isual Search **T**o Tell **C**omputers and **H**umans **A**part). The design of Movtcha takes into account the analysis of human behavior to minimize noise during cognitive feature estimation. Our empirical results suggest that Movtcha can provide accuracy and usability comparable to other established Captchas. Our system is suitable for large scale applications since image selection, challenge generation and response evaluation are automated. Movtcha, unlike other Captchas, surpasses language and experience barriers by presenting both challenge and response in *clear form* and therefore can be used by people all across the world.

1 Introduction

Captcha (Completely Automated Public Turing test to tell Computers and Humans Apart) [1] exploits the difference in the ability of humans and computers in performing a task to tell the two apart. The task is designed such that it cannot be solved by computers using the state-of-the-art computing technologies but can easily be solved by human users. The most commonly encountered Captchas rely on distorted alphanumeric string. The advent of image-based Captcha offered an alternative approach with promising usability and security. However, eventually schemes based on image recognition such as [2,3] were compromised. Captchas exploiting semantic relationships between images [4,5] or between images and words [6], usually claim high security and usability but fail to auto generate the challenge (secret) database, resulting in scalability issues.

Another challenge while designing Captchas which is seldom explored, is the issue of Captcha being language, culture or experience dependent. Text/audio based Captchas are entirely language dependent. Some image-based Captchas [4,7] though language independent, rely heavily on user's past experience or exposure to certain things Sect. 7. One way to remove these dependencies is to present both the challenge and response in *clear form* and use behavioral or cognitive features to differentiate human from machine. We define *clear form* as a scenario where the response is not concealed by the challenge *somehow*, e.g. through distortion. This means that both the challenge and response are

© Springer International Publishing Switzerland 2015
L.C.K. Hui et al. (Eds.): ICICS 2014, LNCS 8958, pp. 290–304, 2015.
DOI: 10.1007/978-3-319-21966-0_21

available to the users as well as the computers. *Clear form* allows both human and machine respond to the challenge with ease. However, such scenario clearly violates the current pre-requisite for security of Captcha systems [1,8]. Movtcha presents both challenge and response to a user in *clear form* and is still able to maintain high security. Another important security challenge in Captcha is preventing relay attack where the attacker (the bot) relays/sends the Captcha challenge to a human user who in turn solves the Captcha [9]. Movtcha prevents such relay attacks.

Movtcha is presented as a Cognitive Task. It estimates cognitive ability of a human, in particular visual search ability. An individual's capacity in carrying out any cognitive task (a task requiring a mental process such as perception, thinking and reasoning [10]) is referred to as the cognitive ability of that individual. We consider serial visual search [11] where each item is inspected in turn in a search set to determine if it is a target or not. For example, consider searching through a list of 100 unsorted names until the desired one is found (or the search self-terminates [12]). The unsorted list aids in sequential search unlike a sorted list where users could have skipped some names. In a serial self-terminating search, if it takes a constant amount of time to inspect each item in turn until the desired one is found then the visual search time is found to have a positive linear relationship with the position of the target item inside the search set [13,14].

We design a game-like Cognitive Task (CT) that takes advantage of this observation. The cardinal notion is to conceal the size of the list or search set containing target item from the bot but keep it visible/comprehensible to a human user. For example, consider Bob and a machine. Both are presented with a list of 10 unsorted names and challenged to find "Alice" which appears at the 9th position. Bob *somehow* acquires a *knowledge* which says "Alice" does not appear in the first 5 entries. As a result Bob searches from the 6th position and continues until he finds "Alice" at the 9th position. If it takes 1 second to inspect each name in the list, Bob will spend 4 seconds to find "Alice". On the other hand the machine being deprived of the *knowledge* searches from the 1st position until it finds "Alice" at the 9th position. The machine searches faster than Bob and both the challenge ("Alice") and response ("Alice") are in *clear form* but it fails to mimic the search time of Bob without the *knowledge*. That is, although the bot can add delays and increase its search time, it does not know how much delay needs to be introduced. Movtcha has a similar design principle where the *knowledge* is conveyed only to a human user.

Movtcha consists of a carefully tailored image and a challenge tile. An image is first divided into θ items (cells) by superimposing a grid like structure. A subset of cells $\theta_{sub} \subseteq \theta$ is modified (the *knowledge*) such that, (1) a bot is not able to differentiate them from other cells and (2) the *modification* process creates random artifacts, conveying no meaning in current context to a human user [11] (Appendix A, Fig. 1(a)). A target tile t_r is then selected randomly from the search set, θ_{sub}, and an exact copy of t_r is presented to the user as the challenge tile t_c. Dragging and dropping t_c (challenge) onto t_r (response) inside θ_{sub} is equivalent to a correct visual search task. A human instantly distinguishes and separates out these *exotic* tiles, θ_{sub}, from the context of the image via parallel search and then performs serial search on the subset, θ_{sub}, to find t_r [15]. Therefore, his search time will vary according to $|\theta_{sub}^{P_{t_r}}|$ i.e. the number of *exotic* tiles that need to be inspected before encountering t_r. On the other hand, a bot is not able to figure out the *knowledge* i.e. θ_{sub}. Therefore, it will not be able to mimic the search time of a human user.

We do not consider the actual visual search time. In fact, we look for *trends*. If the search time grows linearly (roughly, possibly with a few outliers) with $|\theta_{sub}^{P_{t_r}}|$, then the system authenticates the user as a human. Our contributions in a nutshell, (1) Movtcha estimates a cognitive feature to make authentication decision. Our design takes into account human behavioral analysis to eliminate noise during feature estimation. (2) It bypasses traditional pre-requisite for the security of Captcha by presenting both the challenge and response in *clear form*. This makes it language and experience independent. (3) It is resistant against random, automated and static relay attacks. (4) Movtcha is an automated system.

Paper Organization. Section 2: Design of Movtcha, feature estimation and authentication mechanism. Section 3: Search set and challenge generation. Section 4: Security analysis. Section 5: Experiments & results. Section 6: Relay attacks. Section 7: Related work. Section 8: Conclusion.

2   The Cognitive Task as MOVTCHA

Movtcha is a simple and intuitive object matching game. This section provides details on the (1) design of Movtcha (2) extraction of cognitive and behavioral features and (3) the authentication mechanism.

2.1   Design and Execution of Movtcha

An image of size $x \times y$ pixels, (*width* $\times$ *height*), is first broken into a grid, g, containing θ pieces of square tiles of size $k \times k$ indexed as $c_1, c_2, \ldots, c_{|\theta|}$ from left to right and then top to bottom, $|\theta| = \frac{x \times y}{k^2}$. The random set of tiles that is systematically *modified*, to look *exotic* to a human user is referred to as the search set θ_{sub}. The game starts with the user being challenged with a tile t_c at position P_{t_c}. The objective of the human user is to drag and drop t_c onto the corresponding target tile, t_r, inside g. We call this search action/response A_{resp}. On a correct visual search task, the user is rewarded with a *star*, s_r, superimposed on t_r. The user then performs action A_{rew}, where he drags and drops the rewarded *star* s_r, back to P_{t_c}. One *instance* of the game is thus completed. The user is required to play certain number of *instances* in a Movtcha and each time the image, the number of *exotic* tiles $|\theta_{sub}|$, and the position of the target tile is varied.

Constraints and Helpers. The game must invoke serial self-terminating visual search of a human user after the parallel stage. In order to guarantee (1) its invocation *(C1, C2 & H2)* (2) its correct measurement under non-laboratory conditions with the aid of human behavioral analysis *(C2, C3, C4 & C5)* and (3) facilitate the visual search process *(H1 & H2)*, certain *constraints &helpers* have been placed throughout Movtcha.

C1. At the beginning of each *instance*, as the user hovers over a bounded region P_{t_c}, the tile holder and grid "pop up". The tile holder moves randomly within R_{t_c} and the tile is only visible when the user hovers over the tile holder. This ensures no prior exposure of the challenge tile or search set which can bias the search time [11] and ensures a drag and search action from user. Appendix A Fig. 1(a).

C2. Consider the pixel co-ordinate system. As the tile is dragged, if the y-coordinate of the drag event, e_d^y is in between the minimum and maximum y-coordinate of the jth row in the grid, g, then that row is highlighted by two red lines. If e_d^y during A_{resp} crosses the maximum y-coordinate of target tile t_r, then t_r is highlighted signifying a failed search. The user is then presented with a new *instance*. This constraint ensures that user does not skip over and misses t_r while performing serial search from top to bottom and from left to right. Therefore, visual search time, VST collected from a skipped search is avoided similar to [13].

C3. If the time taken in A_{resp} crosses some experimentally set threshold λ (Sect. 5.1), the user immediately receives a new *instance*. This discards abnormal VST caused due to loss of attention by the user and encourages user not to get distracted while completing an *instance*.

C4. A_{rew} action demands smooth movement of star, s_r, since no cognitive thinking in particular, visual search, is required to execute A_{rew}. Large number of pauses during the movement of s_r signifies that the user was distracted. If the amount of pauses crosses some experimentally set threshold ζ (Sect. 5.1) during dragging s_r, then it moves back to t_r inside g.

C5. On dropping t_c anywhere other than on t_r inside g, the challenge tile t_c moves back to P_{t_c} signifying a *mismatch*. The user immediately receives another new *instance*.

H1. We allow some tolerance on the placement of the tile/star. This means that the user does not need pin-point accuracy when dropping t_c/s_r.

H2. A grid is drawn on the image for establishing finer distinguishability among the tiles and forming a structured visual field. This helps in invoking serial search. It also aids in resisting automated *memory* attacks (Sect. 4).

2.2 Cognitive and Behavioral Feature Extraction

We refer to features collected during the execution of a cognitive task as cognitive features. Human behavior do not necessarily invoke any particular cognitive process. We refer to features collected through the observation of human behavior, such as in behavioral biometrics (*while browsing, typing*), as behavioral features.

Visual Search Time Estimation, VST. The time required for the user to visually search, detect and match t_c onto t_r, is referred to as the visual search time VST. The VST is a cognitive feature, calculated by the subtraction method [16]. The subtraction method is an established technique in cognitive psychology that involves subtracting the amount of time information processing takes with the process $(MT_{A_{resp}} + t^t_{RT})$ from the time it takes without the process $(MT_{A_{rew}})$. Therefore, $VST = (MT_{A_{resp}} + t^t_{RT}) - MT_{A_{rew}}$, where $MT_{A_{resp}} =$ time elapsed during A_{resp}, $MT_{A_{rew}} =$ time elapsed during A_{rew}, $t^t_{RT} =$ (reaction) time elapsed between the appearance of the stimulus (t_c) and the user picking it up (responding).

Pause Time, PT. This feature is required to enforce almost smooth movement during dragging the *star* and in turn to provide better estimation of VST. If user remains at the same pixel for more than 0.1 seconds we refer to it as a pause. We measure the number of pauses and derive the total paused time, $PT_{A_{rew}}$. The A_{rew} action does *not* involve any cognitive process. $PT_{A_{rew}}$ should be zero in an ideal condition. In practice, if $PT_{A_{rew}}$ crosses some experimentally set threshold ζ then constraint $C4$ is activated.

2.3   Telling Computers and Humans Apart

We use an accuracy metric $\triangle^A_{VST}$ in order to differentiate between a human and a bot. Let s^h_i and s^m_i represents the two series of observations (VST) at instances $\langle 1, 2, \ldots, n \rangle$ from human user and bot respectively. The two series are first arranged according to decreasing order of search set sizes. A series of plus points s^{h+}_i and s^{m+}_i are then obtained from s^h_i and s^m_i. A plus point p is awarded to an element s_e at index i_e of the sorted sequence s, if s_e is greater than p elements with indices more than i_e. An accuracy metric $\triangle^A_{VST}$ is then calculated as the ratio of the summation of the plus points s^+ and the summation of a strictly decreasing series. If the VSTs follow a strictly decreasing trend with decreasing set sizes then the resulting accuracy metric $\triangle^A_{VST} = 1$ and vice versa. A human or a machine is then authenticated based on two *conditions* (1) the $\triangle^A_{VST}$ must cross some certain threshold α. (2) $VST - MT_{A_{rew}}$ must be least when the search set size $|\theta_{sub}| = 1$.

We provide an example, here, to show how plus points and $\triangle^A_{VST}$ are calculated for $n = 6$ *instances* for a human user and a bot. The bot makes random guesses on the position of the target tile P_{t_r} inside θ_{sub} and generates VST. The VSTs, $s^h = \langle 3.8, 3.3, 1.7, 3.4, 1.4, 0.3 \rangle$ and $s^m = \langle 2, 3, 3.5, 4.5, 4, 1 \rangle$ are first arranged according to decreasing order of $|\theta^{P_{t_r}}_{sub}| = \langle 33, 26, 15, 12, 5, 1 \rangle$. Plus points $s^{h+} = \langle 5, 3, 2, 2, 1, 0 \rangle$ and $s^{m+} = \langle 1, 1, 1, 2, 1, 0 \rangle$ are then used to figure out $\triangle^A_{VST} = \frac{\sum^n_{i=1} s^+_i}{n(n-1)/2}$. $\triangle^A_{VST} = 0.867$ for human and $\triangle^A_{VST} = 0.4$ for bot. Experimentally the value of the authentication threshold α is set. In this scenario, setting α to some values less than 0.867 allows some *tolerance* with few observations being out of place for a human user. Increasing such *tolerance* increases the success probability of the bot. Appendix A Fig. 2(a) shows how the success probability varies with the amount of *tolerance* or $\triangle^A_{VST} \wedge condition(2)$.

3   Nuts and Bolts of Our System

Movtcha consists of the following stages: (1) Selecting the appropriate images to be tailored, (2) Generating the search set and displaying the challenge and (3) Telling computers and humans apart (as described in Sect. 2.3).

3.1   Selecting Images to Be Tailored

The goal is to have some portion of the image look *exotic* to a human e.g. consider the rectangular half of a book being modified to a cone. This modification needs to be done in such a way s.t. (1) the human can distinguish the *exotic* tiles in the parallel stage and then perform a serial search to find the target, (2) the machine is not able to figure out the *exotic* tiles. We use images containing pencil or pen sketches/drawings. All images in our setting are first converted to grayscale. Uncontrolled colors generally hinders serial search and can make some tiles more conspicuous or obscure than others [11,17]. Sketches have traversing edges, or pencil strokes, which can be easily mimicked/modified by new random strokes. We refer to an edge/object that flows across a tile as a traversing edge/object of that tile. The images are first cropped to suitable sizes $x \times y$. For most tiles if the number of traversing edges is outside some certain interval the image is discarded. This image selection process guarantees that most of the tiles contains at least some traversing edges so that any of them can be *modified* to form some random shapes. Any image surviving such constraints is then referred to as the candidate image I_C.

3.2   Generation of Search Set and Displaying an Instance

At each *instance* of Movtcha, an I_C is selected to be tailored to generate θ_{sub}. For each *instance*, we randomly choose a search set size from an interval $[LL, UL]$. This interval is determined by the parameter *AmountOfSeperation*, *AOS*, which ensures that search set sizes differ by some random amounts at each *instance*. Larger offsets ensure sparser estimated $VSTs$, and result into higher $\triangle_{VST}^A$ by eliminating outliers (Sect. 5.1). We then randomly select a subset of tiles $\theta_{sub} \in \theta$. We refer to the boundary of each tile t_i in θ_{sub} as b_{t_i}. We find the continuity points $b_{t_i}^{\{P\}}$ of the traversing edges at the boundary b_{t_i} by applying Canny. If a pair of tiles $\{t_x, t_y\} \in \theta_{sub}$ share the same boundary $b_{t_i}, i \in \{x, y\}$, then they also share the same edge continuity points $b_{t_i}^{\{P\}}, i \in \{x, y\}$. Once the edge continuity points are found, some of the traversing edges in each tile are almost dissolved by minimizing the intensity gradient difference. We then draw strokes connecting those points randomly. These strokes are approximation curves drawn across $\{p_x^i, p_y^i\}$, with varying number of control points randomly set in the vicinity of the center of the *exotic* tile t_i. As a result each time a stroke is drawn, a random shape is formed. A stroke might also end abruptly midway without connecting the points. Details in Appendix A. The grayscale intensities of all the tiles $\theta = \{c_1, c_2, \ldots, c_{|\theta|}\}$ are then randomly changed. And finally a grid like structure is drawn on the image I_C. When presented to the user the image size is scaled with a nonlinear bicubic interpolation and by adding some random noise. At this stage, the candidate image I_C is referred to as the processed image I_P.

Displaying an Instance. If there are n *instances* in a Movtcha, n processed images $\{I_P^1, I_P^2, \ldots, I_P^n\}$ are formed from n candidate images, with $\{\theta_{sub}^1, \theta_{sub}^2, \ldots, \theta_{sub}^n\}$ as their corresponding search sets, where

$|\theta^1_{sub}|<|\theta^2_{sub}|<\ldots<|\theta^n_{sub}|$. From each of these search sets the corresponding t_c are selected s.t. $|\theta^{1,\ P_{t_r}}_{sub}|<|\theta^{2,\ P_{t_r}}_{sub}|<\ldots<|\theta^{n,\ P_{t_r}}_{sub}|$. A random permutation $\pi : [n] \to [n]$ is selected and applied to the processed images $\langle I_P^{\pi(1)}, I_P^{\pi(2)}, \ldots, I_P^{\pi(n)} \rangle$ and the challenge tiles $\langle t_{c_{\pi(1)}}, t_{c_{\pi(2)}}, \ldots, t_{c_{\pi(n)}} \rangle$. At the ith *instance* of Movtcha, a processed image $I_P^{\pi(i)}$ and target tile $t_{c_{\pi(i)}}$ is selected and displayed to the user.

4 Security Analysis

We analyze the success probability of an attacker in random guessing attack and automated attack. Section 7 provides a discussion on static relay attack.

We consider that an automated attacker uses a framework f specially designed to attack our system. It can (1) separate out the background and the foreground objects and identify moving challenge tile and grid tiles centroids in negligible time, and (2) perform A_{resp} and A_{rew} action at a desired speed while mimicking human user's mouse dynamics (such as addition of jitters). At each *instance*, the attacker matches the tiles using f and generates VST by guessing the *concealed* $|\theta^{P_{t_r}}_{sub}|$. In such scenario for n instances there should be $n!$ ways of varying the VST. The probability for a successful attack thus becomes $\frac{1}{n!}$. Movtcha involving 8 *instances* results in 0.0025 % success rate, much smaller than the target probability for a practical Captcha system security of 0.6 % [7]. However, in real settings, we allow some *tolerance* on the VST *trend* and subsequently on $\triangle^A_{VST}$ to accept *trends* with possibly a few outliers. Appendix A, Fig. 2(a) shows a simulation of how the success probability varies with $\triangle^A_{VST}$ for varying number of *instances*. In practice, f needs some processing time (such as separating the background and foreground objects). This and other similar processing time can also be upper bounded based on *condition(2)* (Appendix A, Fig. 2(b, c)). On the other hand, a random guessing attacker drags and drops t_c onto t_r randomly. Since the grid size is θ, the success probability of a random guessing attack, without *tolerance*, is very small $\frac{1}{\theta^n \times n!}$. Even with *tolerance* this probability remains small.

The current challenge in Movtcha is always independent of the past challenges. Since object type (*exotic* tiles) are randomly generated, object recognition or classification is apparently a hard problem in Movtcha. Ideally, the same tile could have produced infinitely many random shapes, as it is processed each time. Movtcha presents unique image at each *instance*, making the challenges independent of each other. The attacker is then left to exploit the low level cues in order to identify the *exotic* tiles. We discuss in details the possible attacks and the associated empirical results.

Attack Using Low-Level Cues. The *exotic* tiles in θ_{sub} might differ in grayscale intensity from its neighboring tiles due to the modifications applied. Considering there is no grid like structure, the attacker can therefore, use off-the-shelf edge detection algorithm such as Sobel or Canny to figure out the boundaries of the *exotic* tiles. A simple approach of hindering such naive attack is to introduce false tiles boundaries by randomly changing the tile intensities across the grid. With the grid structure in position such gradient-based methods detect the whole grid (Appendix A, Fig. 1(b)). So we sought to a customized boundary detection approach similar to [7]. The image is first smoothed by a 5×5 Gaussian filter in order to reduce noise. We consider squares for each location, along the tile boundaries. The squares are then divided into halves at $0°$, $45°$, $90°$, $135°$. The goal is to have a large enough square so that any pair of halves covers portions of the neighboring tiles pixels (grid pixels being symmetric on both halves). The difference in the gray-scale intensity between the two halves of the square is then estimated by calculating $\triangle(h_1, h_2) = \frac{1}{2}\sum_{n=1}^{\#bins} \frac{(h_{1n}-h_{2n})^2}{h_{1n}+h_{2n}}$, where h_1 and h_2 represents the gray-scale intensity histogram of the two halves respectively. Gradient direction and magnitude of a location are set as the direction with the maximum grayscale intensity and the maximum intensity respectively. We then apply non-maximum suppression and threshold the resulting image incrementally until the candidate tile set size, $|C_T|$ converges to $|\theta_{sub}|$, at which point if $C_T = \theta_{sub}$, the attack would be considered effective. Any $c_{t_i} \in C_T$ has a boundary *edge* weight of $w_i > p_i/2$ (p_i is the *shared* perimeter of c_{t_i} with other tiles). Attacks on 100 I_C's with $|\theta_{sub}| = 10$, $|\theta| = 48$ resulted into $\left(\frac{|C_T \cap \theta_{sub}|}{|\theta_{sub}|}\right) = 0.039$(average). Edge density on opposite side of the boundaries remains almost similar due to the false traversing edges constructed randomly among the edge continuation points. Any local artifacts at the tile boundaries, that would have been exploited by an edge traversing algorithm, are concealed by the grid structure (3-pixel width). Besides, finding out the edge continuation points at the processing stage, using Canny edge detection algorithm minimized the distance between actual edges in the image and the edges found. Appendix A, Fig. 1(c) shows a contour plot of an I_P where intensity depth varies across θ providing no useful information to an attacker. On the other hand, scaling and adding random noise before the image is presented prevents the attacker from exploiting any noise or quantization patterns.

Attack Using Memory. We define *memory* as an accumulation of low level features from more than one *instance*. However, since unique images are used for each *instance* the current challenge is always independent of the past challenges, resulting into absolutely *no* accumulation of *memory*. We now look into another attempt of acquiring such *memory* using a Context-Based Image Retrieval (CBIR) system S_C, s.t. S_C retrieves the original image I_C from I_P. However, the amount of irreversible distortion added to the processed image I_P by the grid g, cut-and-scale, random strokes essentially thwart a CBIR system like [18] in retrieving the original I_C (as tested on 100 I_P's).

5   Experiments and Results

We carried out three experiments to evaluate Movtcha in terms of (1) Design and presentation, (2) & (3) Accuracy, efficiency and usability. The first experiment was carried out in a controlled condition to ascertain some parameters and design of Movtcha. While the second and third were carried out in a non-controlled condition, mimicking a real life Captcha solving scenario. We obtained approval from the Research Ethics Board of our Institution for the experiments. All experiments were divided into three phases (1) Phase-I, where participants agreed to the consent information. (2) In Phase-II, they were instructed to solve Movtchas. (3) And in Phase-III, participants were required to fill up an exit survey consisting of the standard SUS (Simple Usability Scale) questions [19] and a few other related questions S_{Fun}.

5.1   Experiment I: Design and Presentation

The goals of the first experiment were to figure out (1) how the *intra-accuracy*, $\triangle_{VST}^{A}$ varies with the size of the grid and (2) the parameters λ for $C3$ and ζ for $C4$. $C3$ & $C4$ were therefore not set in this experiment. The goals required human users to solve Movtcha in a laboratory condition i.e. in a non-distracting environment using a single platform. The experiment consisted of a pool of 24 students comprising of equal number of males and females aged between 21–36. All of them used a PC with 2.10 GHz Intel i3, 4 GB RAM and an wireless optical USB mouse. They used Google Chrome on a screen of resolution 1366 × 768 (96 PPI) in Windows 7 SP1 OS.

Setup. A short video showed how the game is played at the beginning. Participants received no further instructions. Each participant was required to solve 15 Movtchas $\langle M_1, M_2, \ldots, M_{15} \rangle$ each comprising of a fixed number of instances (*#instances = 8*). The 15 Movtchas were divided into three groups. The group G_1 consisted of images divided into $5 \times 5 = 25$ (*Row × Column*) tiles each of size 60 × 60 pixels. Similarly, G_2 and G_3 consisted of the same size tiles with images divided into $6 \times 6 = 36$ and $8 \times 6 = 48$ tiles. t_c holder moved randomly inside the bounding box at 0.1 pixels/frame @60 FPS i.e. 6 pixels/s.

Results. It is observable from Table 1 that the average $\triangle_{VST}^{A}$, increased with increasing grid size. *AmountOfSeperation* increased with grid size, resulting into VST with increasing standard deviation. Noise fail to affect the $\triangle_{VST}^{A}$, when VSTs are sparser. Similar results can be observed in Neisser [13] where sparser target positions P_{t_r} results into VST with larger offsets. Therefore, in order to have larger $\triangle_{VST}^{A}$, Experiment-II & III were carried out using images with 8×6 tiles. G_3 has the highest $\triangle_{VST}^{A}$ and a relatively longer completion time, T_{Com}. T_{Com} decreases with decreasing $|\theta|$ as expected. E_c is the average error rate per click and refers to the ratio of number of times user missed picking up or dropped midway t_c or s_r during A_{resp} or A_{rew} to the total number of actual ($A_{resp} + A_{rew}$) actions in a Movtcha. The observed E_c suggested that users felt comfortable with the moving speed of the tile. I_d refers to the ratio of number of *instances* discarded (due to $C2$, $C3$, & $C5$) to the total number of *instances*. Although the average E_c remained almost unchanging among the groups, the average I_d^{C2} was relatively higher in G_1, an implication that as the users get familiar with Movtcha, they tend *not* to skip targets during search. Further analysis of data from G1, showed that I_d^{C2} was highest for the 1st Movtcha, M_1, for 79.17 % of the users. The average I_d^{C5} remained as low as 0.052 suggesting comfortable visual search task performance in the current visual field.

Fixing Parameters. In an ideal condition $PT_{A_{rew}}$ is supposed to be zero, since dragging the star, A_{rew} action, does not involve any cognitive process. As can be observed from Table 1, the average $PT_{A_{rew}}$ is <100 ms, implying an almost smooth non-distracted movement during A_{rew}. We set $\zeta = 0.2\,s$ of $C4$ to possible extreme outliers using interquartile range $PT_{A_{rew}}^{Q3} + (3 \times PT_{A_{rew}}^{IQR})$, to allow some tolerance in non-controlled condition. The ratio of VST to $|\theta_{sub}^{P_{tr}}|$ is the *true* inspection time, IPT, for each *exotic* tile. The average inspection time of all the participants throughout the 3 *sessions* was 102.1 ms. The parameter λ of $C3$ is similarly set to extreme outliers values for non-laboratory conditions s.t. $\lambda = (|\theta| * IPT') + MT'_{rew}$ where $IPT' = IPT^{Q3} + (3 \times IPT^{IQR}) \approx 0.27\,s$ and $MT'_{rew} = MT_{rew}^{Q3} + (3 \times MT_{rew}^{IQR}) \approx 2.0\,s$ for all *instances* with varying $|\theta_{sub}^{P_{tr}}|$. Therefore, λ provided comfortable time span while searching at any *instance* and only triggered $C3$ when the user is distracted (or "lazy" searching) for a relatively long time.

5.2 Experiment II: Accuracy and Efficiency

The goal of this experiment was to determine (1) how the *intra-accuracy*, $\triangle_{VST}^{A}$, and *inter-accuracy*, $\triangle_{M}^{A}$, varied with the number of *instances* and (2) the efficiency or completion time of a Movtcha. *Inter-accuracy* is the ratio of number of solved Movtchas to the number of Movtcha challenges. Unlike, experiment-I, this experiment was carried out in a non-controlled condition.

Setup. The users were emailed to solve Movtcha on 3 *occasions*. At each *occasion* the users were required to complete 5 Movtchas with (1) fixed image size, 8×6, (2) fixed parameters ζ, λ. They can make a maximum of 3 mistakes happening due to $C2 - C5$ while solving a Movtcha. For each *occasion*, #*instances* is varied from 6–8. They completed the exit survey as well.

Results. We collected complete submissions from 42 participants/workers. It can be observed that the average $\triangle_{VST}^{A}$ in all three cases is around 80 %. However, considering the success probability of a bot is tuned to a particular value, the allowable decrease in $\triangle_{VST}^{A}$ is larger for increasing #*instances* (Appendix A, Fig. 2(a)). This resulted into higher $\triangle_{M}^{A}$ for increasing #*instances*. The average I_d is higher relative to Experiment-I. Activation of $C4$ led to relatively higher click error, E_c. These increases were expected in non-controlled condition. Furthermore, it implies that the constraints proved to be useful in discarding abnormal VST and $MT_{A_{rew}}$ that might have resulted from distractions. Table 2 shows $\triangle_{M}^{A}$ when $\triangle_{VST}^{A} > 80\,\%$. Even when $\triangle_{VST}^{A}$ is set at $\geq 82.14\,\%$, limiting bot success to 0.85 % for #*instance* $= 8$, the *inter-accuracy* $\triangle_{M}^{A}$ is around 81 % (Gmail's Captcha accuracy rate 82.8 % [7]). Mouse type statistics from exit survey include wireless/wired mouse (61.9 %), laptop touchpad (38.1 %). Recall, VST is calculated using subtraction method [16] which allows VST to self adjust for the user's specific environment.

Table 1. Results from Experiment-I

	$\triangle^A_{VST}$	I^{C2}_d	T_{Com}(Std)	E_c	$PT_{A_{rew}}$
G1	67.94(4.81)	0.110	17.19(1.89)	0.058	76.8
G2	78.40(4.28)	0.078	21.90(2.08)	0.051	40.1
G3	85.10(4.43)	0.073	24.96(2.52)	0.062	44.2

Table 2. Results from Experiment-II

inst	$\triangle^A_{VST}$(Std)	$\triangle^A_M$	T_{Com}(Std)	I^{C2}_d
6	80.22(4.76)	67.14	21.57(5.02)	0.21
7	79.97(7.40)	71.9	26.43(7.58)	0.29
8	82.90(6.77)	80.96	28.11(6.03)	0.24

5.3 Experiment III: Accuracy and Efficiency

The goal of this experiment was to observe how random users from different parts of the world perform on Movtcha through Amazon Mechanical Turk [20]. A single HIT was created with 70 assignments to have 70 unique workers. The workers were directed to the website hosting Movtcha. After watching the video, they were required to solve one Movtcha and collect 8 stars (complete 8 *instances* successfully) and in the process can make a maximum of 3 mistakes. Afterwards, they completed an exit survey. There was one demo *instance* at the beginning which was not considered in accuracy calculation. Workers were then required to copy-paste a code (generated on our website) back to Amazon to get paid \$ 0.3. The average *intra-accuracy*, $\triangle^A_{VST}$, is 78.2 % (std 6.03 %). When $\triangle^A_{VST}$ is set at ≥ 75, limiting the success probability of bot to 2.38 % the *inter-accuracy* is $\triangle^A_M = 78.9\%$. The average time to complete T_{com}, is 38.04 s (std 8.63 s). We highlight that these results are reported from unique users solving just *one* Movtcha for the first time. The average time required to complete each assignment was 5.4 min. Workers participated from 7 different countries (based on IP) with 84.3 % using mouse and rest touchpad (user-claimed).

5.4 User Experience

The average SUS score for all the experiments were within the user-friendly industrial software ratings [21]. The average SUS score for Amazon workers was 66.17. The S_{Fun} questions asked the user to rate the game in (1) "fun to play" (2) "easy and intuitive" (1–5, "5" signifying "Strong agreement" and vice versa). SUS and S_{Fun} rating was relatively higher in Experiment-I. This might be the result of users being more "polite" under a supervised condition. Considering Experiment-II & III, 57.1 % & 67.14 % of the participants agreed that the game was fun to play and 71.4 % & 74.2 % felt it was easy and intuitive respectively. This demonstrates that Movtcha is a user-friendly system.

6 Relay Attacks

We consider attacks, where the bot takes snapshots of *instances*, send it to a human solver and subsequently uses the responses to solve Movtcha [8]. In such attacks, the bot needs to consider four time intervals for each *instance*, (1) The communication delay between the bot and the human solver's machine $\triangle^c_t$,

(2) the time taken by the human solver to perform the visual search task and provide P_{t_r} and $|\theta_{sub}^{P_{t_r}}|$. (3) the time taken for the bot to match the tile. (4) the time taken to move the star back to P_{t_c}.

Captchas with dynamic challenge objects are generally resistant against relay attacks because the object co-ordinate sent by the human solver, C_{t_c}, at time t mismatches with that of P_{t_c} of the moving object at $t + k$, $k > 0$ [8]. The probability that $C_{t_c} = P_{t_c}$ at $t + k$ can be given as the ratio of the object area and the bounding box area where it randomly moves. In our setting, there is roughly $1/5$ chance that the bot correctly picks up t_c. Such chance should produce relatively higher E_c and I_d in relay attacks. We carried out a small scale experiment with 10 users from the 1st pool to examine our hypothesis. We considered a *strong* relay attack scenario where $\triangle_c^t = 0$. Therefore, the task of the human solver is to respond with $|\theta_{sub}^{P_{t_r}}|$ and C_{t_c}. To setup the experiment, *snapshots* $(s_1, s_2, \ldots s_n)$ at time $(\tau_1, \tau_2, \ldots, \tau_n)$ of the HTML5 canvas were taken along with the co-ordinates of t_c for 3 Movtchas. During the experiment, users were provided the *snapshots* one by one along with a beeping sound (audio stimulus) for a ready alert, similar to [8]. As soon as s_i is presented with the stimulus the user performed search and clicked on t_r and then C_{t_c} consecutively. If $P_{t_c} \neq C_{t_c}$ then the user is presented with the same s_i and were required to provide *only* a new C_{t_c}. There was a significant increase in $E_c = 2.81$ (avg) resulting into longer VST and $C3$ activations. None of the users were able to authenticate in the 3 Movtchas, with a maximum of 3 mistakes. In a real setting, where $\triangle_t^c \neq 0$, constraint $C3$ puts an upper bound on the distance between the relay bot and the human solver.

7   Related Work

May be the work closest to ours, which claims to consider human behavioral analysis is the dynamic game Captcha owned by a startup company called "Are you a Human" [22]. The company claims to differentiate human and machine based on behavioral data such as mouse events [8,22]. Their system challenges the user to drag-drop semantically related objects such as "baby" & "milk". *Clear form* Captchas are supposed to be inherently language and culture independent, because the response to a challenge is basically the challenge itself. Semage [4] claims to surpass the boundaries of languages but fails to auto-generate the challenge database. IR such as Cortcha [7] can automatically generate the image data-base. However, it also requires prior knowledge on the relationship between the decoy object and the inpainted image. On the other hand, our system demands the user to have the minimum ability of distinguishing the *exotic* tiles, conveying no meaning, from the original image. And this can be done with apparent ease and without establishing any form of semantic relationship [15].

Visual Search in Cognitive Psychology. Neisser [13] carried out an experiment where users were instructed to find the *absence* of letter Z in a list. The list contained 49 items like JZTXVB, DQFJHZ, ZXLSMT and one target item

VXRLFH arranged in a column. 15 such lists (with random target item position and random strings of letters) were given to each human user. It was observed for each user that the visual search time has a positive linear relationship with the position of the target item inside the list of 50 items.

8   Conclusion

We have provided a new approach to Captcha by estimating a cognitive feature. Human behavioral analysis was used to eliminate noise in the feature estimation process. Our empirical results suggest comparable accuracy, efficiency and usability to existing Captcha systems. We have discussed how image selection, challenge generation and response evaluation are automatically accomplished by our system. Movtcha maintains real world security while presenting *clear* answers to challenges. This attribute makes Movtcha language, culture and experience independent.

Acknowledgments. This research is in part supported by Alberta Innovates Technology Futures and Telus Mobility Canada.

A   Generation of Search Set

We refer to the boundary of each tile t_i (to be made *exotic*) as b_{t_i}. We find the continuity points $b_{t_i}^{\{P\}}$ of the traversing edges at the boundary b_{t_i} by applying Canny. The gray values of t_i is changed to be within $[\alpha, \beta]$, until the number of traversing edges fall below $b_{t_i}^{|\{P\}|/2}$. α is set to the min and β to max gray value of t_i. At each step j, $(\alpha{+}{+}, \beta{-}{-})$ any pixel value $> \beta$ and $<\alpha$ is set randomly to $(\alpha, \alpha + \delta]$ and $[\beta - \delta, \beta)$ respectively until $b_{t_i}^{|\{P\}|}$ decreases to $b_{t_i}^{|\{P\}|/2}$. δ is set s.t. $b_{t_i}^{|\{P\}|_{j-1}} > b_{t_i}^{|\{P\}|_j}$. For each pair of edge points $\{p_x, p_y\}$ obtained from $b_{t_i}^{\{P\}}$

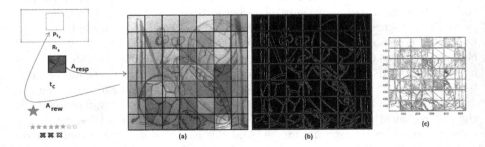

Fig. 1. Best viewed in soft copy. (a) An *instance* of Movtcha where user has collected 6 stars and made 2 mistakes. The search set size, $|\theta_{sub}| = 6$, and the position of target tile inside the search set, $|\theta_{sub}^{P_{t_r}}| = 4$. (b) Edges of I_P using Canny edge detection algorithm. (c) Contour plot of I_P.

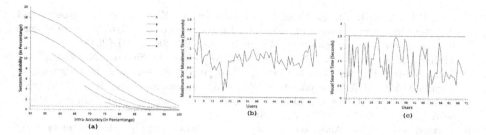

Fig. 2. (a) Simulation of the attacker's success probability for $\#instances$ =5–9. Dotted line represents 0.6 %. (b) Shows the maximum $MT_{A_{rew}}$ of successful Amazon users out of all the *instances* they played (c) Shows VST when $|\theta_{sub}| = 1$. If we restrict $MT_{A_{rew}}$ and VST ($|\theta_{sub}| = 1$) to 1.4 s and 2.5 s respectively as a constraint, we can upper bound the computational time of an attacker by 3.9s due to *condition(2)*. In other words, the attacker needs to successfully complete a visual search task within 3.9 s which involves separating objects from background, locating dynamic t_c, identifying search set size, and dragging-dropping t_c onto t_r. Successful users from Experiment-I and II provides even smaller bounds of 1.6 s and 2.1 s respectively. Most importantly, this constraint/bound can be set without interfering much with user's Movtcha solving activity. On the other hand, limiting computational time of attacker for traditional Captcha systems essentially limits the solving time of that Captcha.

a r-pixel width random stroke is drawn $\langle s_1, s_2, s_3, \ldots, s_r \rangle$, $s_i = Rand(s_i, s_i + \frac{\zeta}{r}]$. $s_1 = minGrayIntensity(I_C)$ and ζ is set as the difference between s_1 and the local (3×3) max gray value of $b_{t_i}^{\{p_e\}}$, $e \in \{x, y\}$. r is varied from 4–6. Each stroke is varied in intensity along its length to give it a sense of natural expression of pencil sketch. We set a small probability at each pixel that the stroke will stop at that pixel before joining a pair of continuity points.

References

1. Von Ahn, L., Blum, M., Hopper, N.J., Langford, J.: CAPTCHA: using hard AI problems for security. In: Biham, E. (ed.) EUROCRYPT 2003. LNCS, vol. 2656, pp. 294–311. Springer, Heidelberg (2003)
2. Elson, J., Douceur, J.R., Howell, J., Saul, J.: Asirra: a captcha that exploits interest-aligned manual image categorization. In: ACM Conference on Computer and Communications Security, pp. 366–374 (2007)
3. Datta, R., Li, J., Wang, J.Z.: Imagination: a robust image-based captcha generation system. In: Proceedings of the 13th annual ACM international conference on Multimedia, pp. 331–334. ACM (2005)
4. Vikram, S., Fan, Y., Gu, G.: Semage: a new image-based two-factor captcha. In: Proceedings of the 27th Annual Computer Security Applications Conference, pp. 237–246. ACM (2011)
5. Chew, M., Tygar, J.D.: Image recognition CAPTCHAs. In: Zhang, K., Zheng, Y. (eds.) ISC 2004. LNCS, vol. 3225, pp. 268–279. Springer, Heidelberg (2004)
6. Esp-pix. http://server251.theory.cs.cmu.edu/cgi-bin/esp-pix/esp-pix

7. Zhu, B.B., Yan, J., Li, Q., Yang, C., Liu, J., Xu, N., Yi, M., Cai, K.: Attacks and design of image recognition captchas. In: Proceedings of the 17th ACM conference on Computer and communications security, pp. 187–200. ACM (2010)

8. Mohamed, M., Sachdeva, N., Georgescu, M., Gao, S., Saxena, N., Zhang, C., Kumaraguru, P., van Oorschot, P.C., Chen, W.B.: A three-way investigation of a game-CAPTCHA: automated attacks, relay attacks and usability. In: Proceedings of the 9th ACM symposium on Information, computer and communications security, pp. 195–206. ACM, June 2014

9. Virtual sweatshop. Accessed 23 September 2014. http://krebsonsecurity.com/2012/01/virtual-sweatshops-defeat-bot-or-not-tests/

10. Sternberg, R.J.: Cognitive Psychology. Cengage Learning, Belmont (2011)

11. Wickens, C.D., Gordon, S.E., Liu, Y.: An Introduction to Human Factors Engineering. Pearson Prentice Hall, Upper Saddle River (2004)

12. Van Zandt, T., Townsend, J.T.: Self-terminating versus exhaustive processes in rapid visual and memory search: an evaluative review. Percept. Psychophysics **53**(5), 563–580 (1993)

13. Neisser, U.: Decision-time without reaction-time: experiments in visual scanning. Am. J. Psychol. **76**, 376–385 (1963)

14. Liu, Y.: Interactions between memory scanning and visual scanning in process monitoring. Ann Arbor 1001, 48109-2117 (1995)

15. Cave, K.R., Wolfe, J.M.: Modeling the role of parallel processing in visual search. Cogn. psychol. **22**(2), 225–271 (1990)

16. Donders, F.: 1868 Over de snelheid van psychische processen. onderzoekingen gedaan in het physiologisch laboratorium der utrechtsche hoogeschool, (1868–1869). Tweede reeks, ii: 92–120. Reprinted as donders, Franciscus, C.: On the speed of mental processes. Acta Psychologica **30**, 412–431 (1969)

17. Treisman, A.: Properties, Parts, and Objects. Wiley, New York (1986)

18. Google search by image. Accessed 23 September 2014. http://images.google.com/imghp?hl=en

19. Brooke, J.: Sus-a quick and dirty usability scale. Usability Eval. Ind. **189**, 194 (1996)

20. Amazon mechanical turk. Accessed 23 September 2014. https://www.mturk.com/mturk/welcome

21. Lewis, J.R., Sauro, J.: The factor structure of the system usability scale. In: Kurosu, M. (ed.) HCD 2009. LNCS, vol. 5619, pp. 94–103. Springer, Heidelberg (2009)

22. Are you a human. Accessed 23 September 2014. http://www.areyouahuman.com/

Security Analysis of EMV Channel Establishment Protocol in An Enhanced Security Model

Yanfei Guo[✉], Zhenfeng Zhang, Jiang Zhang, and Xuexian Hu

Trusted Computing and Information Assurance Laboratory, Institute of Software, Chinese Academy of Sciences, Beijing, China
{guoyanfei,zfzhang,zhangjiang,huxuexian}@tca.iscas.ac.cn

Abstract. The EMV chip-and-pin system is one of the most widely used cryptographic system in securing credit card and ATM transactions. As suggested by the EMV consortium, the existing RSA-based EMV system will be upgraded to Elliptic Curve Cryptography (ECC) based system. In CCS 2013, Brzuska et al. made the first step to analyze the security of the ECC-based EMV channel establishment protocol in a channel establishment security model, and showed that a slightly modified version of the protocol meets the intended security goals. In this paper, we continue this strand of research by analyzing the security of the ECC-based EMV protocol in a strong channel establishment security model which allows the adversary to get ephemeral private keys of the involved parties. We find that the original protocol is not secure in our security model because the adversary can impersonate a Card entity. Then we slightly modify the protocol almost with no addition of computation cost and show that the resulting protocol is secure in our security model under standard cryptographic assumptions.

1 Introduction

As an international specification for debit and credit card payments [1,7,25], the EMV system has been widely deployed in more than 1.6 million credit cards [24]. The current EMV system is based on RSA public key cryptography, and symmetric-key cryptography (such as DES and AES) [9–12]. The system is recognized as of great significance in providing secure transaction and reducing card payment fraud [26].

Due to the practical significance of EMV system, many researchers have made efforts to investigate its security [1,5–8,25,26,28]. Most of the works focused on the RSA-based EMV system, while the EMV consortium are planning to upgraded the existing RSA-based EMV system to ECC-based system. In November 2012, the EMV consortium released a Request-For-Comments [13] on a draft specification for the ECC-based EMV channel establishment protocol, which is used for establishing a common secret seed and a channel to protect all subsequent messages between a Card and a Terminal.

© Springer International Publishing Switzerland 2015
L.C.K. Hui et al. (Eds.): ICICS 2014, LNCS 8958, pp. 305–320, 2015.
DOI: 10.1007/978-3-319-21966-0_22

According to the EMV consortium, the protocols are designed to (i) provide authentication of the Card (the authenticated parties) by the Terminal (the unauthenticated parties), (ii) detect modifications to the communications, (iii) and protect against eavesdropping and card tracking [13].

As far as we know, there is only one work [3] by Brzuska et al. which analyzes the security of the protocol. They suggested minor changes to the protocol by choosing the ephemeral secret key of the Card entity from a larger space, and establishing two keys instead of one key for the authenticated encryption scheme. They proved the modified protocol (we will call it ECC-based EMV protocol in our paper) is secure in a carefully designed channel establishment security model. However, in their model, adversaries are not allowed to get the participants' ephemeral secret keys.

1.1 Security Model

Bellare and Rogaway [2] proposed the first formal security model for key establishment protocols, known as the BR model. The BR model captures basic security requirements for authenticated key establishment protocols such as known key security and impersonation resilience. Canetti and Krawczyk [4] consider the leakage of the parties' static secret keys and sessions' state (i.e., CK model). Whereas, both above two models fail to capture several advanced attacks such as key compromise impersonation (given a static secret key, an adversary tries to impersonate some honest party in order to fool the owner of the leaked secret key), the breaking of weak perfect forward secrecy (given the static secret keys of participants of the protocol, the adversary tries to recover a previous session key) and maximal exposure attacks (an adversary tries to distinguish the session key from a random value under the disclosure of any pair of secret static keys and ephemeral secret keys of the participants in the session except for both the secret keys of a single participant) [15,20]. In order to capture the advanced attacks mentioned above, LaMacchia et al. [22] proposed a well known security model, (i.e., eCK model [14,17,27,29]) which allows the adversary to obtain the ephemeral secret keys.

However, the above security models seem not fit for the practical requirement in real word protocols such as the TLS protocol [3,18]. Therefore, researchers started to focus on the study of more accurate portrayal of the widely used channel establishment protocols. In 2012, Jager et al. [18] defined the security model for authenticated and confidential channel establishment (ACCE) protocol in which they proved the TLS-DHE is secure under the assumption that the TLS record layer is a stateful length hiding authenticated encryption (sLHAE) scheme.

Later, Krawczyk et al. [21] and Kohlar et al. [19] proved the security of TLS-RSA, TLS-DHE and TLS-DH in the ACCE model respectively. Giesen et al. [16] extended the ACCE model to give the formal treatment of renegotiation in secure channel establishment protocols and analyzed the security of TLS renegotiation in the extended model. Li et al. [23] introduced the definition of ACCE security for authentication protocols with pre-shared keys and proved the security of the Pre-Shared Key Ciphersuites of TLS in the model. Following the similar idea, Brzuska et al. [3] analyzed the ECC-based EMV protocol in a channel establishment security model, which captures one-way authentication key agreement followed by composition with a secure channel and unlinkability property. Nevertheless, the model doesn't describe the situations for the leakage of the ephemeral secret keys and leakage of static secret keys for the parties involved in the target session, which seems not meet the practical requirement [14, 20, 22].

1.2 Our Contribution

In this paper, we propose a strong security model for one-way authentication channel establishment protocols and point that the ECC-based EMV protocol is not secure in our security model. Concretely, if the adversary can get ephemeral keys and session keys of the sessions, he can impersonate a valid Card entity to Terminals. We make slight modification almost without addition of computation cost to the protocol and show that the modified protocol is secure in our security model.

In our security model, we strengthen the adversaries' ability by allowing them to obtain the ephemeral keys of the sessions through *EphemeralKeyReveal* queries. In particular, we allow the adversary to obtain either the static or the ephemeral secret keys of the authenticated party involved in the target session, but not both the static and ephemeral secrets of that party. This enables us to capture the forward security property in one-way authentication setting which means that the compromise of the authenticated party's static secret key can not help the adversary to recover the party's previously established session keys. We note that this property is not captured in the previous one-way authentication channel establishment security models [3, 21].

The security proof is given in the random oracle model under standard cryptographic assumptions, i.e., Gap Diffie-Hellman assumptions, the existence of EUF-CMA digital signatures, and the existence of IND-sfCCA secure and INT-sfPTXT secure authenticated encryption schemes (see Sect. 2).

2   Preliminaries and Definitions

We denote $\mathbb{G} = E(\mathbb{F}_p)$ to be a Diffie-Hellman group defined over an elliptic curve of prime order q, which uses a base point $P \in \mathbb{G}$. The prime q is a function of an implicit security parameter λ. Denote with $\emptyset$ the empty string. Assume that messages in a transcript s are represented as binary strings. Let $|s|$ denote the number of messages of s. $Prefix(s_1, s_2) = true$ if the first $|s_1|$ messages (provided not empty) in transcripts s_1 and s_2 are pairwise equivalent as binary strings, and $false$ otherwise. $\xleftarrow{r}$ means that the value on the left is chosen uniformly at random from the set that on the right of the notion.

Definition 1 (Computational Diffie-Hellman (CDH)). *The CDH problem asks that given $P, rP, sP \in \mathbb{G}$, where $r, s \xleftarrow{r} \mathbb{F}_q$, compute rsP. We say that the*

CDH problem is (t, ϵ_{CDH}) *hard if for any adversary* $\mathcal{A}$ *that runs in time* t *it holds that*

$$Pr[r, s \xleftarrow{r} \mathbb{F}_q : \mathcal{A}(rP, sP) = rsP] \leq \epsilon_{CDH}$$

Definition 2 (Gap-Diffie-Hellman(Gap-DH)). *Let* $\mathcal{O}_{DDH}$ *be an oracle that solves the DDH problem in* $\mathbb{G}$, *i.e. takes as input* $rP, sP, uP \in \mathbb{G}$, *and outputs one if* $uP = rsP$ *and zero otherwise. The Gap Diffie-Hellman problem then asks that given* $P, aP, bP \in \mathbb{G}$ *where* $a, b \xleftarrow{r} \mathbb{F}_q$, *and access to* $\mathcal{O}_{DDH}$, *compute* abP *(i.e. solve CDH). We say that the Gap-DH problem is* $(t, \epsilon_{Gap\text{-}DH})$ *hard if for any adversary* $\mathcal{A}$ *that runs in time* t *it holds that*

$$Pr[a, b \xleftarrow{r} \mathbb{F}_q : \mathcal{A}^{\mathcal{O}_{DDH}}(P, aP, bP) = abP] \leq \epsilon_{Gap\text{-}DH}$$

A digital signature scheme is a triple $SIG = (SIG.Gen, SIG.Sign, SIG.Vfy)$, consisting of a key generation algorithm $(sk, pk) \xleftarrow{\$} SIG.Gen(1^\lambda)$ generating a (public) verification key pk and a secret signing key sk on input of security parameter λ, signing algorithm $\sigma \leftarrow SIG.Sign(sk, m)$ generating a signature for message m, and verification algorithm $SIG.Vfy(pk, \sigma, m)$ returning 1, if σ is a valid signature for m under key pk, and 0 otherwise. Consider the following security experiment played between a challenger $\mathcal{C}$ and an adversary $\mathcal{A}$.

1. The challenger generates a public/secret key pair $(sk, pk) \xleftarrow{\$} SIG.Gen(1^\lambda)$, the adversary receives pk as input.
2. The adversary may query arbitrary messages m_i to the challenger. The challenger replies to each query with a signature $\sigma_i = SIG.Sign(sk, m_i)$. Here i is an index, ranging between $1 \leq i \leq q$ for some $q \in \mathbb{N}$. Queries can be made adaptively.
3. Eventually, the adversary outputs a message/signature pair (m, σ).

Definition 3 (EUF-CMA). *We say that* SIG *is* (t, ϵ_{SIG}) *EUF-CMA secure against existential forgeries under adaptive chosen-message attacks, if for all adversaries* $\mathcal{A}$ *that run in time* t *it holds that*

$$Pr[(m, \sigma) \leftarrow \mathcal{A}^{Sign(sk, \cdot)}(1^\lambda, pk) \text{ such that } SIG.Vfy(pk, m, \sigma) = 1 \wedge m \notin \{m_1, \cdots, m_q\}] \leq \epsilon_{SIG}$$

Note that we have $q \leq t$, i.e., the number of allowed queries q is bounded by the running time t of the adversary.

An authenticated encryption (AE) scheme $AE = (\mathcal{K}, enc, dec)$ consists of three algorithms. The randomized key generation algorithm $\mathcal{K}$ returns a key K. The encryption algorithm enc, takes key K and a plaintext and returns a ciphertext. The decryption algorithm dec takes key K and a ciphertext and returns either a plaintext or a special symbol $\perp$ indicating failure. The following two properties are variants of the stateful security models of AE scheme [3]. $enc_\kappa(h, m; st_e)$ is a symmetric encryption oracle for κ, which takes as input a header h, message m, outputs ciphertext c and updated state st_e. $dec_\kappa(h, c; st_d)$ is a symmetric decryption oracle for κ which takes a header h, a ciphertext c as input, outputs message m or $\perp$ and updated state st_d. $LR_b(m_0, m_1)$ for $b \in \{0, 1\}$

outputs m_b. So a left-or-right encryption oracle $enc_\kappa(h, LR_b(m_0, m_1); st_e)$ outputs $enc_\kappa(h, m_b; st_e)$ if $m_0 = m_1$ and $\perp$ otherwise. C-E (C-D) is the set of ciphertexts output by (input to) the left-or-right encryption (decryption) oracle. M-E (M-D) is the set of messages input to (output by) the encryption (decryption) oracle.

Definition 4 (IND-sfCCA [3]). *Consider the authenticated encryption scheme $AE = \{enc_\kappa, dec_\kappa\}$. Let $\mathcal{A}$ be an adversary with access to a left-or-right encryption oracle $enc_\kappa(h, LR_b(m_0, m_1); st_e)$ and a decryption oracle $dec_\kappa(h, c; st_d)$. It is mandated that any two messages queried to $enc_\kappa(h, LR_b(m_0, m_1); st_e)$ have equal length. The ind-sfcca experiment is defined as in Fig. 1. The attacker wins when $b' = b$, and his advantage is defined as*

$$Adv_{AE}^{ind\text{-}sfcca}(\mathcal{A}) = Pr[Exec_{AE}^{ind\text{-}sfcca\text{-}1}(\mathcal{A}) = 1] - Pr[Exec_{AE}^{ind\text{-}sfcca\text{-}0}(\mathcal{A}) = 1].$$

We say that AE is $(t, \epsilon_{ind\text{-}sfcca})$ IND-sfCCA secure, if for all adversaries $\mathcal{A}$ that run in time t it holds that

$$Adv_{AE}^{ind\text{-}sfcca}(\mathcal{A}) \leq \epsilon_{ind\text{-}sfcca}.$$

$$Adv_{AE}^{ind\text{-}sfcca}(\mathcal{A}) \leq \epsilon_{ind\text{-}sfcca}.$$

<table>
<tr><td>

The *ind-sfcca* experiment

$Exec_{AE}^{ind\text{-}sfcca\text{-}b}(\mathcal{A})$
$\kappa \xleftarrow{r} \{0,1\}^k$, C-$E := \emptyset$, C-$D := \emptyset$, $st_e := \emptyset$ and $st_d := \emptyset$
Run $\mathcal{A}^{enc_\kappa, dec_\kappa}$
  Reply to $enc_\kappa(h, LR_b(m_0, m_1); st_e)$ as follows:
    $(c, st_e) \xleftarrow{r} enc_\kappa(h, m_b, st_e)$
    C-$E \leftarrow C$-$E \cup c; \mathcal{A} \Leftarrow c$
  Reply to $dec_\kappa(h, c; st_d)$ as follows:
    $(m, st_d) \xleftarrow{r} dec_\kappa(h, c; st_d)$
    if $m \neq \perp$ then
      C-$D \leftarrow C$-$D \cup c$
      if $Prefix(C$-D, C-$E) = false$ then $\mathcal{A} \Leftarrow m$
Until $\mathcal{A}$ returns a bit b'
return b'

</td><td>

The *int-sfptxt* experiment

$Exec_{AE}^{int\text{-}sfptxt}(\mathcal{A})$
$\kappa \xleftarrow{r} \{0,1\}^k, d := 0$
M-$E := \emptyset$, M-$D := \emptyset$, $st_e := \emptyset$ and $st_d := \emptyset$
Run $\mathcal{A}^{enc_\kappa, dec_\kappa}$
  Reply to $enc_\kappa(h, m; st_e)$ as follows:
    $(c, st_e) \xleftarrow{r} enc_\kappa(h, m; st_e)$
    M-$E \leftarrow M$-$E \cup m; \mathcal{A} \Leftarrow c$
  Reply to $dec_\kappa(h, c; st_d)$ as follows:
    $(m, st_d) \xleftarrow{r} dec_\kappa(h, c; st_d)$
    if $m \neq \perp$ then
      M-$D \leftarrow M$-$D \cup m; \mathcal{A} \Leftarrow 1$
      if $Prefix(M$-D, M-$E) = false$ then $d := 1$
    else $\mathcal{A} \Leftarrow 0$
Until $\mathcal{A}$ halts
return d

</td></tr>
</table>

Fig. 1. The *ind-sfcca* (resp. *int-sfptxt*) experiment

Definition 5 (INT-sfPTXT [3]). *Consider the scheme $AE = \{enc_\kappa, dec_\kappa\}$. Let $\mathcal{A}$ be an adversary with oracle access to $enc_\kappa(h, m; st_e)$ and $dec_\kappa(h, c; st_d)$. The int-sfptxt experiment is defined as in Fig. 1. The advantage $Adv_{AE}^{int\text{-}sfptxt}(\mathcal{A})$ of an adversary is defined as*

$$Adv_{AE}^{int\text{-}sfptxt}(\mathcal{A}) = Pr[Exec_{AE}^{int\text{-}sfptxt}(\mathcal{A}) = 1].$$

We say that AE is $(t, \epsilon_{int\text{-}sfptxt})$ INT-sfPTXT secure, if for all adversaries $\mathcal{A}$ that run in time t it holds that

$$Adv_{AE}^{int\text{-}sfptxt}(\mathcal{A}) \leq \epsilon_{int\text{-}sfptxt}.$$

3   EMV Channel Establishment Protocol

The original specification of the EMV channel establishment protocol can be found in [13]. In this section, the EMV channel establishment protocol modified by [3] is presented. There are two kinds of participants in the system: Card and Terminal. Each Card holds a certificate which is a digital signature of its public key $Q_C = dP \in \mathbb{G}$. The secret key of the Card participant is $d \xleftarrow{r} \mathbb{F}_q$. The protocol uses a hash function H that takes elements in the group $\mathbb{G}$ and maps them onto a pair of keys for the authenticated encryption scheme.

After the protocol has established secret keys, it uses them in a secure channel protocol $(SendCh, ReceiveCh)$. On input an application message m and state st_e, $SendCh$ returns a channel message ch. On input a channel message ch and state st_d, $ReceiveCh$ returns an application message m. The secure channel protocol is based on a stateful AE scheme $AE = \{enc, dec\}$. Assume that all plaintext headers used by the secure channel are unauthenticated, implying that no header is sent in clear as part of the AE scheme. The states st_e and st_d here model the fact that in practice sequence numbers are used to ensure that messages are delivered in order, thus the operations are stateful. The protocol is presented in Fig. 2. The static key of the Card is d, the ephemeral key of the Card is a, the ephemeral key of the Terminal is e, and the session keys are $(\kappa_e^C, \kappa_d^C) = (\kappa_d^T, \kappa_e^T) = H(eadP)$.

Card (C)		Terminal (T)
$a \in_R \mathbb{F}_q$		
	$\xrightarrow{A=aQ_C}$	
		$e \in_R \mathbb{F}_q$
	$\xleftarrow{E=eP}$	
$(\kappa_e^C, \kappa_d^C) = H(daE)$		$(\kappa_d^T, \kappa_e^T) = H(eA)$
$(ch, st_e^C) = SendCh_{\kappa_e^C}(cert_C\|a\|Q_C; st_e^C)$	$\xrightarrow{ch}$	$(cert_C\|a\|Q_C, st_d^T) = ReceiveCh_{\kappa_d^T}(ch, st_d^T)$
		Check $ver_{pk}(cert_C, Q_C) \overset{?}{=} true$
		Check $aQ_C \overset{?}{=} A$
$(ch_1, st_e^C) = SendCh_{\kappa_e^C}(m_1; st_e^C)$	$\xrightarrow{ch_1}$	$(m_1, st_d^T) = ReceiveCh_{\kappa_d^T}(ch_1; st_d^T)$
$(m_2, st_d^C) = ReceiveCh_{\kappa_d^C}(ch_2; st_d^C)$	$\xleftarrow{ch_2}$	$(ch_2, st_e^T) = SendCh_{\kappa_e^T}(m_2; st_e^T)$

Fig. 2. ECC-based EMV channel establishment protocol

4   The Enhanced Security Model

In this section we present a stronger security model for one-way authentication channel establishment protocols which is inspired by the security models of [3] and [22]. We enhance the channel establishment security model [3] by considering $EphemeralKeyReveal$ queries and using stronger freshness definition.

This enhancement enables us to capture the forward security property in one-way authentication setting which is not captured in the previous one-way authentication channel establishment security models [3,21].

4.1 Preliminaries

Let $n_C, n_T, n_S \in N$ be positive integers. Assume that there are n_C authenticated entities and n_T unauthenticated entities in the system. Each party can establish at most n_S sessions. Each party in the system has a distinct identity i.

The protocol description is defined by two efficiently computable stateful (sub)-protocols $P = \{\Pi, \mathcal{G}\}$. The protocol Π defines how honest parties behave and $\mathcal{G}$ is the key generation algorithm. Each execution of the protocol can be modeled as an oracle Π_i^s, which means that the session is party i's s-th instance of carrying out the protocol with some partner j (which is determined during the protocol execution). The oracle has access to its owner's private key and independently maintains a list of internal state information as follows:

- $\delta \in \{derived, accept, reject, \perp\}$ is current state of the key exchange (initialized to $\perp$). When the session owner derives a session key, he marks the session as *derived*. When the key establishment protocol ends successfully (and stipulates that no further messages are to be received), the session owner marks the session as *accepted*. An *accepted* session must be *derived*. $\delta = reject$ means that the session rejects.
- $\rho \in \{initiator, responder\}$ is the role of the participant.
- *pid* is the partner identifier which is determined during the protocol execution.
- *sid* is the session identifier which can be defined by a transcript of all the messages the session receives and sends.
- $\kappa = (\kappa_e^\rho, \kappa_d^\rho) \in (\{0,1\}^* \cup \{\perp\})^2$ is the agreed pair of keys. The order of the keys depends on the role. It is initialized as $(\perp, \perp)$. κ is set to be the derived session key when $\delta = derived$.
- T_i^s records the transcript of messages sent and received by oracle Π_i^s. Initialized as $\emptyset$.
- $kst_i^s \in \{exposed, fresh\}$ denotes the freshness of the session key. Initialized as *fresh*.
- $st_k \in \{0,1\}^*$ is the session state after the session key/channel is established. Initialized as $\emptyset$.

To distinguish the different types of messages that may occur in an execution, there are three different execution "modes" of protocols: establishing a key, sending, respectively receiving messages from the established channel. Formally, the honest operation of a participant is defined by a triple $\Pi = (KeyExch, SendCh, ReceiveCh)$.

Some of the messages sent during the key-exchange may travel over the channel. So, strictly speaking, $KeyExch$ may make use of the latter algorithms. To facilitate the description of the resulting complex interaction we define the algorithm $EstChannel$ which, essentially , is in charge of establishing the channel. This algorithm may make calls to the algorithms defining Π.

During the execution of a protocol an oracle can receive two types of input, an application message (user input) or a channel message (received from the wire). At any point during its execution, protocol Π takes as input a message m and a message type $type \in \{ap, ch\}$ indicating the message was received from the user's application or the channel, respectively, runs the appropriate algorithm, and returns the output of that algorithm. The execution of protocol Π is summarized in Fig. 3.

After the channel has been established whenever the input message type is ch then $ReceiveCh$ will be called. This models messages that are received from the channel (for decryption). It takes as input a message m and state st_d and outputs a message m' for output to the user's application. $ReceiveCh$ rejects and outputs $\perp$ if the received messages are "out of state" messages (e.g., format error, invalid message).

When the message type is ap then $SendCh$ will be called. This models application messages that are input to be sent (encrypted) on the channel. It takes as input a message m and state st_e and outputs a message m' for output to the channel. Note that if keys have not yet been established ($\delta \neq accept$) then such a call to $SendCh$ will output $\perp$.

Protocol $\Pi(m, type)$:
if $type = ch \wedge \delta \neq accept$ **then**
$(m'; st_\kappa) \leftarrow EstChannel(m; st_\kappa)$
else if $type = ch$ **then**
$(m'; st_d) \leftarrow ReceiveCh_{\kappa_d}(m; st_d)$
else $(type = ap)$
$(m'; st_e) \leftarrow SendCh_{\kappa_e}(m; st_e)$
return m'

Fig. 3. Honest protocol execution

4.2 Matching Conversations

Denote $TEstCha_i^s$ and $TEstCha_j^t$ to be the transcript involved in the execution of $Estchannel$ for oracles Π_i^s and Π_j^t respectively.

Definition 6 (Matching Conversation). *We say that an oracle Π_i^s has a matching conversation to oracle Π_j^t, if $Prefix(TEstCha_j^t, TEstCha_i^s) = true$ or $Prefix(TEstCha_i^s, TEstCha_j^t) = true$.*

To keep the correctness of the protocol, two matching sessions which accept should always establish the same session key.

Definition 7 (Correctness). *For any two oracles Π_i^s and Π_j^t that have matching conversation with $pid_i^s = j$, $pid_j^t = i$, $\delta_i^s = accept$ and $\delta_j^t = accept$ it always holds that $\kappa_i^s = \kappa_j^t$.*

4.3   Adversarial Capabilities

The adversary $\mathcal{A}$ is a probabilistic polynomial Turing machine taking as input the security parameter λ and the public information, and controls the communication and network. $\mathcal{A}$ can issue the following queries to oracles Π_i^s for $i \in [1, n_C + n_T], s \in [1, n_S]$.

- $Newsession(i, \rho)$. Create a session for user i with role ρ.
- $Send(\Pi_i^s, m, type)$. Send a message m to Π_i^s with type $type$. As a result Π_i^s will run Π on input $(m, type)$ (as in Fig. 3) and respond with the outputting message m^* (if there is any) that should be sent according to the protocol specification and its internal states. The state information of Π_i^s will be updated depending on the protocol specification. After the session accepted, this query may initiate $ReceiveCh$ or $SendCh$ algorithms. Note that the session will not send message to the channel when it just invokes the $ReceiveCh$ algorithms.
- $StaticKeyReveal(i)$. $\mathcal{A}$ obtains the long-term private key of i if it is an authenticated entity.
- $EphemeralKeyReveal(\Pi_i^s)$. $\mathcal{A}$ obtains the ephemeral private key of session Π_i^s.
- $SessionKeyReveal(\Pi_i^s)$. $\mathcal{A}$ gets the derived session key of Π_i^s if δ is $derived$ or $accepted$, at the same time, kst_i^s is set to be $exposed$. If at the point when this query is issued, there exists another oracle Π_j^t having matching conversation to Π_i^s, then kst_j^t is also set to be $exposed$.

Following the routine of [3], to define the security experiments for message authentication and privacy latter, the following notations for each Π_i^s is maintained:

- Application messages sent $Ap\text{-}S_i^s$, i.e. the list of all messages m input to $Send(\Pi_i^s, m, ap)$.
- Channel messages sent $Ch\text{-}S_i^s$, i.e. the list of all outputs from $Send(\Pi_i^s, m, ap)$.
- Channel messages received $Ch\text{-}R_i^s$, i.e. the list of all messages m input to $Send(\Pi_i^s, m, ch)$.
- Application messages received $Ap\text{-}R_i^s$, i.e. the list of all outputs from $Send(\Pi_i^s, m, ch)$.

Once a channel is established, whenever an application message is input to $Send$, the protocol Π is executed and a channel message will be output and sent on the channel. Similarly whenever a channel message is input to $Send$, the protocol Π is run and an application message will be output to the user. The above lists help us keep track of these messages and facilitate checking necessary in the following security models.

4.4   Security Definitions

In this subsection, we consider the security of one-way authentication secure channel establishment protocols, which is the scenario of EMV channel establishment protocol. The parties in the system are classified into two sets.

Let C be the set of authenticated participants (the Cards) and let T be the set of unauthenticated participants (the Terminals), where unauthenticated participants do not hold long-term private/public key pairs.

In our model, a Terminal $i \in T$ wishes to authenticate a Card $j \in C$ and establish a key (additionally a secure channel) with this Card. For a session Π_j^t owned by party $j \in C$ with public/secret key pairs, the adversary $\mathcal{A}$ needs to obtain both static and ephemeral secret keys to get the session key. But if the session has a matching conversation with another session Π_i^s with $i \in T$, knowing the session's ephemeral key enables the adversary to get the session key. Since all $i \in T$ have no long-term secret, it would always be possible for an adversary to impersonate an unauthenticated participant and establish a session with a real Card. So, in our model, the target session should always be a session owned by a Terminal.

We give the freshness definition for a session of a Terminal as follows. The session that the adversary attacks should keep fresh to make sense. In our model, the freshness definition enlarges the scope of sessions the adversary can attack compared to the previous security model [3]. That is, we allow the adversary to obtain either static key or ephemeral key of the Card party involved in the target session. While in [3], the adversary can ask neither keys of this party. So, the forward security property in one-way setting is captured in our model.

Definition 8 (One-Sided Freshness). *Let Π_i^s be an accepted session held by a party $i \in T$ with other party $j \in C$, and both parties are honest. Session Π_j^t (if it exists) is the matching conversation of Π_i^s. Then the session Π_i^s is said to be fresh if none of the following conditions hold:*

1. *Π_i^s has internal state $kst_i^s = exposed$.*
2. *Π_j^t exists and $\mathcal{A}$ issued one of the following:*
   - *EphemeralKeyReveal(Π_i^s).*
   - *Both StaticKeyReveal(j) and EphemeralKeyReveal(Π_j^t).*
3. *Π_j^t doesn't exist and $\mathcal{A}$ issued one of the following:*
   - *EphemeralKeyReveal(Π_i^s).*
   - *StaticKeyReveal(j) before session Π_i^s accepts.*

As in [3], we formulate three levels of security: Entity Authentication (EA), Message Authentication (MA) and Message Privacy (MP).

Entity Authentication. An adversary violates entity authentication if he can get a session to accept even if there is no unique session of its intended partner that has a matching conversation to it. More formally, the security is defined via an experiment *ent* played between a challenger $\mathcal{C}$ and an adversary $\mathcal{A}$. At the beginning, $\mathcal{C}$ generates the long-term key pairs (pk_U, sk_U) for all the parties $U \in C$ and sends the public keys pk_U for $U \in C$ to $\mathcal{A}$. Then the adversary can issue the oracle queries we defined above to the oracles.

Send query for *auth* game

Send($\Pi_i^s, m, type$) :
$m' \leftarrow \Pi_i^s(m, type)$
if $\delta = accept$ and $type = ap$ then
$\quad AP\text{-}S_i^s \leftarrow AP\text{-}S_i^s \| m$
else if $\delta = accept$ and $type = ch$ then
$\quad$ if $m' \neq\, \perp$ then $AP\text{-}R_i^s \leftarrow AP\text{-}R_i^s \| m'$
return m'

$SendLR$ query for *priv* game

$SendLR(\Pi_i^s, m_0, m_1, type)$:
if $\delta = accept$ and $type = ap$ then
$\quad m' \leftarrow \Pi_i^s(m_{b_i^s}, ap)$
$\quad Ch\text{-}S_i^s \leftarrow Ch\text{-}S_i^s \| m'$
else if $m_0 \neq m_1$ then $m' := \perp$
else
$\quad m' \leftarrow \Pi_i^s(m_0, type)$
$\quad$ if $\delta = accept$ and $type = ch$ then
$\quad\quad$ if $m' \neq\, \perp$ and Π_i^s has a partner Π_j^t then
$\quad\quad\quad Ch\text{-}R_i^s \leftarrow Ch\text{-}R_i^s \| m_0$
$\quad\quad\quad$ if $Prefix(Ch\text{-}R_i^s, Ch\text{-}S_j^t) = true$ then $m' := \emptyset$
return m'

Fig. 4. The *Send* (resp. *SendLR*) query for the *auth* (resp. *priv*) games

Definition 9 (EA). *We say that protocol $P = \{\Pi, \mathcal{G}\}$ is a (t, ϵ_{EA})-secure EA protocol if for all adversaries $\mathcal{A}$ running in time at most t, when $\mathcal{A}$ terminates, then with probability at most ϵ_{EA} there exists a fresh oracle Π_i^s such that Π_i^s accepts, but there is no unique oracle Π_j^t such that Π_i^s has a matching conversation to Π_j^t for $i \in T, j \in C$.*

Message Authentication. The message authentication property ensures the integrity and authenticity of all messages sent over the channel. For any two partner oracles Π_i^s and Π_j^t, the oracle Π_i^s should only successfully receive messages which were output by Π_j^t and vice versa. That is formalized by requiring that for any fresh oracle Π_i^s with unique partner Π_j^t, $Prefix(Ap\text{-}R_i^s, Ap\text{-}S_j^t) = true$. If this does not hold then the adversary successfully fools Π_i^s into receiving an application message which was not output by the partnered oracle Π_j^t.

The authentication experiment *auth* generates public/private key pairs for each user $i \in C$ (by running $\mathcal{G}$) and returns the public keys to $\mathcal{A}$. The adversary is permitted to make the queries $NewSession(i, \rho)$, $SessionKeyReveal(\Pi_i^s)$, $StaticKeyReveal(i)$, $EphemeralKey\ Reveal(\Pi_i^s)$ as well as $Send(\Pi_i^s, m, type)$ with message $type \in \{ap, ch\}$. On querying $Send(\Pi_i^s, m, type)$, the game behaves as in Fig. 4.

The game $Exec_\Pi^{auth}(\mathcal{A})$ between an adversary $\mathcal{A}$ and challenger $\mathcal{C}$ is defined as follows:

1. The challenger $\mathcal{C}$ generates public/private key pairs for each user $U \in C$ (by running $\mathcal{G}$) and returns the public keys to $\mathcal{A}$.
2. $\mathcal{A}$ is allowed to make as many $NewSession$, $SessionKeyReveal$, $StaticKey$ $Reveal$, $EphemeralKeyReveal$, $Send$ queries as it likes.
3. The adversary stops with no output.

We say that an adversary $\mathcal{A}$ wins the game if there exists Π_i^s with unique partner Π_j^t such that they are matching conversations and the list $Ap\text{-}R_i^s$ is not a prefix of $Ap\text{-}S_j^t$. The adversary's advantage is $Adv_\Pi^{auth}(\mathcal{A}) = Pr[\exists \Pi_i^s, \Pi_j^t \text{ for } i \in T, j \in C : \Pi_i^s \text{ is fresh } \wedge \Pi_i^s, \Pi_j^t \text{ are matching } \wedge Prefix(Ap\text{-}R_i^s, Ap\text{-}S_j^t) = false]$.

Definition 10 (MA). *A protocol* $P = \{\Pi, \mathcal{G}\}$ *is a* (t, ϵ_{MA})*-secure MA protocol if for all adversaries* $\mathcal{A}_{auth}$ *running in time at most* t, $Adv_\Pi^{auth}(\mathcal{A}_{auth}) \le \epsilon_{MA}$.

Message Privacy. The message privacy property ensures that the adversary should not be able to determine which set of messages $\{m_{01}, m_{02}, m_{03}, \cdots\}$ and $\{m_{11}, m_{12}, m_{13}, \cdots\}$ has been transmitted on the secure channel.

The message privacy experiment *priv* initializes the states as in the authentication experiment *auth*, except that each session now also holds a random secret bit b_i^s. As before, the adversary can make the queries *NewSession*, *SessionKeyReveal*, *StaticKeyReveal*, *EphemeralKeyReveal*. In addition, the adversary can issue a left-right version of $Send(\Pi_i^s, m, type)$ which is used to model message privacy. Specifically, the query $SendLR(\Pi_i^s, m_0, m_1, type)$ takes as input two messages and returns $Send(\Pi_i^s, m_{b_i^s}, type)$. When $type \ne ap$ these two messages are equal, $SendLR(\Pi_i^s, m, m, type) = Send(\Pi_i^s, m, type)$.

As before, two sessions are matching conversations. On the $SendLR(\Pi_i^s, m_0, m_1, type)$ query, the game behaves as in Fig. 4. Once the channel is established, whenever $SendLR(\Pi_i^s, m, m, ch)$ is called, we allow the protocol to run as normal but check the lists $Ch\text{-}R_i^s$ and $Ch\text{-}S_j^t$. If the message m was a channel output from Π_i^s's partner Π_j^t, then $SendLR$ will not return anything. This allows the adversary to progress the state of an oracle but prevents them from trivially winning the game.

Game $Exec_\Pi^{priv}(\mathcal{A})$ between an adversary $\mathcal{A}$ and challenger $\mathcal{C}$:

1. The challenger $\mathcal{C}$, generates public/private key pairs for each user $U \in C$ (by running $\mathcal{G}$) and returns the public keys to $\mathcal{A}$.
2. $\mathcal{A}$ is allowed to make as many *NewSession*, *SessionKeyReveal*, *StaticKey Reveal*, *EphemeralKeyReveal*, *SendLR* queries as it likes.
3. Finally $\mathcal{A}$ outputs a tuple (i, s, b_0) for $i \in T$.

We say the adversary $\mathcal{A}$ wins if its output $b_0 = b_i^s$ and Π_i^s is fresh (and has a unique partner) and the output of $Exec_\Pi^{priv}(\mathcal{A})$ is set to 1. Otherwise the output is 0. Formally we define the advantage of $\mathcal{A}$ as $Adv_\Pi^{priv}(\mathcal{A}) = |Pr[Exec_\Pi^{priv}(\mathcal{A}) = 1] - 1/2|$.

Definition 11 (MP). *A protocol* $P = \{\Pi, \mathcal{G}\}$ *is a* (t, ϵ_{MP})*-secure MP protocol if for all adversaries* $\mathcal{A}_{priv}$ *running in time at most* t, $Adv_\Pi^{priv}(\mathcal{A}_{priv}) \le \epsilon_{MP}$.

A channel establishment protocol is secure if it satisfies all of the three notions above.

Definition 12 (eEAMAP). *Protocol* $P = \{\Pi, \mathcal{G}\}$ *is a* (t, ϵ)*-secure eEAMAP protocol if it is a* (t, ϵ)*-secure EA protocol, a* (t, ϵ)*-secure MA protocol and a* (t, ϵ)*-secure MP protocol.*

4.5 Unlinkability

In practice, the Card holders may also want to have a property that their two independent transactions can not be linked. Actually, this property is formally captured by a notion called unlinkability. In this paper, we adapt the idea of [3] to define our unlinkability definition (see full version of our paper), which means that it should be hard for an adversary to determine whether two particular sessions are linked with the same Card. Note that this property only holds against an eavesdropper adversary who is not a Terminal.

5   Security Analysis of EMV Channel Establishment Protocol in Our Security Model

In our security model, the adversary controls all the communications and can get the ephemeral keys and session keys of sessions, so he can impersonate a valid Card through the following steps (see Fig. 5):

1. Card entity C chooses $a \in_R \mathbb{F}_q$ and sends out $A = aQ_C$.
2. The adversary $\mathcal{M}$ intercepts the message A, computes $2 \cdot A$ and sends it to Terminal T.
3. The Terminal T selects $e \in_R \mathbb{F}_q$ and sends out $E = eP$.
4. $\mathcal{M}$ intercepts E, computes $2 \cdot E$ and sends it to the Card C.
5. After that, $\mathcal{M}$ issues $EphemeralKeyReveal$ to the Card session and obtains a.
6. After the Card session accepts, $\mathcal{M}$ issues $SessionKeyReveal$ query to the Card's session and obtains its session key $(\kappa_e^C, \kappa_d^C) = H(2adE) = H(2deaP) = (\kappa_d^T, \kappa_e^T)$.
7. $\mathcal{M}$ can obtain $Q_C, cert_C$ by impersonating a Terminal to C in a different session.[1]
8. $\mathcal{M}$ computes and sends $ch' = SendCh_{\kappa_e^C}(cert_C||2a||Q_C; st_e^C)$ which will pass the verification of the Terminal.

So, the adversary successfully impersonates the Card to the Terminal which breaks the EA property.

6   The Enhanced Protocol

The enhanced protocol is presented as follows in Fig. 6. The only difference lies in the computation of the session key. We add the ephemeral public keys of the session to the inputs of the hash function.

---

[1] Note that in this process the adversary can also make no $EphemeralKeyReveal$ queries and just keep and decrypt value ch using κ_e^C to obtain $(cert_C||a||Q_C)$ and extract the value of $cert_C, a, Q_C$.

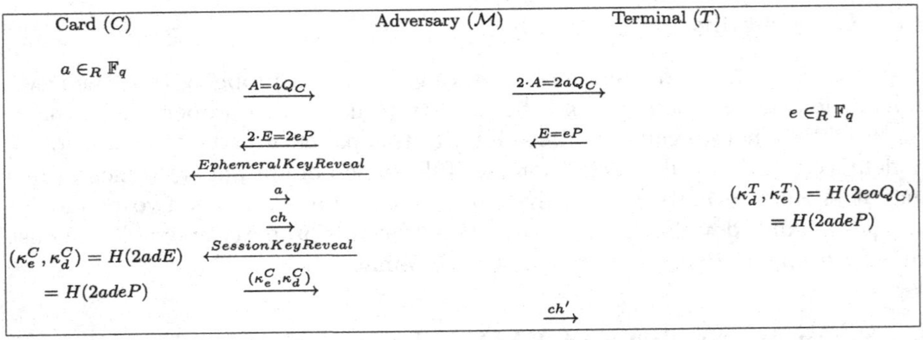

Fig. 5. Security analysis of ECC-based EMV channel establishment protocol in the enhanced security model

7 Security

Theorem 1. *If the Gap-DH problem is $(t, \epsilon_{Gap\text{-}DH})$ hard over $\mathbb{G}$, $AE = (enc, dec)$ is $(t, \epsilon_{ind\text{-}sfcca})$ IND-sfCCA secure and $(t, \epsilon_{int\text{-}sfptxt})$ INT-sfPTXT secure, and the signature scheme (sig, ver) used to produce card certificates is (t, ϵ_{sig}) EUF-CMA secure, then the Enhanced EMV protocol $P = (\Pi, \mathcal{G})$ in Fig. 6 is secure in the sense of eEAMAP and unlinkability.*

The proof of the theorem is given in the full version of the paper.

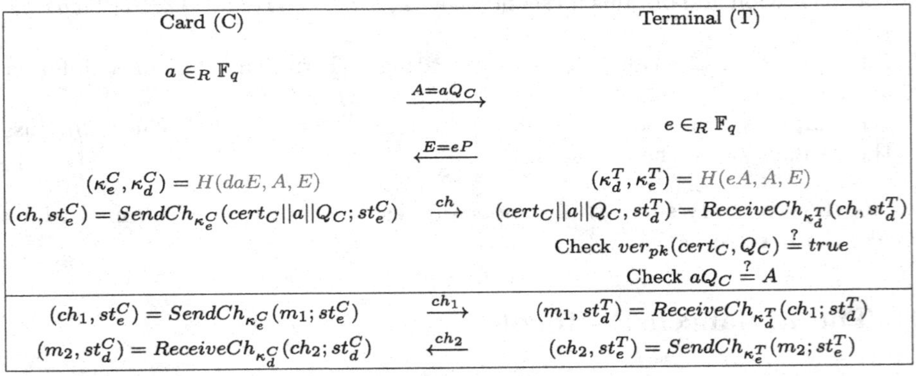

Fig. 6. Enhanced ECC-based EMV channel establishment protocol

Acknowledgement. The work is supported by the National Basic Research Program of China (No. 2013CB338003), the National Natural Science Foundation of China (No. 61170278, 91118006), and the 863 project (No. 2012AA01A403).

References

1. Anderson, R., Bond, M., Choudary, O., Murdoch, S.J., Stajano, F.: Might financial cryptography kill financial innovation? – the curious case of EMV. In: Danezis, G. (ed.) FC 2011. LNCS, vol. 7035, pp. 220–234. Springer, Heidelberg (2012)
2. Bellare, M., Rogaway, P.: Entity authentication and key distribution. In: Stinson, D.R. (ed.) CRYPTO 1993. LNCS, vol. 773, pp. 232–249. Springer, Heidelberg (1994)
3. Brzuska, C., Smart, N.P., Warinschi, B., Watson, G.J.: An analysis of the EMV channel establishment protocol. In: Proceedings of the 2013 ACM SIGSAC Conference on Computer and Communications Security, CCS 2013, pp. 373–386. ACM, New York (2013)
4. Canetti, R., Krawczyk, H.: Analysis of key-exchange protocols and their use for building secure channels. In: Pfitzmann, B. (ed.) EUROCRYPT 2001. LNCS, vol. 2045, p. 453. Springer, Heidelberg (2001)
5. Coron, J.-S., Naccache, D., Tibouchi, M.: Fault attacks against EMV signatures. In: Pieprzyk, J. (ed.) CT-RSA 2010. LNCS, vol. 5985, pp. 208–220. Springer, Heidelberg (2010)
6. Coron, J.-S., Naccache, D., Tibouchi, M., Weinmann, R.-P.: Practical cryptanalysis of ISO/IEC 9796-2 and EMV signatures. In: Halevi, S. (ed.) CRYPTO 2009. LNCS, vol. 5677, pp. 428–444. Springer, Heidelberg (2009)
7. Degabriele, J.P., Lehmann, A., Paterson, K.G., Smart, N.P., Strefler, M.: On the joint security of encryption and signature in EMV. In: Dunkelman, O. (ed.) CT-RSA 2012. LNCS, vol. 7178, pp. 116–135. Springer, Heidelberg (2012)
8. Drimer, S., Murdoch, S.J., Anderson, R.: Optimised to fail: card readers for online banking. In: Dingledine, R., Golle, P. (eds.) FC 2009. LNCS, vol. 5628, pp. 184–200. Springer, Heidelberg (2009)
9. EMVCo: EMV-Integrated Circuit Card Specifications for Payment Systems, Book 1: Application Independent ICC to Terminal Interface Requirements (2011)
10. EMVCo: EMV-Integrated Circuit Card Specifications for Payment Systems, Book 2: Security and Key Management (2011)
11. EMVCo: EMV-Integrated Circuit Card Specifications for Payment Systems, Book 3: Application Specification (2011)
12. EMVCo: EMV-Integrated Circuit Card Specifications for Payment Systems, Book 4: Cardholder, Attendant, and Acquirer Interface Requirements (2011)
13. EMVCo: EMV ECC Key Establishment Protocols (2012)
14. Fujioka, A., Suzuki, K.: Designing efficient authenticated key exchange resilient to leakage of ephemeral secret keys. In: Kiayias, A. (ed.) CT-RSA 2011. LNCS, vol. 6558, pp. 121–141. Springer, Heidelberg (2011)
15. Fujioka, A., Suzuki, K., Xagawa, K., Yoneyama, K.: Strongly secure authenticated key exchange from factoring, codes, and lattices. In: Fischlin, M., Buchmann, J., Manulis, M. (eds.) PKC 2012. LNCS, vol. 7293, pp. 467–484. Springer, Heidelberg (2012)
16. Giesen, F., Kohlar, F., Stebila, D.: On the security of TLS renegotiation. In Proceedings of the 2013 ACM SIGSAC Conference on Computer and Communications Security, CCS 2013, pp. 387–398. ACM, New York (2013)
17. Huang, H.: Strongly secure one round authenticated key exchange protocol with perfect forward security. In: Boyen, X., Chen, X. (eds.) ProvSec 2011. LNCS, vol. 6980, pp. 389–397. Springer, Heidelberg (2011)

18. Jager, T., Kohlar, F., Schäge, S., Schwenk, J.: On the security of TLS-DHE in the standard model. In: Safavi-Naini, R., Canetti, R. (eds.) CRYPTO 2012. LNCS, vol. 7417, pp. 273–293. Springer, Heidelberg (2012)

19. Kohlar, F., Schäge, S., Schwenk, J.: On the security of TLS-DH and TLS-RSA in the standard model. Cryptology ePrint Archive, Report 2013/367 (2013). http://eprint.iacr.org/

20. Krawczyk, H.: HMQV: a high-performance secure diffie-hellman protocol. In: Shoup, V. (ed.) CRYPTO 2005. LNCS, vol. 3621, pp. 546–566. Springer, Heidelberg (2005)

21. Krawczyk, H., Paterson, K.G., Wee, H.: On the security of the TLS protocol: a systematic analysis. In: Canetti, R., Garay, J.A. (eds.) CRYPTO 2013, Part I. LNCS, vol. 8042, pp. 429–448. Springer, Heidelberg (2013)

22. LaMacchia, B.A., Lauter, K., Mityagin, A.: Stronger security of authenticated key exchange. In: Susilo, W., Liu, J.K., Mu, Y. (eds.) ProvSec 2007. LNCS, vol. 4784, pp. 1–16. Springer, Heidelberg (2007)

23. Li, Y., Schäge, S., Yang, Z., Kohlar, F., Schwenk, J.: On the security of the pre-shared key ciphersuites of TLS. In: Krawczyk, H. (ed.) PKC 2014. LNCS, vol. 8383, pp. 669–684. Springer, Heidelberg (2014)

24. EMVCo LLC: EMV deployment statistics (2012). http://www.emvco.com/about_emvco.aspx?id=202

25. Murdoch, S., Drimer, S., Anderson, R., Bond, M.: Chip and pin is broken. In: 2010 IEEE Symposium on Security and Privacy (SP), pp. 433–446, May 2010

26. Ogundele, O., Zavarsky, P., Ruhl, R., Lindskog, D.: The implementation of a full EMV smartcard for a point-of-sale transaction. In: 2012 World Congress on Internet Security (WorldCIS), pp. 28–35, June 2012

27. Ustaoglu, B.: Obtaining a secure and efficient key agreement protocol from (H)MQV and NAXOS. Des. Codes Crypt. 46(3), 329–342 (2008)

28. Van Herreweghen, E., Wille, U.: Risks and potentials of using EMV for internet payments. In: Proceedings of the USENIX Workshop on Smartcard Technology on USENIX Workshop on Smartcard Technology, WOST 1999, p. 18. USENIX Association, Berkeley (1999)

29. Yang, Z.: Efficient eCK-secure authenticated key exchange protocols in the standard model. In: Qing, S., Zhou, J., Liu, D. (eds.) ICICS 2013. LNCS, vol. 8233, pp. 185–193. Springer, Heidelberg (2013)

Author Index

Printed in the United States
By Bookmasters